THE
Green Continent

A Comprehensive View of LATIN AMERICA

BY ITS LEADING WRITERS

Selected and Edited by
Germán Arciniegas

Translated from the Spanish and Portuguese by
Harriet De Onís
and Others

1967   ALFRED A. KNOPF   NEW YORK

PUBLISHED AUGUST 21, 1944
REPRINTED SIX TIMES
EIGHTH PRINTING, JULY 1967

To *Gabriela*

To *Gabriela Mercedes*

CALIFORNIA

1943

FOREWORD

THE PURPOSE OF THIS BOOK is to present a picture of Latin America as seen by Latin Americans. Through these pages the reader will be able to become acquainted with many of the outstanding writers of the southern half of the hemisphere and at the same time inform himself about the principal aspects of its way of life. This book aims to be not only a literary anthology, but an informative work as well.

This is not a work of propaganda. None of the selections was written with a view to exalting the merits of any of our countries in foreign eyes. Quite the contrary. All the excerpts are from books intended for domestic consumption. The greater part of our literature has been a literature of criticism. Writers there, as here, in their attempt to portray the human tragedy in its full depth, tend to select such primitive and violent aspects of life as yet remain. It would be puerile to attempt to evade touching upon these notes, which form an essential part of our reality.

In these last thirty years the progress of Latin America has been enormous. Buenos Aires, which was the least important of all its capitals in colonial times, is today the third largest city in America. Brazil has today thirteen times as many miles of highway and railroad as thirty years ago. In Colombia twice as many tons of freight a year are transported by airplane as in the United States. This does not mean that, for the moment, Latin America has any importance in the world by reason of its industrial capacity or its armies, or because of its weight in international affairs. It is not in the light of the present but of the future that the importance of the Latin-American nations must be evaluated. If the rhythm of the ever increasing progress of our nations as demonstrated in recent years had not been interrupted by the war, and if, as a result of the war, the countries of Latin America manage firmly to establish the bases of their own development, in a few years, perhaps, we shall see in these countries a development similar to that which has served as the foundation for the transformation of countries such as Russia and Turkey.

For the moment our life moves within a gamut that ranges from the almost primitive aspects of the Amazon jungle to the refinement and culture of the great cities. This life, in its scenery, its historic conflicts, the formation of its great figures, and its typical notes of local color, is what the reader is going to find in these pages.

Naturally, this must be regarded as merely an introduction to the Latin-American scene. The great diversity among our countries and the extent of our territory have made it necessary to proceed along certain general lines in this exposition without treating each country as a separate entity. Strictly speaking, in order to form a clear concept of Latin America one must study twenty republics.

I owe thanks to many people for the help they have given me in the selection of material; to the living authors included for their authorization to reproduce the excerpts from their works; to Bruce Humphries, Inc., and Alfred A. Knopf for allowing me to use material already translated into English; to Alfred and Blanche Knopf for their cordial encouragement to undertake the work; to Baldomero Sanín Cano and Erico Verissimo for their contributions, which were written specially for this book; and very particularly to Harriet de Onís, who not only has been an enthusiastic translator, but has given me the benefit of her advice on a number of points.

GERMÁN ARCINIEGAS

MILLS COLLEGE
OAKLAND, CALIFORNIA

viii

CONTENTS *

* This entire volume was translated by Harriet de Onís with the exceptions
noted in this Table of Contents.

CONTENTS

CONTENTS

CONTENTS

The Green Continent

OUR LITTLE BIG WORLD

People are in the habit of looking upon Latin America as a group of similar nations of the same color and appearance. This is a fundamental error. If there is anything contradictory in the world, or a place where the most violent contrasts exist, that place is Latin America. It is a world that has been formed against a twofold opposition: the opposition of nature and of man. Many years must still elapse before these forces, which until now have made our history a convulsed, chaotic record, can be stabilized.

Half of the life of this America exists in the shadow of the Andes. Men subordinate their existence and adapt their minds to the intimate hollows of valleys so narrow that they recall the fjords of Norway, or they live close to the clouds on silent, cold plateaus, nine thousand feet above the sea. At times these valleys broaden out; deep quiet rivers run through hot fertile plains, but man's horizon is blocked by fold upon fold of mountainous curtain. These millions of men have never seen the sea.

The other half of America spreads over low-lying, burning plains that are like motionless seas — prairies that somewhat resemble the steppes of Russia or jungles that still preserve their age-old mysteries. Those who live in these regions are also inland people who have never seen the blue stretches of the ocean.

The gaucho who is the rider of the pampas, and the mountaineer who has cleared the hillside to build his white house in the midst of his cornfields, stand with their backs turned to each other. They have never seen each other; they are like two races of mankind traveling in opposite directions. One day they will come to know each other, but that day has not yet arrived. Even in the cities among people who, with the help of books, have been able to see farther, the Ecuadorian knows Paris, the Argentinean knows Paris, but the Argentinean does not know Ecuador, nor the Ecuadorian Argentina.

In Latin America there are cities where the African darkens the streets, and cities to which the Indian gives his copper hue,

and cities whiter than Berlin. To further accentuate these contrasts, there is the mestizo, the man whose blood is half white and
half Indian; the mulatto, who is half black and half white; the
zambo, who is half Negro and half Indian.

The process that has been going on in this America for four
hundred years is the resolution of this geographic antithesis so
the mountains and the lowlands shall not represent two hostile
worlds, but two mutually helpful, two complementary points of
view and economies. A policy of approximation between the
Latin-American nations cannot be worked out on the basis of their
identity, for this is a false premise, but by accepting the interde-
pendence of nations and countries which supplement one another
and thereby increase their power and solidarity. This is our position toward the United States as well. And just as roads are being
built to join mountain and plain, so a stabilization is taking place
in these dual-souled men, these mestizos, zambos, and mulattoes,
whose first vital reactions were restlessness, bewilderment, and
turbulence.

Alongside the country we have the city. Railroads, highways,
airplanes, books, research, schools have given many of our capitals a resemblance to the great cities of older, more prosperous
nations. Buenos Aires has two and a half million inhabitants, Rio
Janeiro one million eight hundred thousand, Mexico City over a
million. But in these same cities that diversity continues which
makes our map one of typical colors. While Buenos Aires models
itself after Paris in the ornate livery of its servants and in the re-
modeling of its streets, Mexico exalts the memory of the Indian.
And while the capital of the Argentine boasts of its white blood,
through the veins of the capital of Brazil rushes the blood of three
continents.

And what we are seeing now is only the last scene of a history
that from its beginning has been paved with contradictions. Some
of these are purely symbolic, but they seem to have charted us a
confused course from the very start. "Spanish" America was discovered by an Italian. It was conquered and colonized by humble
folk from Andalusia, Castile, Navarre, or Galicia, under the rule
of a king who was the "Emperor of Germany" and belonged to the

Habsburg dynasty. The continent should have been called Columbia, for Columbus, but it was called America for Amerigo Ves-
pucci, an extra who stayed off stage. We speak of Latin America,
but the name is nothing short of laughable in view of the fact that
millions of our inhabitants who speak Guarany, Quechua, Maya,
or Aymará in their mountains, and who are the real flesh of our
flesh, really know very little of the arches of Rome or the beautiful
countryside of Latium.

People from all over the world have come to our lands in search
of the justice and freedom which Europe could not always, or
hardly ever, offer its children. Yet these immigrants have spent a
century here struggling in the throes of anarchy and dictatorship.
The two Liberators who did the most for our independence —
Bolívar and San Martín — were thinking of life-term presidents or
importing a European sovereign to rule us. And yet the "Liberators," by definition, were striving toward the achievement one
day of those two fine things — liberty and democratic justice —
which were the goal the people from all over the world who
came here were pursuing.

In reality the road we have had to travel to reach the point
where we are now, which is not half the distance, has probably
been a harder and rougher one than that of North America. Our
people are more complex, more ungovernable. The problem has
been that of stabilizing the soul of the mestizo, a work of generations. Our nineteenth century was chaos. At that time only a
glimpse of light for the distant future could be discerned. But
there is a sense of direction that encourages us, and that has united
us and made us one for four hundred years. Beyond question we
are marching toward a future of democracy, social justice, freedom, and tolerance, which are the four points of our compass, and
all our peoples know this, the hundred and twenty million of
them. We move in this direction with growing assurance, which
little by little frees us from small dictators and anarchy. With our
blood we are filling in the gulfs that have separated our races
and kept our souls from meeting. No discerning reader with an
ear attuned to history can fail to recognize this. Beneath our dictatorships and civil wars there is an underground stream that

keeps flowing. It is the masses in pursuit of democracy. We have not caught up with it; we still have little tyrants, left-overs from times that have passed. These are facts which all can see, which no one tries to conceal, and which are worth studying to measure the scope of our achievements and our setbacks. Latin America arose from chaos. But its path is lighted by a certain phrase of Bolívar's, who was well aware of the anarchy and unrest through which it would have to pass, but who, just before the Battle of Junín, said these prophetic words to his soldiers: "The freedom of America is the hope of the world."

Reducing the problem of Latin America, and perhaps that of the United States as well, to a simple formula, I have proposed to make a distinction between the America of the Atlantic and the America of the Pacific.

The differences between these two Americas is at least as valid as the geographer's old classification of North America, Central America, and South America. Along the edge of the Pacific Ocean the Andes form a gigantic ridge which runs from Mount McKinley in Alaska to the very end of Chile. Nowhere else in the world does a barrier of this sort exist. Between Chile and the Argentine, between Bolivia and Peru, there is a steady succession of peaks all over twenty thousand feet high. At times the mountain chain opens out into parallel ranges, like the fingers of a hand, and between these lie deep valleys like Colombia and Venezuela. In certain places pleasant plains crown the mountains; in others the craters of volcanoes or lakes like Titicaca, a little fresh-water sea, 12,500 feet above sea-level.

On the other side lie the pampas, the jungles of the Amazon. On the plains of the Argentine there is room for nearly all the large nations of Europe. The Republic of Brazil, which has an area larger than that of the United States, is only a little smaller than the whole continent of Europe. South America is much broader than the Atlantic Ocean it faces. Airplanes cross this in one hop from Natal to Dakar, but it would be a tremendous flight from the coast of Brazil to that of Peru.

On the Pacific slope the rivers have hardly come down from the mountains before they are rushing into the sea. In the east, on the other hand, the waters of the Amazon must travel 4,000 miles to reach the Atlantic; and those of the Paraná, 2,300, and the Orinoco, 1,600. The watershed of these three rivers comes together and they form a network of canals which extends over the whole interior of South America. Through arms like the Casiquiare, which joins the Amazon and the Orinoco, these rivers with their many tributaries unite, and it may be said that the unexplored interior of this green hell of America is an archipelago of jungles. Geographers have spent years and years arguing about the source of the Amazon and the Orinoco and no one can really yet say where they rise.

The inhabitants of the Atlantic coast are reluctant to venture into either the mysterious jungle or the empty pampa. They cluster about the ports. Argentina has a ring of large cities around the pampa where the population is less than one inhabitant per square kilometer. The *porteño,* the inhabitant of Buenos Aires, has lived in a permanent dialogue with Europe.

The behavior of the inhabitants of the Pacific is just the opposite. The ocean that stretches before them is the sea of remote Asia; it touches an unknown world, and no one ventures upon its waters. The coasts are inhabited only by fishermen. All the people go to the uplands to plant their potatoes and their corn, to burrow in the mines, and they know little of the world. In the Andes the Spanish seed sown four centuries ago grows without haste, but without rest or pause, and its shoots intermingle with those of the Indian in affectionate promiscuity.

For four hundred years men from the four corners of the earth — Europeans, Africans, Asiatics — have been mixing with the copper-colored natives of these lands. It is the most amazing experiment in the intermingling of bloods that history has ever witnessed since those remote epochs when something of the same sort took place in Europe. So many circumstances have influenced the color scheme that today the racial map is like Joseph's coat. In the Argentine there are no Negroes, and only two per cent of the population have traces of Indian blood. When the traveler crosses the boundary that separates it from Brazil he finds a nation of forty-four million inhabitants of which five million are as black as stove polish. In another of the Argentine's neighbors, Bolivia, the white population is only thirteen per cent of the total; over fifty per cent are pure Indians and the rest mestizos. After this comes Peru, a contradictory little world where half the population are whites or mestizos, a third pure Indians, and the rest predominantly Negro or Asiatic. In Mexico the whites are in the minority: they number only 2,400,000 in a population of 19,000,-000; the number of pure Indians is twice that of the whites, and the rest mestizos. In Colombia and Paraguay the mestizo predominates, but whereas the racial emphasis in Colombia is Spanish, in Paraguay it is Guarany.

Nor should one have illusions about the language. There has been a great division from the start, for ours is a dual world, one part of which speaks Portuguese — Brazil — and the other principally Spanish — Spanish America. But inland, in the heart of the continent, other accents are heard. One of the best authors of Paraguay, who writes in Spanish, said to me: "I express myself better in Guarany than in Spanish." And he went on to explain that there is no shade of meaning, poetic image, or new word that cannot be carried into that language. Guarany survived the Spanish conquest; in Paraguay it is spoken by the descendants of Spaniards and is used by the masses of the people. During the electoral campaigns nobody speaks to the voters of the smaller towns in Spanish — only in Guarany. Even in the Congress, although the official language is Spanish, in moments of enthusiasm the Congressmen forsake the language of Cervantes for that of the Indians, to establish closer contact with their hearers. I have gone to Ecuador to the weekly fair in Otabalo. It is one of the most beautiful spots in America. The town is ordinarily a deserted village. The streets are empty, not a soul crosses the town square, until the day of the fair. From daybreak thousands of country people in their gay costumes, as picturesque as those of certain corners of Europe — Holland, Austria, or the Balkans — begin to descend from the surrounding hills. By the time the sun is high, flooding everything with light, the three great squares of Otabalo are crowded with this multitude of Indians. They weave the cloth for their garments, make their enormous felt hats, cultivate their lands, and need nothing from the outside world. Fifteen or twenty thousand people gather together at this market, which is a feast of color in the squares and of Quechua music in the inns, where they dance the old dances of the highlands. And in all this not a word of Spanish is heard; as in the days of the Incas, it is Quechua that is spoken in Otabalo, and in Bolivia Aymará, and in certain places in the south of Mexico Maya.

All these differences will explain to the reader the difficulty of reducing to a hasty synthesis a series of nations whose outward appearance is so varied, so differing in air, and whose inner spirit is so secret.

The conquest and colonization of Latin America followed a process diametrically opposite to that in the United States. In North America the colonies grew strong along the seaboard, developed a solid base for expansion, and little by little, in an orderly rhythm, extended their frontiers westward. That is to say, here colonization came first and then the conquest. To us in the south, the way the Europeans established themselves in New England, New Holland, New Sweden, and along the narrow strip of Virginia that lies between the Atlantic and the Appalachians, which they crossed later to push on beyond the Mississippi, seems a miracle of systematic expansion. In the maps of the history of the United States, under each city is the date of its founding; nearly always a year that begins with the two figures 16. . . . Then, when all this had been consolidated, the mountains were crossed and the settlers pressed on toward the river, over the Rockies, to California. The process covers two centuries. In 1830 the frontier was barely across the Mississippi. California was reached only yesterday. As far as the North Americans are concerned, the Pacific Ocean was discovered only two or three generations ago. The Spaniards themselves, who spread so quickly over the south, urged on perhaps by the dream of gold, were less enthusiastic in their northern advance. They founded San Francisco in 1776. In 1844 it had twelve houses and fifty inhabitants. In 1845, somewhat by chance, the American flag was hoisted there. But by that time Mexico had been a city of importance for three centuries.

In Latin America thirty or forty years after Columbus discovered the New World the Spaniards and Portuguese had penetrated to the most remote fastness of our mountains and had laid the foundations of all our cities. First came the conquest – a reckless, ambitious, headlong conquest. Then colonization began to receive thought. For the colonization of North America, trading companies of stockholders were organized which sent out groups of families. In the south it was bands of soldiers whose only flag was that of their captain and whose only women were the Indians they took as their mates. These captains were men of dominating personality, a combination of hero and bandit, who left the history of the conquest stamped with a series of names which dominated at least half a century of our life. The Pacific Ocean was a Spanish sea from 1513. Over it they went to the conquest of Peru, Ecuador, Chile. That hurricane of adventurers that put to sea in roughly built ships climbed mountains and marched through jungles discovering a fantastic world that the hands of proud weak kings were unable to maintain. Our first foundations always bear a date that begins 15. . . . Havana was founded in 1512. Mexico City was Spanish from 1521. On our entire map, from north to south, from east to west, from the shores of the sea to the crest of the Andes, one can read these early dates for the founding of our cities: São Paulo, 1532; Quito, 1534; Lima and Buenos Aires, 1535; Pernambuco, 1536; Santiago, 1541. In the year 1545 a city was founded at 12,400 feet above sea-level: La Paz. Bogotá, which lies at the juncture of three mountain ranges, at a height of 8,600 feet, was founded in 1538.

To be sure, these hasty foundations often disappeared with the wind or in flames, as happened with Buenos Aires. Or the English buccaneers swept down and put the flimsy houses to the torch after raiding the city. They were cities that were born, died, came to life again, at times moved, changed their location, a little Bohemian and restless like their founders. But they were taking root. It suffices to say that in Lima and Mexico universities which still exist today were opened in 1551, and at that time Mexico already had a printing press.

For four centuries we Latin Americans have led a life of internal readjustments; our history has been one of little cities lost in the hills, of petty chieftains who led their bands from one province to another, as happened in Europe during the Middle Ages. It was well into the nineteenth century before the railroads and highways that were slowly being built along the steep flank of the mountains began to unite us. In 1900 we had everywhere short stretches of railroad which went nowhere. About 1910 they began to link up and thereupon the central points of our economic life had a means of communication. The influence of the more advanced cities began to make itself felt. As though by magic, what the day before had been sleepy little towns acquired the proportions of cities. Alongside the old cities, which were often reduced to rubble-heaps by the speed with which engineers, devoid of historical or artistic sense, did their work, new structures rose. These new cities, which are today all the capitals of America, seem to be no more than thirty years old. Our republics are only now awakening to their possibilities, are only now falling into step with the march of the modern world. We are now crossing the frontier that separates our Middle Ages from our Renaissance and our modern age. We are now, at one and the same time, that barbarism and civilization which Sarmiento, the great Argentine writer, tried to divide into two camps one hundred years ago. The nations which have been struggling for years, which have a history of their own and understand such things, know that there are barriers which cannot be surmounted in a quarter of an hour. For four centuries we have been bruising our bare feet against the rocks, but now we believe we are beginning to see over the top of the wall.

PART I

Landscape and Man

THE PAMPAS

A T THE MENTION OF THE ARGENTINE two images evoking its landscape and its life at once flash before the mind: the pampas and Buenos Aires. The pampas comprise nearly all the land of this Republic. Buenos Aires is the city. On the pampas the wheat and the herds grow and multiply. The people are in Buenos Aires. In crossing the pampas one rides for three hundred, six hundred miles along endless, unswerving highways without passing a city, seeing only every fifty miles or so a station of the Argentine Automobile Club, and the traveler is overwhelmed by the solitude. In the distance, clouds, the huge disk of the setting sun, which sinks into the earth without a hill or a rise in the ground to give one the feeling of a limit on which the eye can rest. It is as though the thirteen million inhabitants of the Argentine had fled this empty stage and huddled into the ring of cities that surrounds it. The first group of inhabitants is to be found in Bahía Blanca, a port on the Atlantic, far to the south. Then, still looking out on the sea, Mar del Plata, La Plata, Avellaneda, and Buenos Aires reach out their hands to one another, merging at times to the point where these last three cities with their suburbs form a single block of 3,000,000 inhabitants. After this, in the valley of the Paraná, comes Rosario with 500,000 and Santa Fé with 140,000. In the face of the empty pampas this garland of cities confirms almost violently the dualism of the Argentine, the men on one side, all together, and facing them a landscape, nothing but landscape. The Argentineans personify this dualism in two clearly defined types: the man who takes his chances on the pampas is the "gaucho," the one who lives in Buenos Aires is the "porteño."

Between these two extremes of Argentine life there is an intermediate landscape and type: the mountains and the man of the uplands. These are the farmers who have their small holdings on the slopes of Mendoza, in the foothills of the Andes, crisscrossed by irrigation ditches, people who live caring for their vineyards, watching the peaches and pears ripen. Or the highlanders of

Córdoba, whose colonial city lies among the hills, with its cathedral that is like an old engraving and its university, founded in 1613. In these places tradition has more weight and is Spanish. Córdoba in colonial days was the spiritual center of the country.

The pampas, besides being an Argentine landscape, are an American landscape. They are the same as the plains of Colombia and Venezuela. The *gaucho* has his counterpart in the *llanero* of those countries. They sing the same songs under the palm as under the ombú, the *corridos* or *galerones*, in which, to the accompaniment of the guitar, each tells of his life with humor, irony, and boastfulness, relating deeds of prowess that may be true or fanciful. Nobody can bear out or give the lie to the singer. On the plains man lives with his horse and his star. The rider's sole guide during the day is the sun; at night, the stars. To find a trail on the plains, only an eye trained over generations can read the confused language of prints that the wind blurs or the passing of man or beast effaces. If a storm breaks, or a panther, a bull, or a man attacks the son of the pampas, he defends himself and metes out his own justice. A man is himself and his knife. Martínez Estrada, who has written the best book on the pampas since that of Sarmiento, says: "The knife is of use, naturally, to uphold the right, to talk with sincerity, and in the hands of the child and the woman it is docile to domestic duties. It cuts bread and peels fruit; but it is dangerous to learn the secrets of its use and the complete mastery of its technique. The knowledge of its 'carving art' is fatal, like that of writing a good verse; it leads one further than one would wish. It serves to kill, and especially to kill a man, demanding for this a body-to-body encounter, eliminating any advantage, any impunity due to distance. It is the synthesis of all the arms man has employed since his beginnings. Ameghino found five different classes of small flint knives on our pampas. It is the only arm that helps a man to earn his humble living and which, in its blood-stains, tells of a crime. At times it is swifter than an insult and it is hard to control or measure in the attack, for when the soul would hold back, the hand has already carried out the first impulse, unconsciously; we could say it was swifter than thought itself. It goes in up to the hilt; forefinger and thumb touch the body. This contact,

4

which could make the sign of the cross to pardon, is testimony of a fact beyond repair." On the plains of Venezuela and Colombia the llaneros draw their own portrait in these words:

> Under the sky the pampas,
> Upon the pampas my horse,
> Upon my horse me,
> Upon me my hat.

For reasons that are not without profound human significance, the two Liberators of Spanish America in the south — Bolívar and San Martín — in the decisive hour of the final battle turn to the plains, and upon them and with the plainsmen they form their armies and their cavalry. This happened at the very moment when Spain, restored from the calamities of the Napoleonic invasion, sent over fleets of soldiers to subdue the rebellious colonists. These were the same soldiers that had helped defeat Napoleon at Waterloo under the command of Wellington. For the first time the rebels of America were to pit their barefoot armies against the best-prepared war machine of Europe. Bolívar assembled his troops on the plains of Venezuela, then crossed the Andes with his plainsmen, surprised the Spaniards in the mountain strongholds, and liberated five nations with the plainsmen's lances. San Martín, too, set out from the pampas, trained his men at the foot of the mountains, crossed the Andes, and at Chacabuco, on the Chilean side, fought the battle that decided the fate of the south. So the two plains have been the fulcrum of our independence, the gateways of our freedom.

In the pampas great bandits have taken refuge, dictators have been trained, liberators and heroes formed. Paez, who hurled his squadrons of naked lancers against the Spanish artillery and defeated it in Venezuela was known as "the tiger of the plains." And, curiously enough, Facundo Quiroga was known to the Argentine gauchos by the same name. And the name fitted him well, wrote Sarmiento. When Rosas, the dictator of the Argentine, began to prepare himself to wield the absolute power with which he governed by fire and sword for twenty-three years, he went to the pampas and made himself a gaucho. Bolívar, to prepare himself to be the Liberator, went to the plains and made himself a llanero.

The transformation of America during this century, which has been largely due to better communications, has not changed the life of the pampas as far as man and landscape are concerned, except to make their solitude greater. Perhaps the future will bring other changes, but, for the moment, Martínez Estrada observes: "All along the uninhabited miles of holdings one has the impression that the train is rolling over the same point and that the cars are almost empty. An empty car is a lie on wheels and the passengers who are riding in it with their stamped tickets are ghosts in a fantasy. . . . Our trains are the equivalent in steel of so many pounds sterling and not vehicles to produce wealth; they are set in motion from London; there these branch lines start and end; they travel over their tracks, not through our fields. . . ."

The pampas have given rise to a literature that has the grandeur, the bravery, the naturalness and desolation of the landscape and the life. Together with a wealth of folklore, and utilizing it, there are works like the epic poem, *Martín Fierro* of José Hernández. "Of all the Spanish-American literature I know," wrote Unamuno, "Martín Fierro is the most profoundly Spanish." Menéndez Pelayo thought: "The breath of the Argentine pampas runs through its disheveled, untamed, vigorous verses." The strange thing is that this tale by a gaucho of his life, told with the wit and vaunt that characterize his people, has the most striking resemblance to similar accounts, in ballad form, of the llaneros of Venezuela and Colombia, which proves that there is as much of South America as of the Argentine in the gaucho and his landscape. In another field of literature Ricardo Güiraldes has written a novel of the pampas, *Don Segundo Sombra,* which is already a classic in America.

But no writer has produced so vigorous a painting as that of Domingo Faustino Sarmiento in his *Facundo,* which was published in 1845 and is one of the masterpieces of our literature. Sarmiento (1811–88) may be called the Argentine Jefferson. Besides having been the greatest journalist of his day, he was President of his country from 1868 to 1874, and he made it his mission to see that every Argentinean should learn to read. The character of Sarmiento has been depicted by Lugones in his biography in these words: "Danger was his habit and wrath his beauty; his dimensions became those of a deity, cleaving the air like lightning, riding the tempest with a cloud at his belt and a thunderbolt on his shoulder." *Facundo* was a work of combat and was written as an invective against the dictatorship of Rosas. Many of the judgments expressed in it have been revised by writers as able as Ricardo Rojas, but from the literary point of view the work is unexcelled. The pages that follow have been taken from it.

LIFE IN THE ARGENTINE REPUBLIC
DOMINGO F. SARMIENTO

"The extent of the pampas is so prodigious that they are bounded on the north by groves of palm trees and on the south by eternal snows."
HEAD

THE CONTINENT of America ends at the south in a point, with the Strait of Magellan at its southern extremity. Upon the west the Chilean Andes run parallel to the coast at a short distance from the Pacific. Between that range of mountains and the Atlantic is a country whose boundary follows the River Plata up the course of the Uruguay into the interior, which was formerly known as the United Provinces of the River Plata, but where blood is still shed to determine whether its name shall be the Argentine Republic or the Argentine Confederation. On the north lie Paraguay, the Gran Chaco, and Bolivia, its assumed boundaries.

The vast tract which occupies its extremities is altogether uninhabited, and possesses navigable rivers as yet unfurrowed even by a frail canoe. Its own extent is the evil from which the Argentine Republic suffers; the desert encompasses it on every side and penetrates its very heart; wastes containing no human dwelling, are, generally speaking, the unmistakable boundaries between its several provinces. Immensity is the universal characteristic of the country: the plains, the woods, the rivers, are all immense; and the horizon is always undefined, always lost in haze and delicate vapors which forbid the eye to mark the point in the distant perspective where the land ends and the sky begins. On the south and on the north are savages ever on the watch, who take advantage of the moonlight nights to fall like packs of hyenas upon the herds in their pastures and upon the defenseless settlements. When the solitary caravan of wagons, as it sluggishly traverses the pampas, halts for a short period of rest, the men in charge of it, grouped around their scanty fire, turn their eyes mechanically toward the south upon the faintest whisper of the wind among the dry grass and gaze into the deep darkness of the night, in search of the sinister visages of the savage horde which at any moment, approaching unperceived, may surprise them. If no sound reaches their ears, if their sight fails to pierce the gloomy veil which covers the silent wilderness, they direct their eyes, before entirely dismissing their apprehensions, to the ears of any horse standing within the firelight, to see if they are pricked up or turned carelessly backwards. Then they resume their interrupted conversation or put into their mouths the half-scorched pieces of dried beef on which they subsist. When not fearful of the approach of the savage, the plainsman has equal cause to dread the keen eyes of the tiger, or the viper beneath his foot. This constant insecurity of life outside the towns, in my opinion, stamps upon the Argentine character a certain stoical resignation to death by violence, which is regarded as one of the inevitable probabilities of existence. Perhaps this is the reason why they inflict death or submit to it with so much indifference and why such events make no deep or lasting impression upon the survivors.

Upon the boundless expanse above described stand scattered here and there fourteen cities, each the capital of a province. The obvious method of arranging their names would be to classify them according to their geographical position: Buenos Aires, Santa Fé, Entre Rios, and Corrientes, on the banks of the Paraná; Mendoza, San Juan, Rioja, Catamarca, Tucumán, Salta, and Jujuy, being on a line nearly parallel to the Chilean Andes; with Santiago, San Luis, and Córdoba in the center. But this manner of enumerating the Argentine towns has no connection with any of the social results which I have in view. A classification adapted to my purpose must originate in the ways of life pursued by the country people, for it is this that determines their character and spirit. I have stated above that the proximity of the rivers makes no difference in this respect, because the extent to which they are navigated is so trifling as to be without influence upon the people.

All the Argentine provinces except San Juan and Mendoza depend on the products of pastoral life; Tucumán avails itself of agriculture also, and Buenos Aires, besides raising millions of cattle and sheep, devotes itself to the numerous and diversified occupations of civilized life.

The Argentine cities, like almost all the cities of South America, have an appearance of regularity. Their streets are laid out at right angles, and their population scattered over a wide surface, except in Córdoba, which occupies a narrow and confined position and presents all the appearance of a European city, the resemblance being increased by the multitude of towers and domes attached to its numerous and magnificent churches. All civilization, whether native, Spanish, or European, centers in the cities, where are to be found the factories, the shops, the schools and colleges, and other characteristics of civilized nations. Elegance of style, articles of luxury, dress-coats, and frock-coats, with other European garments, occupy their appropriate place in these towns. I mention these small matters designedly. It is sometimes the case that the only city of a pastoral province is its capital, and occasionally the land is uncultivated up to its very streets. The encircling desert besets such cities at a greater or less distance and bears heavily upon them, and they are thus small oases of civilization surrounded by an untilled plain, hundreds of square miles in extent, the surface of which is but rarely interrupted by any settlement of consequence.

The cities of Buenos Aires and Córdoba have succeeded better than the others in establishing about them subordinate towns to serve as new focuses of civilization and municipal interests — a fact which deserves notice. The inhabitants of the city wear the European dress, live in a civilized manner, and possess laws, ideas of progress, means of instruction, some municipal organization, regular forms of government, and so on. Beyond the precincts of the city everything assumes a new aspect; the country people wear a different costume, which I will call South American, as it is common to all districts; their habits of life are different, their wants peculiar and limited. The people composing these two distinct forms of society do not seem to belong to the same nation. Moreover, the countryman, far from attempting to imitate the customs of the city, rejects with disdain its luxury and refinement; and it is unsafe for the costume of the city people, their coats, their cloaks, their saddles, or anything European, to show themselves in the country. Everything civilized which the city contains is blockaded there, proscribed beyond its limits; and anyone who would dare to appear in the rural districts in a frock-coat, for example, or mounted on an English saddle, would bring ridicule and brutal assaults upon himself.

The whole remaining population inhabits the open country, which, whether wooded or destitute of the larger plants, is generally level and almost everywhere occupied by pastures, in some places of such abundance and excellence that the grass of an artificial meadow would not surpass them. Mendoza, and especially San Juan, are exceptions to this general absence of tilled fields, the people here depending chiefly on the products of agriculture. Everywhere else, pasturage being plentiful, the means of subsistence of the inhabitants — for we cannot call it their occupation — is stock-raising. Pastoral life reminds us of the Asiatic plains, which imagination covers with Kalmuck, Cossack, or Arab tents. The primitive life of nations — a life essentially barbarous and unprogressive — the life of Abraham, which is that of the Bedouin today, prevails in the Argentine plains, although modified in a peculiar manner by civilization. The Arab tribe which wanders through the wilds of Asia is united under the rule of one of its elders or of a warrior chief; society exists, although not fixed in any determined locality. Its religious opinions, immemorial traditions, unchanging customs, and its sentiment of respect for age, make all together a code of laws and a form of government which preserves morality, as it is there understood, as well as order and the association of the tribe. But progress is impossible, because there can be no progress without permanent possession of the soil, or without cities, which are the means of developing the capacity of man for the processes of industry and which enable him to extend his acquisitions.

Nomad tribes do not exist in the Argentine plains; the stock-raiser is a proprietor, living upon his own land; but this condition renders association impossible and tends to scatter separate families over an immense extent of surface. Imagine an expanse of fourteen thousand square miles, inhabited throughout, but where the dwellings are usually ten or even twenty miles apart, and five or six miles, at least, separate the nearest neighbors. The production of movable property is not impossible, the enjoyments of luxury are not wholly incompatible with this isolation; wealth can raise a superb edifice in the desert. But the incentive is wanting; no example is near; the inducements for making a great display which exist in a city are not known in that isolation and solitude. Inevitable privations justify natural indolence; a dearth of all the amenities of life induces all the externals of barbarism. Society has altogether disappeared. There is but the isolated self-concentrated feudal family. Since there is no collected society, no government is possible; there is neither municipal nor executive power, and civil justice has no means of reaching criminals. I doubt if the modern world presents any other form of association so monstrous as this. It is the exact opposite of the Roman municipality, where all the population was assembled within an inclosed space and went from it to cultivate the surrounding fields. The consequence of this was a strong social organization, the good results of which have prepared the way for modern civilization. The Argentine system resembles the old Slavonic Sloboda, with the difference that the latter was agricultural, and therefore more susceptible of government, while the dispersion of the population was not so great as in South America. It differs from the nomad tribes in admitting of no social reunion, and in a permanent occupation of the soil. Lastly, it has something in common with the feudal system of the Middle Ages, when the barons lived in their strongholds and thence made war on the cities and laid waste the country in the vicinity; but the baron and the feudal castle are wanting. If power starts up in the country, it lasts only for a moment, and is democratic; it is not inherited, nor can it maintain itself for want of mountains and strong positions. It follows from this that even the savage tribe of the pampas is better organized for moral development than are our country districts.

But the remarkable feature of this society, viewed in its social aspect, is its affinity to the life of the ancients — to the life of the Spartans or Romans; but again a radical dissimilarity appears when the subject is considered from another side. The free citizen of Sparta or of Rome threw upon his slaves the weight of material life, the care of providing for his subsistence, while he lived, free from such cares, in the forum or in the public place of assembly, exclusively occupied with the interests of the state — peace, war, and party contests. The stock-raiser has his share of the same advantages, and his herds fulfill the degrading office of the ancient Helot. Their spontaneous multiplication constitutes and indefinitely augments his fortune; the help of man is superfluous; his labor, his intelligence, his time, are not needed for the preservation and increase of the means of life. But though he needs none of these forces for the supply of his physical wants, he is unable to make use of them when thus saved, as the Roman did. He has no city, no municipality, no intimate associations, and thus the basis of all social development is wanting. As the landowners are not brought together, they have no public wants to satisfy; in a word, there is no *res publica*.

Moral progress and the cultivation of the intellect are here not only neglected, as in the Arab or Tatar tribe, but impossible. Where can a school be placed for the instruction of children living thirty miles apart in all directions? Thus, consequently, civilization can in no way be brought about. Barbarism is the normal condition [1] and it is fortunate if domestic customs preserve a small germ of morality. Religion feels the consequences of this want of social organization. The offices of the pastor are nominal, the

---

[1] In 1826, during a year's residence at the Sierra de San Luis, I taught the art of reading to six young people of good families, the youngest of whom was twenty-two years old.

pulpit has no audience, the priest flees from the deserted chapel or allows his character to deteriorate in inactivity and solitude. Vice, simony, and the prevalent barbarism penetrate his cell and change his moral superiority into the means of gratifying his avarice or ambition, and he ends by becoming a party leader. I once witnessed a scene of rural life worthy of the primitive ages of the world which preceded the institution of the priesthood. In 1838 I happened to be in the Sierra de San Luis, at the house of a proprietor whose two favorite occupations were saying prayers and gambling. He had built a chapel where he used to pray through the rosary on Sunday afternoons, to supply the want of a priest and of public divine service, of which the place had been destitute for many years. It was a Homeric picture: the sun declining to the west; the sheep returning to the fold and rending the air with their confused bleatings; the service conducted by the master of the house, a man of sixty, with a noble countenance, in which the pure European race was evident in the white skin, blue eyes, and wide and open forehead; while the responses were made by a dozen women and some young men, whose imperfectly broken horses were fastened near the door of the chapel. After finishing the rosary he fervently offered up his own petitions. I never heard a voice fuller of pious feeling, nor a prayer of purer warmth, of firmer faith, of greater beauty, or better adapted to the circumstances than that which he uttered. In this prayer he besought God to grant rain for the fields, fruitfulness for the herds and flocks, peace for the Republic, and safety for all wayfarers. I readily shed tears, and wept even with sobs, for the religious sentiment had, been awakened in my soul to intensity, and like an unknown sensation, for I never witnessed a more religious scene. I seemed to be living in the times of Abraham, in his presence, in that of God, and of the nature which reveals Him. The voices of that sincere and pure-minded man made all my nerves vibrate and penetrated to my inmost soul.

To this — that is, to natural religion — is all religion reduced in the pastoral districts. Christianity exists, like the Spanish idiom, as a tradition which is perpetuated, but corrupted; colored by gross superstitions and unaided by instruction, rites, or convictions. It is the case in almost all the districts which are remote from the cities that when traders from San Juan or Mendoza arrive there, three or four children, some months or a year old, are presented to them for baptism, confidence being felt that their good education will enable them to administer the rite in a valid manner; and on the arrival of a priest, young men old enough to break a colt present themselves to him to be anointed and have baptism *sub conditione* administered to them.

In the absence of all the means of civilization and progress, which can only be developed among men collected into societies of many individuals, the education of the country people is as follows: The women look after the house, get the meals ready, shear the sheep, milk the cows, make the cheese, and weave the coarse cloth used for garments. All domestic occupations are performed by women; on them rests the burden of all the labor, and it is an exceptional favor when some of the men undertake the cultivation of a little corn, bread not being in use as an ordinary article of diet. The boys exercise their strength and amuse themselves by gaining skill in the use of the lasso and the bolas, with which they constantly harass and pursue the calves and goats. When they can ride, which is as soon as they have learned to walk, they perform some small services on horseback. When they become stronger, they race over the country, falling off their horses and getting up again, tumbling on purpose into rabbit [2] burrows, scrambling over precipices, and practicing feats of horsemanship. On reaching puberty they take to breaking wild colts, and death is the least penalty that awaits them if their strength or courage fails them for a moment. With early manhood come complete independence and idleness.

Now begins the public life of the gaucho, so to speak, since his education is by this time at an end. These men, Spaniards only in their language and in the confused religious notions preserved among them, must be seen before a right estimate can be made of the indomitable and haughty character which grows out of this struggle of isolated man with untamed nature, of the rational being with the brute. It is necessary to see their visages bristling

[2] Viscachas.

with beards, their countenances as grave and serious as those of the Arabs of Asia, to appreciate the pitying scorn with which they look upon the sedentary denizen of the city, who may have read many books, but who cannot overthrow and slay a fierce bull, who could not provide himself with a horse from the pampas, who has never met a tiger alone and received him with a dagger in one hand and a poncho rolled up in the other, to be thrust into the animal's mouth while he transfixes his heart with the dagger.

This habit of triumphing over resistance, of constantly showing a superiority to nature, of defying and subduing her, prodigiously develops the consciousness of individual consequence and superior prowess. The Argentine people of every class, civilized and ignorant alike, have a high opinion of their national importance. All the other people of South America throw this vanity of theirs in their teeth and take offense at their presumption and arrogance. I believe the charge not to be wholly unfounded, but I do not object to the trait. Alas for the nation without faith in itself! Great things were not made for such a people. To what extent may not the independence of that part of America be due to the arrogance of these Argentine gauchos, who have never seen anything beneath the sun superior to themselves in wisdom or in power? The European is in their eyes the most contemptible of all men, for a horse gets the better of him in a couple of plunges.[3]

If the origin of this national vanity among the lower classes is despicable, it has none the less on that account some noble results, as the water of a river is no less pure for the mire and pollution of its sources. Implacable is the hatred which these people feel for men of refinement, whose garments, manners, and customs they regard with invincible repugnance. Such is the material of the Argentine soldiery, and it may easily be imagined what valor and endurance in war are the consequences of the habits described above. We may add that these soldiers have been used

[3] General Mansilla said in a public meeting during the French blockade: "What have we to apprehend from these Europeans, who are not equal to one night's gallop?" and the vast plebeian audience drowned the speaker's voice with thunders of applause.

to slaughtering cattle from their childhood, and that this act of necessary cruelty makes them familiar with bloodshed, and hardens their hearts against the groans of their victims.

Country life, then, has developed all the physical but none of the intellectual powers of the gaucho. His moral character is of the quality to be expected from his habit of triumphing over the obstacles and the forces of nature; it is strong, haughty, and energetic. Without instruction, and indeed without need of any, without means of support as without wants, he is happy in the midst of his poverty and privations, which are not such to one who never knew nor wished for greater pleasures than are his already. Thus if the disorganization of society among the gauchos deeply implants barbarism in their natures, through the impossibility and uselessness of moral and intellectual education, it has, too, its attractive side to him. The gaucho does not labor; he finds his food and raiment ready to his hand. If he is a proprietor, his own flocks yield him both; if he possesses nothing himself, he finds them in the house of a patron or a relation. The necessary care of the herds is reduced to excursions and pleasure parties; the branding, which is like the harvesting of farmers, is a festival, the arrival of which is received with transports of joy, being the occasion of the assembling of all the men for sixty miles around and the opportunity for displaying incredible skill with the lasso. The gaucho arrives at the spot on his best steed, riding at a slow and measured pace; he halts at a little distance and puts his leg over his horse's neck to enjoy the sight leisurely. If enthusiasm seizes him, he slowly dismounts, uncoils his lasso, and flings it at some bull, passing like a flash of lightning forty paces from him; he catches him by one hoof, as he intended, and quietly coils his leather cord again.

THE RASTREADOR. The most conspicuous and extraordinary of the occupations to be described is that of the *rastreador,* or track-finder. All the gauchos of the interior are rastreadores. In such extensive plains, where paths and lines of travel cross one another in all directions, and where the pastures in which the herds feed are unfenced, it is necessary often to follow the tracks of an animal, to distinguish them among a thousand others, and to know whether it was going at an easy or a rapid pace, at liberty or led, laden or carrying no weight.

This is a generally understood branch of household knowledge. I once happened to turn out of a by-way into the Buenos Aires road, and my guide, following the usual practice, cast a look at the ground. "There was a very nice little Moorish mule in that train," said he, directly. "D. N. Zapata's it was — she is good for the saddle, and it is very plain she was saddled this time; they went by yesterday." The man was traveling from the Sierra de San Luis, while the train had passed on its way from Buenos Aires, and it was a year since he had seen the Moorish mule, whose track was mixed up with those of a whole train in a path two feet wide. And this seemingly incredible tale only illustrates the common degree of skill — the guide was a mere herdsman, and no professional rastreador.

The rastreador proper is a grave, circumspect personage, whose declarations are considered conclusive evidence in the inferior courts. Consciousness of the knowledge he possesses gives him a certain reserved and mysterious dignity. Everyone treats him with respect; the poor man because he fears to offend one who might injure him by a slander or an accusation; and the proprietor because of the possible value of his testimony. A theft has been committed during the night; no one knows anything of it; the victims of it hasten to look for one of the robber's footprints, and on finding it, they cover it with something to keep the wind from disturbing it. They then send for the rastreador, who detects the track and follows it, only occasionally looking at the ground as if his eyes saw in full relief the footsteps invisible to others. He follows the course of the streets, crosses gardens, enters a house, and, pointing to a man whom he finds there, says coldly: "That is he!" The crime is proved, and the criminal seldom denies the charge. In his estimation, even more than in that of the judge, the rastreador's deposition is a positive demonstration; it would be ridiculous and absurd to dispute it. The culprit accordingly yields to a witness whom he regards as the finger of God pointing him out. I have had some acquaintance myself with Calibar, who has practiced his profession for forty consecutive years in one province. He is now about eighty years old, and of venerable and dignified appearance, though bowed down by age. When his fabulous reputation is mentioned to him, he replies: "I am good for nothing now; there are the boys." The "boys" who have studied under so famous a master are his sons. The story is that his best horse-trappings were once stolen while he was absent on a journey to Buenos Aires. His wife covered one of the thief's footprints with a tray. Two months afterwards Calibar returned, looked at the footprint, which by that time had become blurred and could not have been made out by other eyes, after which he spoke no more of the circumstances. A year and a half later Calibar might have been seen walking through a street in the outskirts of the town with his eyes on the ground. He turned into a house, where he found his trappings, by that time blackened by use and nearly worn out. He had come upon the trail of the thief nearly two years after the robbery.

In 1830, a criminal under sentence of death having escaped from prison, Calibar was employed to search for him. The unhappy man, aware that he would be tracked, had taken all the precautions suggested to him by the image of the scaffold, but they were taken in vain. Perhaps they only assured his destruction; for as Calibar's reputation was hazarded, his jealous self-esteem made him ardent in accomplishing a task which would demonstrate the wonderful sharpness of his sight though it insured the destruction of another man. The fugitive had left as few traces as the nature of the ground would permit; he had crossed whole squares on tiptoe; afterwards he had leaped upon low walls; he had turned back after crossing one place; but Calibar followed him without losing the trail. If he missed the way for a moment, he found it again, exclaiming: "Where are you?" Finally the trail entered a watercourse in the suburbs in which the fugitive had sought to elude the rastreador. In vain! Calibar went along the bank without uneasiness or hesitation. At last he stops, examines some plants, and says: "He came out here; there are no footprints, but these drops of water on the herbage are the sign!" On coming to a vineyard, Calibar reconnoitered the mud walls around it and said: "He is in there." The party of soldiers looked till they were tired, and came back to report the failure of the search. "He has not come out," was the only answer of the rastreador, who would not even take the trouble to make a second investigation. In fact, he had not come out, but he was taken and executed the next day.

In 1831 some political prisoners were planning an escape; all was ready, and outside help had been secured. On the point of making the attempt, "What shall be done about Calibar?" said one. "To be sure, Calibar!" said the others in dismay. Their relations prevailed upon Calibar to be ill for four full days after the escape, which was thus without difficulty effected.

What a mystery is this of the rastreador! What microscopic power is developed in the visual organs of these men! How sublime a creature is that which God made in His image and likeness!

THE BAQUEANO, OR PATHFINDER. Next to the rastreador comes the *baqueano,* a personage of distinction, and one who controls the fate of individuals and of provinces. The baqueano is a grave and reserved gaucho, who knows every span of a hundred and fifty thousand square miles of plain, wood, and mountain! He is the most thorough topographer, the only man whom a general consults in directing the movements of his campaign. The baqueano is always at his side. Modest and mute as a garden wall, he is in possession of every secret of the campaign; the fate of the army, the issue of a battle, the conquest of a province, all depend upon him. The baqueano almost always discharges his duty with fidelity, but the general does not place full confidence in him.

Conceive the situation of a commander condemned to be attended by a traitor, from whom he has to obtain the information without which he cannot succeed. A baqueano finds a little path crossing the road which he is following; he knows to what distant watering-place it leads. If he finds a thousand such paths, some of them even three hundred miles apart, he is acquainted with each and knows whence it comes and whither it goes. He knows the hidden fords of a hundred rivers and streams above or below the ordinary place of crossing. He can point out a convenient path through a hundred distinct and extensive swamps.

In the deepest darkness of the night, surrounded by boundless plains or by forests, while his companions are astray and at a loss, he rides around them inspecting the trees; if there are none, he dismounts and stoops to examine the shrubs and satisfies himself of his points of the compass. He then mounts and reassures his party by saying: "We are in a straight line from such a place, so many miles from the houses; we must travel southwards." And he sets off in the direction he has indicated, without uneasiness, without hurrying to confirm his judgment by arriving at the town, and without answering the objections suggested to the others by fear or bewilderment.

If even this is insufficient, or if he finds himself upon the pampas in the impenetrable darkness, he pulls up herbs from different places, smells their roots and the earth about them, chews their foliage, and, by often repeating this proceeding, assures himself of the neighborhood of some lake or stream, either of salt or of fresh water, of which he avails himself upon finding it to set himself exactly right. It is said that General Rosas knows the pasturage of every estate in the south of Buenos Aires by its taste.

If the baqueano belongs to the pampas, where no road exists, and a traveler asks him to show the way straight to a place a hundred and fifty miles off, he pauses a moment, reconnoiters the horizon, examines the ground, fixes his eyes upon some point, and gallops off straight as an arrow until he changes his course for reasons known only to himself, and keeps up his gallop day and night till he arrives at the place named.

The baqueano also announces the approach of the enemy; that is, that they are within thirty miles; and he also detects the direction in which they are approaching by means of the movements of the ostriches, deer, and guanacos which fly in certain directions. At shorter distances he notices the clouds of dust and estimates the number of the hostile force by their density. "They have two thousand men," he says, "five hundred," "two hundred"; and the commander acts upon this assumption, which is almost always infallible. If the condors and crows are wheeling in circles through the air, he can tell whether there are troops hidden thereabouts, or whether a recently abandoned camp, or simply a dead animal is the attractive object. The baqueano knows how far one place is from another, the number of days and hours which the journey requires, and, besides, some unknown by-way through which the passage may be made in half the time, so as to end in a surprise; and expeditions for the surprise of towns a hundred and fifty miles away are thus undertaken, and generally with success, by parties of peasants. This may be thought an exaggeration. No! General Rivera, of the Banda Oriental, is a simple baqueano, who knows every tree that grows anywhere in the Republic of Uruguay. The Brazilians would not have occupied that country if he had not aided them; nor, but for him, would the Argentines have set it free.

This man, at once general and baqueano, overpowered Oribe, who was supported by Rosas, after a contest of three years; and at the present day were he in the field against it, the whole power of Buenos Aires, with its numerous armies, which are spread all over Uruguay, might gradually fade away by means of a surprise today, by a post cut off tomorrow, by some victory which he could turn to his own advantage by his knowledge of some route to the enemy's rear or by some other unnoticed or trifling circumstance.

General Rivera began his study of the ground in 1804, when making war upon the government as an outlaw; afterwards he waged war upon the outlaws as a government officer; next upon the King as a patriot; and later upon the patriots as a peasant; upon the Argentines as a Brazilian chieftain; and upon the Brazilians as an Argentine general; upon Lavalleja as President; upon President Oribe as a proscribed chieftain; and finally upon Rosas, the ally of Oribe, as a general of Uruguay; in all which positions he has had abundance of time to learn something of the art of the baqueano.

THE GAUCHO OUTLAW. The example of this type of character, to be found in certain places, is an outlaw, a squatter, a kind of misanthrope. He is Cooper's Hawkeye or Trapper, with all the knowledge of the wilderness possessed by the latter, and with all his aversion to the settlements of the whites, but without his natural morality or his friendly relations with the savages. The name of gaucho outlaw is not applied to him wholly as an uncomplimentary epithet. The law has been for many years in pursuit of him. His name is dreaded — spoken under the breath, but not in hate, and almost respectfully. He is a mysterious personage; his abode is the pampas; his lodgings are the thistle-fields; he lives on partridges and hedgehogs, and whenever he is disposed to regale himself upon a tongue, he lassos a cow, throws her without assistance, kills her, takes his favorite morsel, and leaves the rest for the carrion birds. The gaucho outlaw will make his appearance in a place just left by soldiers, will talk in a friendly way with the admiring group of good gauchos around him, provide himself with tobacco and yerba maté, which makes a refreshing beverage; and if he discovers the soldiers, he mounts his horse quietly and directs his steps leisurely to the wilderness, not even deigning to look back. He is seldom pursued; that would be killing horses to no purpose, for the beast of the gaucho outlaw is a bay courser, as noted in his own way as his master. If the gaucho outlaw ever happens to fall unawares into the hands of the soldiers, he sets upon the densest masses of his assailants and breaks through them with the help of a few slashes left by his knife upon the faces or bodies of his opponents; and lying along the ridge of his horse's back to avoid the bullets sent after him, he hastens toward the wilderness, until, having left his pursuers at a convenient distance, he pulls up and travels at his ease. The poets of the vicinity add this new exploit to the biography of the desert hero, and his renown flies through all the vast region around. Sometimes he appears before the scene of a rustic festival with a young woman whom he has carried off and takes a place in the dance with his partner, goes through the figures of the *cielito,* and disappears, unnoticed. Another day he brings the girl he has seduced to the house of her offended family, sets her down from his horse's croup, and, heedless of the parents' curses by which he is followed, quietly betakes himself to his boundless abode.

This white-skinned savage, at war with society and proscribed by the laws, is no more depraved at heart than the inhabitants of the settlements. The reckless outlaw who attacks a whole troop

22

does no harm to the traveler. The gaucho outlaw is no bandit or highwayman; murderous assaults do not suit his temper, as robbery would not suit the character of the *churriador* (sheep-stealer). To be sure, he steals; but this is his profession, his trade, his science. He steals horses. He arrives, for instance, at the camp of a train from the interior; its master offers to buy of him a horse of some unusual color, of a particular shape and quality, with a white star on the shoulder. The gaucho collects his thoughts, considers a moment, and replies, after a short silence: "There is no such horse alive." What thoughts have been passing through the gaucho's mind? In that moment his memory has traversed a thousand estates upon the pampa; he has seen and examined every horse in the province, with its marks, color, and special traits, and he has convinced himself that not one of them has a star on its shoulder; some have one on their foreheads, others have white spots on their haunches. Is this power of memory amazing? No! Napoleon knew two hundred thousand soldiers by name and remembered, when he saw any one of them, all the facts relating to him. Therefore, if nothing impossible is required of him, the gaucho will deliver upon a designated day and spot just such a horse as has been asked for, and with no less punctuality if he has been paid in advance. His honor is as sensitive upon this point as that of a gambler about his debts.

Sometimes he travels to the country about Córdoba or Santa Fé. Then he may be seen crossing the pampa behind a small body of horses; if anyone meets him, he follows his course without approaching the newcomer unless he is requested to do so.

THE JUNGLE

THE JUNGLE IS THE LEGENDARY LANDSCAPE of America. The conquistadors who chopped their way through the wall of green growth that was the shield and defense of our virgin lands left an enduring impression of their exploits in the books of their chroniclers. America, seen from Europe, seemed one solid jungle that men gazed upon in terror, but whose very mystery drew them on, spellbound. It was feared, and yet there was the urge to conquer it. Over the span of four hundred years the slopes of the mountains have been cleared. Axe and machete have gleamed in the hands of the settlers of the uplands until these wild lands of Columbus's day are now tame and submissive. But even today the jungle still spreads over the interior of tropical America and from the foot of the Andes reaches out over the basins of the great rivers. The Orinoco, the Amazon, the Madeira, and the Paraguay form a gigantic flower which opens in the heart of seven nations: Brazil, Venezuela, Colombia, Ecuador, Bolivia, and Paraguay, and pour their waters into seas which extend from the Caribbean to the mouth of the Plata. This jungle, in which the great English writer William Henry Hudson saw only swarms of butterflies and beautiful serpents, has received other less flattering names than that of *Green Mansions* which he gave to his book. Hardenburg wrote about the same landscape, but he called his book *The Devil's Paradise*. Alberto Rangel agrees with Hardenburg, and his novel is entitled *El Inferno Verde* (*Green Hell*). José Eustasio Rivera, in turn, called his book *La Vorágine* (*The Vortex*).

The fact is that since the sixteenth century, when the tyrant Lope de Aguirre descended the waters of the Amazon, the weight of the jungle seemed always on the side of violence and death. Aguirre with his own dagger killed his captain, Pedro de Ursua, and after usurping the command and committing acts which even in those days were considered excessive refused to yield until he had first killed his wife and daughter. He was drawn and quartered. As a precedent the story could hardly be improved upon. Sir Roger Casement once published in London a report on the cruelties of certain gentlemen who milked the white sap of the rubber from the udders of the Amazon jungle with the hands of slaves. His account was so hair-raising that the publishers were unwilling to print the complete report because they thought readers would be unable to endure it. Between 1900 and 1911, says Sir Roger, four thousand tons of rubber were collected in Putumayo at the cost of thirty thousand lives. Seen from an airplane the jungle looks like a mossy carpet that reaches as far as the eye can see; above it the clouds frisk like lambs, and the rivers, which disappear amidst the vegetation, are visible only at times and resemble strings of glass. Seen from within, from the trails, the jungle is a strange fantastic world where many of the notions that men have used to guide themselves by, in the physical or the moral sphere, cease to exist. In a greenish light the tree-trunks rise, swathed in lianas or dead leaves. At midday it is light; as night approaches, little phosphorescent eyes gleam in the shadows, but never a ray of sunlight comes through so a man can tell the hour or the direction. If he wanders a few steps from the trail he is lost, for he will be unable to find his way back to it. His screams of despair will be lost in the perennial concert of songs and whistles of parrots, monkeys, and insects, a concert as bewitched as the jungle itself. This is the world José Eustasio Rivera describes in a fascinating book written a few years ago and which has been translated into English, French, German, and Russian. Rivera was one of Colombia's great poets, who painted the landscape of the country in sonnets. He died in New York in 1928, at the age of thirty-nine.

THE VORTEX

JOSÉ EUSTASIO RIVERA

For the first time I saw the inhuman jungle in all its horror, saw the pitiless struggle for existence. Deformed trees were held imprisoned by creepers. Lianas bound them together in a death grip. Stretched from tree to palm in long elastic curves, like carelessly hung nets, they caught falling leaves, branches, and fruits, held them for years until they sagged and burst like rotten bags, scattering blind reptiles, rusty salamanders, hairy spiders, and decayed vegetable matter over the underbrush.

Everywhere the *matapalo* — the pulpy creeper of the forests — sticks its tentacles on the tree-trunks, twisting and strangling them, injecting itself into them, and fusing with them in a painful metempsychosis. The *bachaqueros* vomit forth trillions of devastating ants. These mow down the mantle of the jungles and return to their tunnels over the wide swaths they cut, carrying leaves aloft like the banners of an army of extinction. The *comejen* grub gnaws at the trees like quick-spreading syphilis, boring unseen from within, rotting tissue and pulverizing bark, until the weight of the branches that are still living brings the giant crashing to the ground.

Meanwhile the earth continues its successive renovations: at the foot of the colossus that falls, new germs are budding; pollen is flying in the midst of miasmas; everywhere is the reek of fermentation, steaming shadows, the sopor of death, the enervating process of procreation. Where is that solitude poets sing of? Where are those butterflies like translucent flowers, the magic birds, those singing streams? Poor phantasies of those who know only domesticated retreats!

No cooing nightingales here, no Versaillian gardens or sentimental vistas! Instead the croaking of dropsical frogs, the tangled misanthropic undergrowth, the stagnant backwaters and swamps. Here the aphrodisiac parasite that covers the ground with dead insects, the disgusting blooms that throb with sensual palpitations, their sticky smell intoxicating as a drug; the malignant liana, the hairs of which blind animals; the *pringamosa* that irritates the skin; the berry of the *curuju,* a rainbow-hued globe that holds only a caustic ash; the purging grape; the bitter nut of the corojo palm.

At night, unknown voices, phantasmagoric lights, funereal silences. It is death that passes, giving life. Fruits fall, and on falling give promise of new seed. Leaves come to earth with a faint sighing, to become fertilizer for the roots of the parent tree. Crunching jaws are heard, devouring with the fear of being devoured. Warning whistles, dying wails, beasts belching. And when dawn showers its tragic glory over the jungles, the clamor of survivors again begins: the zoom of the shrieking guan; the wild boar crashing through the underbrush; the laughter of ridiculous monkeys. All for the brief joy of a few more hours of life!

This sadistic and virgin jungle casts premonitions of coming danger over one's spirits. Vegetable life is a sensitive thing, the psychology of which we ignore. In these desolate places, only our presentiments understand the language it speaks. Under its influence man's nerves become taut and ready to attack, are ready for treachery and ambush. Our senses confuse their tasks; the eye feels, the back sees, the nose explores, the legs calculate, and the blood cries out: "Flee! Flee!"

And yet, it is civilized man who is the champion of destruction. There is something magnificent in the story of these pirates who enslave their peons, exploit the environment, and struggle with the jungle. Buffeted by misfortune, they leave the anonymity of cities to plunge into the wilderness, seeking a purpose for their sterile life. Delirious from malaria, they loose themselves of their conscience and adapt themselves to the environment; and with no arms but the rifle and the machete, they suffer the most atrocious needs, while longing for pleasures and plenty. They live exposed to the elements, always ravenous, even naked, for here clothes rot on one's body.

Then some day, on the rock of some river, they build their thatched hut and appoint themselves "masters of the enterprise." Although the jungle is their enemy, they don't know whom to fight; so they fall upon one another and kill and subdue their own kind during intervals in their onslaught on the forests; and at times their trail is like that left by an avalanche. Every year the rubber workers in Colombia destroy millions of trees, while in Venezuela the balata rubber tree has disappeared. In this way they defraud the coming generations.

The story of El Cayeno symbolizes the fierce urge of these men. He escaped from a celebrated prison that has the ocean as its moat. Although he knew that the guards feed the sharks in order to keep them swimming near the walls, he threw himself into the water without removing his irons. He reached the banks of the Papunagua, attacked a settlement, and subdued the fugitive rubber-tappers. He established a monopoly of the exploitation of rubber, and lived with his henchmen and his slaves on the Guaracu. The distant lights of his settlement twinkled through the heavy foliage one night when we finally drew close to it, and then waited until daybreak before advancing any farther.

Who could have told us that we were to follow the same path of cruelty!

On the trip over this trail to the Guaracu, I had made a humiliating discovery: my physical well-being was only apparent. My body, wasted by fevers, tired very easily. On the other hand, my companions seemed immune to fatigue; and even old man Silva, despite his years and scars, was more vigorous on the marches. Every now and again they had to stop to wait for me; and even though they lightened me of my load, relieving me of my knapsack and carbine, I had to continue forcing myself on, my pride keeping me from falling to the ground and confessing my weakness.

I traveled barefooted, barelegged, peevish, cutting through thickets and swamps in a lofty forest the tangled roots of which have forgotten what light of the sun is like. Fidel's hand helped me as we walked the logs that served us as bridges; and the dogs howled, seeking to be let loose in that hunter's paradise, which even as such aroused no enthusiasm in me.

This physical inferiority of mine made me distrustful, irritable, testy. Old man Silva, of course, was practically in charge of us during the trip, and I began to feel jealous of him. I began to suspect that he had chosen this route purposely, so that he could convince me of my physical inability to handle El Cayeno. Don Clemente, too, lost no opportunity to make me conscious of the horrors of life in that settlement, and how remote was the possibility of escaping from there. Escape — that perennial dream of all rubber-tappers, who see it always before their eyes and yet never attempt it, because they know that death closes all the exits of the jungle.

These warnings found an echo in my comrades, and my advisers became more numerous. I would not listen to them.

"Although you accompany me," I said, "I know I'm going alone. Are you tired? You can walk behind me."

Then, silent, they went ahead; and while they waited for me to catch up with them whispered together, gazed at me askance. That made me indignant. I felt a sudden hatred for them. Probably they ridiculed my pride. Or had they been following a route that did not lead to Guaracu?

"Listen, old man Silva!" I cried, seizing him. "If you don't take me to the Isana, I'll shoot you!"

The old fellow realized I wasn't joking. Nor did he show surprise. He knew the forces of the jungle had gripped me. Kill a man! And what of it? Why not? It was a natural thing, Protect myself, free myself that way? What quicker method for solving the daily conflicts that arose in the jungle?

And that, O jungle! is how all who have fallen into your vortex have been transformed.

Crouching in the thicket, our hands on our rifles, we could discern the flickering lights of the palm-leaf huts of the Guaracu settlement. We were afraid of being discovered. It would be necessary to spend the night in that hiding-place, fireless. A river sobbed near by in the darkness. It was the Isana.

"Don Clemente," I said, embracing him, "when it comes to breaking a trail you're a true genius."

"Nevertheless, there was a time when I lost all confidence in myself. For two months I roamed the rubber forest of Yaguanari, lost."

"I remember your speaking of it. When you fled for the Vaupes . . ."

"We were seven fugitives — latex-gatherers . . ."

"And your companions wanted to kill you . . ."

"They thought I was leading them astray purposely."

"And sometimes they maltreated you . . ."

"And other times begged me on their knees that I save them."

"And they kept you tied up for a whole night . . ."

"Fearing I'd abandon them."

"And then they separated to find trails of their own . . ."

"But they only found one leading to death."

This unhappy old man, Clemente Silva, seemed to have a monopoly of misfortune.

Since that day when on leaving Iquitos for Manaos he had heard of the death of his son, he had realized that to carry out his vow — to bury Lucianito's bones beside his wife's — the only hope was in prolonging his slavery. He had to continue as a rubber worker, until the earth had washed his son's bones clean and allowed him to exhume the remains of that youth he loved so deeply. The jungles indirectly claimed him as a fugitive; but it was the spirit of Lucianito that called him back.

Even had La Madona wanted to free him, what would he have gained from freedom? Physical want would oblige him to sign up with some other rubber lord, who would send him away from the Vaupes. In Manaos he combed the agencies frequented by the "immigrants" seeking work, only to emerge from these slave marts discouraged and heartbroken. The *patrones* he found out were "advancing" men only to the Madeira, the Purus, and the Ucayali. And what he wanted was to go to that accursed river where at the foot of some rapids was a tomb, overgrown with underbrush, marked only by four white stones.

The Turk Pezil was not gathering latex in the Vaupes district, but he offered to take him to the upper regions of the Río Negro — and that was moving in the right direction. But Pezil pretended he did not want to buy Don Clemente, and he finally acceded to the old man's entreaties only on the condition that La Madona would agree to buy him back should the work of "the Colombian" not be satisfactory. He took Silva to his pretentious estate in Naranjal, located across the river from Yaguanari. There he had Don Clemente for some time, giving him simple tasks, treating him well, but always with the vigilance of the disdainful and taciturn Moslem.

But one day some women in the kitchen started squabbling and awoke their lord, who was sleeping his siesta. Don Clemente was on their veranda, studying a map of the jungles hanging on the wall. Pezil, irate on being disturbed, found him there and, shouting loudly, ordered Don Clemente to strip the culprits to the waist and flog them. Old man Silva refused to obey. That same afternoon he was dispatched across the river to Yaguanari as a latex-gatherer.

One of the women involved in the scullery wrangle had been a maid of La Madona's — the one who had known Luciano Silva in the Vaupes region when he was Doña Zoraida's paramour. "She had not seen him dead" — but she knew the grave, near the Yavarate; and she had told Don Clemente how to find it.

The Colombian's disobedience did not spare her a whipping. The savage Turk, lash in each hand, covered her with blood and bruises in short order. Moaning in the pantry, she scribbled a note to her lover, a tapper in the rubber groves, and begged Don Clemente to deliver it without omitting any details of the flogging.

This lover of hers, Manuel Cardoso, was the foreman of a squad on the Yurubaxi. On knowing what had happened, he vowed he'd kill Pezil wherever he might find him; and to revenge himself meanwhile, he started inciting the men to flee with the rubber stores.

Old man Silva, afraid of incriminating himself in what might be only a plot against him, pretended to oppose the idea. Nevertheless, when the men gathered to smoke the latex, he sounded them out. Their reply was always the same: "Cardoso knows that there's no guide able to tackle these jungles."

At night the rubber-gatherers again would take up their foreman's proposal, as enticing as it was impossible of realization. In fact, it was discussed chiefly because there was little else to talk about.

"It's clear that to escape by the Río Negro would be foolhardy; the master's launches are like bloodhounds."

"Yet by following the Cababuri up to its source it's an easy matter to descend the Maturaca and enter the Casiquiare River."

"That's true. But the Río Negro is a couple of miles wide and it would be next to impossible to cross it without being seen. The tributaries on the left bank must also be disregarded. A better plan would be to go up this Yurubaxi River; it's said that two months' canoeing will get one to a small river that flows into the Caqueta."

"There's no direct route to the Vaupes?"

"Who'd think of such a stupid thing?"

The hut was on a rocky elevation, just high enough to survive the annual floods, an only refuge in the jungles when the rivers lost their outlines and spread through the forests. Every month the launch from Naranjal came to load rubber and leave provisions. The workers were few, and beriberi shrank their numbers, not to mention those who perished in the swamps, falling into them, sick with fevers, from the trees they climbed to wound.

Entire months often passed without the latex-gatherers seeing the face of their foreman. Working down the river, they took shelter under rude palm-leaf coverings, coming to the main shack only when they had a shipment of latex ready. They brought it smoked and rolled into balls, floating them down the river. As they seldom penetrated the jungle very far from the river banks, their sense of direction was not well developed. This helped Don Clemente to acquire a reputation as guide. He would plunge deep into the jungle, sink his machete into a tree, and, days afterwards, guide them back to it, starting from any point the workers selected.

One morning at sunrise came unexpected disaster. The sick workers who had remained in the main hut to doctor their livers suddenly heard shouts from the river. They hastily gathered on the rocky ledge. Floating down the middle of the stream, like enormous black ducks, were the balls of rubber; and behind them came a peon in a small dugout, pushing with his pole the spheres that tarried in the eddies and backwaters. As he herded his black flock into the inlet of the little bay, he raised a cry more frightful than any war-cry:

"Tambochas! Tambochas! And the men are isolated!"

Tambochas! That meant suspending work, leaving shelter, throwing barriers of fire across the trail, and seeking refuge elsewhere. An invasion of carnivorous ants, born who knows where, emigrating to die as winter comes, sweeping the hills for leagues and leagues with the rustle and crackle of a distant forest fire. Wingless wasps, with red heads and lemon-colored bodies, scattering terror in their path because of their venomous bite and swarming multitudes. Every cave, every crevice, every hole — trees, shrubs, nests, beehives — everything suffered from the overpowering flow of that heavy and fetid wave that devours young birds, rodents, reptiles, and puts to flight whole villages of men and beasts.

The news spread consternation. The peons of the camp scurried around madly, gathering tools and equipment.

"On which side is the swarm coming?" asked Manuel Cardoso.

"On both banks, it seems. The tapirs and peccaries are plunging into the river from this side, but the bees are swarming on the other side."

"Who are the workers who are isolated?"

"Five in El Silencio swamp — they don't even have a boat."

"What can we do? They'll have to shift for themselves! We can't help. Who'd risk losing himself in these swamps?"

"I," replied old man Clemente Silva.

And a young Brazilian youth named Lauro Coutinho joined him. "I'll go, too," he said. "My brother's there."

Gathering together what provisions they could, and supplied with arms and matches, the two set out along a trail that plunged into the jungle toward the Marie River.

They traveled hastily over oozing mud and through tangled underbrush, eyes and ears on the alert. Of a sudden, as the old man was clearing a path before him, forcing a trail toward El Silencio marsh, Lauro Coutinho stopped him.

"Now's the time to escape!"

The same thought had already crossed Don Clemente's mind, but he gave no sign of his pleasure at the suggestion.

"We should consult the others. . . ."

"I can assure you they'll agree — without hesitation."

And he was right. They found the five men on the following day, in a rude shelter, shooting craps on a handkerchief spread on the earth, drunk from the palmachonta wine they were imbibing from a gourd that went its ceaseless rounds.

"Ants? To hell with the ants! We laugh at tambochas! To escape, escape! With a guide like you — even from hell you could lead us!"

And there they go through the jungles with the illusion of freedom before them, laughing, full of plans, praising their guide, promising him their friendship, their remembrance, their gratitude! Lauro Coutinho has cut a palm leaf and carries it aloft like a banner. Souza Machado will not abandon his ball of crude rubber. It weighs ten pounds, but with its price he hopes to enjoy two nights of a woman's caresses, a white and fair woman, fragrant of roses and brandy. The Italian Peggi babbles of going to a city and getting a job as cook in a hotel where there is an abundance of left-overs and tips are generous. Coutinho the elder wants to marry a wench who boasts an income. The Indian Venancio wants to spend the rest of his days making dugouts. Pedro Fajardo aspires to buy a cottage that will shelter his blind old mother. Don Clemente dreams of finding the grave. It is a procession of unfortunates, a march from misery to death.

And which the route they sought? The Curi-curiari River. From there they would go up the Río Negro, two hundred miles above Naranjal, passing to Umarituba to seek shelter. Señor Castanheira Fontes was a good man. He would help them. There a broad horizon would spread itself before them. In case of capture, the explanation was obvious; they were fleeing before the tambochas. Let them ask the foreman.

On the fourth day through the jungles the crisis began; food was scarce and the swamps interminable. They stopped to rest. They took off their shirts and tore them into strips to wrap around their legs, tortured by the leeches that lurked in the muddy waters. Souza Machado, made generous by fatigue, slashed his ball of rubber with a knife and shared it with his companions. Fajardo would not receive his portion. Souza took it. It was black gold and not to be despised.

A thoughtless one asked:

"Where now?"

And all replied, reproachful:

"Forward! of course."

But the guide was lost. He advanced doubtfully, feeling his way, yet without stopping or saying anything in order not to alarm the others. Three times within an hour he found himself back at the same swamp, but fortunately his companions did not recognize it. Concentrating all his being in his memory, he saw before him the map he had studied so often on the veranda at Naranjal. He saw the sinuous lines, spreading like a network of veins over a spot of palish green. Unforgettable names stood out: Teiya, Marie, Curi-curiari. But what a difference between this wilderness and the map, which shrinks in reproduction! Who would have thought that that piece of paper, scarcely large enough to be covered by his open hands, embraced such vast stretches, such dismal jungles, such deadly swamps! And he, experienced trail-breaker, who so easily passed his finger from one line to another, spanning rivers and jungles, parallels and meridians — how could he ever have been fool enough to believe his feet would move as lightly as his fingers?

Inwardly he began to pray. If God would give him the sun but for a moment. . . . But nothing! Cold grayness — foliage sweating a blue vapor. Forward! The sun will not shine for the sad!

One of the men suddenly declared emphatically that he heard whistling. All stopped. Only a buzzing in his ears. Souza Machado wanted to be in the midst of the others. He swore the trees made uncanny gestures at him.

They grew nervous. Forebodings of misfortune pressed heavily upon them. A careless word and the repressed emotions might be released — in panic, rage, madness. Each struggled to resist. Forward!

Lauro Coutinho made a sorry effort to appear carefree. He bantered with Souza Machado, who had stopped to throw away the remains of his rubber ball. Machado attempted hilarity. They talked awhile. Then someone, I don't know who, asked Don Clemente some questions.

"Silence!" growled the Italian. "Remember that pilots and guides must not be spoken to!"

But old man Silva, stopping short, raised his arms as one who surrenders to captors and, facing his friends, sobbed: "We are lost!"

Instantly the unhappy group, with their eyes lifted to the lofty branches, howled like dogs, raising a chorus of blasphemy and prayer:

"Inhuman God! Save us, O God! We are lost!"

"We are lost!" Simple and common words — yet uttered in the jungles they strike terror in the heart. To the mind of the person who hears them comes the vision of a man-consuming hell, a gaping mouth swallowing men whom hunger and disappointment place in the jaws.

Neither vows, nor warnings, nor the tears of the guide, who promised to find his way again, could serve to calm the men's panic.

"This old fellow is to blame! He lost his way because he wanted to go to the Vaupes!"

"Wretch! Bandit! You were deceiving us. You were taking us to sell us, God knows where!"

"Yes, you criminal! But God blasted your schemes!"

Seeing that his crazed companions might kill him, old man Silva started to run, but the treacherous lianas of a tree caught his legs and tripped him. There they tied him up, while Peggi urged that they rip him to shreds. Then it was that Don Clemente spoke the words that saved him.

"You want to kill me?" he said. "How can you do anything without me? I'm your only hope!"

The men stopped mechanically.

"Yes, yes, it's necessary that he live in order to save us."

"But without letting him loose, or he'll escape!"

And although they would not unfasten him, they knelt before him to beg him to save them.

"Don't desert us!"

"Let's return to the hut!"

"If you abandon us, we'll starve!"

Don Clemente's explanations gradually made them amenable to reason. What had happened, he told them, was nothing unusual in the lives of guides and hunters. It was foolish to give up hope at the very first mishap, especially as there were so many ways of getting out of the difficulty. Why had they scared him? Why had they thought of the possibility of getting lost? Had he not told them again and again to resist all such thoughts, so easily aroused by the accursed jungles that seem eager to bewilder and confuse men? Had he not warned them not to look at the trees, because they beckon to one; not to listen to murmurings because they whisper things; not to speak, because the heavy foliage echoes back the voice? Far from following these instructions, they jested with the forest, and its witchery fell upon them, spreading from one to another as if by contagion; and he, too, although walking on ahead, had started feeling the influence of the evil spirits; the jungle began to move, the trees to dance before his eyes, the undergrowth to resist his efforts to blaze a trail; the branches hid from his knife, or sometimes sought to wrest it from him with a mighty grip. Who was to blame?

And now why the devil start yelling? And what good would shooting do? Who but the jaguar would run to find them? Would they like a visit from him? If so, they could wait until nightfall. He'd come then!

This terrified them and they were silent. Yet had they wished it, they could not have made their voices heard more than a couple of yards — their outcries had parched their throats. They spoke hoarsely, with the guttural pantings of geese.

Long before the sun was pluming with crimson those upper reaches they could not see, the smudge fire had to be lighted, for darkness falls upon the forest early. They cut branches on which to rest, scattering them on the mud, there to await the anguish of the inky shadows. Oh, the torture of a long night of hunger, of thoughts that terrify; yawning, always yawning, knowing that the next day the yawning will be worse! Oh, the depressing effect of the incessant sobbing in the shadows, of comforting words that are in vain, for they only hide death! Lost, lost! Sleeplessness brought its train of phantoms — and the agony of the helpless who feel unseen eyes spying on them from the darkness. The sounds came — the nocturnal voices, the creeping steps — silences as appalling as gaps in eternity.

Don Clemente, his head in his hands, searched his memory for some clarifying hint. Only the sky could help him. Let it only tell him where the light of dawn came. That would be enough to plan another route.

Through a clear space in the lofty ceiling of foliage, a skylight in the forest, he saw a fragment of blue, fractured by the riblike branches of a withered bough. He recalled his map again. To see the sun, to see the sun! That was the key. If those tall cones of green, which every day saw it pass over them, could only speak! Why should the silent trees refuse to tell a man what to do that he might not die? And, thinking again on God, he began to pray to the jungle, a prayer that begged forgiveness for the injury done the forests through bantering talk.

To climb one of those giants was next to impossible: the enormous trunks, the remote branches, dizziness lurking in the foliage to overtake the one who dared. If Lauro Coutinho, dozing nervously, were to try. . . .

Silva was about to call him when a noise, as of rats gnawing on fine wood, scratched across the stillness. It was the teeth of his companions, chewing on the hard seeds of the vegetable ivory tree.

Don Clemente felt a surge of compassion. He would console them, even though by lying.

"What is it?" they whispered, bringing their shadowed faces near.

And anxious hands felt the knots of the cords that bound him.

"We are saved!"

Dulled with joy, they repeated the words: "Saved! Saved!" They knelt down and pressed the mud with their knees, for suffering had left them contrite. Without even asking what it was that offered them salvation, they gave vent to a hoarse prayer of thanks. It was enough that another promised it.

Don Clemente received embraces, entreaties of forgiveness, apologies to amend the wrong they had done him. Some took all the credit for the miracle:

"The prayers of my little mother!"

"The Masses that I offered!"

"The blessed amulet I carry!"

And meanwhile, in the shadows, death must have laughed!

Dawn broke.

The hope that sustained them accentuated the tragedy on their faces. Emaciated, feverish, with bloodshot eyes and fluttering pulses, they waited for the sun to rise. Their actions inspired fear. They had forgotten how to smile, or if they thought of smiling, only a frightful grimace moved their lips.

Vainly they searched for a place where they might see the sun. Then softly it began to rain. No one said a word. They understood. The sun was not to be theirs.

They decided to return, traveling over the trails traversed the previous day, skirting a swamp where footprints left tiny pools into which waters gurgled — and wiped away the traces. Yet the guide stuck to the route. Silently they kept on until about nine in the morning, when they entered a heavy growth of coarse and matted bamboo. There they encountered flocks of rabbits and trogons, which, stupefied, ran between their legs seeking refuge. A few moments later and a sound as of swirling rapids was heard reverberating through the wilderness.

"Good God! The tambochas!"

Flight was the only thought then. Turning, they stumbled back and then plunged into the swamp until the stagnant waters swept over their shoulders. Better the leeches than the ants.

From there they watched the first swarm pass by. Like ashes

thrown from a distant conflagration, clouds of fugitive roaches and coleoptera swept down to the waters, while the edges of the marsh grew dense with arachnids and reptiles, forcing the men to splash the foul waters so that the insects would not come toward them. A continual tremor agitated the ground, as if the vegetation of the jungles were boiling. From under trunks and roots came the tumultuous invaders; over the trees spread a dark stain, sheathing the trunks like a flowing shell that crept upward implacably to torture the branches, plunder the nests, swarm the apertures and cracks. A blind weasel, a tardy lizard, a new-born rat — these were coveted prey for the avaricious army which, grating shrilly, stripped the bones of flesh like some fast-dissolving acid.

How long did the martyrdom of those men last? Buried to the chin in the slimy liquid, with terror-stricken eyes, they watched the swarms of the enemy passing, passing, and again passing. Nerve-racking hours, during which they sipped and sipped the bitter depths of slow torture. When at length the last swarm was sweeping into the distance, they tried to emerge; but their limbs were numb, too weak to wrench themselves from the hungry mud that gripped them.

Yet they must not die there. They must struggle out. The Indian Venancio managed to grasp some plants and began to pull. Then he caught hold of a clump of reeds. Several stray tambochas gnawed the flesh of his hands, eating deeply. Little by little he felt the clammy mold that gripped him loosening its hold. His legs, as they tore from the bottom, cracked loudly. "*Upa!* Once more, and don't faint! Courage! Courage!"

He's out. The waters gurgled and bubbled in the hole he left.

Panting, on his back, he heard his despairing comrades calling on him for help. "Let me rest! Let me rest!"

An hour later, by means of branches and lianas, he had managed to get them all out.

This was the last time they suffered together. Which way had they been going? They felt their heads in flames, their bodies stiff. Pedro Fajardo began to cough convulsively. Of a sudden he fell bathed in frothy blood that he vomited in an attack of hemoptysis.

But they could feel no pity for the dying man. Coutinho the elder advised them to lose no time. "Take his knife from his belt and leave him there. Why did he come if he was ill? He mustn't hamper us." So saying, he forced his brother to climb a copaiba to seek the sun.

The unfortunate youth bound his ankles with strips of shirt. Vainly he tried to grip the tree-trunk. They raised him on their shoulders so that he might catch hold higher up. He continued his efforts, but the bark peeled off. He would slide down, to start anew. They held him up, propping him with long, forked branches and feeling their height tripled in their effort to help him. Finally he grasped the first branch. Stomach, arms, chest, and knees shed blood. "Do you see anything? Do you see anything?" they asked. And with his head he answered: "No!"

They no longer remembered to be silent in order not to provoke the jungle. An absurd violence filled them, and the fury of drowning people surged through them, the fury that knows neither friend nor relative, fighting off those who would clamber into a boat that can hold no more. With their hands they gesticulated heavenwards as they called to Lauro Coutinho.

"You see nothing? Climb higher — and look well."

Lauro, on a branch, clutching the trunk, panted without replying. At such a height he seemed a wounded monkey, trying to squirm into frantic hiding from the hunter. "Coward! You must climb higher!" And those below, mad with rage, threatened him.

Suddenly, however, the youth started to descend. A roar of hate rose from the ground. Lauro, terrified, tried to explain. "More tambochas — coming — com — "

The last syllable died in his throat. The elder Coutinho, with a shot from his rifle, had pierced his chest. The youth fell like a plummet.

The fratricide stood still, his eyes on the crumpled, bleeding body.

"My God!" he broke out suddenly. "I've killed my brother — killed my brother!" Then, throwing away his gun, he fled. The others ran too, not knowing where. And they scattered never to meet again.

Many nights later Don Clemente heard them shouting, but he was afraid they would kill him. He, too, had lost all pity. The jungle possessed him. Then remorse set him weeping, although the need for saving his own life justified his act before his conscience. Eventually he went back to look for them. He found the skulls and a few femurs.

Without fire or gun, he wandered two months, reduced almost to imbecility, deprived of his senses, animalized by the jungle, despised even by death, chewing roots, husks, mushrooms like an herbivorous animal, with the sole difference that he had to watch what kind of fruit or berries the monkeys ate in order to avoid the poisonous ones.

But one morning he had a sudden revelation. He stopped before a cananguche palm, and to his mind came the tradition that tells how this species follows the sun, like a sunflower. Never had he given the matter any thought before. He spent anxious moments watching, and he thought he saw the lofty foliage slowly bending, with the rhythm of a head that took exactly twelve hours to move from the right shoulder over to the left. The secret voice filled his soul. Was it possible that this palm, planted in the wilderness like an index pointing to the blue, was showing him his route? True or false, he heard it speak. And he believed! That was all he needed — belief. And from the course the palm tree followed he plotted his own.

So it was that he reached the banks of the Tiquie. That river, narrow and curving, seemed more like a stagnant pond in the marshes than a stream. He began throwing leaves into the waters to see if they moved. The Albuquerque brothers found him thus occupied and, almost dragging him, took him to the shelter.

"Who's that scarecrow you've found?" the rubber-gatherers asked.

"A fugitive who can only say: 'Coutinho! . . . Peggi! . . . Souza Machado! . . .'"

Then after working there a year, he escaped in a dugout to the Vaupes.

Now he's sitting here in my company, waiting for dawn to break before going down to the shacks of Guaracu. Perhaps he's

42

thinking of Yaguanari, of Yavarate, of his lost companions. "Don't go to Yaguanari!" he's always telling me. But I, remembering Alicia and my enemy, cry angrily:

"I'll go! I'll go, I'll go!"

THE UPLANDS

At nine, ten, twelve thousand feet above sea-level broad plateaus spread out upon the loins of the Andes. There the land is level as a lake, and what today are meadows and tilled fields must have been, in prehistoric times, lakes. After crossing a parapet of rough cliffs and pinnacles, the traveler who climbs the mountains suddenly finds himself gazing upon the landscape of the uplands, which is like a miracle of repose. A chronicler of the sixteenth century tells that when the Spaniards of the conquest saw it they cried: "Good land! A land where our sufferings end!" Surrounding the plain there is a circle of hills like the rim of a goblet. And in the background the snow-covered peaks. On one of these plateaus the Incas founded the greatest empire that existed in America prior to Columbus, and one of the greatest of its day, for it covered 1,200,000 square miles and had a population of 8,000,000 subjects of the Descendant of the Sun. For some ten centuries these same copper-colored men — lightened a little by a late Spanish admixture — have been working this land with solicitous care, even caressing it as they moisten it, mold it, and polish it to make their household utensils: the pot that blackens on the three stones of the hearth, the bowl covered with the white foam of the fresh milk. When the Indian potter wants to amuse himself he makes toys: dolls, horses, chickens, pigs, giving free rein to the image of his dreams with his sensitive fingers. Over the emerald fields shines a sun which gives more light than heat, but which has gilded with a touch of legend the life of these men. When the Spaniards arrived, the Indians of the coast did not say to them: "There among the Andes lives an industrious, numerous people." They said: "There is El Dorado." And the conquistadors scaled the heights in mad pursuit of the phantom of gold. To be sure, they found a people that worshipped the disk of gold that is ushered in by the rosy-fingered dawn. For those Indians who did not know, who do not yet know the sea, God was in the golden light of day, in the lake that mirrors the passing of the cloud, where the breeze and the light play amidst the ripple of its waters; in the lizard and the snake, which are of the land and the water; in the changing moon; in the industrious, early rising and constant sun. The Indian is humble, gentle, and secret. He does not tell the truth because the truth is hard and dangerous, but he bears the truth in his soul. He seeks his God — without wasting words — everywhere. He is at once credulous and ironical. He understood his old God, the God of the golden air that enveloped his opaque world, better than his present one. He could touch Him. He could consult Him himself in the mirror of the waters, and He was a God that befitted his solitary soul. He worships his present Divinity, but with certain mental reservations, the outcome of unpleasant experiences of his life.

Baldomero Sanín Cano, Colombia's great writer and the teacher of America, tells this anecdote, which is in itself a treatise of philosophy: "A peasant who had reached his three score and ten was dying, and a priest was helping him to make his peace with God. 'Do you believe,' asked the kindly priest, 'in Almighty God, Maker of heaven and earth?' 'I believe, father,' answered the dying man. 'And do you believe,' the Lord's minister went on, 'that His son came into this world and suffered death on the cross to redeem us?' 'I do,' answered the penitent. 'And do you believe that He will come on the Judgment Day to judge over the quick and the dead?' asked the clergyman. And the peasant, in full possession of his senses, answered: 'I believe, Father; but your Reverence will see how He won't come.'"

Just as the Indians had built up their greatest Empire on the uplands, so did the Spaniards organize their best colonies there. Anyone who has not visited the uplands and has not seen the flocks of llamas, sheep, or Indians descending the hills, crowding into the fold, the market-place, or the church, huddling against one another when the cold winds blow or soothing themselves with the music of flageolet, harp, or flute, does not know our America. Since colonial days the uplands have been the scene of silent struggles. The revolutions which have been ferocious in the torrid valleys became attenuated on the heights. The man of the cool uplands prefers some kind of working arrangement to dramatic conflict. Justice for him is rather an achievement by intelligence than a conquest of arms. It was in this wise that the Incas built up their Empire, bringing nations together through voluntary federation rather than violent coercion. In the uplands politics is preferred to war.

Ciro Alegría, a Peruvian writer, whose book *Broad and Alien is the World,* received first prize in the Latin-American novel contest sponsored by the publishing house of Farrar & Rinehart in 1942, describes the life of the uplands in several of his books. The following pages are taken from *Los Perros hambrientos* (*The Hungry Dogs*).

THE HUNGRY DOGS
CIRO ALEGRÍA

THE SUSTAINED, monotonous barking of the dogs, ear-piercing in sharpness, sad as a lament, beat against the white fleece of the sheep leading the flock. They moved along, with short steady trot, nibbling at the tough ichu grass, dots of white against the gray roughness of the Andean range.

It was a big flock, for it contained a hundred pairs without counting the lambs. Because it must be known that Antuca, the shepherdess, as well as her parents and brothers, counted by pairs. Her arithmetic went as far as a hundred, then started again at the beginning. She would have said "five hundreds" or "seven hundreds" or "nine hundreds"; but as a matter of fact she had no need to speak of such fabulous sums. And to make the matter still simpler, there were the pairs to help her, a custom-hallowed survival of the native system of keeping accounts. After all, why complicate things? Counting is the business of those who lay up treasures, and it is logical that a people who did not know what money was, and attended to all its needs with the simple system of barter, should not have left descendants capable of dealing with large numbers. But this is another story. We were talking about a flock of sheep.

Antuca and her family were happy to be the owners of so many sheep. And of the sheep dogs, too. Only the tone of their bark was sad, for they leaped and ran about gaily, guiding the steps of the sheep wherever the shepherdess wanted them to go. She walked along behind, silent or humming a song, spinning the hank of wool fastened to her distaff, when she did not have to give orders. The dogs understood her by signs and also perhaps by the few words she used to send them to one place or another.

> Up the dark hills
> Climb my sheep,
> Little white lambs
> Follow the old ones.

The sweet thin little voice of Antuca carried only a few feet in the vast desolation of the mountains, where the hay is the only gift of the rude climate.

> The Sun is my father,
> The Moon is my mother,
> And the wee stars
> My little sisters.

The gnarled hills raised their bluish-black crags. Around them, slowly rising, floated dense clouds.

The hushed, imposing grandeur of the rocks dwarfed still more the sheep, the dogs, even Antuca, a little country girl, twelve years old, who sang to keep herself company. When they reached a patch of hay that looked good, the procession halted and the dogs stopped barking. Then a vast heavy silence bore down upon the virgin breast of the shepherdess. She called out: "Cloud, cloud, clou-oud . . ."

For this is the way of the mountain people. Because everything of nature is part of their intimate consciousness.

"Wind, wind, wi-iind . . ."

And sometimes the wind rushed in, rough and strong, howling against the cliffs, whistling through the hay, disheveling the dogs' hairy coats, and blowing out Antuca's black shawl and red skirt. Then she would say to the dog beside her — one always stayed close to her — jokingly:

"See? The wind came. It minds me."

And she would laugh with a sound like the purling of clear waters. The dog, as though it understood her, would wag its tail and laugh, too, with its bright eyes that gleamed behind its pointed, glistening muzzle.

"Dog, nice doggie. . . ."

Then she would find herself a little nest somewhere in the thick hay and they would snuggle down in it. The wind blew over their heads. Antuca talked to the dog while she spun her wool. Sometimes she would put down her work to pat him.

"Dog, my nice little doggie. . . ."

Occasionally she would look out at the flock, and if one of the sheep had wandered too far, she would point to it and say:

"Look, Sambo, go bring it in."

Then the dog would run to the stray, and barking at it, without harassing it too much — the sheep knew how he would keep on if they did not obey — he would bring it back to the flock. This was important. If a sheep lingers behind or strays from the rest, it may get lost or be caught by some puma or fox, for they are always lurking in the shadows of their den.

After having fulfilled his duty, Sambo trotted back with the agile, effortless gait of the native dogs and lay down again beside the shepherdess. With the heat of their bodies they kept each other warm.

And thus they spent the day, watching the contorted battlements of the Andes, the bleating flock, the sky now blue, now cloudy and threatening. Antuca spun her wool, sometimes talking, calling out, or singing, sometimes in silence, as though she were one with the deep, vast silence of the mountains, all stone and immeasurable empty space. Sambo kept faithfully beside her, prick-

47

ing up his ears at her slightest gesture, ready to obey, though at times he allowed himself to lay down his head and doze lightly against the soft flannel of her skirt.

Some days Pancho, a young half-breed shepherd, would appear, his lean figure silhouetted against the bristling curve of a hill. Antuca would call to him and he would come toward her, happy and eager, after first making sure that his flock was far enough away from hers so they would not get mixed up. The yellow dog which followed him exchanged menacing growls with Sambo until their masters finally scolded them into quiet. Antuca and Pancho, on the contrary, were the best of friends. They talked and laughed together. Pancho would take his pan-pipe, which hung about his neck on a red string, and begin to play, tossing to the wind the notes, half-sad, half-happy, of a *huaino,* or the anguished tones of a *yaraví.* There was one called *Manchaipuito* which tore the heart out of Antuca's breast and even made the dogs howl. She would manage to force a smile and, making a great effort, scold at Sambo:

"Keep still, you fool dog . . . I never saw such a fool dog. . . ."

Then one day Pancho told her:

"That *yaraví* is about a priest who fell in love. . . ."

"Tell me the story," begged Antuca.

And Pancho began:

"They say there was once a priest who had fallen in love with a girl, but as he was a priest the girl didn't love him. And one day all of a sudden the girl died. Then the priest, because he loved her so much, went and dug up her body and took it to his house. And there he kept the body, and he took the long bone of her leg and made himself a flute, and there beside her body he played this *yaraví* on the flute, day and night. And between his love and this sad music, he lost his mind. And the people who lived near by, who heard this *yaraví* day and night, went to see why he played this sad song so much, and they found him sitting beside the dead body of the girl, which was all rotted, crying and playing the flute. They spoke to him, but he did not answer or stop his playing. You see, he was mad. And he died playing this music. . . . Maybe that's why the dogs howl. Maybe the soul of the priest comes to listen to his music and then the dogs howl, for they say they do that when they see the souls of the dead."

Antuca answered:

"It's so sad. . . . Don't play it."

But deep in her heart she wanted to hear it. The grievous lament of *Manchaipuito* ran all through her, producing a pain that was also pleasant, a suffering that was sweet. The last quivering notes of the music went through her like a piercing sword, wounding her, and at the same time agitating her with a secret fear.

Pancho was dimly aware of this and he kept making his pipes quiver with the palpitating notes of the legendary *yaraví*. Then he would say:

"What must love be like, to grieve so! . . ."

For a moment Antuca raised her eyes to his, with the emotion of the female who awaits her mate, but then she grew afraid and went back to her distaff and to scolding the howling Sambo. Her young hands — quick brown spiders — twirled the spindle to reel off the smooth thread from the silky white hank of wool. Pancho watched her with satisfaction and played something else.

Such are the idylls of the mountains. The two were more or less the same age. In the end the ripening flesh would have its way. They would mate, have children, who, in their turn, would pasture their flocks on the hills and meet others doing the same. . . .

But Pancho did not always come, and then Antuca spent the day alone, talking with the clouds or the wind and solacing herself somewhat with Sambo's quiet company. When the sun began to sink they would start toward home. In the rainy season they would have to go back earlier, for the dingy opaqueness of the sky would soon burst into a brutal storm. Antuca got up, calling the dogs, who bounded out of the hay, barking and running to round up the sheep and then slowly driving them home to the fold.

The dogs that helped Antuca were four: Sambo, Wanka, Güeso, and Pellejo. They were excellent sheep dogs, famed throughout the neighborhood, where many of their offspring maintained the fine reputation of the breed. Their master, Simon Robles, was as well known as the dogs, and this was due in part to his being their owner and in part to the fact that he was an excellent flute- and drum-player, in addition to other accomplishments.

Always, when they were herding, Sambo walked alongside Antuca, urging on the stragglers. Wanka went ahead leading the way, and Güeso and Pellejo took care of the flanks, making sure that none of the sheep strayed. They knew their job well. They had never injured an animal; barking close to the sheep's ears was their way of imposing their authority. It sometimes happens that mean dogs get so furious with a stubborn sheep that they finally kill it. Sambo and his mates were patient; they made the sheep obey by pushing against them with their shoulders, tugging gently at their wool, though these measures were used only as a last resort, for when they pressed in against a sheep on one side, it meant that it was to go the other way, and when they barked in its ear it meant it was to give a half turn. They were happy as they did their work, leaping and frisking about.

Not even the storms bothered them. At times, even though it was still early, the lowering sky began to drizzle. If Pancho happened to be around he would offer Antuca his poncho. She would refuse it with a polite "That's all right," and they would start home. The drops grew bigger and faster, and then turned into lashing streams; the thunder crashed and the lightning drove its swift blinding swords of fire into the summits of the peaks. The dogs herded the sheep into a compact mass they could guard easily, and drove them along at a rapid pace. They had to wade the creeks and freshets before the storm swelled them so they could not get across. There was no delay. They pushed on quickly and silently. The eyes of the sheep dilated with fear at every flash of lightning and every clap of thunder. The dogs trotted along quietly, the water dripping from their shaggy coats matted with the rain. Behind them, using her distaff as a staff to keep from falling on the slippery wet clay, and with the brim of her straw hat turned down so the rain would roll off, Antuca walked along, breaking easily through the gray web of the rain.

But as a rule they got back to the village in the calm hours of the late afternoon enveloped in the joyous riot of colors of the sunset. They shut the sheep up in the fold and Antuca went into the house. That was the end of her day's work.

The fact should be mentioned that there were few houses like hers. It had a thatch roof to be sure, but only one of the rooms had a mud and wattle wall; the others were of thick adobe. In the middle room, before the hearth, her mother, Juana, was serving food to Antuca's father, Simon Robles, her brother, Timoteo, and her sister, Vicenta. The shepherdess took her place in the family circle and shared the sweetness of the wheat, the corn, and the squash. The dogs drew near, too, and received their share in a wooden trough. There was Shapra, too, the watchdog of the house. They did not fight. They knew that Timoteo wielded a swift stick.

Night fell slowly amidst violet and blue shadows which finally thickened into blackness. Juana put out the fire, keeping a few embers to start it again the next day, and then they all went to sleep. Except the dogs. Around the fold they broke the silent heavy darkness of the night with their persistent barking. They slept with one eye open. This was the hour when the pumas and the foxes take advantage of the darkness to attack the fold and snatch their prey. The dogs barked at any noise. Even when it grew so light that the beasts of prey give up their hunting, the dogs kept on barking. They barked at the moon. She, the beloved of poets and romantic ladies, full and white, produced the same effect on the dogs as the ravening pumas and foxes.

The voices of Sambo and his companions, and the other dogs of the neighborhood, formed a lugubrious chorus that sent a tremor through the Andean night.

THE LAND OF BRAZIL

IN A TOURISTS' GUIDE-BOOK there is a map of Brazil on which all the countries of Europe have been superimposed with the exception of Russia. And all Europe is very much smaller than the South American Republic. There are only three nations in the world that are larger: China, Russia, and Canada. Within America itself Brazil's importance is no less striking. Half the population of South America is Brazilian, and the country borders upon every one of the other nations except Chile and Ecuador. In reality Brazil is like a continent within a continent. All the problems that in one form or another have agitated the other republics have worked themselves out in a special way in Brazil. Nowhere else can the problem of miscegenation be studied so well. Nowhere else do the political conflicts or their solution afford such dramatic contrasts. The abolition of slavery there constituted a problem which in intensity has been surpassed only in the history of the United States. The economy of Brazilian agriculture, like that in the Southern United States, was based on slave labor. Another point of similarity between the development of the northern and the southern nation was their conquest of the interior. In the United States this was carried out by legions of "conquistadors" rushing from the eastern seaboard toward the west, and in Brazil by the "bandeirantes" who, driving out the Indians, enlarged the territory available to the modern colonists. In Latin America the history of Brazil forms a chapter by itself. Its discovery and conquest, which were carried out under the auspices of Portugal, gave this region a different language. Moreover, Brazil was immensely superior in human and natural resources to the European kingdom in whose name the conquest had been made. During the first century of the colonial period the Dutch invaded several points on the coast and the flag of this nation flew over Bahia, Pernambuco, Olinda, and Recife. The territory that today comprises the states of Sergipe, Algoas, Pernambuco, Parahyba, Rio Grande do Norte, Ceará, Piauhy, and Maranhão fell into the hands of the invaders, and Portugal was unable to send troops to defend its possessions. Whereupon the Brazilians themselves took the situation in hand and drove out the aggressors, at the same time giving Portugal to understand that they were capable of defending themselves without any help from the mother country. At the time of Napoleon's invasion of the Iberian peninsula a phenomenon occurred that was unique in the history of America: the Emperor and his court moved from Lisbon to Rio de Janeiro, and for fourteen years Rio de Janeiro was the capital of the Empire.

Brazil is a land that is largely unknown not only to the rest of America, but to the Brazilians themselves. Like the rest of Latin America it is a world still in the making, whose productive capacity only time will reveal. The virgin forests of Brazil, which extend over the entire central plain of the country, are said to constitute the greatest existing unexplored reserves of our time. Monteiro Lobato in a brief essay entitled "Brazil Seen Vertically," which gives a bird's-eye view of the country, says:

This view from above makes it possible for us to see Brazil as it really is: a great portion of the earth's crust which man has, as yet, hardly dominated. Along the Atlantic seaboard there is just a sprinkling of the freckles of civilization, but this is only a narrow strip compared with the bulk of the country. Here and there in the south this strip advances toward the interior in spots that look like bent coins: coffee plantations. But the rest, the great remaining portion, preserves its pristine verdure. In a zone near the middle the observer from above sees a contorted wrinkling of the bare earth: these are the iron mines of Minas Geraes, the vast, the immense potential wealth of Brazil. The future lies sleeping there. The imagination reels at the thought of that huge mass of iron mobilized, turned into the millions of machines into which it can be transformed like the huge block of marble that becomes Moses in the hands of Michelangelo. . . . Brazil is still the greatest field unconquered by man, and its possibilities of development are fabulous. Who knows the wealth that may be slumbering in its subsoil? The very ones that will permit man on its surface to dominate nature: metals and combustibles; the raw material of the machine and the raw material of the energy to move the machine. Brazil has the millions of potential machines it needs to master nature buried in its subsoil. It possesses them, but for the future. The time will come when it will mobilize them, as the United States did, and then its day will come.

The landscape of Brazil is unique in the world. It has certain natural wonders like the bay of Rio de Janeiro or the falls of Sete

Quedas and Iguassu, which are unequaled. Graça Aranha (1868–1931) wrote a novel, *Canaán,* which has been considered, from the day it was published, the most typical of the life and scenery of Brazil. It has been translated into many languages and is today universally known. It has given direction to a new movement in Brazil's literature. It paints not only the landscape of the country, but also the reaction to it of the European immigrants, especially the German colonists who have contributed greatly to the development of certain regions, and today still comprise one of the strong racial groups in the general population of the Republic.

CANAÁN

GRAÇA ARANHA

Milkau was sitting at the door of the inn at Santa Theresa, where he had spent the night, and was studying nature as it woke up around him, when Lentz, coming out of his room, met him with a happy, jovial expression, slightly excited by the cool, subtle air. Milkau was glad to see his friend and greeted him with a kindly smile. Shortly after, they took a walk through the city, which was already fully awake and shining in its ingenuous simplicity. The doors and windows of the primitive, whitewashed houses, opened in the bright sunlight like eyes that are waking up. The little houses, of monotonous uniformity, lined the streets and looked like dove-cotes on the side of the mountain. Around the city there was a green park studded with trees, through which flowed murmuring brooks that seemed the very soul of the landscape.

The two immigrants felt transformed by a soothing peace and by a consoling hope as they contemplated the beautiful sight the city presented. They could see the people quietly working at the doors or inside the houses, and there the different trades were reborn with all the simplicity of their happy initiation. It was a small industrial nucleus in the colony. While all around them, in the thick of the jungle, others wrestled with the earth, the inhabitants of the town were busy at their humble trades.

Milkau and Lentz walked through the town listening to the lovely joyful music formed by the noises of toil. An old shoemaker, with long beard and very white hands, sat in his shop hammering on a piece of leather. Lentz found him as venerable as a saint. A tailor was ironing a coarse cloth; women were spinning and singing in their rooms; others were kneading dough to make bread; others with graceful movements were sifting corn flour for the *fuba;* always the same light manual work, humble and sweet, without the shrill scream of steam and with no engines, except the contrivance for the bellows of the smith's forge, which the water from a dam kept moving with a sonorous clatter. And all this blessed lively noise was in harmony with the rest. Even the hammering on the iron at the smithy harmonized with sounds of a clarinet with which the conductor of the band at Santa Theresa was giving the morning lesson to his pupils. There was inexpressible happiness in that primitive community, in its retrogression to the beginning of the world. To Lentz's passionate and exuberant spirit, this unexpected meeting with the past seemed like the revelation of a mystery.

"This is heavenly," he said, breaking the silence in which they had been walking. "These poor people modestly working with their own hands, these men who are not stained by coal smoke, who are not brutalized by the noise of machinery, who preserve the freshness of their souls, who are sufficient unto themselves, who sing while they make their bread and clothes . . . these people are simple and natural creatures, and creation with them is the happy satisfaction of the unconscious."

Milkau was also lost in admiration, proud of being a man away up in that mountain where toil had its peaceful setting; but as he discerned in Lentz's praises the opposite emotion of his own mind, he observed:

"Really, this is a wonderful picture we have before our eyes, and the spectacle of free and individual toil makes us drunk with pleasure. But, at bottom, we are only witnessing the beginning of a civilization; it is like a man who has not yet vanquished most of the forces of nature and merely stands at her side in a humble and servile attitude."

"But who can deny that man, the slave of machinery, is gradually sinking into a barbarism even worse than that of the savages?" replied Lentz.

"As far as I am concerned, there is a mirage in that romantic sentiment. Yes, machinery, specializing and eliminating men, has deprived them of the perception of industry as a whole. Today, however, when man has been transformed into a mechanism of peculiar motions, he has freed himself, has gained his intelligence, directing mechanisms which are almost on a level with workmen. We cannot force the mass of civilization to go back to the old times of industry. The poetry in it is the mysterious perfume of the past, toward which we turn with fear; but there is also poetry, more seductive, stronger, in the industrial life of today, and we must look at it from the proper viewpoint. . . ."

"Well," replied Lentz, as he continued walking with Milkau, "I hold these people sacred; they are more worthy of my love than the army of proletarians, full of ambition, hungry, and frightful, who are trying to govern the world. These people at any rate are free from all sins of pride, are kind and ingenuous, and carry their yoke with a smile."

They walked about for some time, feeling a curious difficulty in leaving the place. They walked along the roads that skirt the town. They sought the small elevations, went up and down the park, stopped at the doors of the houses, watched the busy inmates, smiled at the children, and followed with their eyes the handsome girls, who blushed at their attentions. They amused themselves walking about at random, charmed by the simplicity of the natives, which retained them in the little town for some time. But at last they had to tear themselves away. The landlady's daughter took them to the Timbuhy road. They detained her for a few moments with many questions, attracted by her delicate face and her beautiful red hair. Lentz saw in the girl a strange divinity of the green forest, a kindly divinity, like the other inhabitants of Santa Theresa. The girl stretched out her long arm, pointing the way to Milkau and Lentz, and they admired her gesture, her air, her gracefulness, and went away as if in a dream.

At first they walked thoughtfully, without saying a word, as do those who travel toward the unknown. The road went up and down the deserted hills. The wide landscape, fertile and pictur-esque, offered a variety of aspects with its woods, valleys, forests, rivers, and waterfalls. It was a stretch of one of the most opulent and most productive regions in Brazil. Within it was sheltered the multitude of barbarians and foreigners, who had been received with kindliness and love. Milkau and Lentz passed several colo-nists' houses, which they saw for the first time, and stood to ad-mire these shelters nestled in the green and peaceful abundance of the countryside. The little houses were strung all along the val-leys, some sheltered by the projecting spurs of the hills, others perched on the slopes, and all of them gracefully arranged.

One could see everywhere smoke rising from the chimneys, women at their domestic duties, children and animals under the trees, and men under the cool shadow of the coffee plantations that surround the dwellings. The two immigrants, in the silence of the road, united by a common hope and a common admiration, began to praise the Land of Canaan.

They said that she was beautiful in her magnificent garments, dressed in sunshine and covered by a voluptuous and endless blue cloak; that she was petted by nature. The waters of the river turn round and round her neck and bind her waist; the stars, lost in passionate admiration, pour upon her like the tears of some divine joy; flowers perfume her with their strange scents; birds sing her praises; gentle breezes play with her green hair; the sea, the wide sea, with the foam of its kisses, caresses her body eternally. . . .

She was opulent because in her fantastic bosom is hidden an incalculable treasure, pure gold and brilliant stones; because her flocks suffice for the needs of her people, and the fruits of her trees sweeten the bitterness of life; because one grain of her pro-lific soil would suffice to fertilize the whole world and would ban-ish misery and hunger from among men. Oh, how powerful she is! . . .

They said that in her love she tempers the rays of the sun with her shadows, and against the dew of the cold night she offers the heat of her warm skin, and men find in her, so sweet and consoling, instant forgetfulness for the eternal agony.

They said that she was happiest among the happy because she was a mother who could provide for all — the house of gold, the providence of carefree children, who would not exchange her for another, who would never leave her protecting skirts but would recompense her with loving, childish caresses and sing to her hymns with a joyful heart. . . .

They said that she was generous because she distributes her precious gifts among those who wish them; nobody is turned away from her door, her riches have no owner; she is not disturbed by ambition or pride; her soft, divine eyes see no petty distinctions, her maternal bosom is opened to all like a warm comfortable shelter. . . . Oh, cherished hope of ours!

They sang these and other praises as they walked along in the sunshine. . . .

They had been traveling five hours from Santa Theresa when they arrived at the banks of the Doce River. They hardly had time for a look around, for the surveyor, Felicissimo, issuing from a green shed located there, came to them with the brown triangle of his face lit up by a broad, kindly smile.

"Upon my word," he shouted from a distance, "this is a fine time to arrive."

And without waiting for an answer, he went to meet the two Germans, with his hands outstretched. . . . It seemed to Milkau that he was the good genius of the native race which ruled over the land and was appearing to them full of joy and hospitality.

"Ah! my friend," exclaimed Lentz, "we very nearly stayed kneeling down in the road, adoring your wonderful country."

"There is no doubt about it; this is a real paradise," assented the surveyor enthusiastically.

Milkau and Lentz very excitedly began to tell him their first impressions. Felicissimo, however, interrupted them, impelled by his hospitable instinct.

"Where are you going to lunch? I could get you something here to appease your hunger. . . ."

"Thanks very much," said Milkau. "Just as we left Santa Theresa we ate a few things we had brought with us, and afterwards, on the road, we had a lot of oranges from the orchard of an old woman colonist. We even brought you some. Look how beautiful they are."

"That's nothing," answered the surveyor, taking the oranges. "Don't waste your admiration, for there are many things that will make you stand with your mouths open. Look here, there is no part of Brazil like this one, in everything!"

They walked to a shed covered with corrugated iron, where the surveyor had his office. It was arranged in the simplest of fashions; at one side, several agricultural implements; on the table, two or three large folios which contained a register of lots rented to the colonists; and on the wall, a large map showing the lots of land of the district. Not even one book, nor a humble picture nor a photograph; only a bundle of newspapers to satisfy the curiosity of the surveyor. Felicissimo had in the same shed his bedroom, which was of nomadic simplicity. Near by there was a larger shed which was used as lodgings by the immigrants while they were building their houses on the lots they had acquired. It was roomy and arranged like a ward in a hospital, and at one end of it there was a small kitchen. Felicissimo, however, made an exception of the two foreigners and entertained them in the shed where he had his office. His guests thanked the obliging Brazilian, and, sitting in the bedroom, they engaged in a lengthy conversation from which they learned much about the place. At last the surveyor, seeing that the sun had lowered, said to them:

"Come on, friends! Let us go and choose the lots."

They passed into the office and looked at the map, which he had taken from the wall. He went on:

"I have an idea that number ten would suit you best. The land there must be splendid. The devil of it is that it is located right in the thick of the jungle and it'll take a lot of work to clear it up. But I really think it worth while."

And Felicissimo, with a little stick in his hand to point at the map, looked at the other two eagerly. Milkau, without bothering in the least about the selection, and through deference to the opinion of the surveyor, readily accepted the proposal. He felt happy in this glorious day with the mirage of the great and glorious labor ahead of him.

They got ready to go out. When they reached the door, Felicissimo looked at the sky with the air of a connoisseur, reflected a little, and said to his companions:

"It is quite a way from here to the lot. We could not get there and back before dark. But if you insist — "

"Not at all," answered Lentz. "Let it go until tomorrow."

The travelers felt a sweet torpor caused by the journey, and lying down on the turf near the house, they listened to the stories of the surveyor, pondered on vague things, and watched the river lazily flowing by. . . .

A group of men armed with agricultural implements appeared in the distance. They approached slowly, dragging themselves along the deserted road on the river bank. Perceiving at a distance that there were newcomers, they walked silently under the reserved and sinister impulse which is the first advance of man toward man. . . . When they arrived, they saluted half-heartedly and went silently into the store to lock up their tools. Felicissimo, seeing that they were passing in such a queer fashion, was greatly surprised and shouted to them:

"Hallo, friends! Is the ditch finished?"

"All done!" they answered with one voice, which was a combination of all their voices, and they looked at one another, frightened at having answered in chorus.

Milkau and Lentz admired the strength of these men of iron hands, herculean torsos, red beards, and sky-blue eyes, who resembled each other like a group of brothers. There was one young mulatto among them, and he could be distinguished easily. His face was pitted with smallpox; his complexion was bronzed; he wore a short, curly beard and his short hair stood upright on his head. With his bloodshot eyes and his teeth pointed like those of a saw, he had at times the appearance of an evil satyr. But that impression was not frequent and it quickly disappeared in an easy, ingenuous smile. In the midst of the mass of his red, heavy companions, the Brazilian goat [1] had a victorious, spiritualized air.

[1] "Goat" is the name given in Brazil to a half-caste Negro and Indian.

Was there not, after all, a remote connection between him and the land, perpetuated by the blood and transmitted from generation to generation?

By and by the men came cautiously where the strangers were and silently listened to their conversation. Just as the sun was setting, turning the waters of the river blood-red, Felicissimo pointed to the sky, showing Lentz and Milkau the flocks of birds which were flying in the twilight, passing along in thin graceful lines.

"My! . . . what a shot I could have at those birds!" exclaimed the mulatto, enjoying, not without some melancholy, the picture which his imagination, that of an inveterate hunter, presented to him.

"Get out, Joca, you couldn't hit one of them, you goat . . ." said Felicissimo in German, laughing at him.

The man laughed.

"I bet you I could," replied the mulatto pompously. "If I had a good gun, there wouldn't be one bird left flying. I know how to aim . . . and if the gun had a good reach, you would see me . . ."

The birds continued to fly together, serene and proud in their flight. Other flocks could be seen in the distance. . . . Joca looked at them and followed them with his eyes regretfully.

Lentz admired the facility with which the mulatto could speak German, although he interspersed his phrases with Brazilian words. And addressing the Germans, he asked them if they could speak Portuguese. They answered that they could not, and Felicissimo added:

"Listen, don't be surprised at that, for these men have been in the colony only one year. But there are people who have been here over thirty years and can't speak one single word of Brazilian. It is a darn shame. What happens is that all our cattle men and laborers learn German. I don't know. There is no people like ours to learn foreign languages. . . . I think it must be a natural gift. . . ."

Joca agreed with the surveyor and added that he himself could speak more German than his own native tongue, and he also had a smattering of Polish and Italian. In his innermost thoughts Lentz felt some pleasure at these testimonials of the inability of the

Brazilian people to impose their own language upon other men. This weakness, would it not be like a breach through which the Germanic ambitions would in the future take possession of this magnificent country? And he pondered on this idea, with his eyes wide open and shining.

"The day is not far," said Milkau, "when the Brazilian language will dominate the land. The case of the colonies is a mere accident, due in great part to their segregation from the native population. I won't deny that foreign languages will have a great influence upon the native tongue, but from this mixture will result a language whose basis and whose character will be those of the Portuguese, ingrained into the soul of the population for centuries, fixed in their poetry and preserved for future generations by a literature which is determined to live." . . . (And he smiled, looking at Lentz.) "We will be the losers."

This pleased Felicissimo. Joca, who had only caught the last phrase, looked with a superior air at his German fellow workers. The prophecy imbued him already with the pride of a conqueror.

They were thus amicably talking when a thin, tall man passed along the road, close to the river, armed with a gun and carrying on his back a dead animal dripping with blood, which Joca declared was a "paca," a kind of wild boar. The hunter was accompanied by a pack of hounds which preceded or surrounded him, all heated up, their ears cocked or hanging down, exhausted with the hunt, their mouths open and their tongues hanging out, tremulous, nervous, panting, burning the cool air with their ardent and restless breathing, in a combustion which enveloped them in a cloud of vapor. The hunter walked with a hasty step, and the dogs accompanied him barking, excited by the blood which flowed from the prey.

"Ah!" exclaimed Joca, sorrowfully, "if we could get one like that for our pot!"

The hunter passed without saluting them.

"He is a savage," said Felicissimo.

"Does he live around here?" asked Milkau.

"He is our nearest neighbor, but he never salutes us, all the same. . . . He passes us as if we were dogs . . ." answered Joca.

"He must be some hermit," suggested Lentz.

"A misanthrope," explained the surveyor. "He never speaks with anyone that I know of, and lives alone with those dogs, which are as ferocious as tigers."

The old man continued on his way, unconcerned by the group of men who were observing him, until he was lost in the jungle.

They continued to talk about the singular life led by the hunter, when one of the men approached Felicissimo and informed him that they could start their supper. They got up from the turf, some stretching their arms, some yawning, and slowly and quietly they all entered the house.

The workers arranged the table for their meals in the immigrants' dormitory, and it was there that they had their supper. The meal was poor and simple, salt fish and dried meat, which is the food common to men of their occupations, and all enjoyed themselves, some quietly, others, like Felicissimo and Joca, lively and loquacious. Lentz looked at the two races gathered at the table. He admired the solidity and heaviness in the German giants, while the interminable empty talk of the surveyor and the mulatto produced in him the nausea of seasickness.

Meanwhile Milkau was pleasant to everybody and glad to see this mixture of races, foreseeing a bright future for the guests of a table which seemed like a relic from patriarchal times.

The room was lighted by a kerosene lamp. Its light was gloomy and shaky but strong enough to enable the new colonists to distinguish the face of each worker, who, so far, had been confused in a single mass. Some were matured men, experienced in long suffering; others were newcomers and young, generally strong, and exhibiting in their movements an indolent calmness and in their eyes a longing for repose. They ate also in the same way, slowly and cautiously. Besides the general uniformity of their class, a long intimacy had given them many points of resemblance.

Milkau enjoyed himself talking to his countrymen, asking them where each came from. Nearly all of them came from East Prussia, from Pomerania; there were, however, some who came from the banks of the Rhine.

"Where are you from?" inquired Milkau of the nearest workman.

"From Germersheim."

"Then we are almost neighbors, for I came from Heidelberg."

The workman smiled, happy to have found a countryman; but his happiness only found expression in a painfully incomplete gesture, like his own mind. To Milkau, a countryman was the sudden and unexpected apparition of his own past. An incomprehensible remembrance of his first years mortified him for a few moments; it was like repentance at not having been in his first years the same man he was today. It was a desire to go back, to begin anew, to pay in love all the indifference he had shown for the things of his country, for the men of his city, for the surroundings, in fact, where he had spent his silent youth.

"Ah!" he exclaimed, musingly. "Then you are from the land of Sister Martha! Do you know the Rock of the Nun?"

"Yes."

Lentz asked if that had anything to do with any legend. And Milkau asked the workman to relate the tradition, unknown to the rest of the company. They all turned round to the immigrant from the Rhine.

The man remained for a second astonished and embarrassed, unwilling to emerge from the obscure and collective anonymity in which he had remained at the table. At first he did not say a word, merely shook his head.

Joca, for whom a moment's silence was perturbing and painful, turned round to his German companion with wrathful eyes.

"Out with it, man alive! Is it a secret?" shouted the goat.

The German at last decided to speak, looking timorously at the other men, scared at finding himself in such a prominent position.

In his own uncouth language, he told how at the time of the crusades a newly married Duke had to leave his wife and go to fight for the Cross. His bride remained inconsolable at the separation, and fearing that her husband might die, she made a vow that if she saw him again, their first-born would be dedicated to the service of God. The Duke returned, and after some time a daughter was born to them and they called her Martha. The child was of astonishing beauty, and the neighbors of the nobility, who wanted her as wife for their sons, were very sorry to see her born dead to the world. Hardly had Martha reached her girlhood when she entered a convent, where her piety, even more than her wonderful beauty, charmed everyone. The Duke died in another crusade, and the widow, with no other children, remained alone in the castle. Her only comfort was her daughter, who from time to time came to see her, dressed as a nun. One day when she was crossing the wood on one of her consoling visits, she happened to meet a young hunter, son of a Palatine Count. Charmed by her beauty, the lad fell madly in love with the sister and followed her silently to the castle. He struggled with himself to smother his criminal passion, but in vain, and overcome by desire, he planned to kidnap the nun. One afternoon, disguised as a peasant, the young Count knocked at the door of the convent to tell Martha that the Duchess was at death's door. The sister at once set out for her mother's home. The Count accompanied her, and when they arrived at a lonely spot, he revealed his identity, explained his stratagem, and asked her to flee with him and hide their love in other lands. The virtuous Martha, frantic with terror, starts to run. The lad, blind with passion, pursues her. They run like mad through the forest. The sister, losing her way, takes a road which leads away from the castle, and in the fury of her flight arrives at the river, where the Count almost seizes her. . . . A big rock opens up and the young nun takes shelter within its cavity. The Count could not believe that God was thus protecting the nun, and he stubbornly waited until Martha should come out. He remained there days and days, living close to the rock. From within, instead of curses, came the echo of the supplications of the nun for the salvation of her malefactor's soul. Months and years passed; the Count grew old, his white beard reached down to his feet, and finally his heart, softened by the nun's prayers, was freed from temptation, and, penitent and converted, he sang hymns which Martha had taught him from within the inviolable rock. He swore then to consecrate himself to the service of God, and with the intention of founding a religious order he bade good-by to the nun with tears of repentance. He went away, old and full of the divine spirit. The rock opened up again and Martha came out as young as when she had entered it. Comforted and fed by the angels, time had not passed for her, and she had the illusion that she had spent but one day within the rock prison. Confused and timid, she departed for the convent. During her absence the nuns, hearing in her cell a celestial voice, spent all the time kneeling down at the door, charmed, hypnotized by the melody, praying in ecstasies. When Sister Martha left the rock, the voice ceased in her cell, and the sisters, free from the spell which had kept them at the door, returned to their usual occupations. Martha ran to the convent, and on her way the season, which was winter, changed into spring, and the flowers opened up in the desolate fields. . . . She went into the convent and found everything as she had left it years before. . . . Time had not passed there either. The nun threw herself at the feet of the mother superior, explaining the danger she had run during her absence. The poor mother told her that she must have suffered a moment of hallucination, for she had never left her cell, where she had been singing the most beautiful praises to God. Astounded at her words, Martha went to her cell, whence at that very moment issued an angel who had taken her place during her absence and who was her very image.

The supper ended under the vague spell which the evocation of the native legend had cast on the workers. One by one they got up and left the room. They gathered outside, in the open, to enjoy the coolness of the night. Milkau and Lentz also joined them, and in the solitude they felt more and more drawn toward each other. The men lay down on the turf, looking toward the river, which seemed like a phosphorescent tremulous band from which radiated the only light which pierced the blackness of the night. The conversation was slow and broken, stumbling on uncertain subjects, for each mind was absorbed by an idea which had taken possession of it. And one of the men was the common interpreter when he said:

"There are a good many enchantments in this world of God. . . . We must always be ready, for no one knows what sufferings there are in store. There is danger when you least expect it. . . ."

The others thoughtfully assented with a murmur, and they fell into a deep silence. Lentz tried to raise their spirits, and he began to deny that there were any witches, miracles, or enchantments. He spoke at length, but could not shake the convictions which centuries had rooted in their minds. And when he had finished by saying: "The witches have all died long ago and they always were the same women that you love," one of the older men did not like his tone and replied:

"Don't say that, young man. Men ought to be careful whom they love. How many misfortunes have happened because men have trusted the voices and songs of women! . . ."

Each one recalled some story of his native town. There, in the middle of a tropical land, were summoned, by the evocations of the immigrant heroes, Saxon demigods, nymphs from the Rhine, giants with their corteges of fantastic dwarfs. The two Brazilians were intensely interested in these stories from an unknown world which brought to their minds similar European stories handed down to them and adulterated by the whites who had contributed to the formation of their half-caste breed. But now the legends came straight from their origin, purer, clearer, with their character unpolluted by foreign contact; and how they enjoyed the story of the wonderful deeds of Siegfried, son of Sigisbert, and his feats at the castle of Niebelung, his fight with the giant, the defeat of the dwarf Alberic, keeper of untold treasures, and then his fights, his struggles with the witch Brunhilde, Queen of Iceland, in which, thanks to his charmed head-piece, he fought invisible, vanquishing the woman to return her to her husband, until one day the hero died, run through by a lance which found his only vulnerable spot! . . . And with what eagerness they listened to the story of the beautiful Lorelei, now kindly inclined, protecting the men of her neighborhood, now vengeful, making the waters of the Rhine to open up and swallow the daring men who attempted to gaze at her mysterious face and who, before dying, became demented listening to her songs! . . . In that story was related the passion of the Palatine Count for the fairy, charmed by her magic voice, until one day, finding Lorelei on a rock with the lyre in her hand, he fainted and she carried him away to her crystal palace at the bottom of the blue waters. . . . And the despair that seized the castle, the father madly looking for his son until, finding the nymph, he asked her to return his son to him, and she, proud, divine as a symbol, answered as she struck her harp: "My smiling crystal palace is in the bosom of the waves, and there, far away from your world, I have carried my faithful, loyal lover. . . ."

When the story ended, some of the men began to make comments suggested by their foggy ideas. Joca declared that he was not afraid of the mother of the waters. As the others made fun of him, he insisted petulantly:

"You don't feel afraid of any women, devils or witches, after you have had dealings with Currupira."

To Milkau there seemed a rare and beautiful accent in that term; he thought it was one of those words of the Brazilian language, rich in sound, which have been grafted on to the old tongue, but as he did not know its meaning or the native legend attached to it, he asked the mulatto in a familiar tone:

"Tell us all about it, Joca."

"Ah!" he answered, getting ready to tell his story. "It wasn't around here, it was in Maranhao. That's where I belong to. . . . My uncle, Manuel Pereira, in the estate of Pindobal, used to tell me: 'My lad, you'd better stop those trips through the jungle to see your girl, for one fine day Currupira'll get you. . . . Take care!' I was a careless daredevil, with plenty of nerve, and laughed at the old man's words. 'Now, uncle! stop trying to frighten me. I am not a coward . . . Currupira is only a myth.' And Uncle Manuel Pereira used to go on and tell me some stories that always finished up this way: 'My lad! take care.' One day we had just taken the cattle into the corral. My horse was dead tired with rounding up a wild steer, which I finally brought in at the end of my lasso, after a hard struggle. . . . As soon as we arrived I got off Ventania, who, sweating and with his back half-broken, went away to graze. . . . My uncle shouted to me to come to supper. . . . The sun had cooled when we sat down at the table, my uncle, who was the chief cattle man of the state, and we four, his assistants. . . . The goats were so hungry they scared my aunt. 'Now, boys! You seem to be hungrier than the devil,' she said as she was serving us.

'Good gracious!' The fact remains that the *curimatas* quickly disappeared, not a banana was left behind either, and we wound up the feast with a good drink of *branca*. At that hour the cows were bellowing to break your heart, licking the calves that pushed toward them on the other side of the fence. I was as tired as could be. . . . The others were just as tired as I. But Manuel Formosa, he goes and says to me: 'Don't you know that there is a dance at Mary Benedicta's?' Oh, what a head I have! I had clean forgotten about our appointment. . . . The Saturday before I had arranged to meet Chiquinha Rosa at the dance. I was madly in love with the wench; a lass tall as a palm tree, with a head as delicate as a dove. A great desire to see Chiquinha seized me and roused me entirely.

"'All right! Come on, Manuel. . . .'

"But Formosa excused himself with some lies; you had only to hear him to know that he had business somewhere else. . . . The other fellows were old and married and were not in for any fun. I was quite disheartened for a while, but the thought of the girl gave my body new strength. . . . Ah, my blood, keep still! 'Well, seeing that no one will come with me, I shall go alone, for my father's son will not miss a chance of enjoying himself,' I said rather crossly to the lazy goats.

"I got up to go to the pond, and Uncle Pereira, who opposed me in everything, began to growl: 'Lad, you are not well. Don't take a bath at this hour of the day or you'll get sick. Then there'll be more work for the others.'

"I didn't pay any attention to the old man's talk and I went to the pond. It was quite light as I plunged into the water and it chilled me to the very bones. I splashed and kicked the water to scare away any *yacares* that might be prowling in the vicinity. I went in a hurry to my ranch to change my clothes. I put on a white shirt and white pants, and I tied round my neck a red muffler which I had bought from a sailor at the port. I knocked at Aunt Benta's door and asked her for a little of her perfumed pomade, and in two ticks I was ready. Chiquinha had my white muffler from the previous week, for I had left it with her so that she could carry it in her bosom and scent it with the perfume of her own body. She was going to give it back to me at the dance. Uncle Pereira, seeing me ready to start, said to me: 'Come back as soon as you can, for early tomorrow morning, as soon as the moon sets, we are going for provisions to the estate of Marambaia.' 'All right, uncle, don't be afraid. I'll be back in good time and I'll wake you up in the morning.'

"I didn't want any more talk with the old man and I started on my way as fast as an ostrich. From Pindobal to Mary Benedicta's house is a good two hours' walk. I crossed our fields intending to reach the point at Guariba, and I remember as if it were today that everything was dry, and the few lean cattle that stood around had the sad eyes of a dead fish and looked toward the setting sun. You could only hear the grunts of some swine that were digging up manioc with their snouts. When I arrived at the point I went into the store of Joseph, the sailor. 'Well, Joca, where are you going all dressed up?' the Portuguese asked me. 'To dance a little at Mary Benedicta's.' 'Listen, a lot of young people passed here today. There'll be a lot of young people at the dance. And there'll be plenty to drink, for I have sent it all . . . by order of Mr. Peter Tupinamba . . . you know.'

"I don't know whether Sailor Joe's talk heated my blood a little more, but I felt everything turning round, my heart wanted to jump out of my mouth, and my legs were giving way under me. . . . But I made an effort and stood up courageously, and in a little while I was able to say to the landlord: 'I am in a hurry to get there, but people should not take advantage of others; they should carry their own provisions. Please give me one quart of *restillo* and cut me two ropes of chewing tobacco.'

"He did as I asked and I started on my way again. The sun had already set and the glow-worms were beginning to fly about in the still air, but their light was quite unnecessary, for the moon was lighting everything. I started on a path through a coppice which considerably shortened the way to the house. The sand was warmer there than in the open fields; a great heat ran through my body; I walked, I walked; the lizards ran shaking the leaves, and from time to time a woodpecker, perched on a tree-stump, struck the evening hours. There was no living soul around, and I was breathing the dust which I was raising in my hurry to get to the house. I was afraid I was going to find all the couples arranged, and that Chiquinha, tired of waiting for me, had got a partner for the night. 'Shake a leg!' I said to myself. My head, however, was in bad shape; it seemed as if it were going to burst, and I felt very sick in my stomach.

"In the middle of the jungle there was a clearing, and it seemed to me that a form was moving toward me. However, I didn't attach any importance to this and I said to myself: 'It must be Sailor Joe's son going home because his father won't allow him to go to the dance.' Suddenly I heard a sharp whistle behind me. 'Some friend,' I thought, 'who is going to the dance and is calling me to wait for him.' I turned my head, but I didn't see anyone. I looked again and saw nothing. I went on my way. . . . Another whistle came, piercing my ears, another, and another; they seemed to be whistling from everywhere, from the thick of the jungle, from the road, from over the trees. 'What a flock of owls there must be around here! . . . It must be an ill omen.' A cold shiver ran through me, and to gain courage I thought of the meeting with Sailor Joe's son. But I looked in vain ahead of me; I saw no one. 'Where has the little devil gone to?' The whistling kept up around me, my head was dizzy and my heart was beating furiously. Again I saw the youngster in front of me; I took a good look at him, for I was quite close, but he wasn't the son of the Portuguese. 'I bet I don't know this kid.' We stood about one hundred yards from each other, when the little one disappeared again. Then I shouted in a frightful voice, to scare the goat: 'What sort of conversation is that? Why do you keep making faces at me?' He said nothing; but why should I have spoken? The whole jungle began to whistle like the devil and I was scared to death with the noise. The little devil was now about ten yards from me. My blood boiled; my head burned. I'll tell you what I did; I just made for him, blind with rage. 'You devil! You'll pay me for this!' I raised my stick . . . but when I recovered my senses, someone was holding me by the wrists. 'Let go!' I yelled. The little devil was looking at me with his bloodshot eyes. 'Let go!' But I was held firm. I moved toward the goat with more rage than when I fought An-

thony Pimenta, once when we were branding cattle. I remembered how many brave bulls I had knocked down, and to find myself now fooled by a kid! We struggled up and down; I hit his
face with my head, I kicked his shins with my feet, but he always
stood up, hard as nails, the ugly monkey! After a few minutes I
heard a thundering roar, the roar of a jaguar; ah! I thought the
wicked one was going to let me go. But things got worse, for the
roar was echoed all over; the wild boars came snapping their jaws,
wild cats miauled; I heard the rattlesnake rattling away. . . . In
a moment I fell to the ground with the little blackguard atop of
me. All the beasts hustled in the jungle and came toward us; the
very trees bent down making fun of me; the hawks, the urubus,
came to scent my carcass. . . . I felt a terrible fear and my
strength abandoned me. I began to shiver with cold, and the
sweat made my clothes stick to me. 'Oh! . . . blessed St. John
. . . I am going to die!' I exclaimed. And my eyes closed as if I
were dead. . . . I was half-unconscious for a long time, feeling
the beasts, commanded by my devilish antagonist, prowling
about me. . . . Then peace fell over everything; my fists were
once more free; a great heat burned my body; I opened my eyes
cautiously. . . everything stood still . . . all the beasts had disappeared, and the moon shone as if it had been midday. I was
tired with the struggle . . . my tongue was as hard and dry as
that of a parrot. I opened my eyes wide, and didn't see either the
little devil or the beasts. But I felt a great fear and tried to get
away from the place. I passed my hand around me, looking for
my bottle of *restillo* and the ropes of tobacco. To waken up thoroughly, there is nothing like a drink of eau-de-vie and a good
chew. . . . But I couldn't find a thing. I searched and searched.
Nothing. I began to think that perhaps the fight with the kid was
because of my bottle. I remembered some words of my old Uncle
Pereira: 'If Currupira tackles you, give him right away what you
have, drink and tobacco.' And then I knew that I had had to do
with Currupira. I got up with a jump. I wanted to run to Mary
Benedicta: the dance must have been at its best then. I looked
ahead, but the road ended far away, very far away. I was afraid
of a new encounter. I turned back, walking as if I were drunk,

CANAÁN

falling here and there. I went out into the fields bumping up against the cattle; my eyes burned, my blood beat as if it were going to burst out; my tongue was thick and I felt as thirsty as a tortoise . . . but in spite of all, I arrived somehow at the door of my ranch. I didn't want to talk to anyone, so I threw myself into the hammock, which moved with my body as if it had been a canoe at the Boqueirao. . . .

"I woke up when I heard people talking at the door. It was the voices of my uncle and of Formosa. They opened the door and the light of the dawn shone in my room.

" 'Time to get up, Joca! Come on!'

"I tried to get up, but my forces failed me. The old man steadied the hammock with his hand, for it was swinging quite a lot. My body shook as if all my bones were having a dance. My uncle told Formosa to open the door and the windows, and the room was flooded with sunlight. He placed his hand on my forehead and I opened my eyes, which were full of fire, and Uncle Pereira grumbled:

" 'Didn't I tell you? You got it all right! Why should you have gone and had a bath when you were so tired? And at that hour too!'

"I didn't answer. I was too mad to tell the old man that I had been up against the Currupira."

After this yarn the colonists sat thoughtful, without saying a word. Each one went back to the beginning of his life, and the remembrance of the past filled his soul with shadows and regrets.

Felicissimo noticed that it was late and advised them to retire, he himself being the first one to get up from the grass. The others stood up yawning, for sleep was already caressing them. From the Doce River and from the neighboring forest came sweet murmurings, and the silent colonists interpreted these nocturnal sounds either as the voices of the mother of the waters, yearning for the love of men, or as the noise caused by the forays of the wandering Currupira.

THE VALLEY OF MEXICO

WHEN THE SPANIARDS began their conquest of the New World they found two great native empires: that of the Incas and that of the Aztecs. These empires represented centuries of evolution, and the life, thought, religion, language, arts which were developed there gave them an important place in the history of civilization. In size they were larger than any of the European nations that were then emerging as modern states. The two great cities, Cuzco in the south and Mexico in the north, gave the Spaniards the impression that they had not left behind them in Spain any so large or so rich. But these two American civilizations had no contact with each other. They were two separate and, in a sense, opposed worlds. Whereas the Empire of the Incas was based on a communistic ideal, in Mexico there was a deep-rooted caste system, going from the warriors and priests down through the slaves that were sold in the market-place. The separate study of these two worlds shows what the genius of America could bring forth in solitary gestation. The point in common between the two empires was that they both developed in the uplands, amidst the Andes, without seeking other than land routes. The fact that neither of them was a seagoing nation explains their ignorance of each other, and perhaps also why it was here the Castilians, men of the Spanish uplands, sunk their roots deepest. The fact remains that the natives of America settled densely only in the plateaus, and Spain took the same direction in the development of its colonial empire, following the trend of native thought. The two first viceroyalties, which for over a century were the only ones, were located in Mexico and Peru. In the courts that formed about the viceroyalties in Lima and Mexico City an attempt was made to revive the ancient splendor, although, as a matter of fact, a viceroy is little more than a jack in the deck, while Atahuallpa and Montezuma really possessed the pomp of kings.

Where the greatest splendor of the pre-Columbian world lies buried under the greatest splendor of the Spanish colonial world is in the city of Mexico. Even today, as one reads in the letters of Hernán Cortés or in the relation of one of his soldiers, Bernal Díaz del Castillo, the description of the city the Indians constructed in the middle of a lake, one realizes the greatness and originality of this incomparable city. The Spaniards built their cathedral, which is a monument of colonial art, on the very spot where the Indians had dedicated their temple to Huitzipochtli. On no other spot in America did Spain lavish the same jealous affection as on the valley of Anahuac, whose veil of mystery Hernán Cortés rent asunder with his daring lance. For this reason Mexico was given the name of "New Spain," which it bore for centuries, and which seemed to proclaim in the period of the renaissances: "Here is the Renaissance of Spain." There a university was founded in 1551, and some years earlier the city already had its printing press. More than a hundred books were published in Mexico in the sixteenth century, when printing presses were not even dreamed of in what is now the United States. But in this respect Mexico went back even further: the Aztecs were making their painted books before Columbus reached these shores, and in Montezuma's city there was a library when Cortés arrived. It may be said of Mexico that it has twice been the Rome of our America: first as the capital of the old world of America and then as the capital of the new Spanish-American world. Noblemen, artists, captains came from the peninsula to see the "New Spain," and there the Spanish poet whose poem beginning: "Eyes sweet, serene," is the most perfect madrigal that has ever been written in the Spanish language lived out the last years of his tempestuous life. The city repaid the affection lavished upon it by sending to Spain one of its sons, Juan Ruíz de Alarcón, who is reckoned among Spain's greatest writers. Because this city was at one and the same time so Spanish and so Indian, this twofold passion has been transformed into the revolutionary spirit with which we are all familiar and which is the inevitable prologue to the fusion of two races. But overshadowing its history and giving it a setting worthy of the empires that have passed through the streets of the city is the landscape, which the Chilean writer Gabriela Mistral has described in a series of vignettes like these that follow.

SILHOUETTE OF THE MEXICAN INDIAN WOMAN

GABRIELA MISTRAL

THE SILHOUETTE of the Mexican Indian woman is full of grace. She is often beautiful, but with a different beauty from that to which our eyes have grown accustomed. Her flesh has not the rosy mother-of-pearl tint of the shell but the brownness of ripe wheat caressed by the sun. There is a glowing sweetness in her eye, her cheek is finely modeled; her lips are neither inexpressively thin nor over-thick; the tone of her voice is sweet and has a hint of sadness as though there were always a tear in the depths of her throat. The Indian woman is rarely fat; slender and graceful, she walks with her water-jar on her head or resting on her hip, or with her child, no bigger than the water-jar, on her back. Like that of her mate, her body has the austere outlines of the organ cactus upon a hillside.

The scarf, the *rebozo*, lends her a line of Biblical simplicity. Narrow, it does not thicken her figure with heavy folds, but descends like quiet waters across her back and to her knees. Like the rippling of water, too, are the beautiful fringes at the ends: the longer they are, the more beautiful, and exquisitely interwoven.

The rebozo is nearly always blue, flecked with white; it is like the prettiest spotted bird's egg I have ever seen. Sometimes it is finely striped with bright colors.

It enfolds her well, as the long new leaf of the banana sheathes the thick trunk of the tree before it opens out. Often she wears it covering her head. It is not the scalloped coquettish mantilla held in place by a dark butterfly on its wearer's golden hair; nor is it the embroidered shawl which resembles the vivid gardens of the tropics. The rebozo clings soberly to the head.

In it the Indian woman ties her child and carries it gently. She is primitive woman not yet freed from her young. Her shawl enfolds it as within her womb it was held in a fine, strong web woven from her blood. She carries it to the market on Sunday. While she cries her wares, the child plays with the fruits or the bright trinkets. Bearing it bound to her, she climbs the hills, makes all her long trips. She wants her precious burden with her always. She has not yet learned to free herself. . . .

Her skirt is generally of sober hue. Only in certain regions of the tropical lowlands has it the gay coloring of the painted bowls, and as she lifts it to walk, it spreads out like a dazzling-hued fan.

There are two feminine silhouettes that have the form of flowers: one is the broad silhouette of the wide gathered skirt and the full blouse, which is like an open rose; the other is the straight skirt and plain blouse which has the form of the jasmine flower with its long petal stalk. This slender silhouette is nearly always that of the Mexican Indian woman.

She walks and walks, from the sierra of Puebla or the gardens of Uruapan to the cities. She walks barefoot; her little feet have not been spoiled with all her walking. (The Aztecs considered big feet the mark of a barbarous race.)

She walks with her head covered when it rains, but on clear days her dark luxuriant braids are bared to the light and wound high on her head. Sometimes she makes herself a gorgeous topknot, like a parrot's, out of bright-colored wools.

She stops in the middle of the fields and I watch her. She is not the Greek amphora; her hips are narrow; she is a glass, an amber glass of Guadalajara, its surface bronzed by the heat of the firing oven — her Mexican sun.

Usually the Indian walks beside her; his hat casts an immense shadow over the woman's slender shoulder, and the whiteness of his clothing is like a flash of lightning upon the fields. They walk in silence through the landscape, sunk in meditation; occasionally they exchange a word, of which I grasp only the sweetness without understanding its meaning.

They might have been a joyous race; God put them in a garden, like the first couple. But four hundred years of slavery have dulled for them the very glory of their sun and their fruits; it has made the clay of their roads hard beneath their feet, yet it is as soft as fruit pulp.

And this woman, whom the poets have never sung, with her Asiatic silhouette, must be like Ruth the Moabitess who labored so well and whose cheek, bent over the sheaves, was bronzed by the sun of a thousand afternoons.

THE MAGUEY.   The maguey is like an emanation from the earth, a deep sigh, broad as a furrow. Everything about it bespeaks strength: the toughness of its huge leaves and the sharpness of its clawlike points.

Plants seem to me to embody the emotions of the earth: daisies are its innocent dreams; jasmine, its urgent desire for perfection. The magueys are verses of strength, epic stanzas.

It is born and lives close to the earth, cheek to cheek with the furrow. It does not rear itself aloft like the taper of the organ cactus; its leaves open to the side to caress the earth with filial devotion.

The maguey lacks a stem, that spiritualization of the plant which makes it more a child of the air than of the earth and lends it that same idealized quality a long neck gives a woman. The whole plant is like a hard, powerful cup which can contain the dew that falls upon the whole plain in a night.

The heat makes it impossible for it to hold the shade of young green tenderness the grass possesses. Its color has a purplish tinge which deepens in the afternoon. At that hour the purple blotch of the fields of maguey prevails in the Mexican landscape, and it is like an overflow of violets from the far-off hills.

The maguey is to the Indian what the palm is to the Arab, the fountainhead of countless blessings. Its immense leaves make the roof of his house, its fibers serve him in two ways: one makes the tough thread out of which he weaves the honey-colored net he carries on his back, and which also makes the strongest sail shrouds; the other, the fine thread for artificial silk.

Besides, when its heart is gashed, it gives forth its sweet juice, *aguamiel,* which crystallizes into a pale sugar. But the Indian is unhappy and, as Pascal says of man, "he needs the oblivion of his misfortune." Therefore he turns this innocent liquid into that devil's brew, pulque, which gives him a spurious happiness and ferments madness in his vitals, making him love and kill in one and the same impulse.

Maguey of Mexico, give the poor Aztec and Maya Indian, instead of the madness you bear hidden in your heart, a hundred leaves for the sheltering eave of his house; give him the ropes and the sails for the ship in which he must carry away the products of his land to enrich others.

And while the men sail the Pacific in quest of the markets of the world, give the woman the sweetness of your delicate fiber, that her hands may weave from it her wedding dress. Let her not bear along the roads she travels the aftertaste of sadness which five hundred years of enslavement have given her and which makes the corners of her mouth droop in resignation.

THE CAVE OF CACAHUAMILPA. This cave is deep; one geography book says it is almost five thousand feet deep. When one touches the bottom the silence is overpowering, as though one had reached the roots of the earth. From the moment we enter we become aware of an *audible* desolation, almost more tragic than the *visual.* The only sound is that of our footsteps and the slow dripping of the drops of water which gives the cave a deep vibration.

The world has turned upside down before our eyes; outside, the sky is boundless, impalpable, and blue and holds the earth in an intangible embrace; the sky which covers us here is plastic and hard. But instead of the decoration of clouds, changing with every moment, what a sky we gaze upon here! Above our heads hang the hundred thousand whimsies of the water: wreaths, enormous inverted flower pistils, towers.

Through the centuries the lime filtration has peopled the bare heart of the cave until it has become this labyrinth of hallucinations.

The floor of the cave resembles its ceiling. ("Above it is like below," says Swedenborg.) In certain places the formations that hang down meet those that rise up. As I contemplate this contact a tremor runs through me; thus in prayer is the believer joined to the Creator.

The cave is a marvelous cathedral; but a cathedral that has altars not only against the walls, but scattered through the naves as well, and that might serve whole towns. There are thousands of human postures in the stalagmites that rise from the ground, like kneeling crowds whose backs cover the floor; at times they are wild masses, their arms contorted with anxiety. It is a community over which hangs a fateful hour; it resembles the loins of the sea when the wind lifts it up in a convulsive wave.

The valley of Jehosaphat comes to my mind, and the Scriptures become a living, possible thing to me. Here we come upon an immense striding figure, tall and grave, like a god; it might be Moses. A tightly knit mass of figures follows him. I turn a corner and the gaze of an anguished visage meets my eyes: Œdipus or King Lear. Its hair is disheveled by snow and wind, and from its mouth proceeds a cry which never quite emerges and which, in its immensity, would seem to unhinge the jaw. Across from this there is a countenance that is all dark; the only clearly formed thing about it is the eyes; we have to envisage all the rest around them.

We move ahead. . . .

Now the cave is the scene of a fantastic chase, like that of St. Julian the Hospitaler, in the tale of Flaubert: a buffalo rearing up to jump, deer that run lightly before it, and stags with branching antlers, all intermingled and turning upon one another, and crouching panthers and snakes which twist beneath our feet. . . . It is a palpitating bas-relief of the heart of the African jungle.

Or this group, from which I cannot tear my eyes away, with its innumerable figures that might be Adam surrounded by the beasts after the Fall. Creation has turned against him in anger; the animals mill about, looking at him, pressing in upon him. . . .

But in spots the sharp, clearly delineated forms predominate. Then the cave is not a place of violent fauna but of exquisite flora:

80

waving ferns, firmly planted, meditative pines and cypresses, and beneath them a multitude of plants and bushes. Everything is covered over by a snowfall of many hours which gives the foliage a certain density. And before this quiet landscape I feel just as I felt in a snow-covered forest: the urgent need for a wind to come and unshroud the forest and liberate me from that hallucination compounded of whiteness and silence.

The air here is heavy, as in the heart of a tropical forest.

We go on in the rarefied atmosphere of a dream.

These forms rising from the floor of the cave seem at times a thousand arms filled with offerings; it is all one huge offertory raised to an unheeding god — propitiatory goblets, vases, thyrsi — like a judgment on cities that would not pray. One feels the profitless weariness of the slender arms and feels that at any moment one of them may fall, broken with fatigue.

In spite of the absolute quiet this does not seem for an instant a scene of death. Each of these beings is quick, but with a life different from our own. The Golden Legend tells the story of the Seven Young Sleepers whom a mountain covered, without harming them, like a light quilt. Centuries later they were brought to light by an excavation, seven white, undefiled bodies, still drowsy from their fabulous sleep. Their breasts rose and fell almost imperceptibly; there was no rigor of death in their bodies, and the kiss of the sun gently and quietly aroused them. In the same way the immobility of the stalagmites seems like restrained power; it is as though their vast breathing were being held within their bodies. As we leave each room we refrain from looking back; we feel as if the bodies all came to life as soon as we left, and that breasts, backs, and mouths breathe a sigh of relief as they move.

But if I had entered the cave alone, "as man by himself is pure," I would not hurry by in feverish haste like this, and the cavern would want to live for my adoring eyes. I would sit down before each group of figures; I would look upon them in silence hours and days until I had overcome their stubborn silence, and suddenly, as though warmed by my ardent gaze, the trees would emerge from their torpidness, the animals would complete their suspended leap, and from the lips would fall, like a full pregnant drop, the withheld word. The men would climb down their Jacob's ladder, and this moon-dwelling humanity would move about me. And, above all, I should like to be alone in the depths of the cave to hear that perfect silence which is its attribute, a silence un-wounded even by the fall of the drops of water. (They only echo to reveal the miracle of the silence.) I would lave my ears of the impurities with which the agitation of the world has filled them and which has dulled them. It would be a silence like that of ten bandages swathing my head; better still, the silence of death within a body alive to sense it.

And when this complete silence had weighed down upon me, unbearably, like the mass of waters upon a submerged diver, I could also fill the depths of the cave with music. This world of forms can be translated into a symphony: those towers are the high, cold notes; this cupola, a severe sustained note; that clump of grass, a scherzo of tones. I would create a close forest of har-mony when my soul had savored for years the heavenly taste of silence.

I go on observing the patiently carved out groups of figures. Which of those we have known in the other world has been for-gotten? Not one. The water, with the creative power of a Shake-speare, has molded every type. And besides the creations of nature, the human inventions are here, too: this is a fine old arm-chair, there is a suggestion of the smokestacks of a factory. In this cave I have come to understand what is meant by the *imagination of nature.*

The cave, blind like Milton, dreamed the outside world and by its desire reproduced all the beings the water was forming in its vitals. I can believe that in this mass of beings not one is missing; I might even find my dead among them. If I were to stay here a few hours, my mother would come to me from that shadowy cor-ner, and if I were to peer along the walls, clustered with faces, I would find my own there. Yes, this has been a fever-heated dream of the cave, and its days of creation are not done. The pulsation of the drops works on invisibly; that grave, slow pulsation which is everywhere, which seems to follow and mock us.

Electric lights brutally illuminate the stalactites. If the moon could only know the caves, how eagerly it would light them with its silvery blue, or its silvery gold, or its silvery silver.

The whiteness gives an austere chastity to the underground panorama. White and gray: we might be walking astounded through the landscape of another planet. We talk to hear the sound of our own voices, to keep from going mad with amazement.

Some day cities will spring up near this cave, and no matter how many temples are erected, those who are troubled in spirit will come here, to the frozen white interior of the cave, to feel more closely on their faces the breath of death. Perhaps their prayer will be the most perfect that contrite man has ever raised to God. Perhaps the greatest religious hymn of humanity will come to the tongue of man from these stalagmite altars. The sensation of divinity has come to me only in the abyss of the starry night and in this other depth which also makes the soul faint.

When I was a child and asked my mother what the inside of the earth was like, she said to me: "It is bare and horrible." Mother, I have looked upon the inside of the earth; it is like the swelling breast of a great flower, it is full of forms, and one walks breathless through its tremendous beauty.

We emerge from the cave, and the blue of noonday wounds our eyes, which, like those of a sick person, close, blinded. . . .

THE MOUNTAINS

THE PAMPA AND THE JUNGLE are hostile to man. The mountain is friendly. Its flanks are dotted today with towns and villages. When at night one looks down from its heights into the depths of the valley, one sees on its wooded slopes winking lights that tell of the warmth of homes: the ranch-houses or the cabins of the poor. Farther down, on the plains, handfuls of electric lights: these are the little cities. From the days of the Spaniards, marking each step in the traveler's journey when the method of travel was muleback, the villages began to spring up about the inns. These towns with their white church towers, whose roofs of Spanish tile and American zinc gleam in the sun, today adorn the string of highways which encircles the throat of the mountains.

The mountains have always been the focal point of life in our America. The three great kingdoms which existed on Columbus's arrival had as their center the three plateaus of the Andes: the Incas, that of Peru; the Aztecs, that of Mexico; and the Chibchas, that of Colombia. The Spaniards respected the Indians' choice, and the three first viceroyalties followed the same pattern: Peru, Mexico, New Granada. The capitals were hung on the balcony of the mountains. Life, which is horizontal on the plains, is vertical on the mountain range. In much of it the weather is cold in the uplands all year, and the valleys are torrid all year. In these regions a classification of peoples exists that has more meaning than that by races: men are "cold country" or "hot country." They represent two almost completely opposed human types. When the inhabitant of the uplands wants to spend a few days where it is warm, he gets into his car, descends the curlicue of the highway, and in an hour he has to take off his overcoat and exchange the woolen clothing of the uplands for the cotton of the tropics. The trains must creep down-grade so slowly that riders on horseback can outdistance them on bridle-paths that are like waterfalls of stone. In three or four hours the automobile traveler crosses paramos where nothing grows but *frailejon* with its velvety leaves and small plants whose little flowers are like swarms of butterflies. Then he descends to the valleys where the river runs tempestuously along, between dense forests of trees and bamboo thickets, and the air is like that of a furnace. The uplands are splotched with patches of wheat which the August wind blows about like golden banners on the slopes of the hills, or flocks of sheep which are a moving foam on the quiet fields, or llamas, whose fragile necks make a stylized design against the clear air, or lakes, mirrors of steel that reflect the olive-green of the mountains. But as he descends the slopes, the coffee plantations begin to appear, sometimes covered with white flowers, sometimes aglow with the ripe

84

fruit; and orange trees covered with their golden coins, and pineapples whose fragrance perfumes the breeze. Farther down, the air is redolent with the heavy sweetness of the sugar mills and the jasmine flower. Hanging from the cabin eaves, like a brown fringe, tobacco dries.

The mountains break in a thousand different ways. The water hurls itself against the cliffs and bursts in waterfalls. The voices of the women are heard singing in the cabins; those of the men, on the roads and in the taverns. Day begins with the crowing of the cock. There is gold in the Andes. The men dig it out of the mountains. The women wash it from the sands of the river. There are coal, copper, tin. There are the treasure of platinum, the green eye of the emerald, and mountains whose bowels are of salt. Amidst the foliage of the trees, myriads of different birds sing. Over the stones of the roads and the bushes that shade them hover butterflies, dotting the air with their electric hues. There is one bird that is like a cartoon in color of the mountain: the macaw. There are rich Indians whose saddles are embossed with silver. Within the churches the little lights floating on oil and the flames of the candles are like fireflies in a forest of gold. Nowhere are the nights of the full moon so luminous as in the mountains. Nowhere does the sun shine through air so diaphanous: the Indians worshipped it as their god.

The literature of the mountain is rich in songs. In the field of the novel several masterpieces have been written for which it forms the background, such as the works of Tomás Carrasquilla of Colombia, or *La Trepadora* by Rómulo Gallegos of Venezuela. The great works of the Mexican Revolution, those of Azuela, Martín Luis Guzmán, or López Fuentes, are a natural outgrowth of the mountains. The mountains are the refuge of the revolutionary guerrillas.

Flavio Herrera, a Guatemalan novelist, has given this excellent painting of a coffee plantation in these pages from *La Tempestad* (*The Tempest*).

COFFEE: ITS LIFE STORY

FLAVIO HERRERA

Oɴʟʏ those who have had the glory of creating a farm, of starting a plantation, can know that ineffable delight which is the privilege of gods and kings. To create, to found, to sow, to build. Create, create, create. It does not matter what. To create is to be like a god. And to sow? To assume the gesture of the husbandman in its fullest sense, in all its purity and grandeur. To plow a mountainside. To write a heroic tale with seed or carve it out with the axe or spade. To feel the ancestral emotion of the first man who opened the first furrow and dropped the first seed. A silent epic. An anonymous epic. Silent, anonymous, and, for that very reason, the noblest. To spend the night musing, with a head full of dreams, when the hours seem ages because the earth is calling to the soul. To rise drunk with plans, with the will as powerful and efficient as a dynamo. The fields are still dark, but in the east the first hint of the sun is smiling through. There is something like electricity in the air. Suddenly a bell that has the sound of a golden psalm rends the silence. Oh, the farm bell! The mistress of the day's tasks. The first bird of daybreak! And through the cracks of a cabin comes the glimmering flame of a pine knot. Then the other cabins begin to light up. Here and there hearthfires send up hesitant flames. The roosters sing matins. There is the sound of cheerful slapping, and the tortilla sputters gaily in the clay baking-dish. The overseers call the roll of the hands. The peons line up, eager hands clutching machetes or spades, and the air reeks with the foul smoke of their cheap cigars, which, in the shadowy light of dawn, are fireflies. Then the assignment of the day's tasks. The brush-clearers: if one could only go with them into the woods! The noises there seem the echo of a legend. The sun sings on the gleaming blade of the first axe that is raised, and the first stroke reverberates through the whole wood, spreading through the soul an echo of hope. The machetes gleam symbolically as they swing through the air . . . suddenly there is a scream. The peons gather about in frowning agitation. A viper has bitten the first peon. The mountain gives up its virginity demanding a blood sacrifice in return. Tragedy intervenes as always in human aspirations. The Indian's eyes are glazing over in his agony. Brother Indian, nameless hero, the first to fall. One day, five years from now, right here, your blood will well up again, no longer tainted with poison, but transformed into the red fruit encircling the coffee berries with their promise of wealth, and then nobody, nobody, nobody will recall you, nameless hero.

They killed forty-seven vipers in the lands adjoining Paluna when they cleared them. The forty-seven vipers killed two men. They are all rotting below the ground now.

The earth makes them one with it and then sends them forth again in more plants, more flowers.

To feed more men and more vipers.

And this happened on the bottoms of "The Conjurer," which since then people call "Snake Hollow."

The only memory is a name.

Because to the Indians this was a normal thing. Without transcendence.

Tomorrow other men will kill other vipers.

And other vipers will kill other men.

And tomorrow.

And always.

But with the seed of their blood and their bones the dead quicken the road of action. From the mysterious beyond they stretch to the earth in a red chain of heroism. Those who do not die come back with an arm or leg slashed by a machete. With lianas tangled about their heads. Tattooed by thorns. Many with heads fractured by a falling tree. Some, mutilated, go about with a maimed reddish stump where the hand used to be that sowed the grain, or brought forth music from the accordion or marimba, or dragged away some Indian girl into the bushes.

Fields carved out by machete-strokes. Blank staffs on which

the new plants write the notes. Moist bottom lands of rich silty earth, pierced with stakes in the geometrical ceremony that precedes the planting.

Each stake marks the spot for a hole. Overseers with a grave, concise expression, carrying measuring sticks with an air of geodesic efficiency; set in their routine. Indians from Ixtatan, Indians from Cajola, bent over the spade or mattock. Rows of black cradles which May will flood with the first showers to slake the thirst of the plant that is to come, for this hole is the final dwelling-place of the wandering plant. And here its hitherto anonymous and promiscuous history, from seed-bed to nursery, comes to an end. But one must know this history, for it is the reproduction of the dreams and fears of the men of these lands.

The worries begin with the selection of the seed. Every man wise in the ways of husbandry, every true planter knows that this is the problem and the key to the success of a plantation. Those who buy their plants from a nursery! Those who plant from cuttings! Besides there is a kind of pride, and justifiable, too, in watching the genealogical process of a plant which at the same time that it puts down roots in the earth sinks them into our heart. Seed-beds! We say the word and there is implicit in it a sense of hope. Five years from now! . . . And the mind and heart sour agilely from the limbo of vague, confused ideas on the wings of imagination and enthusiasm to contemplate the dreams of success and ease. Enthusiasm! A marvelous dynamo for the hand that sows the seed of healthy, clean, vigorous strain and carefully prepares its nest. Well-worked, loose rich earth. Phosphates and potash. Humus and ash. But the sharp blade of the sun carries the threat of death for the frail and delicate budding shoots, so over the bed — a Lilliputian island like those in the rivulets of Nativity representations — a protecting tree spreads the wings of its shade. But it must be a cool shade, for there are those that are malignant and harmful. Days of concern and anxious hope go by; but one day the surface of the bed begins to be dotted over as though it were breaking out in a rash, and suddenly the whole bed bristles with millions of tiny waving wires, of a tender green hue, little wires shaped like a handle with a knot at the end. Countryfolk call them soldiers. That's it, soldiers of Lilliput, and later on, each soldier will be ordered to the nursery. Lo, each soldier's head has opened and two wings have sprouted from the seed. A butterfly rests on his head, and it was not good to stay on there, crowded, rubbing up against one's brothers. Choking, smothering each other. Now the soldier stands in trim, straight lines. Now he begins to feel chilly, and a hand — the guardian angel of his infancy — raises the cover of the nursery frame so the sun can smile upon him. The friendly sun lengthens his legs and makes him feel very cocksure. He looks smart and dapper in his four leaves, and here he will spend two years of his childhood growing up. During this time every leaf, every shoot is, for the soul, the key to hopes; and every day that passes, a milestone of impatience. The little soldier has grown, has filled out, has become accustomed to the hazards of his environment. He no longer fears the sun and can soak it up for a long time without getting burned. Besides, the sun is his friend and makes his arms stretch out. But now they are getting too long and they brush up against his brothers. He begins to feel crowded. Besides, something strange is pushing and bumping painfully up against his feet, and he has had to move one of his roots away because the brother next to him has thrust his toes down in the same place. It's the same as when they were in the seed-bed. Now here there's certainly going to be trouble. . . . When suddenly the guardian spirit that has watched over his infancy realizes his need to stretch out, and it carries him away with his shoes on, in the very clod in which he has been growing. Another change in his destiny. They take him to another field, and of course it's much better there. More light . . . more sun. He can stretch his arms as much as he likes. He has a lot of arms now. Now his brothers don't step on his feet. And, above all, now he can see the sky . . . the clouds . . . the stars . . . and no cover between him and the sun even when it is hottest. Big trees that live beside him protect him with their moist cloaks. He would like to stay here forever.

And he does.

If the coffee tree only knew that its life is the mainspring and pivot of another life! That each inch of its trunk paces a dream and each shoot it puts forth gives wings to an illusion. That there is a soul whose beat is timed to the rhythm of its sap, that its days are the key to anxiety or hope.

The planting, the planting! May comes in rainy, and keeps on in such a bad humor that it frightens the sun, which comes out only once in a while, timidly, fitfully. You could not ask for better planting weather. If it rains, so much the better. The men are assigned to their tasks, each to his ability. The transplanters, those Indians with gentle, skillful hand who can slip the trowel into the earth without hurting a single rootlet and deftly scoop out a cylinder with the plant. And then the wrappers, who with stolid rapidity put a shirt of *bijague* leaves around the plants, and still others, stronger or clumsier, who carry them in crates on their backs to the field. The little plant now waits beside the hole for its future to be decided. It is thirsty, its leaves droop limply, its feet ache, and it waits and waits. Suddenly an Indian comes up — not that strong Indian who brought him, but another one with a spade, who takes the shirt off and puts him into his hole. How cool! It's damp here. What a relief! The bottom is as soft as though it were made of feathers. Two shovelfuls of dirt around it, the Indian presses it in tight, and that's all. It looks around it and there are its brothers in a row, but farther away. In between them there are some intruders, often those mischievous bananas it saw from the nursery always fooling around, disheveled by the wind, waving their windmill arms.

And now the fight begins, or rather goes on, but harder, on a new front. A protean struggle, long, stubborn, full of ups and downs, some dangerous, some favorable. It has to fight against everything, man and the elements. Creditors, bankers, peons, merchants. . . . Against nature. . . . Every plant is a target. There is the forest, the hostile, dangerous forest, exuding menace and venom. The forest stealthily prepares its attack, awaits the propitious moment, and releases it with all its strength. A treacherous liana — a vegetable snake — writhes its way to the foot of the newcomer — the little coffee plant — kisses its leaves, tightening its coils to strangle it. Under the blaze of the sun everything proliferates. The weeds grow before one's very eyes; they come in from all sides of the clearing, surrounding it, embracing it, suffocating it. They thrust claws between every row. They grow, close in, close in, cover, choke; man watches, works, clears, clears; but the weeds have a malignant stubbornness, a deadly obstinacy, like a fatal curse; blind, implacable, overwhelming, inescapable. Man grows desperate, mad. He clears, he clears more. But there are not enough men, not enough hands. He lets other work go. Hands, hands, more hands. What's the matter with that gang that it doesn't come! Those dogs of Indians. That dog of an agent. Help at any price! Then the frenzy begins. Double wages are offered. In the highways and byways help is sought, implored. Only a fool would condemn this. What would anyone do? The same thing. Save the efforts of two years, three years. Save the planting. Would a father expose his children or leave them unprotected? And the true husbandman feels a glow of fatherly love toward the plants. They are his plants, sometimes planted by his own hand. They are his children. Each one has cost him anxiety and, in the end, sorrow.

Now they are wasting away, choked by the weeds, yellowing, drying up; a little more and all will be lost. Weed them, weed them. Clean them out. And this goes on two years, three years, forever. Every weeding gives a brief respite; but the sun, oh, that damned sun of the tropics, brings back the weeds as if by magic, and once again they are there, crowding in, threatening to devour the plantation. The anxiety is unending, killing . . . and money, money, money. It must be secured in some way, a loan, a mortgage, a bigger mortgage. The day of rest and ease will come. Of course, coffee pays well, but in the meantime one must not get discouraged. . . . And take care of the plants, spending, spending, without restraint, without choice. What a curse! Before the planting has been cleared the weeds are already springing up once more at the end where the weeding began, and all over again. . . . It is a torture worthy of Dante, a refined cruelty, an excruciating tension of the spirit that keeps it morbidly alert. Only at night perhaps comes a pause or a parenthesis. Pause? Parenthesis? It is worse then. At night, when everything lies in calm indifference, under the ecstasy of the stars, the head seems about to burst.

It is impossible to sleep. All worries acquire an acute corrosiveness and a hopeless blackness. Everything would be all right if . . . that is to say, it would be better if the creditor would grant an extension, even if the interest . . . but who can have the money ready on time with so many expenses that won't wait? And everything has been invested right here on the plantation. . . . All well and good, says the creditor, but my interest is due, I need my money! It is enough to make a man lose his mind. The mistake of asking for credit for a year, on terms that cannot be extended, with documents full of snares, legal penalties and tricky phrases and pitfalls, when it takes nearly five years to get the first crop of coffee!

When the time comes to pay, the planter has only future plans to show for the money he has invested.

When finally the first beans appear, the planter is disheartened, downcast, and skeptical. Life, like love, makes use of snares to win its end. Because growing old is not accumulating years or sorrows; growing old is giving up; it is yielding before the first obstacle; it is stepping aside from the first hurdle to be taken. And that never! Not as long as there is hope and enthusiasm. The struggle has now reached its climax, but the worst phase of it is over. Why lose heart now when the future is aglow with promise? If each shoot was a poem of anxiety, each drupe, each seed is a talisman of hope, each grain a badge of triumph and an echo of ambition. Except that there is a specter, a specter which was first a foreboding, and then began to take on shape and outline, growing, growing, always growing, looming up against the horizon of the spirit, overwhelming life, threatening to smother, to strangle. . . . Debt. The interest growing, piling up, like those structures of coral that rise from the bottom of the sea and get bigger and bigger until one day they emerge above the surface and go on growing and form reefs that pile higher and higher. . . .

Then every day there are new demands on the planter. The plantation grows, the trees flourish, but it is a constant drain. The growing industry needs materials, buildings, tools; food must be provided for the help, and therefore additional crops must be planted. Every so often the creditors growl hungrily, menacingly, and one must beg, plead, promise, sign anything. Now the harvest approaches, and what a harvest! The branches bend and split under the weight of the fruit. Is it to be lost? No, never. Letters to the loan-agent. The devil . . . he always wants money, always.

His appetite for money is insatiable. He threatens not to make any more loans. People beg him for advances, and more advances. He talks of other offers. To the planter he is a hobgoblin both fearsome and desirable, necessary and hated. In the mind of the planter he has a zoological resemblance to an octopus.

It is the middle of the year. The reports are good, the rumors optimistic. "Coffee is going to bring a good price this year." That's what they are saying; the news spreads. Some reliable source has brought it from the capital. People's spirits rise. The planter smiles now and he goes to Guatemala City to find out the prices. And sell if he can.

There he wanders about from pillar to post with his pockets full of samples. He spends his time in waiting-rooms and offices. He offers, refuses, bargains, and comes home with a skeptical air. Things are not the way they said. All right, the price has gone up a little, it's better than last year, but not what people expected. The brokers . . . not interested. The coffee market is weak. Since he's an old customer, they'll make him an offer. But the offer is disappointing. However, something was accomplished. He has sold half the crop, only half, in case the price goes up. An ingenuous precaution which the hunter — the broker — is familiar with, knowing the resources of the hunted — the planter — and fully aware of his childish tactics. The quarry doubles back, makes a run for it, but is finally caught. The law of the strongest. Good Lord, what a contract, what a sales agreement! It's the standard contract, says the lawyer. The house isn't included. Just the usual provisions. They are put in for bad customers, but in your case — what an idea! — the house would never be. . . . In the contract the broker seems like one of God's little cherubs, risking his money, while the planter seems like a double-dyed scoundrel capable of everything, against whom every precaution must be used to keep him from wriggling out of his bargain. The ones who are an exception don't count. The debtor must surrender his claims to everything, even life itself, and all this drawn up in a gibberish, an idiotic jargon in which treachery is hidden in a welter of nonsense. Justice is blind, the law helpless, words meaningless, and logic twisted. Don Ramon Castillo uses a picturesque comparison. He calls these contracts "shotgun shells." Cartridges full of shot. Some one of them will find its mark. In the agreement the legal provisos of all contracts are jumbled together, even though they mean exactly the opposite and contradict one another. Each clause may be absurd, invalid, but it works. . . . If one doesn't get the victim, the other does. Shotgun shell! Like the prescriptions some doctors order. If one ingredient doesn't cure, the other will . . . or all together they kill the patient.

But, after all, a man has to live, says the planter, with the long-dreamed-of check in his pocket, or his wallet stuffed with bills. He comes out of the hands of the despoiler beaming, as though he had just picked up a fortune. Now to get ready. A letter to the labor-agent with a check. Let him set his own figure, but get a move on, hurry. Notify the men to get ready to go to work, without delay.

The first berries are beginning to turn. One morning the whole grove appeared dotted with stars. The alchemy of the sun transmuted into gold the snow of the flowers. And now this gold has been transmuted into garnets and rubies. A vision of glory, yes, beside which another vision arises. Each garnet, each ruby is like a drop of blood. Blood of the Indian, blood of the master, fused through time, and fused once more in the trees, through a double osmosis: living and suffering.

Now preparations must be made for the harvest. All harvests rest on two strong indispensable piles: money, corn, which are really only one: money. The pickers are coming. The agent has been notified. The planter is waiting. The plantation is waiting. Everybody is waiting. One day a bright, multi-hued group will appear down the road. A weary procession marching in time to the wailing of a violin played by a young Indian bringing up the rear. Every day is a worry that pierces the spirit like a thorn. The planter curses. There is a letter from the uplands. The men cannot come yet. They are planting their wheat. In a few days. The mail is eagerly awaited. The planter is as tensely uneasy as a criminal waiting to hear his sentence. Finally the gang arrives. "There they come," shouts one of the tenants excitedly. The foreman comes over with a letter for the planter. Damn it! What is this? Not half of the men the agent had promised. It can't be. . . . That dirty dog . . . with all the money he has received. It can't be . . . but it is. There are still some who are hanging back, holding out for more money. But will they come? Of course they will . . . but they never get there. What can be done with so few people? This is a swindle. But finally the planter overcomes his impatience and drowns his disappointment in another swallow of hope. A half loaf is better than none. And now there's no time to lose. The coffee is beginning to fall off; it all gets ripe at once and then a shower, or anything, can ruin it. The planter's optimism was so shortlived. A cloud hides the sun? His smile disappears at the hint of failure. There aren't enough men? Pay them more. The neighboring planter is paying double? Offer them more. Use every enticement and bribe. Corn? All right, increase the rations. Corn . . . corn. The Indian swallows corn like a bottomless pit. He doesn't only eat it. He sells it. He exchanges it for clothes and gewgaws. He trades it. Especially for brandy. And in every town there is a scoundrel, a thief of a saloon-keeper who gets rich at the expense of the plantations in the neighborhood. There is one like Chilolo in every town. The workers on the plantations have a standing debt with him. The Indian supplies him with corn at a ridiculous price. What does it matter? It doesn't cost the Indian anything. It is something extra that he did not count on or wasn't sure about. The planter knows it and puts up with it because it is a link in the chain that binds him. If he complains, the Indian won't work. If he tries to stop it, the Indian runs away. So he pretends not to notice and pours out corn.

The end of the harvest. A casting-up of accounts by subtraction. And another casting-up of accounts: in terms of suffering. That labor agent — the devil! — did not keep his word. He did not even answer the last letters. The coffee fell off and they had to sell what they could salvage at any price. And then, for the finishing touch, bad weather. Everything went wrong, as though on purpose. Who ever heard of a month without rain at this season? The coffee ripened too fast. The result was half the crop on the ground. The planter feels as though a knife were being turned in his heart, and a wave of anger comes over him, an anger that makes his eyes smart as he walks through the rows over a carpet of rotting coffee that gives off a sourish-sweet reek in the air thick with mosquitoes. Casting up accounts by subtraction. The failure of bookkeeping and hopes. Hope that blunts itself against the inexorability of figures. And now the whole crop will go to the creditor, with danger of penalties, padded charges, and even foreclosure. How can he go on now with tasks that are urgent, pressing? Pruning, weeding, clearing. And all this effort for nothing? So many dreams so rudely shattered? Another year of defeat for hope? Another year, but in this year the planter has lived ten. There is more gray in his hair. The furrow between his brows, like a gash, tells of sleepless nights and ceaseless worry. Then there is that pain, here, around the liver. Of course, the tropics. The dog's life a planter leads — poor digestion, problems, on the go for days without any rest. It's not worth it. Still . . . a man can't refuse to stand up to life. He has to live. Who knows — maybe next year. . . . The weather may be better, conditions may improve. They've been experimenting with a new strain. . . . They say the Chinese are going to start to drink coffee. They say there's been a frost in Brazil. And then they're burning it. Yes, yes, one must keep on.

"This is the picture," said Don Ramón to César, reading his pages. "This is a pretty accurate picture. Bitter, isn't it? But one must fight on without weakening. More than that: with illusion, with hope. Who knows but that one day things will take a turn for the better. Though economic success seldom depends solely on the abilities of the planter. There were times when coffee brought in enough for everything, no matter how badly things were done. Remember the saying: 'God give you luck, son'? Look how it works out with that old man who owns La Riqueza, who is just a lucky fool. If he hurries and sells his crop, coffee drops, and without knowing it, he's done a good stroke of business. If he holds his crop, the price goes up until he has a two-year harvest to sell. That has happened several times. And then the neighbors marvel at his ability, his shrewdness. Life is full of grotesque ironies. It sometimes seems as though an evil spirit ruled events, giving them a twist so that everything conspires against honesty and fair dealing. But it is a fact that when a man gets into debt, neither shrewdness, nor foresight, nor caution, nor intelligence is of any use, for the best-laid plans, the most carefully thought-out tactics, fail in the face of a payment that must be met or robbery under cover of law. Happy those who are free of debt, who know not struggle and suffering. Those who have shaken the fist of their economic independence in the teeth of usury. But that is not the worst of this business. It is the social injustice of the thing. Here, because we revert to simian ways, or because of mental flabbiness, we don't think, and one or two think for the lot, elaborating opinions and ideas which pass for Holy Writ and become dogmas in the general mind. As for the planter, he is credited with certain traits that it has become a matter of course to attribute to him: he doesn't plan, he's a spendthrift, he's stupid, he sticks to the single-crop system. . . . Who could ever clear out this accumulation of nonsense and prejudices based on ridiculous unreasoned generalizations? Then they cite examples that are meant to be edifying without stopping to think that the more usual thing is for a rascal to achieve prosperity while a thousand poor honest devils kill themselves working from sunup to sundown all their lives and die in debt. Without thinking that to make a fortune honesty and intelligence are hardly needed at all, but a good dose of spiritual coarseness, deceit, and low cunning, and nearly all great fortunes are stained with blood and tears. In other places rich men are aware of this and try to redeem themselves by acting as Mæcenas, returning part of the wealth they have amassed to charitable organizations and institutions of learning. But not here. The person who makes a fortune — almost always a foreigner — sends it abroad after having exploited the country and its people. I am not moved by stupid local pride or raging xenophobia, nor have I anything against the foreigners who have come to this country to earn an honest living, to employ their energies in our land, to live with us and, in thousands of cases, to identify them-

selves with us, making this their real home. I refer to that band
of vampires that have no country, but that adopt any one where
they can prosper, sucking away our blood with the leeches of
usury."

There was a Biblical echo in the old man's deep voice as he
spoke, and the pathos would have seemed theatrical if he had not
been such a sincere person.

THE CARIBBEAN SEA

ASSUREDLY, THIS IS NOT THE MEDITERRANEAN. When one thinks of
the Mediterranean, the first thing that comes to mind is Sandro
Botticelli's painting, *The Birth of Venus*. The naked goddess, burnished with light, her tresses disordered by the gentle hands of
the wind, with all that equilibrium of grace that was the Greek
heritage of the Italian Renaissance, rests upon the skiff of shell
rocked by the waters of the Greco-Latin sea. The Venus of the
Caribbean is cinnamon-colored. When her sensuous body steps
upon the sand her elastic limbs move to the rhythm of old airs of
Spain and songs of Africa. To be sure, the Mediterranean has its
legends of Turkish pirates, of Phœnician and Greek thieves, and
the Roman galleys were bathed in the blood of slaves; but the
thousand sails of Latin ships and all the marble that was polished
in the days of Praxiteles converted it into the bustling bay that
witnessed the birth of Western civilization. For centuries the
Caribbean knew only the Indian mounted on his little wooden
horse that leaped agilely over the waves. *"Caribe"* meant wild in
the language of the conquistador. The term "Carib Indian" was
synonymous with "wild Indian." The word vibrates like a poisoned
arrow.

Over this sea of ours sweep the most devastating cyclones. It
is a sea sown with islands, islets, keys, which seems to open out
only when its waters look upon the broad Gulf of Mexico through

the straits of Yucatan. It was the first mirror of America that reflected the ships of Columbus. From its islands Cortés set out to conquer Mexico, Balboa to discover the Pacific, Pizarro to dominate the Incas, Quesada to found New Granada, Hernando de Soto to explore North America and slake his thirst for adventure in the waters of the broad Mississippi. The most beautiful history of America was written by Fernández de Oviedo, who heard from the lips of the conquistadors themselves their prowesses and their lies. The Caribbean was the ear in which all the first sounds of our history echoed. Crime and glory were born there together. There Columbus wrote the most poignantly sorrowful letters, and there Governor Bobadilla shackled him with opprobrious chains as a reward for having discovered the New World. The dirty sails of the buccaneers' ships swelled in its gusty breezes. Cartagena and Panama still recall Morgan's and Drake's assaults and pillage, and there can still be seen the girdles of stone the kings of Spain built to defend those American ports. Castles and fortresses, like islands that vomited fire and steel into the middle of these bays, were built into the cliffs by military engineers. For centuries these bays were seas of combat. In the ports of the Caribbean, in Havana, in Cartagena, as in New Orleans, the slave-traders set up their markets. From Africa these hunters brought their boats loaded with wares to be sold at auction, where the families of Negroes were put up on blocks and tables so the buyer could examine them to his satisfaction. The Caribbean was then the sea of slavery. Later it was the sea of liberty. There for the first time Miranda, the forerunner of Latin-American independence, unfurled his flag, and Bolívar, who crossed its waters again and again, found in its islands refuge in defeat and hope in hours of adversity. In Jamaica he wrote the finest of his letters and in Santa Marta, facing the sea, he lived the greatest of his hours, that of his death, when he took leave of his people in a proclamation that has remained as the crown of his life. Bolívar already saw the role Panama was destined to play in the future and said that all the routes of the world would intersect through the canal that would be built there. For this reason he convoked in Panama a meeting of the first Pan-American congress, the dream of his far-seeing mind. And the Caribbean has continued to write the history of liberty and faith. Only yesterday José Martí, the last of the liberators, crossed its waters to seek death in battle for the independence of Cuba. All these memories live on about this wild, blue, gay sea which in the channels of Miami seems a tropical Venice, and as it breaks against the reefs of certain lost islands recovers the air of its tempestuous days. In the canefields of Cuba the voice of Africa is heard, become music in throats of ebony. In Haiti there is a black republic. Beside the Panama Canal, which is the path of peace and war, are the beer gardens where the sailors make merry and where they dance the conga, samba, the cumbia, and the rumba. Smuggling gives wings to the shabby schooners, just as did piracy two hundred years ago. Curaçao, with its drawbridges and its wooden houses, has been a free port where French perfumes and Oriental silks are sold for the price of scented alcohol and sleazy cotton. Carlos Pellicer, the Mexican poet, has an admirable poem which begins: "I will play with the houses of Curaçao . . . I'll put the sea over on the left. . . ."

Castañeda Aragón has been one of the poets of the Caribbean. His best book is *Rincones en el Mar* (*Corners in the Sea*). His love of the Caribbean is revealed in a short proletarian novel called *Castaways of the Earth*. Over against the broad earth, where the man of the coast does not always find a welcome, Castañeda has placed the keel of a little boat which has rocked the best dreams of his life.

CASTAWAYS OF THE EARTH

G. CASTAÑEDA ARAGÓN

O N fine summer days that arm of the sea that thrusts into the rocky waste that lies to the north of the Caribbean coast unveils its deep mirrors to reflect better the graceful curves of the mountains. But in the long rainy season it turns fierce and lowering and hurls against the reefs the mass of its cataract of white foam. The light which struggles in the grip of the heavy clouds occasionally breaks through the thick walls of darkness and, dropping suddenly upon the waters, pours out over the brooding expanse of sky and waves the breath-taking jewels of its enchanted treasures.

At night when the storm has died down, its wild impulse stilled, the inlet seems like a sleeping prolongation of the land, and only an occasional solitary bird, belated by the tempest, traces the scrawl of its weary flight upon the blackboard of the sea.

In the midsummer of this north-lying country those arms of the sea that reach into the wasteland become desolate swamps. The vegetation droops and dies under the pitiless sun, and the flowers of the aquatic plants that hopefully opened languish with unquenchable thirst.

These are hard times for the inhabitants of the region. During the long hot months they search in vain for a green shoot among the rocks, a withered fruit upon the branches, or a rabbit in the ravines. It would seem that nature, which leads a brief, miraculous existence there, had squeezed the last drop of milk from her flaccid, undernourished breasts, and her flesh could flower no more nor bestow the gracious gift of daily bread.

The fecundating rainy season had passed and a brilliant sun fell burning upon the slopes of this remote corner of the Atlantic when a couple from the highlands appeared in the neighborhood. They were strong as the vertebræ of their mountains, impulsive as the wild falls of their streams, and with more optimism in their souls than the flocks of joyful birds that morning and evening turn the dense woods of the mountains to music.

They had come there to live, to clear fields of hope with their own hands, and the future held no fears for them. The future? What shadows could the future hide when here, in sight of the land which awaited them, was all the flower and pride of their youth?

Day by day, with slow but diligent effort, their strong hands opened the furrows, sowed the grain, watered the dour earth, cleared the brush. And in a little hollow where wild palms spread the shade of their tattered parasols that rustle in the sea breeze, they built their cabin. The roof, dry palm fronds that had been blown off by the wind; the floor, rough poles covered with leaves. This was the nest in which Teobaldo and Agueda hid their humble dreams of love and life.

The first night in their improvised home made them feel romantic. They thought of the chill heights of the sierra that had given them birth and to which they would never return as though it were the forgotten land of some old tale. They were no longer two frightened animals that sought refuge in the cleft of a ravine. Now they had a good house, their own, and land — rough and unyielding to be sure, but belonging to no one else either. And they recalled their recent wedding in the mountains, the greediness of the master, their grief at leaving, and finally their love, which suddenly burst upon them and joined and united them as in an unbreakable monogram of fidelity. They were like two young tree-trunks joined at the base that had been uprooted by a hurricane and hurled down the mountainside in the fury of a cyclone or an earthquake.

Ah, who would gainsay them now this sterile field, which was like a wasteland where no one would venture?

Teobaldo was sinewy, with wiry hair like a goat's, startled eyes and hands like the paws of an animal. Agueda, tall, robust, with flesh as hard as a rock. She knew how to smile and endure her lot with resignation. The two were like a single force, and it was because they really loved each other, with the love of the mountains, undefiled by the meanness of the earth.

Morning after morning, sun after sun, between the rough furrows of the plowed land the magic rill of a little brook turned the thorn leaves green, darkened the sun-baked land, until one day the field burst into an Epiphany of green shoots like a flowering of emeralds.

With the first fruits of the sweat of their brow came the first fruits of their blood. Then the cracks of the flimsy walls must be covered with fresh leaves, which the light turned into wonderful stained glass. And the golden curtain of banana-leaf fibers had to be made thicker to keep out the rough winds of the sea, and fires kept burning at night to drive away the buzzing attacks of insects.

Then one day Teobaldo, burned by the sun, drunk with the tropic, like a hero crudely fashioned out of clay, raised with the vigor of his muscles, as in the rude cradle of pleached branches of an age-old ceiba, the weak rosy joy of his first-born.

A son! Agueda, her eyes darkly circled as never before, a little pale, and thinner than when she came down from the mountains, timidly drew close to her husband. It seemed to her that in this good thing she had done the greater share was Teobaldo's. And he, in turn, felt ashamed, depressed. It was she, she who had put this child in his arms. And like a grateful slave who lays an offering before his master, he raised the new-born child aloft in the dim, leaf-tinted light of the princely cabin. Now he was really a king of glory, a conquering king, because he had triumphed over everything. There outside lay the submissive, generous, hopeful earth; here, within his arms, like a living Eucharist, pale and golden like the first fruits of the cornfield, lay this babe which he had harvested without toil, without care, because God had so willed it. How good life seemed! There was the grain of his field to prolong and make pleasant his life. And this grain of his spirit to prolong him, all of him, through time: his spirit and his flesh.

Walking the length of the cove which forms a bright oval here and looks like a silver fountain filled with light, one can see at the same time the far-off hills of Cabo de la Vela to the north, the glittering peaks of the Sierra Nevada de Santa Marta to the east, and to the south, on the beach itself, the sunburned squalid vegetation with its yellowish shadows, its faded green like that of Castile, and the bleak contours of its reddish ravines, which the surge of the tide gnaws at and washes away.

Not far from Teobaldo's little patch, some ten stone-throws from the hidden field, lies a little fishing village. There are thirty or forty shacks of old wood, thrown up rather than built on a corner of the shifting sand, under the lee of a towering cliff scarred with brutal vertical gashes all the way down from its sun-crowned peak. Against a background of thistles and underbrush about a half-dozen little fishing boats sleep their lazy siesta on the beach.

And in the midst of this motionless landscape it is not unusual to see one of the men leisurely smoking as with tar and tow — the salve and bandages of his simple therapy — he calks the cracks of his boat as though he were dressing a wound of the flesh.

Night is not so lonely or quiet here as the day. Noon is bright with sun in the village, which the waves rock with the gentleness of a nurse and which the wind from the sea cools with the breeze it has picked up on its travels over all the oceans. Here, as in the cities, with the darkness comes unrest; because these people of the sea, whom the sun makes heavy and drowsy, as soon as the last glow of sunset fades away and the light has climbed to the top step of the mountains, take their oars and prepare their tackle while all is still touched with the gold from the Andean battlements. Sails begin to rise above the leaden waters and belated pelicans skim by in weary flight, almost brushing the sea, on their way to the distant mangrove swamps or the sheltered coves of the headlands.

On the dark nights lighted by the stars, or, when there is a moon, by the glow of the molten fortune it pours through space, the fisherman makes for the high seas with the joy of a conqueror.

A boy at the gunwale, the look-out, announces with a shout the approach of a school of fish, and the canoe flies to meet them, cutting the waves and raising a gleaming torch of foam at the prow.

As he approaches, the fisherman grasps the harpoon and takes aim at the largest of the school; as the harpoon flies through the air it comes loose from the handle but remains tied to a rope held fast on the boat. It buries itself deeper and deeper in its victim until the *alacha*, worn out and unable to fight any longer, floats to the surface or slowly sinks.

Sometimes the *alachas* grow to enormous size, and it is no easy task to fish for them; but the boats nearly always return heavily loaded, and after a satisfactory night's work, about dawn, the fishermen come back to shore with their catch.

What a sight then to see the beach, with the women gathered there waiting for the fish, glowing in beauty under the first rays of the sun. The burnished gold and silver scales of the magnificent haul is like the enchanted river of a fairy tale emptying out on the sands.

Every morning Teobaldo and Agueda, carrying the baby, make their way to the village. They dally along the beach, make their purchase of fresh fish, sell their produce — fruits in season, vegetables — and return to their farm, their hearts full of joy, that innocent joy of the simple-hearted who have no contact with people of the city.

In the village they had come to know Julian, a dark young fellow who lived by himself and who owned nothing in the world but a canoe which was swifter than the breeze and safer than the rocky shore where he beached it each day. Teobaldo had often advised him to find himself a wife, but Julian just smiled and answered that there was no room in his heart for any love but that of the sea. When he was on the water he felt happier than anyone on land, and when he came back to shore he had enough to do taking care of *La Celosa,* his slim little fishing craft, which he had to clean every morning and calk every so often and protect all the time from the burning sun. And then, too, he had to mend his nets and replace his harpoons, or repair his paddles and sail. Why should he look for a wife? He did not feel that he could really love a woman. He even felt a certain fear of their arms, which he considered dangerous. The sea was better. Its love truer. More comforting. And as for beauty, what can compare in charm with the waves, feminine in their curves and movements, whose subtle caresses are unforgettable? Who has a sweet word and a song for the bad hours, and croons to you like a baby and kisses your face with lips that are always young and cool?

In his love Julian could discern details of coquettishness and was aware of the colors of the dresses his beloved donned to please his eyes. For instance, in the mornings she appeared before him in a thin, voluptuous tunic of gauze, as though she had just risen from the nuptial couch. At midday he admired her in her clear blue gown with snowy borders of foam, so delicate that only the enchanted hands of fairy nuns in their undersea convent could have woven them. In the afternoons her dress was of an ambiguous hue, between pearl-gray and pale black, trimmed with the subdued colors of the sunset; and at night she wore a loose robe of changeable colors, and a crown of stars like a queen. Sometimes it pleased her to fasten her hair with the sumptuous, glowing comb of the moon.

Teobaldo smiled as he listened to him. He looked at his wife, covered the little one's head with kisses, and felt no envy. He did not seem to understand such things. For love, these two, he said, and his little remote corner of the earth, which paid him a drop of honey for each drop of sweat; which soothed his fatigue with the cool shade of peace, and when he lay down to rest at night on his rude bed, comforted him and lulled him to sleep with the peaceful music of its unfathomed silence.

After the burning heat of June the rainy season set in once more. The sea covered the swamps, bristling with rushes again, and the rains painted with new shining varnish the branches of the trees and darkened the rocks that jutted out of the hills and the sand of the dunes.

The eyes of Agueda and Teobaldo, which had learned to look deep, saw the sky darken and the sea cloud and they awaited with frightened pleasure the kindly help of the season which would lighten their anxious care. They would not have to spend the nights guiding the little brook by hand from patch to patch to moisten the furrows and bring new life to the plants. Everything would come from above. The earth lay passive under the miracle of fertilization and tomorrow would return the gift multiplied a hundredfold.

"Now," thought Teobaldo, "that dreamer of a Julian won't be able to fish except just once in a while. The *alacha* goes away in the rainy season, and all there is are the little fish the tide brings in as it sweeps against the rocks. How good he would find the warmth of a woman and the joy of children in these days of enforced idleness! Because when a man most needs family affection is when Nature, in an unpleasant mood, seems to abandon him to his fate and hampers his work and makes him stand with idle arms, awaiting her pleasure."

Really, hardly a boat dared venture out between thunderstorms in that weather. Only rarely on those afternoons when sky and

water seem to meet in a tragic embrace did the villagers see, struggling against the wind, a coastwise sloop or an occasional schooner,
which in good weather sail by in the distance, some twenty or
thirty miles from the shore, like shy birds.

The smoke from the hearth, where the fire had to be coaxed
from the damp wood and brush gathered up along the shore —
for during the bad months the sea vents its ill humor by washing
up on the beach everything the flooded rivers have snatched
away from the farmers in the valleys — rose from Teobaldo's
cabin, Georgic and blue in the damp morning, filling the rain-
pocked air with the pleasant smell of food.

Agueda was nursing her baby beside the fire, beneath the dripping eave. Clean and smiling, she recalled the figure of the poem:

> . . . bountiful, in the bright dawn of morning,
> she puts her bared breast, like a fruit of glory,
> into the baby's mouth, which is a flowering rose.

Teobaldo, talking over the work of the day with the monotonous
accent of the country people, was preparing the meal. He had
crushed the aggressive heads of the shrimps on a hollowed-out
stone, and the whiteness of the rice was taking on color as it
simmered over the slow fire, crowned with the bright rubies of the
tomato and the emeralds of the young garlic, when another
shower, brightened by occasional flashes of lightning, began to
fall with sleepy monotony. To one side of the hearth, wild plan-
tains, which have more honey in their heart than a beehive, were
browning over the embers on a grill made of a barrel hoop. A
little farther away, spread out on the floor, with the silvery side
up, were banana leaves, which make the fine tablecloth of the
countryfolk.

Beyond doubt everybody had a good appetite. But the one who
seemed to feel the most urgent need of food was Nero, the mastiff,
who lay stretched out full length beside the fire. Every time Teobaldo lifted the lid from the pot he blinked his sleepy eyes.

At twelve, when the sound of the bells of the distant town came
leaping from cliff to cliff through the transparent air, swept clean

by the storm, they sat down cross-legged before their food. Teobaldo sat at Agueda's side; she held the baby in her lap, and near all of them sat the dog, his drooling tongue hanging out.

The weather had cleared. The trill of a bird, like the tinkling of crystal, emerged from the dripping branches of an almond tree. Agueda and Teobaldo crossed themselves. And a pale, watery ray of sun, filtering through the cracks of the cabin, glorified the scene.

Many days had gone by, days of rain and storm, and the roads were still furrowed by the rush of the storm's runnels. One morning when the sun had come out early, as though it were going for a swim, wrapped in its filmy robe of mist, the inhabitants of the fishing village heard horses coming down the ravine.

The confused shouts that reached them, together with the noise and clatter of the iron shoes on the road, startled the hearts of the two mountaineers. They were just getting ready to gather the vegetables to take to the village. They could not say why, but that unusual event filled them with a foreboding of something that might be coming to destroy forever the nest of happiness which, with so many sacrifices, they had hidden from the eyes of the world.

They stepped to the door and looked out at the slopes down which they thought the cavalcade might come. They stood motionless, but their souls were beating in painful expectancy.

A vivid polychrome of wild flowers, brightened by the sun, covered the flanks of the foothills. The sky, bluer than the sea, now clear of fog, had that healthful relaxation one sometimes sees in the eyes of certain women when they smile after they have been crying. And a young donkey, its hide still furry, which was tied to a tree in the garden, raised its hairy ears and let out a loud, ringing bray that rose through the hills like the call to arms of a trumpet.

In a little while the riders came into view. They were six men dressed in baggy khaki suits, shining leggings, and cork helmets. The one in front, who seemed to know the lay of the land well, was dark and spoke in Spanish; the others had light hair and blue eyes. Teobaldo and Agueda caught bits of the conversation in a language they did not know and their uneasiness became terror. Their fright was so great that their nerves, taut as the strings of a guitar, allowed only a mumble of blurred words to come out in answer to the "Good day" of the first traveler, who had now alighted beside the door.

His companions slid lightly from their mounts, tied them under a shed, and sat down in the shade of the banana palms. Then one of them took a roll of papers from a metal tube, spread them out on the grass, and they all began to examine a shining parchment sheet on which were geometrical lines traced in red ink.

Teobaldo in his bewilderment said nothing at first. But pricked on by Agueda's glittering eyes, he ventured to clear his throat and then step forward and say to the visitors:

"The gentlemen are welcome here. If you would like something to eat we can fix you some coffee. You're looking for oil, aren't you?"

"Thanks," said the one who looked like a native. "We had breakfast in town. What brings us here is not exactly what you're thinking. These foreign gentlemen have come to look over their property."

A silence dense with unspoken hostility floated thickly in the air.

"This land, sir," said Agueda timidly, rocking the baby in her arms, "has never belonged to anybody. It hasn't any owner. It was just wasteland and we have cultivated it."

"Oh, it's the same old story," said the dark man. "Nothing belongs to anybody, but a day comes when everything has its owner. This land is part of a concession made by the government to the company these gentlemen represent. This is nothing to be surprised at. In Colombia there are lots of people like these who own land. Now you folks can't be considered tenants or anything. You might even be accused of trespassing on other people's property, and the best thing you can do is go back where you came from without saying a word."

"That's right," the voices of the others, who were standing near, agreed.

Teobaldo wanted to say something but he couldn't. He felt dizzy and he had to rest against his wife's shoulder; she, with tears in her eyes, was leaning up against the door jamb. The lees of old ancestral injustices, demanding retribution, began to work in the depths of his heart. But he kept silent.

One of the foreigners spoke up: "Read these people the copy, doctor."

The "doctor" pompously reached into his coat pocket, brought out a pair of horn-rimmed spectacles, and, unfolding the official document brought along for the purpose, began to read in the tone of the town crier. He emphasized the phrases he considered important, looked over his glasses at every paragraph as though to please the Yankees, who were paying no attention to him and were talking quietly among themselves in English. When he had finished he walked over and put his hand on Teobaldo's shoulder.

"As you can see, it is the simplest thing in the world." And he added: "It's better for you not to wait to be evicted. The police are on our side."

But Teobaldo did not listen to him. He jerked away and lunged into the cabin.

The order gave him two weeks' notice to leave the place. It allowed him to harvest whatever crops might be ready during that time. But that was all. If he refused to get off he would be put in jail.

"Where does it say all that?" Agueda ventured to ask. And the foreigner who had ordered the notice read answered: "Here," pointing to the document. "Your husband can sign at the town hall."

The words of the law clerk and the Yankee had fallen like sharp stones on Agueda's heart. She did not know what to do with her reddened eyes, swimming in tears, like those rainy sunsets she had often watched with Teobaldo. Her tears, bitter baptismal waters of sorrow, fell on the baby asleep in her arms.

Teobaldo came silently to the door once more. Not a single gesture revealed the tragedy that was taking place within him. And nothing could rouse him from the kind of stupefaction that had come over him. He heard the horses trotting off down the path without a sign of rebelliousness or even protest. Only when the law clerk called back to him from the distance: "Maybe these gentlemen will give you work," did his pent-up silence burst out in a savage roar of despair and impotence:

"Thieves!"

Two weeks after the tragic day they were ordered from the land, Teobaldo and Agueda were still there, not knowing what to do. They had gathered their pitiful little crop, sold the donkey, and packed their few belongings into two or three bundles. Where were they going? They had not even thought about it. It was like the first time when they came down from the hills, urged on by the need of finding the open roads. From there to here, from here who knows where, inch by inch the earth cast them out, refused them refuge.

The morning they departed was the warm awakening of the new season. Once more, almost overnight, summer was here again and the trees were beginning to get dusty and the ground was drying out. The twisted, curled-up old leaves of the mango trees were torn off by the light northeast wind. And as Teobaldo had not irrigated the garden for days, the plants were turning yellow and some of the vegetables, still green, were rotting beside the little ditches, dying of thirst.

Teobaldo, with a malicious delight of which he would not have believed himself capable, was tearing down, board by board, the little house where he had once been happy. He piled up the ruins, set fire to them, and fanned the flames. Nobody — and least of all those hateful people who had come from afar to rob him of what was his — should find shelter beneath the happy roof that had covered the three of them. His hatred toward these oppressors was boundless, and now he understood the reason for revolutions, which had never been clear to him before.

He recalled that in the last civil uprising a guerrilla band had marched over the mountains destroying everything in its path like a hurricane. And they had recruited him, who had never hated anybody, without his understanding then the reason for that barbarous warfare. Where were they going, what were these farmers

111

seeking who had abandoned the iron that opens the earth to fertility for the iron that kills? Ah, but now he, too, would wield it. Not against his own, his brothers in misfortune, but to drive out of the country those foreigners, and those others who were even more despicable, for they were the ones who turned the land over to the foreigners. Now that all the happiness of his heart had been destroyed, one road was as good as another.

And Teobaldo was just about to finish his thoughts with a curse when the voice of Agueda, praying and holding the baby out to him, halted him. Transfigured, his gesture turned gentle and his face, twisted with rage, softened as he approached them. The heads of the three together against the morning landscape were like the miraculous flowering of a new and fecund life.

The words of the prayer — "Give us this day our daily bread" — still floated in the deep quiet of the hour of peace as the sad group made their way along the coast. In the back of his mind Teobaldo was wondering if perhaps the machete at the right moment might not be more useful than the prayers advised by religion, but nevertheless the sweetness of those words on Agueda's fresh young lips filled him with confidence in the future. Nero followed behind them, sniffing at each footstep they left in the damp sand, which disappeared almost at once as though nothing of these exiles should be left.

They looked back and in the distance they could still see the column of smoke from their destroyed cabin, which seemed thus to be bidding them farewell. The air of the morning was so still and the sky was so clear and enamel-bright that the white column rose straight, without twisting or feigning those changing shapes of monsters in which some claim to read the future. And they walked on.

Step by step they reached Julian's village. The beach was alive with the shouts of women and children who crowded the beach at that hour awaiting the return of the boats with their catch. Teobaldo and his wife could see in the distance *La Celosa*, which rose and fell with the movement of the waves, like the pelicans that let themselves be floated in to shore after a long flight.

Julian saw them and made for shore. He reefed in his sail and then, standing in the water up to his knees, brought his boat up on the shore with a surge of the tide.

His face gave evidence of a successful night. The haul had been a good one. One only needed to see him smile, especially when he buried his hands in the bottom and pulled up, for the admiration of all, the biggest fish of the whole catch. It was an *alacha* with scales of embossed silver, belly the color of the sea, and fins and tail like open fans of mother-of-pearl.

With the vanity of the deep-sea hunter, he waited for his friends, to offer them his prize. But one glance at their faces told him that something tragic had happened, and his expression became as serious as when he expounded his theories to Teobaldo.

"What is the matter? What is in the bundles? What has happened?"

And they told him their story. They had lost everything; they had no place to go. They were going where fate led. Perhaps they could find something to do in town. There was nothing for them here. But they had to feed the little one. They didn't care about themselves. It was for him, only for him, the dawn in which all the shadows of their night had melted away, that they had to live and face everything in the world, even death. . . .

Julian lighted his pipe, sat down on the edge of his boat, and with his peculiar intonation, calm and grave, said to them:

"No, your life is here. Forget your mountains and your fields. You will have another cabin on this shore and a little boat like mine. The mountain cast you off into the furrow, and now the furrow casts you on to the strand. You are the castaways of the earth, and only the sea, my sea, will give you the refuge you seek. It hasn't taken you long, Teobaldo, to see that I am right. I, too, lost all I had on land. The men there robbed me and degraded me. And here I have redeemed myself. Now I laugh at them and am happy. The earth is theirs alone. Let them keep it. One day the sea will swallow it up."

With his bearded face, his serene eyes looking off into the horizon, Julian recalled the prophets of old.

Teobaldo and Agueda said nothing, but a smile of hope lighted up their faces. It was the truth: the farther they were from the earth, the better. It had been cruel to them. At least no one would drive them away from here.

Comforted by the promise contained in the words of the fisherman, they held out their grateful hands to him, and he clasped them in his own damp salty ones.

In the village a bell began to ring.

Nero, with a bound, leaped ahead on the sand, barking joyously, as though he wished to be the first of the castaways to reach dry land, and Agueda and Teobaldo followed him.

The serious little group, under the blazing sun, against the serene landscape, aroused in Julian's memory the recollection of another group, long lost in time, which he had once seen in a book. Perhaps it was in one of the saints' lives.

At this childhood memory tears filled his eyes, and his knife made the bright scales fly through the air as though he were sowing stars.

THE LAKES OF THE SOUTH

"THE SWITZERLAND OF AMERICA" is the name generally given the lake region in the southern part of Argentina and Chile. Those who have visited it agree that it may well be considered one of the most beautiful in the world. Nevertheless, it has only recently been incorporated into the national life of these countries. Its conquest has been one of the last in America. Where today stand luxurious hotels for rich Argentineans and tourists from all over the world, yesterday the Indians roved wild. In the days of the tyrant Rosas these Indians were so strong that they came up the pampas to the outskirts of Buenos Aires and sowed terror among the whites. Rosas began the first "desert campaign" to subdue them. But the person who really extended the frontier, in a manner similar to the winning of the West in the United States, was General Julio A. Roca, beginning in 1879. As a result of this campaign, in which thousands of Indians were killed, over 100,000 square miles of territory were opened to Argentine settlers. After the army came the scientists, the engineers, who drew up maps, built roads, and discovered the Bariloche Pass, which leads to the region of Nahuel Huapí and the lake world where the landscapes of Chile and the Argentine come together. The process was similar on the Chilean side. President Bulnes (1841–51) decided to extend the boundaries of Chile to the Strait of Magellan. The city of Punta Arenas, which overlooks the strait, was founded at this time. Bulnes wanted to settle this region, too, and encouraged European immigration. This was the beginning of the German settlements. Bernardo Philippi, a German, whom Bulnes appointed governor of the territory, was largely instrumental in bringing in families of settlers. The Indians assassinated him some years later, but the Germans were established by that time and soon business and industry were in their hands. The greater part of the population there is of this origin.

Before reaching the lakes there is the desert to be crossed. It is a great dark plain. It is almost impossible for travelers to protect themselves from the dust which sifts into the train through the tiniest crack. There is Huecubu Maipu, which means Land of the Devil. But then come the lakes. Guillermo Estrella has written: "If the Argentine has a garden in the north, it has a park in the south, in this hallucinatory lake region of the south, which emerges from the most dismal desert of the world, as though it had been created for the purpose of giving plastic form in rock, plant, and water to the totality of Dante's vision: Hell at one end and Paradise at the other." On the Chilean side are Lakes Llanquihue, measuring 290 square miles, Todos los Santos, Puyeyue, Rupanco, Chapo. And on the Argentine side, Nahuel Huapí, Huechulauquén, Lacar, Traful, and others. Julio Navarro Monzo says: "I know the lakes of Scotland and Switzerland. And those of Canada. Not all, of course, but the most famous, and others less so. Lake Menteith, for instance, in the middle of an island; Inchmahome, where 'our' Don Roberto, the never-to-be-forgotten Cunninghame-Graham, lies. I have lived in remote corners of these beautiful regions as I am now living in a quiet spot near Nahuel Huapí. When I think back on all I have seen in Europe and America, and also in Africa along the banks of the Nyasa and the Zambesi, I can find nothing to compare with this in beauty. For there are views here that remind one of the Alps and the Swiss lakes seen from Geneva, Neuchâtel, or Zürich; scenes, too, that recall the Trossachs, Lake Lomond, and other Scotch 'lochs.' But this is unique. It has all this and more, too: a primitive aspect which the others lack."

Victoria Ocampo, the founder and editor of one of the most important magazines of the continent, *Sur*, wrote the following pages on her return from a trip to the lake country.

THE LAKES OF THE SOUTH
VICTORIA OCAMPO

Mauriac in *Les Maisons fugitives,* which is illustrated with photographs recalling the places in which he spent his youth, says he belongs to that species of goat, and their name is legion, which fret at having to graze in the spot where they are tethered, but which remain there even after the rope is broken and never leave the stake that has decided their fate for all time.

Beyond question I belong to the same species. When, for instance, I try to analyze what "Argentina" means to me, I discover something that is neither grand nor involved: the smell of certain plants and certain trees through which, in certain months, I look upon a certain river from a certain terrace; the noise of a certain train that passes, breaking the false silence filled with birds, crickets, and frogs.

This limitation has kept me, until a short time ago, ignorant of my own country (but aware of my ignorance), and when people were surprised that I did not know the beauties of the Iguassu or Tilcara, of Villa Nogués or Nahuel Huapí, and reproached me as lacking in patriotism on this account, I always felt like answering: "Those falls, valleys, mountains, and lakes are admirable, I have no doubt; but it is my own peculiar way of striking roots in the place I was born that keeps me from them. My real native land consists of some unassuming willows, a few thick ombus, an *aguaribay*, as mournful and romantic as the willow, *tipa* trees that spit like guanacos at certain seasons of the year, lilac *paraisos* which pervade the air with their scent in November, jasmines, honeysuckles, *tumbergias*, on a high bluff of the Plata River; it is this river, these trees, these flowers whose shape, perfume, and feel I knew before I knew their name. My physical homeland is the meeting between this piece of land and my infancy. I can neither add to it nor take from it.

But I said nothing and kept a shamefaced, contrite silence.

In spite of the fact that I so disliked leaving my little corner that for a long time it made me "a monster of indifference and heedlessness" with regard to all the Argentine landscape aside from the banks of the San Isidro or the breakwater of Mar de la Plata (two loves of which I am not ashamed), I have finally — against my will — left my province (and when I say province I am exaggerating; I really mean the few miles of land where I have returned to pasture, after the tether was broken). I have seen and enjoyed the varied beauties of my country, to which I had been the indifferent heir. Because I loved too well the mud of the brown, turbid river in which, as a little girl, I had sloshed my feet with delight, for a long time I neglected the promised transparence of far-off lakes; and because my eyes were too used to play over the horizon without meeting any obstacles, to wander over the pampas of the land or flat, lazy waters, I did not miss the luxuriance of the forest or the snows of the Andes.

Yet, in spite of myself, I have finally taken trains and automobiles which carried me to my unexplored domains. Trains and automobiles that I hated, but to which I owe a debt of gratitude.

Cheating at solitaire, swallowing dust and irritation, I have wiped with countless damp towels and napkins the forks and spoons of the dining-car, my dirty face, the hermetically closed windows of the compartment, through which, notwithstanding, the dust entered with the greatest ease.

Whatever remarks all these things may have elicited at the moment, and which, out of respect for the reader, I shall keep to myself, I have never regretted enduring these passing annoyances which the born tourist suffers with secret satisfaction (for it makes it possible for him to display his stoicism).

I fear nothing could make a real tourist of me. The minute I bite off a few miles too many, I cannot digest them. Local color — which is generally nothing but a thick coat of dirt on buildings and people — fails to arouse my interest or throw me into a trance of delight. What can I do if I have no vocation for this?

On the contrary, the more I see of a place (if I like it), the richer it grows to my eyes, beneath my gaze, the more beauties I discover in it, and with greater pleasure. In short, I do not believe one can really love a place without returning to it (with certain exceptions). And if one goes back a thousand times, one loves it a thousand times more for a thousand reasons.

A person who has not watched and waited for the changes of season in a little, well-known bit of the earth, as one watches on a face one loves the play of happiness, sadness, deceit, or anger, has missed something which all the miles gulped down can never substitute.

Every place that we see for the first time seems to us bare and empty unless we have lived in it for a long time with the mind, the imagination, or the desire. And it is books that help us to people the unknown. Writers are the great builders of bridges, of railroads and ocean liners. So true is this that we go by preference to the places where they have already taken us. For this reason Europe has an irresistible attraction for us. Its charm is not that of the unknown, but of something already seen in dreams.

The natural-born tourist is a new species of animal who likes to graze only where he has never grazed before. It matters little to him whether the place he visits is peopled for him or bare; the important thing is to be seeing it for the first time. His ambition is to swallow the greatest possible amount of new scenery. The born tourist collects landscapes as others collect stamps or coins.

For the anti-tourist, of which I am one (I should like to find some other expression, such as own-corner-lover, because I have never liked this use of "anti," so much in vogue; it seems to me purely negative and sterile), it is as impossible to collect land-

scapes as to collect human beings. For the anti-tourist the landscape is a person. He has to get used to it. He has to devote his
time to it, a great deal of time, if he really loves it. He has to talk
with it, leisurely and alone.

When an anti-tourist travels, it is usually for reasons which have
nothing to do with adding to his stamp collection. His obligations
take him past landscapes where he regrets not being able to stop.
For a person of this sort, essentially a creature of routine, to feel
at home in a place he must find in it a minimum of recollections
and habits.

In this manner, because I had something to do there, I have
known and admired the cornfields of Santa Fé, the miles of flowering cactus of Santiago del Estero, the gorges of Entre Rios, the
fragrant sierras of Córdoba, the canefields of Tucumán, which are
splashes of such delicate green seen from Aconguija.

It was a waste of time for them to talk to me about the lakes of
the south. I had no call to go there except as a pure and simple
tourist. And since I do not give a snap of my fingers for salmon-
fishing, it took me years to make up my mind to go.

But finally last November I took the train at Constitución. There
was the endless procession of hours and the everlasting ceremony
of the damp towels against the windows, on a train that picked
the most desolate places to stop, and maliciously halted there for
hours on end, and where, instead of thirst-quenching fruit, I was
offered chunks of petrified forest at ten cents apiece. And, into the
bargain, I was ashamed to complain of my first-class accommoda-
tions after seeing the second-class; but at last one morning I found
myself in Bariloche just as I had lost all hopes of ever arriving.

A few minutes before we entered the pleasant stone station I
forgot my fatigue. The lake had come up to meet us. How blue it
looked against the background of the snow-capped mountains,
beside the bushes covered with flowers so red that they seemed
land coral reefs! These bushes, the harbingers of spring in the
Andes, whose name and existence I was unaware of (we call them
ciruelillos; North Americans have given them the name of fire-
bush), gave us a dazzling welcome all along the way, like Lake
Nahuel Huapí itself. Not a breath of wind stirred it that day; vast

and calm, it looked up at the sky without blinking, while the sky descended to its very depths.

By noon, on the road from Bariloche to Llao-Llao which skirts the lake and grows in wonders as it advances, I asked myself if I was on another planet. This seemed the only explanation. The sky without a cloud, the branches of the trees and the water motionless, in a calm (rare in this region) which emphasized the colors just as silence and immobility emphasize the slightest sound. I said to myself: "If there were only the lake, it would be extraordinary. If there were nothing but the mountains or the trees, or the special quality of the air and the light, that, too, would be extraordinary. And here we have everything together." I thought this on a stretch of road from Bariloche to Llao-Llao, before I had seen anything else. This road, which I feared might suddenly end at every turn, so incredible it seemed, took me in the afternoon to the forest of Llao-Llao. Even the acres of trees charred by the forest fires, which one sees along the way, have their attraction. The remains of a forest become there the ruins of a temple, and the wood of the trunks lopped off at different heights, fallen or standing erect like columns, take on a silvery-gray tone that I have never seen anywhere else. But, then, was there anything in the lakes of the south that I had seen anywhere else?

The giant *coihues* of the forest of Llao-Llao, those huge columns that terminate in a few small-leaved branches, seem trees that belong to another geological age, and it would not surprise us to see the long neck and tiny head of a dinosaur peering out from the bamboo-like *colihues* growing at their feet. Here amidst the *coihues* no other animal seems to fit in except these gigantic herbivores with their lizard-like paws. It strikes me that the antediluvian animals of Conan Doyle's *Lost World* would have been better preserved in this forest than in ice. I had a feeling all the time that I was an intruder and that I had miraculously slipped into a world that was not yet ready for man.

But if the forests of *coihues* and *lengas* amaze and almost frighten one, seeming, as they do, monuments of another age, the forest of myrtle of the peninsula of Quetrihue leaves one disconcerted. The trunk of these trees is reddish, smooth, and extremely soft to the touch. The leaves are small, like those of all the trees of the region, shiny and of an intense green. There are myrtles grow-ing scattered around Lake Nahuel Huapí, but it is in Quetrihue that one sees them in a compact assembly. The effect is over-whelming. Within the forest everything seems bathed in rose-colored light, as though the tree-trunks were illuminated from within. These trunks seem at times legs and arm with the muscles tense, the arms and legs of Nijinsky when, in *The Specter of the Rose*, he rose like a human tree in motion, freed at last from its roots.

On the road to Traful we passed a place called Enchanted Val-ley because of the strange forms of the jagged, broken rocks, in which, as in the clouds, one can see whatever one fancies. The forest of Quetrihue is more deserving of the name Enchanted. It would even be worthy of a legend. What Apollo has flayed all these young Phrygians to death in punishment?

> . . . *Si comme quiando Marsia traesti*
> *della vagina delle membri sue!*

I keep coming back to this air of almost mythological inveri-similitude, for it seems to me typical. The waters of the Limay River, for instance, roll slowly like molten metal. One would hardly dare put one's hand into them. As soon as we ascend a hill — Otto Hill, for example, where one gets a panoramic view of the lakes — the trees display a strange pale-green beard (lichens? moss?). The road from Llao-Llao to Tronador, past amazing Lake Mascardi, or from Bariloche to Correntoso, to Traful, to San Mar-tín of the Andes, to mention only what we were able to see during a brief stay, are like nothing we have ever seen elsewhere.

Another agreeable surprise for the visitor to the lake region is that man's intervention — I refer to the National Parks — has not spoiled nature's work. It has respected all its grandiose, untamed elements, but at the same time has rendered it accessible. In this sense the work of the Department of National Parks seems to me perfect. Not once have they betrayed or affronted the spirit of the place. And that is saying a great deal. We must remember that this is a country which abounds in colored fountains, pergolas, and monuments to match. The lake region is still undefiled by such horrors and it would be a great pity if it did not preserve this purity, this virginal quality for which our eyes so often gave thanks to Heaven (and to the Department of National Parks).

Now I dream of books on Patagonia, on its forests, its wild flowers, and its lakes. I dream of words that shall do it justice.

I have returned to the stake that has decided my destiny forever, as Mauriac would say. I cannot say that I have been converted into a tourist. But I have fallen in love with the lake country. I wonder if the same thing has not happened to all the others who have visited it. Neither wind, nor rain, nor distance can keep me from it now.

We possess only what we really love. We possess things only to the extent that we love them. All other possession is illusory. I have discovered that my trip to Patagonia, where I thought I had nothing to do, has not been just travel. I went there to take possession of a piece of land that belonged to me, for I have loved it with that special love that pays the price of things better than money. Now I have lakes, forests, falls, mountains whose beauty I had never imagined. The mysterious lake country is mine. I should like to see it belong to all those Argentines who do not know it yet, and since it is now mine, my first impulse is to share it with them.

THE OCEANS OF CHILE

Benjamín Subercaseaux has written an excellent book which bears the title *Chile, a Mad Geography*. If the description is not wholly exact, at least it can be said that Chile has a unique geography. It is the maritime nation of Latin America. It is a narrow shelf of the Andes that projects over the Pacific and reaches from the torrid zone to a latitude in the south that corresponds to Alaska or Labrador in the north. It has 2,900 miles of coastline, twice as long as that of the United States on the Pacific. On the other hand, inland, Chile is not as wide as the state of Oregon. Chile is like a California stretching from Mexico to Alaska, like a Norway with several times as much seacoast. And with a profile like Norway's, too, full of islands, coves, fjords. There man, his life, and his songs are all of the mountain or the sea. But not an international sea, for the Pacific has never been like the European waters; ships flying the flags of all nations have not furrowed its plains. The sea of Chile, like that of Norway, has been a domestic sea, full of local color and fishermen's tales. It is a provincial sea which takes on a worldly air only around the fashionable watering-place, Viña del Mar, to which, nevertheless, the sea-food and the wines of Chile give a local stamp. Facing the sea lies the desert or the mountains. The desert leads to the copper and nitrate mines; the mountains, to the highest peaks of the world, which are covered with perpetual snow. Out of the thick, ancient forests came one of the bravest races of America: the Araucanians; one of the most beautiful trees botanists have classified: the araucaria; and the greatest epic poem of the conquest: *La Araucana*. The common root of these three names, which evokes a race, a landscape, and a poem that are unique, is the root of Chile. Anyone who visits Chile today can eat the most delicious grapes in America and enjoy the fine climate. Whoever writes about Chile nearly always mentions California; there have been periods when intimate contacts have been established between Chile and the northern state, and masses of Chilean workingmen threw in their fate with that of North Americans in the tumultuous days of California's settlement. But Chile, too, has had a hard life and it has taken tremendous efforts to dominate a nature that did not yield easily.

Torres Rioseco analyzes the historical development of his country thus: "Chile is a country 'made' by its inhabitants. Peru, Mexico, Venezuela, Cuba were the same when they were discovered as now: abounding in natural wealth, favored by nature, promised lands. Chile is still a country difficult to subdue; this is the reason that in colonial days it offers nothing comparable in display of luxury, wealth, splendor, and refinement to the courts of Lima and Mexico City; its colonial history is a continual struggle against the Indian and nature. The first Spaniard who set foot on our soil — Diego de Almagro — knew how grim this crossing of the mountains and the desert could be, for he left the corpses of his best soldiers upon them. Later the conquistador Pedro de Valdivia was eaten alive by the fierce Araucanians, whom the Spanish legions were never able to subdue. The early days of the conquest and the colony were hard and the life of the Spaniards in Chile never had the charm of the sumptuous viceregal courts or rich centers. In these three centuries of unremitting struggle the repose needed to create a literature was lacking; there were only isolated cases, like the miracle of Don Alonso de Ercilla, who 'wrote by night what he did by day,' adding the note of music to the clamor of conquest."

Mariano Latorre, who stands out as one of Chile's great writers today, has portrayed the mountains and sea of Chile with great fidelity.

CAPTAIN OYARZO

MARIANO LATORRE

I HAD just sat down at my desk that pleasant afternoon of the month of June. As usual, I had got there five minutes before time. My life had grown so mechanized in this English importing firm that I could have put down on my calendar (a gift of the house) what I was going to do every day of the year, and every year that still stretched before me.

I was smoking my Capstan cigarette (genuine) and absently watching the swinging door give its sharp creak, catching the light on its beveled glass window, as the entering employees pushed it open: young girls of the port city, smartly dressed, the office stenographers; young Chileans who imitated the English employees; slow-moving gringos, with their bony shoulder-blades, baggy vicuna sweater jackets, and their fragrant pipe tobacco. All this busy multitude hurried to their different compartments like honeybees to their cells in a hive. My mind, which had dozed for a minute, slipped back into gear again. There were some letters to be answered, I had to go to the dock to see the customs inspector and hurry through the landing of goods that was already loaded into the company's barges. In a few minutes the tall, lanky figure of Mr. MacKenzie, my boss, would appear with his red face, his red nose, his pipe between his teeth, to ask: "What's on today?" referring to the notes on the memorandum pad two inches from my hand.

Through the broad window unwonted sunlight poured in, the reluctant sun of the seaside winter. I had just sat down when the office boy, making his way through the labyrinth of wooden compartments, came to tell me that there was somebody to see me.

I looked up to see a weatherbeaten old fellow, enveloped in a frayed coat and an air of strange timidity. He kept turning the brim of his old hat between his thick, dirty fingers.

"What can I do for you?" I asked with a brusqueness I could not hide.

I hated to admit it, but it annoyed me to have a man who looked like that come to see me.

The old man must have seen this from the expression on my face and he said nothing. An inexpressible air of suffering lay upon him like a halo. At last he seemed to make up his mind. His decayed teeth showed themselves in a pitiful attempt at a smile, almost a grimace.

"Don't you remember me, Mr. Sánchez?" he asked.

His voice gave me an odd sensation. It was firm, almost youthful; it had not aged. It seemed to me that I had heard it before, and it called up the perfume of a memory that vanished before I could get hold of it. The man went on, lowering his voice timidly:

"I have changed a lot, Mr. Sánchez. It's been twenty years. I am José Oyarzo, sir, Captain Oyarzo."

A flood of recollections rushed to my memory. A swift, unthinking emotion made me reach out toward the old man and grasp his dirty hand, which I took almost against his will.

"I wouldn't have remembered you, Oyarzo. You look like a different man. You've aged a lot."

Then, quickly, to wipe out the impression of arrogance I might have given him, I said:

"I thought you were at sea. They told me you owned a schooner over in Lebu."

My friendly attitude seemed to bring him back to normal. His voice lost its pathetic, mournful tone.

"Yes, sir, I did. I bought it at Corral, a little after that trip, but the German steamers ruined the coastwise trade. Naturally the cargo traveled safer in the steamers. It didn't pay us to take the risks we had to, so I went back home again, to Talcahuano."

And as though he were eager to get to the matter that had brought him there, the tone of his voice changed again. It clouded over once more and he began to mumble with a whining intonation that made the image of the former skipper of the Milnes Company recede in the distance again.

"That's why I've come, sir. I've just got in. I had to stow away on one of the Sud-Americana boats. Please excuse my taking the liberty; but I happened to remember that you, the only person I knew in Valparaiso, were in the firm."

He hesitated and I asked him to sit down. Over the top of the partitions the clerks and stenographers were watching the scene. I could see the smiles on their stupid faces.

"Go ahead. Tell me what I can do for you, and I'll be glad to do whatever I can to help you."

"I'm old, boss, and they want me to go. The rheumatism, you know how it is, it cripples you up sometimes. . . . So many years in the water . . . and by myself. My only son — you remember — he'd be a man now."

Old Oyarzo stopped. His voice clouded over and hoarsened on the last words. I remembered other instances. It was a common occurrence, this throwing overboard of the old skippers, like useless ballast, after a lifetime of work. It was before the day of labor unions and the protection of labor laws.

"All right, Oyarzo, I'll see what I can do. Unfortunately, Mr. Merry is dead. Mr. MacKenzie is a splendid man, and I think he can find you something, though it will probably be on land. How would that suit you?"

"Thanks an awful lot, sir. When shall I come back?"

"Tomorrow."

"You can't think how grateful the old lady and the girls will be."

There were tears in his voice. It was plain that this same scene had taken place many times.

"There are five of them, and they've got only what I make to live on," he added.

No question about it, he was a defeated man. There was not much left of the Oyarzo I had known twenty years before — strong, powerful, commanding, like one of the trees of his native island. Oyarzo was from Chiloé. He held out his hand to me with an impulsive gesture of gratitude, but quickly drew it back in embarrassment. His watery little eyes reflected a childlike happiness when I put my hand on his stooped back as I walked with him to the waiting-room. He was, beyond all doubt, a defeated man. I followed his shrunken, timid, insignificant figure until it disappeared behind the swinging door. My imagination attempted to restore that withered frame, blow the spark of life into it, but recollection followed recollection, and like a stream in flood my whole youth rushed to my memory, with all its privations and heroism, its wild desire for life and its mortal disappointments, its reckless generosity and its unbounded selfishness.

I saw myself that far-off afternoon in early January hurriedly stuffing my shirt and socks into the suitcase I had borrowed from a friend to take passage on one of the Braun and Blanchard boats. I had been with Milnes for a year and this was my first vacation. With patient determination I brokenly repeated my first English verbs; I smoked nothing but Virginia cigarettes and even my walk copied Mr. Merry's Anglo-Saxon gait. My whole psychology had so molded itself to their way of life that I liked only slender blonde girls who played tennis. I could not endure the Creole laziness, the thick ankles of the Chilean girls gabbling in Victoria Square every afternoon. My ideal woman was one who wore a bright scarf in the afternoon, practiced hymns to sing at the Protestant church, and prepared tempting puddings for the convalescents of the colony. And so I fell madly in love with that golden-tressed girl, Ruby Thompson, the daughter of a Yankee merchant, a friend of Mr. Merry, who had made up her mind to teach me to talk English. Those monotonous lessons were to me the sweetest, most idyllic experience of my life. To be sure, when summer came we went swimming together at Torpaderas and I made strenuous efforts to keep up with my friend Ruby, who in the black bathing suit which molded the white splendor of her body, and her rubber cap trimmed in blue, swam out to the open sea.

At the beginning of January the Thompsons left on a vacation. Mr. Thompson had some relatives who lived on a ranch near Concepción and they took passage on the steamer *Chiloé*. I hurriedly asked for my vacation and I, too, embarked that far-off afternoon at the beginning of January. I had only a little money with me. In this respect I certainly was not thinking Anglo-Saxonly. My heart, overflowing with tenderness, left the immediate future a little to chance. These were Latin residues that still fermented in my soul, the racial lack of foresight which little by little would disappear through contact with the stern regime of the House of Milnes. On board I had to do my share of the spending, like my friends the Thompsons, and when we went ashore at Talcahuano, I had only enough money left to spend a few days there. My beloved left that same afternoon. Not a word did she say about the future of our relationship. Not the slightest insinuation that I come to see her in the country. I saw her drive off in her relatives' car and disappear down the road to Concepción in a cloud of red dust. My amorous passion came to an end there. It was as though the chill of ten years of experience had sunk into my young heart. Within me a new man seemed to come to life, more calm, of better judgment. Unflinching, I swallowed the bitter draught of my first disillusion. Who was I, a Creole nobody, working for the rich firm of Milnes, in the eyes of this girl of another race, rich, spoiled, beautiful, whom I was never to see again, for, as I later learned, her father sent her to Europe in June of that same year.

I was on the point of writing to the firm to ask for an advance, though I did not like the idea at all. This would seem, to the rigid Anglo-Saxon system of the management, a foolish lack of foresight, although I knew I could count on the support of Mr. Merry, who was married to a Chilean and who always came to the defense

of the native employees of Milnes. I was thinking how to word
my request when I met an old friend of mine from Valparaiso at
San Vicente. After some years in the port city he had taken the
job of manager of the Lebu Company. In an outburst of frankness
I told him the fix I was in, without asking him for money. My
friend told me without beating around the bush that he would not
be able to let me have any money. He was married and did not
have much of a salary. But he wanted to help me if he could, so
he suggested that I come to Lebu's with him. Two days later a
barge and two lighters were leaving for Valparaiso with a cargo
of coal. That was what had brought him to Talcahuano. José
Oyarzo, the captain of the tug *Caupolicán*, would be glad to take
me north.

"So day after tomorrow you can be in Valparaiso without it
costing you a cent. The quarters won't be too comfortable, for
they're alongside the engine room, but don't ask for an advance,
for it will give you a bad name, even though Mr. Merry does
think a lot of you. After all, he's an Englishman."

I accepted gratefully. It was an unexpected solution and the best
of all. That afternoon I went to Lebu's with my friend. The
next afternoon I met Captain Oyarzo at the company's docks. The
Caupolicán was tied alongside with steam up. It was a modern
type of tug for use on the high seas, almost square, with a powerful engine and a tremendous screw propeller. Its wood and
brass shone and its gleaming black funnel had the gray ring of
the boats of the Milnes Line painted round its middle. There was
a strange resemblance between the captain, the Oyarzo of those
days, and the boat. He was square and stout and radiated
strength. He had a fine air of prosperity, in his plain suit with
the thick gold chain that hung in two loops across his knitted
woolen vest. A frank pleasant expression shone from his small blue
eyes. He made no objections to my friend's proposal. He merely
said with a firm gesture:

"Get right aboard, sir. If we don't run into a wind, we'll be in
Valparaiso tomorrow afternoon."

A man wearing soot-stained blue dungarees picked up my suitcase and disappeared with it down the single hatchway on deck.

I said good-by to my friend and went up to the bridge beside Oyarzo. The tug slipped away from the wharf and the dark hawser of the towline began to play out, as though with a strange life of its own, from the very heart of the boat, as the tug moved out to sea. Two men in the stern were in charge of the operation. The heavy-stranded cable slapped against the thick green water with resounding smacks. The two barges, loaded with tall pyramids of coal, remained motionless some distance off — black, clumsy, unwieldy. They looked a little like old beasts of burden. In the stern of the nearest one a young fellow, dressed in oilskins and rubber boots, was handling the tiller of the improvised rudder. In the farthest, a black-bearded man.

When the warping hawser was completely played out, one of the men shouted to the boy:

"Watch out, Baucha, she's going to jerk."

Oyarzo, with his hands on the treenail of the rudder, watched the figure of the little helmsman as it was left behind. A tender smile played around his red lips. His frank eyes turned toward me confidentially.

"That's my son. This is his first trip. He's getting his baptism at sea."

I could feel the engine panting under my feet like a person with asthma. The noise of the pistons was deafening; nevertheless the propeller revolved in vain in the quiet water. The tug stood still. At last with a great effort it began to move ahead once more. Against the black prow of the barges two arcs of thick white foam appeared. The convoy began to inch out of the bay. The old hull of an abandoned sailing vessel rose and fell with the waves. A red-funneled steamer of the Compañia Sud-Americana came slowly up the bay.

It was a hot day in early February. The faintly wrinkled sea stretched out to meet the horizon where the deep blue of the sky faded to the pale tint of a watercolor. The gulls along the black border of the shore were bands of fluttering whiteness. In the deep trough of the waves that formed about the ship's prow the heavy bodies of the albatrosses moved up and down as they indifferently watched the ship go by.

In the pure diaphanous air of the morning, drenched in summer sun, the tug, with its thick smoke curling heavenward, and the lumbering black coal barges struck a dirty, discordant note.

When the coast had melted away in the distance and the sea surrounded us on all sides, Oyarzo left the rudder and, sitting down beside me, began to tell me about his life. His soul was as clear and open as the sea. Satisfaction with life vibrated in his words, confidence in the future, which in certain men is like a powerful magnetism. In this way I found out that he had risen from sailor on schooners and barges to steamers, and from that to master of a tugboat with Lebu. He was around forty. When he was twenty he had married a cousin of his, who lived in their home on one of the little islands of Chiloé. He had six children, and it was the oldest, the only boy, who was making his first trip to sea as helmsman on one of the barges. Oyarzo was going to buy himself a schooner. That was the dream of his life — to own his own boat and build up a trade with it.

I watched evening fall that day at sea. Into the gently rippling leaden sea, striped with shadows, the sun sank with the glow of a live coal. The sea remained aglitter for a long time. The crests of the waves were bordered with tremulous red. Night swept in with a rush of cool breeze.

Gray waves smacked against the sides of the tug as though they were kissing it. The barges were two charcoal sketches in the darkling air. A vast clear sky burst into stars above our heads.

I did sleep pretty badly in my narrow bunk below decks. The steam of the boilers filled the tiny cabin with its hot breath. The throbbing of the engines reverberated right in my ears. The little boat was nothing but a piece of strong machinery. The hull contained only what was needed to house the crew and defend itself against the sea.

The sailors and boiler-tenders got up almost with the dawn to change watches, but I did not go on deck until after the sun was up. As I came out of my cabin, I felt the violent rush of the south wind. The sea was a white boiling sheet of foam. Small dancing waves broke against the sides of the ship, the prow, the stern, giggling wildly. I called Oyarzo's attention to the color of the sea.

"It's dirty, all right," he answered. "If it doesn't get any worse . . ."

"Do you think it may?"

"Can't tell. We often get southers this time of year."

"Is there any danger?"

"With the tug, yes. You can't put its nose against the waves, and the sea along the boards can be treacherous. It's liable to break off a blade of the propeller. It wouldn't be the first time. When I was in the navy a souther caught us up around Corral. It loosened the blades of the destroyer so we had to hoist them on board and that way, with the help of a towline, we managed to make Talcahuano."

Beyond doubt the sea was losing its playful appearance. There was not the slightest strip of green water to be seen; it was all white, foaming, heaving. I saw the prow of the tug go down in the water. A wave had hurled its load of foam over the stern. The propeller spun around in space in the boiling foam. I noticed, too, how a shiver ran through the hull at every jerk of the towline, which interfered with the ship's agility. I thought of the barges and looked back at them. Through the windows spattered with spray they could barely be seen in the distance, lumbering along, their black prows awash with white foam. The souther was coming on in full fury. Although I was unable to judge its growing violence, I could tell it by the face of the captain and the short quick phrases that passed between him and the mate.

"The sea, hitting alongside, may ruin the propeller, and the barges will pile up on us," observed the captain, looking through the porthole.

"If we try to turn, the water will smash against the barges from the side," the other answered, hanging fast to the railing while the water streamed off his yellow oilskin.

"We'd better wait," said Oyarzo.

"I guess so," replied the other, ducking down the black mouth of the engine room.

Ahead of us the sea, broken into millions of little white furrows, formed a strange contrast with the dull immobility of the sky. Not a single cloud disturbed its opaque serenity, as though the wind from the Pole, like a huge emery board, had buffed off the velvety polish of calm days. The line of the horizon grew still clearer; and far, far away, to the south, a dark blur made one think of the hurricane gust that was piling up the waves and tearing them to bits as it pleased.

Under the strong squat hull of the tug one could feel the fury of the sea. The waves raised it up like a bit of board, to let it fall the next minute among the furious white furrows of water. It was growing unsteadier all the time. The frame was creaking sharply; the iron plates were rattling. The smoke, snatched up by the wind the moment it left the smokestack, had taken that characteristic straight line in the direction of the bow. It looked like a huge tail touching an animal's head.

Captain Oyarzo was nervous. Through the thick glass of the cabin portholes he kept looking to the stern. His experienced eye could foresee the dangerous waves and by a quick turn of the wheel he managed to reduce to a minimum the attacks of the foaming monsters. The sea had become so rough that at times the curve of a wave blotted out the serenity of the horizon at which the souther seemed to snap in vain with its frozen teeth. It was no longer one sea. It was many, rushing, tireless. It was no longer possible to see the barges through its wild heaving; but with each rise and fall the thick, dripping hawser appeared, only to vanish again as though someone had given it a jerk from the bottom of the sea. Just then a huge wave broke over the ship. The wind instantly pulverized it and we were enveloped in a white spray which ran madly down the windows; a lurch of the boat sent it to larboard and it returned to the sea through the scuppers. As we slid down the mountain of water, we could hear the noise of the engines and the propeller churning up the foam. I could see the hawser writhing as though in the throes of a convulsion. It made me nervous. Oyarzo's face was grim and paler. Only his fingers, obedient to the cold, steely eyes, kept moving over the spokes of the wheel continually. The implacable souther had blotted out all sight of the barges. His son was in the first of them, and he was his only son. I recalled the pride in the father's eyes as he watched the lad in the stern of the lighter with the tiller in his hand. The boy was the continuation of himself, his successor in the barges of the Milnes Company, and even more, perhaps.

The quick, melodious chime of the ship's bell rang out.

The pilot who had the duties of first mate on the barge and shared the watches with captain appeared. Oyarzo's voice was strangely weak:

"Can you see the barges from the stern, Pérez?"

"Once in a while I can catch a glimpse of the first one."

"Have they given any signals?"

"Not a one."

The state of nervous tension I was in made me seize upon these scattered remarks and build them into a fantastic structure. But I did have a clear idea of the danger we were in and of the anguished wordless torment that was going on inside Oyarzo. New waves, no longer foaming and noisy, but sly and insidious, were wrapping their tentacles about the hull of the tug. They rose over the deck as high as the bridge and ran down the sides like torrents of rain. One crest of foam rose as high as the black cloud of smoke which spread out like a fan over the captain, fading away into the sea. The voice of the pilot called out again. Oyarzo opened the starboard porthole.

"The tug is shipping water."

Oyarzo answered: "We'll have to put about."

At that moment one of the machinists, sweaty, sooty, wiping his fingers on a piece of dirty waste, put his head through the hatchway leading to the engine room. His voice rang out brutally, without any trace of consideration:

"There's nothing to do but cut the towline. We'll have to let the barges go, and whoever sinks sinks."

Oyarzo slammed the window shut. His teeth gnawed his lip in a gesture that was at once helplessness and rage. It was the only outward sign of what was going on inside him. His well-cut features, which recalled the remote Spanish ancestry of the inhabitants of the islands, remained steady. But a pallor spread over them, like that of the immense vault of the sky swept by the south wind.

Once more the ship's bell rang. The arm of the quadrant had

swung around to its maximum tension. The nose of the tug began to swing northeast. This was the only hope of saving the barges and the helmsmen, whom it was impossible to give help of any kind. In a little while the roaring, rushing waves were breaking against the side of the *Caupolicán* and spewing their chill, noisy vomit over the deck. With every roll of the boat this water, dirtied by its contact with the ropes and chains, poured over the gunwale. The little boat was not holding its own too well against the waves. It gave one the sensation of a bird tied by one foot that beats its wings in vain trying to fly away. Beyond question, it was the dead weight of its tow-load that was sapping its vitality and hampering it from outriding the storm. It was rolling in a way that was frightening. Every two seconds the varnished square of the deck-house lost its horizontal line, tipping first to one side, then to the other, to form an obtuse angle with the horizon.

I was beginning to feel the nausea of seasickness. My whole body was wet with cold sweat. I sat down on the little bench fastened to the wooden wall and, holding on to the edge, closed my eyes for a minute. Despite the veil of semi-consciousness that slipped between the outer world and myself, I was aware of certain details which made it possible for me to piece together what happened later. I heard urgent angry shouts which I learned afterwards were telling Oyarzo that one of the barges, the very one his son was steering, was making distress signals. During a moment of calm the little red flag could be seen on the crest of a wave. This could mean either that the tiller was broken, or that the joints had loosened and water was coming into the hold, or that one of the barges had already sunk. They threw out life-preservers in the hope that some helmsman might be able to grab one as his barge sank. I can remember the sweating head of Oyarzo, disordered and wild-looking as it leaned out of the window and, in a hoarse voice, pronounced his son's death sentence:

"Cut the towline."

I did not hear the blow of the axe that severed the hawser and left the barges to their fate in that avalanche of white foam, beneath the indifferent serenity of the summer day. But as long as I live I shall not forget the disheveled head of that man, with his forehead resting on the rim of the steering wheel, and the convulsive heaving of his powerful back.

Once it was free of that weight that dragged it down, like a swimmer with his leg in the clutch of a drowning man, who then suddenly gets loose, the tug rose agilely on the waves, as though rejoicing in its freedom. Its iron prow, perforated by huge hawseholes which spewed forth a continuous stream of water, plowed through the white mass of the waves with all the force of its powerful lungs.

At daybreak the next day the wind had died away in a faded dawn, as though worn out by its efforts of the previous night. The tug put around to look for the shipwrecked victims. There was not a sign of them anywhere. One of the life-preservers that had been thrown out the day before was hoisted aboard. There was still hope. They might have been washed ashore. At noon we came into Valparaiso. At one o'clock the tug tied up at the Milnes dock. From behind the huge derrick that was getting ready to go to work I saw my friend Pedro González, the clerk who had taken my place, appear. His square red face stared at me in astonishment.

"What? You here? Where are the barges?"

I made a warning gesture.

"Shsh. I'll tell you later."

And I pointed to Oyarzo, who, last of all, after the sailors and engine-room men, was coming up the little cement stairway on to the dock, accompanied by the port official who had come down to check the *Caupolicán*. His eyes were glazed with sorrow; his step, tired and unsteady.

The *Caupolicán*, whitened with its film of salt, rocked calmly, fastened to its buoy at the stern and anchored at the prow.

After hearing my story and the crew's, the company congratulated Oyarzo.

Milnes had lost its coal barges and two hundred tons of coal. What was that? Oyarzo had lost his son, for nothing was ever heard of the helmsmen.

Mr. John Merry, at that time in charge of the freight section, spoke a good word for Oyarzo to the management. Two days afterwards he returned to Lebu with a tow-load of silks and liquor. Some time later I met the pilot who had made the trip in the *Caupolicán*. I asked him if he had seen anything of the barges as he cut the towline.

"The last one sank first," he said. "She sprang a leak and went down like a plummet. The other one with poor Baucha, I almost saw it sink. The boy had climbed on top of the pile of coal. Then a big wave rose up and covered everything."

This episode I had witnessed seemed like something that had become a part of my life, mine and my race's. I felt a deep pity for this man, aged before his time and sick, who humbly begged not to be dismissed from his job, his only recourse being to appeal to the pity of his employers. He was like one of those old worm-eaten mud-scows that are broken up for wood because they cannot even keep afloat. Nervously gesturing and muttering incoherent words, to the amazement of the stenographers, I rushed out to find Mr. MacKenzie.

OUR RIVERS

THE MAP OF SOUTH AMERICA seems to rest on a tree of rivers. There are rivers that shatter their waters against the mountain crags, or run deep and quiet beneath the foliage of the jungle, or hurl themselves down in monstrous cataracts, or spread out over the defenseless plains. Transparent rivers, red rivers, black rivers, honey-colored rivers. On the plains the valiant cut across them swimming; in the mountains the Indians cross them on swaying bridges of withes. Along these rivers the conquistadors made their way, and at times they swallowed up whole armies in their seething, wool-like waters. They were the route that missionaries, scientists, and bandits followed; they have traced the profile of our history and formed the bewitched background of our legends. Whoever follows the course of our rivers will penetrate to the heart of our life, the depths of our valleys, our mountains standing aloof. The mouth of the Plata River tempted the navigator Solis in the sixteenth century; he believed it to be a "fresh-water sea." He sailed up it and met his death. They say the Indians there ate him alive. But the river continued to exercise its spell over men. In its headwaters they hoped to see the White King who lived in caves of silver. It was this that gave the Argentine its name. In search of the White King went Ayola and Irala, the conquerors of Paraguay. And up the mouth of the Magdalena, which empties into the Caribbean, went Jiménez de Quesada; he was to find, far inland, the kingdom of the emeralds. Federmann, another conquistador, followed the course of the Meta in search of El Dorado. Those ambitious dreamers nearly always met with frustration. Not a few of them died, like Solis, between the jaws of the Indians. El Dorado was a mirage. In the valleys, on the heights, in the summits of the mountains where the rivers have their source, the only thing to be seen was the gray mirror of the lakes, and the only gold was that of the sun which bathed in their waters and received the adoration of the Indians. But the mystery and attraction of the rivers persisted.

The legends about them possessed those soldiers who fought bravely, one against a hundred, but who believed in spirits and witches. The legend of the Amazons, the warrior women who cut off one breast the better to handle the bow, took root in the minds of the Spaniards as well as the Germans. Their kingdom was in the heart of the greatest forest of the world, through which the broadest and longest river of the world runs: the Amazon. Ulrich Schmidl, who took part in the adventure of Paraguay, talks of them with the same assurance as Federmann, who was one of the discoverers of Venezuela. The Amazon was the puzzle of America in the sixteenth century, and it remains so today. In the old maps it is not painted as a river; it is an inland sea. The boldest of the conquistadors descended from Peru to explore it; Gonzalo Pizarro, great bandit though he was, hesitated at the entrance to the jungle and left the enterprise in the hands of Francisco de Orellana. Orellana lost an eye on the way, but with the one that was left he finally beheld the waters of the Atlantic. For years the

Amazon was known as the Orellana River. Yáñez Pinzón, who had seen it from the Atlantic, had given it the musical name of Santa Maria of the Fresh Waters. But the soldiers who accompanied Orellana called it the Marañón. Because its many tributaries form a huge web — *marañón* — of streams. The Amazon and the Orinoco are really one river, joined by the arm of the Casiquiare. It was here that Lope de Aguirre, that incredible figure, was defeated and stained the broad expanse of the waters with his blood. For generations it reflected the red trail of the Spaniards more than it did the tropical skies. Along it sailed bandits, Jesuits, scientists, poets, traders.

These were the Jesuits of the missions: Father Fritz of Bohemia, who drew up the first map of the region with an authentic outline of the river; Father Acuña, author of the delightful account of *The New Discovery of the Great Amazon River;* and those Jesuits of Paraguay who descended the waters of the Paraná at twilight, with boatloads of Indians chanting in Latin and accompanying themselves on harps. How strangely this chorus must have fallen upon the silence of the primitive, tropical jungle! Later came the scientists — Humboldt, the most eager of the Europeans; and Godin, the companion of La Condamine, who came to measure the Equator and wound up exploring the Amazon. He spent nineteen years along the banks of the river. Mme Godin, his wife, was waiting for him in Quito. When she finally got tired of waiting for news, she started out to search for her husband. She set out with a group of servants; she wandered through the jungle, sailed a canoe, saw those with her perish; and alone, without a compass, without a friendly oar to help her along, she finally found Godin in Pará. She was the first white woman to explore the jungle. Perhaps the only Amazon of the Amazon. After the scientists came the historians, the novelists, the poets — Gumilla, the entertaining author of *Orinoco Illustrado;* José Eustasio Rivera, who has painted the terror of the jungle; Hudson and Rómulo Gallegos, who have described the sunsets of the Orinoco. After the poets, the traders. The voracious rubber-gatherers who extracted more blood from the veins of the Indians than sap from the trees. Ford, who has founded Fordlandia of miraculous future. The hunters of *barbasco.*

the poison herb with which the Indians daub the points of their arrows and which is now used by chemists for the diabolical arts of war. Rivers of prayer, adventure, crimes, dreams, science, which those who know them never want to leave, enslaved by their magic charm. Rivers that know the secret of our America, where all the waters intermingle and flow together, the dark and the clear, but whose final scene is one of those twilights Rómulo Gallegos describes: "Beyond the banks of the river, the far-reaching vista of the plains, the deep perspective of the rising hills, without the smoke of hearthfires, or the slash of roads, vast silences to be filled by the tumult of future nations; overhead the magic scenery of the sunset; fleeces of gold and lakes of blood and a rain of fire between dark heaped-up cloud masses, and beneath the dramatic pomp of this display in the wilderness, broad, majestic, gleaming, the full Orinoco! The great Orinoco!"

Of all our river scenery, none is so impressive as the Iguassú when it descends in the most beautiful display of waterfalls to be found on any of nature's stages. Three nations, Brazil, Paraguay, and the Argentine, come together to see this wonder. José Vasconcelos, the Mexican writer, describes the cataract in these pages from his book *La Raza cosmica* (*The Cosmic Race*).

THE WATERFALLS OF SOUTH AMERICA
JOSÉ VASCONCELOS

WE reached Posadas in the early morning. A large reception committee accompanied us to the park. In a pavilion that had been erected there and adorned with flowers we sat to watch a parade of school children and their teachers. Some two thousand children marched by, neatly dressed, carrying their blue and white flags. Afterwards we went to the home of the prefect, where on the veranda of a colonial house, like those of Orizaba or Puebla, we were served breakfast. The authorities and the teachers made speeches of welcome and expressed their good wishes for a pleasant journey. We were touched by so much affectionate courtesy in that remote provincial nook. The boat left at ten o'clock, so as soon as we had thanked the committee for its attentions we started out on foot to the dock, accompanied by a number of young men and girls. The streets, the houses, the country were redolent of the tropics; we might have been in one of the river towns of our torrid zone, like Tlacotalpan, except that Posadas had more inhabitants and was larger. At the end of a street we saw below the bank the bright shining expanse of the river. On the far-off opposite shore, against a background of forests, we could see the houses of Concepción, in Paraguay, which we could not visit then because it was besieged by the rebels. The sight of Paraguay aroused in us a great but futile desire; so near and yet we could not set foot on it. Three days going and three coming we sailed past it without being able to go ashore. Though, as a matter of fact, it was the idea, rather than the fact itself that caused our disappointment, for we really had very little time at our disposal.

Even after we reached the landing, our conversation with the people of Posadas went on for more than an hour. The boat was ready to cast its moorings, but the younger members of our party were still exchanging compliments and agreeable phrases with the young ladies of Posadas. We all felt a touch of that sorrow with which one leaves his home town; not so intense, perhaps, but deeper, for we knew that we would probably never see most of those pleasant people again. If we could only have stamped those moments indelibly on some broad slate, for the stuff of memory is so fragile, its stream so shifting! At that moment Buenos Aires was forgotten, Rio de Janeiro, our native land, our own past life; the sorrow we felt was at leaving Posadas. In a few hours that little city had stolen our hearts away. Finally the exasperating maneuvers involved in getting a ship under way were completed, forerunners of the torturing delays of every trip by water. We had left the train, that marvelous invention that runs along with a change of scenery and emotion every moment, for this imitation of a sea voyage. Though less hateful than the ocean trip, where it seems that the boat makes no headway, and the scenery never changes, and thinking ceases. Life on an ocean liner: eating all day, dancing now and then, like bears in a circus, like animals being fattened for the market.

The impression at first, however, was new and interesting. The mysterious Paraná River has an average width of more than half a mile and runs along walled in between high wooded ravines which afford a wild, splendid sight. In a short time we were far from all human habitation; at intervals of several hours we would catch a glimpse of a little wooden house high on the bank or of logs brought in from the forest and fastened together to be slid into the river, which carries them free of cost to the ports. The first day went by swiftly and not unpleasantly. The landscape was amazing and the glowing golden sunset filled us with joy.

Along either bank were the famous plantations of yerba maté. The tree, which is cultivated here almost in the form of a shrub and is not nearly so large as in Rio Grande do Sul, covers a considerable acreage which has been wrested from the jungle. We were told the history of nearly all these farms. The majority of them belong to foreigners who have managed to buy a piece of land from the great land-holders of Buenos Aires. After a more or less difficult start they have prospered; but there are not many of these small farmers, for all this land, from Posadas to Iguassú, belongs to no more than twenty "patrician" families, who will neither cultivate nor sell it. And yet in this region alone there is room for millions of people. Today it is nothing but a wasteland, exactly as the Spaniards found it in the days of the conquest and exploration. Among the passengers on the boat there were a French couple and several Spaniards and Hollanders, who had settled on the left bank of the river. They all had the same complaint: these lands could feed the whole world, but they do not prosper because of the curse of latifundism. When to this is added the irregularity and abuses of the steamship lines, whose rates are exorbitant, one understands why the Argentine is in danger of losing this territory of Misiones, wedged in between Paraguay, which, under the influence of a military government, dreams of expansion, and Brazil, whose vast prosperity may one day make it a dangerous neighbor. The rich Argentines are betraying their nation and their lands. They are like the fabled dog in the manger, who neither eats nor lets anyone else eat.

The second day of our voyage we advanced slowly over the broad stream of waters, which grow clearer as we move upstream. The high banks formed walls of trees and foliage. With the heat of the morning, swarms of bright-colored butterflies appeared — yellow, red, blue; flags of the tropics, they seemed. Some of them dropped on deck. There was one kind that is called 88 because on each wing there is a black and red marking that looks exactly like two eights. The earth along the bank is reddish, soft alluvial soil, completely covered with lush growth. It is warm, but not unpleasantly so. All life pulses with plenitude.

On the right we gradually leave behind us the region that belonged to the Jesuit missionaries. The tourist who has time can get off at one of the landings to visit the ruins of San Ignacio, which was the capital of this old political-religious community. The achievements of the Spanish Jesuits, the Franciscan and the Dominican friars here, as in California and in the rest of America, were stupendous. The efforts of the Jesuits were greater here than in California; yet there the seed fell on fertile ground, while here the traces of civilization have been wiped out, swallowed up and buried by the jungle. The first attempt to establish a colony in these parts was in 1588, under the Spanish captain Nuño Cabeza de Vaca. Before this there had been Cainigua and Guarany Indians here, but the Indian's was a primitive existence, adapted to the jungle, and his life was carried on in keeping with the natural laws of the forest, like that of the monkeys and other animals. He felt no need to modify his surroundings to suit his purposes; on the contrary, he turned the natural configuration of the land to his advantage. The leafy boughs gave him shade and shelter; the thick trunks, protection; the streams were his pathways, so he hardly needed to build houses or open clearings. As he had no definite goal in his wanderings, his movements were adjusted to the elements, to the paths the waters marked as they followed the law of gravity to the lower levels and the canebreaks. Civilization, from the first moment, established a new rhythm. It rebelled at the blind acceptance of its surroundings as it found them and against the slow measures nature employed. It created a set of new methods and values. It was then that the stubborn struggle began to open roads, which the jungle gradually closed up; to raise upright walls in defiance of the law of gravity, which tends to flatten everything and make it homogeneous again. A wall is a fundamental violation of a natural law; it outwits this law by utilizing it, and by putting one stone on top of another makes gravity serve man's purposes. But if man is not continually on the alert to keep his work in repair, nature, which knows no rest, takes its revenge, undermining the foundations of the wall with the roots of its potent trees and bringing down the stones if they depart in the slightest from the cunning device of the vertical line. To fight the elements and subdue them to man's will, to utilize them for human ends, what greater incentive can there be for the heroic heart! At first it is sheer audacity and the spirit of contradiction; then it becomes concord, as in the great feats of engineering, where, without further violence or struggle, the forces of nature are geared to man's purposes, as when the waterfall moves the wheels that produce the power for factories, cities, nations. But at the beginning, skill is not enough; it takes heroism, and there was never a greater display of heroism than that of the conquistadors and *bandeirantes*. Even today, on a pleasure trip, to clear a trail through the forest, we take panting turns and are soon exhausted and it requires an effort of the will to keep going, for the instinct of our weary feet is to turn back. Think what it must have been in the early days of the conquest in this vast wilderness. To achieve this conquest of nature, to subdue it to our will, all that is heroic in a man must gain the upper hand of the beast in us to keep alive our ambition and impulse, lest we accept things as they are instead of imposing on physical resistance the higher law of the will.

By the year 1623 the Jesuits had founded populous and prosperous towns such as Candelaria, Santa Ana and San Ignacio, in what is now the territory of Misiones. But all this region was the center of the boundary disputes between Spaniards and Portuguese. Few Ibero-Americans are familiar with the history of the terrible encounters which took place between conquistadors and *bandei-rantes* before the boundaries which today delimit the field of action of these twin civilizations were finally fixed. In that glorious period of Spain's history, only a Portuguese could defy a Spaniard. The great achievements of England later on were possible only because Spain and Portugal did not unite. If the two heroic kingdoms had had the wit to join forces, there would be no British Empire in Asia, or America, and certainly not in Africa. Instead of an English-speaking world, we should have a Latin world.

Besides having to defend themselves from the Brazilians, the new settlers had to fight off savage Indians and combat environment and disease. Yet out of this struggle emerged a civilization that grew and thrived. The expulsion of the Jesuits did away with this. The Indians returned to their nomadic life and primitive nature invaded the cities, overran clearings, streets, and squares, undermined walls, rotted roofs. In one place a vigorous tree embraced a carved pillar, enveloped it in its fibrous growth until it was covered over. The visitor can hardly distinguish it any longer. The pillar has become famous in collections of rare photographs, under the name of "the stone-hearted tree." The majority of the Jesuit settlements disappeared. Some of the centers have prospered again, and new colonies are springing up under the auspices of the Argentine government. But the greatest interest lies in the ruins. One sees magnificent doorways, fluted striate columns sculptured in stone foliage, animals and fruit, with something Hindustani in the richness and profusion of the ornamentation. The art of the tropics, like the civilization produced there, is always a total thing. To express itself it utilizes all forms and all rhythms. The primitive peoples of the cold and temperate zones call this barbarous, because the penury of their surroundings reflects itself in their judgment.

Since we could not visit San Ignacio, we had to content ourselves with the accounts of travelers who had been there.

Every afternoon at three o'clock the captain of the boat, a bronzed Indian wearing the regulation Argentine service uniform, used to send me maté in his own luxurious maté-cup, embossed in gold and silver, with a brand-new sipper. The tea is agreeable, sweet and pungent, and its stimulating and diuretic effects explain its widespread use. Once it becomes known in the world market, it will probably be drunk everywhere. At maté time, after the siesta, the poor passengers get together on the lower deck, countryfolk from Paraguay, sailors, sometimes with a girl or two, dark and well built. They say hardly anything; they sing in a melancholy voice, accompanying themselves on the guitar. The dark, slender Paraguayans resemble the Mexican Indians of the tropics. They wear a red handkerchief around their necks, a knife in their belts, a knitted shirt, and pants. They have the air of a fighting race.

The afternoon moves along slowly, like one of those tedious acts of Wagner's tetralogy, yet imbued with poetry and meaning, too. The river, far larger than the Rhine and with greater promise for humanity, gleams in the sunlight; there are little wooded islands where some day castles in the shape of hotels, with all modern improvements, will be built for the pleasure of the public with enough money to spend, that collective, capricious master of our democracies today. There are also marvelous spots in which to rest and dream, where the modern magicians, the engineers, will build themselves enchanted palaces after working the miracle of harnessing the power of the waterfalls. Their palaces will be like towers standing guard over the genii of agriculture and industry. But for the moment there is only this vast pristine growth like Siegfried's own forest; through the golden glow of the setting sun at times one seems to catch the faint sound of a hunting horn, echoing the theme of the famous opera.

In other spots the river widens until it is like a bay. Nevertheless, the pilot steers cautiously, because the river is not navigable at all points. The solitude in which we travel is so complete that we might be the first discoverers; suddenly a deer appears, slips into the water, and begins to swim across the river. Only its head can be seen above the water, and its nostrils, dilated with its effort. The waves are transparent, but virginal; no water fairies have yet been born here, man's fantasy has not yet been at work here. As there are no men, the complement of all landscape is missing: poetry, which is the wedding song of the soul and nature.

The golden delight is fading away in a ruddy clarity that floods the horizon. The tragedy of all beautiful afternoons is played out with grandeur. Shadow begins filtering into the very substance of light, breaking it up, overpowering it. The reflections grow thinner, paler, and fade out one after another until the sun itself seems a heap of glowing embers. It is no longer that stupendous fire which the eye was unable to contemplate. The night closes in, the shadows grow thicker, everything is blotted out, and the forest sleeps. Mystery penetrates the very waters of the river, turning them black. The only protest is that of the stars with their bright but impotent pricks of light.

And yet there is another rebel, man, who challenges the darkness. He lights the boat's lanterns and proceeds on his way. Suddenly ahead of us, out of the blackness of the river, there appears another light, and the sound of a whistle is heard; it is a little boat which approaches and then slips past our black mass, perforated here and there with light from within. The two boats salute each other and then separate, each going its own way, carrying along man, man who has invented lights, little lights, but enough to outwit the night. There are times when man pays dearly for his audacity; not far behind we have left the ruined hulk of a boat; it was carrying oil, which caught fire through someone's carelessness and the water was covered with burning oil. The passengers who threw themselves overboard attempting to swim ashore were burned, too, and nothing was left but the iron hull foundered in the sand. Those who died will be replaced by the millions who are left, just like the ants and the bees. Without knowing who directs us or where we are going, we move, we toil like those industrious insects. After all, there are as many worlds as there are organisms; and what we call the world is only one of the thousand forms of existence which lie in the bosom of infinite mystery.

The morning of the third day was fraught with that emotion which precedes great events. We had been told that at one o'clock we would put in at Port Aguirre and would arrive, after an hour's ride by automobile, at the cataracts. At one of the wharves where we stopped on the way, several Scandinavians came aboard who owned a farm and the hotel at Port Aguirre and who gave us detailed information about the falls and about the life in those parts. Port Aguirre is a little village on a high bluff which juts out into the river where the Iguassú joins the Paraná. The boat veered into the stream of the Iguassú and in a little while tied up at a small landing wharf. It could not travel very far up the river because as one approaches the cataracts the current becomes very swift and the bed of the river is rocky.

It must have been about two o'clock in the afternoon when we stepped ashore on the damp red earth of the right bank and climbed up the hillside between trucks and an occasional Ford. For a moment there is an imitation of traffic which surprises and thrills us a little after three days of quiet. We do not stop at any of the wooden houses, nor is there any need to do so. Before, the hotel used to be here; now it is on the other side, in full view of the falls. Our party is distributed in several Fords, and for an hour or so we go bouncing along on a road that makes its way through the tangle of trees. Every moment it seems to us that we can hear the rushing of the waters; but after listening intently for an instant, we realize that it is only the beating of our hearts as the sublime moment approaches. Suddenly we draw up before a fairly large building, one story high, white, with steeply pitched red roofs, in the modern Scandinavian style. It is the hotel. We get out of the cars and go inside. From the big wooden doors we can see the esplanade of green lawn framed by the forest. We turn left, and in a moment, as we make our way through the right wing to the end of the glass-enclosed porch, looking off in the distance we see it. There it is always, making no noise. We gaze at it in rapt amazement. It is like a long, blue, snow-covered slope which without pause drops into another mass of liquid which rolls along in silent majesty until it is lost in the abyss. The foam boils, first white and then yellow toward the bottom; it is like two or three levels of falling water; above is the clarity of the sky and all around the green of the forest. Only after looking at it for a moment does one realize that it is an immense thing which is falling, which has been falling for ages. It gives one the impression of an unending, melodious catastrophe.

We sit down because both legs and will are weak with emotion. This must be seen again and again; it must be seen slowly and also in rapid glimpses. The mind must adapt itself to the awe and magnitude of this unbelievable reality. We have to learn our way about as though we had entered into a new world, so difficult it is to grasp the vision at once in its full grandeur; our awareness must grow to match the spectacle.

After the first impression the guides advise us to take advantage of the afternoon light to take a walk through a little natural, rustic park which lies along the slope of the ravine across from the falls. We cross the green esplanade which is the lawn of the hotel and begin to make our way through huge trees — bamboos, palms, and bushes. We jump over innumerable little streams and cross other wider ones over improvised wooden bridges. We see rivulets, brooklets, and rivers that fan out to pour themselves through the defiles of the steep ravine where each liquid string adds its note and its rainbow color to the symphony of falling waters. The place is immense and picturesque, and, with very little in the way of improvements, could be made into one of the world's tourist centers.

Gently at first, and then abruptly we follow the downward path that skirts the ravine until we reach the very foot of Bossetti Falls; behind us we have left Lanusse; farther ahead, veiled by the mists from the rich stream of Bossetti, can be seen the waters of San Martín, divided into a succession of cascades, some of which break at two levels while others drop in a sheer fall around a vast amphitheater. In places the streams of falling waters resemble an immense organ with liquid pipes playing celestial music.

Going down to the bottom, we stand on an almost triangular surface, hemmed in by the broad stream which carries away the waters of San Martín and, at the back, by the ravine. At the other end rises the cliff called Bella Vista, from whose height we can see, behind us, the Lanusse and Bossetti Falls. On the other side, across from the river, which is fed by the lateral streams from the different falls, rises the high, rolling bank of the wooded Brazilian shore. To the right, in the distance, another triple fall is barely visible. It is known as the Three Musketeers. Beyond this nothing can be seen. The islands, the palm trees, and the mist hide the great cataract, Union Falls, which together with Belgrano is lost in the background. On the other hand, at the end of the opposite bank the great Floriano Falls is clearly visible, a shining mass which plunges down and then, as it hits the rocks at the bottom of the ravine, breaks up into a great steam of white foam. Seen from a distance, over the slope of the rocks, it might be the beard of some titanic forest god.

At seven the next morning, equipped with machetes and preceded by six guides, we set out. The automobile carries us about three miles into the woods, following the river, so we can cross the stream at the upper level of the waters. Every few minutes the majestic view of the river reappears as the road winds in and out of the forest with its infinite variety of trees, vines, ferns, bushes, and flowers of rare beauty.

The moment comes when we have to leave the automobile. We follow on foot behind the guides. We help them in their task of clearing a path with the machetes, chopping through the interlaced branches or cutting down the high grass. The narrow breach through the heavy undergrowth follows the course of the river, parallel to its banks, for two or three miles, which grow fatiguing because of the heat which drenches us with sweat, while swarms of gnats bite us. We try to frighten them away, slashing about us with our machetes, and the tender branches that fall give off a delicate fragrance. Sometimes the blows of the machetes stir up and irritate the gnats, which make straight for the bare skin. There are all kinds and all sizes, some as large as mosquitoes, with a sharp sting that causes instant swelling; others small and slow of movement, which seem harmless, yet when they bite they leave reddish, burning lumps which itch unbearably. The only cure is to get used to them; the first days are bad, but afterwards one seems to acquire a certain immunity, as though in time one became vaccinated by the sting. On the way the guide has explained to us what we are looking for: a high place where we can cross the river in a canoe and then walk back the way we have come, but on the opposite shore, to the Brazilian hotel, right across the river from the Argentine hotel, on top of the highest cliff. By one o'clock, after about a five-hour walk, we should be eating *feijoada* at a Brazilian table.

In a clearing in the forest the guides pause to examine a spoor which leads to the edge of the water. It is that of a wild boar which has come down to drink, says one; but when we examine it closely, it turns out to be that of a hunting dog. The men of the country tell us what seems to be a common story: the peon who wants to leave, and the landowner who invents debts to hold him prisoner; one day in despair the worker runs away; then he is hunted by a search party, armed and with hounds, which harass the fugitive until he falls, dead or alive, into the hands of his pursuers. The ranch-owners, meanwhile, are in Buenos Aires, gambling at the Jockey Club or betting on the races at the Hippodrome. Part of what they have left over is spent on poor young things who learn to talk French and dress in the Parisian manner for the pleasure of these gentlemen who hunt down a man for a debt, real or trumped up, of half a peso. Even there in the midst of the jungle we would have preferred the tracks to be those of a wild boar. Boars are more decent than men.

Drenched with sweat and covered with mud, we reach the dock and climb into a large canoe. The river is awe-imposing. On both sides it is hemmed in by masses of branches and foliage; the Brazilian bank looks a little the higher. We had to go pretty far upstream to find the zigzag route across. While we were crossing the river, someone told a half-forgotten story of a Guarany chief who was coming down the river with a fleet of piraguas pursuing a defeated enemy tribe. Drunk with victory, he failed to notice that the current was sweeping them along, and he and all his warriors perished in the whirlpool. A group of herons stands silhouetted along the edge of a distant bank. The forests and river banks are full of birds. Confidence in human skill can grow so boundless that we did not give a thought to the fact that this immense expanse of water on which our boat was floating emptied, only a short distance away, with everything in it, down a chasm, to be reborn again as another huge river foaming over the rocks of its bed below. The boatmen displayed their great skill, carrying us with perfect accuracy to the improvised dock of boards laid on posts

151

driven into the bank. We stepped joyously ashore on Brazilian soil, recalling that in a certain sense it is ours, too.

Our legs have gone to sleep and it is with an effort that we climb a winding trail that loses itself in the splendid forest. We walk slowly to save our strength and to enjoy the fragrant cool air. There are no limits to imagination's delight, in spite of physical discomforts which now and then become acute. How pleasant a pair of dry socks would be, for our feet are soaking wet. We are no longer tired or hungry; all we want is to get off these wet socks. After a fairly long walk we reach the hotel. At first it seems that there is nobody there. Finally a boy who looks after the house manages to find us some towels and dry clothes and starts to get us something for lunch. We note with satisfaction that there are chickens in the barnyard, and some cans and bottles of wine in the pantry. While all this is being prepared, we go to look at the incredible panorama.

All that we saw yesterday from the ravine below, almost from the back, now extends before us in all its magnificence. From the moment one steps on to the terrace of the Hotel Faz do Iguassú, one sees in front and a little below the magic fringe of the green woods and the white jets and curtains of water. The first thing that catches the eye is the little Argentine hotel with its red roof, set in its emerald lawn. Then as the eye sweeps the horizon, a succession of miracles appears. The sensation is so powerful that there is nothing to say, the sight imposes silence. Instinctively we feel that any word would shatter the spell. We move like sleep-walkers in a world of dreams. Only the solidity of the floor under our feet convinces us that this is real, and one of the most sublime realities the forces of the Cosmos have brought into being.

At first we see our old friends across the way in all their clarity: Lanusse in the form of two white ribbons separated by a cliff crowned with trees. We can divine the music in the movement of the waters and foam. Near it is Bossetti, with its slim and elegant perpendicular drop to an outcropping of rocks, over which it flows smoothly to drop again in a wider fall and quickly melt into the waters of the river; then the clear stream disappears from sight amidst rocks, palms, and lichens. On one side of Bossetti there is another fall, which in the distance, and by comparison, looks small, but in reality pours out a great volume of water. It has been forced to separate from the main fall by a blockade of trees, palms, and vines which form a wedge at the edge of the abyss. Its impetus counterbalances the descending gravity of the other mass of waters, which threatens to level and tear down the crag itself.

Following the edge of the ravine and looking across it, beyond Bossetti, we see a palisade of steep cliffs over which a series of ribbons and curtains of water descend by stages to form finally one fall that is lost from sight in the depths, to reappear below in a single stream that empties into the river half-way through the gorge. This open hemicycle of waters forms San Martín Cascade.

These falls we are passing in review come from a great lateral bifurcation of the Iguassú, which divides into a number of streams seeking a channel. They drop over the precipice and all come together again at the lower level. On both sides of the main San Martín Falls we can count twelve tributaries, some narrow, others broad, which either fling themselves into the abyss or flow to the edge of the cliff and slip majestically over. The view of the main fall is obstructed by a crag that juts out and makes it impossible to see the final descent, but one senses that there the stream spreads out and comes together anew.

Still looking downstream, we see not far from the San Martín group the graceful triple falls of the Three Musketeers. Beyond this the gorge fills up with trees, and above its rocky crenellation rises the plumy forest, crowned with the tall tufts of the palm trees. Then again, through the forest growth, Miter Falls emerges, narrow but full; and farther on, Belgrano, broad and voluminous. Almost at once the serene central semicircle of waters appears, drops first to a platform which boils with foam, then hurls itself into space again in a mass whose impact makes the earth shake. From where we stand, it is impossible to see this gigantic downpouring in all its extension — only the swollen masses of water which roll incessantly. As they fall, the streams intermingle, intertwine, or come together in a single mass; they boil and quiver, crash, and send up clouds of foam and mist which envelop everything as on the first day of creation. Something of primeval chaos persists in this spot, which from time immemorial has been known as the Devil's Throat. The fall which fills this maw is known as Union, because it belongs to both countries and is the junction of the waters, the mother fall, which has a perimeter of almost a mile and discharges the greatest volume of water of any fall in the world.

Along the edge of the declivity the river shows itself treacherously smooth, with that paralyzing calm that precedes the catastrophe.

But the picture is not yet complete. To the left of Devil's Throat and at the prolongation of the same incline on which we are standing we can see and feel the thundering downrush of the great overwhelming Floriano Peixoto Falls.

Our obliging guides lead us down a pathway cut in the stone, to one side of the Floriano, which splashes us with its waters, to a spot where it seems as though the whole Brazilian waterfall were coming down upon us. Now, seen from below, it gives the impression that with the eye one might plumb the depths of mystery. Peering amidst brilliant flashes as from a blurred Mount Sinai, and through curtains of mist which open for a moment and then come together again, we look into the Devil's Throat. In the middle there are vertical columns which are inexhaustible and at the bottom a swirling, boiling mass which has never stopped moving throughout the ages. Through the mist one can sense the great volume of water that is descending, the powerful streams that slide over the black rocks, polished by the furious, unending rush of the waters. Nothing but rock and water in this magnificent chaos of forces, seemingly sterile, yet mysteriously potent, for this friction can generate the power that life can utilize. After long contemplation of these awesome depths, we swerve our eyes to the left to gaze upon the Floriano, in all its powerful majesty, its convex length bathed in light after its life-giving journey through the jungle, a prodigy of whiteness as it drops into space. Seen in its totality, it looks like a sliding mountain. Compared with Union, it seems more human, like an impetuous force, but one that could nevertheless be mastered, whereas the other exceeds the grasp of our powers and imagination.

Down below, in the river, the waters spread far out, breaking against rocks and islets, but now they inspire pleasure, not fear.

We have to clamber back the side of the cliff, clinging to roots and branches, to return for lunch. The emotions we have experienced have dulled our appetites, and as soon as we finish we repeat our excursion, but this time more quickly and synthetically. It was as though we were trying to fix the vision on a mental photographic film and engrave it on our soul for all eternity. We no longer feel fatigue; it is as though something important had been added to our lives forever; even beyond death this vision of the cascades would never leave us completely.

Our last trip was to the brink of the Devil's Throat. From a point known as Canoas we set out in Indian pirogues. From there, in an almost straight line, we sailed downstream. The trip is, if not exactly dangerous, certainly exciting. The river broadens out enormously in this great bend we are sailing through and rolls along almost unbroken by islets or rocks. It is not very deep here, but the great slabs of stone, the cliffs, and the crenellated rocks that jut out into the waters make the swift-flowing stream most picturesque. The main body of the river empties over the brink of the deep abyss, the Devil's Throat, which we approach through a tributary channel in order to view it from the side. We have to row up a broad arm, through a fan of smaller streams, which in places are deep and in others run very swiftly, forming little cascades. Two or three times our boat leaps perhaps as much as a yard above the changing levels of the water, as in that well-known picture of the Indian maid in her canoe familiar to all who have visited Niagara Falls. We hold our breath as though we had really overturned and then we laugh at our fears. And so we advance until the joining streams grow deeper and swifter; but the guides, with great skill, keep out of the dangerous currents by hugging the rocks and clinging to the branches that hang over the edge of the islets, and bring us safely to the edge of the abyss. There we get out of the canoe and proceed on foot through the water, leaving the boat tied to a tree. Slowly wading through the water or hopping from one stone or islet to another, we finally reach the crag that overhangs the abyss. It is of black basalt, covered in part with thick green moss and iridescent slime, and over it the waters have been pouring for centuries. An occasional bush has managed to cling there, gnarled and almost stripped of its leaves by the rush of waters in the flood season. Without realizing it, we have taken our vantage point at a dead end between the thick ribbon of Belgrano Falls and the great torrents of Union Falls. The noise is deafening and the sight makes the head swim.

By lying face-downward and stretching out the neck it is possible to look into the depths of the maelstrom and see such a falling of waters as that of the Biblical Flood. The thick impenetrable curtain of waters is made up of streams which come together, hurl themselves down, and become mingled in one. As they hit the bottom they disappear in a crash, then seem to rise again in angry waves, boiling bubbles, and a rainbow of misty spray. Without end, without rest, the liquid masses pour over the brink and the chasm is never filled, never satisfied. It would seem as though here were the end of everything, and yet life laughs at this elemental power, this physical power, and above the boiling floods pass the birds in their flight. One of these fragile, innocent creatures comes to rest on a branch that hangs swaying above the abyss. Within the waters something sings, something that is like the cry of the life that bathes in its depths and emerges strengthened to bring cooling relief to the forest and a tremor to the breast of man, who for a moment is overcome by doubt and fear as he feels within his soul an inversion of the forces of the universe. He trembles at the thought that perhaps his inner scheme of things may not always be able to triumph over the enormous capacity for destruction and chaos of the elements.

When all is said and done, one says to oneself at the thought of going down into the depths with the waters that it would be a death like any other, from which the soul would emerge amidst the gleam of the waves. But the body is reluctant and fearful; it feels its weakness, its inability to protect its brief moment in the face of the eternity and indifference of creation.

One must check the imagination, rest for a few moments, stop thinking, to be able to view this prodigy again, clearly devise its outlines, learn the secret of its rhythms, steep oneself in its melodies. One of our party amuses himself by pushing a log into the stream, hoping to follow it with his eyes into the maelstrom. The log floats along, slips gently over, and is suddenly gulped in and disappears amidst the waters.

Looking up, now one can see the semicircle of the exuberant central falls pouring itself evenly above a boiling bed of foam and waves; then immediately the mass broadens out to hurl itself over the brink overwhelmingly and unrestrainedly. And as it plunges into this profound space, it rolls first, then roars and expands, fills the bed, breaks into fragments, atomizes its contents, which in this fashion return to chaos and then go up in mist and disappear in the air as though transformed into fluid.

With so much gazing there comes a moment in which the head droops wearily and there passes through the mind the idea of the futility of the moment which each of us represents in creation in the face of the eternity of its processes. What are we doing on this incomprehensible planet, slaves that we are of we know not what strange powers? The peak of our achievements is condensed in words, perhaps, because the word is the essence and the fiat of our acts. Words that say Life, Love, and Beauty, but the idea of eternity passes us by without our being able to lay hold of it. It passes as the waters pass and destroys us like these waters. Why this unceasing interplay of building up and tearing down, without ever being able to restore the moment that has passed? I perish, but another is born, and I am born again in him and in all those who come after us. There come moments in which it seems that all this is words, words. Wise men of India, of Greece, theologians, there is only one certainty, the certainty of the words Love, Beauty, Life, perhaps Soul, too; but what we cannot know, what we cannot ever hope to discover, is how to combine these words which are realities. We lack the connecting nexus; Love thinks it can join them together, but Nature tears them apart, tears us to pieces as well, and once more these tremendous words stand separate: Life, Power, Beauty, Soul, Virtue. Whoever is sincere must say: I do not understand. Nevertheless, it has given me infinite happiness to have known the essence of these great and sacred words: Nature, Virtue, Power, Beauty, Love.

PART II

The March of Time

SIXTEENTH CENTURY: THE CONQUEST

THERE IS NO PHENOMENON in the history of the world to compare with the conquest of America. In some, curiosity; in others, love of adventure; in nearly all, the thirst for gold and treasures moved fleets and armies with a speed that is amazing. In less than thirty years the Pacific Ocean was discovered; Mexico, Peru, Central America, Chile, the Argentine, Paraguay, Brazil, Colombia, Venezuela, were conquered; the great rivers, the Mississippi, the Amazon, the Plata, the Orinoco, the Magdalena, explored. Magellan's ships had sailed round the world; cities were founded whose names have been forever incorporated in the history of mankind: Buenos Aires, Rio de Janeiro, Mexico, Lima, Bogotá, Santiago, Quito, Panama. . . . The whole range of the Andes had been traversed and cities had been built nine, twelve thousand feet above sea-level. And all this was done by discoverers and conquerors who came in a few little boats that did not hold fifty men each and that creaked and seemed on the point of splitting asunder when a strong wind filled their sails. Or they hacked their way through the web of the jungles with machetes so men and horses could climb the virgin flanks of the Andes. Alonso Niño and Cristóbal Guerra put to sea in a single caravel with thirty-three men. They set sail from Spain for the Caribbean when all that had been discovered of the Caribbean was a few islands. They discovered nearly all the coast of Venezuela and returned to Spain laden with gold and pearls. The conquistadors were this breed of men.

The conquest was not the work of the government but of the people of Spain. In the majority of the cases all the monarchs did was to give their approval to deeds already accomplished by obscure soldiers. When the armies were struggling through the heart of the jungle the ones who took charge were not those who bore the King's seal but the most daring, who seized command and laughed in the teeth of the agents of the crown. Neither Hernán Cortés, who conquered Mexico, nor Pizarro, who conquered Peru, nor Quesada, who conquered New Granada, nor Balboa, who dis-

161

covered the Pacific, left Spain invested with any authority. But their daring knew no limits. Cortés conquered Mexico, which was the size of several Spains, with four hundred soldiers; Pizarro conquered Peru with two hundred and twenty-seven. It was a struggle of life and death; the soldiers were brave and the King was far away. When the Spaniards had to be cruel, they wasted no compunctions. With their clothes in tatters, they arrived at the place they set out for, covered with mud as well as blood. Only thus could Spain and Portugal, with a population of less than ten millions, have conquered a world inhabited today by more than one hundred and thirty million people and thirty-five times the size of the Iberian Peninsula.

It was not groups of families that came to the conquest, nor companies like those that were later formed to establish the new colonies of North America. The soldiers arrived without women and for that reason they soon mixed with the Indians, making Latin America a world of half-breeds. The aggressive individualism of the Spaniard found in the conquest the finest stage imaginable and produced a generation of heroes such as had never before been known in the history of the peninsula. There were fifty years of adventure, blood, and glory in which thousands and thousands of Spaniards participated, leaving the conquering nation depopulated, impoverished in spite of the gold of America. The workingman left his industry in the belief that he could pick up gold in handfuls on the shores of America; with the same hope the peasants left their fields. But the gold that was sent back as the price of these sacrifices was handed over by the kings to shrewd bankers who were waiting across the frontier. And the men of Spain who came to America did not return to Spain. They fell in love, some with the land, others with the Indian women, and finally, after the men, came the women of the mother country. And the conquest was over and the colony began.

The history of the conquest is full of dramatic episodes. Two of the culminating incidents were the taking of the city of Mexico and the imprisonment of Montezuma; and the conquest of Peru and the imprisonment and death of Atahuallpa. Of the many admirable books on the conquest of Mexico, the account of Bernal

Díaz del Castillo is outstanding, ranking as a classic in the literature of Spain and America. Benjamín Carrión, a leading figure among the younger generation of Ecuador, has written an excellent book on the life of Atahuallpa, of which the last chapter follows.

CAXAMARCA
BENJAMÍN CARRIÓN

"Atabalipa was a man thirty years old, well formed and of goodly aspect, corpulent; his face was broad, handsome, and fierce; his eyes bloodshot; he was grave in speech, like a great lord. His reasoning was very acute, and when the Spaniards understood his words they recognized him for a wise man. He was gay although harsh; when he talked with his people he was very severe and gave no sign of happiness." — FRANCISCO XEREZ: A True Relation of the Conquest of Peru and the Province of Cuzco.

CAXAMARCA means the "place where there is ice." Xerez states that the day the conquistadors entered Caxamarca "in a little while it began to rain and hail." The sun, which had been shining all morning, disappeared, and after a clashing overture of thunder, lightning, and black clouds came a torrential cloudburst, with hail, one of the kind so typical of the tropical uplands.

During the downpour Pizarro ordered his troops to take shelter in the great houses that surrounded the central square of Caxamarca. When the rain was over — not for one moment did he abate his attitude of intrepidity and self-assurance — he called Hernando de Soto, the youngest and most intelligent of his captains, and ordered him to take a group of fifteen mounted men and go to Atahuallpa's camp to present the greetings of the commander of the white men and to say that he was eager to see him and speak to him in the name of his sovereign lord, the King of Spain, to offer him friendship and help against his enemies.

Soto set out, his horse prancing down the broad highway, flanked by trees, flowers, and growing fields, that runs straight from Caxa-marca to the hot springs of Cónoc, where at that moment the Inca resided, surrounded by his court and thousands of Indians from this region.

The sun was about to set and Captain de Soto had not yet re-turned. Pizarro — and the other Spaniards with him — began to grow worried, and he sent for his brother Hernando, famous for his bravery and daring, to go after de Soto and give him help if he needed it.

Meanwhile Hernando de Soto had arrived before Atahuallpa, courteously aided and guided by the Indians themselves. But in spite of the fact that he had been received almost affectionately, he had not been able to get one word of reply, not even a look from the Inca. In the words of Francisco de Xerez, Pizarro's sec-retary: ". . . the Inca was sitting at the door of his dwelling, on a low seat, with many Indians in front of him and women standing beside him so he was almost completely surrounded. Over his fore-head hung a fringe of wool that looked like silk, crimson in color, two handbreadths wide, tied around his head with cords, which reached down to his eyes; this made him look even graver than he is; his eyes were fixed on the ground, and he never raised them. The captain — de Soto — appeared before him and told him through the interpreter, the *faraute*, he had brought with him, that he was a captain of the governor, who had sent him to visit him and to tell him in his name that it would make the governor very happy if he would come to see him. He said a number of other things, to which the Inca did not reply, nor did he raise his eyes to look at him. Instead one of the councilors answered what the cap-tain had been saying. At this point the other captain, Hernando Pizarro, arrived where the first had left his men, and when he in-quired about the captain, they told him he was talking with the Indian chief. He left his men there, crossed the river, and when he came near the place where Atabalipa was sitting, the captain who was with him, de Soto, said: 'This is a brother of the governor; speak with him, for he has come to see you.' Then the Inca raised his eyes and said: 'Maizabilica, a captain of mine on the Zuricara River, has sent me a message telling me that you have been treat-

ing the caciques badly, and putting them in chains; and he has
sent me an iron collar and says that he has killed three Christians
and a horse. But I shall be pleased to go to see the governor tomorrow and be a friend of the Christians, for they are good.' Hernando
Pizarro replied: 'Maizabilica is a scoundrel, and a single Christian
could kill him and all the Indians of that river. How could he kill
Christians or horses when he and his men are all a chicken-hearted
lot? Neither the governor nor the Christians treat the chiefs badly
as long as they do not fight with them. They treat the good ones
who wish to be friends with them very well; but with those who
want war they fight until they are destroyed. And when you see
what the Christians do to help you in your wars with your enemies, you will realize that Maizabilica lied to you.'

"Atabalipa spoke: 'There is a chief who has refused to obey
me; my men will go with you and you will make war on him.' Hernando Pizarro replied: 'For a chief, no matter how many men he
has, it is not necessary for you to send your Indians. Ten Christian horsemen can destroy him.' Atabalipa laughed and invited
them to drink. The captains said they were fasting, so they would
not have to drink. But when he insisted, they accepted. Then
women came bearing corn liquor, *chicha,* in goblets of gold. When
Atabalipa saw them, he looked at them without saying a word,
and they went away swiftly and came back with bigger gold goblets, and in these they gave them to drink. Then the captains took
their leave, and Atabalipa agreed to come to see the governor the
next morning."

On their return from the visit to the Inca, Hernando Pizarro and
de Soto set forth their impressions of Atahuallpa, his probable intentions, and the forces he had at his disposal. Their information
was definitely pessimistic, although they emphatically insisted
that the good intentions Atahuallpa had expressed seemed to them
sincere. The numerical superiority of the Indians was incomparable; there were probably over thirty thousand. And the Spaniards
were less than two hundred. Not even the swashbuckling boastfulness of Hernando Pizarro could hide his real concern.

This was the climax of the venture. They had to make a decision. The governor called a council of the friars, the fiscal agent, and the leading captains. And he outlined his plan, the only one, in his opinion, that could save the situation. This was to persuade the Inca to come to Caxamarca. And once he had reached the middle of the great three-sided plaza, "larger than any in Spain," take him by surprise in the midst of his Indians — not all of whom could come into the square because the only entrance was narrow — and make him a prisoner.

The reports of Hernando Pizarro and de Soto had cast the adventurers into a deplorable frame of mind. "The Spaniards were all gathered together in a building in mortal fear and not one showed himself in the square," relates Pedro Pizarro, and then he goes on to add: "for I saw many Spaniards so terrified they could not hold their water." The decision of the governor produced surprise and bewilderment among the men in this state. But Pizarro explained his reasons. To turn back, revealing their "fear and terror" to the Indians, would be suicide. They would be pursued through roads and hills unknown to them, hunted down like wild animals, and wiped out. If they were to continue on friendly relations with the Inca, whose reputation for ferocity was notorious, it would weaken their position, destroy their prestige as supernatural beings, which was what gave them their strength, turn them into men like the Indians, and expose them at any moment to the wrath or suspicions of Atahuallpa, for as mere men their number was ridiculous in comparison with the natives. On the other hand, he recalled to their minds the marvelous success they had achieved through surprise, by decisions made on the spur of the moment: Pueblo Quemado, Atacámez, Puná, Túmbez. His speech grew oratorical and heroic — a tonic for Spaniards — and reawakened courage in the hearts of his men.

The plan was worked out. Foot-soldiers, arquebusiers, archers, and horsemen were assigned their positions. A guard was to be set at the entrances to the square. When the Inca, with his personal retinue, came in, the friar, Vicente de Valverde, was to approach Atahuallpa, followed by interpreters and soldiers, making a gesture of peace. Whereupon Pizarro would step forward to receive

him, and at the same time would make a sign, and with the cry of
"St. James and at them!" they would begin a noisy attack, to the
sound of fifes, drums, and shots. Pizarro himself would take the
Inca prisoner.

That last vigil of the conquistadors was a night of tense and
sinister bravery. Hardly anybody slept. The friars spent the night
hearing confessions and muttering prayers. And at daybreak, in
the middle of the square, Brother Vicente de Valverde intoned
before the kneeling Spanish legion:

"*Exsurge, Domine, in ira tua* — Arise, O Lord, in Thy wrath."

And the fanatical, hate-filled prayer went on: "Behold the day
foretold by the angel of the Apocalypse; this is the corrupt land
where the kings have become prostituted and the people drunk
with fornication; the Devil stands upon their altars and with his
evil light hides the true God. The dragon will march against you
spewing blasphemies from its mouth, but fire will descend from
heaven upon the earth. Then you shall hear the sound of harps
and behold the new Jerusalem, with its walls of jasper, its palaces
of shining gold, its streets paved with precious stones, and its gates
of pearl.

"Arise, O Lord, in Thy wrath. Descend in all Thy majesty in
the midst of Thine enemies."

From the top of a tower a look-out called down that Atahuallpa's
camp was being broken on the hill of Cónoc and that he must be
getting ready to set out for Caxamarca. But at that very moment
an emissary of the Inca appeared to say that the visit would not
take place until the next day.

This change of plan visibly displeased Pizarro, for he knew that
a long wait would release the nervous tension his men had worked
up, and that, given time for reflection, their fear would return.
A psychologist without knowing it, Pizarro instinctively felt that
the nervous pitch to which his men had been raised by his
speeches, if prolonged too far, would bring about a reaction of depression, a close neighbor to fear, of pessimism sicklied over by
thought which would stand in the way of daring, reckless action.
Therefore, by the Inca's own messenger, he begged him most

courteously to do him the favor of not delaying his visit and of accepting his invitation to dine with him that same afternoon in his camp.

Shortly afterwards Atahuallpa's affirmative reply was received.

The sun was beginning to sink. The hosts of Atahuallpa began to move toward Caxamarca. In the vanguard were the servants who cleared the road of stones and fallen branches. Then the singers and dancers keeping their monotonous rhythm. Surrounded by generals, councilors, officials, and priests — their ornaments of plumes and metals gleaming in the sun — came the Imperial litter, made of solid gold, "which weighed a hundred pounds," carried on the shoulders of sixteen members of the Imperial clan. In it the Inca Atahuallpa, proudly unarmed, was on his way to his city to receive the homage of the foreigners. His eagle perspicacity — overcast perhaps by the pride of his recent victories — failed to see that this little group of strangers which he had permitted to enter his dominions would attack him and take him prisoner in the midst of his followers.

The descendant of the Sun reached the square of the good city of Caxamarca, whose narrow gates were opened to receive him. With the Emperor entered the Indians of his immediate cortege, some five or six thousand. The others as they arrived remained outside. Not a Spaniard was to be seen in the square.

"Where are the strangers?" he asked those who stood near him.

And in answer Vicente de Valverde, the Dominican friar, chaplain of the band of adventurers, "a restless, dissatisfied, dishonest priest," Oviedo calls him, advanced toward the Inca holding out the cross and the Bible, accompanied by Felipillo, the sly Indian interpreter. He talked to him of God, the one God in three persons; of the passion and death of Jesus; he exhorted — demanded as the Inquisitors say — the descendant of the Sun, of Manco and Viracocha, to abjure his "savage idolatry" and embrace the only true religion, Christianity. He told him of the vast power of the Spanish King, to whom Atahuallpa owed fealty because the Pope, the successor of St. Peter, had bestowed upon him all the lands of the Indians, from one ocean to the other. So tactless was

168

the friar's speech at Caxamarca that, according to a reliable historian, a Catholic bishop, González Suárez, "it would have been ridiculous if it had not been so absurd and criminal."

Atahuallpa's eyes gleamed with haughty pride and he disdainfully answered the mischievous, tactless, ominous friar: "I am the first king of the world and I owe homage to no one. Yours must be a great king, for he has sent his servants so far across the waters. Therefore I shall treat him as a brother. Who is this other king or god you are talking about who has bestowed on yours lands which do not belong to him because they are mine? Tahuantinsuyu [1] is mine and mine alone. What you say about this god of yours seems foolish to me, this god whom the men he had created murdered. I adore no dead god. My god is the Sun, who lives and gives life to men, animals, and plants. If he were to die we would all die with him, just as when he sleeps we sleep, too. And finally," concluded Atahuallpa, "by what right do you dare say to me these senseless things you have spoken?"

"By that which this book gives me," answered the friar, holding out the Bible to the Inca. "When he did not manage to open it, the friar stretched out his hands to open it, and Atabalipa scornfully hit his arm, because he did not want him to open it, and he finally managed to open it himself, and without showing any surprise at the letters or the paper, he threw it five or six feet away from him," relates Xerez.

The outraged friar ran to Pizarro and said: "Do you see what has happened? Why do you waste courtesy or restraint on this dog swollen with pride, when we are surrounded on all sides by Indians? Go on. I absolve you."

Pizarro gave the sign. Shots rang out from muskets and arquebuses. The deafening clamor of war. The governor — in person and alone — approached the Inca's litter and took him prisoner. In the face of the fury of the Spaniards, all of whom sought the dubious honor of maltreating the Inca, the voice of Francisco Pizarro was heard — a voice truly Spanish in that grave moment: "Let no one who values his life lay a hand upon the Inca."

A delirium of slaughter followed. The Indians struggled to flee,

---

[1] Native name of the kingdom of the Incas.

like a flock of sheep set upon by dogs. And as the gate was too narrow, by sheer weight of numbers they knocked down one of the
walls of the square which faced the open country. Hundreds of
Indians were killed. One would-be Spanish hero, Estete, probably
the historian of this same name, snatched the Imperial hood from
the head of the Inca of Tahuantin-suyu. The only Spanish blood
shed in this brutal, inglorious struggle was that of the governor,
Don Francisco Pizarro, who received a sword-thrust while protecting the descendant of the Sun with his own body.

His Lordship the Marquis Don Francisco Pizarro achieved his
desire that the Inca of Tahuantin-suyu, the Emperor of Peru,
should dine with him that day.

There, at his mercy, impassive and silent, sits Atahuallpa the
Inca. His only comment on the terrible events of the day was his
remark to Hernando Pizarro: "Maizabilica lied." With a haughty
gesture he brushes aside the hypocritical consolation of the governor, who says "that this is the way of war, one either conquers or
is conquered." He does not refuse the solicitous attention lavished
on him by his host, for he accepts it as his due. He eats the enemy
food with good grace and drinks the foreign drinks.

Hernando Pizarro, the swashbuckling hidalgo, mindful of the
uses of court etiquette, demands for the Inca the treatment due
his rank. The Marquis orders that the best rooms of the House of
the Snake, the royal palace of Caxamarca, be made ready for him,
and he reserves for himself a room next to these, that he may keep
watch over the prisoner. He sends word to Atahuallpa's relatives
that they may stay with him, and orders that the Inca's table and
bed be served by all his many concubines.

Outdoors the spectacle is depressing. The monotonous shouts
of the sentries who stumble over Indian corpses at every step. The
gloomy prayers of the friars. And through the countryside, along
the roads, the terrified, cowering flight of the stunned Indians,
who understand nothing of what has taken place, who perhaps
subconsciously refuse to understand.

At daybreak Pizarro's first care was to send a party to search
the headquarters of Atahuallpa at Cónoc Springs. "It was marvelous to behold the goblets of silver and gold that were in that camp,

170

so many and so good, and many tents and clothes and other articles of value. The golden dinner service Atahuallpa had brought with him was worth more than sixty thousand gold pesos, and more than five thousand women that traveled with the army came to the Spaniards of their own free will," says Zárate. "Five thousand women who, though sad and forlorn, accepted the advances of the Christians," comments Gómara.

But life must go on as usual in Caxamarca after the massacre. By the command of the Inca the inhabitants are to return to their daily routine of work. A familiar coexistence is established between the Spaniards and the natives. There is no visible resistance or hostility toward the intruders. The Indians give them their indolent, unprotesting service; the Indian women, their bodies on which to procreate, without affection.

Despite his shrewd sagacity Atahuallpa cannot fathom his strange situation. He does not know whether these men are friendly toward him, for they have taken him prisoner; but if they are his enemies, why have they not killed him? His religious training has shaped his conception of the world as a single ascending spiral which ends in the sun. He has no other explanation for events than the theistic. Any obstruction in the straight line of his thoughts disconcerts him. Not knowing how to rebel against the unexpected, he resigns himself in silence.

The relations between the Spaniards and the natives have taken on a plant and animal sort of calm. From among the sisters of the Inca, Pizarro has selected his woman; her name is Intip-Cusi — the servant of the sun — and she is firm-fleshed, terracotta in color, and broad of hip and breast. She is to be called Doña Inés, and will serve the *machu capitu*. Gonzalo and Juan Pizarro — the two youngest members of the dynasty — select their women among the most desirable of the princesses and become members of the family of the Inca. The rest give their inclinations free rein; Alcón and the other younger ones pursue the shy Indian girls, slow of smile but easy of possession. Riquelme and the friars make inquiries about the riches. Pedro de Candia discovers the delights of *chicha*. Valverde, possessed by a mystic fury, unlike the gentle evangelism of Motolina or Gante, relates to the poor Indians, forsaken by their sun, the tragic aspects of the Christian legend. And in the name of the Christ of the scourging and the Crucifixion — not of the wedding in Cana or the Sermon on the Mount — he baptizes, baptizes, baptizes.

With Spanish courtesy, de Soto and Hernando Pizarro have done all they can to make the life of the Inca less severe. With the help of Martinillo they have taught the intelligent Indian enough Spanish for his everyday needs. The Inca initiates the captains in the life of his people, so different from that of individualistic feudal Spain, which is the only world they know. De Soto and Pizarro feel the moral superiority of these "savages" who live their religion of the sun and work; who esteem cleanliness and the uses of water, and who passionately love their land, because it is really theirs.

Hernando Pizarro and de Soto entertain the Inca with accounts of knightly exploits in Flanders, Castile, and Italy. The Inca tries to understand these strange men for whom, at times, deception is a virtue and at times must be paid for by death. The duel interests him as a monstrous thing, and he asks for repeated explanations of what the Spaniards call "honor."

De Soto, the Pizarros, the other captains, and friars teach Atahuallpa the games that are played in camp: cards, chess, dominoes. Chess fascinates him more than any other. In a few months he is a better player than his teachers.

In his daily association with them Atahuallpa has noticed that, above such good and beautiful things as wool, the llamas, corn, these strangers love gold, the *cori* out of which goblets are made for the Inca to drink his *chicha*, and ornaments for the princesses. In this the Inca sees his only hope of salvation. He talks to them of the gold of his dwellings, of the temples, of the House of the Virgins of the Sun. Atahuallpa delights to see how the eyes of these men burn with greed, and then, with all naturalness, he says to Francisco Pizarro that in exchange for his freedom "he would fill a room twenty-two feet long and seventeen wide up to a white line half-way up the wall almost three yards high; and in addition to this he would fill the room with different articles of gold, vases, jars, plates, and other things, and of silver he would give a whole cabin twice full, and he would fulfill all this within two months."

Pizarro, astounded at the dimensions of the rooms, and hardly able to judge the probable value of the fabulous promise, had little faith in it. But with the inveterate gambling spirit of an old soldier, whose god was chance, he gallantly accepted the Inca's offer, as one who bets the contents of his purse in a gambling house on the turn of a card.

In addition to his offer, and to gorge his jailers with gold and wealth, the Inca insinuated the value of a trip to Pacha-Camac, in the territory of the Yungas, where the temple of the great god of the shore-dwellers was to be found. The men of his race had never really believed in this god and had accepted him only as a mark of respect to the regional gods for the sake of the unification of Tahuantin-suyu. He told them that great quantities of gold in ornaments and offerings were to be found there; and as a guarantee of his good faith he sent a messenger to bring before him the priests of the temple, so they might accompany the Spaniards on their trip for these treasures. When the priest and the augur arrived, Atahuallpa, pointing to the priest, said to the Spaniards: "The god Pacha-Camac he serves is no god, because he lies. I would have you know that when my father, Huayna-Capac, was sick in Quito, I sent to ask what we must do to cure him, and he answered that we should lay him in the sun. This we did and he died. Huascar, my brother, asked him if he would be victorious in the war that we two were waging; he said yes and it was I who won. When you came, I consulted him and he assured me that I would defeat you, and you triumphed over me. A god that lies is no god." This is González Suárez's account.

The governor sent his brother Hernando with a group of soldiers. He told him that while on his way to seek the treasure he should try to find out the attitude of the Indians and whether there seemed to be any signs of "rebellion brewing." Hernando set out, and after a long, adventurous trip he returned to Caxamarca with a herd of llamas loaded with gold and the horses shod with gold for the long journey. With him came Chalcuchima, one of Atahuallpa's most famous generals, the conqueror of Huascar. The old warrior, when he saw the stranger arrive accompanied by Indians of the Inca's entourage, instantly made up his mind to go with Pizarro to be with his sovereign.

On his return to Caxamarca Hernando gave the Marquis a quick summary of his trip. He told him that he had seen no signs of plotting either in the villages or along the way. That he had been well received by the Indians, and that the great general Chalcuchima had come with him, submissive and obedient, and was waiting for permission to see his captive King once more.

The interview between Atahuallpa and Chalcuchima was touching and tragic. The warrior entered, his back bowed low under the ritual weight with which the Inca must be approached. His knees shook with emotion. When he saw that the Inca was a prisoner, the tears ran down his cheeks. "These men of Caxamarca did not know how to defend you. If I had been here with the Puruhas and the Caranguis this would never have happened." The Inca smiled.

During Hernando Pizarro's trip to Pacha-Camac a conspiracy of greed, fear, and suspicion began to grow up around the prisoner. It was rumored that in Guamachucho the Indians were secretly gathering — either of their own accord or at Atahuallpa's secret order — to attack the Spaniards and free the Inca. Pizarro asked Atahuallpa about it. The Inca's reply was sarcastic: "Do you think I am so foolish as to order uprisings when I am in your power and you could kill me at the first sign of a revolt? Besides, the rooms are almost filled with the gold for my ransom. I have confidence that you will keep your word. I shall soon be free, and your friend and ally." To prove the truth of his words he suggested that a Spanish party be sent as far as Cuzco, thus passing through most of Tahuantin-suyu, so that all might be convinced that no revolt was brewing and also so they might bring back as much gold as they could from the sacred city.

Pizarro accepted his offer — his eyes gleaming as if with the reflection of the gold of Cuzco — and sent a party of soldiers under the command of Hernando de Soto, Pedro del Barco, and a fiscal officer of the crown. They traveled for days. And on one of these days they met a squadron of Indians who had the captive Huascar in charge. De Soto talked with them. And he quickly realized that if the complaints of the legitimate Inca reached Pizarro's ears through some other channel, the situation of his friend, the prisoner of Caxamarca, would become still more difficult. So he decided to turn back and report to Pizarro that, as far as Jauja, he had detected no signs of revolt. Also that he had met Huascar, who made the most generous offers to the Spaniards in return for his freedom, but that the whole Empire was behind Atahuallpa and recognized him alone as the real Emperor.

During these trips an event of the greatest importance had taken place which changed the whole aspect of the situation. This was the arrival of Don Diego de Almagro, on the 14th of April, "Easter Eve," from Panama with reinforcements of men and horses. To all appearances the reunion of the two captains was friendly, but this was only on the surface. Pizarro knew that Almagro had come to claim his share of the booty, by the terms of the tripartite agreement between the two of them and Luque, who had died by that time; but he, and even less his men, the heroes of the episode of Caxamarca, were unwilling to admit any such equality. The first civil war of Spanish America had begun.

It was perfectly clear who was to be the victim of this war: Atahuallpa. Gold for the ransom was coming in from all directions in Tahuantin-suyu; the rooms the Inca had designated were almost full. Gold was to be followed by blood. The Inca's eagle eye had discerned that the arrival of Almagro, the one-eyed, was baleful to him. And so it was. Almagro and his men — backed up by the black-hearted Riquelme — were plotting against Atahuallpa with the object of hastening the division of the ransom gold — which they assumed they would not share and share alike with Pizarro and his men — so they might the sooner be free, once they were rid of the need of guarding the Inca, to proceed with the conquest to Cuzco, where a future of gold and adventures awaited them.

Valverde and the friars were plotting, too, in their hypocritical fashion. The Dominican could not forgive Atahuallpa's disdainful reception of him in Caxamarca and his manifest dislike for listening to him or having anything to do with him. Nor could he forgive him the luxury in which he lived nor his women, while he was obliged to keep up before the soldiers the tormenting farce of his chastity.

Another conspirator was the sly interpreter, Felipillo, Valverde's creature and inseparable companion. Felipillo was from Túmbez; he had been reared in the most complete devotion to Huascar. He detested everything Quitu. His Christianity was only skin-deep; there remained in him a subconscious, totemic recollection of Pacha-Camac, the god of the Yungas. For this reason, Atahuallpa's harshness toward the priest of Pacha-Camac and his encouragement of Hernando Pizarro to sack the temple aggravated the traditional hatred he felt for the descendant of the Caras. And knowing that he would be upheld by the Spaniards, who needed his services, he set about making Atahuallpa's life as unpleasant as he could with his disgusting plotting and spying. He acted as a go-between for the Spaniards with the Inca's concubines, and, that the outrage might be complete, he seduced and ravished one of them himself. When the Inca heard about it he complained to Pizarro. The old veteran of love and war laughed. . . . But Felipillo knew that Atahuallpa had demanded his head, and fearful lest the Spaniards — whose changeability he had come to know — might accede to the prisoner's demands, he decided to accelerate his campaign against him.

The nagging insistence of Riquelme and Almagro about the division of the ransom wore down the resistance of the governor, and they proceeded to the rapacious division of the great prize of the adventure. To make the division easier and fairer they decided to melt down the nuggets of gold, the marvelous vases, pitchers, and idols. "Twenty-seven loads of gold and two thousand marks of silver," from Pachac-Camac; "178 loads of gold, and the loads are *paliqueros* that are carried between four Indians," from Cuzco . . . besides the overflowing rooms. A few things were saved out — golden ears of corn, golden dishes holding birds on them of the same metal — to send the Emperor in Madrid. To the governor, Don Francisco Pizarro, went the litter of gold. The balance of the treasure — the greatest spoils of war known up to that moment — was divided, in public, with a crier carefully calling out the shares, after deducting the royal fifth.

And now at last the dreamed-of treasures were in the hands of the Spanish adventurers. But the great illusion did not bring happiness. They learned — without understanding it — the truth of the Midas myth — that one may be poor and lack everything one needs even though one's hands are buried in the deceitful gold that passes for wealth. De Soto, cursing with rage, had to pay a pound of gold for a sheet of paper on which to write his mother a letter. Pedro de Candia was on the point of killing one of Almagro's men — one of the new arrivals — who demanded fifty gold pesos for a pair of boots.

NIGHTFALL AT NOON. Before dividing up the gold, Pizarro formally declared that Atahuallpa had complied with the terms of the ransom pact. But the Inca remained a prisoner, more closely guarded than before. Everyone felt that now the episode of Caxamarca was approaching its end. It was impossible to continue it without endangering the success of the conquest. But the great problem was still unsolved: Atahuallpa. Three possible solutions suggested themselves: to send him to Spain with the custodians of the royal share of the treasure; to take him along to Cuzco; to kill him.

The first two were favored by Hernando de Soto, Pedro de Candia, Hernando Pizarro, Blas de Atienza, Anton de Carrión, Pedro de Ayala, the brothers Chávez, Alonso de Ávila, Francisco de Fuentes, Juan de Herrada, and some of the other true hidalgos. The third was supported by Riquelme, Almagro, and his men. The moving spirit of the murder plot was Felipillo, the interpreter. And the one who counseled Atahuallpa's death as a Christian duty to Pizarro's reluctant ears was Valverde.

The governor set great store by Hernando Pizarro's opinion. He was the older of the two and better educated. Almagro, who had hated him ever since Panama, resolved to remove him from Francisco's side. To achieve this, the "one-eyed" began to extol his fine qualities, his honesty, his distinction, and to proclaim that he was the one who should be sent to Spain with the royal treasure and the gifts for the King. And he suggested that in return for carrying out this delicate mission he should receive a larger share of gold than the other captains. The Marquis was too shrewd to be taken in by the "foxiness" of his old partner; but this time it was to his interest to heed him, for he realized that the bluntness and uncompromising honesty of Hernando would make his relations with Almagro difficult. Therefore it was decided that Hernando should go to Spain to carry to the King "the gold of Peru." When Atahuallpa heard of this from Hernando himself, he was unable to conceal his distress: "Captain, once you are gone, I am sure your comrades will kill me. That 'one-eyed one' and that 'fat one' will persuade your brother to kill me. Don't leave me, captain. . . ."

Hernando did everything he could to reassure him. He promised that he would not leave until the governor had given him his word anew that his life would be respected. But Atahuallpa was not reassured. And, in fact, Hernando spoke sternly to the Marquis about the matter and even asked to be allowed to take the Inca with him to Spain. But Francisco did not want to take the risk and he did not consent.

After Hernando's departure the conspiracy against Atahuallpa grew like wildfire. There was no argument that Almagro or the friars did not invoke: offense to God, ill service to the crown, betrayal of the Indians. Felipillo added fuel to the flame. He was always reporting supposed conversations he had overheard among the Indians, plots to overthrow the Spaniards; finally, taking advantage of the arrival of some Indians from the south, partisans of Huascar, he invented a tale of a tremendous plot to free the Inca. The center of action and the gathering-point was Guamachucho.

Confronted with a specific accusation of this sort, Pizarro grew frightened. He did not trust the passivity of the natives. His forthright, one-sided mind, the mind of a soldier, could not understand how thousands of men, in their own land, did not work out some plan to save their King and drive the invader from their country.

Atahuallpa's case was upheld by Hernando de Soto and a few others. To get de Soto away from Caxamarca, Pizarro sent him to Guamachucho, to find out whether such a plot really existed. When de Soto left, certain that he would be able to return with proof of the Inca's innocence, Atahuallpa saw his case completely lost. And, to be sure, Felipillo managed to have him put in chains and he was much more strictly guarded. And then, without any real opposition any longer, Pizarro ordered the Emperor of Tahuantinsuyu brought to trial. The grotesque hearing began. Pizarro and Almagro acted as judges; Sancho de Cuellar was the clerk. As a sop to the small group of dissenting hidalgos, they were allowed to appoint Juan de Herrada to defend the prisoner.

As the trial of the Inca was getting under way, a new group of natives from the south arrived. To the accompaniment of ululations of grief, they told the Spaniards that the legitimate Inca of Cuzco, Huascar, had been drowned in the Andamarca River by the band of Indians who had him in their custody. Felipillo, who was handling the matter, added that the order for the assassination had been secretly issued by Atahuallpa, who was afraid that Pizarro might come to an understanding with Huascar and give him his support. This sealed Atahuallpa's doom. Almagro's men and the friars hypocritically found this testimony irrefutable evidence; they who had stopped at nothing, and who were later to kill one another, professed to be horrified by this accident of war, for which Atahuallpa's direct responsibility has never been even remotely proved.

The prosecutor Riquelme, aided by the charlatan Sancho de Cuellar, accused the Inca of being guilty on twelve counts. The most outstanding of the charges were: that Atahuallpa was a bastard and a usurper; that he had ordered his brother Huascar assassinated; that he had squandered the state's funds; that he had been guilty of idolatry; that he was an adulterer, for he openly lived with many women; that he had incited the natives to revolt against Spain. . . . Valverde pronounced one of his most lurid speeches and — quoting savage texts from the Bible — demanded the death penalty for this savage, this living incarnation of the Devil, who had himself been publicly worshipped by his people; who practiced the most revolting idolatry, and one of the most abominable of all sins: polygamy.

In vain Juan de Herrada invoked every human and divine law on the Inca's behalf; idle for him to tell them that the Emperor alone was qualified to judge a defeated monarch; that he was defending the innocence of a man who had observed the tenets of his own law, and who was unable to disobey laws or religions of which he was ignorant. . . . The case had been decided beforehand. Pizarro and Almagro — hypocritically observing the legal provisions — condemned Atahuallpa to be burned to death unless he accepted Christianity, in which case burning would be commuted to garroting.

Pedro Pizarro claims to have seen tears in the eyes of his brother Francisco as he came out of the room where the murderous trial was held. . . . Be that as it may, the same night, the 29th of August 1533, Atahuallpa was to be put to death in the public square of Caxamarca before de Soto could get back with proofs of his innocence. In a final effort the Inca's defenders made a last appeal to the whole group of the adventurers. In vain. Blinded by religious fanaticism and greed, these Spaniards of the "Black Spain" voted ten to one against the prisoner. At the end Pizarro, to satisfy some last scruple of his conscience, and to have a defense in case this act should be frowned upon in Spain, asked Valverde to sign the death sentence. Without hesitating, he affixed his signature, preceded by a cross, this "restless, dissatisfied, dishonest priest."

When the news of his sentence was brought to Atahuallpa, he upbraided Pizarro for his treachery; reminded him that — according to Pizarro's own public statement — he had fulfilled the terms of the ransom agreement; and he told him that while he and his people had treated the Spaniards with consideration and affection, they were repaying him with death. . . . Seeing that all his reproaches were in vain, he recovered his outwardly serene attitude and asked the conqueror to look after his children and his wives. Then he talked for a time with his priests and his ministers who were with him. They reminded him that the spirit of an Inca cannot rejoin the sun if his body has been consumed by fire on earth, and they advised him to accept baptism so his punishment might be commuted.

This was the hour of Valverde's sinister revenge. In the square, between the gallows and the faggots waiting for the torch, stands the group composed of the Inca and his executioners. The sun has already set. A few flickering torches light up the tragic scene. Valverde mumbles prayers, and after the Inca has stated — and his desire has been put into Latin by the acolyte — that he wishes to abjure his infamous idolatry and embrace the Christian faith, Valverde pours the baptismal waters over the head of the great King, and with the anointing and the salt grotesquely christens him Juan Francisco. . . .

The execution of the sentence follows. The friars intone the prayers for the dead; the soldiers kneel. Huddled in the corners of the square, "as though they were drunk," the Indians listen to the death agony of the descendant of the Sun.

When Hernando de Soto returned with the news that the report of the plot at Guamachucho was completely false, he found that the crime had already been committed. The young captain, filled with righteous indignation, upbraided Pizarro for his precipitate act, his cowardice, his injustice. He told him it would bring upon him the anger of the crown, for the Emperor alone was entitled to judge another great king. Pizarro, dismayed, put the blame on Valverde and Riquelme. The latter hurled accusations and insults at one another, each trying to absolve himself from any share in the assassination. History has had little trouble in arriving at its verdict; with their mutual recriminations, their accusations, these three principal actors in this sinister drama declare their own guilt.

A native woman of the confederation of the Zarzas, when she heard the tragic news, uttered the greatest funeral oration that could be pronounced upon the Inca and the Empire: *"Chaupi punchapi tutayaca:* Night fell at noon." The young, virile Inca died with his life span but half completed. And the great Empire of Tahuantin-suyu, which had built up a vast, solid civilization and a political and social organization wiser and more just than any the Western world has yet known, was cut down at the height of its development. For although the great Huayna-Capac, through his love for Atahuallpa, had yielded to the division of the Empire, the mistake was already being corrected by this strong, wise son of his, alive to the values of both innovation and tradition.

After this came the ridiculous comedy of the viceroys, a system all imperialisms have practiced and still follow to give the conquered peoples the ridiculous gratification of a mock independence. Then came Vilcabamba and his protest, and finally the heroic cry of Tupac-Amaru.

Today is the fruitful hour for Indo-Hispania. All its voices which express themselves in Spanish without exception affirm their desire to live in justice and equality. From the undying Mexico of Zapata, through the Peru of Mariategui, to the south alive with affirmation and hope. Atahuallpa has no words of hatred for Pizarro in these pages. Four centuries have passed. Atahuallpa and Pizarro together await and will achieve the hour of the earth and of justice.

SEVENTEENTH CENTURY: THE COLONY

ALL THE MOVEMENT, the daring, the valor of the conquest became quiet, submission, meekness in the colonial period. History has never known a longer period of peace. Almost three centuries elapsed without a single war. In the days of the conquest, scaling mountains, discovering new lands, risking their lives on land and sea, every conqueror had traveled through half of the continent, and it even seemed as though all America were too small for their ambition. Under the colony it became rare for a man to leave the fields his eyes had beheld from infancy. The hero of the conquest is the soldier who shouts, roars, drowns out every other sound. In the colony it is the *oidor*, the magistrate, who hears, listens, and passes judgment. It is the transition from violence to reflection. Between the two epochs which open and close the cycle — the War of the Conquest and the War of Independence — the colony is our first Middle Ages, the night of creation. It is then that the parent races cross and adapt themselves to each other, and the mestizo is born, like a confused plan of a man, with a white soul — Spanish — and a coppery soul — Indian. The writers of this period no longer relate turbulent tales like those of the days of the conquests, but picaresque narrations, sermons, a little poetry. Sometimes mystic poetry. Some of the greatest Spanish poets of the Golden Age came to America: Tirso de Molina, Balbuena, and, later, Gutierre de Cetina. Cervantes himself sought a post in these lands, though unsuccessfully. A son of the Sevillian Bartolomé Esteban Murillo comes to Santa Fé de Bogotá to paint. In the small cities and convents people gossip. There are books that have preserved part of this life and gossip and bedroom scandal, in which the suspicion of witchcraft was not unknown, and the "unco guid" were duly shocked. The Inquisition takes a hand when the gossip becomes too bold, and the archives are full of trials that were held in Mexico and Lima. It is the time of altarpainting in America, those altar-paintings of gold that make the inside of our churches gleam like an enchanted cave and where the polychrome figures shine like brilliant birds in a golden wood. In the sixteenth century man spreads himself over a world that has no limits. In the seventeenth he withdraws into a little world, a cell. Our saints make their appearance and for the first time a breeze of American air blows through the gardens of Christian mysticism. Saint Rose of Lima is, above all, a flower of Peru. Ventura García Calderón draws this parallel between the mysticism of Spain and that of America:

> The Spanish Saint Theresa talks of war and loving combat, of the divine conqueror. For her love was "hard and relentless as hell." Less equatorial is the tone of the Peruvian saint, so gentle, so resigned, so Creole in her ejaculation of upbraidings when Jesus is overlong in keeping His tryst in the garden. "Where is the fortunate one who delays him?" she complains. Even while reading the account of her divine rapture and ecstasy which her biographers have set down, we never for a moment can forget that she was Catholic, Apostolic, and from Lima.

A Peruvian friar of the seventeenth century, Juan Meléndez, wrote in his *True Treasures of the Indies* a life of Saint Rose of Lima from which the following excerpts are taken.

SAINT ROSE OF LIMA

JUAN DE MELÉNDEZ

THAT the city of Lima, the mart and metropolis of the vast and powerful kingdoms of Peru, might have nothing to envy the rest of the world, there was born there around the year 1586 one of the most extraordinary women the New or the Old World has ever seen: Rosa de Santa Maria. The Church was then under the rule of His Holiness Sixtus V, and the Kingdom of Spain under His Majesty Philip II.

She was born in the month of April, the month of the joys of spring, when the flowers unfasten the green button that has been holding them close, to adorn and celebrate May. This Rose was born to be the ornament of the May of the Church of my religion and of its blossoming and pleasant gardens. Her felicitous birth took place on the 20th of April, when the heavens and the stars are in their most peaceful and auspicious conjunction and the waters flow most crystalline and clear, the winds are most gentle and restrained, when the earth brings forth new plants and flowers, and the heat of the fire on high is still tempered.

Her parents were Gaspar Flores and Maria de la Oliva. Her father was born in the city of Puerto Rico of the Windward Islands, in the domain of Hispaniola; her mother, in the city of Lima itself. They were of respectable and honest origin, though not over-blessed with worldly goods. But by the designs of Providence they were endowed with far greater riches, with the incomparable treasure and priceless jewel of such a daughter.

Close beside the Hospital of the Espíritu Santo, in Santo Domingo Street, lived her father when the Virgin Rose was born. Here we see the happy augury of the ardent spirit she was to inherit from her glorious father Santo Domingo, which would enable her to achieve thirty-three years of triumph over nature, with the help of grace, in silent struggles between the spirit and the flesh, following from so early an age the path of such extreme perfection;

184

treading the strait road of virtue with all the power and breath of her life, with that joy and happiness in its progress which we shall contemplate and admire.

From childhood everything in the Virgin Rose was love, and for this reason she went to the lengths she did. She had no fear of suffering, because she had no fear of loving. She began her discipline with the severity with which others end, because she began with a love which is to be found in few. She grew in years and in love, in fasting, mortification, and penitence. When she entered upon her new obligations in the Third Order of Santo Domingo, she employed new forms of discipline. Out of two iron chains she made a scourge, and to follow in the steps of our Father Santo Domingo, she flagellated herself every night until her blood watered the ground. She followed a plan in these bloody scourgings, setting forth the end for which they were employed: one night for her many and great sins, providing they were not mortal or among the graver venial sins; another night for public calamities, to appease the wrath of God, temper His justice, and implore His mercy; another night, and this most frequently, for the misfortunes of the Church, offering herself as the victim, being merciless with herself so that God might take pity on the state of the Church and cure its wounds with hers.

Another night for the kingdoms of Peru and her beloved natal city of Lima, in the hope that the Divine Bridegroom, beholding her back bathed in blood, would remember that He had suffered likewise for us, and that His mercy, which the many sins of its dwellers had benumbed, would be aroused at the sight of the severity of her discipline and He would not visit His wrath upon the city. Another night for the souls of the departed in purgatory, in the hope that her blood might slake that raging, devouring fire. Her love and discipline were spurred on by the desire to bring them some comfort in their burning torment, and she poured out streams of blood in the hope that the great quantity of blood might extinguish the great fires.

Another night for the dying, so that in that dangerous but inevitable transaction they might have the aid and succor of Heaven, which all those in that state so greatly need, for all eternity hangs on a moment's repentance. Another night for those in mortal sin, that God might give them light and knowledge of their miserable and perilous state, the more perilous because they are sure to be lost and their souls lost if they are not reconciled in time to God. She asked this with many voices because her desire was so great, and to this end she furrowed and laid open her flesh with the greatest severity until she was become Job the patient and Lazarus the beggar, without friends to console her or dogs to lick her wounds. What pious impiety! To endanger her life to win souls for God, seeking their conversion with her own blood! The scourgings she gave herself were cruel, and applied with greatest harshness to those parts of her body most sensitive to pain.

THE CROWN OF THORNS.   In order to know many kinds of suffering, the Virgin Rose tried to make herself a crown; and as all the just seek, with pious ambition, a crown of thorns in this life, leaving the crown of gold for the other, this aspiration, which is fortuitous in others, was very natural to our Rose. Because what rose is there, or has there ever been, that is not crowned with thorns? The rose and the thorns that are to crown it are born together. The thorns remain blunt until the rose bursts its green bud. Little by little it breaks through the narrow prison cell of its leaves, and the thorns grow finer and sharper. The Virgin Rose was born and at the same time the blunt thorns of the Rose; she began to free herself from the first afflictions of nature and began to give off the sweetest fragrance of virtue. The thorns grew and the Rose grew because with the passing of the years her penitence increased. She had come to love crowns since once when her friends had put a garland of flowers upon her head; she put a pin in it, so the Rose might never be without thorns, and the pin pierced her brow. From that time she vowed in her heart to make a crown that should serve as a penitence, because the one she put on that time had done very well. These desires had been engendered by experience and love; and her grief at beholding a sorrowful image of an *Ecce Homo* so strengthened them that she immediately put them into effect. She looked at the image, pity filled her and sorrow and gratitude, and her heart was afflicted to see that precious head pierced with thorns. And she said with great emotion: "Why should I be so delicate a member, when my head is so severely wounded and pierced?" And moved by this tender consideration, she made herself a crown of tin, interlaced with string to which she tied some little nails on the side that was to rest against her head. She put it on, the nails pierced her temples, and it pleased her so much that she never again took it off — if not this same one, another like it — from the day she put it on until she died. Death took away her life and her crown, so that God might crown her life with a better life, and her crown with a better crown.

As tin is a soft metal, and obedient to the hands, it lacked that firmness that the Virgin Rose needed to hold the nails in place, for they would come loose and not wound her as she wanted them to do. She decided to make one of harder, stronger metal and found silver to be the best, both because of its cleanliness as well as for the purpose she had in mind. She ordered a narrow strip of silver to be beaten out and three rows of nails to be soldered into the strip itself. Each row was to have thirty-three nails to commemorate the years of Christ Our Lord, making ninety-nine nails all together, and this crown she wore with great delight of her heart.

And because her hair might interfere and prevent the nails from piercing her head as she wished, she shaved off all her hair, and this she did whenever it grew back, leaving a few locks on her forehead to cover the crown, for the rest of it was covered by her wimple, so she was a crowned victim under the folds of her wimple. It is difficult to understand or even conceive the pain and suffering she underwent with this strange penitence. How it wounded her delicate head! How sharply the nails pierced her! If one alone was more than enough to pierce her brain, what would so many do and so close together? It was not as though the pain were confined to her temples, forehead, and brain, for as all the senses and acts of the body are dependent upon that higher force by which they are governed, all the members and parts of the body feel the pains suffered by the head. From this fact comes the proverb that when the head suffers, all the body suffers. Her eyes felt it most because of their proximity; then her mouth, talking or eating; her breast when she coughed; so that every natural movement she made was one of torture and martyrdom.

Ninety-nine strong immovable nails pierced her delicate head day and night; and to this cruel martyrdom she added still another.

Every day she changed the crown around so the nails would open new wounds each day. On Fridays she pushed it toward the back so it would encircle her ears, which, after her eyes, were the most sensitive part, and there she would leave it until Sunday, thus accompanying the Blessed Virgin, the mother of anguish and suffering, who lies pierced with grief at the foot of the cross. A tender and devout meditation for the day! She kept this mortification hidden from the eyes of her parents, her brothers and sisters, and the other members of the household for a long time, for it did not occur to them that under the folds of her wimple the prudent virgin had such a fierce torment concealed. Only her confessor knew about the crown, but he did not know what kind of crown she wore. He did not know about the nails or the things she thought of to make the pain of her penitence greater. She never gave him a clear account of it nor did she explain how she had come to make such a strange invention. But Divine Providence, whom every creature obeys, did not permit silence to lock away a thing so marvelous and rare; and breaking down the walls that imprisoned it, let it be known of all for Its own honor and glory and the great credit of Its omnipotence.

FERVENT EXERCISE OF PRAYER. In her early years, when the only study of children of that age is how to amuse and entertain one another, since it is the natural condition of childhood to play together, for this is all their concern and occupation, the neighbors of the Virgin Rose came with their dolls and played with them and dressed and undressed them, with that instinct for beautification they display so early. They called to the Blessed Girl and coaxed her to bring hers out; she excused herself, saying she had none, nor did she want them, either. "But why don't you want them?" asked one of her neighbors. And she answered: "Because they say the Devil sometimes talks through the mouth of dolls." And this was true, because most of the idols worshipped by the Indians look like dolls. All the little girls in the neighborhood were absorbed in playing with their dolls while the wise little Rose thought only of how to slip away from them and withdraw to the secret place of her house where she could pray and commend her soul to God. Her brothers and sisters, who amused themselves and played with the other children of their age, often missed her. One of them, seeing that she had slipped away from the games and was not to be found anywhere, went to look for her. He found her in a room full of dust and rubbish in the cellar, where she sat in a corner by herself praying. He began to laugh at her and tease her, saying: "Sister, is it better to sit amongst this rubbish and dirt, alone and hidden, than to play with the other girls with your dolls?" To this she answered with a prudence and judgment not to be expected of one of her tender years: "Leave me alone here with my God, for I know that He is here, and I do not know whether He would like to be where the dolls are."

SOLITUDE. This tender love of solitude grew in her as she grew in years. She was now older, and was entering upon new obligations, free now from those of childhood. She asked an older brother, called Fernando, to build her a shrine and a little altar among some banana trees that grew in the garden beside the walls that encircled it. But it was to be done so secretly that the family should neither see it nor know about it. He told her he would and immediately set to work at it as his sister had desired and requested, covering it all over with banana fronds, and this was easy to do, for the altar was small and the leaves are so large that they are sometimes two yards long and two thirds of a yard wide. He put a cross on it painted in many colors, and beside it many pictures of saints to keep it company, and he arranged it so it could be used as an oratory in keeping with the wishes of his sister Rose.

It seemed to her that in this little piece of ground which she had consecrated to her solitude all the pleasures and delights of the world were to be found. She did not want to leave it all day long.

All the time she had left from her work, her duties in the house, and sleep she spent in the garden, at the altar praying, and this was her conversation, her play, and her amusement. She lived apart from all, yet living with all; like David, who being with many was with none, and, like an angel in human flesh, praised God at all hours. She grew so fond of this little retreat that it became her center of existence and she was ill at ease, as though lost, when she was not there. She knew no greater moment of pleasure than when she was at prayer in her shrine. "If you want to find Rose don't look for her in the garden," her family would say; you will not find her anywhere else because the Blessed Girl was nowhere else.

ROSE AND THE MOSQUITOES. At night, especially when the sky was serene and the wind blew stronger after the sun had departed from the horizon, many more mosquitoes came, seeking refuge in her cell. But the senseless little beasts were so polite that they made no noise nor bit her.

If her mother or some other visitor came to see her they bit their hands and faces so much they had to go home, so much did they suffer from the bites and the swelling they caused. They were amazed to see that in spite of the army of mosquitoes by which she was surrounded, Rose had no marks on her hands or face. They spoke of this to her and she smiled and answered: "When I moved into this house the mosquitoes and I made a friendly agreement: I would not bother them or drive them away and they would not bite me or make a noise; and we live in such friendship that they neither bite nor annoy me; on the contrary, they help me to praise the Lord with the hum of their buzzing." And this really took place, for as the first rays of dawn appeared, she would open the door and window and say to all the mosquitoes: "Come, my friends, let's praise God, let's praise God."

They would come out, obedient to the Virgin Rose's voice, and grouping their squadrons as in a choir, some of them would intone a gentle buzzing and others would answer them, and the sound of their buzzing made so gentle and pleasant a music that it seemed as though they had the gift of reason. She sent them out to seek their food, the choir and the music ceased, and they departed. They would return in the evening and she would say to them: "Now, friends, it would be good for you to sing God's praises with me before we go to bed, for He has cared for you today and He cares for us all." They formed a choir the same as in the morning and began the sonorous music of their noisy buzzing, but in such perfect time and rhythm that it seemed as though they were trying to make a most agreeable harmony. Then she would tell them to be quiet and go to sleep; they would obey without making another sound all night.

ROSE'S BIRDS. Accustomed now to the plants' obeying her, submissively doing as she bid them, she wanted the birds to obey in the same way. It was easy for her to achieve this, for all animals render obedience to whoever serves the Lord truly and with a pure and perfect heart, as the ardent voice, aflame with charity, of St. Francis of Paul asserts. A year before she died, being a guest of the Treasurer, Don Gonzalo de la Maza, this singular thing happened throughout one Lent: She would sit with her work beside a window which overlooked the greater part of the beautiful garden of the Treasurer, in which there was a huge tree that gave it shade. Every night, an hour before evening prayers, a bird came and sat on a branch in view of Rose, whetting its beak, fluttering its wings, and breaking into gentle warblings. Rose left her work and sang to it:

> Come, little nightingale,
> Let us praise the Lord.
> Raise a song to your Creator,
> I shall sing unto my Saviour.

The stanza had metrical defects, but although many saints have composed elegant verse, the ardor of the spirit often pays little attention to the correction of the syllables but seeks the harmony of the feelings. The spirit does not work for the perfection of the meter, but only that the words may tell its love.

THE SAINT SINGS. The Virgin Rose sang and sang well, for she had an excellent voice and could modulate it in trills, arpeggios, and changes of tone. When she stopped, the nightingale began. For this bird not only sings, but has taught human beings its art, for it loves them tenderly and only displays the full gamut of its talents when it knows they are listening. When the nightingale had completed its harmony, the Rose entered, breaking her silence, and they sang to each other in turn, so beautifully and rhythmically that all who heard them marveled. This sweet melody of music and singing lasted for a whole hour, because it began when the sun was going down. As night closed in, the nightingale departed, and the Virgin Rose closed her window, a mourning dove that before was a gay linnet, pouring forth sad lamentations to the Lord:

> How shall I love You, my God
> When I am but Your creature
> And You my Creator?

In gentle lament she poured forth the burning desires of her heart to His Majesty, to whom the music and concert were directed every afternoon, for the nightingale came daily to help her sing, obedient to her command, like the trees and the flowers. And the lamentation and pleasure went hand in hand, for even in the most spiritual persons, like this one, joy is never complete and as a rule sorrow walks beside delight. And she bemoaned the absence of those divine ardors with which to follow the ascent of love until she should be consumed in them. But she contemplated her lowliness, the lowliness of a being whose love, however much it ascends, has limits beyond which it cannot pass. She longed to love God with the love with which His Divine Majesty loves Himself, and she piteously lamented this impossible struggle, seeing how her love was finite and that of God infinite.

Then she turned to those who had been drawn by the new music, who were the members of the household and many from outside, gathered together by this unusual prodigy, and continued her laments:

> The little bird departs and leaves me,
> Flying away in the night,
> But my God remains beside me,
> Blessed be His name.

Then she withdrew to continue in sweet colloquies the occasion of her song and her sad lament in the oratory, toward which all her thoughts and actions were directed. She pondered greatly how a little bird without the gift of reason praised its Creator, and accompanied her with its music, merely because she told it to do so; and how men, supposedly endowed with reason, persuaded and obliged by all the tongues God has given them and the manifold reasons for praising Him, neither heed the one nor fulfill the other, deaf to the example and exhortation of creatures devoid of reason. As she burned in a fire of divine love, she would have burned the hearts of all, like the seraphic virgin St. Catherine, so that they might serve, praise, and glorify Him who by so many rights deserves to be served and reverenced.

EIGHTEENTH CENTURY: THE REVOLUTION

In Spanish America the War of Independence broke out in 1810. Brazil separated from Portugal in 1822. But for many years before, from the second half of the eighteenth century, the spirit of revolution had been gathering. The Creole, the mestizo, and even the Indian and the Negro, who had withdrawn in meditation during the seventeenth century as they took possession of the land under the new colonial order, began to see clearly. They wanted to be the masters of their own fate. At first this was in the nature of a vague desire, a subterranean stream. Then came a moment when America's soul could no longer fit in its body, and the cry of liberty rang out. Many factors contributed to arouse the Spanish Americans: among the lower classes, the growing abuses of the great holders of land grants and officials who exploited the Indians and the slaves, and the new taxes levied to help Spain in her war with England; in the upper classes, the desire to eliminate the Spaniards from government posts, the need to free trade from the monopoly exercised by Spain, the example of the United States, which had just declared its independence of England, the writings of the French Encyclopedists, the reverberations of the revolution that had placed Louis XVI upon the scaffold, the interest in science which began to manifest itself in the universities. During the reign of Carlos III, the Bourbon King who brought many new things from France into Spain, Spanish America was visited by scientists like Humboldt, La Condamine, Jorge Juan, Antonio Ulloa. The younger generation became infected by the scientific and political preoccupations of Europe; Rousseau and Voltaire were read; certain ports began to trade with England; the study of economy was encouraged; chemists came from France to improve the methods of working the mines. Without intending to, the Bourbon kings placed in the hands of the Americans the tools they needed for their freedom. Then came the revolution.

But the original thing about our eighteenth century was that the ones who first thought of freeing themselves were the people of the lower classes. It was the Indians, the Negroes, those of the "community" in Paraguay who rose against the Jesuits, in Peru against the officers of the crown, in New Granada (today Colombia) against all those who represented the colonial system. At times these rebels had brilliant leaders, like Antequera and Mompox in Paraguay, who had studied law and had read the French writers. Other times their leaders were the descendants of the old native monarchs, as in Peru and Bolivia, where José Gabriel Tupac-Amaru and his brother headed the first great war of independence. In New Granada, Ecuador, and Venezuela the masses went into the struggle almost without anyone to guide them, or with some bold guerrilla leader like José Antonio Galan.

The documents of the period describe the process of these revolutions, which have been called the risings of the "comuneros," better than any literary work. A collection of documents dealing with that led by Tupac-Amaru in Peru was published in Buenos

Aires in 1836, and from it the four following excerpts have been taken. They were written by different civilian and ecclesiastical authorities of the colony, and they reveal both the importance of the popular uprising and the rancor with which the Spaniards viewed and punished it. Tupac-Amaru was defeated by the King's soldiers, but his name continued to be a talisman, which Bolívar used later as he led his armies of liberation to victory.

REBELLION AND DEATH OF TUPAC–AMARU

THE UPRISING

THE PUBLIC funds were gone, because all the money in the royal treasury had been taken to Lima a little while before. The citizens were impoverished and those who had means found all sorts of excuses to refuse to contribute to the daily upkeep of the troops. There was no gunpowder or other ammunition in the stores, for the thought of a catastrophe of this sort had never entered anyone's mind. And since it was imperative to supply this help at once, it seemed proper to me to assemble the clergy and the priors of the various religious orders and lay before them the need of raising a subscription to attend to the needs of the country and the King, and I set an example by subscribing 12,000 pesos in my name and in that of three convents, and the other groups did the same, according to their means, so that we raised close to 30,000 pesos, besides 14,000 in church funds which I loaned, without interest, and the priest of San Jeronimo gave 40,000.

The enemy had the advantage over us, for our forces were weak, and the members of the so-called Council of War spent their time fighting with one another, arguing over everything and deciding nothing. If, by chance, they agreed upon some measure that would have been helpful, it was never carried out. And so, to leave no stone unturned to help our country and put down the rebellion, I became a soldier myself, without ceasing to be a bishop, and when things looked blackest for us I armed the regular and the secular clergy, and, as a last resort, appointed the dean of my cathedral, Don Manuel de Mendieta, commander of these church troops, set up barracks, and formed the priests and the students of the two seminaries into four companies, with their respective officers, with arms and munitions which I provided, and they began their military training and drill under the command of an army officer. And there Your Reverence has the clergy of Cuzco, armed with sword and rifle, waiting every moment to meet the attack of the rebel Tupac-Amaru on state, religion and crown. They have already appeared in the market-place, under the sign of the banner of the Christ of the Earthquakes, the image of the Virgin of the Rosary, the portrait of the King and his arms, prepared to lend their assistance to the regular troops in the first encounters with the Indians at Chita, three miles from the city. They have conducted themselves like seasoned veterans, and by their example have put heart into the masses, a different attitude into the nobles, and raised the spirits of our scanty troops.

At the same time that they were lending this aid, the clergy stood watch in the towers, patrolled the streets, guarded the most dangerous posts, without omitting the most routine duty of the soldier, as they stood guard, night and day, with their arms in their hands, over the convents of nuns. I devoted my attention to all this, untiringly, for this was my rest.

Critics have not been lacking who have frowned upon this determination I took, and to justify their defamations they have circulated among the people a letter, purporting to come from Your Reverence's hand, saying that, even in the case of an insurrection, the clergy must not take up arms. I have paid no attention to this imposture, which brought forth a statement from the University of Lima that in such circumstances the clergy could and should take up arms; this is based on the doctrines of the greatest authorities in canon law, but apparently the impostor lacked this knowledge, and even that supplied by history. There have been many popes, since the days of St. Gregory, who have taken up arms, not in defense of the faith, but for purely temporal motives, even against Catholics. We have the case of Julius II leading an army, not for religious reasons, but to defend his states; Cardinal Cisneros directing the campaign for the conquest of Orán; Juan Cara-muel, Suffragan Bishop of Prague, conducting the defense of that city in 1648, and, before that, against the French and the Dutch; and if we want to go back to more remote times, we see Prince Sancho of Aragon, son of King Jaime, a member of the Order of La Merced, and later Archbishop of Toledo, who raised an army and went to Andalusia to fight the Moors, and as he was killed in battle the historians of his order consider him a martyr. And, leaving aside other examples of prelates and friars who have commanded armies, and have died with them, we have the case of Don José Dávila Falcón, judge of the ecclesiastical tribunal of the see of Lima, who, at the orders of the Royal Council of that city, raised a troop of 850 clergymen when the capital was threatened by the English.

This bloody conflict has made it plain that the Indians are Christians only superficially, or as a mere rite, and that, if the truth be told, they are hardly less barbarous than their ancestors, though more cruel; and at the same time they have shown themselves to be irreconcilable enemies of the Spaniards. Therefore if it is not wrong for a priest to kill to defend an innocent person when there is no other way of saving his life, as Covarrubias, Lecio, Suárez, Bonocina, and others have held to be just, legitimate, and holy, as proved by Deuteronomy, chapter ix, verse 23, where Moses kills the Egyptian, how much more justified was the clergy of Cuzco in taking up arms against the Indians, who, aside from having given indubitable proof of their hostility to religion, were savagely attacking so many innocent persons, without sparing even the children. Besides, as I have pointed out, theirs was only a secondary aid, for the occasion never arose for them to take the field.

And what would Your Reverence say if he knew that in addition to all these cares I have laid upon me one which is far greater, and superior to my strength, which is that of preventing the inhabitants of the towns from fleeing, and making them remain where they are, as happened in Calca, Colla, Lamay, Pisac, San Salvador, etc., to guard the bridges and accompany the priests on their expeditions of spiritual reconquest, for the commanders of the troops have advised me that the people do not feel safe or respectable without the comfort of the divine services. All this fell upon me, and the most trying thing of all was safeguarding the town of Urubamba and its surrounding villages, because of the reckless order that had been issued to burn its bridge of withes which was its only means of communication with the neighboring provinces. I opposed this order, determined to station members of my army to guard it, because if that had ever been done, the enemy would have been left in undisputed possession of the impregnable fortress of Vilcabamba in the province of Abancay and of all the others as far as Lima, and all this help would have been lost if we had destroyed the bridge, as Tupac-Amaru planned to do; and once Urubamba was in his hands, Cuzco would have been left without the abundant supply of grain from its fertile fields and exposed to frequent attack.

It is common knowledge how the priests of that valley of Urubamba worked to defend it from the raids of the enemy; for although they reached the neighboring village of Incay, they were thrown back with heavy losses and were unable to penetrate into the rest of the province. The zeal of the priests of Cotabambas is equally praiseworthy; they worked hard to strike at the root of the evil that was spreading through all that province and the bordering one of Chumbivilcas; for when the sacrilegious Bermúdez and Parbina, Tupac-Amaru's principal lieutenants, had been defeated and killed, the evil disappeared completely. Neither were the clergy of Paucartambo contaminated by this evil; they took up arms and strengthened the ranks of the inhabitants of that rich settlement, without excepting the women, who also served, thus throwing back Diego Tupac-Amaru, a cousin of José's, who tried to overcome it with a powerful army in order to go to the help of the rebel, who was laying siege to Cuzco, an attempt that was unsuccessful although the first time he besieged it for more than three months, in which time there were more than sixteen combats. I shall omit giving you further details about the priests and ecclesiastics of the rest of the diocese, because the account would be too long.

(*From Juan Manuel, Bishop of Cuzco, to the Reverend Gregorio Francisco, Bishop of La Paz*)

PORTRAIT OF TUPAC–AMARU

Some of those who have recently fled here from the province of Azangaro say that when the rebel entered that province he was accompanied by four masked men who had nothing to do with any of the others, and this piece of news has been repeated by many, and it agrees with that given by Zavala, which is as follows: "The army was very large, and, besides the infantry, there were a thousand cavalry troops, Spaniards and mestizos, all armed, and on Tupac-Amaru's right and left two fair men, of goodly aspect, who looked as though they might be English. Tupac-Amaru was riding a white horse, with handsome trappings, and had two blunderbusses, a pair of pistols, and a sword. He wore a suit of blue velvet, embroidered in gold, a red cloak of the same material, a gold galloon about his forehead, a three-cornered hat, and, over all his clothing, a surplice like that of a bishop, without sleeves, richly embroidered, and around his neck a golden chain and, hanging from it, a sun of the same metal, the insignias of his princely ancestors."

(From a newspaper of Arequipa)

THE DEFEAT OF TUPAC–AMARU

The night of the 7th of the present month [April], a little before eight o'clock, we received reliable word of the capture of the rebel José Gabriel Tupac-Amaru, with his wife and children, who were accompanying him, and who have been with him throughout the war he has been making on us. It would be too long to give you a detailed account of the engagements between our troops and the rebels, nor have I time, for a soldier is leaving on horseback in a few minutes, at the order of the circuit judge, to carry these glad tidings to the capital, so I shall give you only the principal facts.

On March 31 the heads of two of the rebel's famous captains, called Porvida and Bermúdez, were brought to this city. They had been killed in a battle between our men and a rebel column of from five to six thousand men. Over a thousand of these were killed and the rest completely defeated. These two captains fought so fiercely that they died beside the cannon which they were firing upon us. This action took place in the province of Chumbivilcas near Tinta. The commander of our troops, who was marching along another road to this province with a considerable force which was to be joined by four other columns near Tungasuca, where the rebel had set up his court, entered the town of Quiquijana with an army of 16,000 men, and there took prisoner the rebel's chief justice and another chief, named Pomiaca, who were both hanged immediately. From there we marched toward Tungasuca, and on the outskirts of the town the rebels came out to meet us and give battle. But it was one of the showy sort he fights, with great uproar and movement, and the six cannon and other firearms he shot off were so badly handled that they killed only three men of our regiment. One of ours, comprising from three hundred to four hundred men, which was closest to the enemy, attacked them with such fury that they completely routed them, with such slaughter that Tupac-Amaru was horrified. His consternation grew when he saw that they captured his cannon, supplies, munitions, equipment, and all the booty he had stolen. He managed to escape without being taken prisoner because of the fine horse he was riding, and when he saw that all was lost he sent word to his wife and children to flee as best they could, and he plunged into a swiftly flowing river and managed to swim across. But when he got to the other side the man he had made colonel of Langui, took him prisoner in the hope of saving his own skin, and turned him over to our men, and the same thing happened with his wife, children, and other allies. Tomorrow our commander will leave this city to bring back the prisoners so that they may receive their just reward.

At six o'clock this morning Francisco Tupac-Amaru, the uncle of José, together with another chief named Torres, both famous captains of the rebels, were brought in prisoners. The first wore the royal garments the Incas used, with the arms of Tupac-Amaru embroidered in silk and gold on the corners.

This city is in a state of wild excitement over the capture of Tupac-Amaru and his family. The bells are pealing and the common people of the city are rejoicing, although two trunks of papers that were found among the rebel's possessions will keep some folks from sleeping soundly at night. Among the treasures that have been captured with the rebel are twelve coffers of embossed silver, many jewels of gold and diamonds, and many other things that cannot be listed here, for they say the inventory will take many days.

(*From the Journal of the Army that left Cuzco to fight Tupac-Amaru under the command of Field Marshal José del Valle*)

THE DEATH OF THE REBEL LEADER

On Friday, the 18th of May 1781, the soldiers of this city of Cuzco were formed in a hollow square around the plaza, with their lances and their shotguns, and the four-sided gallows was surrounded by a squad of mulattoes and Indians, all with fixed bayonets. Nine prisoners were led forth, who were the following: José Verdejo, Andrés Castelo, a half-breed, Antonio Oblitas (who was the executioner of General Arriaga), Antonio Bastidas, Francisco Tupac-Amaru, Tomasa Condemaita, the woman chieftain of Acos, Hipólito Tupac-Amaru, the son of the traitor, Micaela Bastidas, his wife, and the rebel José Gabriel. They were all brought out together, their hands and feet shackled, in big baskets of the kind they use to bring maté leaves from Paraguay, and dragged along behind a harnessed horse. Accompanied by priests to administer the last rites to them and by guards, they were brought to the foot of the gallows, and two executioners meted out the following deaths to them:

Verdejo, the half-breed Castelo, and Bastidas were hanged. Francisco Tupac-Amaru, the rebel's uncle, and Hipólito, the rebel's son, had their tongues cut out before they were thrown down the steps of the gallows. The Indian woman of Condemaita was garroted against a post that had been fixed up with an iron screw for this purpose, which was something that had never before been seen in these parts. And Tupac-Amaru and his wife saw these torments with their own eyes, even that of their son Hipólito, who was the last to go to the gallows. Then the Indian woman Micaela

201

was taken up to the scaffold, where, in the sight of her husband, her tongue was cut out and she was garroted, and her sufferings were unspeakable, because as her neck was very slender the screw was not able to strangle her, and the executioners had to tie ropes around her neck, and each pulled in a different direction, and with kicks in the stomach and breast they finally killed her. The spectacle ended with the death of José Gabriel. He was brought into the middle of the square and the executioner cut out his tongue. Then they unshackled his hands and feet and laid him on the ground. They tied four ropes to his hands and feet and fastened the ropes to the girths of four horses, and four mestizos led them in four different directions, a sight this city had never before beheld. Either because the horses were not very strong, or because the Indian was really of iron, they could not possibly tear him apart, even though they tugged at him for a long time so that he was stretched in the air in a way that looked like a spider. Until finally the commander, moved to compassion, to end the miserable wretch's sufferings, sent word to the executioner that he was to cut off his head, and this was done. Then his body was laid under the gallows and his hands and feet were cut off. The same was done with the women, and the heads of the others were cut off and they were sent to different towns. The bodies of the Indian and his wife were taken to Picchu, where a huge fire was built and they were thrown into it and reduced to ashes, which were thrown into the air and the stream that runs through there. And this was the end of José Gabriel Tupac-Amaru and Micaela Bastidas, whose pride and arrogance were so great that they called themselves King and Queen of Peru, Chile, Quito, Tucumán, and other regions, even including the Great Paititi, and other follies of the same sort.

A great many people had gathered that day, but nobody uttered a cry or spoke a word. Many observed, and I among them, that in all that assembly there were no Indians to be seen, or at least not in their customary garb; if there were any, they were disguised in capes or ponchos. Sometimes things happen in such a way that it seems the Devil must have a hand in them to confirm these Indians in their abuses, beliefs, and superstitions. I say this because, although the weather had been fine and dry, that day dawned overcast, without a sign of the sun, and threatening rain; and at twelve o'clock, when the horses were tugging at the Indian, a strong wind arose, followed by a sudden downpour, so that everybody, even the guards, had to run for shelter. As a result of this the Indians are saying that the heavens and the elements were lamenting the death of the Inca whom the cruel, impious Spaniards were putting to death so inhumanly.

(From a contemporary account)

NINETEENTH CENTURY: ANARCHY AND DICTATORSHIP

THE VICTORY OF AYACUCHO in 1824 may be said to have ended Spanish rule in America. Only Cuba had to wait a number of years to win its independence. The passion for freedom was as intense at the end of the war as when the first proclamation of independence was launched. But the people were untaught and unprepared to grasp the complicated processes on which a democratic government must rest; and the leaders who had triumphed in the war with Spain, many of whom were as ignorant as they were brave, had acquired a taste for power. The Spanish tradition, based on the principle of absolutism, was of no help in settling the problems that sprang up. There was the example of two republican systems: that of the United States and that of France. That of the United States was still too new. Napoleon had reduced that of France to rubble. The liberators themselves were perplexed. Bolívar thought of a life-term president; San Martín, of a monarchy. Brazil decided in favor of an emperor. In its search for a democratic formula, Latin America has had to waste a century — a century of unremitting struggle in which the people have grouped themselves around two parties which represented the two apparently irreconcilable needs of America: the need for order and the need for liberty. The struggle has been a bitter one because there were many special privileges left over from the colonial period that, in certain cases, could be abolished only by violence. These were medieval privileges which Spain had preserved and which, in the case of the Church, for instance, placed their very discussion on dangerous ground. There also existed the other factor of inequality which the United States did not have to face: the social struggle of the mestizo. Under these circumstances our turbulent nineteenth century was our second Middle Ages. Once more the night of creation, but this time not in the peace and withdrawal of the seventeenth century, but filled with cries and shots, with guerrilla bands crowned with machetes. The *caudillo,* the chieftain, comes into being as the natural product of these disorders. They are sensual men with a lust for power and they derive their strength from the people. What they really are is "democratic" agitators, in whom the trusting masses see their redeemers. The first thing the caudillo does when he enters public life is to talk of the "sacred rights of the people." The seizure of power follows. But with the swing of the pendulum typical of political life, dictatorship has been followed by revolution. It is the struggle between the brutal power of the master and the hopes of the people who fought their wars of independence to be free.

And the nineteenth century brought us, together with the second Dark Ages, a second revolution: the revolution against this tyranny which was the war of the romantics. These impassioned friends of liberty recited Victor Hugo's poems by heart, and at night, by the flickering light of tallow candles, feverishly drew up burning pamphlets or new constitutions or battle plans. All Latin America was one huge bonfire. Sociologists called us an ailing people, a race that had been gutted by useless conflicts. The image of the time is that of a holocaust. And the struggle lasted in places until the twentieth century, which seems to have reached us a little late. Only as this century advances do the cries of the caudillos die down; then the machetes are sheathed and a younger generation that begins to see clearly raises its head. The dictatorship of Porfirio Díaz in Mexico lasted thirty-four years; that of Dr. Francia in Paraguay, twenty-seven years; that of Gómez in Venezuela, twenty-four years; that of Rosas in the Argentine, twenty-three years. There were educated dictators like Dr. Francia, or almost illiterate, like Melgarejo of Bolivia. Dr. Francia was somewhat Voltairean in his ideas; García Moreno of Ecuador governed with the counsels of the Jesuits; Carrera of Guatemala went into battle with his bare breast covered with scapulars. The passions of the people who took up arms against these men knew no limits. The intellectuals, when they were unable to take part in the actual fighting, could say with Montalvo: My pen killed the dictator.

Few people have painted a more violent, savage, and therefore more accurate picture of the dictators than Alcides Arguedas, the Bolivian writer, in his book *Los Caudillos bárbaros* (*The Barbarous Chieftains*).

MELGAREJO
ALCIDES ARGUEDAS

THE SOLDIER who had so boldly taken the leading role in the overthrow of President Achá was a man without the most rudimentary notion of the functions of government, who did not even represent any political ideology. Nor was he supported by anyone who, of his own accord, could have raised a banner that would have captured the sympathies of the masses. Therefore, at the beginning, nobody could say what Melgarejo's program was, or what he intended to do with those military chieftains who had been helping him in his race for the presidency, especially Ballivián, to whom he was linked by strong bonds of gratitude and friendship. For the moment there was only one indisputable fact: Melgarejo had engineered a revolution. But for whom?

This doubt was dissipated, however, the very next day, when it became known that the soldier had made Don Mariano Donato Muñoz his general secretary.

The two men were of mutual assistance.

A man of humblest origin, whose education was the training he received in the degraded atmosphere of the barracks, Melgarejo's whole life was compounded of treason and crimes, each more vile and detestable than the other. He began his career as a common soldier in times when blind bravery and cynical audacity were looked upon as great virtues, and he soon was made an officer and received special distinction, for he possessed those qualities, accentuated by his exuberant, restless nature, to an unusual degree. Completely devoid of all intellectual attainments, powerful, uncouth, inured to hardships, he began to make a name for himself as a consequence of his rascalities during Ballivián's administration. The latter, who was well aware of his turbulent nature and his ascendancy over the troops, kept him in his service, but shifting him continually from one battalion to another, before he had time to carry out some scandalous atrocity. In this way he came to know the most remote corners of the Republic without ever leaving in any the memory of a single good deed. In 1857, now a colonel, he put himself at Linares's service, and two years later betrayed him. He did the same with Belzu and Achá.

He was tall, solidly built, with a small head that was bald, a retreating forehead, thick sensual lips, prominent cheek-bones, and a long thick black beard. His voice was hoarse and his manners brusque, without a vestige of charm. His tastes were gross and sensual. All his background of poverty and coarse associations revealed itself in his every gesture, for they all bespoke vulgarity, low origins, and lamentable ignorance.

"Devoid of the most elementary idea of history, he insisted that Napoleon was superior to Bonaparte and that Cicero was a second-rate general of antiquity. But he was as presumptuous as he was ignorant. He considered Bolivia a first-class power and so, as soon as he heard about the Franco-Prussian War, he called a meeting of his cabinet and decided to remain neutral in the war."

His general secretary, Don Mariano Donato Muñoz, was a not over-successful lawyer, skilled in the art of low intrigue, whose past would not bear too close a scrutiny. Not long before, in 1863, he had been accused of being one of the leaders of an uprising in Potosí against General Achá's government. He was a Congressman at the time, and waiving the immunity of his office, he defended himself against these charges in the newspapers with great heat, which was later to kindle a blush of shame on his face. In the name of his "probity and loyalty" he denied the accusations made against him and said that his duty as a loyal citizen, his recognition of the merits of General Achá, "the anchor of national salvation," made it incumbent upon him to "defend this government against any threat of revolt." "Affiliated as I am with the constitutional cause, of which the illustrious President Achá is the legitimate representative, it becomes my duty and my honor to defend it and support it, whatever my walk in life."

The statements he made were of such a nature that a historian of the period has called them a "classic document of political corruption." And, as we now know, he was a hypocrite and a traitor.

Before it had been in power thirty days the new government issued two decrees which by a stroke of the pen abrogated the Constitution of 1861 and did away with all municipal autonomy, centralizing under Melgarejo's authority and personal will all administrative functions.

The country began to show manifest alarm, for it plainly saw that this soldier, who, feigning gratitude and loyalty, had overthrown the man to whom he owed the rank he had attained, was prepared to trample underfoot all its institutions for the sake of defending the powers he had usurped. And, naturally, armed protests began to break out, in the name of upholding the Constitution.

But Melgarejo was prepared to defend his spoils resolutely. He levied a forced loan on Cochabamba to defray the pay of his troops and he marched upon La Paz, which he believed not too favorably disposed toward his ambitions. However, the local pride of the city had been wounded by Achá's indifference toward it, so Melgarejo was able to enter "without animosity on the part of the lower classes, although the better element remained aloof and even hostile." Melgarejo wanted to win over the goodwill of the population and, by advice of his general secretary, he issued several decrees designed to flatter their local pride. One of these ordered "the erection of a monument to the Revolution of the 16th of July 1809," and the other returned to the people "the right to hold carnivals, which a municipal ordinance had forbidden as unbefitting a civilized country." In addition he held a number of gatherings in the palace to which he invited many of the most important people. At one of these, having drunk too much, which was his greatest vice, he answered a guest who had made some allusion to the end of this rule of force: "I'll rule in Bolivia as long as I feel like it, and if anyone tries to interfere with me, he'll find himself dangling in the middle of the public square." And a similar scene took place at an official banquet when he insolently cut short a member of the higher court of La Paz who, in a toast, ventured to insinuate a reference to the ideas and principles of the Constitution, with these words: "Look here, the one who rules, rules, and whoever doesn't like it knows what he can do."

In the meantime there had been armed movements of protest in Cochabamba, Sucre, and Potosí, which were put down by his troops, part of which were under the command of Colonel Morales. But fearing that the movement might spread, he left La Paz on March 6 for Sucre and Potosí, leaving Don Casto Arguedas in command of the national guard. He had gone no farther than Oruro, however, when he learned, to his consternation, that La Paz had revolted in favor of Belzu and that it was preparing to resist under the command of this popular leader, who, on learning of these latest developments, had managed to get back into the country.

Belzu was morally and physically a wreck. He had dissipated his fortune in his unfortunate experiences in Europe and in the hardships of exile and he returned to his country avid of honors and riches and persuaded that still sterner measures were needed to root out what he called merely political corruption, but which was more the absence of moral sensibility and an utter indifference to the concepts of good and evil, an indifference that came from the deplorable ignorance of the people and their complete lack of education.

"That country," he had said to Campero on board the ship that was bringing them both home after a long absence, "is so corrupt and the immorality so great that it will take a Nero to straighten it out."

Campero and Belzu reached Tacna in the middle of March and both of them, taking different routes, proceeded to Bolivia, the one, Campero, to offer his services to Melgarejo, and the other to launch a revolution against him.

Belzu was in La Paz on the 22nd of March. Melgarejo learned of this and suddenly decided to countermarch his troops, without allowing them to rest, to the point from which they had started.

The trip was wearisome, but not at all arduous for the troops, accustomed as they were to incessant marches up and down the vast territory of the Republic. Each soldier carried in his haversack some pieces of jerked beef and a little frozen dried potato known as *chuño*. At his side hung a canteen of water or liquor; his bare feet were protected by crude sandals, his pants were rolled up to his knees, and the white sheet he wore over the upper part of his body was fastened at the waist. The officers rode small mounts they had taken by force from the Indians, and not one of them, from the commanding general down, carried a tent or even a simple folding cot to protect him from the night dew.

The country through which they marched was deserted, for the Indians had taken their produce to the city to sell it to the leader of the revolution, and the soldiers had to live out of their haversacks and saddle-bags.

Dawn was just breaking on the 24th when Melgarejo ordered his men to begin the last lap of their trip. A little after daybreak they reached the height that overlooks the city, where by the wan light of lanterns breastworks were being thrown up and trenches dug, and the people preparing for a battle which they guessed would be stubborn and furious. At the head of the troops rode Melgarejo and Campero, engaged in a conversation that boded good for no one. The leader complained angrily of the inhabitants of La Paz, manifesting special displeasure toward the brothers Barragan, who were journalists, and Lieutenant-Colonel Cortés, whom he had left in command of a division and who was said to have been one of the first to pass over to Belzu.

At that moment an enemy guerrilla squad appeared on the brow of El Alto, fired a few shots, and disappeared into the hollow of the city. A little while later several individuals who were loyal to Melgarejo presented themselves: they had fled the city and come to join his forces. Among these was the abovementioned Lieutenant-Colonel Cortés. At the sight of him Melgarejo cocked his revolver and rode toward him, shouting fearful threats. Cortés, terrified, threw himself at his assailant and, clinging to one of his legs, impeded him from using his gun while at the same time, in an anguished tone, he pleaded for his life and tried to vindicate his behavior.

The other would not listen and made an effort to "fire off his revolver at the poor wretch's head." Meanwhile, in the face of the impassivity with which Melgarejo's staff looked on without daring to intercede for the victim, Muñoz, the secretary, sprang from his horse and, "pale and wild-eyed, begged the general, in the name of God, not to do this with his own hand," Campero relates.

Melgarejo, "replacing his revolver in its holster, tried to dismount on the side on which he always got off his horse, but as his victim impeded him, clinging frantically to horse and rider, General Melgarejo, with an effort, managed to get down on the other side, and said:

"'Come on, riflemen. Fire on him, horse and all!'

"He had no more than spoken when one of the riflemen sprang on the man like a flash, grabbed him by the neck, pulled him loose from the horse, dragged him a few steps off, and fired a shot at him point-blank. As he did this General Melgarejo and the rest of us in his retinue moved on," continues Campero. And he adds this gruesome detail: "Mechanically I looked back to where the deed was being consummated, and I saw one of those sights which cannot be contemplated without horror even in the fury of combat. The wretch had not yet even completely fallen to earth and was flapping his arms like a drowning man when the riflemen, who at that moment were two, picked up their rifles by the barrel and pounded the dying man's skull to a pulp with their gunstocks."

The caudillo was deliberately carrying out a plan, for discontent had spread among the troops on learning that they were going to fight against Belzu, the best-remembered of the popular idols, and many soldiers had begun to desert and join the revolutionary ranks. It was a serious situation and Melgarejo, the soldier, saw that the only way to halt the complete defection of his troops was to offer them a bloody example. And he sacrificed one of his best friends. . . .

The attack on the city was begun at once, with unsuccessful results for Melgarejo. His soldiers fought without conviction and even against their will, and they began deserting to the enemy, abandoning their leader. Whereupon Melgarejo, giving his cause up for lost and thinking he would not be able to save himself by flight, attempted to end his life. Campero dissuaded him from this and advised him to make one last attempt, however desperate it might seem. Melgarejo yielded to his advice, and gathering about him a small group of lancers, he made his way to the palace through the mob which was joyously celebrating the victory of Belzu. In the crowd were many of his own soldiers who had gone completely over to the other side. Thus, runs the official communiqué prepared by Olañeta, "he entered the square with six lancers. His unexpected presence so astounded the crowd that for a few minutes the only sound that was heard was the clatter of horses' hoofs. He rode up to the palace, dismounted, and ascended the steps leading to the reception room."

As he reached the last flight he was stopped by one of Belzu's servants who was a fanatical enemy of Melgarejo's. "He instantly pointed a rifle at him, saying: 'Now what are you going to do, you black devil?'

"With one hand Melgarejo pushed aside the weapon of his assailant and with the other fired a shot at him," leaving him stretched out at his feet. At the sound of the shot, several people, their wineglasses still in their hands, came out of the reception room, where they had been drinking a toast to victory while Melgarejo had been giving orders to his men to search the rooms on the first floor. At that very moment Belzu, in utter consternation, appeared at the head of the stairs arm-in-arm with a friend. As the two leaders met, for a moment there was stupefaction in their escorts. Melgarejo lifted his arm again to fire on Belzu, but Campero stopped him. There was a brief exchange of words, punctuated and interrupted by ripples of agitation among the on-lookers, and then a shot rang out and Belzu was seen to fall, mortally wounded, into the arms of one of his escort.

Fright paralyzed some and put the others to flight. Melgarejo strode over to the window and, stepping out on the overhanging balcony, shouted to the dense crowd that was still cheering the victorious chieftain:

"Belzu is dead. Now long live who?"

And the mob, subdued and conquered, answered in fear and admiration: "Long live Melgarejo!"

Such an instant radical change on the part of a crowd was never seen before. There was no time for an idea to be born or for an opinion to make any headway: everything was abrupt and instinctive. The thing imposed itself through its reality and its brutality.

Melgarejo was instantly surrounded by those who, brief moments before, had deserted him, and he set out with them to ride through the city, to the very outskirts, accompanied by the applause and shouts of the mob. In the afternoon he returned to the palace, but now he did not want to take up his quarters on the first floor, where the body of Belzu lay alone, abandoned even by his family. . . . Night was already falling when Señora Juana Manuela Garrita, Belzu's widow, appeared to claim the body of her husband, which had been stripped of all its jewels and other valuables.

The funeral was a solemn one and never had so many people been seen following the remains of a leader to their resting-place. At the cemetery an endless number of funeral orations was pronounced, in which the acts of the usurper were boldly condemned; curses were invoked upon his daring exploit, and the virtues of the dead were disproportionately extolled. The crowd went wild when at the end of the funeral a fanatical follower of Belzu's raised the dead man's hand to bless the gathering, in which there were many who believed that Belzu, like Christ, would soon rise from the dead. . . .

Melgarejo took the wise precaution of not persecuting the orators, but he made careful note of their names, for within the rude depths of his untamed soul he felt a profound aversion rising toward the better-class people of the city who had not hastened to lavish the attentions on him they had shown toward Belzu. This aversion revealed itself in bitter complaints, which those who surrounded him took care to enlarge upon to ingratiate themselves with the victor. This desire for absolute power led his general secretary to counsel him quickly to organize a cabinet made up of men whose personal loyalty to him was unquestionable as the only means of overcoming the resistance of the people of La Paz and guaranteeing the permanence of his rule.

It was ill-advised counsel.

Public opinion was hoping that the chieftain, now that he had imposed himself by his unexampled daring and by force of arms, would try to atone partially for his illegal seizure of power by surrounding himself with the best elements in the country. Its disillusionment and astonishment were great when they saw him select as his advisers men who had always acted with utter selfishness, such as Jorge Oblitas and Donato Muñoz himself, who were notorious, especially the first, for their shifting political affiliations.

The void which surrounded Melgarejo grew more hostile. As a result he "limited himself more and more to the circle of his cabinet, his army leaders, and a small group of citizens who still visited the palace, but who were not among the best, certainly, nor the most influential members of the community," writes Campero.

When Melgarejo saw that he could not break the ice about him and that his collaborators showed an atavistic willingness to carry out and submit to his most arbitrary decisions, he gave free rein to his natural inclinations and turned the governmental palace into the abode of free and easy pleasure. Nearly every night there was dancing to the music of the army bands, and drinking; he paid no attention to the advice of his few friends, who wondered uneasily what the outcome of this dissipated, reckless life of his would be.

About this time the illicit relations between Melgarejo and Doña Juana Sanchez began. She was a young woman of humble family, poor, quite pretty, extremely vain, ignorant, as were nearly all the women of her epoch, and warm-hearted.

Their meeting was a chance one and perhaps fortunate for both of them; certainly it was fortunate for the country, for Doña Juana stayed Melgarejo's arm from many crimes and dried the tears of many an unhappy person.

When Melgarejo seized the presidency he did away with a number of state subsidies to utilize the money for his own purposes. Among these were the widows' pensions and the grants allotted by Achá to the victims of the revolution of Cortés. Complaints poured in, as was to be expected, but no attention was paid to them, despite the meekness and persistence of the complainants, among whom was a young woman of attractive appearance, pale, slender, and about twenty-three years old. This was Doña Juana Sanchez, who had been left in the most abject poverty by the death of her father and who, following the shrewd advice of her family, undertook to collect the pension due them.

The girl's attempts were fruitless, for Melgarejo remained inaccessible. Whereupon Avila, one of his aides-de-camp, the very one who had spurred him on to the revolution against Achá and who, as a reward, was now chief of staff, knowing his master's inclinations and the secret intentions of the young solicitant, decided that all this might redound to his personal benefit, and advised the seductive young woman to talk with the President personally and to behave with kindness and indulgence if she hoped to achieve her desire.

The interview took place and the results were those the pandering aide-de-camp had foreseen. The girl came out of Melgarejo's office with her petition signed and, above all, having captivated and enslaved the heart and senses of this inflammable man, who from that moment on began to commit the wildest follies and to squander the depleted funds of the country on magnificent gifts for her.

Naturally the news of this intrigue, an outrage to the marriage vows, further irritated the God-fearing spirit of the people, who were already shocked and horrified at the soldier's effrontery, and the reserve with which he was regarded grew still greater. And it grew into open conflict, for Melgarejo, in his desire to humiliate these people for their attitude toward him, gave banquets at the palace, parties to which no lady was invited, and arranged dances and gatherings at which only men were present. The only couple there were he and Doña Juana; occasionally, as a mark of special distinction and an act of supreme favor, he would cede his partner to some high official or officer whose loyalty and bravery were beyond doubt.

Meanwhile the funds of the national treasury were dwindling away and there was no money to provide for public services. But the thing that worried Melgarejo most was that he was unable to pay his soldiers, in whom he saw the only real support for his cause. This often made him uneasy, but not so much so that he gave up his dissolute habits. On the contrary, it seemed to stimulate his desire to enjoy while he could what might soon come to an end.

Despite this situation, and notwithstanding his crass ignorance of everything and particularly financial matters, he began to think up a thousand wild schemes, conceived in the heat of his orgies, which grew progressively grosser and in which, unmindful of his high office, he reverted to the habits acquired during his wandering, poverty-stricken, insecure existence. He liked to drink until he could not stand up, and he would fall to the floor, an inert mass. When he was drunk he would flourish his inseparable revolver, threatening to kill himself or one of his friends, swearing that he would put a bullet through his brain if they started a revolution against him, and firing wildly into the air and at the furniture and mirrors of the room. He usually slept on the floor, with no sheets, and he spent day after day locked in his bedroom, lying down, drinking with his boon companions or given over to a frenzy of sexual excesses.

One day when he was a little less drunk than usual he sent for Colonel Campero, who was the prefect of the city. When Campero arrived he was received with marked deference; Melgarejo even invited him to sit down on the bed with him, which, as has been said, was on the floor, and the two began drinking. At this moment an aide-de-camp announced the arrival of the ministers who had come to submit certain matters for the President's consideration. The ministers were shown in and one of them, Bustamante, began to unroll some papers he was carrying under his arm and explain the matters that had brought them there. They were serious and urgent: General Santa Cruz had managed to secure a favorable offer in Europe to exploit the guano beds recently discovered in Mejillones; the contracts . . .

Melgarejo did not let him finish. All this talk about guano beds, contracts, and so on, was just the vaporings of visionary learned men. What he wanted right away was money to pay his troops and keep them satisfied; otherwise they might get out of hand and loot the city. And that was something that had to be avoided. How? By a very simple plan which anyone but his ministers could understand: declaring war on Peru. That way they could raise money by forced loans and the army would have something to do. Otherwise disaster was imminent and they would all perish in it. War with Peru would be the solution to the problem of securing funds, for at the moment nobody had a cent, not even he, whom his unprincipled adversaries accused of squandering the state funds, when the truth of the matter was that he did not even have sheets for his bed.

And throwing aside the covers, pointing to his bare bed, he said to his amazed ministers:

"A fine kind of President I am! I haven't even got any sheets. And I'm going to get myself some in Peru."

This wild nonsense left the ministers in a state of bewilderment, especially in view of the conviction with which Melgarejo spoke. Two of them, Dr. Muñoz and Bustamante himself, tried mildly to interpose certain objections. Whereupon Melgarejo, Campero relates, "flew into a rage and, snatching off his cap, embroidered in red velvet and with a raised design in gold, threw it on the floor, shouting:

"'This is all ministers are good for. To make objections and put stumbling-blocks in your way. Damn the day I formed a cabinet. If I didn't have one I'd issue a general mobilization order and tomorrow I'd be marching with my army on Desaguadero.'"

Behavior of this sort, at times terribly tragic and at others absurdly clownish, was frequent in those days of faint-heartedness and pusillanimity on the part of the public. But no amount of tricks or buffoonery nor all the thought-taking of his advisers could solve the problem of paying the troops, whose discontent was now manifest. It was decided to levy a loan on the provinces of the interior, and the army was ordered to make ready for the trip. But as the officers had no horses of their own, a herd of mules was secured which was divided up among the officials, who "the day after receiving them were on foot once more. For they had sold them at half and even a third of the prices for which they had been bought," relates Campero.

The departure of the troops was hastened because word had been received that the departments of the south had revolted against Melgarejo, who set out from La Paz the 13th of May 1865, leaving Campero in charge.

The latter found himself in an awkward situation. The treasury was low in funds; the soldiers and officers had not been paid for three months, and among the lower classes a determination to avenge Belzu was spreading and becoming an obsession.

The 16th of May a commission of workingmen appeared before Campero to ask permission to hold funeral services for Belzu. The ceremony was impressive. Bitter speeches were pronounced against Melgarejo the murderer; the governor had to pretend that he knew nothing about them, for he lacked the means to punish these outbursts, which, encouraged by their impunity, were assuming a frankly revolutionary character.

The name most frequently to be heard on the lips of the mob was that of Colonel Casto Arguedas, who at the time was the subprefect of Cercado and who was already well known for his restless contradictory temperament, a characteristic frequent in the epoch and in the spirit of the race. He had carried out the revolution in favor of Belzu, and as he was unable to display a blind enthusiasm for the conquering idol, Melgarejo, he was exiled to the coast and named captain of this department, which at the time was the farthest removed of all those directly under the central administration; of the others that comprised the national domain only the vaguest, most remote notions existed. The adherents of Melga-

rejo accused him of disloyalty, for they knew him to be a friend
of Ballivián, which constituted a heinous crime in official eyes,
and they did not forgive him those independent inclinations which
had always characterized him.

Arguedas, who by reason of his official post could not lend his
support to any subversive movement, planned to leave the city
and so notified the governor; but on May 25 a crowd besieged the
prefecture and, after constituting itself a popular primary, proclaimed Arguedas captain-general of the province.

Alarm verging on panic began to spread from the first moment,
because everyone knew that as soon as Melgarejo received word
of what had taken place, he would return with his troops and go
to the lengths that were typical of him. As a result a swift exodus
to the near-by valleys took place. "They left in terror," one witness
relates, "mothers and fathers, young people, children, some riding, others any way they could; some of the young ladies were
riding donkeys, and not a few shanks's mares. . . ."

That same day, May 25, Melgarejo set out from Oruro in the
direction of Potosí, where the revolt against his absurd domination
was really serious; it was not until the third day that he learned
of the rebellion in La Paz. When he reached Potosí he received
the news of that of Oruro, too, which on June 1 had, with significant unanimity, like La Paz, proclaimed the Constitution of 1861,
to the wild enthusiasm of the people, and had put Don Francisco
Velasco and Dr. Vazquez, the former a journalist and the latter a
lawyer, both among the most distinguished people in Oruro, at the
head of the government.

Melgarejo who made the trip "in a state of almost steady intoxication, given over to the wildest behavior," for, adds the proper
Campero, "one of those women who are the shame of their sex
and a disgrace to their family had got him into her clutches." He
did not want to retrace his steps and he entered Potosí in triumph, allowing his troops a brief rest there. On the way he
ordered his brother-in-law, Colonel Rojas, who was a polite com-
placent witness of Melgarejo's infidelity to his sister, to Cochabamba, but he was unable to enter because of the hostility of the

valley city, and he had to retreat to Oruro, which had already been evacuated by the revolutionary troops. On the 8th of June these latter marched toward La Paz, where, with these valuable reinforcements, Arguedas felt himself strong enough to overthrow Melgarejo's domination, even though among the instigators and adherents of the revolution in the different departments serious difficulties were already cropping up because of petty conflicts of pride. Most of these men were devoid of any idea of well-bred social relationships, lacking in all refinement, and possessed of the most rudimentary education; the one satisfaction they felt was the gratification of their vanity, and they were quite capable of sacrificing not merely a group but the nation itself to their personal aggrandizement.

The leaders of La Paz feared that their action might be hampered by the ambitions that would inevitably spring up among the leaders of the auxiliary division, and this idea aroused jealousy and suspicion among certain second-rate figures, especially the Barragan brothers, who lost no opportunity to show their aversion toward the men from Oruro. On the very afternoon of their arrival at La Paz, at a banquet Arguedas gave for his allies, when the customary libations had stimulated feelings to a high pitch, Cirilo Barragan proposed a toast to the bravery of La Paz, "which needed no help to do away with Melgarejo's domination," thus crudely offending the touchy sensibilities of these allies.

On July 9 Arguedas was unanimously proclaimed the Supreme Head of the Republic in a certificate of election signed with the best names of the representatives of Oruro and La Paz. To this Arguedas replied with a proclamation addressed to the nation in which, invoking the time-honored procedure of all caudillos, he promised that his acts would uphold the principles of the Constitution and that only the imperative need to restore these desecrated institutions led him to accept this high mandatory post. His plan was to call upon the people "to organize the power, for all authority that is not based on the will of the people is usurpation and cannot endure," and he concluded with the promise that he would consider himself happy the day he was able to convoke a national representative body "after the political hatreds engendered by the use of force, which we should renounce forever, have subsided."

In another proclamation to the army, as encouraging as the preceding, he voiced, among other things, what was a theme of unfailing concern to him:

"Our fathers fought for fifteen years to give us independence; we shall fight as long as need be to give ourselves a Constitution."

On the 10th of July Arguedas issued his first decree, calling for a general election.

In August Cochabamba once more rose as a man against Melgarejo, the usurper, and with this revolt the whole Republic was in arms against this soldier who, rejected by the country and confronted by the confusion of his own men, seemed to grow in boldness and desire to rule.

Melgarejo decided to move quickly, beginning his campaign with an attack on Cochabamba and in two days his troops covered the hundred miles that separated them from the rebellious city. He showed great determination in putting down this insurrection because his soldiers were completely without food and it was Cochabamba that supplied the toasted corn which was the only nourishment provided his men, admirable in their frugality, resignation, and indifference to life. . . .

It was not necessary to subdue the garrison because the revolutionists had left their valleys in mass to join the ranks of the opposition in Sucre and Potosí, where dissension was smoldering among the leaders for exactly the same reasons as in La Paz. . . . The trouble was that the prospect of the coveted tricolor presidential ribbon seemed to lure on all the caudillos, and none of them wanted to be less than the others or to play a secondary part. On the contrary, each passionately longed to be known by the high-sounding, longed-for title of Supreme Chief of the Revolution of the South, as Arguedas was of the north and so, with Melgarejo at the gates, the only recourse was to resort to the inglorious tactics of "heel warfare." They met with a disastrous defeat at Potosí in a battle that was fruitless and criminal by reason of the brave men who were ignobly sacrificed to covetousness and jealousies.

After this first barrier had been breached, Melgarejo remained in Potosí for three months, repairing his finances and giving his troops a much needed rest before beginning his northern campaign, which he knew would be difficult, for the revolution there had acquired increment and presented a more solid front than in the south.

But here, too, it was handicapped by the incompetent leadership of its directors.

The ambitions Arguedas met at every turn and at all times made it impossible for him to operate with the independence he would have wished. He was surrounded and advised by schemers who were seeking means of furthering their own plans, and he could not conceal his own ambitions, which gave way to duty when he learned that Melgarejo had defeated the forces of Potosí at Cantería, where the tragic death of the noble poet Nestor Galindo took place. Then, on the advice of his counselors, and believing himself strong enough to meet the victorious caudillo in the field, he started out toward Oruro, which he entered on December 17 at the head of an army of two thousand men.

He remained in Oruro a few days, but on learning that Melgarejo was advancing on the city, he made a hasty and disorderly retreat to La Paz, thus weakening the discipline and morale of his troops, who on December 24, after wandering about with Arguedas on the upland plains without plan or purpose, met with miserable defeat on the fields of Letanias a few miles from the turbulent city.

And so Melgarejo tightened his grasp on the power, triumphing over short-sighted ambitions, inordinate thirst for power, and incompetence.

After this easy victory Melgarejo signed, on the very field of his prowess, a decree convoking an assembly, within a short time, and he established himself in La Paz, where, yielding to his shameful thirst for vengeance, he had a number of his enemies shot who had candidly believed in his promise of amnesty and who lacked the means to flee their native soil following the leading figures among the vanquished to the hunger, poverty, and humiliation of exile on the shores of Peru.

It was then, in the face of the inevitability of events, that the whole country gave up and submitted to the caudillo. And the same men who in secret censured the imposition of force yielded too and forsook their principles. They even went further: many, and not the worst, rushed to offer their services to the victor, who found himself surrounded, through servility and fear, by the best elements in the country. . . .

At this time it was very fashionable to drink many toasts at the palace banquets, where the wine flowed like water. Each of the guests was eager to display his indubitable allegiance to the head of the government and there were as many toasts as guests at the table.

When his turn came, one of the guests, thinking, no doubt, to flatter the dictator's lip-service to legality, spoke in words of fulsome praise of the new political charter which would surely govern the acts of the illustrious Melgarejo, the flower of all rulers past and future.

The instant response of the cynical, drunken soldier was brutal and unqualified:

"I want the gentleman who has just spoken and all the honorable deputies gathered here to know that I have put the Constitution of 1861, which was very good, in this pocket" (pointing to his left trouser pocket) "and that of 1868, which is even better in the opinion of these gentlemen, in this one" (pointing to his right pocket) "and that nobody is going to rule in Bolivia but me."

TWENTIETH CENTURY: AMERICA TODAY AND TOMORROW

THE TRANSFORMATION Latin America has undergone in the last thirty years constitutes one of those processes of rapid change which can happen only in our times. The Western United States, Soviet Russia, and Turkey are three examples of these sudden leaps of history. Russia and Turkey have made greater advances in the last fifteen years than in the preceding fifteen centuries. The case of Latin America is similar. Thirty years ago these republics lacked the means of communication with one another, and in the field of international relations they were regarded as almost primitive countries. Only Argentina and, to a certain extent, Mexico had a system of railways at that time. To judge from the highways, one would have thought that the wheel had not yet been invented in those countries. Instead of having for our railbeds the solid, fertile plains of the Mississippi Valley, we had the jungle and the swamps and the steep slopes of the Andes. It was impossible for us to exploit the natural wealth shut up within these walls. Agricultural production could not be linked to the life of the city. The guerrilla leaders barricaded themselves in this isolation that made them invincible, and democracy was but a dream that appeared for an instant between the flashes of machetes. For the school to find the pupil it had to push its way through underbrush and desert.

For the past thirty years these conditions have been changing and our America is beginning to take its place in modern civilization. The cities have suddenly grown large. Ranchers who for two or three centuries led a medieval existence on their vast domains are now drawn to the urban centers, where they make their homes without forsaking their agricultural interests. A new society is springing up with a broader cultural life linked to that of Europe. The wealthy class in Brazil still lived on their ranches at the beginning of this century; their country homes were more sumptuous than those of the city, and could house a hundred guests for weeks and even for months. As electricity was introduced into the capitals, theaters opened, and the cities became transformed into stars of steel by the railroads, the center of gravity shifted. A comparison between the number of inhabitants in our capitals in 1910 and now reveals the swift tempo of this growth. In 1910 these cities were almost four hundred years old, and they had not yet lost their colonial air. In the thirty years that followed, some doubled, others tripled, and still others quadrupled their population. In the old census reports, even as late as the beginning of this century, the number of inhabitants was counted by "souls," and souls indeed they seemed as they scurried past one another on the empty streets and retired to their houses with the curfew bell. But now it is no longer said: "Santa Fe de Bogotá has a hundred thousand souls," but "Bogotá has four hundred thousand inhabitants." The number grows with such rapidity that the count cannot keep up with reality. The figure published today is inaccurate by tomorrow. The growth of the cities is a direct consequence of the development of the means of communication. Brazil, Colombia, Peru have thirteen times as many miles of railroads and highways as thirty years ago. This means that the ability to travel, to work, to produce are multiplied by at least this same figure. At least, because in cases of this sort the proportion of growth is in geometric, not arithmetical progression. It is a proportion that has several dimensions. In certain countries the change has been from travel on muleback to travel by airplane. Nowhere in the world has the use of the airplane become so general and so necessary as in certain mountainous regions of Latin America, where regular passenger, mail, and freight services by air have been in existence for over twenty years.

As can be seen, this is a process of today, one might almost say of tomorrow. To be sure, the nineteenth century is still alive among us. The school has not yet reached the remote mountainous regions, nor have political rights — rendered less effective by ignorance — brought all men equality of citizenship. Never has so much been done as in the last thirty years to open more schools, to redeem the Indian from his backward state, to bring the land under cultivation, thereby fulfilling its social mission instead of lying fallow in the hands of its idle owners. Deep changes of this sort cannot be brought about overnight, but they make up the program of twenty-one nations in which a new world is coming into being that will be the shield and buckler of future democracy. For four hundred years the America that was settled by Spaniards and Portuguese moved at a slow pace. The creation of a new human type from the differing races took generations. The jungle and the mountains yielded only when man could bring the resources of modern techniques to bear against them. Now the countenance of this world is beginning to emerge. In a few more years its outlines will be clear.

The writers of today are defining its characteristics, bringing its blurred lineaments into focus. Latin America cannot be interpreted by journalists who are ignorant of its history and lack the imagination to see into the future. To understand it one must see it in its natural perspective. Setting oneself up as a prophet is as risky as it is ingenuous. But no one can doubt that our twentieth century is moving. A snapshot taken by a tourist in a moment of pause is a mistake. Two writers, the most thoughtful and trustworthy of our days, Baldomero Sanín Cano, of Colombia, and Alfonso Reyes, of Mexico, have evaluated this present world of ours in the two essays that follow. That of Alfonso Reyes is a revision of the famous address he delivered at the international meeting of the PEN clubs in Buenos Aires in 1939. That of Sanín Cano has been specially written for this book.

THOUGHTS ON THE AMERICAN MIND
ALFONSO REYES

My observations are limited to what is known as Latin America. The need for brevity obliges me to be sketchy, imprecise, and exaggerated to the point of caricature. My function is merely to stimulate or arouse discussion without attempting to touch upon all the problems involved and much less to suggest their solution.

I have the feeling that, using America as a pretext, I am merely skimming over the surface of certain universal themes.

2. To speak of American civilization here would be out of place. It would lead us into the field of archæology, which lies outside the scope of our topic. To speak of American culture would be misleading. It would lead us to consider only one branch of the tree of Europe, which has been transplanted to the soil of America. But we can speak of the American mind, its vision of life and its reaction to life. This will allow us to define, even though only provisionally, the particular tonality of America.

3. Our drama has a stage, a chorus, and a leading character. By stage here I do not mean space, but time, time almost in the musical sense of the word, a beat, a rhythm. America reached the feast of European civilization late. It has had to bridge epochs, rushing and hurrying from one form to another, without allowing sufficient time for the preceding one to ripen thoroughly. At times the gap to be bridged has been so great that the new product resembles a dish that has been taken from the fire before it was done. Tradition has weighed less oppressively here, and this explains our audacity. But we have yet to learn whether the rhythm of Europe — which we are trying to overtake by forced marches since we cannot catch up with it at a normal pace — is the only possible historical "tempo." Nobody has yet proved that there is anything unnatural about a certain speeding-up of the process. This is the secret of our history, our politics, and our lives, whose watchword is improvisation.

The chorus — the inhabitants of America — have been recruited principally from the old indigenous populations, the mass of Iberian conquerors, missionaries, and settlers, and later the influx of immigrants from all parts of Europe. There are clashes of races, problems of miscegenation, attempts at adaptation and absorption. Depending on the region, the predominating hue is that of the Indian, the Iberian, the lightened tint of the mestizo, the white of the European immigrant, and the broad splotches of the Africans brought to our shores in other centuries by the old colonial administrations. Every tone of the scale is present. In the unceasing melting-pot of America these heterogeneous elements are little by little becoming fused, and today there is already a distinctive American mankind, an American spirit. The leading character or actor in our plot is the mind.

4. The American mind has been faced with a series of dilemmas. Fifty years after the Spanish conquest — that is to say, during the first generation — we already find in Mexico an American psychology. Under the influence of new surroundings, a new economic organization, contact with the sensibility of the Indians, the sense of possession which comes from having arrived earlier, the Spaniards of Mexico had developed a sense of colonial aristocracy which clashed sharply with the *nouveau riche* impulses of the later-arriving Spaniards. There is abundant literary testimony to bear this out, in the satirical popular poetry of the day as well as in the shrewd observations of thoughtful Spaniards like Juan de Cárdenas. Literary criticism has centered this phenomenon, as though it were its focus of light, on the figure of the Mexican playwright Don Juan Ruiz de Alarcón, who through Corneille — and through him on Molière — exercised a great influence on the modern French theater. And what I say of Mexico, because I am more familiar with it and know it better, could be said to a greater or less degree of the rest of our America. This early incompatibility already held the first seeds of America's long aspiration to independence.

The second dilemma: no sooner had independence been achieved than the inevitable conflict began between Americanists and Hispanists, between those who put the emphasis on the new reality and those who stressed the hallowed tradition. Sarmiento is, first of all, an Americanist; Bello, a Hispanist. In Mexico there still exists the memory of a controversy between the Indian Ignacio Ramírez, and the Spaniard Emilio Castelar, which hinged upon similar discrepancies. This polemic often turned into a duel between liberals and conservatives. Independence was still so recent that neither father nor son knew how to adopt a sensible attitude toward it.

The third dilemma: One of our poles lies in Europe, the other in the United States. We receive inspiration from both. Our Utopian constitutions combine the political philosophy of France with the federalism under a president of the United States. The sirens of Europe and the sirens of the United States woo us at the same time. By and large, the mind of our America (without denying the affinities between it and the most select spirits of the other America) seems to find in Europe a more universal vision of human problems, more basic, more in keeping with its own feelings. Aside from historic misgivings, fortunately ever less justified and needing no mention here, we are not in sympathy with the tendency toward race distinctions. To speak only of the Anglo-Saxon world, we like the natural way in which a man like Chesterton or George Bernard Shaw regards the people of all climates, ascribing to them equal standing as human beings. Gide does the same in the Congo. It displeases us to regard any human type as a mere curiosity or an interesting exotic case, for this is not the basis of real moral sympathy. The first preceptors of our America, the missionaries, lambs with the heart of lions, terrible in their independence, embraced the Indians with love, promising them the same heaven which had been promised themselves. The first conquerors established the principle of equality in the delights of miscegenation. Thus, in the Antilles, Miguel Díaz and his Cacica, whom we meet in the pages of Juan de Castellanos; thus that soldier, one Guerrero, who but for this would have been unknown, who refused to follow Cortés's Spaniards because he liked it among the Indians, and, in the words of the old Spanish ballad, "he had a beautiful wife and children like flowers." And in Brazil the famous João Ramalho and El Caramuru, who fascinated the Indian women of San Vicente and Bahia. Cortés himself grasps the secret of his conquest as he rests upon the bosom of Doña Marina. Perhaps it is there that he comes to love his prey as other colder-hearted captains never learned to do (Cæsar of Gaul), and in his soul certain dreams of autonomy began to spring up which, behind closed doors and in the bosom of his family, he was to communicate to his sons, who later suffered punishment for plotting against the mother country. Imperial Iberia did far more than govern us; she continually poured out her blood over America. For that reason here, in our lands, we still consider life as a generous transfusion of blood.

5. These are the stage, the chorus, the leading character. I have spoken of the principal dilemmas in our behavior. I spoke of our watchword as being improvisation, and now I must try to make myself clear. The American mind is of necessity less highly specialized than the European. Our social structure has brought this about. Our writers here have greater connections with society. It is rare for a writer to be only a writer; he is almost always a writer and something else, or several things else. A situation of this sort has its advantages and disadvantages. The disadvantages: when called to action, the mind discovers that the norms of action are the norms of compromise, and this is not pleasant. Hampered by constant interruptions, the intellectual output is sporadic, the mind tends to wander. The advantages come from the special state the world is in today. In this crisis, in this overturning of values which has affected us all and which demands the efforts of all and particularly of the intelligence (unless we are willing that ignorance and despair shall chart mankind's future), the American mind is more accustomed to the open air; we do not have, there is no place among us for ivory towers. This new hard choice between advantages and disadvantages at the same time admits of a synthesis, an equilibrium which resolves itself into a special manner of understanding intellectual work as a public service and a duty to civilization. Naturally, and fortunately, this does not eliminate the possibility of a pause, the luxury of a purely literary diversion, which is a spring in which it is good to immerse oneself as often as possible. Whereas in Europe the pause was the normal state of affairs. The European writer is born, as it were, on the top floor of the Eiffel Tower. With but a slight effort more, he frisks about on the intellectual mountain tops. The American writer is born in the inner region of perpetual fire. By a titanic effort, in which he is often helped by a feverish vitality which almost seems like genius, he barely manages to emerge to the earth's surface. My colleagues of Europe: concealed under this or that mediocre American there often lies a storehouse of qualities which really warrant your interest and attention. Consider him, if it so please you, from the angle of the profession which, in the words of Guyau and José Enrique Rodó, is superior to all others: the profession of

being a man. Viewed thus, there is no danger of science losing touch with its surroundings in its isolated conquests of a millimeter to this side or to that, dangers whose consequences Jules Romains has so lucidly set forth. Nor is there, in this peculiarly American aspect, any threat of losing touch with Europe. On the contrary, it is my feeling that the American mind is called upon to fulfill the highest complementary function: that of establishing syntheses, even though they be of necessity provisional; that of applying the results quickly, testing the truth of the theory on the living tissue of action. In this way, just as European economy now has need of us, so will the mind of Europe need us as well.

6. For this beautiful harmony which I envisage the American mind is peculiarly suited, for our mentality, at the same time that it is deeply rooted in our soil, is, as I have said, by nature international. The explanation of this lies not merely in the fact that America is fitted to be the crucible of that "cosmic race" of the future which Vasconcelos has dreamed of but also in the fact that we have had to go to the great centers of Europe for our cultural equipment, and in this way we have become accustomed to handle ideas of foreign origin as though they were our own. Whereas the European has never had to approach America to construct the system of his world, the American studies, knows, follows Europe from the time he starts to school. Out of this comes a curious consequence, which I cite without vanity or rancor: in the computation of errors or partial misunderstanding in the European books dealing with America and the American books that deal with Europe, the balance is in our favor. It is a professional secret among American writers that European literature frequently misquotes us, spells our names and those of our geography wrong, and so on. Our innate internationalism, based, fortunately, on the historic brotherhood which links our numerous republics together, gives the American mind an indisputably peace-loving inclination. This intervenes and overrules the threat of armed conflict with an ever more skillful hand, and in the international field it makes itself felt among those groups which are more contaminated by the political pugnacity now in fashion. This will facilitate a

gracious junction with the pacifistic idealism of the greatest North American minds.

Our America should live as though it were always making ready to realize the dream which its discovery gave rise to among the thinkers of Europe: the dream of Utopia, of the happy republic which lent peculiar warmth to the pages of Montaigne as he contemplated the surprises and marvels of the New World.

7. In the new literature of America there is a clearly marked tendency toward autochthony, which is deserving of the deepest respect, especially when it does not stop with the easy achievement of local color but attempts to plumb the depths of our psychological realities. This warmth of youth comes to rectify that hereditary sadness, that uneasy conscience with which our forebears looked out upon the world, feeling themselves the offspring of the great original sin of the *capitis deminutio* of being American.

The generation which immediately preceded us still believed it had been born within the prison walls of several concentric fatalities. The most pessimistic felt that the first great fatality was that of living, the maxim of Silenus, repeated by Calderón:

> Because man's greatest crime
> Is to have been born.

Inside this came the second circle, which consisted in having arrived too late in a world that was old. The echoes had not yet died away of that romanticism which the Cuban Juan Clemente summed up in two verses:

> My days are those of ancient Rome
> And my brothers have died with Greece.

In our world of letters a sentimental anachronism held sway over the majority of our writers. This was the third circle, in addition to that of being a human being and being modern, the very specific one of being American, born and rooted in a soil that was not the real center of civilization, but a branch office. To use the words of our Victoria Ocampo, our grandfathers felt themselves to be the "owners of souls that had no passport." And besides being an American, another handicap in life's race was being a Latin or of Latin spiritual formation. It was the epoch of *"A quoi tient la supériorité des Anglo-Saxons?"* It was the epoch of submission to the existing state of things, without hope of a definite change or faith in redemption. Only the noble frank exhortations of Rodó carried a word of hope. And not only did we belong to the Latin world; within it, it was again our fatality to belong to the Hispanic world. For a long time the old lion had been on the down-grade. Spain, skeptical and destitute, seemed to have abjured its former greatness. The sun had set on its domain. And, to cap the climax, the Spanish Americans did not get along well with Spain. This was the case until a little before Spain's recent suffering, which has wounded us all. And even within the Hispanic world we were a dialect, a derivation, a second-rate thing, a branch once more: Spanish-American, a name that is joined by a little hyphen like a chain. Within Spanish America the ones to whom I am near-bred complained of having been born in a region full of Indians. The Indian, then, was a burden, not yet a proud duty and a strong hope. Within this region others even closer to me had reason to lament the fact that they had been born in dangerous proximity to a strong, powerful neighbor, a sentiment which has now been transformed into the supreme honor of representing the race on one front. Of all these specters which the wind has been sweeping away or the light of day has transfigured into, at the very least, realities that can be accepted, there are still a few left in corners of America, and they must be hunted down, opening the windows wide, calling superstition by its name, which is the way to drive it off. But, on the whole, this has all been rectified.

8. Having made the foregoing claims and after this hearing of the case, I venture to assume the style of a legal summing up. For a time now between Spain and us there has existed a feeling of similarity and equality. And now I say to this jury of international thinkers before me: recognize the right to world citizenship which we have achieved. We have come of age. Very soon you will get into the habit of including us in your plans.

THE TRANSFORMATION OF AMERICA IN OUR TIMES

BALDOMERO SANÍN CANO

U NTIL 1914 the twentieth century was an extension of the nineteenth, which, as is well known, began·long before 1800. When the first World War broke out, America was living on the ideas, the experience, the discoveries, and the will of the previous century. Up to the year 1914 the only real difference between this century and that which had preceded it was the increased speed of transportation. Metallurgy had provided engineers with a substance as strong as steel but far lighter; a pneumatic sphere that greatly reduced friction; and the ability to utilize the explosive force of internal-combustion engines which raised the speed of communication to an astonishing degree. The application of these ingenious devices to life in general and to business in particular brought about the close approximation, almost a real contact, between America and Europe, and between the Saxon and Latin divisions of this continent. The strong barriers of habit and thought which existed between the most advanced nations of Europe and Latin America began to disappear. The first reaction of the Latin of Buenos Aires, Lima, or Bogotá who visited Europe about the middle of the nineteenth century was one of surprise and bewilderment. Life in Europe was different in almost every respect from life in Latin America, especially in the material details of daily living. By the twentieth century these differences were less sharply accentuated and, in certain aspects, the Latin American from the southern countries of the continent could find a basis for favorable comparison between the material civilization of his country and Europe.

To the material reality of the so-called Iberian-American republics, occupying one continent, and the historic reality of their common Iberian origin and their having followed parallel lines of development during the first years of their existence is due the fact that in Europe and North America, and even in some of our own countries, the illiterate masses, certain dilettantes, and even people of sound preparation and training in other fields assume that the words Latin America, Spanish America, or South America refer to a unified whole that can be grouped under a general heading as having identical or at least similar traits and contours. This assumption, which gave rise to misleading and dangerous conclusions a hundred years ago, still confuses the ideas of certain historians, expounders of sociology, travelers, and correspondents of European and Saxon-American newspapers. It is impossible to reduce to a social, economic, or even geographic formula the total meaning of this continent. The region, the climate, the variety of soils, the character of the original inhabitants, the sources of immigration, the prevalent ideas in matters of order, education, and international relations; the trade routes, products, even the area of its territory have already created differences which demand the careful, documented study of each country in order to grasp its historic, social, and political significance. All these nations are republics or are at least so nominated in their constitutions. Four are, according to their statutes, republics of a federal type; the others are, theoretically, centralized governments of democratic type. Today only Colombia, Costa Rica, Venezuela, Chile, Mexico, and possibly Uruguay may be considered to have a purely democratic type of organization.

These considerations should be borne in mind when reading the following pages, which deal with the Latin-American republics in the forty-three years of the present century that have elapsed. I know my own country well, have lived for seven years in the Argentine and for thirty years have had connections of various sorts with it. I know all the republics of South America, with the exception of Paraguay and Bolivia, and have visited Cuba. For many years I have studied the literature of all these nations, but I do not believe myself qualified to pass opinion on this phase of their development except in the case of Colombia, my own country, and the Argentine. I have always been a watchful observer of the political activities of the continent, with my thoughts on the possibility of a spiritual union between the nations that inhabit it.

The Argentine Republic and Colombia, the two countries of which I feel qualified to speak, are diagonally opposed on the map of South America; by reason of their geographical characteristics, their soil, and the course followed by their governmental policies they are even farther apart. Argentina is a southern region, which lies almost wholly in the temperate zone, with the exception of a small portion that extends into the torrid zone along its boundary with Bolivia.

At the beginning of the present century the various republics of Latin America had acquired marked characteristics of their own. The political and economic situation of the southern nations, Argentina, Chile, Uruguay, gave promise of years of peace and active economic development. There was the danger that hostilities might break out between Argentina and Chile over the question of boundaries, but the timely and civilized friendly intervention of Great Britain prevented what would have been the greatest calamity that could have afflicted the continent. This splendid proof of a deep and genuinely American sentiment aroused an echo in all the republics and set a precedent of singular efficacy.

The natural wealth of the Argentine, intensively exploited, had created bonds of great intimacy with the fine products of European civilization, and with the development of this natural wealth came a keen interest in scientific and literary studies and in all aspects of art. The first years of the century revealed a rich flowering of all branches of intellectual activity in the Argentine Republic.

In the political field, during the second decade of the century a certain restiveness began to manifest itself. The party which had governed the nation and had presided over the development of its great wealth and the growth of its intellectual life was at heart aware of the fact that an injustice lay at the base of its political structure. A great and wisely directed plan had extended public education and had considerably reduced the percentage of illiteracy, which had increased with the ever growing immigration from Europe. The increase in the number of citizens able to read and write was not in keeping with the democratic reality of the ballot. A noble soul, who became President in 1910, Dr. Roque Saenz, recognized the need of reforming the electoral law and presented a plan to Congress which was approved in 1912. With the passage of this law, which introduced the secret ballot, those parties which until then had refrained from voting decided to participate in the elections. The Radical Party won a great victory which kept it in power by a majority vote until 1930, when a military uprising overthrew the legitimate government. The effect of this refusal to recognize a legally constituted government was largely to blame for discrediting all Latin America in the eyes of Europe. Other smaller nations, less well known in Europe, for half a century had been affording the sorry spectacle of their continual revolutions, many of which were of military origin; but Argentina had seemed a model of orderly political procedure. This subversion of order through a military coup in a country so rich and well organized caused a deep impression in Europe and great disheartening among the true democracies of America. Since then Argentina has continued to progress; its trade has grown to large dimensions; its industry has developed by leaps and bounds; science and the arts are widely cultivated in its universities and special centers with praiseworthy results, but the political malaise caused by the military *coup d'état* of 1930 had not disappeared when another of the same or worse character took place in 1943.

In this connection it is worth noting that to a large degree the World War of 1914 had a hand in weakening the political situation of these southern nations. Before this happened in the Argentine, the unhealthy effects of the World War had made themselves felt in Chile, a nation which was recognized as an example of order by the rest of America before the revolution against Balmaceda and afterwards.

With all this, the international peace of the continent has suffered few disturbances during the twentieth century. The only war between nations which darkened the moral horizon of these countries was that which took place in 1935 between Paraguay and Bolivia, which fortunately was ended through the mediation of friendly American powers and the persistent efforts of the League of Nations.

Europe and North America have eloquently deplored, and not

without repercussions in their relations with Latin America, the harm ensuing from these South American revolutions. It is true that these disturbances of order temporarily paralyzed the progress of these countries and undoubtedly contributed to discrediting the democratic system, but it is a fact well recognized by statisticians that the disasters of a century of wars and revolutions in South America represent less in the way of destruction of wealth or even in cost than two days' effort to restore democracy in Europe in these painful moments of the breakdown of civilized life.

In spite of the upsets and at times inversions of the constitutional order in certain countries, the American continent has been a region of peace. The disturbances of an international order that have occurred during the present century have had their origin in Europe, and this consideration brings home the fact that if a powerful state had not existed in the north of this part of the world, capable of matching itself against older and more aggressive nations of the Old World, the peace of the continent would have been seriously menaced. In struggles as desperate as those of 1914 and 1939 our countries would most certainly have been involved in the hostilities. Viewing the matter dispassionately, it is evident that without the strength and the resources of the great Saxon Republic of the north, the rest of the continent would have ceased to exist as the seat of free republics on both these frightful occasions, as has happened in Africa and Asia when the peace of the world has been less profoundly disturbed. The instinctive awareness of this historic and geographic state of affairs has rallied all the nations of America, with one exception, around the strongest in these years of liberty's desperate struggle for survival.

The ease and rapidity of communications were largely responsible for creating the wealth of Spanish America and helped to alleviate the tension among the less fortunate classes of Europe. By reason of its geographic conditions, the geology of its lands, the distance of its larger centers from the coast, and perhaps because of the persistence of its traditions, Colombia has benefited less than other nations of America from the advancement and inventions of science. Its contact with Europe was not as close as that of certain of its sister republics. Nevertheless, its culture was, until

1914, deeply and almost exclusively European in origin, form, and content.

The twentieth century found Colombia somewhat isolated but not wholly without communication. It received from Europe and from the most advanced nation of America a bitter lesson of painful and enduring memory. Colombia gave France, on extremely favorable terms, a concession to dig a canal through its territory linking the Atlantic and Pacific Oceans. The climate, the inefficiency of those in charge, and the tortuous machinations of the French financiers brought the enterprise to grief. By 1903 the ambitious undertaking had become a complete fiasco. In twenty-five years the French company to which the concession had been granted had hardly made a beginning and its financial situation was as desperate as its technical capacity was wanting. It is beside the point to give an account here of the schemes employed to arrange for the transfer of the enterprise to a Saxon-American company, the mutilation of Colombia's territorial integrity, and the accomplishment by the government of Washington of an undertaking which meant so much for civilization. In reviewing the facts connected with this adventure it is a signal injustice to lay upon the shoulders of North America all the moral responsibility. The idea, the treachery involved in the sorry business, were purely of French origin. The French company which was to have built the Panama Canal was unworthy of the confidence of our government and of its own stockholders. It set out to find technical assistance for its devious plan and finally found a buyer for its bankrupt holdings.

It was from Europe, the fountainhead of civilization and the model of culture, that Colombia received the first and rudest shock it has suffered in the course of its relations with that world. To which must be added the fact that at the beginning of the century, too, as a result of deplorable political training and administrative customs that were in conflict with traditions of decency, the twentieth century found Colombia involved in a civil war which, because of its duration and severity, was most harmful to its financial credit and prosperity.

In 1910 the Constitution was revised and the nation began to

adjust itself to new political habits. The civil war and the territorial mutilation served as a hard but sound lesson. Its citizens
decided to live in peace and to adopt an administrative procedure
based on equality of representation and tolerance. The nation
had lived from 1902 until the trying year of 1943 in absolute
peace, both within its frontiers and with the other nations of the
world.

The transformations that came about as a result of the Allied victory of 1918 were felt strongly in Colombia, although less intensely
than in other American countries, precisely because its political
and ideological links with Europe were weaker than those of other
nations. For reasons of geography, expediency, and perhaps necessity Colombia detached itself somewhat from Europe politically
and economically. Its commercial connections with the fatherland
of Lincoln became greatly intensified as the links with Europe
weakened. As a result of the economic difficulties of the Old World
which followed the war, and also as a consequence of the crisis
caused by the terrible depression of 1929, Colombia directed its
trade routes toward North America. It did not say, as did other
countries: "We will buy from those who buy our products"; but
in the natural order of events, as England, France, Spain, Italy,
and other countries of Europe refused to buy its principal export,
which is coffee, its purchases in North America grew as those from
Europe shrank, despite the difference in prices. This shifting of
the currents of commerce toward the United States has had a considerable influence on the direction and nature of Colombia's intellectual activities. Writers are prone to scoff at the merchant. It
is an accepted attitude without basis in fact. Whatever the vices
and moral shortcomings of the business man, it is a historical fact
that he carries his civilization to the regions with which he deals
and helps to modify the customs and the thought of the countries
with which he trades. Together with the manufactures of Man-
chester and the whisky of Scotland, Great Britain brought to our
countries the Bible, the works of Shakespeare, Richardson's novels,
Byron's poetry, Bentham's philosophy, and, later, Darwin's painstaking studies and Spencer's labored reflections. In spite of the
difficultly surmountable barrier of language, trade with England

has had a noticeable influence on the intellectual formation of New Granada. Side by side with the commercial products of Paris, the French brought in their writers and their philosophers and stamped the literature of Colombia with those transmissible and easily imitable characteristics of their rich and contagious literary culture.

As the direction of the trade routes changed, certain aspects of our outlook on the world changed. In the case of trade with North America the language makes a frontier difficult to cross. Yet English is supplanting French in the program of our schools, and every day the number of Colombians who can read with profit the books written in the language of Emerson, Poe, T. S. Eliot, and Hemingway grows.

Since 1918 the United States has drawn closer to Colombia at an ever increasing pace. At the end of the nineteenth century it normally took from twenty to twenty-four days to travel from New York to Bogotá. This time was cut to about half by the use of swift steamship lines. The airplane has brought us together at a dizzying pace. The distance between the two cities is now only a matter of a little over two days. There are those who say that at the end of World War II the southern shores of the Caribbean will be so close to New York that it will be possible to travel the distance between them in ten hours. This will bring about marked changes in the customs and thinking of the Colombians if the cost of air travel diminishes with the same velocity.

Colombia's culture was almost exclusively French in character until the end of the nineteenth century, with a few enduring notes of English origin. Spain had given it its initial impulse with the conquest and the colonization; but the struggle for independence on the one hand, and the inferiority of Spain's literary, scientific, and industrial culture on the other, compared with that of France and England, made the Spanish influence much weaker in these aspects than that of the other countries, despite the ties of blood and language. During the first decade of this century there began a revival of Spanish culture in Colombia, due to the effort of certain publishing houses of the peninsula and to the propaganda of the governments looking to better cultural relations. The sale of Spanish books increased greatly in our country. In the majority of libraries of modern books there was a preponderance of French authors during all the nineteenth century. It has been said that the colonial government took care to prevent the entry into our countries of all except a few books, carefully inspected first by the authorities. There has been a certain amount of exaggeration in this. At the end of the eighteenth century many of the French authors who were most frowned upon by the censorship and were among the most advanced of their time were known to us. In certain cases it was the viceroys themselves who were instrumental in having these books included in the public libraries.

The growth of the sale of Spanish books at the beginning of this century had as an immediate consequence a falling off in the sale of French books. The publishers of Madrid and Barcelona began to supply reliable Spanish translations of French, German, and English works to South American booksellers. This enterprise, which proved successful, managed partly to dislodge French books, and in addition brought about a certain coolness toward the study and use of the French language.

The war of 1914 had other surprises in store. The trade routes changed and with them the literary influences. French literature, which during the last thirty years of the nineteenth century had had a gorgeous flowering, incomparably greater than that of the other nations of Europe, ceased to produce masterpieces on the scale and of the quality to which the genius of its writers had accustomed us. The violent economic crises which paralyzed commercial relations also deflected the cultural relations. Europe could no longer fully satisfy the new aspirations and the thirst for knowledge that characterized the youth of Colombia in these moments. And at the same time, although the crisis was very severe in North America, its proximity and the enormous powers of recuperation of the Saxon Republic helped to reroute our trade to a very large extent toward that powerful nation.

The resentment engendered by the unpleasant incidents having to do with the separation of Panama disappeared with the treaty of 1922, by the terms of which Colombia and the United States put an end to their mutual complaints. At the same time the Colombian nation entered upon a period of relative prosperity and a settled political life, dominated by institutions of frankly democratic type and meaning. This internal peace lasted for twenty years; the different parties had arrived at a tacit agreement to respect the country's institutions and a firm determination to maintain peace under all circumstances.

In 1930, in an absolutely free and honest election, the party that had governed the country for twenty-five years was defeated at the polls. The losers accepted the decision of the voters and since then a government of liberal tendencies, sincerely democratic, has ruled the nation in accordance with its principles and aims. This party has had the good fortune to see the rise in the United States of a new attitude toward the rest of America. The "Good Neighbor" policy, whose continuance would seem to be guaranteed by its initial success and by its basis on international ethics, makes the political action of Colombia with relation to the other nations of the continent much simpler.

Mutual respect is the basis of the relations between the nations of the continent. Colombia followed the clear route of its destiny in favor of peace. The war has had a deplorable influence on the general life of the Republic, as was to be expected; but it has not affected in the least the basis of its institutions nor caused it to deviate from its habit of devotion to democracy.

Our closer relations with the United States have made us appreciate better its marvelous progress in the fields of techniques as well as in art and literature. The young people who used to go to Europe to round off their professional preparation or to complete their studies in specialized branches of knowledge now go to the northern Republic.

It must be said, however, that we are still the most unknown Americans on the continent. We occupy a space on the globe as large as Arizona, New Mexico, Montana, and Wyoming put together. The press of North America seems surprised to learn this. Colombia has a population of more than nine million inhabitants and has room for sixty million. In normal times its exports amount to 120,000,000 pesos colombianos ($68,500,000) and its imports to 80,000,000 ($45,700,000). It has an Atlantic and Pacific seaboard, and through its territory flow the Orinoco and the Amazon, an inland sea that separates it from Peru where it borders on Brazil. In its valleys all the fruits of the tropical zone flourish, and on the Andean plains those of the temperate zone. A great part of its territorial expanse is relatively uncultivated. By reason of its abundant supply of coal, oil, iron ores, copper, lead, and other metals and its numerous waterfalls it offers a vast field for the development of many different industries. Its production of gold and silver at present amounts to 30,000,000 pesos colombianos ($17,-000,000).

Its language is Spanish, and it is said to speak it with great correctness. The press of Bogotá and of certain provincial capitals has acquired a great industrial and literary development. The literature of Colombia occupies an outstanding position in the literary history of Spanish America.

Public education, which for a time was the chief concern of the government, declined dangerously during certain periods of this and the past century. In keeping with the nation's demands and its historic precedents the government has again interested itself in the matter, and the number of illiterates is decreasing noticeably.

Peace has come to be the aspiration of the greater part of Colombia's citizens. The rare *coups d'état* of its history are of unpleasant memory. The attempts to establish a dictatorship, which have been less than three in its hundred and twenty-four years of life as a republic, have been frustrated by the unanimous sentiments of the nation. The watchword of the governments that have ruled for the past twenty years has been probity in the administration of public funds. The caudillo, that unhealthy growth of the tropics, and in recent times the scourge of European nations, has completely disappeared from our political scene. Democracy, which was the aspiration of the founders of the Republic, and a difficult venture for many years, has become second nature.

Studied attempts have been made and are still made abroad to ignore the existence of Colombia, and not entirely unsuccessfully; but little by little the world is becoming aware of the fact that in the northwest of South America, looking out over the Caribbean and the Pacific, there lives a Republic, modern in character, greatly favored by nature, which will play its part in the civilization of the future, whose dawn is already breaking through the frightful shadows of the present.

PART III

Bronzes and Marbles

SIMÓN BOLÍVAR (1783–1830)

For three centuries Spain ruled the American colonies. Under her maternal wing a racial intermingling took place and a new spirit was coming into being. By the end of the eighteenth century, when the United States won its freedom from England, France was broadcasting the seeds of revolution through the world, and in Spain the monarchy came to grief in the reign of Charles IV, this new spirit was already formed. Salvador de Madariaga has portrayed the Spanish monarchy well in these words: "Charles IV through his stupidity, Ferdinand VII through his cruelty and unscrupulousness, dishonored the crown when they identified it with their unworthy heads." The peoples of America who then, for the first time, gazed upon the outside world felt that all this was urging them on to the conquest of their liberty. The masses began to revolt in the fields and the mines. The students sounded the first tocsins of rebellion in the cities. The day it became known that Napoleon was holding Ferdinand VII prisoner and had sent his brother Joseph to Spain as King — the drunken Pepe Bottles, famous in the songs of the Madrid populace — war broke out in America. There was no government in Spain, and the Creoles here knew more of the art of politics and local administration than was known in Madrid.

Declarations of independence were signed. From Mexico to Buenos Aires in the same year, 1810, and almost the same month, without any previous accord, everybody was talking of independence and everyone took up arms. This time many of the whites were foremost among the leaders. Bolívar — known in our America as the Liberator — arose in Venezuela, his native land. His flaming spirit aroused the peoples; he was the scourge of the royalists; he seemed to conjure up armies out of the thin air, he breathed new spirit into the defeated after every royalist victory, encouraging and regrouping the troops until, under his command, they finally liberated Venezuela, Colombia, Ecuador, Peru, and Bolivia. On mule or horseback, on cockleshells of sailing ships, time after time he crossed the Andes, time after time he crossed the seas, determined not to die until he had driven Spanish rule from America. Dismounting only to sleep on the bare ground, often wrapped only in his cape, he scaled the mountains, traveling from the tropical lowlands to the bleak heights covered with perpetual snow, driving on the armies by the force of his will. They were armies of Indians, Negroes, and mestizos, which he disciplined with his genius until they could face the regular Spanish troops that had fought against Napoleon in Europe. No horseman has ever ridden so many miles over such bad and such varied roads. No man has ever sunk so deep in the abyss of defeat to rise so high in the glory of triumph. He was rich among the rich of his country and of a family connected with the nobility of Spain. He staked all he had on a single card. And he lost. He was twice completely defeated in his own country and had to take refuge in the Antilles, penniless. In these refuges, and under circumstances like this, he wrote the greatest political documents of his day and he grasped the problems of America with such prescience that he foresaw the Pan-American policy and the role of Panama in the coming world. His writings, rich as they were in profound judgments upon the realities of his day and the future of America, achieved moments of lyric heights which closely recall those of Napoleon. They contain phrases which seem written for our own days, such as this he addressed to the soldiers of America: "Liberal Europe looks with delight upon you, for the freedom of the New World is the hope of the universe."

When his days as a soldier were over and Spanish America was free — San Martín had sealed the independence of Argentina and Chile and, in the north, Mexico had proclaimed its freedom in the Plan of Iguala in 1821 — Bolívar saw that the countries which had achieved liberation under his banners were rending themselves asunder in internal struggles that were the prelude to the civil wars to come. His conception of life-term presidencies — as a bulwark against chaos — left the road open to dictatorship, and the people rejected it. At the same time the disorders and instability made it impossible for anyone to govern peaceably. The Great Colombia split into three nations: Colombia, Venezuela, Ecuador.

Peru declared war on Colombia. In Bolivia the presidents that he had dreamed of as governing for life occupied the chair for only a few hours. Disheartened and ill, Bolívar saw the world he had created crumbling between his fingers and he died, grief-stricken, at Santa Marta on the shores of the Caribbean, which had witnessed his great moral conflicts, issuing a last proclamation, which closes with these words: "If my death helps to bring to an end party strife and consolidate union, I shall go to my grave in peace."

Jules Mancini, a Colombian writer who spent most of his life in France, wrote a book on Bolívar that is considered one of the best of the abundant literature on the subject. The pages that follow describe the development of Bolívar's first campaign in Colombia, immediately following the failure of the first Republic of Venezuela. With this campaign, the most complete and successful within its limited scope, Bolívar's military career begins. In it, as he himself said, his glory was born.

BOLÍVAR'S FIRST CAMPAIGN
JULES MANCINI

From the house of the Marquis of Casa León, where he had taken refuge, Bolívar followed, with impotent despair, the bloody reprisals his enemies were carrying out during the days that followed Monteverde's entrance into Caracas.

The Spaniards, the Canary Islanders, the adherents of the crown, known as *godos*, rallied around Miranda's conqueror as soon as he assumed the temporary governorship of the province, and urged him to take the severest measures against all who had been involved in the revolt. Monteverde, who was weak of character and cruel and suspicious by nature, allowed himself to be persuaded.

He had twice solemnly promised, in proclamations dated the 3rd and 5th of August 1812, not to employ violence against the patriots. But the fear that the people might again revolt against his authority led him to adopt the measures that his inner council claimed were necessary for the safety and the very existence of the restored regime. A secret committee, composed of the most fanatical of the *godos*, was empowered to draw up a daily list of suspects. Monteverde passed these lists as submitted, and sinister police agents, *prendedores* as they were known, even added, at will, the names of Creoles, innocent or guilty, who had refused to pay them the ransom fee they demanded.

On the 15th of August the military governors of outlying cities in the province received orders to arrest all those suspected of liberal ideas and send them to the capital, Caracas. In a short time the prisons were filled to overflowing with these unfortunate victims, who were put to death without distinction of age or sex. As there were not enough public executioners for the work, the troops were called upon. Mass shootings began. An eyewitness of the events, J. F. Heredia, wrote: "A group of despicable mulattoes, who had taken part in the rebellion, won the confidence of the authorities and were made *prendedores*. They took advantage of their position in the most shocking manner, bringing shame upon the good Spaniards before whose eyes countless horrors were being perpetrated in the name of the most generous nation and the greatest King in the world."

At this point one of these Spaniards, Don Francisco de Iturbe, for whom Monteverde had the highest respect because of his irreproachable character, intervened with the governor to secure a safe-conduct for Bolívar, to whom he was joined by the bonds of an old, devoted friendship. Monteverde gladly acceded to this request. The role Bolívar had played at the time of Miranda's arrest gave him a claim on the gratitude of the Spanish leader which the latter was only too glad to honor, especially as it seemed good strategy to employ toward the most influential and active Creole in Caracas. The governor hoped to be able to utilize Bolívar's valuable co-operation; but as he had promised to give him proof of his friendliness toward him, he did not want to go back on his word when he learned that the young officer wished to leave the country.

So he sent him an order to appear at the palace, and Bolívar presented himself on August 26, accompanied by Iturbe. "This is Don Simón Bolívar, the commander of Puerto Cabello, for whom I am willing to go security," said Iturbe, nobly presenting him to Monteverde. "If he has been found deserving of punishment, I am willing to suffer it; my life for his."

"Very good, sir," replied the governor. "He will be granted a passport in return for his services to the King in bringing Miranda to prison."

Bolívar, who until then had observed silence, spoke up quickly to say that "he had arrested Miranda because he was a traitor to his country, not to serve the King."

This answer almost spoiled everything. Greatly angered, Monteverde was about to stop the hand of his secretary, Bernardo Muro, who had the passport all ready. "Now, now, don't pay any attention to this hot-head. Give him his passport and let him go."

"So be it," answered the governor tartly, "I have given my word."

Had the Spanish commander been less gentlemanly that day, it is probable that Bolívar would have paid the price of his brave but rash words, which nevertheless he could not do less than say. To be sure, Monteverde was aware of the blame to which he was laying himself open in permitting this dangerous enemy to escape, and he felt obliged to justify his act to his superiors. In a dispatch addressed to the Secretary of State in Madrid that same night he said: "I could not ignore the services we owe to Casas, as well as to Peña and Bolívar. For this reason their persons have been respected. To the last alone have I given a passport to go abroad, for his influence and his connections might be dangerous under existing circumstances."

The next day Bolívar embarked in La Guayra with his cousin José Felix Ribas on the Spanish schooner *Jesús María José*, bound for Curaçao. In Santa Ana, where he arrived September 2, he spent days of tribulation and penury. The ship's papers were not in order. The authorities of Curaçao attached Bolívar's baggage, in which he was carrying some ten thousand dollars in negotiable securities. At the moment this represented his entire fortune. The legal proceedings he instituted to recover his property dragged on interminably. As a result this dashing Creole, whose lavishness had aroused the admiration of his associates at the Palais Royal years before, soon found himself with barely enough to keep from starving to death. Meanwhile his plantations in Caracas and Aragua were about to be confiscated by Monteverde's government. He was confronted with complete ruin.

But this could not make the Liberator lose heart. In a letter to Iturbe during those days he said: "The upright brave man must be indifferent to the blows of fortune, and I have armed myself with steadfastness and look with contempt on the missiles of misfortune. The sole master of my heart is my conscience, which is at peace and untroubled." Bolívar had reached a decision: now more than ever he was determined to devote himself to the freedom of nations, as he had said on another occasion to his teacher Rodríguez, and he no longer believed that for this it was necessary to be rich.

A profound change had been wrought in him through misfortunes, war, and catastrophes; and the dreadful events with which, as a disciple of Miranda, he had been associated had tempered his will and strengthened his judgment. He now saw with amazing insight the reasons for the failure of the work undertaken by the first champions of American liberty. He distinguished clearly the abilities and the defects of those men, the characteristics of the masses they were trying to win to their cause. With a sort of clairvoyance which from this moment was to be one of the distinguishing traits of his many-sided genius, Bolívar saw, beyond time, events, defeats, and victories, the goal that was to be won and that he would win. He never for a moment doubted that this supreme task had been reserved for him.

At the beginning of November, giving up all concern for financial consideration in his eagerness to get on with this work, he sold a few jewels he still owned and, together with Ribas, Pedro Briceño Méndez, and several other Venezuelans, took passage in a brigantine bound for Cartagena, where the flag of independence still waved. He was received by President Torices, who immediately confirmed him in his rank of colonel and ordered the commander-in-chief, Labatut, to make use of his services. On December 1 Bolívar was assigned to the command of the outpost of Barranca, on the banks of the Magdalena, and he entrusted to his fellow countrymen Salazar and Vicente Tejera the publication of a manifesto he had prepared during the tedious days of exile and poverty in Curaçao. This document, which was printed at the press of the "citizen Domingo Espinosa," was published fifteen days later under the title: *Proclamation of Colonel Simón Bolívar, Venezuela, to the inhabitants of New Granada.*

It rejoices the spirit to hear, amidst so much confused, prejudiced, incoherent thinking as was going on at that moment, the eloquent ringing tones of truth and reason:

> The most fateful mistake Venezuela made when she appeared on the political stage was beyond doubt the adoption of a regime of tolerance. The law codes by which our magistrates were guided were not designed to teach them the practical science of government. They were the compilation of certain amiable visionaries who, with an imaginary republic in mind, aimed for political perfection, and assumed the perfectability of mankind. As a result, we had philosophers for leaders, philanthropy for legislation, dialectics for policy, and sophists for soldiers.

> The determined opposition to calling up veteran troops, disciplined, trained, and ready to take the field in the defense of liberty with glory and success was the second cause of our misfortunes. Instead, many bodies of raw recruits were formed. This not only depleted the national treasury, by reason of the salaries that had to be paid the ranking officers, but ruined agriculture by taking the farmers from the land. A republic, argued our statesmen, has no need of hirelings to protect its liberty. All its citizens will spring to arms when threatened by the enemy. This unpolitical, mistaken reasoning proved alluring to the simple-minded. The squandering of the public funds for frivolous, futile purposes and especially on salaries to a host of clerks, secretaries, judges,

magistrates, local and federal legislators, dealt the Republic a mortal blow, for it was forced to resort to the dangerous expedient of issuing paper money.

But the thing that weakened the government of Venezuela above everything else was the adoption of the federal form of government. Even though the federal system is the most perfect and best designed to further the happiness of human society, it is, nevertheless, the most contrary to the interests of our new-born states. The earthquake of March 26, to be sure, was both a physical and a moral disaster and may be properly called the immediate cause of the ruin of Venezuela. But it would not have had such tragic consequences if there had been a sole authority at the head of the government of Caracas who could have taken quick decisive steps to counteract the harm that had been wrought without the interference and delay which allowed the misfortune to acquire such proportions that it became hopeless. The influence of the Church after the earthquake was largely to blame for the uprisings in villages and smaller cities and for opening the country to the enemy. It took sacrilegious advantage of its position to foment civil war because it could commit these crimes with complete impunity.

These instances of mistakes and misfortunes will not be lost upon the peoples of South America who are seeking their freedom.

The necessary steps for correcting this situation become self-evident from Bolívar's foregoing remarks.

It is imperative for the government to identify itself, in a manner of speaking, with the nature of the circumstances, the times, and the people among which it moves. If these are prosperous and serene, the government can be mild and indulgent, but if they are dangerous and turbulent, it must be severe and employ such measures as the dangers require, without regard for constitution or laws, until peace and quiet have been restored. Only trained armies can cope with the initial setbacks of a campaign.

As for the political doctrines which have been in force up to this time, they are incompatible with our present mentality.

Our fellow citizens are not yet capable of making full use of their rights for themselves; they lack the political virtues which characterize the true republican.

New Granada has seen the collapse of Venezuela; it must therefore avoid the reefs upon which the latter came to grief. To this end I propose, as an indispensable measure for the safety of New Granada, the recapture of Caracas. At first sight this plan may seem inconclusive, costly, and perhaps even impracticable. But after carefully and thoughtfully weighing it, with an eye to the future, it becomes impossible not to recognize its urgency or to take the necessary steps for carrying it out. The first argument in favor of this operation is a realization of the cause of the loss of Caracas, which was none other than the indifference with which that city tolerated the existence of an enemy it considered insignificant, which, in the true light of the facts, was not the case.

To be sure, Coro could not have represented a threat to Caracas if we compare merely the size of the opposing forces. But, in the course of human struggles, it is not always the physical weight of numbers that turns the political scale, but their moral superiority. Therefore the government of Venezuela should not have neglected to destroy an enemy which, though apparently insignificant, had valuable auxiliary forces: the support of the province of Maracaibo; of all the provinces which accepted the Regency; the money and support of our inveterate enemies, the Europeans who live among us; the clerical party, which is always the ally and supporter of despotism; and, above all, the unswerving adherence of all the ignorant and superstitious within our states. To put it in the form of a proportion, applying the example of Venezuela to New Granada, we find that Coro is to Caracas as Caracas to all America.

The manner of stating the problem could not be more logical; and it seemed clear, as Bolívar later proved beyond doubt, that "as long as Spain possessed Venezuela, she could easily draw on it for men, food, and munitions which would make it possible for her experienced officers, operating from the provinces of Barinas and Maracaibo, to invade all South America."

Moreover, the author of the proclamation foresaw the expeditionary force that Spain would send against the New World once she herself was free from foreign invaders. It was therefore imperative, he concluded, to frustrate these plans.

> Our rebellious provinces must be quickly pacified so we can turn our arms against the enemy, and in this way train officers and soldiers deserving of the name of defenders of the nation. . . . The honor of New Granada demands that these bold invaders be punished and driven back to their last redoubt. And her glory rests upon her willingness to undertake the march to Venezuela to free the cradle of Colombian independence. Let us hasten to strike off the shackles of the victims who lie in the dungeons awaiting liberation at our hands. Let us not fail them. Do not turn a deaf ear to the laments of your brothers. Rush to avenge the dead, to restore life to the dying, to bring freedom to the oppressed and liberty to all.

The preciseness and clarity of these observations and conclusions, and, above all, the general plan of operations to which they inspired the future Liberator, have never received all the praise they deserve. At one glance Bolívar took in the theater and the actors of the drama in which he was to play the leading role. He outlines to us beforehand the program that he will carry out in full, overcoming the greatest obstacles any human being has ever encountered in his path and rising above them without ever a sign of discouragement. To pacify, as he said, those states torn by anarchy and lack of political experience; to employ the forces drawn from them to break the fetters of those regions still under the heel of the old tyranny; then to make use of the released energy of the provinces thus freed one after another to embark upon ever greater conquests as his resources for the enterprise of freedom grow; to begin and begin again a hundred times over with sublime perseverance this work he feels is his mission; and finally to give liberty to half a continent; this is the superhuman plan that Bolívar is to carry to fulfillment, and that he clearly envisaged in this Manifesto of Cartagena.

Moreover, at that moment Bolívar was clearly aware of the difficulties which lay ahead of him. He knew that in addition to the opposing armies, incomparably superior in number to his own, he had to face the hundred times greater resistance of American nature and man. Both seemed equally inconstant, equally hostile. The treacherous climates, the overpowering exuberance of riotous plant life, the lurking stealth of cruel animals, were a counterpart of the fickle character of the inhabitants, their generous but uncontrollable surges of emotion, and the evil forces of selfishness.

To wrench from their fields and homes the necessary masses of peasants and workers, whose will to liberty was too faltering and sluggish to make them eager for a direct part in winning it; to dominate and subdue the undisciplined, turbulent volunteers; to make a whole nation follow where he led, was nothing compared with what he still had to do. The will, the persuasion, the steadfastness he had to employ to make those men endure, without deserting or giving up, the torrid, fever-breeding climate of the coast and low-lying valleys, deadly to the dwellers of plateau and plain, and the chill wind and rains of the mountains, fatal in turn to the inhabitants of the coast!

Then in the interior of the country there were virgin jungles to be traversed, roads that were little more than paths crawling along the mountain slopes, skirting precipices, broken by gorges which swallowed up man and beast, by swollen streams. "These roads," one explorer writes, "are unbelievable to anyone who has not traversed them. One makes one's way with compass and machete. On the continuous ascent there is the ever present threat of sliding over cliffs that are practically vertical and slippery with decayed vegetation and plants." Travel along them is in the nature of "ceaseless gymnastics in which the hands play a greater part than the feet. Every moment there is the danger of encountering snakes of every description, centipedes, the soldier snail, whose bite is fatal, tarantulas, *arañas bravas* — huge, squat purple spiders whose bite can kill a horse — and swarms of locusts and mosquitoes. At night this is aggravated by the vampire bats which are found in the regions along the coast, and by countless savage insects attracted to the campfires lighted to frighten off the pumas."

Apart from the cities or towns, usually scattered at vast distances from one another, these difficulties and dangers were the same that had beset the path of the intrepid adventurers of the conquest. In the period that is to follow, souls like those of the conquistadors are going to be needed. Bolívar undertakes the incredible task of forming them. The audacity and enthusiasm he radiates are so great that his people become charged with his spirit and rise to the most exalted manifestations of bravery. But — and this is the greatest proof of the Liberator's prodigious political genius — at the same time that he revives and stimulates the martial instincts of the people, he keeps constantly before them the ideal for which he is leading them to battle. His is the stirring eloquence which the heart of the people, if not their spirit, admires and understands. He expresses the magnificent thoughts which rouse an echo in the souls of them all and of which he is the incarnation. He can inspire his soldiers to unbelievable lengths of heroism and sacrifice; he becomes their idol.

His teachings, patiently repeated whenever the occasion offers, become stamped on the minds of those who form his most intimate circle and who, in turn, spread them. Not only has he the instincts of a warrior: that of the military leader shows itself, too. The moral influence of a struggle inspired by the noblest of sentiments gradually has its effect on the masses. They acquire the sense of true patriotism and come to know its virtues.

To be sure, this goal was to be achieved only in part, at the cost of repeated effort and sacrifices over the course of many campaigns and years marked by tragic days. To be sure, also, the ancestral vocation of adventure and war, thus unleashed and drunk with the wine of battle, its only sustenance, went beyond the goal the Liberator had envisaged. Cruelty, ambition, and discord, the inevitable reverse of the medal of South American virtues, had free rein and paved the way for the civil wars, the insurrections and military uprisings which finally brought about the ruin of

Bolívar's plans. There is no doubt that the civic education of the people was still in a feeble, precarious state at the end of the struggle for independence, yet from that moment the work of liberation was completely and finally accomplished, and the Liberator's titanic concept was on the point of becoming a reality. In the flush of his triumph he dreamed of setting up on the former continental domain of Spain a vast, enduring, powerful state, united in brotherhood.

Nevertheless, the contrast between the actual moment and these radiant, far-off dreams was enough to dishearten the most sanguine and gifted of heroes. The *próceres* had been decimated and their petty ambitions were everywhere undermining their hesitant aspirations. Many of the Creoles, fearing the threat of the revolution to their economic interests, had withdrawn from the struggle. On the whole, the people, deeply influenced by the Church, to which the terms "country," "liberty," and "independence" were but synonyms for the most dangerous heresies, were hostile, or at least inert. Everywhere ignorance, cruelty, and anarchy held the field. It seemed impossible to raise an army. Only a few half-breeds from the dregs of the nation, ruined farmers, or half-savage Indians volunteered to serve under the discredited banner of the revolution. They were troops without discipline and almost without equipment, barefoot, their only clothing a pair of patched pants, a square of tattered blanket with a hole in the middle for the head and a broad-brimmed, frayed hat. This was the kind of soldiers Bolívar was not ashamed to command.

And this was the most extraordinary and perhaps the most impressive proof of the man's genius. He submitted to the discouraging, disagreeable conditions which the leader of a revolutionary army must be prepared to accept. This aristocrat by birth, accustomed to all the refinements of comfort and luxury, instinctively inclined toward lofty and resounding enterprises, gave himself over body and soul to the wretched life of a guerrilla leader. Interminable marches on foot and horse, eternal vigilance, constant threat of ambush, encounters in which quarter was neither given nor asked, brutal reprisals — on both sides, to be sure — by command of the leader, although perhaps in his heart he condemned them; panic-stricken routs when everything seemed lost, alternating, in the reddened dust of the afternoons of victory, with the savage cheers of the excited hordes. This existence of grim and heartless savagery, was willingly accepted by the great man, to temper still further his iron will, sustained by an unfaltering conviction of his great destiny.

Bolívar had barely set up his headquarters at Barranca, which he reached about the second week of December, when he began to lay plans for immediately taking the offensive. The regions of the lower Magdalena, in the approximate center of which lay the post of Barranca, was in the power of the Spaniards. The detachments stationed by them along the river made all communication with the interior of New Granada impossible. Nevertheless, Bolívar calculated that by a bold, swift attack he could dislodge the enemy, and he began to make preparations. But Labatut would not even hear of it. He ordered his young adjutant to remain in Barranca awaiting further orders, and himself set out on an expedition to Santa Marta. Thereupon Bolívar made up his mind to appeal directly to President Torices. The latter granted his authorization and on the 21st of December Bolívar was all ready for the undertaking that he alone believed feasible.

The next day, at dusk, the two hundred men Bolívar had selected and equipped, who were willing to follow him, embarked in ten sampans, long flat punts with a thatched reed canopy, rowed by the sturdy boatmen of the country, the *bogas*, who, standing on each side of the boat, pushed it along untiringly with long poles resting firmly against their breast. On the 23rd of December the republicans were but a short distance from Tenerife, the first enemy outpost, which was manned by a force of five hundred. Bolívar sent one of his officers to the Spanish commander, ordering him to surrender. The commander had barely spoken his refusal when the sampans drew up before Tenerife. The republicans leaped ashore, fired on the bewildered soldiers, and the survivors fled in disorder, abandoning this stronghold to what they believed to be a stronger enemy force. The capture of Tenerife, then a thriving, prosperous city, where a small but well-stocked arsenal was found, gave Bolívar the armament he needed. A number of recruits joined him; he strengthened his little fleet, and that same night he set out for Mompox.

This was the beginning of a series of dazzling successes. Mompox received the liberators jubilantly when they disembarked there on December 26. Some twenty young men belonging to the best families and about three hundred volunteers joined him. Fifteen boats armed for war now precede the sampans loaded with arms and munitions. Bolívar finds himself at the head of five hundred men. Two days later he reaches El Banco, from which the Spanish commander, Capdevila, has fled to the interior in the direction of Chiriguana on news of his approach. Bolívar pursues him, overtakes him on January 1, 1813, defeats him, and immediately moves against Captain Capmani, who is in command of the near-by fort of Tamalameque. Another victory. On January 6 the republicans occupy the town of Puerto Real without encountering resistance, and two days later finally enter the important city of Ocaña, which receives them with cheers and acclamation. In fifteen days — that is to say, in less time than it would take a courier to go from Cartagena to Ocaña — Bolívar had routed ten times as many enemies as he had soldiers and had liberated a whole province.

As a result of this brilliant campaign prosperity returned to the government of Cartagena. General Labatut had managed to make himself master of Santa Marta. Once the city had declared itself in favor of independence, not over-enthusiastically, to be sure, Torices immediately had the city council, now headed by General Labatut, proclaim the Constitution of Cartagena. At the same time Torices had sent safe-conducts to the many pirates who operated in the Caribbean, causing considerable damage to the Spanish convoys, which proved highly beneficial to Cartagena. Nevertheless, the errors into which that short-sighted government soon fell paved the way for disastrous setbacks. Only gentleness and persuasion could have made the new regulations imposed by President Torices popular in Santa Marta, and Labatut showed himself a brutal, grasping dictator. He had the principal residents of the city, the majority of whom were Creoles and sincere partisans of the liberal cause, arrested and maltreated because they had dared to ask for a less oppressive regime. He obliged them to hand over to him, making payment in the paper currency Cartagena had introduced into Santa Marta, land, merchandise, securities of every kind, under pretext that the government was in need of them.

This procedure aroused the greatest discontent. The Spaniards, who still held three fourths of the province, sedulously fanned the opposition of the city council and the residents of Santa Marta to their governor. The result was that less than three months after its return to independence, Santa Marta was once more proclaiming the authority of Spain (March 1813).

This type of activity on the part of the Spaniards was not limited to the coast, where, as a matter of fact, they had never lost their predominance. Monteverde, who had managed to extend his authority over nearly all Venezuela, was now considering invading New Granada, just as Bolívar had foreseen. Since the end of 1812 some five thousand excellent troops were stationed at different points in the region of Barinas and the valley of Cúcuta, actively threatening the frontiers of the New Granada provinces of Socorro and Pamplona. The former naval captain Don Antonio Tizcar, whom Monteverde had promised to appoint viceroy of New Granada if they were successful, directed the movements of the army from his headquarters at Barinas. Colonel Ramón Correa was in command of a division of over a thousand men, and early in January 1813 he took up positions at Rosario de Cúcuta.

To oppose the imminent invasion of that dangerous assemblage of superlatively armed and trained forces, the republicans had only the feeble garrisons of Tunja and Pamplona, one comprising slightly more than 500 men, the other, barely 300. The troops at Cundinamarca which Nariño was holding in reserve against a possible thrust from Pasto numbered less than 1,500.

It is not hard to understand the delight of Colonel Manuel del Castillo, commander of the garrison of Pamplona, at the news that Bolívar had reached Ocaña. Without losing a moment he sent a message asking him to come to his aid. It was a source of great satisfaction to Bolívar to comply with this request, for he saw it as a step toward the consolidation of the alliance between the different provinces of New Granada which he considered so essential. He went through the formalities of requesting permission from President Torices, still assuming the role of the latter's military representative, for the troops of Cartagena to co-operate in the defense of the territory of the Confederation. He also notified the President of the United Provinces of New Granada and immediately set about planning the new campaign.

At the head of 500 men, well supplied and armed, Bolívar left Ocaña on the 9th of February, one hour after receiving the authorization he had requested from the government of Cartagena. The column first covered the twelve leagues of desert-like plain seamed by deep ravines that leads to the mountains, and then started up the steep road of Salazar de las Palmas. "To appreciate this undertaking in all its magnitude," writes General O'Leary, "one must have traveled that sinister rock-ribbed road. On the slopes of that endless chain of mountains where, aside from the occasional miserable cave of an Indian, no human trace is to be found, the incessant rains have washed deep gullies. The rays of the sun can never pierce the heavy mists that float above the huge trees whose interlacing branches make even darker the muddy path, which seems always on the point of disappearing. If the explorer ever reaches the summit of the mountains he finds himself on the brink of horrible chasms in whose depths boil roaring rivers. One false step and he is lost. And so height follows height, where night is only a little darker than day, and the raging of the storm and the crash of thunder never cease."

The majority of Bolívar's soldiers were accustomed to the tropical climate of Mompox and Cartagena, and they suffered terribly from the icy winds of the mountains. Only their devotion to their leader kept them from succumbing under the burden of their misery. And despite this they advanced by forced marches. The battered remnants of the expedition had no more than emerged from the mountains when the forces at the command of General Correa tried to ambush them. But Bolívar, avoiding the trap, managed to surprise a Spanish scouting party at Aguada Pass. He hid his men and sent out spies to warn the enemy that he was advancing with a great army.

This stratagem worked perfectly. The Spaniards evacuated Aguada and then all the points they held on the road to Pamplona. While Correa, fearing a full-scale attack, concentrated his troops at San José de Cúcuta, Bolívar joined forces with Castillo, swiftly crossed the Zulia, which was considered impassable, advanced to within ten leagues of the enemy camp, and attacked suddenly on the 28th of February. The battle was a savage one. After a four-hour barrage, bravely withstood by both sides, a furious bayonet charge turned the scales in favor of the republican forces. The royalists left behind them several field pieces and a huge store of arms. Correa managed to escape to La Grita.

This campaign was to have far greater consequences than the one which had preceded it, aside from the tremendous effect it produced in New Granada. Despite all obstacles and suffering, and although all during the passage across the mountains the young Venezuelan colonel had suffered wasting attacks of fever, he had won a victory over the Spaniards as important as it was unexpected. This success constituted a surprising and impressive lesson in resolution, and its stimulating effect was very great. Now that they were free of the nightmare threat of invasion, the people of New Granada recovered awareness of their former hopes. Patriotism, which had become bogged down in civil struggles, raised its head once more. The Congress of the United Provinces was the richer by a million pesos in goods the Spanish merchants had assembled in Cúcuta, counting on the prompt return of the old regime. Besides, Bolívar's and Castillo's victories gave the assembly of Tunja a prestige which would permit it henceforth to consolidate the union of the confederated provinces.

Then, too, Bolívar had found in Camilo Torres, under whose intelligent guidance Congress, in the measures it enacted, was steadily showing a clearer understanding of the country's needs, a whole-hearted admirer. Although he was an ardent advocate of the federalist system, which Bolívar opposed, Torres, nevertheless, had been impressed by the clarity of thought and vision that characterized the Manifesto of Cartagena. The achievements of its author, who had demonstrated his ability to carry out successfully the measures he had advocated, aroused the admiration of the President of the Union. From that moment he became Bolívar's sponsor and attorney at the bar of public opinion of New Granada. On receiving Bolívar's report from "Liberated Cúcuta," in which he gave him the news of his victory over Correa, Torres hastened to communicate the good news to Nariño. "Whatever the present state of our affairs," he wrote as he sent him a copy of Bolívar's report, "I know that you and the illustrious city of Santa Fe de Bogotá will be interested in the news of this report, which I take great pleasure in communicating to you."

And so Bolívar's campaign had the most salutary effect on the dissensions that existed between the Congress and the government of the state of Cundinamarca. Several months later, conferences were opened at which both the delegates of Santa Fe de Bogotá and Tunja showed an equal desire to reach an understanding. It was then that Cundinamarca declared its complete independence from Spain and it seemed as though the period of civil discord was ended.

Yet it seemed to Bolívar that he had done nothing, for there was still so much left to do. The steadily growing forces which President Montes was mobilizing at Quito for a drive against the frontier of New Granada represented a threat of invasion through the Cauca valleys. Don Juan Samano, a sterling officer, who despite his sixty years had lost none of the vigor and bravery that made him a dangerous adversary, had assumed command of the royalist troops quartered near Popayán. He was only waiting to reorganize his forces preparatory to marching on Santa Fe de Bogotá. It was to be hoped that the improved morale of the provinces of New Granada would facilitate their defense, on which Nariño and Congress were jointly at work. It seemed certain that this collaboration, now assured, would make certain the defeat of the royalist troops from that direction. But it was imperative that the Confederation be guarded against all possibility of attack from the north, for Don Antonio Tizcar still held the province of Barinas, and though his forces had been considerably weakened by the defeat of Correa, he still represented no small threat. For all these reasons Bolívar was eager to carry to completion the vast plan of which his two recent campaigns were, from his point of view, but the prelude.

Engage the enemy, disperse his forces, and liberate Venezuela — this was the order of the steps to be taken as he had already outlined them in his program at Cartagena, and the moment had arrived to carry them out. According to the plan he had worked out, Bolívar was counting on the support for his enterprise of each of the several groups that had been organized in New Granada: the Congress of the Union, the government of Cartagena and of Santa Fé. But although he had been assured of the support of the President of the Confederation, Bolívar was not entirely sure that the provisional government headed by Torices would support him without reservations. And Cundinamarca had not yet expressed itself one way or the other.

The truth of the matter was that the patriots who shared the power with Torres, Torices, or Nariño in Tunja, Cartagena, and Santa Fé were not so convinced as their leaders of the bravery and strategic ability of young Colonel Bolívar. His grandiose plans exceeded at least their present ambitions, if not their understanding. Besides, Cartagena and Santa Fe de Bogotá felt themselves in immediate danger, the former from the royalist troops at Santa Marta, the latter from the forces of General Samano. It seemed to them unwise to weaken their garrisons by drawing off troops, and they turned a deaf ear to Bolívar's petition.

Although no material aid was forthcoming, necessary as this seemed, nevertheless the Liberator-to-be insisted that the governing groups of New Granada at least give their formal approval to the liberation of Venezuela. Bolívar's boundless energy, his unlimited faith in victory, made the enterprise seem feasible, regardless of the means at his disposal. The work that he proposed to carry out did not end with the defeat of the Spaniards, however gigantic the task might be, nor even with the liberation of a vast portion of the American continent. These were but the cornerstones of the monument that from that very first moment he planned to erect. The durability and the strength of these foundations would depend upon the fundamental participation of all the elements of which the future edifice was to be built.

So it was that, while requesting President Torices's authorization to lead the troops of Cartagena to the liberation of Venezuela, what Bolívar really wanted above all else was an official order to that effect. His plea to the Congress of the Union was even more urgent, for this body represented the most important coalition of the province of New Granada. On March 1 Bolívar's cousin, José Felix Ribas, left for Tunja carrying several messages to Camilo Torres and one for each member of the assembly. From there he was to proceed to Santa Fe de Bogotá to win over Nariño.

Meanwhile Bolívar had crossed the frontier of Venezuela. He set up his headquarters in Tachera. The booty he had seized in Cúcuta made it possible for him to pay some money to his soldiers, which improved their discipline. He armed them, he instructed them, he drilled them, and he harangued them:

Soldiers: Your liberating arms have reached Venezuela and now one of its cities draws free breath again under your generous protection. In less than two months you have completed two campaigns and you are now undertaking a third, which begins here and which shall end in the land which gave me birth. You republicans are marching to liberate the cradle of Colombian independence as the crusaders delivered Jerusalem, the cradle of Christianity.

. . . The gleam alone of our triumphant arms will clear the Spanish armies from the soil of Venezuela as the mists vanish before the rays of the sun.

All America awaits its liberty and salvation at your hands, you invincible soldiers of Cartagena and the Union. Haste to crown yourselves with glory and win for yourselves the sublime title of Liberators of Venezuela.

These glowing, expressive words, so perfectly suited to the emotions and imagination of his listeners, were addressed to the peoples and authorities of New Granada and America as well. Besides winning for him the absolute devotion of his soldiers, their classic tone and their religious allusions enchanted the spirit of the Creoles, who had been nurtured in these very traditions.

It is impossible not to point out the striking similarity between the attitude of Bolívar at this moment, the arguments he employed, his grasp of the confused aspirations of his countrymen, his passionate desire to win over the opinion of the nation, and that of Bonaparte, general of the army in Italy, "talking to the soldiers and the peoples, but, above both of them, to Paris and to all France . . . rising above the Directory with the authority due the man who talks after accomplishment, not before."

JOSÉ DE SAN MARTÍN (1778-1850)

OF ALL SPAIN'S POSSESSIONS in America none led a more precarious existence for two and a half centuries, to enter suddenly upon a growth as swift as it was unforeseen, than what is today the Argentine Republic. In the beginning, while the monarchy had attempted to exercise a strict control to ensure the Spanish monopoly of trade with America, the port of Buenos Aires had been kept closed. Trade had to be carried on by trans-shipping all merchandise from Panama to the Pacific and then carrying it over the roads that crossed the mountains. This was the situation until the end of the eighteenth century. But when the Bourbons ascended the Spanish throne they reacted against this Habsburg policy. The Plata region, with Buenos Aires as its capital, was made a viceroyalty. The first Viceroy entered upon his duties in 1777; Mexico had been a viceroyalty since 1535. Following the creation of the viceroyalty came freedom of trade: first with Spain, then with foreign colonies. A consulate was opened to handle matters of trade, and the consulate authorized commerce with English ships. Buenos Aires really became a seaport. A new life began for the residents of the city. The growth of the city and its ambitions were simultaneous. The Argentineans felt from that moment that in the future any restriction on their new-found liberties would be an intolerable obstacle to the progress which was delighting them. Farmers and great landowners began to make ever more ambitious appeals to the crown. One drawn up by Mariano Moreno, a man of university training formed in the new trends of thought, contained statements that implied a revolution in the field of administration. From this to the Argentineans' wanting to be the masters of their own destiny was only a step; or a declaration, which was that of May 25, 1810, and the War of Independence had begun. San Martín, the Liberator of the South, the leader in this war, was the son of Spanish parents and had been born in a little town in the interior of the Argentine, Yapeyú. When he was seven years old his parents had taken him back to Spain, and at the time of the Declaration of May he was far from his native land, serving in the Spanish army. His education and the early years of his military career had had Europe for a background. From the Academy of Nobles in Madrid he had gone as a cadet to Africa, when he was only thirteen, to take part in the Battle of Oran. He went later with the Spanish army into France and fought in the victorious Battle of Roussillon. In the naval combat of San Vicente he suffered defeat with the Spaniards at the hands of the fleet commanded by Nelson. He was therefore a soldier of Spain, with a high rank and a fine record of service. But in his heart he felt drawn to the land where he was born, and when he heard of the war in America he laid down the King's sword, made his way to London, and from there embarked for Buenos Aires to offer his services to the rebels. From then on, his figure is fused with the history of the first years of the Argentine Republic. It was he who organized the armies, conceived the strategy of the campaigns, realized that the place to attack the Spaniards was beyond the Andes, crossed over to Chile, fought the Battle of Chacabuco, which meant independence for Chile and Argentina, marched on to Peru, planning to inflict final defeat upon the Spaniards who had been retreating from the north under the blows of Bolívar's implacable sword. San Martín entered Lima in triumph. He then went to Guayaquil for an interview with Bolívar to plan the final blow. San Martín ceded this honor to Bolívar. He left America. In France where he lived the last years of his life, at Boulogne-sur-Mer, nearing seventy, almost blind, he listened while his daughter read him news of America. Accounts of savage guerrilla leaders, revolutions, and a seeming landslide threatening to engulf the liberty won by his grenadiers, that gallant troop of horsemen which he had formed when he reached Buenos Aires and which had covered itself with glory throughout the War of Independence. His own fellow citizens forgot him and even embittered his last years in his country. But he, a soldier of few words, a simple, stout-hearted man, said: "I have a deep faith in the future of America." When the hour of his death drew near he said to his daughter: *"C'est l'orage qui mène au port."* No one in the little city of Boulogne-sur-Mer knew when the two Sisters of Charity crossed his hands upon his breast and knelt with his daughter and grandchildren to pray for his soul.

Don Ricardo Rojas has written a life of San Martín, *El Santo de la Espada* (*The Saint of the Sword*), glowing with fervor and admiration. The pages which follow and which describe San Martín's greatest exploit, the crossing of the Andes, are taken from it.

THE ARMY OF THE ANDES
RICARDO ROJAS

"THE ORIGINAL nucleus of the army known as the Army of the Andes consisted of no more than 180 men from Battalion 11, without any training at all and very poorly disciplined. Eight months before we undertook the march on Chile the government sent out Battalion number 7, which had a strength of 450 foot-soldiers and 220 mounted grenadiers. The rest of the army was recruited in Mendoza. No words can pay fitting tribute to the patriotism and sacrifices of this city during that period."

These were the words of San Martín when, as an old man, in Europe, he recalled the events of his Andean campaign.

For six months Pueyrredon had fulfilled the promises made in Córdoba, sending him all the help he needed in spite of Argentina's lack of resources. In November 1816 the Supreme Director sent his final contribution, and even through the jocular tone in which he advised him to this effect, one can see the strain of the effort he had been making for six months:

> In addition to the 4,000 blankets Córdoba was to send, I am sending you now 500 ponchos, which is all I have been able to get hold of. . . . I have given orders to send you 25,000 pounds of jerked beef by the middle of December. I am enclosing the documents of authorization you requested for the council of that city and for the others in Cuyo. I am sending the dispatches for the officers. I am sending the clothing you asked for and many shirts. If by chance they did not have the blankets in Córdoba, try asking for contributions of blankets, ponchos, or old quilts from the people there and in San Juan. There isn't a family that can't let you have an old blanket. When there's no other way, you have to beg. I am sending you 40 saddles. By mail today I am sending you in a little box the only two clarinets I was able to find. In January of this year 34,675 pounds of jerked beef will be shipped to you. . . . Here are the 2,000 swords you wanted for replacements. Here are 200 campaign tents, and that's all there is. Here is the World. And the Flesh. And the Devil. And I don't see how I'm ever going to get out of the debts I've piled up to pay for all this. Unless I declare myself bankrupt, cancel all my debts and join up with you so you will have to feed me on the jerked beef I am sending you. Damn it, don't ask me for another thing unless you want to get word that my body was found dangling one morning from one of the cross beams of the Fortaleza.

The government of Buenos Aires was in a state of abject poverty, unable to send Belgrano in Tucumán to the north the supplies he needed for his soldiers nor to Güemes in Salta those for his gauchos. The troops of both were half-naked. There was a scarcity of arms and munitions, for there was also fighting going on against the Spanish and Portuguese in the Banda Oriental (Uruguay) besides the internal squabbles. The diplomatic missions the country had sent to Brazil, England, and France called for certain expenditures as well. The budget could not take care of so many drains on it; but ways were found to satisfy San Martín, at least partially, inasmuch as his plans for the Andean campaign carried the seal of approval of the Masonic Lodge, Lautaro, and had been accepted by the government, in which the Masons wielded a strong influence. It was not for nothing that the slogan of this undertaking was "for the complete independence of America and to the glory of the United Provinces." These made the sacrifices although the exploit was San Martín's.

San Martín wrote Guido about his plan in 1816, and he himself anticipates the latter's comments: "I can hear 'my lancer' saying: 'That is the plan of a top sergeant.'" But he knew it was not the plan of a top sergeant.

At the beginning of 1817, the moment set for the march on Chile, the army San Martín had managed to assemble in Cuyo comprised more than 5,000 men, almost the equivalent in numbers of the royalist army against which they were moving. The patriot's army was made up of 3,000 infantry troops, 700 mounted grenadiers, 250 artillerymen, 120 sappers, 1,200 cavalry troops to convoy food and supplies, besides those for medical service, maintenance, quartermaster duty, and communications. No army so well disciplined and equipped had ever been seen in America before, nor had so large a force ever undertaken mountain operations.

The recruiting of all this force was the work of the initiative, ingenuity, skill, devotion, and persistence of San Martín. He had to arouse to action the inhabitants of this sparsely settled region even as disaster was threatening the cause of revolution from without and its champion with political intrigues from within. His own heroic conviction spurred on the faith of the people of Cuyo in his bold enterprise, imbued them with the will to sacrifice needed to fight in far-away regions. Thus he made every man a soldier, personally indoctrinating him, in keeping with his system, in the technical and moral concepts necessary to carry out a concerted military action. The Creole population responded to his call and for two years his ranks were swelled by new recruits.

For his ends he employed the most varied means, and when personal persuasion failed to bring results, he appealed to public pride, as in that proclamation of Mendoza, which reveals the instinct of the popular military leader in him:

"There are 130 swords gathering dust in the barracks of the mounted grenadiers for lack of brave men to wield them. Let those who love their country and their honor come and gird them on."

The 130 volunteers that he needed came to join him, leaving behind their duties and their families on their Argentine farms to follow their illustrious leader, with whom they crossed the Andes, pushing along the Pacific past Ecuador, where a number of them died in combat.

Out of the young men of Spanish descent and good family he formed his officers; of the gauchos, who were of mixed blood in different degrees, he organized his mounted troops, and used the slaves he had liberated for the infantry. To raise the spirits of these last to fighting pitch he showed them, in the camp at Plumerillo, some papers he claimed had been sent him from Chile, saying:

"Here they tell me that if they defeat us the *godos* are going to sell our free Negroes at public auction in Lima. But they won't be able to sell those who are good fighters. . . ."

And how they fought, dying by the thousand in Chacabuco, Marpu, and on the coast of Peru, as Miller admitted in a letter written ten years afterwards!

He incorporated the Chilean émigrés into the Army of the Andes, organizing them in corps which should form the groundwork for the new army of Chile as soon as the country was reconquered. With them he formed the cadres of two regiments of infantry, one of cavalry, an artillery battalion, and, I think, besides, a mobile unit of dragoons known as "the Patriotic Legion of the South." He appointed a committee of outstanding Chileans empowered to act as a provisional government. He entrusted O'Higgins with the major responsibility of this task, thus preparing him for his future duties as Supreme Director of the neighboring country. He discovered in Mendoza, where he had emigrated, Juan Ignacio Zenteno, an innkeeper, whom his compatriots called "the philosopher," and took him from his obscure calling to make him his secretary. So happy was his choice that afterwards Zenteno held important public offices in his country. He put Freyre and Portus in command of the flying squadrons that were to harass the enemy from the south. He addressed all the Chilean émigrés in a manifesto of 1816 in words which touched their hearts:

> Chile, enriched by the blessings of nature, mistress through its geographic position of the Pacific Ocean, fortunate in its population, its industry, and its ease of communication with the neighboring provinces, may be practically called the center of this section of America, and its restoration will establish the basis of our political existence. Peru will yield to its influence and the continent will become one. . . . Nothing must deflect us from our primary object: universal independence. . . . The Chilean army now being constituted will complete this work.

Thus San Martín won over the sympathies of the Chilean soldiers to his plans for America.

There were in Cuyo a number of foreigners from neutral countries, among them a hundred or so Englishmen, mostly émigrés from Chile. These latter interested San Martín most keenly and he contrived to win them over to his cause, not by haranguing them, but through personal conversations, which were his most efficacious method. San Martín was an admirer of British institutions, he knew London, he spoke English fairly well, and he knew the strength of English commercial and naval influence in Valparaiso and all along the Pacific coast toward which he planned to direct his operations if successful in Chile. The names of the British residing in Cuyo at that time have come down to us. They were called Rich, Tuckerman, Lynch, MacGregor, Ferguson, Rowe, Hering, Forbes, Humphrey, Browsen, MacEachan, Wise, Smith, Martin, Holmes, Knowles. . . . They all presented themselves before San Martín to say that "out of gratitude for the hospitality they had received and of their enthusiasm for the rights of man, they could not view with indifference the dangers which threatened the country and were prepared to take up arms and shed their last drop of blood, if necessary, in its defense." San Martín accepted this gallant offer, authorizing the formation of a company of chasseurs, at their own expense, the British Legion to name its own officers. The men met on January 24, 1815 and elected John Young captain, James Lindsay second in command, and John Hefferson lieutenant. Of course the importance of this small group of volunteers was moral rather than military. But in this San Martín followed the policy of Belgrano: "Wars are fought not only with arms but with public opinion." San Martín's aim was that no one in Cuyo should be a foreigner and that the American cause should show its character of universality. Some of these good Britishers left descendants in our countries.

Among the Chilean émigrés there were some supporters of Carrera, O'Higgins's rival, who were trouble-makers. He managed to send them away or reduce them to insignificance. He did the same with the Spaniards and Portuguese whose loyalty had not been clearly demonstrated, taxing them heavily or putting them into confinement. By the end of 1815 he had written to Godoy Cruz: "With regard to the foreigners, do you know they've all left here, and tomorrow the bad Americans and a few Portuguese are going? That is making a clean sweep." In this way San Martín improved public opinion in Cuyo, brought about unity of spirit among all its inhabitants, without overlooking even the Indians to the south, reshaping them all in the mold of a single ideal, his own, until he had recruited the 5,000 men he needed for his army. From the plains of La Rioja in the north to the banks of the Diamante in the south, all along the Andean range, the invincible will of the great leader disciplined the spirit of the people, organized the forces and laid the plans for invasion.

In the carrying out of this enterprise it is difficult to know whether to admire San Martín more as the leader who assembles his forces, the strategist who trains his soldier, or the scrupulous, painstaking administrator which he shows himself to be in the preparation of his transport services and materials of war.

The supplies for the army were prepared partly in Buenos Aires and the rest in Mendoza, where San Martín had appointed Fray Luis Beltran quartermaster. This strange personage had been discovered by San Martín in a monk's cell in Mendoza. He was a native of that city, son of a French father, and former chaplain of the Chilean army. He was self-taught in mathematics, physics, and chemistry, a man of keen intelligence who knew the country well, and he displayed in the performance of his duties as quartermaster a resourcefulness and activity comparable only to his patriotic zeal. In 1816 he left his order, donned the uniform of a colonel, and crossed the Andes with the army. He melted down the church bells to make cannon and bullets; he made powderhorns out of cows' horns; for months he manufactured gun carriages, knapsacks, brogans, saddles, horseshoes, bayonets, swords. In the workshop he set up, lighted by the glow of the forges, the sound of hammer and saw never ceased day or night. San Martín wanted cannon equipped to cross the ravines and rivers that lay ahead of them. "You want cannon with wings — you shall have them," said Fray Luis and he built portable bridges and invented an apparatus consisting of a capstan and cables which later proved very useful.

San Martín found other collaborators in Mendoza. One was Major José Antonio Álvarez Condarco of Tucumán, who knew something about engineering, to whom he assigned the manufacture of gunpowder, making use of the water power and the deposits of saltpeter which are to be found in this region. Major Plaza and Captain Picarte were put in charge of ordnance, and great strictness was enjoined in the care and inspection of arms. He ordered the miller Tejeda of Mendoza to set up a fulling mill run by water power to mill the cloth woven of goat hair in San Luis for the soldiers' clothing. The cloth was dyed blue and the women sewed the uniforms for nothing. Dr. Vera y Pintado of Santa Fé was entrusted with the administration of military justice in accord with the ordinances that had been issued. Dr. David Parossien, an Englishman, and Zapata, a Peruvian, were put in charge of medical services. José Gregorio Lemos was made responsible for the scrupulous administration of the army's finances. In the fever of his dream San Martín utilized every resource that he could lay hand upon. Nobody in Cuyo but felt the spur of his powerful will. There was nothing for which his ingenuity could not devise some use. The army was short of money and shoes. They could make sandals and brogans for the soldiers from the hides of the animals that were slaughtered for the city's meat supply, which had been allowed to go to waste before.

Cuyo responded generously to San Martín's appeal, more than justifying the warmth with which he described to the government the sacrifices these provinces had made when he had finished his preparations for the expedition in 1816. "It is amazing," he says, "how a region with relatively little population, without public revenues, without commerce or large cities, which lacks lumber and basic materials, has been able to raise by its own resources an army of three thousand men, stripping itself even of its slaves, its only man power for agriculture; provide for their pay and maintenance and that of over a thousand émigrés; build up stocks of supplies, manufacture saltpeter and gunpowder, ordnance, munitions, cloth, set up barracks and camps; requisition over three thousand horses, seven thousand mules, innumerable head of cattle; patrol the Andes with its soldiers; give the services of its workmen. . . . America is free. Its enemies cannot stand up against such solid virtues."

The virtues of Cuyo, despite its poverty, were sublime; but the moving spirit of Cuyo was San Martín. Because of his initiative, and the care he took in every phase of its realization, the army of Cuyo was the work of his genius. A master of souls and a craftsman of wills, he worked for years at its creation, until the sun of America bathed it in its glory.

Álvarez Condarco, the engineer of Tucumán, was assigned the drawing up of maps of the Andes. San Martín said to him:

"Major, I am going to send you on a very delicate diplomatic mission to Chile."

"You're sending me, general?" the surprised officer replied.

"Yes. But your real assignment is to make a mental map of the Los Patos and Uspallata roads. You must not take any notes, but you must not forget one stone."

Álvarez Condarco had an extraordinary topographical memory, which explains why the choice fell on him.

"I'll send you by the Los Patos road, which is the longer and more remote of the two; and since it is certain that as soon as you hand over the papers you are to carry, they will send you out of the country without further consideration, by the shortest possible route, which is that of Uspallata — that is, if they don't hang you — you will have made the round trip and can draw up a sketch for me on your return."

Álvarez Condarco bowed with an air of patient resignation.

"Go get ready, and remember that secrecy is of the essence."

Álvarez Condarco's mission ostensibly was to present himself before President Marcó in Santiago and deliver to him a communication from San Martín in which the latter, as governor of Cuyo, advised him that the Provinces of the Plata had declared their independence. Marcó received the sheet, ordered it burned in the public square, and dictated a haughty reply. It is told that as he signed his answer he said:

"And the hand that signs this is white, not black like that of San Martín," alluding to the dark skin of the insurgent general.

In consideration of the quasi-diplomatic nature of his commission, Álvarez Condarco was not clapped into prison, but was ordered to leave Chile immediately. He returned to Mendoza and there drew up the maps San Martín needed, for, as he said, "We cannot go on making war as though we were Hottentots."

In his archives there is to be found the fullest and most detailed documentation of the march of his enterprise. This contains the most minute instructions regarding the handling of animals and equipment, and even how the arms must be cared for in the inclemency and cold of the mountains.

San Martín was not content with building up his material resources in the gifted manner described. He employed equally ingenious methods to disconcert Marcó, having patriotic agents supply false information to the royalists, and letting letters designed to that end fall into the hands of the Spaniards.

He utilized every moral force he could command, without overlooking the religious sentiment which is so important in the Spanish-American countries, and which it is so difficult to turn to political advantage without using sound psychological instinct.

San Martín was born and brought up in a Catholic family and trained in the army of Christian Spain; he lived in countries that were ingenuously superstitious; yet he belonged to the "age of

Enlightenment"; he had come under the influence of the doctrine of regalism of the ministers of Charles III and the contagion of the liberalism of the French Encyclopedists.

In an answer that was written but not sent to José Miguel Carrera, explaining the death of the Carrera brothers, San Martín said: "I swear before God and America." God and America were his two divinities.

He believed in God, whom he always invoked, and respected the religion of his parents; but in his capacity as leader he used the Church shrewdly for political purposes. He was neither clerical nor anticlerical. His genius kept him from going to either extreme. As an illustration of how far this freedom of spirit went, I shall cite two instances.

On May 13, 1815, in Mendoza, he issued a letter resembling a pastoral to the "priests and prelates," in which he decreed that priests in their homilies and sermons shall point out the justice of America's adoption of the liberal system, that "they go into the matter at length," explaining "the legitimacy of a government established by the will of all and the punishment that will be meted out to those who disobey it," including the clergy who will be punished "if they fail to fulfill this sacred duty."

On another occasion, July 5 of the same year 1815, he wrote to the prior of the Franciscan Order in Mendoza advising him that the friars Agustín Muñoz, Miguel del Sar, Francisco Yares, and Joaquin Carao "are unsympathetic to the sacred cause of our political regeneration" and ordering them "incapacitated to hear confession or preach," adding that "they are to be confined to the cloister until further notice."

This communication to the prior, signed by San Martín, concludes: "This government, which is well aware of your fervent patriotism, has no doubt that this order will be scrupulously carried out."

It was not unknown to him that preachments were being made against him from the pulpits in Chile. There the royalist clergy, at the service of Marcó, called the patriots of Cuyo "detestable heretics, spawn of hell, emissaries of Satan, thirsting after blood and rapine." One friar, by the name of Zapata, said that he should not be called San Martín because he was not a saint, but just Martín, like his namesake Luther, for like him he was a heretic. The laying down of rules regarding preaching and the separation of a priest from the confessional are acts of the ecclesiastical authorities. San Martín exercised this episcopal prerogative without a scruple. Someone said that free America would triumph "unless God is a reactionary." But God is not a reactionary. And for this reason San Martín believed in God.

In his determination to utilize all the elements that could help further his plan of emancipation, he did not disdain even the collaboration of the Indians. There are Araucanian tribes to the south of Mendoza which inhabit strategic points in the mountains. Through these passes in the south he was able to establish contact with the Araucanians of Chile and upset the royalist authority there.

The winning over of the Indians to the cause of emancipation was, from the beginning, a part of the plans of the Argentine revolution. As early as 1810 Moreno had announced it in the Junta, as had his representative Castelli when he proclaimed the liberty of the native peoples from the pre-Incan ruins of Tiahuanaco when he entered Upper Peru. Argentine manifestos, written in Quechua and Aymará, were circulated among the Indians of the north. Belgrano addressed the peoples of the coast and Paraguay in Guarany. San Martín used Araucanian for the Pampas, Pehuenches, and Mapuches of the mountains south of Mendoza. On the other side of the Diamante River, at Fort San Carlos, the natives had been convoked in the name of the government of Buenos Aires to appeal for their support. The Secretary of the Treasury, Don Alexo Navarro, distributed gifts among them and harangued them in this fashion: "Your fortunate descendants will not see the rule of tyranny and despotism in our America. We and you, who were born on this soil which has so often been stained with the blood of our forefathers, will be the rulers. We shall restore the compassion and justice which characterized the rule of the Incas." This sentiment of historical continuity made the war of liberation seem in the nature of a revindication, and in 1816 it gave rise to the plan to restore the Incas in Cuzco. San Martín utilized these measures, whether out of conviction or expediency we cannot say. The fact is that in 1816 he made a trip to the banks of the Diamante and at the above-mentioned Fort of San Carlos called together the chief and headmen of the region to confer with them. More than fifty of these chieftains held sway in these Andean valleys of the south. The names of some of them were Calimilla, Millatur, Antepan, Jamin, Huanguenecul, Manquipi, Peñalef, Goyco, Marilinco, Epiman, Aucai, Neyancari, Necuñan. The last named acted as spokesman; he was an old man with long white hair and he spoke in Araucanian. Friar Ynalican, the chaplain of the converted Indians, acted as interpreter to San Martín. San Martín's idea was to form an alliance with the Indians and have them guard the passes to the south of Chile, and at the same time make the royalists on the other side believe they planned to invade them there. San Martín took to San Carlos from Mendoza several mule trains carrying brandy, wine, cloth, sweets, saddles, and glass beads for his new friends. The Indians celebrated the visit with bacchic feasts which lasted six days, at the end of which San Martín returned to Mendoza with the pact of alliance he had set out to secure. The chiefs lavished attentions on San Martín and each one embraced him when he left, to the accompaniment of libations and dances, ceremonies in which the hero resignedly played his part.

At the close of the year 1816 several chiefs came to Mendoza bringing news to San Martín, who received them in his camp at Plumerillo. The general and the chiefs sat gathered together in a circle on the floor, and he spoke to them through the interpreter Guajardo:

"I have gathered you together here to inform you that the Spaniards are going to come from Chile with their army to kill all the Indians and carry off the women and the children. Therefore, *as I, too, am an Indian,* I am going to make an end of these *godos* who have stolen the lands of your ancestors, and to do this I shall cross the Andes with my army and with these cannon."

In his *Memoirs* Manuel Olazabal, an eyewitness, who heard that significant phrase: "I, too, am an Indian," writes: "The army was drilling with great show at that moment and the artillery was firing with a racket, which made a great impression on the Indians."

"I shall have to cross the Andes to the south," added San Martín, "but for this I need your permission, for you are the masters of this region."

He did not intend to go by the south, but said this to deceive Marcó, who weakened his army by deploying it on two fronts.

The Araucanian emissaries, brawny, naked, "smelling of horse," broke into cheers and applause for the "Indian" San Martín, whom they embraced, promising to die with him.

With skill and patience San Martín worked for two years in Cuyo until at the end of 1816 he had built up the Army of the Andes with its full complement of men and materials. The only men not under arms were the essential farmers, shepherds and workmen; but the whole country was a supply depot and camp. Even women, children, and friars took part in the work of those last feverish days that preceded the expedition.

On the eve of its departure the expeditionary force of the Andes had over 10,000 saddle- and pack-mules, 1,600 cavalry horses, and 600 head of cattle to be slaughtered on the march. All these "self-propellers" filed away along the narrow winding mountain trails. San Martín and the 5,200 men who accompanied him in the crossing of the Andes were mounted on mules. There were other mules for replacements or carrying the munitions: 9,000 rounds of ammunition for rifles and carbines, 2,000 cannon balls, 2,000 charges of grapeshot, 600 grenades. The cannon were dismounted from their carriages on to special carts, and the apparatus invented in Mendoza was carried along to hoist them across the ravines. The beasts of burden also carried the provisions: corn, flour, jerked beef, in strips or ground up with fat and red pepper, hardtack, cheese, wine, brandy, all that was needed for the frugal maintenance of 5,200 men during the two weeks calculated for the crossing until they descended to the plains of Chacabuco. Food was stored at posts along the road in case of a retreat. Fodder also had to be carried for the animals, corn, barley, and even wood for fires, because of the lack of vegetation on the arid heights of the Andes. A supply of drugs was necessary, too, and onions and garlic in quantity for the chills, nausea, and nose-bleeding caused by the altitude. All the mounts had been wintered in the alfalfa-fields of Cuyo and newly shod before they started. The army also had guides and messengers.

When the moment came to leave, that great machine of men, animals, and objects swung into motion, directed by the genius of San Martín and driven by his irresistible will. What a difference between this and the war of the Plata and the coast which the rivalry of its leaders had turned into anarchic confusion, or that of northern and Upper Peru, bogged down from lack of preparation and reverses. This enterprise of Cuyo and the Andes was to be carried out with mathematical precision, the logical outcome of its disciplined organization and its material preparation. To this end San Martín had prepared maps of the mountain range; he had learned from cattle-drovers and guides the exact lay of the terrain; he had adapted his plans to the geographical situation; through the work of secret agents he had undermined public opinion in Chile; he had split the enemy front through misleading news about the possible points of attack, and he made Marcó, the royalist leader, fight a war of surprise attacks which destroyed him morally and materially.

Everything was ready for the "Let's go," as San Martín would say, when he added to all the preliminaries the final touch: an appeal to the æsthetic and religious emotions, which are patriotic forces, too, by reason of their effect on mass psychology. With this in mind he formed his army in camp at Plumerillo in their dress uniforms and, riding at their head, he led them into the city of Mendoza through the cañada and they marched to the cathedral along streets bedecked with flowers, banners, hangings, and national emblems. He proclaimed the Virgin the patroness of the army of liberation, as Belgrano had done in Tucumán; and then in the main square, before the assembled soldiers and populace, he raised the flag of the Andes on high, calling for the oath of allegiance. The flag, which had been embroidered by his wife and the ladies of Mendoza, was white and green, with a shield showing two hands holding on high the cap of liberty of the French Revolution above the peaks of the Andes, flanked by branches of Andean laurel and olive, and over the shield a rising sun. A profound silence fell upon the crowd as they saw the banner raised aloft by the leader. San Martín from the platform where he stood, his head uncovered, holding up the flag he planned to carry to Lima, called out with a thundering voice:

"Soldiers, this is the first flag of the independence that has been blessed in America."

He waved it three times through the air and its folds fluttered in the breeze from the near-by Andes.

The crowd and the troops cried out together: "Long live the nation!" And San Martín added laconically:

"Soldiers, swear to support it and die in its defense, as I do."

"We swear!" answered ten thousand voices as one.

The salvos of the cannon, the shouts of the crowd, the pealing of the bells, re-echoed through the city to the mountains with a tumult unheard since the Andes were created by the fire and water of some geological cataclysm.

The afternoon of the same day there was a great celebration, with bull-fights and riding exhibitions and a dance at night in the bull-ring. Groups of Indians, gauchos, mulattoes, and Negroes, mounted and in costume, took part in the bull-fight. San Martín and his wife were present at both the festivities, and as San Martín watched the zest with which they fought the bulls, he said to one of his officers: "The country can make good use of these madmen."

A young officer threw a bull in the ring; with his knife he castrated it and offered the testicles (which are considered a great delicacy) to Doña Remedios. It was an embarrassing moment, but San Martín, who was sitting in the box with her, told her to accept the gift, which she blushingly did.

The busy year of 1816 was over; early the following year, one hot afternoon in January, a peddler came to the house of Solar in Santiago de Chile, entered the patio, and shouted through the silence: "I have fat hens to sell, master."

The master of the house got up from his siesta and went out into the patio at once, to the surprise of his wife, and when he came back he told her he had bought some chickens.

Years later a son of Solar, who told the story, learned that the peddler was a disguised spy of San Martín's whom the latter had sent out from Mendoza on the eve of his crossing of the Andes. With the chickens he had handed Solar a note from San Martín saying:

"January 15. Brother S.: I am sending 4,000 pesos by way of Los Patos; in a month your brother José will be with you."

These were ruses "brother José" frequently employed; the 4,000 pesos were 4,000 soldiers.

A few days later the Army of the Andes set out from Mendoza toward the mountains.

DOM PEDRO (1825–91)

AMONG THE VARIOUS FEATURES that characterize Brazil within the Latin-American world, not the least is that of having been the only monarchy that managed to subsist during almost the entire past century within a republican America. Mexico had two ephemeral monarchies, that of Iturbide (July–December 1822) and of Maximilian (1863–7), whereas Brazil was a monarchy from 1822, the year in which it proclaimed its independence and Dom Pedro I was crowned King, until 1889, when Dom Pedro II abdicated and the republican spirit of the nation prevailed. In the last years of the colonial period, as a result of the Napoleonic invasion, the Portuguese court was transferred to Rio de Janeiro. In this way the country became acquainted with court life, of which certain traces still exist in the nation, as, for example, in its elaborate diplomatic procedure. When the country was ripe for freedom, it was the Prince Dom Pedro who gave the cry: "Independence or Death," waving his hat in the air. He was crowned Emperor. He tried to be an absolute monarch and he finally lost the affection of his people. One day, in the ninth year of his reign, he was received in the capital with the cry "Long live the King if he rules by the Constitution!" There were disturbances. A battle broke out between his partisans and his opponents, to which history has given the name of "Garrafadas" because the weapons they employed were bottles. It was impossible for Dom Pedro to try to continue in power and he abdicated in favor of his son, Pedro de Alcantara, who was only six years old. A regency followed (1831–40). The Regency, in turn, was unpopular, and when Dom Pedro was fourteen years old, he was petitioned to take over the power. He replied: "I'm ready now," and ascended the throne.

Dom Pedro II ruled forty years. They were all years of strife. A long struggle with Uruguay and the Argentine of Rosas made the international situation difficult, and it was highlighted by the war with Paraguay. While an attempt was being made to stabilize the southern frontier, the country on the home front was developing upon the great stage nature has built it. The "bandeirantes" were extending their conquest of the interior. Railways were being built. Coffee plantations and rubber-gathering were begun. Faced by such vexing problems as those with the Church, and with the Freemasons, headed by the Minister Viscount of Rio Branco, carrying out a policy as debatable as it was debated, Dom Pedro presided over the growth of his country with all the enthusiasm of a real ruler and, above all, with the spirit of a liberal philosopher. There have been few heads of state in America who have shown such a marked predilection for letters, arts, and sciences. His determined stand in favor of the emancipation of the slaves brought him into conflict with the great landholders, who had based the economic life of the country on the work of the Negro. The struggle in Brazil might have been as fierce as that in the United States. Perhaps Dom Pedro saved his country from a civil war, but he forfeited to his ideas the future of the monarchy, which had clashed with the leading families and the rising middle class. Moreover, the monarch's own ideas did not constitute a defense of the crown. When the hour of the Republic arrived, it did not meet an obstacle in Dom Pedro — not even an adversary. His grandson's tutor and his own close friend Benjamin Constant, the zealous advocate of Positivism, was the mind of the republican revolution. When Manoel Deodoro da Fonseca engineered his *coup d'état*, Dom Pedro quietly left the throne. He withdrew to Europe and, until his death, maintained the dignity and nobility of the last Emperor of Brazil.

In the following pages from the *History of Dom Pedro II*, by the Brazilian diplomat and historian Heitor Lyra, the quality of the Emperor's intellectual interests can be gauged.

HISTORY OF THE REIGN OF DOM PEDRO II

HEITOR LYRA

THE INTEREST and patronage the Emperor accorded to artists, men of letters, scientists — the sages, as they were generally known, the *doctors* the Empress called them — aroused great comment. A famous caricature of the time shows the Emperor landing at a foreign port; he has no sooner stepped ashore than he turns, with a worried, half-disappointed expression to the local authorities who have come to receive him, saying: "Where are the sages? Aren't there any sages in this country? I want to see the sages."

The Emperor, to be sure, was not a sage, although, to annoy him, it was said that it was his ambition to be. Certain papers which were in the possession of the Viscount of Siminbu contain a sort of self-defense in which he confesses, exaggerating somewhat, his lack of formal education: "To accuse me of claiming to be a sage is as groundless as if I were accused of aspiring to personal power. Moreover, the duties of my position leave me little leisure for study. I read what I have time for, but can this give me what I would need to know to become a sage?"

And farther on: "Anyone who has been made the head of a government at the age of fourteen — and I may say here that if I had not been little more than a child at the time I would not have acquiesced — cannot have learned enough to consider himself wise, if he has good sense."

He was not a learned man. Not because in his childhood he had received only the secondary education that was usual among children of his day and age, but because sages are never made by schoolmasters.

But just as he found time in the midst of his many and absorbing duties, to complete his education and raise it to an unusual level, he might have become, with the patience and perseverance that characterized him, and with the help of his prodigious memory, a true sage in some special branch of human knowledge.

But if he never came to be a sage, neither was he merely an educated man. He was more than that: he was a real scholar. He possessed the insatiable thirst for knowledge of the scholar, an unflagging interest in everything having to do with intellectual matters.

"If I were not Emperor," he said on one occasion, "I should like to have been a teacher. I know of no nobler calling than that of directing the young mind and preparing the men of tomorrow." This inclination toward teaching was to remain with him all his life. Besides, his chief concern, from the beginning to the end of his reign, was to teach the men of public affairs in Brazil to govern the country in accordance with a constitutional, representative system. If his teachings did not produce the results that might have been expected, the fault did not lie with him; if the plant did not sprout, it was not because the seed was bad or the sower careless, but because the ground was not prepared for a product of this sort. The Emperor had bent his efforts to teaching us to govern a democracy. But he forgot that, in the last analysis, Brazil lacked the principal requirement for this: true democracy. This led people to say, with perfect justification, that he spent fifty years pretending to govern a free people. It would perhaps be closer to the truth to say an educated people; for liberty cannot flourish where education does not exist. And Brazil at that time was not an educated nation, as it is not now, nor will be for some time.

It was said of the Emperor that his learning was shallow but covered a wide range. That is true. In this respect, as in many others, he was an exception among our statesmen, who were interested only, or principally, in party politics. They lived exclusively, or almost exclusively, by politics, for politics, with politics — in the worst sense of the word. Outside of that nothing interested them. Public life, then as now, formed an impassable barrier to any scholarly activity. The great majority satisfied their thirst for knowledge with a quick leafing-through of newspapers or magazines.

José Verissimo says that the Emperor was perhaps the only person who was interested in anything except elections, political intrigues, distribution of favors, appointments, or similar matters. "His ministers were not always able to conceal their disapproval of his attitude, and there were some who must have found it extremely bewildering when he began talking to them about Renan's latest book or some recent publication of the Academy of Science."

Neither could they understand the value of certain acts of the Emperor, who made a point of honoring the outstanding intellectual figures of his time. He was never lavish in bestowing honorary decorations of the Empire, especially among foreigners. His selection was always rigorous. Nevertheless, he did not always have the approval of his ministers when he conferred a distinction on a scholar or scientist who really deserved it. On occasions of this sort he had to defend his candidate with the most cogent arguments. This was the case, for instance, when the Emperor proposed Renan's name for the Order of the Rose, and was opposed by the Ministry of the Viscount Rio Branco.

Moreover, there is a certain incongruity in that this Ministry, headed by the Grand Master of Freemasons of Brazil, enemy of the Catholic bishops, who had two of them imprisoned, should have objected to conferring a decoration on Renan on the grounds that his doctrines were too materialistic.

The Emperor was, above all, a great reader. When he was not attending official ceremonies or in session with his cabinet, he spent almost all the free time at his disposal with books or journals. He would pass hour after hour in one of the rooms of the library at São Cristovão — unquestionably the finest private library in the Empire and possibly one of the finest in the world — leaning back in an armchair or bent over the table with an open book, the famous horn-rimmed pince-nez slipping off his nose, a pencil in his hand, taking notes on the passages that interested him most.

He read everything — religious and political history, philosophy, geography, medicine, law, anthropology, geology, astronomy, natural science, literature, history of art. He had an insatiable desire for knowledge. "My father read a great deal and read everything," his daughter said of him; "one of his favorite books and one that he always recommended was Bossuet's *Variations*."

Above everything else he loved to read the Bible. That great book seemed to him not only the basis of our religion but one of the finest examples of writing. He called the prophets the first poets of the world. Whether it was Jeremiah lamenting the fate of his people, or Isaiah describing the downfall of Babylon, or Daniel foretelling the coming of the Messiah and the destruction of the four great empires, all those pages filled him with profoundest emotion. "These are pages," he said, "which might well fill the human heart with pride even if they were not divine revelation."

Among the historians of antiquity his favorite was Thucydides, "Demosthenes' model," he called him, as he might have been of all historians because of his method and the good judgment with which he analyzed what the Emperor called the origins, the motives, and the consequences of events. He spent considerable time translating the great Greek historian, and in his enthusiasm he wrote Gobineau: "In my moments of leisure I translate Thucydides; how I should love to re-read his funeral oration before the ruins of the Acropolis." Tacitus, in his opinion, was "concise, impartial, honest, philosophic." He admired his conciliating, tolerant nature, especially because he was, said the Emperor, "the eloquent disciplinarian of crime and tyranny."

He loved to write verses. He was afflicted, like most of the Brazilians of his day, with this harmless weakness. He dashed them off, on any scrap of paper that came to hand, without much thought as to form or content.

Being of a modest nature, he never considered himself a poet in the true sense of the term. For this he really lacked many qualities. His poems are, except for an occasional verse, really mediocre. "I know perfectly well that I am not a poet," he confessed on one occasion. "I write verses once in a while as an intellectual pastime when I have nothing else to do. But they cannot be called poetry. I show them to my close friends, but I should never want to see them in print."

His translations of certain poets, generally French, are no better, from the point of view of poetry, than his own verses. Nevertheless, some of them were warmly praised by their authors, although, of course, allowance should be made for their natural feeling of gratitude.

Longfellow, for example, wrote him in connection with the Emperor's translation of his *Story of King Robert of Sicily:* "The translation is very faithful and very successful. The double rhymes give a new grace to the narrative, and the old legend seems very musical in the soft accents of the Portuguese."

One of the Emperor's great enthusiasms was the study of foreign languages. In this respect he was justly recognized as the greatest linguist of his country and perhaps one of the greatest of his day. "I love the study of languages, especially their comparative study," he remarked, and added, without false modesty: "I can translate at sight Latin and English, both of which I speak fluently, Greek and German, which, however, I speak badly. I have spoken French since I first began to talk, and Italian and Spanish from childhood. As for other languages, I have studied them only in connection with philology, although I have translated them."

His interest in foreign languages, especially those known as dead languages, lay, to him, in their general cultural value. Perhaps for this reason he did not trouble to study them exhaustively. It was enough for him to know them. Renan said that everyone should know thoroughly two languages: Latin and his own; but that he should be able to understand all those that might be useful to him in his occupation and for his education.

It was possibly with this idea in mind that the Emperor set out to study the language of the Tupi and Guarany Indians, Arabic,

Provençal, Hebrew, and Sanskrit. "I have found a German who is very well prepared in philological studies," he writes Gobineau in January 1875, "Dr. Henning, and I have begun the study of Sanskrit."

Of these languages, it was perhaps Hebrew and Provençal that interested him most. His curiosity about the history and literature of the Jews was so keen that he acquired a thoroughgoing knowledge of Hebrew, and in the Central Synogogue of London and in that of San Francisco, California, he was seen translating at sight from the Talmud or old Semitic documents. The proof of the progress he made in this language is his translations of Hebrew-Provençal poetry, which were later published in France, during his exile.

Hebrew began to interest him during the war with Paraguay, during the long weary evenings in Petropolis. His first teacher of this language was a Swedish Jew, Akerblom. Later he had another, a German Protestant minister, Koch, who was the tutor of the children of Countess Barral, Princess Isabel's governess. When Koch died he was replaced by Dr. Carlos Henning, who began to teach him Sanskrit, and a little later by Dr. C. F. Seybold, a highly learned man, professor of Oriental languages.

Seybold also taught him Arabic, the study of which he had begun in 1875 with the Austrian Minister in Rio, Baron Schreiner, whom the Emperor had met four years before during his first trip to Egypt. "The Emperor comes for his Arabic lesson every day, and he did not omit his lesson even today, which strikes me as being very interesting," wrote Dr. Schreiner on the day of the birth of Dom Pedro, Princess Isabel's first child.

To people in general, and especially in political circles, the Emperor's fondness for exotic languages was the source of comment, cruelly sarcastic, when not frankly derisive. But none of this deterred him from his purpose, which he carried out with the perseverance that characterized him. He knew that this opposition came from envy, spiteful ignorance, bad faith, lack of understanding of things of the spirit. His friend Gobineau said to him once, referring to the hostility with which Renan's book on Semitic languages was received in France: "In such a society as the French have become, anyone who knows Arabic is guilty of insolence because he knows something no one else does."

The Emperor's interest in intellectual things manifested itself early, almost from youth. When he was not yet thirty years old Alexandre Herculano called him "the Prince who, in the general opinion, is one of the foremost of his time because of his spiritual endowments, and because of his application of these gifts to the cultivation of science and letters." Nothing proves this better than the love — and the expression is used advisedly — he lavished from boyhood and all the rest of his life on the Brazilian Institute of History and Geography.

This institution was, so to speak, his own creation. In 1839, when he was barely fourteen years old, he decided to put one of the rooms of the city palace at the service of the Institute for its meetings. In 1842 he founded prizes for the best works dealing with the history and geography of Brazil. From there on, his interest in the institution was unflagging. He gave it the library that had belonged to von Martins, which was a treasure house of works on America; the collection of manuscripts which had been assembled for the Imperial government; the library he had collected during his travels in North America, as well as many other rare books and manuscripts, his own collection of coins and medals, and copies of documents bearing on the history of Brazil which had been taken from Portuguese archives. Out of his own pocket he contributed to defray the Institute's expenses of installation, and hardly a session was held that he did not attend, encouraging with his presence all those who devoted themselves to the study of the history and geography of Brazil.

He often took part in the discussions. He gave his opinion modestly, not to overawe the others, about the topics under consideration. He also intervened in the naming of new members, a matter he watched over with the greatest care, with the same scrupulousness that went into the appointment of government officials, that *tyrannical morality* Oliveira Lima refers to. When the meetings were over he generally stayed on for a while. It was a common sight to see him surrounded by a group of the members, unaffected and at ease, talking animatedly, answering, questioning, with a simplicity and modesty rarely seen.

His inquiring spirit was manifold in its interests. He had inherited from his mother a taste for natural science, as well as a plant collection, which he devotedly kept in the Boa-Vista Park. On the beautiful nights of the tropics he would go up to the observatory he had built in the top of the palace, from which he could observe and study the mystery of the stars. He was the discoverer of a new comet.

This interest of his in astronomy was one of the aspects of his activities that most attracted the shafts of satire and criticism, partly to embarrass him, partly to amuse the public. One year during the carnival in Rio, there was a float that became celebrated, showing a puppet, meant to be the Emperor, looking through a telescope, trying to discover the secrets of Venus gleaming enticingly on the horizon.

The Emperor was accused of not being sincere in his interest in intellectual matters and persons. There were those who alleged that this was pure snobbishness, the attitude of a poseur whose ambition it was to appear, particularly abroad, as a monarch who was the patron of arts and sciences, a new Augustus who had arisen in the rude lands of the New World.

Up to a certain point there was a touch of this vanity in him. "Oh, happy Augustus, who knew, rewarded, and inspired great Horace and Virgil," he exclaimed on one occasion. But what should be borne in mind is the part this so-called vanity played in the development of arts, letters, and sciences in the Empire, to the improvement of the cultural level of a nation like ours, which stood in such great need of this. In this respect, as in the field of politics and public administration, the Emperor exercised a civilizing influence upon us.

To help artists, to raise them from obscurity, to stimulate the study or diffusion of their work was in the Emperor's eyes almost an obligation. At any rate, he understood it as a duty that was incumbent upon him as head of the state.

When the family of the great actor João Castano was left in great distress and difficulties, almost poverty-stricken, the Emperor assigned them a pension, which he paid from his own funds, of 800,000 milreis, which was a considerable sum in those days.

In December 1877 he wrote to Gobineau, who was then living in Rome: "I would ask you to find out for me what you can about a painter who was born in Brazil, of Italian parents, who is studying with Monteverde. I hear that he shows great talent." Gobineau promptly secured the information for him. He went in person to see the artist: "I saw in his studio a large bas-relief which he has begun, and which is for the Academy of Rio — *The Martyrdom of St. Sebastian.* The work reveals great talent." The Emperor replied: "What you say about young Bernardelli makes me very happy." The artist in question was to become Brazil's greatest sculptor and the Emperor discovered him, poor, obscure, and still a boy, in Monteverde's studio.

Pedro Americo de Figueiredo was another artist the Emperor helped develop. The monarch met him on the occasion of a visit to the Pedro II School, where he surprised him during a class in mathematics furtively drawing a sketch of him on a sheet of paper. He was impressed by the boy's ability and sent him to study at the School of Fine Arts, paying all his expenses. Some time after this he sent him to study painting in Europe, still at his expense. This was in 1858. In May 1860 the Emperor wrote asking for "a report on the work of the student of painting Pedro Americo de Figueiredo, so he may judge whether it warrants the continued favor of His Majesty's support."

Carlos Gomes, at the age of twenty-three, left his parents' home in Campinas and came to Rio. From there he wrote to his father: "It is my intention to see the Emperor in the hope of securing his assistance to study in the conservatory here." He entered the conservatory, headed then by Francisco Manuel, and two years later his first opera, *O Noite no Castelo,* was presented, followed in 1863 by *Joana de Flandres.* The Emperor was present at both performances. He conferred upon the composer the Order of the Rose, and decided "that he should go to Europe to complete his studies and that he was to receive a pension of 180,000 milreis for a period of four years." It seems that the Emperor, who at this time was coming to know the music of Wagner, would have preferred to have Carlos Gomes study in Germany, and he agreed to Italy only because the Empress insisted. The fruit of this first stay of Gomes's in Europe was *O Guarany,* the finest work of Brazil's lyric theater.

O Guarany was first presented in Rio in December 1870. Its success was overwhelming. The work had to be repeated on several successive nights, amidst the thunderous applause of the audience. The Emperor was present at all the performances. A little later, hailed as one of the greatest composers of his day — the "Brazilian Meyerbeer," Rebouça called him — Gomes returned to Italy, counting on the promise of João Alfredo, one of the Imperial ministers, that he would receive a pension from the government. But Gomes soon discovered, after he had settled in Milan, that the Minister's promise had no basis in reality; he had been completely forgotten and, what was worse, left almost without means of support. João Alfredo had promised him, besides a pension of a thousand francs a month, decorations for his friends and patrons in Italy. But as soon as Gomes had left the Brazilian shores he forgot everything.

In the face of these difficulties, Carlos Gomes turned to the Emperor once more. "If it had not been for that explicit promise," wrote the composer, "I would have remained in Campinas, thus avoiding this awkward situation, and without responsibility to my fellow Brazilians, who undoubtedly expect further works from the author of *O Guarany.*"

Thanks to the efforts of Viscount de Taunay, who took the matter up before the Congress, a government pension was obtained for the composer. "It was very difficult to secure," Taunay said afterwards. "If it had not been for the able, though indirect, efforts of the Emperor, the attempt would surely have met with failure."

His purse was always open to those in need, great or small, famous or obscure. Out of his own funds he gave pensions to many Brazilians, poor and as yet unknown, to study in Europe. Some of these were later to be an honor to their country in the fields of science, literature, or art. He gave Pedro Americo 400 francs a month to study painting in Rome, 200 francs to Castagneto to study painting in Florence, and 300 francs to Almeida Junior, Daniel Berard, and Francisco Franco de Sa to study painting. He sent Luiza, the daughter of Vitorino Leonardo, and José de Lima Fleming 300 francs to study music in Paris; 100 francs to Henrique Oswald, a student of music, for "as long as the difficult circumstances in which he finds himself last." He also pensioned Manoel Caetano Silva de Lara so he could study civil engineering in Paris, as well as José Gomez Calaça, to the sum of 300 francs. Julian Cesar Ribeiro de Sousa received 100 francs a month to study the steering of balloons at the School of Aeronautics in Paris and submit his theory and findings to the Academy of Science. Adolfo José Soares de Melo received 300 francs a month to study medicine in Louvain, and Pedro Gonçalves da Silva 250 francs to study medicine in Graz.

In 1857 Gonçalves Dias was traveling in Europe. He had been sent on a mission, arranged by the Emperor, for the official purpose of collecting documents of interest for the history of Brazil — which he faithfully executed, sending back to Rio some forty volumes of copies — but really to help the poet get his works published and to see if the change would improve his wife's health. When years later, seriously ill, Gonçalves Dias was obliged to return to Europe in search of relief from his ailments, it was the Emperor who came to his aid again.

Another great poet who enjoyed the Emperor's protection was Domingo José Gonçalves de Magalhães, the future Viscount of Araguaia. The Emperor paid for the publication of his *Confederacão dos Tamoios;* arranged and paid for two translations from the Italian, one of Ricardo Cerani and the other of L. de Simoni; and when a group of critics and writers, among whom was young José de Alencar, attacked Magalhães's poem with the violence which is customary among us, the Emperor was one of the first to come to his defense.

Gonçalves Dias, Magalhães . . . these were the poets. Beside them there is the historian Varnhagen, the future Viscount of

Porto-Seguro, with whom the Emperor was in correspondence from the time Varnhagen began his basic work on our historical formation, *Historia Geral do Brasil.*

In July 1857 Varnhagen completed his task. He had concluded the work on which he had spent years of perseverance, study, investigation, and ceaseless labor. He hastened to write to the Emperor:

> The hour has arrived when I can humbly appear before the throne of Your Imperial Majesty bringing with me the second volume of the *Historia Geral do Brasil,* on which I have spent at times twenty hours a day, so that I almost feel as though these last six years of my life were as long as the thirty-odd years that went before. When I saw the work ended at last I did not exclaim, full of pride: *"Exegi monumentum ore pecunius,"* in return for my sad peregrination upon this earth. Nevertheless I give thanks to God on bended knee not only for having inspired me with the idea of so great a service to this and to other nations, and for having granted me the health and life to complete it, but also for having permitted me to write it during Your Imperial Majesty's reign.

Araujo Porto-Alegre was another of the Emperor's protégés. He was one of the most interesting men of his time, the whole man, as Max Fleuiss called him. Poet, architect, stage-director, painter, decorator, he wound up as Consul-General in Lisbon and, like so many others of his kind, became completely disillusioned about life and mankind. The politicians could not stand him, less because of the diversity of his genius than because of his haughty, indomitable nature.

The Emperor was among the few who understood him, and if he did not consider him as a friend, nevertheless he held him in high regard, something which Porto-Alegre esteemed at its full value. His admiration for the Emperor was all the more sincere in that he made a point of never asking him for favors or benefits in spite of his difficult financial situation. "At times I am tempted to apply to the Emperor," he confessed to a friend, "but then I say to myself: No, one should go to the sovereign with important things." And he never was able to hit upon the important thing.

Perhaps because he understood the artist's pride, it was the Emperor who took the first step. Knowing the straitened circumstances of his life, he sent for him and asked him to draw up a revised plan for the Academy of Fine Arts. This was, at bottom, a pretext to appoint him professor and director of the Academy.

The Emperor's purse was open, without distinctions, for everybody connected in any way with intellectual matters. Wherever he heard that a plan was on foot to honor the memory of a poet, an artist, a man of science, or a statesman of distinction, who by his works or his acts had contributed to the moral or material betterment of mankind, he was among the first to subscribe.

Nothing pleased him or attracted him more than his association with men of letters, artists, or scientists, whether Brazilians or foreigners. They could always be sure of finding in the Emperor the most sincere and cordial reception. "The civilized world," Agassiz wrote him in a letter dated July 17, 1862, "admires in Your Majesty not only the kind, paternal sovereign of a nation that repays him with love and devotion, but also the man of learning, the protector of science and letters, the friend of all that tends to ennoble the human race." Referring in a later communication to letters he had received from the Emperor, he says that as he read them they made him forget that they were from a sovereign because they seemed impregnated with the air of the philosopher's study.

Quatrefages, the great naturalist, wrote him from France: "To be in direct communication with D. Pedro de Alcantara is a privilege which is an honor, and if we were to follow our inclinations, we would be tempted to abuse it."

This correspondence with the learned men of his time was, besides, one of his favorite pastimes; it gave him real spiritual pleasure. On such occasions the monarch disappeared to make way for the friend of writers, artists, poets, scientists; he treated them all on the same terms of equality, with simplicity, with warm cordiality, "the way two neighbors talk, when the sun is setting, after a day's work in the fields," to use one of his own phrases in a letter to the novelist Herculano.

The interest with which these men kept him informed of the progress of their work, of what they had finished, what they had planned to do, their successes, their problems, is eloquent proof of how their letters were received by the Emperor. They were like communications from one comrade to another, filled with the desire, one might even say the need, to talk about themselves and their work, as happens between members of the same profession. For instance, reading this letter of Renan's nobody would say that it was not addressed to a fellow member of the French Academy who, like himself, worked in the field of ancient history:

My principal work is a history of the people of Israel, from the time that definite data about them begin to emerge, to the appearance of Christianity. Will I have the time and strength to finish such a work? At times I doubt it. However, I intend to devote all my activity to it. I think the work will consist of three volumes. The two I really hope to be able to write will deal with the most brilliant period of the prophets, between 800 and 500 B.C. It is, in my opinion, the epoch of the real founding of Judaism, the moment in which the folk of Israel becomes an autonomous people and enters upon a path which no other Semitic people travelled.

In the fall of 1874 Gobineau was revising his *Fleur d'or*, a long survey of men and events in Italy at the time of the Renaissance. From his retreat in Stockholm he writes the Emperor a letter steeped in melancholy, lamenting the distance that separates them and that prevents him from exchanging opinions with his cherished friend, as on those well-remembered Sunday afternoons in São Cristovão:

In my present frame of mind, how I feel the loss of those Sundays! Think of the pleasure it would give me, how it would stimulate and help me in my work, if I could talk with Your Majesty about the nature, the quality, and the temperament of Machiavelli, Julius II, Leon X, and the artists. I shall never forget those Sundays.

Shortly before this, Gobineau had written to the Emperor encouraging him not to forsake his literary occupations. He feared the ever growing affairs of state might interfere with them. "I should like to see Your Majesty's work in the intellectual field brought to completion. It would please me for two reasons: first because the tree should bring forth its fruit, and because this would be a real, a completely personal glory."

Twenty years earlier Alexandre Herculano had lamented the fact that "the laborious duties of the head of the state" did not permit the Emperor to "devote himself to work of greater importance," referring to the literary activities of the twenty-nine-year-old monarch.

His literary production was neither abundant nor of great value. It consisted of some poetry, mediocre for the most part; translations of foreign poets; travel notes, notes on the Tupi language, and marginal notes on certain of the books he read.

"I should like to know how Your Majesty's work is proceeding," Gobineau wrote him in April 1873. "It has been a long time since the Emperor has given me any news of his Travel Notes. I hope the ordering of all these documents is progressing satisfactorily. This should not be too long delayed in order that the impressions which gave rise to them may not fade or, and this is more serious, become distorted."

The Emperor had been working for a long time on a free translation of Æschylus' *Prometheus*. "Your Majesty has not said anything more to me about *Prometheus*," writes Gobineau in July of that same year. "It is a pity to interrupt a work so well advanced, one might almost say finished." The fact was that the translation in prose was finished and the Emperor was planning to put it into verse, which he did not manage to do. He finally entrusted this to Cardoso de Menezes, Baron of Paranapiacaba, the poet who wrote *Harpa Gemedora*, and it was published in the *Journal* of the Brazilian Institute of History and Geography.

Politics and the affairs of state were the Emperor's great enemies and consumed nearly all his leisure. "Political life is for me but the painful fulfillment of a duty," he wrote to Gobineau on the anniversary of the day he came of age. "I feel it keenly this day, thirty-three years now that I have been bearing my cross."

How the Emperor envied the good fortune of his friend, free of such burdens, whose shoulders were not bowed under the weight of these unremitting daily tasks, and who could make the use he liked of his hours and his moments! "How fortunate you are to be able to devote yourself with all your heart to such things!" exclaimed the Emperor, referring to Gobineau's intellectual activities. "How fortunate you are," he said to him again on another occasion, "to be able to apply the activity of your spirit to new literary and artistic creations!"

How fortunate you are! How fortunate you are! was his constant exclamation, the leitmotiv of his every moment, lamenting the narrowness of the life he led in Rio. "What a comfort your love of the fine arts must be to you," he wrote to Gobineau, "and what a pity I cannot take refuge in them once in a while!" And again: "How fortunate you are to be able to devote yourself wholeheartedly to your artistic inclinations! I have almost no time for those studies which delight me so much. I do what I can to save myself from politics, which at times smothers me."

Politics! Always politics! "The foul reek of politics," to use his own expression. Gobineau urged him to complete his literary labors and, to encourage him, pointed to the example of his own works. The Emperor answered: "You understand that, in my position, I am obliged to keep in touch with so many things that I can hardly take any thought for myself." And in another letter: "Ah, if my occupations did not force me to lead such a different existence, how happy I should be to harmonize my readings with yours!" He sighed for the calm, independent life Gobineau led in the Eternal City: "When you tire of the society of Rome you can go to Paris. And I? I have almost no other recourse but my books — when I have time to read them."

To compensate for the limitations of the intellectual life of Rio, and to forget for a while the unpleasantness of politics and government, the Emperor sought to attract foreign scholars. Not always being able to meet them outside, to enjoy their company and the spiritual atmosphere they carried with them, he would invite them to be his guests at the palace.

It would have been his desire to live surrounded by artists, men of letters and science, scholars like himself, and turn the dull, barren atmosphere of the palace of São Cristavão into one of refinement and culture, a kind of academy which should receive the men of thought of all parts of the world.

He resembled those Italian princes of the Renaissance who wanted to be and were, in addition to rulers of the state, great patrons of human thought. Like them, he liked the company of writers, poets, thinkers, philosophers, mathematicians; and beside his throne, in the rooms of the palace, he maintained libraries, a museum, a laboratory, and an observatory. And like those princes, too, his ambassadors and ministers abroad had standing instructions to acquire and send him whatever appeared that might favor the development and enrichment of human thought.

In 1880 he instructed Salvador de Mendonça, our consul in New York, to invite Edison, in his name, to visit Brazil. Though greatly honored by this invitation, Edison, nevertheless, was obliged to decline, because of the many occupations that made it impossible for him to leave the United States, "which leave him no free time at the present," wrote Salvador de Mendonça, "but it is his intention to visit Your Majesty as soon as he is at leisure."

At the same time Mendonça gave him a report of another visit he had made in the Emperor's name, this one to Longfellow, for the same purpose:

It was only last week that I was able to leave New York for a day to go to Boston to visit Mr. Longfellow in Your Majesty's name. I went to Cambridge and transmitted to him Your Majesty's invitation to visit Brazil. I told him that Your Majesty recalled the conversation you had had on the veranda of the poet's home, and that at the palace of Boa Vista there was another veranda where Your Majesty would like to talk with him. I told him that if it were necessary Your Majesty would write the poet a description of the bay of Rio de Janeiro to persuade him to come and see it. Mr. Longfellow, who still strolls through the roads of his country place with long, firm strides, told me that his age forbade him the pleasure which this visit to Your Majesty would give him, and then he recalled in detail all the incidents of the visit with which Your Majesty honored him. He told me that since then his house, which for a time had been the residence of Washington, now treasured the recollection of our august ruler, and that it was his great good fortune, given to no other, thus to be able to associate the memory of two illustrious heads of two American nations. He asked me to tell Your Majesty — which I now do — that the memory of your visit to that house remains as great as the gratitude of its master for the cordiality Your Majesty showed him then as now.

If all were not able to accept the invitations of this friendly, attentive Emperor, there were many who left home and family to visit him. Among these were Castelneau, Per Lund, Jacques Arago, and Louis Agassiz.

Agassiz visited Rio in 1865. He came with his wife and a group of artists and scientists. This trip to Brazil was a desire he had cherished for a long time, since in 1828, while a student at Munich, he had had occasion to read the works of Spix on the Amazon basin. The Emperor, with whom he had been in correspondence for a long time, never ceased to urge him to undertake the trip, inviting him, also, to visit him at his palace of São Cristavão. But Agassiz's health, always delicate, and his many occupations in Cambridge did not permit him to carry out the Emperor's twofold desire until that year of 1865.

"Dom Pedro received Agassiz in the warmest, most gracious manner," relates Jules Marcon. "It was a great pleasure for him, the dilettante scientist, to receive a naturalist like Agassiz under his roof and in his Empire. From their first meeting the two men came to be friends. The Emperor highly esteemed Agassiz's knowledge, his brilliant spirit, his delightful conversation, while, for his part, Agassiz was amazed to meet a 'crowned head' so well versed in geology, in the glacial theory, and in other scientific matters. Dom Pedro II did everything in his power to help the expedition; and from the day Agassiz set foot on the soil of Brazil until he left it the Emperor showed the greatest interest in the success and comfort of Agassiz and his companions."

At the Emperor's request Agassiz gave a course at the Pedro II School. These lectures, honored by the presence of the monarch and his family, were a real event in Rio. It was not merely a scientific, but a social occasion as well, thanks to the presence of ladies, a thing that had never occurred in Rio before. "It is worth pointing out, as proof of his unpretentiousness," wrote Agassiz's wife, "that although he and his family were urged to occupy the seats on the platform that had been reserved for them, the Emperor preferred to sit among the public, thus demonstrating that science recognized no categories or distinctions among persons."

FRANCISCO MIRANDA (1750–1816)

THE LAST YEARS OF SPANISH RULE in America were times of great stress. The university students were beginning to devour the books of the French Encyclopedists. In Mexico the Inquisition put Juan Francisco Ramírez on trial for reading Voltaire, d'Alembert, and Rousseau; in New Granada, Antonio Nariño was sentenced to prison and exiled for translating *The Rights of Man,* the Decalogue of the French Revolution; in Peru, Pablo Olavide, translator of Voltaire, carried his intellectual probing to Spain and was imprisoned there by the Holy Office for his *Evangel of Triumph;* when Belgrano, of the Argentine, was only nineteen years old he obtained permission to translate Montesquieu, Voltaire, and Rousseau; in Chile the sexton of Coquimbo was accused of reading revolutionary books. There was not a nook or corner of America where books were not smuggled in and plotting was not going on. It was the period of the precursors.

Among these, none had a more dramatic career than Francisco de Miranda, the Venezuelan. He traveled through four continents, he read everything he could lay his hands upon; he was the friend of kings, princes, and republicans; he commanded armies in America and Europe, and he finally died in a prison in Cádiz, where the Spanish crown confined him because of his devotion to the cause of American independence. He came to the United States to become one of the soldiers who fought for its freedom, and he was acquainted with Washington, Hamilton, Lafayette. He went to Europe and became a great friend of Catherine of Russia, who tried to persuade him to remain at her court. The King of Poland invited him to be his guest; in Sweden, Norway, and Denmark he talked with kings, and at his suggestion Denmark introduced reforms in its prison administration. He conversed with philosophers and statesmen, collected works of art. At the dinner tables he was the center of attention because the account of his travels and adventures was the most entertaining conversation to be heard in the drawing-rooms of Europe. He had amorous engagements in every city, in every court. But his interest in reforms, his absorption in the great political problems of the hour, made it impossible for him to remain long in one place; he must keep on seeking support for his efforts on behalf of freedom. In the France of the Revolution, the Republic made him a divisional commander. It was there that his life reached its greatest intensity and he knew dramatic triumphs and reverses. In Antwerp, with two thousand Frenchmen he defeated six thousand Prussians and captured the city. A crown of laurel was not far from his brow. But envy and treachery brought him before the Council of Public Safety and his neck was not far from the guillotine. In casting up this epoch of his life, the balance could not be more satisfactory: his name is carved on the Arc de Triomphe as one who had served France well.

But his dream was the freedom of America. He was the friend of the great English and North American statesmen. After planning in a thousand different ways an expedition of liberation to Venezuela, he finally left the United States with a handful of men who, when they embarked, did not know where they were bound for. The Spanish Ambassador divined his intention, the expedition failed, and Miranda returned to London, where he met Bolívar and returned with him to take command of the troops of Venezuela after the country had launched its proclamation of independence. Ill fortune and his fellow countrymen's lack of confidence in him brought him to disaster. He was captured by the Spaniards, who sent him to prison in Cádiz. On July 14, 1816 Pedro José Morán gave this account of his death in a brief letter: "This morning, at five minutes past one, my beloved Don Francisco de Miranda yielded up his soul to its Maker. The priests and friars have not allowed me to hold any funeral rites for him, and just as he had died, with mattress, sheets, and the rest of the bedclothes, they snatched him up, carried him away, and buried him."

The most unusual chapter of Miranda's life was his friendship with Catherine of Russia. The Venezuelan writer José Nucete-Sardi tells of this friendship in the following chapter from his book *Aventura y Tragedia de don Francisco Miranda*, which has just been published in English under the title *Caballero of Destiny* (Ziff-Davis, 1944).

DON FRANCISCO MIRANDA IN RUSSIA
JOSÉ NUCETE–SARDI

As he set foot on Russian soil Miranda began one of the most interesting chapters of his life. The growth of his personality was perhaps stimulated by the setting of imperial splendor and the exotic stage on which all his activities were to take place and the unusual personalities with whom he was to deal and live.

He is one of the first South Americans whose thirst for knowledge and high adventure led him to the steppes of Muscovy and to the study of that human group in which strongly opposed crosscurrents were to clash and open up unsuspected routes for the world in the future.

The journey through the Black Sea was not too pleasant, but

the storms were unable to distract the attention of the traveler from his readings, which alternated between the works of M. Guis and the Abbé Sestini.

His first contact with Russia was disagreeable because of the annoying quarantine he had to suffer, but even during this time he received many attentions from persons of standing. In the midst of his discomfort Miranda made good use of his time and brought his diary up to date. But he fumed with impatience to reach Kherson.

After a long delay in quarantine — to allay the suspicions with which the officials of Imperial Russia regarded all travelers arriving from Turkey — Don Francisco was able to stroll about the muddy streets of Kherson and began to make contact with people of importance, among these Van Schooten, for whom he had letters of recommendation and who had already sent him, while he was in quarantine, a good stock of wines, hams, herrings, and other supplies. Walking through the streets of Kherson was something of a trial because of the mud and because of a pain he had developed in the small of his back from the hard bed in his room at quarantine.

Don Francisco had done a good amount of interesting reading about the country and he picked up a lot of gossip in his conversations with the French merchant M. Rioux, a "famous epicure."

He met Prince Vyasemskoy, who called upon him at once, and he was introduced to the Metropolitan Eugenio Vulgaris, a man of great learning who had been a professor at the University of Leipzig. Princess Vyasemskoy invited him to her salon, where he met the nobility. He was invited to dine daily at the table of princes and he read with the Metropolitan Vulgaris the latter's Greek translation of Virgil.

The Vyasemskoys took notes and routes from Miranda's diary for a trip to Greece and Turkey. He was the first Venezuelan, probably the first South American, to visit the Crimea and make friends throughout the region. He was warmly received and entertained by all and plied with questions about his far-away country of America.

In the company of the princesses of Wallachia and Moldavia —

those heroines of Lehar operettas — nobles of Athens, enchanting nymphs of Greece, he dined, danced, and talked. Accompanied by high officials and officers he visited fortifications, reviewed regiments, inspected ships and arsenals, and impressed the plumed, brilliant courtiers of the Empress Catherine with his command of languages — he spoke Spanish, French, Italian, English, and Latin and read Greek, German, and Portuguese — and his expert knowledge of military affairs.

At the insistence of Prince and Princess Vyasemskoy he moved into an apartment in their mansion. His friend Rioux bored him with his bouts of drinking and at times he was really annoyed with the insolence of this Frenchman, who sang songs he had picked up in brothels before the fifteen-year-old daughter of his Russian friend Rosarovich.

In the fortress in which she lived Princess Gica received him with the greatest cordiality and asked him to tea with her. From General Samoilov he learned of the expected arrival of Prince Potemkin and the coming visit to the Crimea of the Empress Catherine, on whom he was to make such a favorable impression.

He indulged in card games that cost him dearly, and he noted the fact that he found more intelligence among the masses in Russia than among many members of the upper classes in other countries of Europe. From that remote corner he acquired a variety of information about the country, its possibilities, its resources; and he spent the cold winter days reading what had been carefully selected.

He met the most distinguished members of Potemkin's retinue, who had preceded the favorite in order to arrange for his reception, and the Prince of Nassau, who had been in Spain, showed him great marks of consideration.

On a grayish afternoon, the 28th of December, as the setting sun threw its purplish rays over the white steppes, a salvo of cannon fire announced the arrival of Prince Potemkin.

The next day Rokasowsky, an aide-de-camp, took Miranda to an audience with the Prince of Nassau, in the company of Prince Dolgourosky, his friend from Kherson. Nassau, who was surrounded by sycophants and scoundrels, says Miranda, received him with pleasure and invited him to the evening gatherings at his house. And as he departed, the colorful escort of Kalmuks, Cossacks, Greeks, and Jews saluted the future soldier of the French Republic, who from that moment was to be one of the favorites in Potemkin's and Catherine II's suites.

That evening Potemkin, as he drank his tea with vodka, inquired interestedly about Miranda and talked eagerly with Prince and Princess Vyasemskoy about the Venezuelan.

The year 1786 is drawing to a close. On the afternoon of the last day Potemkin sends one of his aides-de-camp to Miranda to invite him to his house. Don Francisco has had a special costume made to please a princess; with it he wears a gleaming sword, and as he approaches the mansion of the favorite, the guards make way for him. The aides-de-camp conduct him into the presence of His Highness, who rises to greet him and makes him sit beside him. With him and the Prince of Nassau, in a cordial tête-à-tête, Don Francisco drinks out the old year with tea prepared and served by this master of Russia, who asks him a thousand questions about South America and his native Venezuela.

The Countess of Sievers, all gossip and ambition, who follows the Prince as his paramour — bitch, the retinue dubs her — comes into the room and the conversation ceases. Potemkin kisses her and presents her to the traveler. They listen together to a concert of chamber music by the Prince's orchestra and at nine o'clock Miranda returns to his lodgings in the carriage the Prince offers him.

The next day — the New Year of 1787 — Miranda is jotting down in his diary the impressions of that meeting when an aide-de-camp of Potemkin's arrives at his house to inform him that His Highness "has greatly regretted that he did not stay to dine the evening before" and invites him to spend the first evening of the new year in his company.

A bitter cold Russian night in January. Francisco de Miranda stands before the palace of the wielder of supreme power in Catherine's court. As he descends from his carriage, snow begins to fall upon his Don Juan cape. Within there are music, dancing, and courtiers. Gregory Alexandrovich Potemkin, Prince of Muscovy, receives him with warm welcome and introduces him to the emissaries from the Caucasus. At dinner-time he seats Miranda beside him. Liquor and good food enliven the conversation. There is talk of Spain, of the Marquis de la Torre and the European political situation. There is also talk of love; warm words fall from the red lips of the princesses. In the pauses, the haunting melodies of Moldavia.

The prestige enjoyed by Miranda among the lofty personages who surrounded Potemkin, and the Prince's constant attentions, aroused the jealousy of many courtiers. Envy is a plant that flourishes in all climates, and whoever rises above the common level by his own superiority is sure to feel the slime of the frogs upon his heels.

Miranda was not at all set up by the position he had achieved and continued to devote his days to study. In the morning he took long walks through the snow and, in the company of a group of officers, watched the regiments at maneuvers. One of his good friends was an officer from Naples, a colonel of cavalry, by name Ribas. At night he attended the Prince's gatherings, and the palace jealousy mounted on seeing the persistence with which Potemkin inquired about Miranda if for any reason he did not come.

Ribas told him that Potemkin wanted to invite him to accompany him to Kiev. Miranda, while appreciating this mark of favor, advised him that he was "traveling only for the purpose of learning," thus avoiding attentions that might lend themselves to malicious interpretation.

On one of his visits to Potemkin he made friends with the son of Prince Heraclitus of Georgia and with the nephew of the dethroned Khan of the Crimea. Nearly every afternoon Mme Sievers served him tea and sometimes, in his honor, Potemkin himself prepared a fricassee. The man from Caracas observed and studied these people; he was always a philosopher, even when the highborn were showering their attentions upon him.

When he insinuated to the Prince that he would like to continue his travels, the Prince told him to wait and travel with him, for he would not find a better guide. Miranda accepted and traversed the frozen steppes in Potemkin's own carriage as his favorite companion, muffling himself in the fur coat which was the gift of the Prince.

They traveled all through the Crimea, which was almost in its vast expanse the favorite's holding, and in one of the villages they met a direct descendant of Genghis Khan. During the trip he shared Potemkin's bedchambers. He hunted with him, and as they traversed the region of Sudak, Miranda found that it greatly resembled certain parts of Spain. This gave him an opportunity to draw comparisons between the procedures employed by the Russian government in its dominions and those of Spain.

He had long discussions with the Prince of Nassau on different topics of politics and customs in Potemkin's presence. One afternoon, over the steaming cups of tea, the Prince of Nassau made some remark about the wantonness of Spanish women. Miranda defended them warmly. And commenting on Figaro's *Travels in Spain*, he and Potemkin remarked how inaccurate the French were in their observations of other nations. Nassau persisted in his attitude and added that when he met the Duchess of Alba she was rotting with syphilis, as were the majority of Spanish women. Miranda sharply replied that not even professional prostitutes behaved in the manner he had described. The discussion grew hotter, and when the Prince of Nassau made some remark about the dirtiness of Spaniards, Miranda answered that in matters of cleanliness the French were hardly fit judges.

After they had separated, Prince Potemkin was deeply worried, for he was afraid something more serious might occur between the two gentlemen. But Nassau took good care not to provoke Don Francisco any further.

The evening concluded with Tatar dancing girls, the same that had entertained the old Khan, in Count Valentine's house in the pleasant company of Ribas and Kisselow. And the traveler learned then what the love of the Circassian women was like.

Ivanov, a famous Russian artist, was painting a portrait of Prince Potemkin, and while he was posing he found out how matters had concluded between Miranda and Nassau. A little later the two men were engaged in a discussion of art, beside the crackling fireplace. Glasses of strong Kurdish brandy warmed the spirits and animated the discussion in the comfortable office of Catherine's favorite.

The trips to neighboring villages and estates continued; the burly Cossacks paid honor to the travelers, who were deep in a serious historical discussion, trying to determine whether the crossing of Pylades and Orestes took place near Balaclava, and the episode of Iphigenia, on the coast at a place called "Partenza," where there are still Greek ruins to be seen. The travelers were also remarking that the capital of the Kingdom of the Bosporus, which was founded by Mithridates, had been somewhere near Einkale.

As Potemkin was obliged to go ahead, he ordered that a special sleigh be prepared for Miranda and that he be shown every courtesy. Several times the Prince stopped to wait for him, and in the evenings they listened with delight to the Ukrainians singing their folk-songs in chorus.

They reached Kremenchuk. Mme Ribiskow was a new feminine acquaintance, and Miranda met the metropolitan of the city, with whom he held long conversations, "half in French, half in Latin." The governor of Kremenchuk sent him his own carriage so he could visit certain advanced teaching centers in the city.

One day he went to bid Potemkin farewell, as he wished to continue his trip to Moscow. But the Prince told him that as he had formed a part of his retinue, and as the Empress was so near by, it would be a breach of etiquette if he did not go to be presented to her. So Miranda went — in Potemkin's company — to the Imperial court, where Catherine had arrived a few days before. He had only the "threadbare frock-coats with which he had left Greece and Turkey," but he had to comply with the Prince's request, since he owed him so many and such delicate attentions.

Colonel Ribas helped him out of his difficulties, lending him money until his own arrived, and Miranda ordered the cloth for a court suit. A German tailor came with his samples and Miranda selected a blue broadcloth — there was no other choice — and ordered an aide-de-camp's uniform made up; he found an embroidered waistcoat for his vicuña suit, a hat, and a fine sword. That night he attended a banquet which the governor gave in honor of Madame Samoilov, where Prince Potemkin was waiting for him, and had ordered dinner delayed an hour so as not to sit down at the table without the traveler.

During the festivity he returned to his house to pack his bags and there he found that his servant — who has shown his uncouthness on other occasions — had brought to his room a beautiful Russian girl, warm, loving, "as ardent as an Andalusian brunette."

He returned to the party, where Mme Kramina was going through the steps of a Russian dance, voluptuous, sharply rhythmic, reminiscent of the fandango. The next day, with letters of recommendation in his pocket, in Nassau's company, he followed the Prince.

The travelers had difficulties on the frozen steppe, but they must reach Kiev as quickly as possible. Two days later they were in the city, where the court had been set up. Potemkin introduced Miranda to his family and told him that he had spoken of him to the Empress. That same night he was taken to the salon of the Countess Branitzka, a woman of exceptional beauty. He also met the Countess Skabronsky, the Minister of War, and the Minister of Foreign Affairs — Prince Bezborodko — and many Polish aristocrats and ambassadors from different countries.

The Imperial Steward, Narichkin, received him and they dined together, to the accompaniment of Cossack dances. With the enchanting Countess Potocka he drank the fine Hungarian wine she had stored in her old cellars.

One morning the Empress was to receive Holy Communion. Miranda was present at the ceremony, watching it from a distance, as he had not yet been presented to her, but that same day Potemkin notified him that he was to be presented the next day.

February 14. It is a morning of royal splendor. At eleven Miranda enters the Imperial palace. Prince Bezborodko is waiting for him, and when Her Majesty enters the room he is presented to her. Don Francisco bends gallantly and kisses the hand of the Empress, "who with a charming gesture took it out of her muff" and held it out to the Venezuelan. After a deep bow Miranda withdrew to an antechamber where it had been arranged that he was to have an audience of a few minutes with the Empress, a privilege not enjoyed by all those present.

After this general paying of respects Her Majesty returned to the antechamber. And as if by contrast, as a pleasant thought in the chill of that Russian day, or else because nearly all conversations between strangers begin with the time-honored theme of the weather, from the Imperial lips the following question falls:

"How low does the thermometer go in your country when it is coldest?"

Miranda answers her question; they exchange a few polite phrases and proceed to the table where a banquet for sixty has been prepared. Count Tchernichev, the Minister of War, is seated beside Don Francisco, and lavishes attentions upon him. Her Majesty does not neglect him either, and twice she has him served from dishes beside her place. She shares several delicacies with him and asks him more questions. This is the beginning of one of the most interesting friendships in history. And from that moment on, this Empress, the patron of artists, philosophers, and scientists, is to lavish her attentions on this philosopher of the New World, "a cross between Don Quixote and Don Juan" a poet has called him.

One afternoon there was a dance in the salons of the palace. Beautiful ladies were there in sumptuous court costumes. At night the gaming tables were crowded. Rich duchesses surrounded the traveler. The Empress asked him more questions:

"Is it true that the Inquisition still exists in your country?"

Miranda sorrowfully confirmed this. The sovereign continued:

"In Russia there are some Dominican friars like those who make up that tribunal. Whenever I see them I say to myself: 'Lord save us.'"

There was a chorus of laughter, and play was resumed. When the game was over, Catherine II left the room amidst bows and curtsies.

An intensely cold morning. The Imperial party visited the Pecherskoy Church. The Empress was in charge. They descended to the catacombs and Don Francisco visited the tomb of Nestor, the oldest Russian historian.

At the Branitzkys' one night there was a lavish festival. The Tatar dances and the music of the Ukraine spread their charm through the gay night. Now Catherine talked with Miranda about his travels and about the political situation in the countries he had visited. When Miranda — a master of courtly behavior — took his leave, the Empress confided to Count Cobenzcel that the Venezuelan was "honest and learned," and that she liked people of that sort.

Naritchin had opened his splendid salons. The Empress, who was present at the gathering, called Miranda to her side to talk with him. Her Majesty was interested in Moorish architecture; she inquired about the gardens of Granada and then returned to the topic of the Inquisition, which she, with her open mind, could not understand. And the conversation closed on a literary note while the beautiful Countess Galovkin danced a Russian dance with a gentle swaying of shoulders and hips.

"She could bring the dead back to life," whispered Miranda to his close friend General Momonov.

One day Nassau told him that Potemkin had said that if he did not leave soon he would find it impossible to cross the rivers. Unquestionably the Prince was growing jealous of the influence that Miranda might acquire and of the marked interest Catherine was showing in him. Therefore Miranda had to leave immediately not to further impose on Potemkin's hospitality, and he began to make preparations for his departure.

But the next day, as the Venezuelan, busied with his departure, did not come to the palace, the Empress inquired about him and Nassau made haste to tell her he was leaving. Potemkin apologized for him. That afternoon Miranda told the Prince he would be leaving in two days, and Potemkin answered indifferently:

"Then you will want to kiss Her Majesty's hand before you leave?"

"Certainly, that is my wish."

"Then it will have to be this very night, for the Empress is not receiving tomorrow; I will arrange everything and I will give you a messenger who will arrange for the horses and accompany you to Moscow."

"A thousand thanks for everything, Prince."

What was the reason for this coldness? Don Francisco recalled that one night Count Stakelberg jokingly criticized Potemkin for always having foreigners around him. The Prince had answered that he trusted Miranda and was glad to have his opinions. All this praise would turn Miranda's head, said the courtiers among themselves. A little later, when the Prince came into the salon, Miranda, who was talking with some ladies, did not rise and several Poles followed his example. This annoyed the favorite.

But the day after that stiff conversation, in which Miranda's departure was arranged, it was Potemkin himself who told him that the Empress was unwilling for him to leave, for the crossing of the rivers was already dangerous.

That night the Empress attended a great ball in her honor at the German Embassy. On leaving she singled out Miranda among those who were waiting for her and, smiling, said:

"Do you want to get drowned? I'll never permit that."

Miranda expressed his gratitude for her interest in him, and thought of the growing coldness of Gregory Potemkin.

But there at the Embassy Potemkin's attitude had already shown a change. He spoke to Miranda with great affability. And in the brilliantly lighted salons, surrounded by the beauties of the court, Catherine resumed her conversations with Don Francisco: Italian painting, French art, the activities of the Jesuits, gossip of the Madrid court, the campaign in Algiers, the health and ability of the Spanish Crown Prince, were topics discussed.

The Count de Ségur, the French Minister, was green with envy because the sovereign had not addressed a word to him. The Prince of Nassau came up to offer Miranda anything he might need, even money. Many ladies of the court fell under Don Francisco's spell. Countess Branitzka was always at his side, and they carried on a discreet flirtation to the measures of the polonaise.

While confined to his bed with a cold, Miranda read Machiavelli and set down his impressions. He did not approve of his doctrines, but he found them true. When he could go out again, the Empress remarked that he had grown thinner. The cold came back and he decided to try a Russian bath. The Prince and the

Empress inquired how it agreed with him and made him take another to hasten his recovery.

On another visit to the palace he was introduced to Prince Stanislaus Poniatowski, the nephew of the King of Poland. The Empress remarked to him with an ironical smile:

"Don't let them find out in Spain that you have been associating with schismatics. The Inquisition will burn you."

It was the beginning of March. The German Embassy was celebrating its Emperor's birthday. There was a dinner and a dance; while the young people danced, the older people played whist. The Empress was playing, too, and she called Miranda to her side, as she did whenever she met him at any gathering.

Catherine was wearing an exquisite dress of finest tulle. During the conversation she told Miranda to feel her dress, which though it seemed very costly, was of material manufactured in Moscow.

Miranda touched the delicate fabric that covered the august body. His attention seemed to have wandered as a wave of perfume and fragrance enveloped him. Suddenly Catherine, smiling, said softly:

"But what is the matter? You are pensive this evening."

JOSÉ MARTÍ (1853–95)

Cuba was the last of the colonies in America to free itself from Spanish domination. Much earlier the three great focuses of independence — Mexico, Greater Colombia, and the Plata countries — sent their armies marching through the continent. But the Caribbean islands remained outside the war. As the Spanish-American republics affirmed themselves, the Cubans felt the urge to expel from their territories the last representatives of the Spanish crown in America. The struggle was long and hard. At the time of the War of Independence on the continent, Spain had to fight against all America. Now it was a single small island upon which it could concentrate all its affection and all the power of its army. After several futile uprisings, in 1868 war broke out that lasted for ten years. Old families long established on the island, representing both tradition and wealth, joined hands in the fight with the humble, the former slaves, the countryfolk, in a romantic crusade that gave birth to the national flag and the national anthem. But the Spanish power was too strong. The leaders of the insurrection were shot and many families emigrated to the United States, Mexico, Colombia, bearing with them the germs of sympathy toward the cause of Cuba's freedom, which at the close of the past century was one of the most popular causes in America. In Key West, as in New York, in Mexico, in Bogotá or Caracas, *"Cuba libre"* was a popular slogan. Even in Spain the liberals pleaded for Cuba's independence. It was the period when the generation of 1898 in Spain renewed its complaints against the blunders of the Spanish crown.

Don Luis de Zulueta, one of Spain's great writers, who at the same time had connections with Cuba, says in a recent book: "Spain to the men of 1898 was a problem. It was not an accepted, admitted, indisputable thing as the fatherland generally is for the majority of people, but, on the contrary, something to be discovered and brought into being. Spain was not merely a problem, it was *the* problem. The generation of 1898 turned its back upon the traditional interpretations of the history and character of the nation. It realized that Spain itself was responsible for its state of disaster — official Spain. Underneath it, as below the withered skin of a fruit, the seeds of the other Spain, the living Spain, had to be found. It felt itself historically aligned with Simón Bolívar and not with Ferdinand VII. It openly extolled Martí and condemned Weyler." (Weyler was the Spanish general who took such brutal reprisals against the Cuban revolutionists.)

The Spanish crown stood firm, however, and the struggle was fierce. The last hero of Cuban independence was José Martí. In his veins ran Spanish blood. His father was from Valencia. But in the hour of emancipation no one else was so eloquent as Martí, so unswerving, so tireless, so convincing in his exaltation of the ideals of country. He was, besides, a poet in the fullest sense of the word, combining the last echoes of romanticism with the new notes of modernism. In his youth, when he first began to scribble for the newspapers and wrote his first drama, he was thrown into prison because he early revealed the spark of the agitator. He was seventeen years old and he was put to work in the rock quarries, at hard labor with criminals. From prison he was exiled to Spain. There he began his career as agitator and journalist. From Spain he returned to America. In Mexico, in Havana, in Guatemala he was the incarnate word of the revolution. All America listened spellbound to his voice. Finally war broke out. Martí, who had planned and kindled it, returned to take his stand beside his people. By a miracle he reached the island alive. Carried away by his enthusiasm, in his frenzy to see the final triumph of his ideals, in the first battle, in a rapture of daring, he fell under the Spanish bullets. But his name continued to be the emblem of the struggle, and afterwards the symbol of the Republic.

Jorge Mañach, a Cuban writer, is the author of a biography of Martí, from which the following pages are taken. They deal with Martí's imprisonment when he was seventeen years old.

MARTÍ IN PRISON
JORGE MAÑACH

THE DEPARTURE of his master, Mendive, to the exile to which the military tribunal had sentenced him left Pepe like a bird without shelter. He had reached the age when life must take on a meaning for the adolescent if his vague yearnings are not to become unbearable. By imbuing him with his own apostolic devotion to country and beauty, Mendive had provided Pepe's spirit with its first handholds. He offset the rough paternal authority, serving as an ideal at a moment when the young soul demands perfection in the object to which its heart goes out.

Now all this security had departed. Pepe was left to the devices of his own impatience at the very moment when, along with his burning eagerness for knowledge, a dramatic sense of responsibility was developing in him. He unavailingly tried to get in touch with the conspirators. The most important were outside of Cuba, exiles or refugees. The ones who remained were surrounded by an almost impenetrable wall of secrecy, and they were not too well disposed toward that excitable, talkative lad, son of a police agent.

The students? San Pablo, the school directed by Mendive, had been ordered closed, and Martí's father, Don Mariano, refused to allow his son to go to the Institute lest — as he explains later in a legal petition — "the excess of liberty after class hours should distract his son from his studies, in which he has achieved such success."

Don Mariano had made up his mind to tie the boy short. Before sundown Pepe must be in the house at Guanabacoa where the family now lived. People called the police agent "Blackmouth," because of his heavy black mustache, and perhaps, too, because of his proficiency at swearing.

Ever since the publication of his poem *Abdala*, Pepe had had to endure this violence of language and even worse. His father's continual watching, spying, and scolding grew intolerable. In October he wrote to Don Rafael Mendive: "I am so miserable over all this that I am telling you, with the blunt frankness you are familiar with in me, that the only thing that has kept me from killing myself is the hope of seeing you again. Your letter yesterday saved my life. Some day you will read my diary, and you will see that this was not a childish impulse but a carefully thought-out determination."

Doña Leonor tried to make up as best she could for the heavy-handed vigilance of her husband. But Pepe needed more understanding comfort. He found it in Fermín Valdés, his former schoolmate at San Pablo. The latter had in his room a picture of Pepe with an inscription referring to his "hours of tears," in which Fermín was "his best friend, his devoted brother."

In the house of the Valdés Domínguez family, on Industria Street, he was always treated like a son. The well-born Guatemalan gentleman and his wife were fond of this poor boy whose speech and manners were as refined as though he had been born in the lap of luxury. And Pepe, in turn, derived a melancholy comfort from the gracious, dignified well-being of that Creole household. He went there every day to listen to the French lesson M. Fortier gave to the children. There, alongside Fermín's desk, he devoured his friend's books, discussed the revolution, and made plans to join the rebels.

Then Don Mariano decided that, until certain difficulties standing in the way of his going on with his education were ironed out, the best thing for Pepe was to find himself something to do. So then he worked at Don Cristóbal Madan's office "from six in the morning until eight at night, earning four and a half doubloons, which he turned over to his father."

So he was not at the Valdés Domínguez's that afternoon of the 4th of October when the incident of the Volunteers took place. Standing behind the grille of one of the windows that faced the street, M. Fortier was talking with Eusebio Valdés, who had just been admitted to the bar, and his friend Sellén, while he waited for Fermín. The pretty neighbor who lived across the street had been drawn to her window by the music of the brass band that was leading a parade of Volunteers to the near-by Campo de Marte, and gallant phrases and gay banter flew back and forth between the windows. The men laughed, the girl laughed. A squadron of the First Battalion of Light Infantry happened to be passing on their way back. They were marching along, proudly enjoying their new-found military status. They heard the noise of smothered laughter at one window and the other and considered themselves insulted. The threatening gesture that ran through the column augured reprisals. M. Fortier and Sellén took their leave.

When Fermín, who had been at Martí's office, returned a little after this, his mother barely had time to tell him what had happened. A squad of Volunteers burst into the hallway, arrested the boy, and took him away. That night Fortier and Sellén were ordered to prison, and the house of the Valdés Domínguez's was searched. In a drawer of Fermín's desk a letter was found dated that same day and addressed to a certain Carlos de Castro y Castro. The letter read:

Comrade: Have you ever dreamed of the glory of apostasy? Do you know how the ancients punished apostates? We trust that a pupil of Señor Rafael María de Mendive's will not fail to answer this letter.

José Martí   Fermín Valdés Domínguez

After considerable investigation the sluggish military intelligence discovered that Carlos de Castro, a former pupil of Mendive's, was a young Cuban who had enlisted in a Spanish regiment, and deduced that the object of the letter was to throw this honor up to him as a disgrace. Pepe was ordered arrested, and the indictment brought against his friends "for insults to the company of sappers of the First Light Infantry Volunteers" was made to include Don José Martí and Don Fermín Valdés Domínguez "on suspicion of malfeasance," a very elastic offense in those days.

Months and months in a foul, promiscuous jail, where the two friends cared for each other with brotherly affection and by their amiability touched even the flinty heart of the jail-keeper.

Finally one day, his voice breaking with pity, he read them the accusation of the military court, which alluded to the death sentence. The two boys attempted to smile. On October 4, one year after the so-called "crime," they were summoned before a court martial. The guilt of all was indisputable; the only point to clear up, as far as Martí and Valdés Domínguez were concerned, was which of the two wrote the letter in question. The experts had not been able to decide, for the handwriting of both was very similar.

Upon being called to the witness stand, Fermín confesses that he is the author of the letter. Martí, when his turn comes, insists that he wrote it. The judge advocate warns them that the one found guilty will suffer the extreme penalty. The accused stick to their statements. A confrontation of the two is ordered, and when Fermín tries to speak, Pepe interrupts him, steps to the table at which the tribunal is sitting, and vehemently repeats his confession. The confident, terse, clearly modulated phrases rise in smooth curves and drop into the void of official amazement. Fermín and his companions are electrified. The defense attorney for a moment forgets his official rank and smiles. The witnesses from the First Light Infantry Volunteers twist nervously at their mustaches. Pepe goes on dauntlessly, exuberantly, carried away with his own words, as though he has discovered a secret spring within himself.

Finally the colonel in charge comes back to earth again and with a sharp thump of his fist on the table declares the trial concluded and passes sentence. Fermín Valdés, six months of confinement; José Martí, six years in a military prison.

> I am going to the big house where I have been told
> Life in death is to be my fate.
> My country sends me there. Even death at her
> Hands is still sweet.

Pepe had written these verses a few hours before being taken to the military prison. While in jail he had heard about, and, as a matter of fact, he had often seen as they passed his house at the close of day, the gangs of weary, stooping men, their jackets slung over one shoulder, their clothes tattered and dirty with lime and red mud, with a chain hanging from their waist to their ankles. He had seen them march along, somber and silent, the harsh voice of the guard goading on their fatigue. In the cafés, buzzing with the sound of dominoes and politics, a sudden hush fell as the chain-gang passed by, a silence underscored by the clanking of chains, the sound of shuffling footsteps, the curt voice of the guards.

Martí had often witnessed scenes of this sort with a shudder of pity and indignation. But he had not plumbed the depths of horror of the black hole of prison where the colonial authorities segregated and buried from sight the dregs of its inhumanity, where injustice was to reveal itself to him not as a political act or a civil abuse but as a deliberate offense against the essential human rights of every man.

On the 5th of April he was taken to prison, his head was shaved, and he was given a plate and a pallet. He was at once set to working the rusty handle of the pump. He was all alone. The rest of the prisoners had gone to the rock quarries at dawn and would not return until sundown. There by the well coping, under the ironic eyes of the guard, he watched the bright swath of sun on the high walls of the prison yard shrink until the eaves lay in darkness, the sparrows ceased their chirping, and a melancholy quiet descended.

Finally voices were heard in the distance, oaths, the muted sounds of men and iron. It was the prisoners returning from the quarries. He saw them throw themselves upon the ground, drop their whitened faces between their knees or lift them longingly to the sky. In bewilderment, Martí fixed his gaze on an old man who suddenly pitched forward as though the last spring of the mechanism that kept him going had suddenly snapped. He hurried to his side. The man looked like a ghost. His hair had turned white, his feet were white with lime dust, and his face was colorless. What ailed him? The old man glanced out of the corner of his eye. He took in Martí's youth, his air of a novice, and murmured faintly: "Poor fellow." When Pepe insisted upon helping him, the man turned over, pulled up his tattered shirt, and showed his back, zebra-striped with furrows, each furrow a wound.

"Have they done this to you here? But why?"

He shrugged his shoulder. Then he murmured: "Son, you might not believe me. Ask anyone else. They'll tell you. . . ."

The next morning when Martí saw the quarries for himself he hardly needed anybody to tell him anything. They were a good three miles from the prison, in a rough hollow, rudely hacked out of the limestone cliffs. In the bed of the quarry, heaped high with piles of broken limestone and lime, the air was like a bake-oven and the shimmer of the sun was blinding. The convicts had to dig out the rock, break it into small pieces, and haul it to the dump-heaps or the furnaces on the top of the quarry. Bent over the rock, loading the boxes or big pieces of rock on their shoulders, they had to be always on the alert for a sudden rock-slide or the whip of the overseer which kept them relentlessly at work. There were whites, blacks, and Chinese, old men and boys, all shackled with chains from the waist to both ankles, which hobbled them as they stumbled through the ruts filled with stagnant water. As they climbed over the piles of stone, the quicklime seared their feet and the fine white dust burned their lungs. The air, the men, the tools, everything was permeated by that inexorable whiteness which irritated eyes and nerves, turning people into ghosts and making of the whole landscape a kind of infernal winter.

That morning they told Pepe the story of the old man, Don Nicolás Castillo. One afternoon his lacerated feet could no longer hold him up. They beat him. He could not get up. Two of the prisoners piled him into a cart, half-dead. At the infirmary the doctor scornfully looked him over and prescribed "more treatments at the quarry." Stretched out in a dump-cart, his white head bumping against the floor-boards at every step, they hauled him back to the rock-pile. Not even the tough yaya-wood sticks could get him to his feet. He lay there all day in the water and the sun.

When Martí asked the reason for this brutality, Cubans and Spaniards alike explained to him that the Volunteers believed Castillo to be one of the leaders of the rebels, and the influence of the Volunteers was very great.

No, Pepe could not believe it. He had to see with his own eyes the case of the child Lino Figueredo, a political prisoner at the age of twelve. He was a country lad, the son of *"pacíficos,"* who had made no open protest against the existing situation; but unfortunately his father's name was Figueredo, like that of the rebel of ballad fame. The boy had no idea of what had happened to his parents. They had taken him to prison. He carried his load of stone like the rest; they beat him like the rest. One day he got yellow fever and smallpox. He kept on working until the disease carried him off. And the case of Ramón Rodriguez, and of Juan de Dios, a poor old idiotic Negro who was charged "with treason"; the little Negro boy Tomás; and that other grim and silent youth who, driven mad by the whiteness, had tried to commit suicide by throwing himself from the top of the quarry, but who had been picked up and treated because it was the captain-general's saint's day, and they did not want the unpleasant news to get around. One morning he was back at work, and when he took off his black

convict's hat, which was known as "the badge of death" three
long, white scars across his head gleamed in the sun.

Martí saw all this. He himself felt the bite of the lime and the
sun and the whip. He dug with the water to his waist. He wore
chains that scarred his ankles. His eyes, inflamed by the blazing
whiteness, oozed pus. He had tried to keep the "old folks" from
knowing what he was suffering. But Don Mariano managed to see
him during the rest hour. Under the iron leg band he slipped some
pads Doña Leonor had made. He told him that she and the girls
were using all the influence they could muster with anyone who
might be able to bring about a lightening of his sentence. Pepe
said nothing; he had no illusions, but he could not blast the old
man's hopes. When the rest period was over and the overseer's
stick prodded Pepe back to the loading boxes, the father stayed
kneeling there in the sun, his eyes blazing with anger.

But Pepe's greatest suffering was for the others. He was sustained by a glowing pride. "A slave of his age and his beliefs," he
wrote on a picture he sent to his mother in his prison garb. And he
begged a friend to see in his effigy "the robust image of his soul
and a beautiful page of his history." But his soul was touched far
deeper by a bitter compassion for the suffering by which he was
surrounded than by his own martyrdom. Don Nicolás and Lino
and all the others knew the comfort of his encouraging word,
his generous hands which helped with the heavy load, bandaged
the wound, or moistened the scorching skin in time. One afternoon
a Chinese prisoner fell down in a convulsion, his face livid and
his mouth foaming. As usual they attempted to get him up with
the whip. A fellow countryman shouted frantic monosyllables in
his defense. They could not understand; they did not want to understand. They had to prick one of the fallen man's veins and see
the drop of black blood ooze out to be convinced. It was cholera.

From that afternoon on there were many who pitched forward
on the stones. It was always Martí who came to their help, picking
them up, bending over them, to rub their arms and legs. The guard,
depending on his mood, either let him do it or shoved him away.
"You keep on with your doctoring, my lad, and you'll see how fast
you get it, too."

Still vaguely loyal to his Spanish blood, Martí believed that all this was done in the name of Spain but that Spain knew nothing of it. No, it was not possible that the liberal statesmen of Madrid could sanction this. Perhaps not even those hardened authorities, upholders of the principle of unity in Havana, really knew what was going on. They could not be this vindictive. This was a secret of the colony, a blot that the good Spaniards in the island did not even suspect. And yet this white hell was in plain sight of all. Had hate dug its claws so deep in their conscience that the most upright tolerated this in the name of unity? Was it possible, for instance, that a man like Don José María Sardá, the owner of the quarries, did not know the crimes by which his profits were produced?

And Sardá seemed like a good man. One day he passed by La Criolla quarry and asked for Martí. He took in the seared cheeks, the inflamed eyes. He put his hand on the boy's shoulder; then he took the guard to one side and talked with him. From that day Pepe received special treatment.

In a week he was transferred to La Cabaña fortress. Sardá, the wealthy Catalonian, who was a friend of the captain-general's, moved perhaps by Don Mariano's pleas, achieved what Doña Leonor's supplications had been unable to do. Pepe's prison sentence was commuted. He was to be transferred provisionally to the Isle of Pines, in Sardá's own custody, while his deportation to Spain was being considered.

He had spent six months in the departmental prison. He emerged half-blind, and with a groin injury caused by the blow of a chain, paler, thinner, his smile sweeter than ever. Three months later he wrote Mendive:

"I have suffered a great deal, but I have known how to suffer. And if I have had strength to endure and if I have the strength really to be a man, it is to you alone that I owe it, and everything good and tender in me comes from you and only you."

THE VOW. Madrid was bleak and gray those early months of 1871. The famous piercing north wind of the Guadarrama, now that there were no leaves left on the aspens, amused itself blowing scraps of the *Gaceta* about the sidewalks or swallowing up the little white puffs of breath as soon as they emerged from behind mufflers or the raised folds of tightly wrapped capes.

Another chill hung in the air. Amadeo I was making his debut and the people of Madrid were reluctant to accept this substitute King who had been imported from Italy after General Prim had put in his bid at all the European courts. Now that his manager was dead, how would *Macarronini I* comport himself on the throne vacated by the Bourbons, Isabel II?

The young man who, with the air of a convalescent, in a closely fitting greatcoat, strolled through the chill streets of Madrid was brooding on near and far-off matters. Madrid. . . . So this was the city on which the Creoles lavished their unrequited love? This was whence the military governors of Cuba and the royal edicts came? Why was it this oppressive city was not disliked there? He recalled how he himself had always associated it in his mind with the idea of a careless grace, a sort of political frivolity which in no way resembled the unyielding fanaticism of the transplanted Spaniards. The Creole delegates to the Cortes came back charmed by Madrid's warm smile. It was a fact. He, too, had felt it even through the bleak winter. Even though Don Rafael, who had been lured away by Paris, was not there to welcome him, he did not feel as though he were in a strange city. It was like a relative whose acquaintance he had just made.

To be sure, Pepe's literary inclinations had predisposed his attitude. His first violent reactions as he neared the shores of the peninsula had been calmed not a little by the thought of the splendid famous writers to be found there. During the three months on the Isle of Pines he had been able to judge the future and sound himself. How considerately Mrs. Sardá and her daughters had left him to himself, punctuating his solitude with delicate gestures of tenderness! He had read the Bible. And *Les Miserables*. In the little breeze-swept house of El Abra, at the foot of the marble-bosomed hill, or along the path to New Gerona, which ran through young pine groves, he had often felt an inner sensation of abundance and great clarity. He had felt a confident urge to write.

Now in Madrid, in contact with a richer, older life, hope began to triumph over memory. For him, a Cuban, Spain was still the model and the standard of culture. In Cuba he had not made much progress with his French, not even in his liberal readings. Mendive himself, although he had entertained Lamartine's literary agent in his house, remained loyal to his traditional culture, without yielding to the flattering message of gratitude the French poet sent him, praising the culture of "the lovely land that produced the poetess Avellaneda and the poet Heredia." Only when, at the gatherings presided over by the master, literary themes were touched upon had Pepe heard Madrid spoken of with respect, and even Martinez de la Rosa.

Now all this — orators, literary clubs, poets, beautiful paintings — were within reach of his curiosity, whetted by long fasting in the tropics. Exile had its compensations.

Making use of the bountiful advice and the slender financial aid his father had been able to give him when he embarked, Pepe decided to enter the University of Madrid and get all the good that was possible from Madrid.

Carlos Sauvalle helped him over his first loneliness and introduced him to the city and its people. They had known each other slightly in Havana. Sauvalle had been obliged to leave Cuba after the Villanueva Theater disorders, although his only active participation in the affair had been to leave his coat in the grasp of the Volunteer who seized him as he was leaving the theater. In his fellow countryman's album Pepe wrote:

> Cuba brings us together in a foreign land,
> Our love sighs for Cuba's gentle breeze,
> Cuba is your heart, Cuba is my heaven;
> Let the word I write in your book be Cuba.

It was indeed the word they caressed at all their meetings: an amulet against homesickness and cold. And the word still called up pleasant memories: childhood, the countryside, palms, the mysterious whispering of the trees.

That winter was a rest cure and a temporary forgetting.

Spring quickened his Creole blood and awakened memories.

The lesion he had received in prison was troubling him again. Carlos Sauvalle was his only bedside companion, Sauvalle, tall, fair, with the blue of his Norman ancestry in his gentle eyes. He supplemented Pepe's slender resources and brought in doctors to operate on him.

In the delirium of fever Martí had visions of old Nicolás Castillo with his white hair and his wounds. The sheets recalled the blinding whiteness of the quarries. When, finally, he got up he was all a living memory. The city received him, more winsome than ever, with its smile of spring. But that friendly glance which people exchanged as they met, as though congratulating one another on the fine young sunshine, that very brotherhood between men and things aroused a bitter gnawing recollection in him. He was suddenly torn by a desire to stop the passers-by and confound them with his terrible secret.

One day, coming toward him up the slope of Atocha, he saw another Cuban in exile, Carlos Fraga. He was with a young man whom Martí did not know. Fraga introduced him: Zeno Gandia, South American. Martí was in no mood to go through the conventional rites of courtesy, and when Gandia held out his hand, he uttered these strange words:

"You do not know me. Before you give me your hand, think whether a man whose dignity has been outraged and who has not yet received satisfaction is worthy to clasp it."

Fraga burst out laughing. But Pepe, in dead earnestness, drew the astonished Creole into a doorway, and, unfastening his shirt, showed him his prison scars.

His memory was a "basket of flames." He had to pour them out on paper to see if they could burn the official consciences to which "Ultramar" was nothing but a treasure chest that was falling apart and an unflagging topic of parliamentary debate.

When he reached his boarding house Martí sat down to write his report entitled *Political Imprisonment in Cuba.* Without hatred, for he "did not know how to hate" — and hiding his own suffering — "Why talk of myself when I speak of sufferings, when others have suffered more than I?" — he poured out the white heat of his indignation in fifty pages of grief and pity, of dramatic truth and apostrophes and antitheses in the manner of Victor Hugo. Through his words marched with a tragic rhythm the shocking examples of imprisonment, all Cuba itself in its unending Calvary.

The printed accusation reached the Congressional desk of Labra and reminded him that in Cuba there existed a still blacker slavery than that which he had condemned in his magnificent speech of April 3d. It reached Don Francisco Díaz Quintero, the director of *El Jurado Federal*, and aroused the republican contingent to noble indignation. Canovas, lying politically fallow at the moment, deplored the fact that a rebel should be endowed with such vigor as a pamphleteer. López de Ayala in the Colonial Office frowned and took note of that new name: José Martí. Doña Barbarita, the Creole widow of General Ravenet, wiped away more than one tear that fell on the pages of the pamphlet that Carlos Sauvalle had distributed among all the Cubans residing in Madrid. The aged, illustrious Calixto Bernal, the soul of the Cuban expatriates, called on Martí to clasp him to his breast.

His illness and the printing of his pamphlet had made heavy inroads on Martí's slender resources. It was useless to think of further help from his father, who had difficulty keeping his head above water in the impoverished island. There was Sauvalle to solve his difficulty. His father was rich. His generous monthly remittances arrived regularly and he begged his friends to share them with him. But Pepe refused. He permitted Carlos to help pay for certain patriotic publications with money that would otherwise have been spent on frivolous amusements. As far as he himself was concerned, he would manage.

He burned his bridges and enrolled at the University of Madrid. The extremely tolerant plan of studies then in force made it possible to take specialized courses before completing the bachelor's degree. And Pepe, like every young Creole with an easy flow of words, studied law, although the bar did not particularly attract him. So in a short time he was studying *res mancipi* and how to pay his next week's rent.

Fortunately, Doña Barbarita Echeverria, who was so moved by his pamphlet, learned of his situation, and once when Pepe went to see her in search of the warmth and accent of Cuba, this widow "with the soul of an angel" asked him if he would be able to tutor her children.

So then in the mornings he attended his law classes and in the afternoons he reinforced with gravity and affection the none too impressive authority Doña Barbarita's children found in his eighteen years. The children's progress was amazing and Doña Barbarita sang Don Pepe Martí's praises from the housetops and said he had no equal at bringing out children's interest and intelligence. These praises reached the ears of Don Leandro Álvarez Torrijos, who likewise entrusted the education of his brood to this beardless youth.

And so he was able to earn a living. Not a very good one, but enough to satisfy his landlady's demands and even to enable him to go once in a while to the gallery of the Español or Real Theaters. Occasionally there was a windfall, as for instance the translation of a certain English contract, "full of strange and technical terms." It came most opportunely, for Pepe's shoes were in a sorry state. The tedious work paid him eight dollars. But instead of spending the money on shoes he bought photographs of famous paintings.

At the university his fellow students quickly made a friend and comrade of this pale young Creole, so generous in his poverty. In respectful silence they had listened more than once to his tales of prison and he had heard phrases of indignation from their lips and protestations of faith in the not too distant coming of the Republic. Although every shade of opinion was represented, from the radicals to monarchists and even young reactionaries, the majority belonged to the forces of Figueras and Pi y Margall.

In this forum of university corridors and in the editorial rooms of certain liberal little news-sheets Pepe learned the inside details of the existing Spanish political scheme of things. The neutrality and discretion of the substitute King were unable to restore peace to the warring Hispanic family. Sagasta and Ruiz Zorilla were at each other's throats. Carlism had broken out again in the north, and while the monarchists were grooming the young Bourbon heir, Alfonso XII, the Republicans were feverishly working for their hour of victory. From the reporters' gallery of Congress Pepe had witnessed jousts of eloquence and wit. Manterola, that master of dialectics, Castelar with his polished phrases, Canovas, and Moret often made a deep impression on him with the eloquence of their words. The shrewdness of Sagasta, the telling thrusts of Romero Robledo, the "young cock of Antequera," both amused and disgusted him.

All that spectacle — and was it really anything but a spectacle? — left in him forever the deplorable sense of a meaningless void. Spain was divided by barriers of words and by petty jealousies. Everything, even politics, became a matter of party spirit, like the divisions between the admirers of Lagartijo's or Frascuelo's style of bull-fighting. In the midst of this eternal discord, which rendered the best intentions impotent, parasites, inertia, and rhetoric flourished. Martí began to see clearly that the problem of Cuba was a product of the problem of Spain, which would be settled only when a solution was found to that of the mother country — unless before that there came a parting of the ways.

Don Calixto Bernal, to whom Martí confided these impressions, on the whole agreed with him. Some of the young man's opinions seemed to him too mystical, especially those having to do with the colonies. Pepe was a poet, whereas the old gentleman from Camaguey, who had been fighting for the dignity of Cuba since the time of Tacón, had a logical, legal, positivistic mind. Before the Investigation Committee his clear reports, urging a gradual policy of home rule for the colonies, had touched on many a sore spot. Despite his moderation in insular affairs, he had bold original ideas in the field of politics. He often discussed with Martí the weaknesses of the parliamentary regime, the need for restoring "true democracy" through government directly by the people, and other of the favorite theses expounded in his books. He somewhat confused the young student with his more elaborate theories: the absolute necessity for a future society of nations, the rise of a "Fourth Estate," the proletariat, as the outcome of a great revolution far beyond any the world had yet seen.

There was no one with whom Pepe would rather talk than that "theoretical practical" old man, as Bernal described himself. They were often seen together: Don Calixto, a little bowed with the weight of years; Pepe, slight, nervous, talkative. Don Calixto was the master of his apprenticeship in democratic ideology. He was to him in the field of politics something of what Mendive had been in literature.

As regards Cuba, however, his ideas left the young author of *Political Imprisonment* in Cuba disconcerted. Bernal, who advocated home rule for reasons of "conviction and legality," held the aspiration to independence premature. He considered preferable Cuba's annexation to the United States, which would assure it internal peace and prosperity until the moment came for it to join the confederation of the Antilles, when the United States, as he considered inevitable, should break up in a series of small republics.

These bold prophecies kept Pepe's imagination working at top speed, training him to project his thought far beyond existing conditions. As yet his objections to Bernal's home rule were somewhat weak. He still found himself on the horns of his own dilemma — Yara or Madrid. His memories and his youthful enthusiasm inclined him toward the first; in the scales of the second weighed the secret voice of his blood, the ties of affinity, and the cultural satisfactions he derived from the Spanish background. If only the republic were to become a reality! If only Spain herself under a worthy government should finally decide to redeem Cuba!

Other exiles often joined the discussions of the old and young Cuban, forming lively groups around a café table or in the editorial rooms of some friendly organ. The conversation would grow heated over the latest news from Cuba, transmitted by letter from Havana — the progress of the revolution, the execution of the poet Zenea, the terrible reprisals of Valmaseda against the rebels of Oriente — or the petty activities of the Colonial Office in Madrid.

Malicious echoes of these discussions reached the offices of *La Prensa*, an insignificant paper affecting a liberal policy, probably supported by the Cuban fortune of Manuel Calvo. So *La Prensa*, which had been making veiled allusion to the "filibustering" hidden "behind the smoke-screen of advanced ideas and radical principles" of Bernal, decided to play up these meetings in a sensational, penny-dreadful fashion, warning the government that the Cubans living in Madrid were nothing but "disguised rebels, hypocrites, and unnatural sons of Spain."

The publication of this and similar outbursts in the same strain led Martí and Sauvalle to publish a vehement denial in *El Jurado Federal* signed "A group of Cubans." It was not Martí's hand that penned the ungainly reply; but it contained several observations about the possibilities of revolutionary action. If any one among the Cubans in Madrid harbored an idea of this sort, he was well aware that Spain was not, and could not be, the place to work toward this end.

La Prensa, spurred on by this denial, persisted in its attack, calling the signers an "organized company." The controversy continued with a pleasant exchange of vituperation between the two papers, and when *La Prensa*, which had expressed its charges as the anonymous voice of public opinion, accused the "Group of Cubans" of being ashamed to sign their statement, Martí stepped openly into the ring to settle "a matter which insults had turned from a public into a private question." Sauvalle, too, signed this final communication to *El Jurado;* but the ringing words and severe lofty tone recalled the pages of *Political Imprisonment*.

Although *La Prensa* muttered grimly of civil suits and even duels, the casualties were negligible.

At the end of November Martí became ill again and had to be operated on once more for the removal of the tumor which had developed in prison. Sauvalle insisted on taking him to his own lodgings to see that he got better care. There Spanish and Cuban friends gathered around his bed to talk. The special topic of conversation was certain dispatches from Cuba stating that students in their last year of medical school had violated the tomb of Castañón, the fanatical spokesman of the Volunteers who had been killed the year before by a Cuban in Cayo Hueso. According to the brief dispatches, public opinion was at fever pitch.

Castañón . . . Volunteers . . . students. The ingredients could not have been more inflammable. The group at the patient's bedside gave itself over to speculation and memories. Pepe, pale and worn, tried to restrain his fever-heated imagination. Something serious must be happening in Cuba. He had had no news since the

28th of November. And among those medical students was Fermín Valdés Domínguez. . . . "Is there any news today, Fraga?" Fraga went out to get a paper. In a few minutes he came back, his face grim, a copy of *El Jurado* in his hand. "They have shot eight." Rising up quickly, Martí snatched the paper from him and read the brief notice, to which *El Juardo* had not dared to give much space. Eight shot; thirty-five sentenced to prison. The silence of stupefaction hung over the room. Pepe fell back upon his pillow. The rest sat gloomy and motionless.

He asked them to leave him by himself that afternoon. From the next room Carlos could hear him repeating at intervals the name "Fermín." What he could not hear was the unspoken oath that severed, once and for all, such inherited loyalty as he possessed and replaced it with the purpose and decision that was to endure the rest of his life.

DOMINGO FAUSTINO SARMIENTO (1811–88)

SARMIENTO WAS THE GREATEST JOURNALIST America has produced, not only because of his forceful analysis of the problems of his day, but because of the imperishable accent of his writings, which has saved them from the dust of oblivion. At least two of the basic works of our literature — *Facundo* and *Recuerdos de Provincia* — are the fruit of his journalistic activity. He was an impetuous man, a fighter. He needed the newspaper columns as a means of direct contact with his people. He crossed pens with Don Andrés Bello in a polemic in defense of romanticism which has been famous among us. Bello was our great humanist of the nineteenth century and stood for method, the balanced organization of intelligence, the serenely disciplined ambition to reorganize independent America in keeping with and aided by the sciences that were coming into being at that time. Sarmiento was violent. His pen placed the Argentine and America face to face with a dilemma which had the simplicity and directness of the new world that had just achieved its liberty: *civilization or barbarity*. In this attitude of Sarmiento's, in his burning zeal, there is a decisive factor of circumstance.

Sarmiento came to manhood under the dictatorship of Rosas. He was one of the many exiles who had to seek safety for their lives, liberty for their minds, in foreign lands. During the long rule of the tyrant Argentine letters flourished as never before, but in Montevideo or in Santiago de Chile. The romantic poems and the socialist creed of Echavarria; *Amalia*, the novel of José Mármol; Alberdi's writings, Sarmiento's books, appeared in cities beyond the reach of Rosas's *Mazorca*, the forerunner of the German Gestapo. And Sarmiento, who cherished in his soul the dream of seeing his Argentina a civilized nation, moving freely down the avenues of progress which was the religion of the liberal minds of the day, leveled all the power of his pen against the dictator. In a sense, Sarmiento is the perfect specimen of a human type that was common in America in that period: the intellectual in exile, the revolutionist of the pen.

But in Sarmiento's many-faceted work, this was only one phase of his life. The Argentine selected him as its President once it had regained its freedom. And then the champion of civilization against barbarism had one thought around which all the others revolved: to elevate the Argentine through the school. His name is forever associated with everything that has been done in his land to extend education, to cultivate the spirit. In his travels through the United States and Europe he had always one predominant concern: to see how a nation can be saved by means of its schools. As one reads the history of his life, one thinks: "There was once a schoolmaster who was the President of the Argentine." Few things pleased Sarmiento so much as the fact that during his administration the importation of paper increased from 12,000 to 200,000 reams. "People wrote more, especially to attack him. But what did that matter? He was born for the woodman's axe, like his own stout trees."

At the end of his long life he went, not exactly to seek repose but a new field of battle, to the backwoods of Paraguay. "Carapachay," writes Lugones, "was the picturesque period of Sarmiento. Three cabins of hand-hewn logs, which were later replaced by a more adequate building of the same wood, plain and unpretentious; a garden, a barnyard presided over by several white ostriches which the soldiers of the garrison had caught for him so he could study the transmission of this sporadic albinoism; several nurseries of eucalyptus trees, and a small experimental farm for his own use, made up his modest holdings. There he trained his birds, those other children with wings, which had always been dear to his soul. There he spent his days contentedly, drinking beer with his visitors, rowing in his punt, studying, even exploring the thick swamp growth a little, mounted on his old brown pony with his heavy boots, his braid-trimmed cashmere coat, a present from Urquiza, his straw hat, and his brush machete, like a rustic general of that little Far West. But his chief delight was to contemplate the nature he loved so dearly with the happy fatigue of a creator and the instinct of an artist. 'How many times we have gone to the islands of the Paraná Delta to see the light of the full moon upon the silent waters!' "

Sarmiento is one of Argentina's most beloved symbols. His work is known and admired all over the continent. Some of his books, like *Facundo*, which Mrs. Horace Mann translated into English, have a universal reputation. Auguste Rodin made a bronze statue of the teacher, which today adorns an avenue in Buenos Aires. Leopoldo Lugones, the Argentine writer, has written a life of Sarmiento, from which the following chapter is taken.

SARMIENTO THE EDUCATOR

LEOPOLDO LUGONES

Pity for ignorance and love of the truth made an educator of Sarmiento.

From seeing the soldiers of the guerrilla bands turned into fanatics by their own leaders, who took advantage of their deplorable state, and certain youths of San Francisco del Monte, stalwart and illiterate, he got the idea of teaching them to read and write. He was born with the gift of teaching, for even when he was small, it amused his relatives to see him doing it, and they rewarded his skill with praise and little presents. Thus the future inventor — the word is used advisedly — of the great system of popular education, which was still to a great extent new, was self-taught. His experimental conception of this discipline was based on the experience of living and the society in which he grew up, and this gives him singular importance as an educator of South America.

The Socialist Dogma of Echavarria and its commentators had formulated the principle, which derived in turn from the liberalism of the day: people should be educated to be free. This idea was in many of Echavarria's writings; in Alberdi, the proponent of manual-training schools as opposed to the colonial teaching of literature and theology, which he criticized with typical insight: "Work is the best remedy for restlessness. It is useless to fill the minds of young people with abstract ideas on religion if they remain in idleness and poverty. Work is a great force for morality. Remind our people that the nation is not just the land. We have had land for three centuries; we have had a nation only since 1810. Liberty, like the civilization of which it forms a part, is essentially an artificial creation in the sense that it is nature cultivated and trained."

But nobody had formulated the program, which is the essential thing, nor hit upon the method, which is everything. The *Manual of Teaching* which the government of Montevideo requested Echavarria to prepare is a hollow liberal ritual. The teaching of the émigrés in Chile followed the Lancastrian method or confined itself to specialized schools. Only Sarmiento really conceived the idea of popular education as the basis of democracy.

I said that this came about also from his love of truth.

The false ideas of the primary schools, where they were still teaching that the earth stands still in the midst of the firmament;

the dogmatic books of his childhood; the odious perceptive system of clerical teaching, which reinforces its conclusions with the threat of damnation, all convinced him that liberty is impossible without the use of reason.

This was the point of departure of his apostolic mission, which began with the Colegio de Santa Rosa, after those first attempts in the Andes, at Pocuro and Copiapó, where he taught the miners of Punta Brava with spelling book and drawings. It should be noted here that this courageous pioneer possessed a very broad education. He had acquired by himself French, English, a fair knowledge of mathematics, a large if unorganized amount of literature, and drawing, already mentioned, the pedagogical importance of which he fully recognized: that of a direct language.

His plan to found a school for girls in San Juan, taking advantage of his reconciliation with Benavidez and the latter's favorable attitude, was the result of long thought and consideration. Sarmiento believed education for women to be of capital importance. On this, said he, depends the fate of nations. For this reason one of his first steps in the field when he came to power was to create normal schools for women. The connection between the school and motherhood was one of his favorite themes. He wanted to found nurseries where working women could leave their children while they were employed: a beneficent institution we do not yet possess. These matters were correlated in his mind with the proper equipment and installation of the schools, which should be places where the future citizen received his first lessons in matters the state should teach him: the example of comfort and cleanliness considered as duties. Also he saw in the education of women the best method of propagating freedom in spiritual matters. For this reason he selected the Woman's Normal School of Montevideo in which to deliver his famous speech against clericalism in 1883. His articles entitled "School without My Wife's Religion" were the result of the polemic occasioned by that speech and initiated the campaign of the liberals which led to the law of secular education.

His famous conflict with the Charity Organization of Buenos

Aires sprang from the same source. The great man wanted to incorporate the schools for women into the general educational plan, and he finally succeeded.

The Colegio de Santa Rosa was finally installed in the cloister of a convent for nuns of her same order which Father Justo de Oro, an uncle of Sarmiento's, had planned years before as a school. This arrangement came about as the result of a suggestion by the aforementioned priest to his sister, Doña Transito, that she put the education of her daughter in the hands of their nephew when he returned from Chile. This explains both the name of the school and the important place of religion in its plan of studies. This was a concession that had to be made to the ideas of the society and the government of the day, for it is well known that the federal leaders were fervent Catholics.

The curriculum of this boarding school included primary education, French, Italian, life drawing, music, dancing, and domestic science: the ideal education for women, yesterday as today. No mystic work was included among the readings, which signified no small advance. The directress of the school was Doña Transito de Oro, and her assistant, Doña Benvenida Sarmiento,[1] who from then on devoted herself so disinterestedly to teaching that on her ninety-sixth birthday, after sixty years spent in teaching, the government of the province of San Juan did not know what pension to assign her, as she had never received a salary.

The program of this boarding school, drawn up by Sarmiento, has been preserved. Discipline was severe as regarded study and recreation. The latter included, in addition to the usual pastimes and weekly excursions, group visits to families of the better class, so the students might learn how to behave in society: a clever linking up of home and school by means of courtesy and good manners. These young ladies went to church also on the holy days of obligation and the saints' days.

One can imagine how the small old city was enlivened by the sight of this flock of candid young doves in their simple uniform. It consisted of a white blouse with sleeve and over-sleeve, lest

---

[1] Doña Transito de Oro was Sarmiento's aunt; Doña Benvenida Sarmiento, his sister.

the transparent cambric might, with the excuse of summer, permit the tempting rosy freshness to show through; a skirt, white, too, that came half-way below the knee, and, like a prolongation of its narrow hem, pantalets of the same color, which descended in a froth of lacy ruffles to the shining kid slippers. A scarlet sash tied in front completed the costume, and the color was repeated in the double bows tied low on the sides of the head to the braids that were combed back smoothly and then fastened like handles under the ears.

This was their Sunday attire. Their everyday uniform was two dresses of printed or blue cotton with apron of nankeen, and in the winter they wore pretty little caps with veils.

They were given a weekly, a monthly, a quarterly, and a final examination. This last was a solemn event which was held in public with the governor as guest. The prizes consisted of rings, necklaces, and small pieces of jewelry.

Sarmiento loved this institution with all his heart, and many years later he still lamented its failure.

Let us examine his vast work in the field of education as contained in the articles he wrote on the subject, in the institutions he founded, and, above all, in his voluminous work *Popular Education*, which describes in detail his pedagogical invention, as he called it.

In 1852, directly on his return from Caseros, he had founded in Chile the *School Monitor*, an officially sponsored publication. In 1855 he published in the same country *Elementary Education in the State of Buenos Aires*, and in Buenos Aires itself the *Yearbook of Elementary Education*, which, as Supervisor of Schools, he had begun to edit. This is the beginning of pedagogical publications in South America.

His plans provided for other organizations.

Among the first of these were the summer lectures or vacation courses for teachers which he organized in Chile in 1854, under his own direction. Rosas had already fallen from power and the political concern about the "future President of the Republic" was so great as to be oppressive. His quarrel with Urquiza was like foundering in sight of port; but nothing could swerve him from his educational crusade, which knew neither limits nor country. Thus he stimulated the vocation of the great educator of Uruguay, Varela, as he later kindled the apostolic fire of General Terreros of Venezuela.

The construction of schools was another of his obsessions. He wanted them built large and pleasant, to accommodate three hundred children, which was the number that could be handled with maximum efficiency.

His instructions to school supervisors are models which have not been surpassed in this field.

The students' savings banks, part-time schools for pupils unable to attend regularly, and schools for backward children were all included in his program. And above all, the vast concept of the educator who wants to make teaching the supreme blessing of humanity, including even the most poverty-stricken: the sun that should shine on all.

"The state should allow every worker employed by it two hours of leisure a day to learn how to read." This was a splendid way of putting into practice the humanitarian eight-hour workday: two to study in the traveling school the state should set up near the work in progress; and two to eat and rest, which would make up the working day.

"The prisons should be schools. The prisoners are sick people who need curative treatment." The "healthy" prisons provided for by the Constitution would seem to have been influenced by this therapeutic idea. "We must make the whole Republic into a school."

During the time of his diplomatic duties in the United States, this idea was uppermost with him. There in the American Institute of Education, over which Emerson presided, he made his famous address: "The Schoolteacher." Later he published the book entitled *The Schools of the United States*, which was a report on the subject for his government. He founded the review known as *Ambas Americas*, dealing with pedagogy, bibliography, and agriculture. He translated the *Life of Lincoln*, the rail-splitting President. . . .

It is idle to point out that in a man as upright and efficient as

344

Sarmiento these ideas were carried out to the full extent of his power.

Two years after the first normal school was founded in the United States, he founded the first in Chile (1842). It must be said here, to give credit where credit is due, that the idea originally came from Don Andres Bello, although the first institution of this sort in America was founded by Rivadavia, who appointed Don Palbo Baladía its director (1826), while the same year the government of General Urquiza in Entrerrios asked the legislature to pass a law providing for two such institutions, although they were never established.

Sarmiento's trip to Europe and the United States was most fruitful. He talked with Guizot, he visited the Normal School at Versailles, he studied Morin's method and did some practice teaching at the Levi Alvarez school. In Spain he investigated the changes that had taken place in spelling through a first-hand study of old manuscripts and he became a member of the Teachers' Association of Madrid. In Holland he observed the system by which they were able to handle a double number of students, although it was not suited to his country. In Italy he visited a number of institutions for the blind and for deaf mutes. In the Prussian seminaries, which were preparatory schools for teachers, he observed the methods of advanced training for teachers; and the United States confirmed his clearest intuition of democratic teaching.

Intuition is precisely the word. He had formulated the system before reading about it or seeing it at work. His *Popular Education* was the literary outgrowth of these trips.

The book sets forth the qualitative and quantitative concepts of education, conceiving it as an integral thing many years before this was adopted as a system. It upholds the principle that teaching is a total which cannot be broken up into successive divisions. The system must be a complete one, with the different parts properly integrated, for the object of the school is to form the complete citizen. For the first time in South America this basic law of democratic teaching was formulated as a duty of the state, without restrictions. The state owes the citizen the maximum of possible instruction, for its primary interest is to form citizens with the greatest number of aptitudes. The methods of accomplishing this are, from the social and pedagogical point of view, free instruction throughout the school career and the correlation of studies.

For all this the establishment of a special budget for education, independent of the direct control of the state, to keep it free of politics, was needed. This was the idea behind the self-governing boards, which were one of the aims he most assiduously pursued. Educational funds were to be kept separate, both at their tax source and in their administration.

It is superfluous to state that his teaching method was rationalistic. His domination of this field was so great that at times a single paragraph of his is the equivalent of a book. The system can be formulated in a few words. First, the rationalist principle of proceeding from the known to the unknown. Then the gradation of difficulties; the opportunity of applying acquired skills to the ideas the student already possesses; the elimination of mechanical routine, making learning interesting.

With his conception of life as an integral thing, he believed that intellectual education and manual education should go hand in hand. Learning by doing constitutes the basis for this. To this end he encouraged the establishment of student museums, which were still rare in our schools. His lesson on a piece of flint, a stone which abounds in Chile, is a model from this point of view.

The plan of that first normal school, however, had great defects. It made no provision for natural science, which is indispensable for objective teaching, and it lacked a practice school. This kept pedagogy, which is essentially practical, theoretical. Although, to tell the truth, it must be admitted that teaching was no better anywhere else.

Among the shortcomings of this pedagogy was the use of corporal punishment and the system of penalties and rewards. The educator put off their abolishment until "the art of teaching has progressed further." This means that he regarded the procedures as fundamentally wrong. On the other hand, he wanted to do away with examinations, which he considered of value only for the higher studies, and substitute for them the constant action of teaching, which, after all, is the real discipline.

But reading and writing — that is to say, the two indispensable instruments for acquiring and transmitting knowledge — made enormous strides. There is no doubt that Sarmiento was a specialist in the field. Up to the day of his death he believed that man's supreme duty to his fellow men was to teach them to read. Every servant he had was also his pupil. He hated bad handwriting, which he said reflected bad breeding and selfishness. On the contrary, good handwriting, in his judgment, was the sign of frankness and love of the good. "It is formed in the soul." He wanted to inculcate this moral graphology, which has a real scientific basis, in children. With this in mind he thought schools should exchange their notebooks, maps, and drawings. When he was President of the Republic he used to visit the schools without warning to see their copybooks.

His famous reformed spelling, based only on the endings and roots of words — that is to say, omitting the etymological vestiges represented by the silent letters — is well known. This was all designed to simplify writing by using only such elements as were strictly necessary. But he overlooked the fact that spelling is the physiognomy of a language and that the living quality of the whole cannot be reproduced by rules. The scientific appearance of this literalist plan was the negation of science; its presumed rationality, impracticable. Letters are conventional, empirical symbols, not rational growths. They proceed from primitive, hieroglyphic reproductions which convey a feeling, not an idea. Sarmiento's ideas on the subject were so convincing that the Faculty of Philosophy and the Humanities of Santiago, headed by the purist Bello, adopted this reform, which lasted for seven years in Chile (1844–51).

But the importance given to reading by the educator initiated a real reform. "A country's civilization depends upon its reading." The construction of American unity on the basis of reading was one of his constant preoccupations.

At the same time he preached the reform of the language. Even before Bello he formulated the rational designation of the parts of speech and sentences.

Arithmetic became completely practical on the blackboard and in the exercise-book. He introduced into this subject the use of the abacus, the decimal system, the objective method which links it to the general positivism of science and mental calculus.

In the same way geography, one of his favorite subjects, had as its field of experiment and as its basis the map. The study of the universe was thus systematized.

Sarmiento was also aware of the difficulty of texts written from the adult point of view and in adult style, which is still one of the great handicaps in teaching. The author of school texts should write as though he were a child himself. In this way the process of learning to read would keep pace with the normal difficulties of childhood.

Finally, drawing, at which he was quite proficient — one can teach only what one knows — lay very close to his heart. For him it was not an adornment. It constituted one of the branches of popular education; that is to say, æsthetic training was a primordial part of teaching. His whole concept, as one can see, was one of integration: manual, æsthetic, and intellectual education. The curriculum of the Colegio de Santa Rosa included music and dancing.

When Sarmiento was elected President, public education was the fundamental plank in his platform. In the provinces he instituted advanced primary education and awarded prizes to the school that graduated the largest number of children. This system was in effect throughout his term of office, and ten prizes were awarded.

The educational grants for this purpose rose from 15,000 pesos in 1864 to 64,000 pesos in 1869. The qualifications required to receive such grants were fixed by decree, and a law of 1871 regulated their distribution by provinces. Free education included free textbooks, and 12,000 pesos was spent for this purpose; but unfortunately the method of their acquisition and distribution was not up to the level of the idea.

Since, according to Sarmiento's beliefs, citizens were entitled to the maximum education at the state's expense, he did not limit his activities to elementary instruction. The secondary schools received great attention as well. Their course of studies was modified, though retaining a predominantly literary character. Only during two of the six years the course covers were physics, chemistry, and mathematics studied. The rest of the time was spent on Latin, French, English, and history. In San Juan and Catamarca, because of local conditions, courses in mineralogy were given. In Buenos Aires there were elective and evening classes in geometry, mechanics, chemistry, and stenography.

In 1869 the development of normal teaching began with the creation of special courses in the secondary schools of Corrientes and Uruguay, where practice schools were set up. The government established ten scholarships. A law was passed the same year authorizing the creation of two normal schools. The next year that of Paraná was founded, with seventy scholarships. Its plan was too vast and badly balanced. Provision was made for seven branches of mathematics, including surveying, but natural history was omitted. The course covered four years, as at present. The minimum age for entering was sixteen, which was a wise provision, for thus the teachers were not too young when they graduated.

Sarmiento's liberal ideas extended to the clergy as well. Among the teaching institutions he founded or organized were theological seminaries. The fact that a citizen is to be a priest in no way invalidates his right to an education. Quite the contrary. It is a matter of maximum interest, for his is a cure of souls.

During his presidency the military and naval academies were founded. The latter was first set up on board the steamer *Brown*.

While he was directing the war against the guerrilla insurgents in 1862, and shortly afterwards, as governor of San Juan, Sarmiento had founded in this province and in Mendoza two experimental farms for the teaching of agriculture and arboriculture. As President he set up similar institutions in Salta and Tucumán. He ordered the first official investigations of plant pests and established the first veterinary school. It was under his government

349

that plans for a school of mines were drawn up, and a prize established for the discovery of soft coal.

He was greatly concerned about the education of deaf-mutes and of the blind, for whom the famous Braille system of raised letters was coming into use. He ordered the first student census, the basis of any organic plan of public instruction, and the compilation of the statistics on elementary education, which is the natural complement of the other. When it was drawn up he could point to its figures with justifiable pride. Under his administration the number of students reached the hundred-thousand mark.

In the field of higher education he founded the Museum of Natural History and brought Burmeister, Darwin's illustrious opponent, to head the institution, even though Sarmiento was a great admirer of Darwin. Burmeister, who was inclined to be overbearing and hard to get along with, had a high regard for Sarmiento's scholarly attainments and dedicated to him his study *The Sea Nettle (Physalia arethusa); an Unusual Marine Animal*. This constituted a signal honor in view of the cross-grained nature of the author.

Sarmiento founded the Faculty of Science in Córdoba, and engaged a staff of foreign professors in Europe who began the study of our natural science, making notable contributions. Lorentz began the classification of plants, dedicating to Sarmiento, with felicitous poetic intent, as is the habit of the followers of Linnæus, whose beautiful Latin floral nomenclature is like verses from the *Georgics*, the noblest of our dicotyledonous trees, the lignum vitæ, with its fragrant heart and rough exterior, like the man for whom it was named: *Bulnesia sarmienti*. Kaiser studied the fossils of the Silurian era in the sierra of San Juan, and gave one of the snails he found the name of *Maclurea sarmienti*. Bodenbender and Brackebush carried on the study of our geology begun by Bravard, who was also a friend of Sarmiento.

The founding of the observatory of Córdoba was the continuation of the enterprise and linked his name to one of the most important scientific contributions of our country: the mapping of the heavens of the southern hemisphere, in the *Argentine Uranometry* of Gould, whom Sarmiento had brought from the United

States for this twofold purpose. He realized that this entry of his country, with its land and its sky, into the world's science would do more to raise its standing among nations than any other thing. And thus his genius made into a gigantic constellation all the stars of his nation's firmament. A poor man all his life, without other human riches than his genius, he was the millionaire owner of the diamonds of eternity.

The general map of the country was also his idea. Sarmiento, always Sarmiento. He had a divine ubiquity, for genius is an emanation of God.

After he had served his term as President of the Republic, he accepted with exemplary democratic modesty the position of General Supervisor of Schools of the province of Buenos Aires, for the second time; and the next year, 1875, the law of elementary education was passed there. A General Board of Education, which had been the object of ceaseless endeavor on his part, was established under this same law. In 1876 he drew up the statutes for the schools under his supervision and founded the fortnightly publication *Public Education in the Province of Buenos Aires.*

In 1881 the national government appointed him Superintendent of Education, which made him the chairman of the National Board of Education, which had been created to replace the commission of the same name. Sarmiento's first measure revealed a characteristic trait of his enterprising nature. He summoned the teachers to give them a lesson in reading. This organization and his appointment lasted barely a year. The work was rendered fruitless because of internal conflicts due to its unsatisfactory organization. Sarmiento could not work well under the supervision of committees, however well-meaning they might be. At the same time his qualifications were such that matters pertaining to education could have been turned over to him to do as he saw fit. An artful, unjust decree, in which the clerical prejudice of the Minister of Public Education, Dr. Pizarro, is apparent, did away with the whole thing, only to create almost at the same time a new National Commission headed by Dr. Benjamin Zorrilla.

Sarmiento suffered one of the great disillusionments of his life, though his generous soul forgave this grave offense which the misguided President and his Minister had chosen to inflict upon him. Finally there remains his other great educational achievement: the founding of public libraries.

The fixed school, the teaching of reading are not enough. They must be carried to the remote spots off the paths of civilization. They must be cast abroad like the bread of supreme charity, imitating the sublime diffusion of the preaching of the apostles. The spirit must imitate the sun, which shines upon all without being summoned.

The traveling school followed the ox-cart route of the old theatrical companies which carried the gift of entertainment to the peasants. It went through the countryside carrying the basic ideas of agriculture, good seed, and elementary textbooks. And together with this the civilizer brought to the distant towns the little library, which put the poor farmer into communication with the inspiring words of great men. Sarmiento knew by his own experience that these glorious creators had worked for these anonymous readers, too, and he wanted to share with them those good things which had delighted his own soul. A patriot in the most sublime sense of the word, with its connotation of love and heroism, he reserved his greatest tenderness for the poor, the forgotten, the unknown. He carried to them the seeds of liberty, as one might carry food to a caged bird.

There is no education possible for the people without books. He knew this from his own bitter experience of having to read whatever came his way. "Books demand schools; schools demand books." "The schools prepare people to read, but they do not read for lack of books." For this reason he wanted all institutions to be open to the public, even the libraries of the technical schools. He sacrificed everything to this end. The government of Chile had heeded him, and in 1856 founded public libraries in the capitals of all the provinces.

But in our country his undertaking met with failure. Sarmiento had no collaborators and he lacked the ability of an organizer. The bookkeeping and the distribution of funds were badly done, and the appropriation was wiped out by the depression of 1876. There was no system in the distribution; the selection of the books, on the whole, was bad. The Commission for the Maintenance of Public Libraries, which Sarmiento organized as an autonomous body, which shows how important he considered it, was not equal to its task.

It would be a mistake, however, to think that all this seed that was scattered broadcast was lost. I can cite an instance which concerns myself, to prove the contrary.

In 1882 I was living with my parents at Ojo de Agua, a small village of Santiago del Estero, which lay almost on the frontier. The local school still had some books left from one of those libraries: the familiar green cloth-bound volumes with the Argentine shield stamped in gold on the cover. The teacher once lent me one of those books — *Insect Metamorphosis*. That was the first light in my spirit, the upwelling of a deep fountain which aroused in me the love of nature through its scientific contemplation. And I know that this was the determining factor in my intellectual life. My predilection for the natural sciences, which I helped to establish as a requirement of education, comes from this childhood study. From this came my observations of the ghoulish nest of the burying beetle, the honeycomb of the angry wasp, the blue sheath of the scarab, which has a sky-blue arch, like the vault of the world, on its black belly. Thus I learned to understand the life of the water, above whose crystal surface the dragonfly hovers like a mad compass needle. And the industry of the untiring ant, and the occupation of the bumblebee, which carries messages from flower to flower, as busy as a rural postman.

During the evening, while my mother's hands moved gently and swiftly over her sewing, my father read another book from the mutilated library: *Jerusalem Liberated,* by the renowned Tasso. And I can recall how deeply I was moved by the tale of the enchanted forest, with its bleeding trees and its terrifying illustrations. Thus I came to know poetry, and the melody of Italy entered my soul in that little mountain village, in the rich silence of the night while the little ones, Ramón and Santiago, slept in their cribs, the one as yellow as a newly hatched chick, the other as brown as a young partridge.

To how many others may the scattered books of this premature undertaking have revealed similar things! And is it not perhaps its justification that the great man should thereby have aroused in an unknown child the ideas of truth and beauty, now placed at the service of the task of relating his heroic life?

JUAN MONTALVO (1833–89)

DURING THE NINETEENTH CENTURY — that is to say, during the epoch of anarchy and dictatorship — in the Republic of Ecuador there rose to power one of the most extraordinary dictators America's history records: Garcia Moreno. He was a man of strong character, learned, but, above all else, a fanatical Catholic, who imposed upon his country a theocratic dictatorship, officially consecrated the nation to the Sacred Heart of Jesus, governed with the help of the Jesuits, persecuted every attempt at freedom, and held that the only link of national unity, above parties or race, was religion. Nobody could be elected to office or enjoy civil rights if he belonged to any sect the Church condemned. He was of the fiber of Philip II and Torquemada. Every night he read the *Imitation of Christ.* He was cruel and unforgiving with his enemies. The Catholics considered him one of their great heroes. Father Berthe said of him: "He is a Christian Hercules, a successor to Charlemagne and St. Louis." Even today there are those who extol his achievements in the warmest terms, like the Argentine writer Manuel Galvez, who is also the panegyrist of Rosas.

Juan Montalvo, on the contrary, a contemporary of Garcia Moreno, devoted the most ardent pages of his life to combating him. As vehement as was the dogmatic spirit of Garcia Moreno was the love of liberty in Montalvo. And if Garcia Moreno was the last of the crusaders and Inquisitors, Montalvo was in his day the clarion voice of America. The ideological combat between the two Ecuadorians is one of the most admirable chapters in Latin-American history. Montalvo was, besides, a great artist of the language, and his book *Chapters Cervantes Forgot* is one of the classics of the continent. Exiled from Ecuador by the dictator, Montalvo wrote, from a little border town of Colombia, pamphlets that aroused the youth of his country. Until the day came that brought the inevitable consequence: Garcia Moreno was assassinated in the public square of Quito, near the cathedral. Montalvo could rightfully exclaim with pride: "My pen killed him."

The Uruguayan writer José Enrique Rodó, who was one of the recognized masters of the youth of Spanish America at the beginning of the century, wrote an essay on Montalvo that is considered one of his short masterpieces. The following pages are taken from it.

MONTALVO

JOSÉ ENRIQUE RODÓ

In the public and militant aspect of his activities Montalvo was the enemy of Garcia Moreno. What Sarmiento was to Rosas, Montalvo was to Garcia Moreno. The two were not unevenly matched and the struggle between them was not devoid of intellectual interest. Of all the despotisms that have cast their oppressive shadow over Spanish America, this of the tyrant of Ecuador had the most originality and character. It was based on religious intolerance and perhaps never among modern nations has the reaction to a theocratic system been marked by such outspokenness and determination. The man who conceived and imposed upon his nation this monstrosity of reaction was far from being a contemptible person, from the standpoint either of energy and ability or of intellectual endowment. To mistake him for one of the upstart, barracks dictators would be to belittle him, thereby minimizing the extent of his responsibility and his aberrations.

Of excellent family, by his own efforts he had achieved civil and social prestige; the possessor of a superior education, scientific rather than literary, which had been rounded out by visits to Europe and which in his youth made him a fit companion for Wisse on his ascent of Pichincha, Don Gabriel Garcia Moreno stepped from a university professorship to the triumvirate and presidency of his country. In his administrative plans there were great things which survived him, either theoretically or actually accomplished by him. Alongside his inquisitorial aberrations, he reorganized the treasury, greatly increased the institutions of learning as well as beneficent and loan societies; he opened up roads from the ports of the Pacific to the heart of the Andes; he gave his country a railroad and tried to give it telegraph communication. Neither was he perverse by instinct or grossly selfish in his ambitions. He was a religious fanatic and that was the root of his evil, as it is the key to his bigoted personality. His sole and sublime idea was how the human clay could be metamorphosed into the ideal transfigurations of sainthood and how to hurl it into the most frightful abysses of hatred and madness. It was the same concept that during the colonization of America became the polar force of the thought and historic action of a whole nation, and was incarnated in the will of one man, Philip II. It was the idea that sank its talons into his conscience. Like the monarch of the Escorial, this President, on his smaller stage, believed that he had been chosen as the instrument of God to execute His judgments and vengeance.

The realization of this dream was a system of government in which it seemed that a shoot of the Spain of the conquest, which had escaped the revolutionary fires, had come to life and put out leaves anew. Ecuador was no longer a sovereign nation and the arbiter of its own fate; it was a dependency of Rome. This submission was sealed by a humiliating concordat. Tithing was restored in a form that had never been seen before. The tenth part of all income had to be set aside to support the Church and to swell the funds of St. Peter's successor. The right of appointing the higher clergy, which had come down from Their Catholic Majesties and in which they had always upheld the equality of their rights with those of the Church, was abrogated by the Republic as a schismatic abomination. There was a censorship of everything that was read or written. Not a book came through the customs or from the presses without the approval of the

Church. Behind the President, like the Venetian Senate, was the Company of Jesus. Public instruction was in the hands of the Jesuits and at times the Minister of Education was chosen from their tonsured ranks. It was a land flowing with milk and honey for the clergy, and from a dozen different directions there came a flood of monkish immigration, the offscourings of all the monasteries of the world, to infect the cities with the plague of their parasitic laziness, while in the small country towns the priest exchanged his spiritual authority for the powers of a tribal headman or military leader. The divisions and regiments of the army were given the names of religious sodalities; they were known as the soldiers of the Infant Jesus, or of the Five Wounds; the Volunteers of the Cross; the Sons of His Holiness; the Guardians of the Virgin. All immigration from Protestant countries was regarded as an abomination. The government prided itself on protecting what it called "the New Jerusalem," destined to be the custodian of the "Ark of the Faith," from this tainted brood. When the victorious armies of Italy marched into Rome, the Republic of Ecuador sent an angry protest; later on, it was planned to consecrate the country to the Sacred Heart of Jesus in a solemn ceremony. To give plastic form to the spirit that informed all this, official acts of devotion employed the trappings of primitive ceremonies. On Good Friday the head of the state walked through the streets, his back bowed beneath the weight of a cross; he was surrounded by his ministers and followed by the multitudes, flagellating themselves and groaning. This patriarchal ingenuousness did not exclude the horrible contradiction in which fanatical piety has always culminated: fratricidal fury in the name of the love of God. Every new attempt to shake off the hateful yoke, to restore the nation to a life of human dignity, ended in the cruelest repression. The gallows wrote the final chapter to prison cell and lash, and streams of blood of generous victims affronted the noble land of the Rocafuertes and the Moncayos.

This had been, in part, or was to be in its forthcoming revival, the system which the vengeful pen of Montalvo was to challenge in his paper *El Cosmopolita.*

For the reader from this region of America where I write, it will not be an easy task to understand this system. In the countries around the Plata religious intolerance has never been a force in government or the platform of a party. Here tyranny never used the mask of faith, and civil strife was motivated by other passions, other interests, and other ideas. When, on the occasion of any legislative reform or other problem that touched upon matters affecting the lives of all, religious controversy has passed from the academic halls to the disputes of the market-place, the resulting agitation has never given rise to any dominant political alignments or organizations. Whether this was due to the special nature of our social body, which from the days of the Spanish domination had been marked by a certain liberal and democratic bent that differentiated us, or to the way we lie open to the winds of the world, owing to our geographic situation and the steady flow of cosmopolitan immigration, with the tolerance engendered through so many differences and contradictions having to live together, the fact remains that the habit of freedom of thought flourished without difficulty among our human groups. Even within the camp of orthodoxy itself, and using the degree of clerical fanaticism in other countries of America as a standard of comparison, we have enjoyed a relative tolerance, a certain freedom of opinion in matters pertaining to religious belief which, at least as far as the social and political realities are concerned, has prudently tempered the logic of pure dogma. This is borne out when one compares the spiritual quality of men like Estrada, Zorrilla de San Martín, or Goyena with that of certain other outstanding and famous churchmen beyond the Andes.

The propaganda of Montalvo was like flashes of lightning amongst the still-living memories of the past regime and the sinister presage of an immediate and intensified restoration. Only the person who can faithfully represent to himself the scope of this ignominy, on the one hand, and the vindictiveness and generosity of a soul like Montalvo's can comprehend the fierce heroism of his fighting pen.

The year 1867 was fraught with great and ominous uneasiness. Garcia Moreno, whose influence was still strong, was elected senator; but the validity of his election was falsely impugned, vigor-

ously assailed, and finally nullified. In his stead the candidate who
ran against him was sworn into office. At this moment liberal opinion acquired vigor and hope. All saw in the decline of the once
powerful man, which they thought conclusive, the ratification of
Montalvo's propaganda, the triumph of *El Cosmopolita*. But the
agitation of that year did not end with this. The dishonest intervention of which the representatives of authority were accused
during those elections gave rise to a conflict between the President and Congress, and the passions aroused in trying to find a
solution to the dispute over the candidacies went far beyond the
original problem. An attempt was made to bring about an understanding between the two branches, but when one of the inter-
ventors was ordered imprisoned and exiled on the grounds that
he was obstructing an agreement with seditious purpose, the opposition decided that matters had gone far enough, and without
further delay moved that responsibilities be demanded of President Carrion. The discord grew, threats to dissolve Congress began to be heard. There were stormy sessions in which the President defied Congress, and on November 5 the latter issued the
severest kind of statement, charging the President with being unworthy of his high office. At this violent extremity Garcia Moreno
stepped in, demanding that Carrion renounce the authority he
could no longer wield. This forcible resignation was accepted and
feelings subsided, for the time being, to their normal level.

The President who had been removed from office was replaced
by Dan Javier Espinosa, no less upright and determined than he.
The approach of the end of the term of office brought up the problem of the coming campaign. Garcia Moreno's election seemed a
foregone conclusion in view of the multiple resources of his
barely disguised influence. Against him there were the candidates
of the liberal groups. There was Don Pedro Carbo, who embodied
outspoken energetic reform tendencies and whom Montalvo would
have preferred, but his very radicalism, excellent as it was, was a
barrier. To combat successfully the threat of reaction a coalition
of all the forces opposed to it was needed, around a person whom
all would support, and to this end Don Francisco Aguirre was
settled upon, a man steeped in liberal ideas and for whom all had

the highest respect. This was the way the electoral contest shaped up, and as it approached its end the unequalness of the opposing factions revealed itself more clearly, the weight of power being with the reactionary leader. Feelings began to rise again.

At this time Montalvo came to the city frequently or lived there. His proud, serene figure as he walked through the streets attracted glances sometimes of hatred, sometimes of admiration. Spies watched his every step. More than once the arm of the fanatic or hired assassin was not far from his breast. Once when mobs threatened to assault his house, a group of devoted young men stood guard over it. This fever of heroic excitement, this stimulus of danger and outrage, kindled the fires of *El Cosmopolita*. It was at this moment that its protests take on the noble, virile accents of *El Nuevo Junius*. In this he denounced the persecutions and acts of violence, the menace of the gallows, the shamelessness of the libeler, and he revealed the omnipotent hand of the arch-instigator behind the deposition of the President. He analyzed in detail the true character of the candidate of the reaction and held him up to abomination, fear, and shame. And when the candidate let his own voice be loudly heard, Montalvo called attention to the true import of his words, which promised that the norms of the government would be the points of the *Syllabus;* its instrument, unrelaxing severity. Now he addressed the parties, urging them to greater unity; now he harangued the officers of the army in the hope of saving them from the abyss of seditious disloyalty to which the state of mind which was the real ruler of the Republic was rushing them at breakneck speed. "Officers," he said to them, "I am not your enemy. In a great nation I would have been a soldier." He also tried to win over those whose innocent piety was being unwittingly yoked to the intrigues of fanaticism; and recalling a talk he had had, real or imaginary, with the gentle soul who was the Archbishop of Quito at the time, he opposed to the objections of cautious timidity the laws of reason, which are encompassed and supported by the integrity of the faith itself.

But all this failed of effect in the face of Garcia Moreno's personal ascendancy, which the force of circumstances rendered hourly more invincible. Urbina, from his place of exile, was threat-

ening an uprising, or at least this was noised about with the intention of arousing suspicion, and this danger was utilized by the
supporters of the reactionary party to work upon the fears of the
friends of law and order, to accuse the government of being weak
and remiss in its measures, and to call for the iron hand of deliver-
ance. Garcia Morena had laid aside all pretense of being a humble
bidder at the polls. A prætorian guard watched at his gates. All
the elements of material power were now in his hands.

The year 1869 began with a conflict that could no longer be post-
poned between a weak central power and a subversive force that
was closing in upon it with insolent assurance. On January 17 the
military uprising finally took place which threw President Espinosa out of office and conferred upon Garcia Moreno the powers
of dictator. All this happened and was over in a moment, as
though it had been inevitable. The restored despot immediately
undertook a revision of the Constitution which should give legal
forms to the dictatorial, theocratic dream he proposed to revive
with even greater perfection. In May of that year the Constitutional Convention met. The chief purpose which informed its
measures was to increase the subjection of the state to the yoke
of the Church and to strengthen the attributes and power of the
executive authority in the distribution of public office. On these
bases that extraordinary man entered upon the exercise of his
new and most typical domination. Freedom of expression, freedom to live in one's native land, had withered at the first breath
of dictatorship. The voice of *El Cosmopolita* was choked in its
throat, and Montalvo took the road of exile.

Over the border of Colombia, on the summit of one of the mesas
which the Andes form on both sides of that sheer frontier, lies the
town of Ipiales, where for seven years Montalvo found refuge. It
is a beautifully situated spot though the cold of the uplands blew
over-chill on the heart of an exile.

He arrived there without books, he remained there without
books. Yet despite this, it was during this village exile that he
produced the greater part of his work and that which most re-
dounds to his glory, and this is the place to speak of Montalvo the

writer. His outward life, practically bounded by the walls of his little garden, was uneventful — an occasional dispute with an annoying neighbor or some coarse, rapacious priest, one of those who were the eternal target of his pen. And all the while his imagination bubbled over with dreamed-of adventures, swarms of ideas, the caprices and music of forms.

There is something typical of Montalvo's entire destiny, like a magnified image of the mishaps of his whole life, in the fact that he produced the best and the most highly literary part of his work in the solitude of a village. Grasp this clearly: not in the solitude of the desert, which is complete, splendid emancipation, the love of the vast freedom of space, which the divine fire of the imagination peoples with nymphs and satyrs; but the solitude of a poor, mean village, the abode of neither gentleman nor savage, but merely of the rustic lout; where the clarion call of the cock is the signal for gossip to begin, and the setting of the sun its hour to spy in the dark; in the solitude of a village, without the association of people of his own sort, and without books. He alludes to his situation in his vehement, amusing manner: "Without books, gentlemen, without books. If you have any compassion in your bowels, you should melt into tears." For his writing, which by its very nature and character was so in need of daily contact with books, and the easily accessible instruments of checking and reference which books are, he had to be content, for a task as difficult as the parody of Don Quixote, with the fancied library his memory and his imagination stood against the bare walls of a village house.

But even in the city or near it, and in the company of his books, the obstacles he had to surmount were great, owing to the unstable structure of his nation's culture. He tells us of the heroic effort required to find a printer. Only with the greatest difficulty and the help of friends was he able to bring out the issues of El Cosmopolita. Yet in his Calvary this was the smallest and most endurable suffering; there was the isolation and spiritual abandonment, which was what hurt most, the general lack of understanding: from that which bristled with envy in the face of superiority, the besetting sin of small democracies, to that which shrugged its shoulders with coarse disdain at the disinterested labor of style and research, and that which, in this very field, turns a deaf ear on all that is new and original, or, affecting to understand, understands nothing. . . . In a word, all those bad traits of the village, as a result of which, as far as the higher things of the spirit go, all Spanish America has been, on a varying scale, like the corner where Montalvo composed the most difficult of his works. One can see the scar of this cruel wound in his admirable introduction to *Chapters Cervantes Forgot*. And there is probably not a single gifted South American who at some time or other has not voiced similar feelings, or in the muted vibration of whose writings it cannot be felt. This attitude toward those of superior capacity is universal; it is rooted in the clay of which Adam was fashioned; but it reappears in an exaggerated form in the nations of South America because of the precarious, unequal basis of its civilization. Although the person endowed with exceptional ability and knowledge can rise as high there as in the great cultural centers, the state of interest and attention on the part of the public is greatly inferior, with the result that the gulf between the elect and the masses is increased a hundredfold. This is the cause of that restlessness which comes from a lack of adaptation to one's medium, and a certain nostalgic yearning for that ancestral, spiritual fatherland which the civilization of Europe has built beyond the sea, so common among Spanish Americans of literary or artistic bent. Expatriation, which Montalvo always longed for, then becomes a natural and inevitable step; but to expatriate oneself, as he did, with thought and memory ever fixed on the homeland, the sweeter for being distant, and dreaming of the day of return, with the fruits of culture assimilated, which shall pay the native land the price of absence. To *remain* thus, in spirit or in actuality, maintains the necessary and fruitful link with the common work of one's brothers, and in America only those who have managed to preserve this link, and in the degree to which they have been faithful to it, have been great. Only those have been great in America who have developed, by word or deed, a consciousness of America. No one can usefully co-operate in the world order who does not accept with stoic resolve — nay, more, with a joyful spirit — the post God was pleased to assign him in His hosts when He gave him a land in which to be born and a period of time in which to carry out his life and his work. Inability to adapt oneself becomes a condition of progress, in social as in organic evolution, only if it turns into a healthy reaction which adjusts itself to the needs of its own superiority to its surroundings, and can be fatal to those incapable of adaptation through weakness or inferiority.

Montalvo's thought often reflects the rhythm of an undisguised aversion to the transient reality of his country and a deep feeling for its enduring, ideal being. Speaking of his dismissal from the post of diplomatic secretary which he had held in Paris, he said: "Fate suddenly turned hostile and with a savage gesture threw me back to this corner." On another occasion he added: "If the day ever comes when I can return to Europe, I promise my fellow citizens that I will give them little cause to complain of me." On occasions he shows his detachment with biting harshness: "My one regret is not having a good, noble, great country where I could be a noble, good, great patriot." Referring to the disorder of the Spanish-American countries, he exclaims: "Oh, Balkan republics! Heaven grieves, Hell smiles when they turn their eyes toward this part of the world." But he has words of faith and hope that offset the foregoing: "America, young, strong, intelligent, enamored of everything great, will fulfill its destiny, will become civilized, will be free, happy, and will enjoy without hindrance the great gifts nature has bestowed upon it." While he was in Paris, he was a constant visitor to the Botanical Gardens and he liked to stop before everything that recalled to his spirit the image of his native land: "the condor of the Andes, the thistle of America, the coronilla, the *gallo tanisario* with its solemn melancholy call."

The integrity of the American conscience, the integrity which prophetically grasps the measure of the greatness of our destinies and, by the same token, of the greatness of our past, is present in his work, and this moves him to make in one of his *Seven Treatises* that bold affirmation of the superiority of Bolívar over Bonaparte, an affirmation that in its day was to startle sober, conservative souls, and would surprise them even today, though fortunately not so much. Who has ever spoken words of deeper compassion for the fate of the conquered native races? And as for the originality of the nature of America, he could feel it, too, and has often left an impression of it for all time. Nothing was ever said more fitting for the ears of a mountain than the words in which he called down the wrath of Heaven upon the majesty of Mount Pichincha in tones which we imagine must still be reverberating about the slopes of the giant. There is nothing more impregnated with the aroma of the earth and divine humility than his praise of corn, the wheat of the poor, the amasser of that energy which moves the arms of the toiling Indian as, bent over the soil which is the dust of his forefathers, he converts his gentle patience into gold for the master. . . . Each time this note of Americanism, in feeling or in color, appears to preside over the harmony of a prose so chaste, so limpid, so cast in the classic mold, there comes to my memory the impression of the Inca Garcilaso's *Comentarios reales,* in which this child of a conquistador and an Incan Princess, who combined within himself the twin nobility of his rank and the privilege of style, gave us in the purest language of the conqueror and in the richest, most elegant prose of his time the most enchanting, ingenuous portraits of the American soul, which resemble the traces of the blood of the Indian on the gleam of a Toledan blade.

The *Seven Treatises,* which was not published until ten years later in Europe, were written, or at least the first draft of them, during 1872 in Montalvo's retreat of Ipiales. It is here that the most characteristic and elevated expression in his writings is to be found. The different sections are entitled: "On Nobility," "On Beauty in the Human Race," "Reply to a Pseudo-Catholic," "The Heroes of South American Freedom," "The Banquets of the Philosophers," and "The Hint." The last was reprinted as the introductory study to *Chapters Cervantes Forgot.*

PART IV

The Cities

RIO DE JANEIRO

THE PORTUGUESE PURSUED a different policy from that of the Spaniards in organizing their colony in America. They founded no large cities in the interior. First they used the port of Bahia as their capital. Later they divided the administration of Brazil into two divisions, with one capital in Bahia and the other in Rio de Janeiro. As a result the two cities suffered the hazards of war and piracy, and their history is a far more troubled one than that of cities like Mexico or Lima. It was only after considerable delay that the Portuguese took advantage of the unique beauty of the bay to found the city of Rio de Janeiro there. It may have been that the settlers were awed by the very magnitude of the natural surroundings, as is already manifest in the early chronicles of the sixteenth century, when Gonzalo Coelho and his astounded crew first beheld it. Magellan stopped there fourteen days on his voyage round the world. From then on, the fate of Rio was linked to the fortunes of war. The French sought refuge there; the Portuguese fortified themselves to resist them. A Huguenot tried to establish the stronghold of Calvinism in America there, and founded the city of Henriville. The Portuguese drove him away. Finally the nephew of the governor of Bahia founded the city of San Sebastian de Rio Janeiro. When it was made the capital of the *capitania*, in 1608, it had only 2,500 inhabitants. At the beginning of the eighteenth century it was captured by the French under the command of Duclerc. Some of the inhabitants and the students rose against them, drove off the invaders, and killed Duclerc. The next year one of his countrymen arrived with a fleet of warships to avenge his death. In order to pacify him the *cariocas* had to give him 610,000 crusados, 500 crates of sugar, and many hundredweight of meat. Seventy years later Rio was made the capital of the viceroyalty. And before fifty years had elapsed the court of Portugal had disembarked at its gates and set up there the capital of the Empire. From 1808 to 1821 a unique thing in the history of America took place: the monarchs of one of the nations of

Europe that had written some of the most brilliant pages of its history established the seat of its government there. Rio grew into an Old World court, and the transition to the monarchy was not difficult. A year after the King of Portugal had sailed for Lisbon, Don Pedro I was proclaimed Emperor of Brazil. The nineteenth century in Brazil is a century of royalty, uprisings, amazing development which ended in the birth of a Republic. Presiding over this complicated web of evolution was Rio, one of the most beautiful cities in the world, the largest in South America after Buenos Aires.

The following description of its character and setting was written especially for this book by the Brazilian novelist Erico Verissimo.

SUN, SEA, AND SAMBA

Impressions of Rio de Janeiro

ERICO VERISSIMO

IN the words of my friend the poet Damasceno Ferreira, there are three basic attitudes a writer can assume toward the landscape of Brazil, and of these Machado de Assis, Graça Aranha, and Olavo Bilac are typical examples. The first is the husband of our scenery: he is reserved, due either to modesty or to jealousy; he never describes it, does not even mention its name before strangers. This accounts for the absence of landscape in the work of this great novelist. The second is the ingenuous wooer of Brazil's natural beauties. He never wearies of embellishing them with vivid adjectives, of adorning them with flowers and colors, in a transport of lyric passion. But Bilac is the lover of the native scene; he proclaims its charms at the top of his lungs, he disrobes it with hot words of delight, he exhibits it before the eyes of all, shouting: "Look at her, see how beautiful she is, and she's mine!"

These reflections come to my mind as I sit down to write the following impressions of the city of Rio de Janeiro.

Why — I was asked the other day — is there no description to be found of this enchanted city? Is it because the *cariocas*, as the natives of Rio de Janeiro are known, are jealous husbands and assume the same attitude as Machado de Assis, taking for granted the beauty of their city, but, out of modesty, avoiding talking about it before strangers? Or is it that they look upon the city as their mother rather than their wife, and in this case their modesty goes even deeper. Or can it be that the beauty of its setting overpowers them, reducing them to silence and leading them to the conclusion that Rio and its landscape are completely and irretrievably beyond the powers of description? Personally, I think the explanation is a simpler one, and comes from the make-up of the cariocas. Why should we describe it? they ask. It is much pleasanter, easier, and more natural to live the city. A man who had a delicious fruit in his hands would be silly to describe it or paint it instead of eating it. And there is still another reason. The carioca is bohemian by nature, and shrewd and acute, and there is nothing he dreads more than making himself ridiculous, as would be the case if he were to be guilty of literature of the picture-postcard type.

And to bring to an end an introduction that has already become too long I may say that it is very possible that the idea, and even less the necessity of describing the surroundings in which he lives, has never crossed the mind of an inhabitant of Rio de Janeiro.

The natural setting of Rio is really breath-taking. The city stretches out lazily in all directions, between the mountains and the sea, winding about the hills, skirting the bay, at whose entrance Sugar Loaf Mountain stands guard. It almost always has a festive, holiday air. If it were painted scenery, one could say that the artist had overdone the color and decorative effects and had deliberately assembled in a single landscape all the varied beauty that God had scattered with thrifty hand over the whole surface of the globe.

The waters of the bay are a smooth green dotted with islands, boats, beacons, buoys, sails. . . . Over it gulls and airplanes trace their flight; often bands of strident-voiced green parrots cross the sky. The spendthrift sun flings handfuls of golden coins over the waters. And on certain days a luminous blue mist, lightly tinged with rose, hovers in the air, giving the city the appearance of a toy wrapped up in cellophane.

How can one remember the names of the countless mountains, or describe their appearance? The light plays tricks with the shape and the color of these hills. We go to bed at night certain that we know the name of these stone walls, and we wake up the next day to discover a new peak, a new chain of mountains, to find that during the night some mischievous invisible sculptor has stayed up working for the sole purpose of changing the landscape or to invent some new wonder. There are days on which the clouds hide the peaks or invent plumes, wigs, and veils for the mountains' heads. The air smells of sun, sea, and forest. The visitor to Rio is immediately infected by this holiday spirit, by an almost pagan attitude toward life, as though suddenly all his inner gloom had been dissipated under the influence of this blazing sun, these fragrant perfumes. For there is magic and music in the air, a caress in the wind, a bright mystery in this luminous city of São Sebastião do Rio de Janeiro.

On the summit of Corcovado, His arms extended toward the sinful city, stands the statue of Christ the Saviour. As one stands at the base of the monument and looks out over the city and the sea, one gasps, as though wounded by so much beauty. Gasps and almost blushes. The scenery is overpowering, almost indecent in its beauty. Those who have a sense of economy are somewhat irked at such a riotous excess of colors. Those whose æsthetic sense leans toward restraint and the golden mean feel almost offended by this lavish display of colors and forms. An ascetic would be inclined to close his eyes, as though he had suddenly come face to face with a naked woman. Because Rio is a woman. Everything about it suggests femininity — breasts, soft flesh, perfumed hair, languid caresses, allurement. . . . Rio is a sun-browned woman adorned with flowers and stretched out in the sun on the sands of the Atlantic. . . .

The first time I looked down upon Rio from the heights of Cor-

covado the beauty of the landscape hit me like a blow in the
solar plexus. It was something far beyond the power of words,
paintings, picture postcards, and the phrases employed by tourist
agencies.

Blues and greens dominated the scene, in an indescribable
gamut of shades. It was both painting and music. A symphony in
blue and green, in perfect counterpoint, a wealth of melodic
variations upon a central theme. The bottle green of the tranquil
bay, the paler, brighter green of the sea beyond the harbor, the
whole scale of green of the vegetation, the bluish tinge of the far-
away hills, the indigo of the more remote sky, the milky purplish
gold of the mist, the lilac of the shadows and the fading distances
. . . all these colors sang together down below and came at me
in a glory that was frightening. I gazed upon the sight in dizzy
amazement. Who was the creator? Some impressionist painter.
There was in it something of the savage beauty of Gauguin's canvases, in the leaves of the trees, in the red and yellow of the hills,
in the form of the bluffs, and in the violence of certain of the
lights. But there were parts of the landscape that were definitely
from the hand of an academic painter, given to detail and realism.
And there were other reminiscences in that startling picture. The
trailing mists were from the brush of Corot. And those jarring yel-
lows were certainly the work of Van Gogh.

My eye followed the curve of the beaches beginning at the
bay, at Gloria, then following along Longo, past the perfect curve
of the beach of Botafogo, to linger over the miniature charms
of Urca, which is like a toy city, at the foot of the huge cliff which
gives it its name. Then, beyond the harbor, I saw the beach at
Copacabana, enormous, surrounded by skyscrapers, and bordered
by a walk of black and white tiles in fancy patterns, on whose
white sands rested people and bright parasols, and where the
waves broke in bouquets of rainbow foam. Between mountain and
sea lay the Rodrigo de Freitas lagoon, as calm and bright as a blue
mirror. Beyond Copacabana, to the south, Ipanema, Leblon, Ga-
vea. And in a line with the beach, red, brown, gray, white roofs.
. . . Bungalows, mansions, cottages, chalets, country places, skyscrapers, gardens, squares, forests. And flooding all a hot, cheerful

sun, lazy and caressing, a sun that is, at bottom, responsible for all those colors, a friendly, indulgent sun, ready to share in everything.

To the west lies the center of the city, the compact group of large buildings. Plate-glass windows glisten in the sun. The streets branch out, black with asphalt, not in the studied symmetry of the avenues of Washington, but in a more bohemian fashion, picturesquely, carelessly, as the spirit moves them. As I look, my eyes keep encountering every minute the hills covered with poor shacks over whose sordidness the distance throws a deceptive cloak. These barren hills are of a reddish brown. The sun which beats against these tawny rocks is not that same agreeable sun which gilds the beaches, the sea, the mountains, and the dwellings of the rich. It is a tragic sun, an implacable sun. It beats pitilessly upon the tin patches of the cabins, upon the faces of the people who live there, who seem to have stepped out of one of Portinari's paintings.

Thus in a succession of skyscrapers and private houses, hills, woods, squares, parks, the city spreads out, far-flung yet always solid, varied, and rich in colors and forms, in sounds and shades. It looks like a sampler. And as scenery and humanity goes, it could really be considered a kind of sampler of Brazil.

Every type of landscape, every kind of city can be found in Rio. For those who like them, there are the boulevards with their sidewalk cafés, around whose tables people who have plenty of time on their hands gather to take their coffee or cool drinks and talk leisurely with their friends. For those whose taste runs that way there are buildings which recall the *art nouveau* or the glory of the last decade of the nineteenth century, such as are to be found on the Avenida Rio Branco and the streets about it. Those to whom the aerodynamic line appeals may find on the Morro do Castelo Esplanade, just a few steps beyond the European city, certain reminiscences of modern Russian construction, public and private buildings of bold outlines, some resembling huge boxes of cement, others bird-cages, others ships, all of which serve as an excuse for endless discussions of an æsthetic and political nature between academicians and revolutionists, between right- and left-wingers. If you want to see something that recalls Miami or Biarritz, there is Copacabana, the magnificent. There you will find what is perhaps the most beautiful beach in the whole world, backed by a long, solid row of skyscrapers, modern hotels, apartment buildings which house wealthy families, those in whom the carioca traditions are weakest, the newly rich, important public officials, and refugees from Hitler and the war who managed to bring money with them. These people, together with the tourists, whose number is not small, fill the bars and the terraces of the hotels and cafés, sun themselves on the beach, and walk about in light, thin clothes, or, in midsummer, almost naked. They are people who seem to have no worries at all, and they contribute to that holiday feeling which the city gives the newcomer. The sound of the old sea is overlaid with a murmur of voices speaking fifty different languages. It is a new tower of Babel built by men too wise to try to reach heaven because they have discovered that paradise, ladies and gentlemen, is here on earth, in this city of Rio de Janeiro.

Between Urca and the southernmost tip of Copacabana are the casinos which pride themselves on having the best shows in the world and where roulette and baccarat are played for high stakes. Men and women from all parts of the world swarm about the green tables. Among the flotsam washed up on this strand by the war are old habitués of Monte Carlo. The local moneyed aristocracy frequents these places too. And petty officials and clerks show up there on certain nights to try their fortune. There are also visitors from the provinces, professional men, cocottes, and always, always, the tourists. There is the rattle of chips, the click of the spinning roulette wheel, the voice of the croupier. . . . Smartly dressed women, blazing with jewels, smoke. The atmosphere is reminiscent of everything except Brazil. In the grill-room people dance to the music of good orchestras. Together with the native music, foxtrots, Argentine tangos, blues are heard. Everywhere one notices the influence of North America, which makes itself felt through the movies and the radio — whisky and soda, boogie-woogie, crooners, soft lights. . . .

But the real Rio is outside all this, in the suburbs, in the hills, in the old sections, the traditional, unspoiled Rio. If you want a whiff of true Brazilian air go to Larangeiras, to Cosme Velho, to the cool heights of Santa Tereza, or seek the friendly shade of the trees of Tijuca. In these places, in the houses that seem transplanted from Portugal, in the appearance of the streets, the gardens, the shops, and the people, you will find the true local flavor. What they eat, what they like, what they say, the way they dress there, everything they do is typically Brazilian, and above all carioca.

The suburbs are like cities apart, with their clubs, their movies, their parks, and their own shops. One can nearly always find a merry-go-round there. In their local theaters third-rate companies — "*mambembes*" — put on the old tear-jerkers that make the young girls and soft-hearted ladies weep, or shows and spicy comedies that bring whoops of laughter, jokes, and applause from the gallery. Along the suburban sidewalks stroll pairs of lovers, with their arms around one another's waist or holding hands. And women lean out of the windows, "watching the crowds go by." Among the passers-by the red coats of the marines make a bright splash of color; they enjoy great popularity among the waitresses and shopgirls. And there are also amusement parks, carnivals, soccer matches, at which the whole suburban population turns out to applaud and encourage the local players. Meyer . . . Madureira . . . Vila-Isabel . . . Bangu . . . these names are famous in the history of the city. From these suburbs more than one hero has emerged — a composer or singer of sambas, a soccer champion, a movie or radio star.

If the city should bore you — which I doubt — you have the country only a little way out. If the heat is too much for you, you can go up to Petropolis, high in the cool mountains, beyond the reach of summer. If the stones tire you, go to the woods, which is only a few steps from the boulevards. And remember that the sea is always at your feet, with its enchanted islands and their smooth beaches of white sand and their green palms.

Plain, mountain, forest, beach, capital, province, present, past, and even the future — Rio de Janeiro offers us all this on its magic, lavish tray.

You like the picturesque? Visit the antique-shops, the *rehos* of Rua São José, where second-hand books are for sale. Wander through the old streets where the sidewalks are hardly a yard wide, and where the houses, the doorways, the stones recall the days of the viceroys. Go into the old churches. Or watch the markets which open every morning in the squares of the suburbs and outlying districts. Stalls are set up where vegetables and fruits, poultry, cheap clothing, and knickknacks of every sort are displayed for sale. Housewives and servants of the neighborhood come with their baskets on their arm to do their marketing, for the prices at these open-air markets are lower than in the city. Onlookers with nothing more pressing to do gather around to watch. The gathering is colorful, lively, and noisy. People argue, haggle, compare prices, all enlivened by laughter and jokes. And when the markets close — there are strict police regulations about the closing-hours — and the stalls are put away, the crowd scatters, and all that remains is a silence dotted with fruit skins, scraps of paper, the spoor of a gathering of people.

And if your thirst for the picturesque is not yet satisfied, there are the amusing cries of the street-venders. "Select oranges!" "Empty bottles!" "Roasted peanuts — nice and hot!" Portuguese, dark old women, kids cry their wares. Each one has a slogan of his own, a special way of talking, for Rio is a land of individuals who loathe standardization, and who freely cultivate their personality. Some sing, others proclaim their wares. The language is twisted, mutilated; but it takes on new shades of expression, through incorrect usages, slang, and musical modulations.

The street-cars of Rio — like those of San Francisco — are relics of the past. They are small, old-fashioned in shape, ugly, but quiet, and they fulfill their function satisfactorily and have even come to form part of the landscape.

The trees of Rio are unforgettable. They fill the air with a forest perfume, sweet and evocative. Their shape and colors are a constant treat to the eyes. There remains engraved on the memory the delicate pattern of the almond trees that border the sidewalks of certain districts and adorn the gardens of the seacoast. And the jacarandas, which in the spring are covered with purple flowers.

And the acacias with their feathery leaves, and the *bicos de papagaio* and the flamboyants with their riot of scarlet flowers, and the towering royal palms which stand so straight along the Avenida Paisandu. . . .

But there is a mobile element in the landscape of Rio which is of prime importance. This is man, perhaps the most colorful feature in the whole setting. The carioca is the great bohemian, the pleasant philosopher, the natural humorist. The climate has made him almost a pagan and a nudist. The samba is the natural language of these people who spend their life between the sun and the sea, singing. To be sure, there exist in the city all types of people, moved by every kind of ambition, the slaves of every sort of prejudice. But the greater part of the population, the people, properly speaking, is made of a different clay. The spirit that moves them is an amused unconcern, delight in a good story, an easy life, and being in the street. A carioca's house is his city, whose roof is the sky and whose furnishings are the mountains, the sea, the streets, the squares. The younger generations go in for sports, bathe in the sun and the sea, take lots of exercise, and live on the beaches, in a state of semi-nudity like that of the garden of Eden. And when they have to dress, they do so as simply and concisely as possible. They have given up hats, and have lost the superstition of the collar and tie. They are sun-browned boys and girls, slender and shapely of body.

Rio is the mouth of a river into which all the human currents from the other states of the country flow. In Brazil an alarming exodus from the farms, the country, and the small towns to the cities is taking place. And Rio de Janeiro is a great, powerful magnet. As a rule all those who aspire to become writers, painters, sculptors, actors, musicians, journalists, and who find the provincial atmosphere of the cities in which they were born too limited for their ambitions make their way there. Rio also attracts those who are looking for large-scale business opportunities or exciting amusements, for the erotic fame of the city is known throughout the land. Old people from the southern states come to Rio for its sun, fleeing from the severer winters of the south.

The number of government employees to be found in the capital of Brazil is appalling. Not less alarming is the size of the army of go-betweens, the "fixers." There is a horde, too, of those whose existence is a mystery, who are always to be found in the streets and wherever anything is going on, but who never seem to work and have no visible means of support. Together with the tourists and the petty officials these people of leisure crowd the streets, drinking in the cafés, exchanging the latest story, filling the coffee-shops, the movies, the restaurants, the sidewalks.

In the midst of all these birds of passage the carioca lives his own life, oblivious of all influences. He is his impermeable self. And in the end it is he who transmits to the others his tastes, his habits, his inclinations. He is not small- or local-minded, he does not boast about his city, he is not suspicious or hostile toward outsiders who come there looking for work. He has a pleasant smile for all. For the carioca is affectionate, polite, somewhat in the feminine manner. It is not at all unusual to hear one man call another "my darling" quite as a matter of course and with the most decent and masculine intentions. A gaucho of Rio Grande do Sul would be outraged at such treatment. In Rio it is coin of the realm. It is of a piece with the carioca's singsong intonation, with his sibilant s's in the Portuguese fashion, and with his affectionate diminutives. But one should never forget that a vein of irony runs under this affectionate manner. For the story, the "wise-crack," is the arm of this extraordinary people. Nobody knows how they start, and nobody knows how they spread like wild-fire throughout the whole country, through some mysterious grapevine system. The majority of them are witty anecdotes, a blend of the Spanish picaresque, French *esprit*, and the British sense of humor. One day a new type of omnibus appears on the streets of Rio. The next day the carioca has thought up a funny name for it, or has invented some yarn about it. And so he goes, baptizing things and people with names that tickle his fancy, poking fun at customs, ridiculing or hero-worshipping politicians, artists, public figures. . . . Nothing is sacred to him. Yet it is interesting to observe that there is no ill will in his jokes. Just a spice of malice, which at bottom is affection.

The hero of these anecdotes is as a rule the Portuguese who is supposed to be dull-witted and the natural butt of jokes. Or else it is the parrot, which is the symbol of bohemian existence, sagacity, and wit. Two friends meet in the street, shake hands, and this question immediately follows: "Have you heard the latest one about the parrot?" Then comes the story, told with wit and grace. And one story leads to another, about politics and politicians, taxes, football players, happenings in the city. All amusing, witty, well told, with a keen sense of humor and acute psychological insight.

From all this one fact stands out clearly. The hero of the carioca is never the fighter, the man who employs force and violence. The great popularity of President Vargas in Rio de Janeiro is due to his poise, his sense of humor, his political shrewdness. The reason for this esteem is to be found, it seems to me, in Brazil's folklore. The hero of the native tales is the jaboti, a kind of small turtle. This little animal always triumphs over the great beasts of the forest through his shrewdness, his coolness, and his trusting to time. It is the spirit of the parrot and the jaboti, not the jaguar or the tapir, that rules in Rio.

The carioca lives on stories, sun, sea, and samba. He cannot get along without his daily ration of these basic elements.

The samba as a rule is born in the hills. One of the tenement-house dwellers starts out from home one day with a melody running through his head. He begins to mold it, to give it form. . . . He comes down the hillside toward the city humming it to himself. At the coffee house, around a table, as he sips his coffee, he whistles to his friends the samba he has just composed. The others listen, collaborate, make suggestions, beat out the accompaniment on a match-box or the stiff crown of a straw hat. It is not unusual for some anonymous composer to sell the melody to a professional musician to work into shape. And in a little while this samba is being sung over the radio, recorded, spread "by word of mouth" all over the country. The wit of the carioca is to be found in the words, in the rhythm of the music, full of sun and sea, his easy-going, sensual spirit. There is jungle in it, Africa, Indian drums.

And the lyrical Portugal of the *fado* reveals itself in a trace of sadness in the melody.

At carnival time the city goes mad, pandemonium reigns. For three days and three nights the cariocas dance, sing, mill and bustle about without stopping, wearing costumes of the most fantastic, absurd, grotesque varieties. There is dancing going on all over the city. Floats pass down the streets. The *ranchos*, those groups of men and women in disguise, parade through the streets, singing, showing off their costumes and lanterns and banners and dances. The most respectable citizens of exemplary life fail to show up at home for three days together. Modest employees spend the whole year saving for the carnival, and spend their savings in a few hours. There are elopements, divorces, shotgun marriages, meetings and partings. It is a form of mass intoxication which arouses slumbering instincts. During these days the whole city is a huge music-box conceived and set in motion by a madman's brain. The natural surroundings themselves seem to have been painted especially for a bacchanal. The heat, the sun, the smell of the sea, the breeze, and the perfumes all contribute to the intoxication. This is when the jungle — which, according to Waldo Frank, is in the soul of every Brazilian — makes itself felt with greatest vigor. There is the throbbing of African drums, the rattle of Indian maracas, savage dances, voodoo, and war-whoops. And even a hint of cannibalistic fury, which reveals itself in bitten lips, in bone-crushing embraces.

When it is over, the city resumes its normal rhythm. But without any "hang-over," for always, like the good daily bread, they are there: sun, sea, and samba.

In all this incongruous, delightful mixture may there not be, perhaps, the germ of a new world?

BUENOS AIRES

THE ROLE OF BUENOS AIRES as a center of attraction in South America is similar to that of New York in North America. It is not only one of the great centers of population of the world but a beautiful city as well, hospitable, cordial, where people work but at the same time converse and leave room for friendship. When a tourist comes to the intersection of the two most important streets of Buenos Aires, Florida and the Diagonal, two steps from his hotel, he finds something almost unique in the world. Down the wide Diagonal, through a channel of towering buildings, flow waves of automobiles giving a metallic gleam and a mechanical vibration to the city. Florida is narrow; motor traffic is not allowed there; two dense streams of humanity move leisurely along it in opposite directions. Both sides are lined with the show-windows of smart shops; the women are all well dressed, the trousers of all the men are impeccably creased; the smiling crowds recall the streets of certain Spanish cities where everything has a human quality: the gay greetings between friends; the satirical observation that circulates like a lampoon through the air.

Buenos Aires has a beautiful history, which begins in 1535, before North America was even outlined. The city was born Santa Maria del Buen Aire, and was the fruit of one of the adventures of those days that was led by a dour, sick conquistador. It was a dramatic episode, about which Enrique Larreta has written a play in verse. The conquistador departed this life, and the settlement became smoke, ashes, dust. The city was reborn, but it lived poorly. It was the farthest outpost of the Spanish colonies. It was centuries before it had its day. In 1807 the people drove out the English who had invaded the city. Three years later this same people gathered before the city hall. It was a raw day and a steady drizzle was falling; but the people did not move until the proclamation of independence came from the city fathers.

After liberty came slavery. Rosas made himself dictator and

ruled with the whip, flaunting his pose of white gaucho. The men had to wear red vests, the women red cockades, the *divisa punzó*. The houses were painted red. It was the color of the dictatorship. At night the call of the town crier was heard: "Death to the foul Unitarians! Long live the Holy Federation!" The secret police, the *"mazorqueros,"* prowled about to punish anyone who disagreed in any way with the government. This domination seemed unshakable, and at Rosas's court his daughter, Manuelita, played the part of a princess. But under the hard official exterior the heart of the Argentine still beat. Rosas fell, and Buenos Aires rose again to its life of contrasts, with reverses as great as its strokes of fortune, while every year there reached its port eighty, a hundred, a hundred and fifty thousand immigrants from Italy, Spain, Poland, Germany, England, Russia. And Buenos Aires became a web of steel, with its railroads reaching out to the farthest corners of the pampa. Its streets and avenues grew beautiful. Rodin, Bourdelle, Le Corbusier, sent their marbles and bronzes, laid out its parks, changed the lines of its mansions. The wealthy inhabitants, who went to France every year, filled their homes with paintings, museum treasures, and gave life there a European air. Beneath this exterior development of the city its intellectual activities have flourished. There are poets who effortlessly catch the unperceived charm of the commonplace, like Fernández Moreno. Or an essayist with the subtle penetration of Eduardo Mallea, who has expressed the anxiety of his generation confronted by the complex, contradictory problem of this city on the sluggish river. Two of the largest and best newspapers in the world are the newspapers of Buenos Aires. The cafés are full of poets, dramatists, painters, journalists. They know all the routes of the world, and they are anxiously, painfully seeking their own.

Some time ago the Argentine Committee of Intellectual Cooperation published a book dealing with the country. It is a beautifully edited book that was published in both Spanish and French. The following pages of Julio Rinaldini were written for it.

BUENOS AIRES

JULIO RINALDINI

Situated on the western bank of the Plata River, a body of water 125 miles across at its widest point, and sprawled over the vast pampas from which it has wrested, slowly at first and then at a vertiginous pace, room for its growth, the city of Buenos Aires contains a population of 2,473,400 within its area of 46,749 acres. These figures refer to the city proper. Greater Buenos Aires — which extends without let or hindrance over 113,666 acres beyond the actual precincts of the city — contains approximately 4,000,000 inhabitants. Four million people linked through their activities to what in the original plans comprised the city, today the heart and the pivot of a tentacled metropolis which has become a cardinal point in the economy of the modern world.

In what is now its nucleus the city began one day as a modest foundation upon a rectangle 2,416 yards wide and 360 yards deep, with an initial population of three hundred souls. The plan traced in 1580 by Don Juan de Garay has been the pivotal point about which the prosperous city has developed, as though in obedience to a legal decree.

This fact alone defines the special position of Buenos Aires in the life of the Argentine Republic and in world economy. It would be impossible to explain the existence of our capital and the increment its development took on at a given moment without bearing in mind its geographic situation, and its position with respect to the rest of the Argentine and on the map of international economy. Buenos Aires is a city of destiny, foreordained by factors which long, if intermittent resistance to this growth was unable to counteract. This is its strength and the basis of its prestige. The idea of its founders, especially in its first settlement,[1] was that

[1] The expedition that set out to conquer this region of the River Plata, under the command of Don Pedro de Mendoza, founded in 1536, very near the spot later selected by Garay as the site of Buenos Aires, the port of Our Lady of the Good Air. Mendoza left behind a group of settlers large enough to

384

Buenos Aires should be a way-stop, or, to be more exact, a post on the fabulous route to the land of gold, that ambition and mirage of the conquest. But this post which they had reached in the course of their navigation was situated, as by the hand of Destiny, at the meeting-point of the country's natural routes, facing the sea on the banks of a river which is practically an inland prolongation of the Atlantic. It was situated at the edge of the most fertile region of a territory which gave promise of immense natural wealth, at the point of convergence and outlet for the true wealth which the colonial enterprise was to discover once it awoke from its feverish dream of mineral wealth. It was a slow, difficult discovery, but a certain one, which, when it took place, would adumbrate the character of the coming nation. An economic center, a natural port, Buenos Aires was to become, by the extension of its sway and as a result of its functional value in the future of the Republic, the civil center, the political capital. It was to be the great city that enveloped all in its tentacles, and also the outward manifestation of civic spirit.

The policy of the conquest consistently opposed the designs of Fate. The provinces of Upper Peru, and in general the lands of the Pacific, were looked upon as the Promised Land, where fabulous riches lay open to the hand. The greed of colonial immigration settled them, and to them was carried the culture of Spain. For the very reason that they were politically the strongest provinces of the Spanish Empire in America, they set the standards of living for all the other regions, and controlled the commerce of the continent and the travel routes of this commerce. This policy left Buenos Aires isolated. This natural port for all this immense territory was nipped in the bud through the ban on

---

keep open the routes he planned to use to discover the fabulous lands of the White King. After five tragic years of exploration and delay, which hastened the death of Mendoza, who was already ill, and during which, according to the accounts of witnesses, the settlers were finally driven to eat the bodies of those who had suffered the death penalty, the settlement was abandoned and the buildings destroyed. Other accounts say that the settlement had managed to establish itself and that dissensions among Mendoza's officers were responsible for its destruction. But there is no document in existence to prove that a plan or a settlement existed, properly speaking. The real, indisputable founding of Buenos Aires took place forty years after this unfortunate experience.

trading with foreign nations. For two centuries this promise of a city had demanded this vital freedom of trade, first in order to clothe and feed itself, and then to maintain the prosperity it had achieved in spite of all legal restrictions.

But the city which was being smothered in this fashion was to find a natural ally in the daring enterprise of those adventurers who, with permission or without it, charted their course through these waters. Seven years after its founding Buenos Aires received its first visit from a pirate ship. Later the English would come, the Portuguese, the Dutch, the French, the Danes. The city spent its early years in fear of these over-bold visitors, who nevertheless showed it the road to prosperity. The freebooters found little to plunder in the needy city. Its first settlers had no gold; neither had they had time to acquire wealth through trade. Their settlement was confined to a small strip of land, the brief point of intersection between the virgin pampas and the unnavigated river. Their only resources were those they could wrest from the land, which fear of the Indians obliged them to limit to the commons of the city. The only materials they had to build their homes were adobes and the rushes of the canebrakes. And we can assume that the only thing that sustained their moral courage in the face of such loneliness and privation was the fascination of the wilderness or the cohesive force which came from their isolation.

There was little of which the pirates could loot them, but they did accustom them to the idea of trade routes, to sailing the seas, and to the sea's relation to overland routes. In a manner of speaking, they taught these people to whom commerce had been forcibly banned the advantages of contraband. It was to prove the city's life-saver, and it needed no persuasion to take full advantage of it. All this vast territory, where the hostility of the Indians had thrown up a kind of frontier of fear, abounded in a wealth that was to become the basis of its fortune: great herds of stray cattle, the descendants of the first animals brought over by the conquistadors, which had multiplied in the wilderness. The city has no deposits of gold in its surrounding territory, nor can it cultivate on any scale worth mentioning the products of the land, but it has the hides of these animals. This is to be the produce of the country, the first, which the same ships that bring in the supplies the people of the city need, and to which some of its inhabitants owe their wealth, will carry away in exchange. And it will be primarily this clandestine trade, in which the duly constituted authorities of the city, showing good political judgment, have a share, that will permit the city to fulfill its destiny.

The trade in hides will lead the man of the city to conquer the pampa. Trade in hides and contraband will bring the city into communication with the outlying territory and will create the social types which are to control the economy of the nation. Work with the herds will shape the figure of the gaucho — semi-barbarous, ascetic, at one and the same time worker, nomad, and soldier in the armies of the War of Independence and the civil conflicts. This type will spread to all the coastal provinces and will overflow into the provinces of the north, where the results of the crossbreeding of Indian and Spaniard are still preserved in their pure form. The exploitation of the cattle will give rise to the rancher, the *estanciero*, a kind of feudal lord, rich in vast acres and countless herds. It is he who has developed the wealth of the pampas, a land of great natural fertility, but in the beginning a wasteland, where everything has been created by the hand of man. It is he who has made the land to bear and has improved the primitive wild stock until it has become the superb herds of today, without equal in the world's markets. The contraband trade was to give rise to the large and small business enterprises of the city and the country, at present among the most upright to be found anywhere. These various factors have paved the way for the future of the Republic. They will create the sense of the whole and will establish the lines of communication with the hinterland which in turn will assure the life of the city. The trade in cattle and contraband merchandise will lay out, all over the country, the routes of travel. As time goes by, the natural routes will define themselves on the economic map of the Republic, and the location and consequent function of Buenos Aires will become evident. This interchange will create, to the city's advantage, the idea of a nation.

When the permanent assault to which international covetousness had submitted the city, beginning as piracy and continuing as smuggling, took the more spectacular and ambitious form, around 1806, of a full-fledged foreign invasion, the country rose as one man in defense of the city. A great deal has been said about the heroic resistance of the people of Buenos Aires to the English invasions, but another and perhaps more important fact has not been sufficiently stressed: the spontaneous support offered the city by the other inhabitants of the territory. The minutes of the city council for December 22, 1806 record proof of this sort:

A communication has been received from Juan Gómez Roldán of Córdoba in which he offers to pay the expenses of two infantry soldiers who enlist in the defense of our native land.

A communication has been received from Don Ramón Delgado stating that he is ready to come down with the troops at his command as soon as he is notified, and that it will give him the greatest satisfaction to assist this Illustrious City in the defense of our native land.

And farther on:

While this was going on, the doorkeeper sent word that ten Indian chiefs from the Pampa had requested permission to come into the meeting hall, and this having been granted, they came in, sat down, and delivered the following speech through an interpreter.

And in the course of the speech, which rewards a reading, they offered "twenty thousand of their followers, all of whom are experienced warriors, each with five horses, because they want to be the first to charge those Redcoats who it seems are still trying to annoy you."

The ranchers, for their part, sent a declaration to the city council in which "they manifest their loyalty and patriotism and their desire to see the defeat of the enemy in case of a new invasion. And they suggest the advisability of driving herds of bulls and cattle against them to disorganize their army, which seems to them an effective measure, for no force can resist a stampeding herd."

Argentine history books have taught us that the English invasions awakened our spirit of independence in all its intensity, because the inhabitants of Buenos Aires were thus made aware of the existence of a desire for self-rule. But we have been told nothing of this general movement in defense of the homeland which sprang to life at the threat to Buenos Aires. Nothing is said of this general rallying to the defense of the city, which in the hour of danger becomes the symbol of the nation. For the first time the word "patria" is heard on all lips, and through a significant combination of circumstances it crystallizes around the image of Buenos Aires. Buenos Aires, which had always been shorn of all its rights, was doubtless unaware of the fact that a political unity had grown up around it. The fact is that at the same time that it was becoming a center of urban population and a trading mart, it was gradually becoming the political pivot of the vast territory. Under the impact of international piracy, the not too edifying ups and downs of contraband dealings, the arbitrary decisions of an incompetent civil administration, and the hostility of the Indians, there was developing in this beginning of a city, by a process of elimination and selection, a sense of independence which was to manifest itself when the occasion demanded. An awareness of the city comes into being, and as the population grows, it becomes a cultural center with European influences, which, when the time comes, will be of value in counteracting the anarchic and excessively rustic tendencies of the people in the hinterland.

Just as Buenos Aires lacked available natural resources for its daily living, it lacked the natural elements that are needed to form a culture. In the rest of the colonial empire of America the conquerors found appropriate materials: stone, metals, magnificent lumber for building-purposes, through which to transmit their civilization to us. Architecture on a grand scale flourished from Mexico and the Antilles to Peru, Bolivia, and the north of the Argentine, and developed a genuinely continental style. Nothing of the sort is to be found in Buenos Aires. The Indians who lived in our pampas have not left a trace even of the ceramic arts. In this respect also Buenos Aires was isolated. The Spanish culture came down along the Pacific to the northern provinces, and as soon as it reached Buenos Aires it dissolved in the universal waters of the

Plata. Buenos Aires received its culture over the same routes as its trade. In this, too, it is a port that lies open to all the contributions of international life. If smuggling and the trade in hides did not enrich the badly administered city, it did enrich certain of its leading citizens, who were thus able to acquire the objects and materials for study required for the formation of a private culture. In this way they could go beyond the scope of the higher education of colonial days, which in its most flourishing moments was limited to grammar, rhetoric, scholastic philosophy, theology, and canon law. Buenos Aires fed upon the products of the most refined European culture. If Buenos Aires did not create culture, at least in the course of its dealings it developed a taste and awareness of the liberal trends of thought in the world; its citizens acquired great independence and acuteness of judgment toward all forms of culture. It developed, in the cultural as well as in the political field, standards which, under the influence of the rest of the country, were to become fixed national characteristics. So the city as it grows acquires a dual personality: that of an urban center and a political and cultural center. Its location, at first glance so unpropitious, is responsible for this miracle. Buenos Aires acquires form and meaning in the reaction between pressure and resistance. It grows and becomes consolidated. And so it becomes the compact and yet elastic conscience of the Republic. Thus it plays the role Destiny had assigned it in national and in world economy. Because in trying to understand Buenos Aires we must never lose sight of the primary fact of its predestination. To understand its role within the nation we have only to look at the map of the Republic; in the universal field the reasons are very similar, but here I am going to venture upon a hypothesis.

There was a moment in Argentine history when Buenos Aires was in open conflict with the rest of the country. After national independence had been achieved in 1810, in all the territories that made up the new Republic, there awoke an equal and spontaneous will to political domination. But it is this city which is the gateway of the nation, which has lived in constant communication with the ideas of freedom rife in the world at that moment, that can appreciate better than any other the disadvantages of being ruled by a mother country so far away and so blind to the colony's real needs, that was the cradle of independence. Here the attempt was made to create the national unity, to establish, as by virtue of a natural right, the capital of the new state. The rest of the country viewed this as a threat to its political rights and rebelled against the preponderance of the city. The "Federalists" rose in arms against the "Unitarians." The fact that there were people from the city in the ranks of the "Federalists" does not alter the case. The struggle is between the city and the territories, between the urban agglomeration and the country.

And with the passage of time we can see that this struggle between the city and the country, which is the leitmotiv of one period of our history, is the belated equivalent, allowing for the difference of time and ideas, of a phenomenon that is universal in the development of the modern world. Our civilization is characterized by the predominance of the city as the center of the vital activities in the life of the nations. According to Ortega y Gasset this sense of its importance on the part of the city is a Greco-Latin heritage, a survival of the fecund spirit of the early agora. Be this as it may, the first step in this special process of character-fixing takes place in the royal courts at the end of the Middle Ages. There, in those rising centers of social refinement, the seeds of our cities begin to sprout. As soon as the European world begins to acquire stability, the spirit of the city manifests itself as a will to organization and domination. As soon as the state supersedes the municipality, the city demands all its privileges, and rivalries spring up between the cities. With the advent of the Renaissance a peculiar process begins in which the centers of economic and political supremacy shift about, as though Europe were seeking to localize its permanent centers of relation and balance. First it is one city, then another, in which the currents of political, intellectual, and economic pre-eminence converge. Naples, Venice, Milan, Antwerp, Amsterdam, Lisbon, Paris, each has its turn, between the sixteenth and the end of the seventeenth century, in this system of natural precedence. But here we can already see how reasons of a universal nature are, for practical purposes, replacing the political criterion of each nation or region.

The location of the city, its position on the travel routes that are of importance to all, gradually becomes the determining factor in the destiny of each city. A new development begins to manifest itself in an increasingly forceful manner: the universal type of city, the city with tentacles reaching out in all directions, begins to take a commanding position in the organization of the modern world. It begins to take its place over the whole face of the globe, as a point of relation and contact, in a sort of total geographic readjustment.

For this reason Spengler's pessimism is mistaken in regarding the development of the great urban centers as a symbol of the supposed decadence of the modern Western world. The modern city, unlike the ancient city, whose fate this pessimism points to with a warning finger, is not the expression of nationality or a creation of a political nature. That which in the ancient world was a symptom of the decay of the national spirit — the overwhelming development of the urban centers — in the modern world is the crystallization of new forms of life. The modern city develops as a center with universal ramifications, a point of relation and inter-play on the earth's surface. It lives on what in Spengler's thesis was the cause of the decay of the cities of the ancient world: its cosmopolitan character, not its intrinsic importance. As the city's predominance grows, it exceeds the limits of the nation and sup-plants it in importance in the field of international relations. The nations talk with the voice of their actual or virtual capitals. Under their auspices the specialists chart the course of world economy.

It is within this new economy that Buenos Aires acquires its true meaning. If it has played such a decisive role in the nation's history; if, despite all opposition, it has become its principal eco-nomic and cultural center, if it has achieved such extraordinary development, it is because in the lottery of this total geographical redistribution, brought about by the economic-political reshuf-fling of the contemporary world — which occurs regardless of all national conceptions — it has been its fate, because of its location and as part of a wealthy nation, to become one of the great centers of communication.

The proof of this fact can be found in the process of its development. During the colonial period, which continues beyond the epoch of Independence, almost until the end of Rosas's tyranny in 1852, its growth is normal. It is the growth that is proportionate to its natural forces, to its ability to withstand the adverse circumstances which beset it. But these hostile contingencies are of no avail against the favorable ones which Fate has in store for it and which are only awaiting the propitious hour to reveal themselves. It is an hour that will favor the development of all the great urban agglomerations.

Already in the sixteenth century the inhabitants of Buenos Aires were vainly asking the mother country, so obtuse in matters of colonial policy, for at least "four ships a year" because the products the city has to sell are "of great bulk and weight." Two centuries later the development of means of transportation will take good care of this need. The city will be able to load its bulky products without difficulty in its own port. And from then on this port, situated as it is at the junction of the great natural routes of communication, will ensure the amazing growth of the city and its power, the power of absorption, which will in turn completely guarantee its economic, political, and cultural predominance. After that the city is to grow by leaps and bounds. In 1852 it has a population of 76,000; twelve years later, in 1864, it has increased to 140,000. In this short space of time the population, which had slowly settled within the city's perimeter from 1580 until the downfall of the tyrant Rosas, a period of 272 years, had doubled. From then on (1864) its growth shows an ascending curve unequaled in the development of any other contemporary city. In 1875 the population is 230,000; in 1887, 437,373; in 1904, 979,325. What was merely an outpost in the vast expanse of America is on the way to becoming the great city, with international ramifications, which absorbs people from without and within. Not only the people and the routes of the Argentine, but men of all the world converge there. In 1887, of a population of 437,373, foreigners numbered 228,641.

But it is time for us to tell how this city of cosmopolitan formation has kept and still manages to keep a character of its own, a national character. The truth is that these 228,641 foreigners were not felt in the city as it was then constituted. It is evident from the manner in which they were assimilated that they had come under the influence of an irresistible power of conversion. Unquestionably, with the passage of time, in the slow struggle of the city to consolidate itself, a strong social consciousness had formed, or a type of society having definite characteristics. From the beginning Buenos Aires had a group of outstanding residents which was to produce the leading families. These citizens, who were without the benefits of a liberal education unless they acquired it on their own initiative, nevertheless received a rigid moral training of Christian character, which the political authority accepted as the standard and which regulated the most intimate acts of their life. They grew up, moreover, in a ceaseless struggle to ensure their unity and that sense of what destiny had put in their hands in the form of a land devoid of civilized life. They grew up as though in search of salvation, which was to produce within the territory of the Republic, as a consequence of this attitude, those strong men of lofty ideals who were to assure us our independence and, later on, the political greatness of the nation. These patricians, as it has become the custom to call them, form the groundwork of our society and the spur of our nationality, which will counteract the influence of our great immigration.

The immigrants found a country which offered itself without reserve "to all men of goodwill who may wish to inhabit our land" (preamble to the Constitution of the Argentine). This immediate possession acted as a direct incentive to assimilation; but the returns from the land thus acquired awakened in the immigrant a desire to become assimilated to the representative social group descended from the patricians. "Society" as it has developed here becomes the ideal to which the immigrant aspires as soon as he begins to make money. In the life of the Argentine the spirit of imitation is one of the distinguishing characteristics. The assimilative force of the country creates the desire to resemble others, which expresses itself in an effort to find the "tone" of the medium in which one lives.

One of the strongest traits of the Argentine character is its dislike of extravagance. It may be that occasional manifestations of display have given foreigners the impression of extravagance, but among us tendencies of this sort are considered in bad taste. The Argentine is greatly concerned with fashioning himself in the image of a definite social type which this very concern helps to shape and which, in the last analysis, is conditioned by secret telluric forces. The immigrant eventually is assimilated to this type. Of the 228,641 foreigners registered in the census of 1887, Italians made up 138,166. The Italian immigration has been the largest in the country. Yet this great human contribution which has played such a valuable part in the development of the Argentine's economy has not stimulated or encouraged the spread of Italian culture. The children of Italians, as in general the children of all immigrants, have been greatly concerned with overcoming such barriers of origin as might hamper them in their determination to be hundred-per-cent Argentines. And this is true notwithstanding the efforts of those who by virtue of *jus sanguinis* would claim for the country of origin the descendants of immigrants. Or restore them to their culture. In their culture the Argentines have always followed their natural inclinations. And in this respect the culture of France has beyond doubt occupied first place, from the political writings in the days of the Independence, which were full of Gallicisms and the ideas of the Encyclopedists, to our own predilection for modern French art and literature, which we know in such detail as to leave no doubt as to our preferences.

If I said earlier that the modern city differs from the ancient city in that it is not a creation of a political nature nor a blueprint of nationality, it is because I have been considering it in its international aspect. As a matter of fact, I believe that the function of these urban developments has been so predetermined from their beginnings that they will in time come to constitute an independent system of international union, contributing in a greater or smaller degree to the cultural trends which have formed and which are the life-blood of the countries in which they happen to exist, but independent of them. I believe that the special character of these centers tends to differentiate them more and more from those things which in the life of the nation represent the essence of its spirit or the genius of its culture. But for the time being, I think they can represent both things simultaneously: a center with universal connections and the political and cultural pivot of the nation. Buenos Aires profits by this dual role, and if we Argentines have a problem at this moment it is that of not confusing the two, of knowing which of its manifestations belongs to the spirit of the nation, and which to its functions as the universal center which it has come to assume in the world's economy.

The spirit of the Argentine throbs within this great tentacular city, and despite the fact that the city would seem to be confined within the high cement walls of its compact structure, it is in contact with the rest of the nation, if through no other factor than one which is ever present: the winds. This is not a figure of speech. The winds are a determining factor in the economy of the Argentine. The chill damp winds of the Pacific discharge their contents as they travel across the mountain ranges to become the dry chill winds which raise the moisture-laden clouds of the hot regions of the north and the center of the Republic and bring on the heavy rains which water these areas. This same damp wind of the Pacific blows through the regions of the far south into the territory of the Argentine and maintains the great forest fertility of this other region of the Republic. Buenos Aires has always been the playground of the winds. It knows the lassitude of the hot, heavy north wind, the relief of the southwest wind, the *pampero,* the cool wind of the southeast, which sweeps the sky clear and raises the atmospheric pressure; and it knows that these brusque changes of climate stimulate and promote the wealth of the nation. The changeable climate of the city is like an ever present reminder of the fortunes of the Republic, the natural agent through which the city controls its destiny.

Naturally a city that has grown so abruptly and so quickly, a city of such unstudied formation, would hardly have a definite architectural character. Buenos Aires has preserved its primitive chessboard lay-out, as prescribed by the laws of the Indies for the foundings of the conquest, in keeping with the Roman tradition. The system has not changed with the growth of the city except that its fan-shape with the original vertex on the banks of the river has grown to a series of converging arteries which in practice modify the working order of the chessboard. The entire city converges toward the point where the essential activities of its economic life take place. As a result this is the most thickly built-up part of the city and the part which, being most active and wealthy, has achieved the greatest architectural unity and splendor. Yet we cannot consider its appearance as definitive, either. The "center," as we call it here, changes countenance, too, and in moments like this, radically. In its very heart an avenue 460 feet wide is being opened up. The first section of this was opened to the public in October 1937. The luxury trade which centered in this zone is steadily moving toward the northern section of the city (a residential district, and wealthy, too) in a process similar to that which took place in Paris, where the rue de la Paix, the Place Vendôme, and part of the boulevards have given way to the Champs-Élysées. If every city is a living organism governed by the laws of evolution, how much truer this is of our city, whose great growth took place under the sign of new modern speeds.

Despite its enormous development, Buenos Aires continues to be a city in the process of formation. Its essential urban character, and the most striking, is its latent power. Latent power, vigor, which here are tantamount to beauty and which little by little generate that other beauty of detail which characterizes the little corners and the vast perspectives of a city. It is taken as a matter of course in Buenos Aires for a six-story apartment house to be torn down after five years to make way for a larger one, or in the broadening of a street — as happened with Corrientes Street, which was widened to eighty-five feet from thirty — for a building constructed the year before to be demolished. Lack of foresight? Certainly, in some cases, but no one can gainsay the vitality of a city where in a single year 15,654 building permits were issued involving a ground surface of 2,129,497 square yards and representing an outlay of about 153,700,000 dollars.

At this dizzy speed Buenos Aires has been molding itself into a great city, great in size and great in the dignity of many phases of its existence. Great in the attention it devotes to the most refined forms of culture and — why not admit it? — in the appearance of its inhabitants: its women who have learned how to dress in

Paris, and its men in London, well set up, physically conditioned by sports, and healthy. It abounds in expositions and artistic activities of every kind. It is visited periodically by the outstanding world figures of science, arts, and letters. It is great in what it has accomplished and in its promise for the future, which the reality of today fully justifies. A city which, despite its rapid natural growth, thanks to the peculiar character of its inhabitants, pursues, if not always successfully, always actively an ideal of order and balance which approaches that of the cities of Europe.

Buenos Aires has experimented with the skyscraper. The experiment was a natural temptation to its vital strength. But everything would seem to indicate that this attempt will not flourish in the future. Not only the great territorial extension of the city would seem to advise against this type of construction (under existing building ordinances Buenos Aires can accommodate 30,000,000 inhabitants), but also the inclinations of the city itself, which tend to follow the more conventional and harmonious forms which prevail in Europe rather than those of North America.

After the federalization of Buenos Aires in 1880, a political question which had been a subject of debate ever since the Independence, the city, which has been chosen the legal capital of the Republic, came of age. When its great growth began in the second half of the nineteenth century, it was still the rectangular city of embryonic colonial design, with narrow streets, without sanitary improvements, without running water. It had its charm, as the accounts of the day and the pictures bear witness, but it was doomed to disappear under the pressure of new conditions. The city as we know it had to start from the beginning. In 1871 the project for supplying the city with running water was authorized. In 1874 the first measures of public sanitation were begun. The average width of the streets was still 315 feet, and remained so during the first stage of the great city. Soon the rise in real-estate values stimulated the building up of all available space, and the large patios which adjoined one another in the old type of construction and formed healthy open spaces in each block disappeared. Although the streets were narrow, the city had room to breathe in the center of the built-up blocks. Now the city had to find this, until the building regulations limited the area that might be built up, in the creation of green open spaces: parks, squares, gardens; in the broadening of its principal avenues of communication; in the creation of great new arteries of traffic, both in and around the city; in the recovery of its magnificent river, which the increase in construction had been shutting off from the view of its inhabitants. This has been and is the program of the great city. Private architecture, too, has played its part in this steady renovation. People understood the advantage — economic, primarily — of not building up all available space and of recovering, by means of the new building techniques, air and light. Buenos Aires is one of the cities where the greatest number of buildings are constructed in the modern style, and, according to European experts, very well done. The average modern apartment, equipped with all the latest improvements, including air conditioning, is probably one of the best in the world. The steady growth of the city and its economic resources permit the constant adoption of the newest techniques of building and the application of all the developments of modern invention which make for greater living-comfort. The residents of Buenos Aires, to whom a lease of more than two years is unknown, are always ready tenants for houses that are new and embody the newest technical achievements.

For this reason the houses of Buenos Aires have passed almost insensibly, except for a brief period of the Second Empire manner, from the colonial manor house of one or two stories and large interior patios to the modern type of apartment house. Probably this type of house, having large and small apartments, would prevail throughout the city if time and private economy had permitted. There are still great mansions as well as an occasional house of one or two stories, with large patios, tucked away among the large apartment houses or in the outlying neighborhoods. Still farther out, in the suburbs, where the city extends to meet the pampa, the small private dwelling flourishes.

But Buenos Aires has no interest in preserving anything. It goes on building and developing as a consequence of its thirst for life and in keeping with the standards created by its vital impulses.

Its life keeps pace with the times. Every day through its brokers, its great banking corporations, its stock exchange, its newspapers of more than thirty pages, with five or six pages of foreign news, it keeps in contact with the world, registers its pulse-beat, and utilizes all the latest manifestations of its activity. It is a keen, eager city whose spirit of criticism leads it to say every unpleasant thing it can think of about itself. But this harsh critical spirit is the direct outgrowth of its eagerness, its determination to play its part. It is an ambitious spirit which frets at the delay in carrying into practice its vital impulse to master the better forms of life.

Beneath the city's great economic activity, its prosperity, its pleasant existence, the benefits of its easily acquired wealth, its well-being, lies this restlessness, this tension, this vigilance of spirit — its fine Latin and Christian heritage — which we feel on luminous days like another attribute of its climate.

THE CITY OF MEXICO

THERE HAS NOT BEEN only one city of Mexico. During every phase of history in this region a great city has flourished here. It is a city of marked individuality, which has embodied the aspirations and art of many different peoples. It has been colored by the characteristic tint of each century, yet in it the most contradictory attitudes have been blended and harmonized by the vigor of the Mexican character. It is the oldest city of America, and it has served as the bridge between a fabulous past and the new world discovered by the Europeans. When Cortés saw it, in the days of the conquest, it was a great flower of stone in the middle of a lake. Bernal Díaz del Castillo, one of the conquistador's soldiers, drew a painstaking and loving picture of it, with its markets, its temples and palaces, which were a vision of enchantment. In our own days Alfonso Reyes, on the basis of these descriptions, has re-created the image of the city in the sixteenth century in a little book,

400

Visión de Anahuac, which is a masterpiece. As one reads it one realizes that here in America, before the arrival of Columbus, a world was already in the making which was a presage of the future of this hemisphere. During the next period of the life of Mexico the cathedral was carved out; this was no longer the lotus flower of stone Cortés had seen, but a lamp hewn of rock which lighted up three centuries of our colonial night. And so each of the different cities Mexico City has been has bequeathed to posterity works of art, for this has been the fortune of this capital. Even the shortlived Empire left us the castle and park of Chapultepec, and in our times the renaissance fostered by the revolution is leaving its images stamped on the walls through the powerful art of men like Diego Rivera. Genaro Estrada, a Mexican artist of delicate perception, gives us in the following pages a painting of Mexico in the days of the colony seen from the vantage point of our own day.

THE COLONIAL CITY
GENARO ESTRADA

Fʀᴏᴍ the towers of the cathedral the city of Mexico is seen as a vast gray plain crisscrossed by the straight or curving lines of its streets. Its outer limits are hardly visible to the naked eye and at times the last of its houses seem to blend with the horizon. In late afternoon, at twilight, when the sun's rays linger only on the upper part of the buildings and the streets begin to grow blurred in the gathering shadows, Mexico becomes the old colonial city of centuries ago. From our vantage point the contributions of modern life are lost; the details stamped by new civilizations disappear, and all that remains, as on a faded canvas, are the gray masses of buildings and the green clumps of trees and foliage. But against the waning light of the afternoon everything that rises above the roofs and the angles of the buildings stands out in relief, sharp and clear.

And behold! Everywhere there are towers, the old towers of the churches, convents, chapels, hermitages; the high, twin-spired towers, slender and soaring, pierced by the lights that shine through their windows; the low towers, like stone cubes, that contain only a single bell; pyramidal towers with their cross of iron; round towers, with their cross of stone; gray towers, darkened by centuries of weather, or white, white and dazzling with sun, inhabitants of the humble districts, neighbors of the simple people, of the miracle-working images and of the bees that store their honey within them in secret hiding-places. Some have heavy bells on which time has left its green patina; others, sets of bells which swing in their brightly painted wooden framework, and little bells that never cease calling, rung by the devout as they enter and leave. There are gleaming towers covered with bright tiles; towers of multicolored glazed porcelain with iron grilles, like an Arabian jalousy; towers whose niches house dusty terracotta saints; or abandoned towers, become the haunt of bats; or gay ones, adorned with paper flowers and wreaths of oak leaves.

And the cupolas! The cupola of La Santisima which looks like a compote-jar; the cupola of La Soledad, solid and solemn, with white medallions against the dark stone; the cupola of Señor de Santa Teresa, slender and high, with its light inside like a Chinese lantern; that of Loreto, which is a snail with the two sharp horns of its spires protruding; that of Santa Inés, which always wears its holiday dress trimmed in orange and blue; that of La Enseñanza, which wears the cap of a doctor of theology; that of La Encarnación, which raises to heaven prayers of white enamel; that of Santa Caterina, broad and flat, with a garland of windows; low, polygonal cupolas; cupolas with a belt of pilasters; egg-shaped cupolas; vast domes made to house beneath them, amidst the cypresses of the churches, the sumptuousness of the ritual and from whose concave walls the thunder of the organ re-echoes; or unassuming and simple cupolas, to welcome the voices of the children in the white afternoons of the month of Mary and the cooing of the doves of the valley of Mexico in the sultry mornings of July.

On all sides the eye finds the vision of the colonial city in the cornices that rise above the façades of the buildings, the old schools, the churches. Those are of the house of some conquistador, these of the viceregal palace, of the Seminary of San Ildefonso; in that direction those of the house of the Count of Valle de Orizaba are still visible. See how they stand out, like little Chinese towers of porcelain, those of the tile-faced house. They are all of stone, white, gray, black; some look like the hats worn in the old university; there are Franciscan cornices, made to crown fortresses with their rough crenellation and furnish loop-holes for the muskets that defended the faith; Baroque inverted pyramids, floridly ornamented; rude battlements carved by heavy-handed workmen, cornices of flames, leaves, balls, censers, urns. . . .

Down below the outlines of the city have disappeared; the people are shadows that slip swiftly by. The Angelus calls; from the streets rises a dull noise of objects that talk and objects that roll on wheels. Only in the jagged foothills is there still a violet glow, which is fading away. The towers, the cupolas, the cornices are picked out against the sky like silhouettes on a screen. At this hour from the tower across the way Don Francisco Cervantes Salazar must be looking down on the city, his old city. And below there passes the shade of Don Carlos de Sigüenza y Góngora, on his way to his home in the near-by street of Hospital del Amor de Dios. There are armed men about the viceregal palace, probably halberdiers standing guard. Across the way, in the city hall, they are discussing the granting of water rights to Antón Gallo, the mason, who has made application for this concession.

Suddenly, as though a curtain had been raised, ten thousand electric lights go on all over the city.

LIMA

Havana, Rio de Janeiro, Montevideo, Buenos Aires, the capitals of Atlantic America, are coastal cities, fanned by the breezes of the sea, where every language can be heard and life somewhat resembles that on the deck of a transatlantic liner. On the Pacific side the cities are inland: they look to the hills rather than to the sea; they cherish their four centuries of tradition, preserving the same well-known names, the same old tales, and a smile that seems to belong to the days of the viceroys. Lima typifies this better than any other city. Spiritually it is like an old book of chronicles. Moreover this book exists, and is known as *Tradiciones Peruanas*. It was written by Don Ricardo Palma.

The city was founded in 1535 by the most mettlesome of all the conquistadors, Francisco Pizarro. He began life as a swineherd and died a marquis. He was a complete barbarian, and his life was one long flashing of swords and daggers, to the accompaniment of virile oaths and epithets. Besides he was a hero. On one occasion, when he was on his way to the conquest of Peru, his troops, ravaged by hunger, fever, and doubt, revolted on a desert island in the Pacific. They wanted to turn back to Panama. Pizarro drew a line in the sand. "That way," he said, pointing to one side, "you can go to Panama, to poverty and shame. This way," pointing to the other, "to Peru, to wealth and glory. Let him who is a good Castilian choose." Thirteen crossed the line, and with them he began the conquest of Peru. Glory was their portion, and the line that Pizarro drew in the sand has not been effaced by the shifting winds of the centuries. And Pizarro went to Peru, founded Lima, filled his coffers with the treasures of the Indians. Then came the viceroys, and all the intrigues of a court: stories of beautiful women, heroines with whom Lope de Vega fell in love from a distance and who turned the heads of the viceroys close at hand.

The city has grown. Today, with its residential districts which extend to the sea, it is several times larger in area than it was in colonial times. It has a population of nearly half a million. But in the heart of the city the old houses still stand. Past the beautifully carved wooden balcony of the Torre Tagle palace centuries of history have flowed by. There is the same old courtyard, the stone stairway, the same arcades bearing the imprint of the past. And this which is true of Lima is true also of Mexico City, Bogotá, Quito, Chuquisaca. There are those who give to this America the name of Spanish America. The Peruvian writer Raúl Porras Barrenechea has compiled a *Pequeña Antologia* (*Little Anthology*) of Lima. He is the author of the brief study which precedes it, from which this excerpt has been taken.

LIMA, PAST AND PRESENT
RAÚL PORRAS BARRENECHEA

PRIMITIVE LIMA

On the left bank of the Rimac Pizarro selected the site for the city. As can be seen from the old plans and according to the annalists, he gave it a triangular form, the base resting against the river, leaving between the stream and the first houses a space of a hundred feet for the city commons.

Pizarro himself, accompanied by the first of the city fathers, traced its historic circumference with the sword made famous on the Isla del Gallo. His clairvoyant genius foresaw the torrent of life and passions that was to be harbored within this space, beating and breaking against its sides like an imprisoned sea. On three sides of the town square, like unscaleable walls, he erected the palace of the governor, the cathedral, and the town hall. God, the King, and the People, the three leading characters of the Spanish drama of the sixteenth century, were the spirits invoked by Pizarro to preside over the destiny of the city and look down upon the adventure of its history like eternal, impassive caryatids. The area of the city was divided like a chessboard into 117 islands or squares. Each block of 18,762 square yards was divided into four lots. The broad, straight streets were laid out from southeast to northwest so that at every hour of the day there would be shade on one side, and at the same time the trade winds, which blow steadily from the south, would enter obliquely, to ensure a moderate circulation of air. This wise arrangement of the streets adopted by the Marquis, at the advice of "experts and people of understanding," made it possible to see the countryside from the Plaza Mayor, and, in the distance, the sea. History has handed down to us the names of those who shared in the founding of the city with Pizarro. Thirteen they were, including himself, the same number that followed him on the Isla del Gallo. Apparently this was his lucky number. The names of the founders of Lima were: Nicolás de Ribera the elder and Juan Tello, the two first mayors; Alonso Riquelme, comptroller; García de Salcedo, supervisor; Nicolás de Ribera the younger; Rodrigo de Mazuelas, Ruiz Díaz, Alonso Martín de Don Benito, Cristóbal Palomino, Diego de Agüero, Antonio Picado, secretary to the governor, and Alonso Tinoco, who was the first priest of Lima.

In addition to the founders there were thirty Spaniards who had come from San Gayán and twenty-five Indians from Jauja. Building sites were apportioned to these settlers, for which, in the absence of money, they had to pay a number of chickens annually, an arrangement which was modified five years later.

Thus laid out and divided, the new city began to grow and become populated with an urge for life and grandeur. It would be a long story to tell of the slow rise of the city, into which the first founders infused the austere Castilian soul of the sixteenth century. Reserved, silent, frugal, and stern was Lima in the days before the viceroys. What it lacked in wealth, which the horn of fortune was not yet pouring out upon it but was depositing in the powerful hold of Spain-bound galleons, it made up for, from its birth, in honors and heraldic pomp. Charles V, in 1537, magnanimously allowed it to display on its coat of arms crowns, which are the symbol of royalty; columns, in tribute to its unswerving loyalty; and a star, to preside over its brilliant future. It was also known in the language of heraldry as "the very noble, very illustrious, and very loyal city of the Kings of Peru."

During its first century the broad and silent city grew about the Plaza Mayor. Without pomp and without vanity the humble façades of the houses arose. The buildings, of a single story, were rudely constructed, according to Father Cobo, "covered with rushes, thatch-roofed, built of rough mangrove wood, with little beauty or grandeur in their doorways or courtyards, though large and spacious." The only thing on which the city laid special emphasis was its churches. Piety erected churches without interruption and every year a new tower reared itself aloft, from which yet another bell might call to endless prayer. Pizarro himself had begun them, laying "with his own hands the first stone and the first beams" of the church which later was to be the cathedral of Lima, consecrated to Our Lady of the Assumption. Hernando Pizarro a little later ordered the Convent and the Church of La Merced built. This was shortly followed by that of San Francisco, in 1535; the Chapel of Vera Cruz, endowed by Pizarro, in 1540; the Sagrario in 1541; Santo Domingo in 1549; Santa Ana in 1550; the beautiful Church of San Agustín in 1551; La Encarnación in 1558; La Caridad in 1559; San Sebastián in 1561; San Lázaro in 1563; La Concepción in 1573; La Trinidad in 1580; the Church of Santa Clara, to which San Toribio made the gift of his heart, in 1596; San Carlos in 1597; San Pedro and San Pablo in 1598; Las Descalzas in 1603; and La Recoleta Dominica in 1606.

The Convent of San Francisco, said a French traveler given to hyperbole, occupied an eighth of the city. The space given over to the churches was greater than that of all the other public buildings put together, in spite of the fact that by 1562 the population had begun to spread to the other side of the river, in the district of San Lázaro, and that in 1571 the walled Cercado had been founded as a dwelling-place for the natives.

Meanwhile the city was devoid of palaces and avenues. In front of the viceregal residence was a group of filthy shacks known as "waterfront boxes," and the Plaza Mayor, the only one in the city, was also the market-place, or *tianguez* as it was called at the time, the gathering-place of "venders, scriveners, and sextons": the center of commerce, justice, and religion; the bull-fighting ring on the occasion of great festivities; the walk of the aristocracy in the evening, and the agora of backbiting and gossip of the Creoles at all hours. But the city gladly suffered these shortcomings for the sake of seeing more stone-carved church porticoes and the silhouettes of more slender towers rising above the flat surface of its buildings.

The city indulged its leisure with another whim, according to Friar Reginaldo de Lizarraga and Father Cobo, in the laying out of the large, perfumed gardens with which it surrounded its buildings. The heavily fruited branches of the trees displayed their verdure and their fragrance above the high adobe walls. Father Cobo, with his eye for detail, says that "all the houses are roomy and large, with great patios, barnyards, orchards, and gardens." And Friar Reginaldo, in flowery phrases, says that "from the outside it does not look like a city but a grove, with its many orchards filled with orange trees, grapevines, pomegranates and other fruit trees of the kind that grow there, and the irrigation ditches that crisscross it."

Sixteenth-century Lima put its heart and soul into its churches and its gardens. It was built of rough materials, devoid of all improvements, without water, police, light, or sanitation, lacking in civic pride and the, as yet unknown, pleasures of comfort; yet it could boast that the melancholy sound of its bells soothed the soul and the wafted perfume of its honeysuckle and jasmine intoxicated the spirit.

The phrase of José Galvez has a twofold musical and floral meaning: "Lima, the city of church bells and flower bells."

LIMA IN THE SEVENTEENTH CENTURY

By the beginning of the seventeenth century Lima had already acquired its own peculiar physiognomy. Its belfrys and its domes gave it, from a distance, a Mohammedan grace that surprised its visitors. And as its religious spirit had not declined, but had been stimulated by astounding examples of sanctity, and this was the golden age of the viceroys, the masons continued to erect arches and vaults to accommodate the growing devotion of the faithful. In this work the most intense religious fervor went hand in hand with the most extravagant display.

The city had been extending toward the south and the east, we are told in an interesting study on the plan of Lima by the architect Tizon y Bueno. Southward it had taken in the hermitage of Guadalupe, located at a distance of three hundred paces, and had reached Belén and La Recoleta, founded in 1604 and 1606 respectively. To the east it extended to Santa Clara, Los Descalzos, San Ildefonso, and El Carmen. The churches mark the advance line of the city. The census taken by the Marquis of Monteclaros shows out of a total of 26,441 inhabitants ten per cent of priests, canons, monks, and nuns. Juan María Gutierrez could say of Lima that it was "a huge convent for both sexes." The cloisters brought forth Saint Rose of Lima, San Francisco Solano, Friar Martín de Porres, and, in the episcopal chair, San Toribio de Mogrovejo.

But Lima was not only this in the seventeenth century; it was also the most important commercial center of the colonies, where all the products of Europe that were to be distributed through South America came in, and whence the fleets carrying millions of ducats to the Main and Spain set out. With the increase of wealth, building and the outward beautification of the city flourished. Finer materials began to be employed for houses. Beautifully carved beams and wainscoting of oak were introduced; stone was brought in from Panama for the doorways of the houses, wood from Guayaquil, and red ebony from the Main and Mexico for doors, lattices, bay windows, balconies, chairs, tables, and inlaid desks. The lack of stone quarries near the city, which prevented the use of stone in the great majority of buildings, diverted the artists' inclination for plasteresque ornamentation toward wood carving. The result was the altars, the pulpits, the choir stalls, the winding staircases, the embossed ceilings, the fretwork balconies, all the marvels and beauty of colonial marquetry.

Personal luxury grew more widespread among the inhabitants of Lima. Father Cobo in 1629 exclaims over "the vanity of attire, the display and pomp of servants and livery." That year there were more than two hundred coaches in the city, all of them most lavish, "trimmed most beautifully with gold and silk." Nobles and ordinary citizens wore clothes only of silk. Inside the houses there was a wealth of damask and the finest cloth and laces produced by the weavers of Holland, Venice, Brussels, and Flanders. "There is nobody," says the chronicler quoted, "even among the poor and lowly, who does not possess some jewel or goblet of silver or gold."

All the worldly pomp, however, was subordinated to the divine service. It was on the occasion of some religious procession that the gold, jewels, tapestries, and silks were displayed to their fullest. The holy images, covered with jewels, were carried through streets that devotion and pride have paved with bars of silver. The outstanding festivals of the seventeenth century were on the occasion of the canonization of Saint Rose and Saint Toribio de Mogrovejo.

But the saints and the Illuminati of the colony, who performed such childish miracles as causing the holy images to sweat or making a dog, cat, and mouse eat out of the same dish, did not save the city from the scourge of earthquakes or the attack of pirates. In 1687 Lima was destroyed by a terrible earthquake, and in 1685 the Duke of La Palata, a zealous custodian of its treasures, built a strong wall, with thirty-four bastions, to defend it against the terrible corsairs. In spite of its faith, these are the two most notable events of Lima's religious century.

LIMA IN THE EIGHTEENTH CENTURY

In his lush description of Lima in the eighteenth century José Guillermo Leguía tells us that despite its commercial reverses as a result of pirate raids, the abolishing of the *encomiendas,* the splitting up of the viceroyalty, and the earthquake of 1746, all of which had a hand in the impoverishment of Lima, the splendor of colonial days continued unabated.

Outwardly the city was still as austere and somber as a convent. The old mansions, with their imposing entrances, their gloomy halls and the high walls of the monasteries gave shade and silence to the streets. The church bells — as in the vision Rodo evokes of Quito — alone raised their voices in the city, which was enveloped in the "double haze of incense and the Rimac," to use the words of Vicuña Mackenna.

But behind this grave appearance the soul of the city smiled, like the faces of its women half-hidden behind their shawls. Within the lordly mansions the women of Lima lived gaily in the bright inner patios, full of geraniums and the trills of canaries, yielding to the fortunate waters of the ornamental pools the envied secret of their beauty. Behind the walls of the convents there was a gay riot of gardens and mosaic tiles, and in certain of them there was more license than prayer. "In spite of religion, which was inflexible; in spite of honor, which was tyrannical," says Ventura García Calderón, "the delightful abandon of Versailles was not unknown."

Life and culture reached their zenith, says this flowery chronicler. But not under the sway of the solemn doctors or the monsters of learning that flourished in the shadow of the university. The interest, the pride, the indulgence of the city crystallized about the most enchanting of its characters: the woman of Lima, *la limeña*. She embodied everything that was most typical of the period in her soul, her customs, even in her dress. Nobody incarnated as did she the wit, the vivacity, the malice, and the shrewdness of the Creole mind. Because of her mischievousness and cunning, and because she shared with them the scepter of wit and often wrested it from their hands, she was the butt of attack of two of the most caustic talents of the epoch: the Indian Concolorcorvo and the Spaniard Terralla y Landa. But in both the former's *El Lazarillo de ciegos caminantes* and the latter's *Lima por dentro y fuera* she is, despite the resentment of the two satirists, the center of attraction. Coquettish, superstitious, extravagant, enamored of luxury, perfume, and flowers, she rules the home, the salon, builds churches with her piety, and in questions of love, honor, and politics is the shrewdest counselor, when she is not the leading actor, obliging the wavering to keep their promises or defying the Viceroy himself. The only one who ig-

411

nored her and kept her in her place was the dour Viceroy nicknamed by the women Pepe Bandos, but it was at the cost of great
unpopularity.

Her greatest originality and most genuine charm were displayed
in her attire. The full skirt and the head shawl were used only in
Lima. Foreign visitors were always intrigued by the picturesque,
enigmatic garb of the "veiled women." The skirt clung seduc-
tively to the hips and reached half-way to the ankle, revealing the
silk stocking and the tiny foot of its wearer. The shawl left only
one eye visible, and from its glance the passer-by could deduce
the hidden charm of the face.

Concolorcorvo scoffingly said of the classic dress of the women
of Lima: "All their charm resides in their lower limbs, from the
garter to the sole of the foot." The tantalizing effect of the veiling
shawl and the wearer's artful manipulation of it gave the streets
the appearance of a masked ball. And this pleasant tyranny during
the eighteenth century reached a point where the city itself
seemed to have been built by the imperious caprice of woman and
under the orders of her implacable coquettishness.

There is a close correspondence between the atmosphere of the
city, its very architecture, and the soul of *la limeña*. Its exterior
severity and aridness are in contrast with its inner gaiety and
sprightliness. Blank walls and dark doorways conceal the Andalusian riot of the gardens, just as the enveloping shawl hides the
mischievous smile of *la limeña*.

Venetian blinds, bay windows, screens, all that architecture
ever designed for watching and spying would seem to have been
invented by that same diabolical fancy that thought up the shawl
and managed the perfidious arm of the fan with such mastery.

The leading figure of the eighteenth century is not the polyglot,
erudite Pedro de Peralta y Barnuevo, despite his brushes with the
Inquisition, but the saucy actress Miquita Villegas, "La Perricholi," who stole the heart of a senile Viceroy who paid for his
belated passion with a country seat worthy of Versailles, where
an avenue of water served the lady as a mirror.

REPUBLICAN LIMA

With the Independence the pampered city of the viceroys was transformed into the "heroic and valiant city of the free men of Peru." For a moment one might have believed that a radical transformation had occurred in the soul and atmosphere of Lima. And from 1810 to 1816 life there took on an unwonted uneasiness. The first insurrections in the neighboring colonies led the Viceroy to embark upon a revolutionary counter-offensive. For some years Lima was the general headquarters of Spanish resistance and the strongest bulwark of the King. In and out of it marched peninsular and Creole troops on their way to destroy the patriot armies of South America.

The newspapers which were allowed to be published were avidly read. Sedition had penetrated to the very palace of the Viceroy. New plots were discovered every day among his favorites and advisors. The typical meeting-place of the period was the café. There, around the tables, gathered gamblers, churchmen, government officials, idlers, and students to drink, gamble, and argue, and sometimes only the last. The news of *La Gaceta* was the subject of discussion, and sometimes items which the censorship had suppressed. In the crowd there was often some stranger who passed for a merchant and was perhaps a secret agent of San Martín, who encouraged the malcontents against the government and applauded the hot-headed remarks of some young student of the new liberal schools, who might well be Sanchez Carrión. The discussion, which began timidly and in a whisper, soon became an uproar, giving rise to angry arguments which threatened to end in violence and involve many of the participants, when the sudden sally of some friar would dissipate all that angry excitement in mirth. Lima, that capital of wit, from 1810 bent its efforts to becoming independent, employing its favorite arm, the epigram.

With the arrival of the liberating armies of San Martín and Bolívar life became even more upset. "That placid city of mystic love," says Vicuña Mackenna, "began to hear the oaths of foreign soldiers in its streets; the convents became barracks; that para-

413

dise, a wasteland; and fragrant Lima . . . reeked with the smell of gunpowder and the sweat of Spanish soldiers still garbed in the rags of peninsular prisons."

But the change was only momentary. Once the revolutionary squall had passed, the city recovered its characteristic air and its colonial habits.

Social life became once more that of the eighteenth century. The quiet, the monotony, the inertia, the boredom were the same when Seralla y Landa wrote his *Week of a Dandy in Lima* in 1790, as when Don Felipe Pardo described the exceptional "Voyage" of Niño Goyito for the *Espejo* in 1840. Radiguet, who visited and described Lima four years later, was amazed to discover the persistence of old customs there to a greater degree than in any other South American city in dress and architectural fashions. The rigid caste distinctions had not disappeared with the Republic; the "veiled women" still wore their typical dress, although they had learned to take part in conspiracies; and as the military uprisings and the political din left no time for innovations, the city remained unchanged.

The improvement in the government's financial situation brought about by the discovery of the value of guano, together with a few years of internal peace, finally brought the capital out of its long stagnation. President Castilla gave it a railroad which linked it with the port of Callao, a water-supply system, which it had lacked until then, and he paved and lighted the streets. In addition he beautified it by refurbishing the Alameda of the Barefoot Friars and putting up monuments to Columbus and Bolívar.

The city's second advance came in 1870, under the presidency of Balta. The engineer Meiggs, who drew up the plans for Peru's largest and most difficult railroad lines, secured permission to raze the confining walls thrown up by the Duke of La Palata, which until then had been limiting the growth of the city. It immediately began to grow by leaps and bounds and the old walls were replaced by broad streets. Meiggs's clear, long-range vision was ably abetted by the artistic spirit and tireless activity of Manuel Atanasio Fuentes, whose good taste and inspiration were responsible for the plans of the palace for the Exposition of 1872 and the gardens around it, where the Zoological Gardens and the Park of Neptune are now located.

Piérola, who, according to Gálvez, had "the Hellenic cult of the representative city," opened new paths to urban improvement. During his term of office, from 1895 to 1899, development companies were organized which took charge of building up new sections and extending the area of the city to estates which had formerly been the country homes and meeting-grounds for the chase of the colonial nobility and the no less presumptuous republican aristocracy. In the old Victoria Gardens, where President Echenique gave magnificent balls, workers' homes were built, and to the east of the city the middle class developed the gay spacious section of Cherimoyo. But the outstanding achievement of Piérola's ædileship was the opening of the two great central avenues, the Paseo Colón, today the most beautiful in the city, which divides the parks of the Exposition and from which many streets branch off, and the broad La Colmena Boulevard.

The last and greatest stimulus to the modernization and beautification of the city came from the Leguía government. From 1919 to 1930 Lima was transformed. The city surged out toward the south. Broad asphalt highways connect Lima with Callao, La Punta, Miraflores, Chorrillos, La Magdalena, Chosica, and its other suburbs. A new Lima has come into being, spacious, bright, surrounded by trees and lawns, somewhat reminiscent of North America in its "comfort" and its asphalt highways, but in certain aspects faithful to its traditions. In the summer resorts about Lima there is a preponderance of houses in the Spanish manner or reminiscent of colonial and Moorish styles. Jalousies and balconies persist, the charm of mosaic tiles flashes everywhere, inside the houses the furniture is antique or copied from the antique: inlaid desks, marquetry tables, leather chairs, old articles of silver, which the revived industry of Lima copies faithfully. Tradition is invincible in Lima and imposes its norms upon the most modern buildings. The new palace of the archbishop, the Country Club, the Hotel Bolívar, and the buildings about the great San Martín Plaza are all in the Spanish style. The names of the streets still evoke picturesque recollections; there are old melancholy corners, and in certain little forgotten squares, lying in the shadow of a church tower, a fountain still murmurs the mystic prayer of long ago. In the section lying below the bridge and in the very heart of old Lima there are still open flower-filled courtyards and balconies as confidential as the confessional. The visitor will prefer the archaic flavor of the Convent of San Francisco and the Palace of Torre Tagle, the enervating perfume of the retreat of La Perricholi to the headlong trip along the asphalt roads that lead to Lauro or the Country Club.

THE PATRONS OF THE CITY

The city has had its tutelary deities, who raised it from its humble beginnings, granted it lofty titles of nobility, brought it back to life from its ashes, and lent dignity and grandeur to its architectural being. Those who are not commemorated by a statue or a memorial tablet, the name of a street or institution, have, nevertheless, left an indelible trace of their passing.

Pizarro is the first of all. He is the Capitoline Jupiter, from whose brow sprang, full-armed and panoplied, the wingèd-helmeted goddess. He did more than draw up the plans for the city, design the Plaza Mayor, and lay the cornerstone of the first church. He bequeathed it the episode of his death: its greatest anecdote.

Charles V gave it for its glory the coat of arms it still displays, on which the eagle and the crown alternate upon the heraldic azure of loyalty. Gerónimo de Loayza, that admirable shepherd of souls, founded the first hospital, in which, that he might share its history and its suffering, he reserved the last bed for himself. The Marquis of Cañete built the first wooden bridge over the river. A romantic death surprised the Count of Nieva as he was constructing the arches of the portico. Viceroy Toledo inaugurated the University of San Marcos, that glory of colonial life, and opened the fountain in the Plaza Mayor, supplied by water brought in by the first aqueduct. Montesclaros rebuilt the city after it had been destroyed by an earthquake; he built the stone bridge which still bears his name and opened the first theater. Salvatierra installed the magnificent fountain in the Plaza. The

Duke of La Palata and the Count of Monclova rebuilt Lima after its destruction in 1687; Nevarra and Rocafull encircled the city with a wall to defend it from the covetous eyes of pirates, and Portocarrero restored its portico. The third person to rebuild the city was the Count of Superunda. Lavalle regards him as its second founder and insists that the Lima of today is not the one Pizarro founded, but that which this Viceroy founded upon the ruins of the other. Amat, the Viceroy of pleasure, built the first bull-fighting ring, and, for the protection of the night-owls of Lima, instituted street-lights and night patrols. Moreover, he expelled the Jesuits. To Viceroy Croix fell the glory of founding the College of San Carlos, and to Gil y Lemus, that of sponsoring the *Mercurio Peruano,* the most illustrious publication of Lima. O'Higgins, because he was the only English Viceroy, and because the viceroyalty was approaching its end, built a highway. And it seems a symbolic coincidence that Abascal, who was really the last of the viceroys and the most outstanding of them, should have bequeathed the city a cemetery.

To the viceregal roster there would have to be added the names of the republican city fathers. San Martín founded the National Library. Bolívar created the system of municipal administration, dividing the city into districts. Castilla, Balta, Meiggs, Fuentes, Piérola and Leguía represent the advances of civilization already mentioned.

THE SOUL OF LIMA

One chapter would be missing and one essential attribute of the city if we did not speak of the soul of Lima. I shall merely mention it, since to attempt to define the intangible would be a presumptuous undertaking.

It consists in something impalpable, but real; gone, but still present; something that is like the wake of the glorious moments of its existence, or perhaps merely a suggestion found in history books. But the fact is that strangers and natives all note in the aspect of the city, in the atmosphere, in its streets and out-of-the-way corners a vague nostalgia. The past lives on in Lima and has an irresistible power of attraction. Everything about it has a history. The name of a street, the inscription on a wall or a doorway, commemorate some episode, trifling or important, remembered or forgotten, but with a longing for survival that makes it cling to some last vestige of life. Historians and chroniclers have exalted, dwelt upon, and disseminated this cult of the legend of the city to the point where it constitutes its finest and most genuine ornament.

But it is not only in tradition that the charm of Lima resides and its soul persists. It is in the light, mocking character of its inhabitants, in the delicate grace of its women, in the mordant wit and keenness of its men that travelers perceive the most typical notes of our character. It would be redundant to insist further in the praise of this pungent Creole wit that is to be found everywhere, in the streets and the newspapers, on the lip and on the pen, which gives conversations, verses, and newspapers an epigrammatic flavor. They say that this thoughtlessness of Lima has been harmful to the country, this "always jesting" condemned by *El Discreto*. In literature, however, this mischievous inclination gave rise to a special type of writing, gay, spontaneous, which has been called Creole when, by rights, it should be called Liman.

With a sigh for the past and a smile, the loyal sons of Lima wrote their works, interpreting and evoking the city, thanks to whom it lives in history and literature. The greatest of them all, the one who joined tradition and wit in a subtle alliance to perpetuate the ephemeral soul of Lima, was Don Ricardo Palma. His roguishness and that of the city were so linked together, just as was the tradition he novelized with real history, that it is impossible to say whether it was the city that shaped him or whether he gave the city its Puckish character, whether the traditions he relates really happened in Lima or only in the viceroyalty of his witty fantasy.

CARTAGENA

BETTER TO DEFEND the vast empire it had conquered in a few years, Spain located the capitals of its viceroyalties and colonies far inland, high in the mountains, and limited the ports of entry to two or three. For over three centuries it fortified these with walls and battlements of stones hewn and joined one by one by the arms of slaves under the blaze of the tropical sun and the rough voice of the sergeant. Portobello in Panama, San Juan de Ulua in Mexico, Cartagena in New Granada, were the strongholds. Their thick gates opened to admit wares of all kinds from Seville, and Negroes trapped in Africa; and from them sailed the galleons loaded with bars of silver, bars of gold. These were the places about which the buccaneers sniffed hungrily. The English, French, Dutch, and Danes turned the Caribbean into a pirate sea. The memory still lives of Hawkins's exploits and his defeat in San Juan de Ulua, Drake's and Morgan's raids on Panama, Ducasse's and François LeClerc's (Peg-Leg's) on Cartagena. Looking out today upon the ruins through the loop-holes of the fortresses, one can see in the mind's eye the axes battering down the cathedral doors, hoarse-voiced sailors blaspheming in English as they burst into the convents amidst the wild fluttering of terrified nuns, traders rushing to take refuge in the hills, Negroes laughing and showing their white teeth as the pools of blood rose higher about the pirates' feet.

Cartagena is the compendium of all these cities and legends. It was founded, as might have been expected, by a swashbuckling Spaniard, Don Pedro de Heredia, who left his nose behind him in the peninsula in an affair involving swords and ladies. The date of its foundation was 1533. Two hundred and sixty years later four hundred and eighty cannon, four hundred and eighty mouths belching fire, crowned its walls. The fortresses of San Fernando and San José stood grimly in the midst of the bay; those of Pastelillo and San Felipe kept watch from the coast, and they

419

were linked to the other fortifications by a maze of underground passageways. They can still be seen there by sightseers. And there are the old white-walled streets, where flowers hang like bright shawls and pour through the wrought-iron grilles like those of Seville.

It is told that once a courtier of Felipe II saw the monarch standing on tiptoe peering at something he seemed unable to make out. The scene took place in the Escorial. "What is Your Majesty looking at?" inquired the courtier. The King replied: "I don't understand why we cannot see the walls of Cartagena from here, with all the money they have cost us." What a good thing it would have been for the King to have embarked on one of the ships sailing to America and to have seen not only the broad wall upon which automobiles now run, the dungeons where the prisoners bewailed their sorrows, the horde of Negroes who dug the canal which made it possible to travel from Cartagena to Rio Grande, and, better than all of this, from Don Felipe's point of view, the palace of the Inquisition, with its imposing door like a carved rock, and its stout iron bars, whose purpose was to help show heretics and backsliding Jewish converts the errors of their ways! The city walls were high and thick. Nevertheless at times bold intruders violated the fortified citadel. The timid fled to the hills. Then later they returned with the treasures they had carried away to pay the ransom and beg Drake not to put the city to the torch. Finally the city made itself invulnerable. An English admiral, Vernon, who was cheered in Parliament in London as he described how easily Cartagena could be attacked, lost his reputation and his men in the bay, having reckoned without his host. The Basque Blas de Lezo, who was in charge of the defense of the stronghold, was a soldier who resembled a fortress in ruins. In youthful combats he had lost his left leg, his right arm, his left eye. But one-armed, one-eyed, and one-legged as he was, he made the English admiral retire in confusion, with fever snapping at his heels and the sea gulping down his men.

Armando Solano, a Colombian writer, has painted Cartagena in his book *Ciudades de Colombia.*

CARTAGENA

ARMANDO SOLANO

Is there any form in which the praises of the city of Cartagena have not been sung? Poems of bronze, resounding and undying, have recited its glories. Severe pages of musical prose, sober and measured in rhythm, have told of the religious awe, the admiring evocation, the feeling tribute, the touching impressions aroused by the old city surrounded by its inexpugnable walls, defended by the towers and fortresses raised by the arrogant power of Spain. There has never yet been a traveler, however limited his knowledge of history, however dry his heart, however poor he be in the generous capacity of admiring and paying tribute to impressive beauty, who has not made special mention in the record of his travels of this venerable relic of the past, which is at the same time a rich promise for tomorrow.

To the eager visitor who reaches its gates Cartagena is like a vision of the Orient. It is a white city, whose roofs and façades are wildly ablaze with violent colors of African intensity. Cupolas, balconies, windows, under the vivid light of the sun, make the sight one of aerial festivity. In its upper stories the city lives a fantastic life, a fitting counterpart to that of its narrow streets flanked by broad windows with grilles of wrought iron, high sidewalks, storied doorways which permit a glimpse of the dewy shadows of broad, flowering Andalusian patios with the dark and green mirrors of their thirsty cisterns. Neither Toledo nor any other city of old Spain can have preserved a purer or more genuinely Spanish air than this quiet city of Colombia where the colony left such a deep and indelible trace. There is not a single detail that breaks this exquisite harmony. Even the language of the populace, even the graphic exclamations and insults which the Negroes hurl at one another from the driver's seat of their little carts when they get in one another's way, have the most typical and genuine flavor that can be imagined. These people use words of old Spanish, words that are no longer in circulation in the language of the educated people and which are rollicking and dashing in their old age. And the agreeable impression this causes wherever one goes, in the market-place where the glittering fish are strewn upon the sand and the turtles paddle in little fenced-off mud puddles, at the doors of the churches, in the public square, is intensified and reinforced by the background against which it is set. There are dark, gloomy shops which offer for sale delicious traditional confectionery and pastries; the poorer classes — in Cartagena, as in the other cities of the coast, Barranquilla, Santa Marta, there are no beggars, that degrading humiliation to be found in the interior — understand good food, possess a pleasant, primitive sybaritism, and often indulge in Homeric culinary satisfactions undegraded by the excessive use of alcohol. The mass of the people love easy, comfortable, abundant, gay living. And as they are not corrupted by certain modern influences, their manifestations take on the most picturesque forms. Here there are customs, traditions; and the people take pride in keeping alive the festivals they have always observed, as, for example, the gay celebration of the Feast of the Candelaria.

The same thing occurs among the upper classes. The greatest social distinction, the most delicate mark of breeding and good taste, lies in the cult of the archaic, in fidelity to the old ways in every walk of life. In Cartagena, whose proud decorum is unassailable, there is no free and easy living in the street, no light, easy friendships, none of that doubtful promiscuousness which filters into other coastal cities in the guise of modern freedom from convention. Here family life is secluded and austere; everyone knows everybody else, with his defects, virtues, and background, and society tends to observe rigid caste distinctions. There are occasions, however, such as certain popular celebrations, when the social extremes meet and fraternize with that typically Spanish sense of democracy, frank, unassuming, jovial, but where there is no confusing who is who among these participants momentarily gathered together. In Cartagena the importation of Africans left a particularly dense sediment. The percentage of colored blood in the population is too high. Yet no racial dilemma exists here, there are no clashes of any kind, and it would seem that a type of human being completely adapted to his surroundings will be fused in the melting-pot of the maternal city. At present that race, with its noisy, vivid inclinations, its amusing laziness, its volubility, and its vehemence, gives to the varied aspect of this city, which is without question one of the most beautiful of America, a refreshing, picaresque, lively touch. Those who maintain as a scientific dogma the unalterable inferiority of the Negro are due for a surprise when they see in Cartagena the obedient, clean school children, wide awake, clear-eyed, intelligent, well-behaved, friendly, and attractive in appearance.

With the partial and barbarous demolition of its precious walls, built as the proud boast of Spain's omnipotence when the city was a jewel coveted by the pirates of the whole world, Cartagena has begun its adjustment to modern exigencies. It is constructing great factories of cement, breaking the massive denseness of its sacred walls with bright windows, and the strident notes of jazz have penetrated the rich splendor of its drawing-rooms and clubs, where the charms of its pale, conventionalized ladies held sway. But in general the colonial type of architecture predominates and endures: broad, solid, the great houses with their whitewashed arches, the old churches with their treasure of pious relics and their towers which throw their long shadows across the blue waters of the bay. The bay of Cartagena! Who can ever forget it? It is repose after exertion, serenity after the storm, eternal peace after unending restlessness. The sea sinks to slumber there, it grows gentle and yields itself up in humble tribute at the feet of the proud sultana. This quiet gulf which clasps the city in an embrace of chaste love holds the key to its future far more than the smoking factories. To it will come, seeking refuge and new activities, the ships of all the world: those carrying the tourist curious to know the monuments of history, the crumbling fortresses, the alert watchtowers, and the cells where the saints prayed; the merchant with his wares; the captain of industry who comes to load his black tankers with the prodigious oil which sows rivalry between nations and crime among men. The bay of Cartagena, as the commercial axis of the world moves westward, will be the magnificent bazaar of mankind, a vast, busy fair where the conglomeration of masts will darken the vision of the sky.

Meanwhile the glorious, heroic, lordly martyr city, lost in its own thoughts, continues to live its life of memories and of hopes. Its severe and learned university disciplines emulate those of the venerable centers of the peninsula from which they sprang; and among the taciturn, aloof patricians of the proud city there abound the cloistered wooer of the muses, the disinterested student of history who pores over old documents that crumble away at the touch, the jurist learned in pandects, codes, and records. And among all of them there stands out that disillusioned, sarcastic poet, master of the epigram and the caricature, Luis C. López, whose imitators are legion and whose equal has not yet appeared. It may seem a paradox, but this mordant poet, in whom satire reaches perfection in incredible malice, embodies in his complex personality much of the soul of the polite, stately, ceremonious city which will tolerate not even the slightest blot on its escutcheon. In López's poetry the plangent note of the tragedy of decadence is heard on muted strings: the contrast between the romantic past and the drab reality of the present; between the stoicism of yesterday and the flabby softness of today; between the virtue of the grandfathers and the middle-class priggishness of the grandsons. López is no superficial wit, no gay jester. He is an avenger, a wrathful archangel who cracks his whip, made of thongs of laughter, over the head of the desecrators of the temple.

On a radiant morning of the pleasant summer, as one looks down from the top of La Popa hill and takes in the complete panorama of the city, one feels such a complete, unqualified pleasure, so in keeping with one's thirst for beauty and light, that there is a moment of such intense sensation as to be almost unbearable. This is an overwhelming symphony of color. On one side lies the open sea, the open, billowing sea with its green depths. On the other, the blue bay, so dark it almost looks black, suddenly furrowed by long striations of sun which tint it in a manner that baffles description. The water penetrates the city in many places, licks its streets, undermines its defenses, forms islands of mangrove swamps, engulfs branches of trees. And the red and blue and white roofs, and the marble slenderness of the Moorish villas, with their decoration of lacy fretwork, together with the dingy gray of the factories combine to make up an enchanted vision which is suddenly dominated by the appearance on the remote horizon of a solitary ship, defenseless, weak, which moves ahead like a soul, like all our souls, at the mercy of the elements, uncertain whether it will reach port in safety. This first impression, heart-lifting, stimulating, is gradually dimmed by the reflections that follow this feast of the senses. We find ourselves suspended between sky and sea, and before our eyes there spreads a city charged with history, evocative, enigmatic, which has suffered the cruelest martyrdoms, which has opposed superhuman resistance to countless enemies, which has in the different periods of its history fought epic battles for freedom, which imprisoned in its dungeons of evil memory romantic champions of the right. The past that impinges upon us is an impressive one, and it overwhelms and engulfs us like a rising tide. What new hazards does the future hold? Will these walls stand firm or will they be razed by the attack of the freebooters? Will the modern conquest, sly, insidious, golden, whose aerial boats come to rest almost in the heart of Cartagena, make use of its power to turn into a mere refueling station what was once an invincible stronghold, immune to humiliation and outrage? Who can tell? Even more than the mind, the heart rejects the idea of the fall of this fortress which protects not so much the Roman strategy of its silent batteries as the unfailing pride and bravery of its inhabitants, the imperious voice of honor that calls from the tombs, from the walls, from all the spots hallowed by the blood of heroes.

The daily life of Cartagena is losing its stiffness, its conventions, its anachronisms. People are gradually accepting the fact that it is impossible, in this climate, to go on wearing frock-coats or formal dress at all ceremonies; as everywhere, though more reluctantly than anywhere else, protocol is losing force and being dispensed with. As a result social gatherings gain in cordiality and ease what they lose in pomp. On the white terraces of the clubs which reach out over the sea, the dances and gatherings are lively and informal. Swift motor-boats come from outlying districts to leave their elegant cargo at the very foot of the stairway that leads to the ballroom. And in the shimmering perfumed night the swaying lanterns produce the impression of a Venetian scene. A more indolent Venice, sleepier than that enchanted city of the doges.

There exists in Cartagena, not as the product of the decay of aristocratic habits, but as a lineal descendant, a green offshoot of the old trunk, an impenitent bohemianism, generous, devoted to matters of the spirit, which makes wit its occupation and is a pleasant oasis for whoever comes to the serene city. These bohemians gather in noisy agapes, recite verses, offer lyric toasts, laugh with childlike ingenuousness, and gossip harmlessly about local matters. They form a fraternal circle, where one may find solid citizens who have spent the day in the law-courts, or paying bills in the stuffy office of some warehouse, or checking shipping invoices at the docks. For it is unusual to find a bohemian who spends the day in complete idleness, leaning against the cannon that adorn and defend the corners. People work hard in Cartagena even though, faithful to its tradition, the city looks upon this as an unjust punishment. Any visitor of intellectual standing is modestly honored by these ingenuous circles which profess the cult of copious libations and traditional dishes, prepared with painstaking authenticity.

Their homage takes the form of those delightful trips around the bay where the visitor feels himself free from the tyranny of having to breathe and lets the iodine-impregnated air fill his breast with its life-giving pulsation; lets his hands trail in the warm heavy water; lets his eyes widen, and learns what it is to gaze upon horizons that have no limit. Or the even gayer visits to the Boquilla, that rustic fishing center, where the fried shad perfumes the air with its delicate smell and the guests dispense with all the inventions of civilization in consuming their due portion.

The isolation in which we still live prevents the people of the highlands from coming to Cartagena as often as they should to fortify their nerves with sea baths, to clear their heads of gloomy thoughts, to establish immediate contact with the past and the future of the country. Here men think, feel, and act differently from in our uplands, which are the home of pessimism, dullness, and gloomy introspection. Here life is not tragic. People gaily spend all they make and perhaps a little more. There is a dignified idea of comfort and the consideration each man owes to himself; this idea is even more evident in centers of rapid growth such as Barranquilla, and in the banana-raising zone of the Magdalena it becomes a senseless squandering of the shower of gold the Colombian workers make there. For our way of life, Cartagena, modest, devout, is the happy medium. It is a city which we are in duty bound to visit, in a sort of spiritual retreat, each year, as a measure of health to bring us into contact with the origins of our Republic and launch us freely on the boldest visions of tomorrow.

For my temperament, Cartagena is the ideal dwelling-place. I know many of the shrines of the republican faith, many of the relics of our history. Yet it seems to me difficult for a person to feel himself as much of a Colombian anywhere else as in Cartagena, which is at once the cradle and the destiny of our country, its legend and its reality, its poetry and its enduring action.

PART V

The Color of Life

THE SERTÕES

BRAZIL IS A CONTINENT within a continent. The other countries of America are beginning to form an idea of the unlimited resources and even of the territorial expanse of this vast empire which the Kingdom of Portugal once held in its tiny hands. The present war — which has taught us so much geography — has helped to discover this new world, whose influence will be a decisive one in the future of America. But it is not only outsiders who are in this state of ignorance. Brazil has been a stranger to itself. Far inland, across deserts where the relentless sun dries up every drop of water and only plants without foliage or sap can subsist, lie better lands. It is toward these lands that the economic frontier of the nation has moved in times not far distant from our own. But in the background of these conquests, which paint the life of America better than any other episode, great human dramas took place. That of *Os Sertões* embodies all the rest. People crossed the desert in search of more hospitable natural surroundings. They were led by a man possessed: Antonio *Conselheiro* (the Counselor). He was followed by people outside the law, outlaws who, dominated by the strange figure of the leader, knelt in prayer and built churches. Out of this mixture of fanaticism and barbarism came one of the strangest cities in the world. Its story was ignored for a long time, despite the fact that in order to overcome Conselheiro the government was obliged to embark upon one of the bloodiest civil wars in the history of Brazil. As a matter of fact, the rebels never gave up, and only after wiping them out completely was the government able to re-establish authority in Canudos. Euclydes da Cunha has told the story of this episode in his book *Os Sertões*, which was published in 1903, and which is today a classic of Brazilian literature. It has just been published in English translation with the title *Rebellion in the Backlands* (University of Chicago Press). The following pages give a portrait of Antonio *Conselheiro.*

DESCRIPTION OF ANTONIO CONSELHEIRO
EUCLYDES DA CUNHA

AND there appeared in Bahia that somber hermit. He was terrifying to behold, with his hair hanging down to his shoulders, a
long, unkempt beard, a face like a death's-head, glittering eyes,
garbed in a habit of blue cotton, and in his hand the classic pilgrim
staff.

For a long time nothing was known of his existence. An old
caboclo, who was imprisoned in Canudos during the later days
of the campaign, gave me a little information about him, but
vague and imprecise. The sertões of the inland of Pernambuco
knew of him a year or two after he left Crata. From the words of
this witness I came to the conclusion that while still a young man
Antonio Maciel had made a vivid impression on the imagination
of the dwellers of that region. He appeared among them without
any definite purpose, a wanderer. He made no reference to his
past. He rarely spoke, and when he did, it was in brief phrases or
monosyllables. He roved about aimlessly, from one ranch to another, indifferent to life and danger, eating poorly and irregularly,
sleeping in the open air beside the road, in a prolonged, severe
penance.

He gradually became something supernatural or bewitched to
the minds of those simple people. When this strangely aged man,
who was only a little more than thirty years old, appeared among
the cattle-herders, their songs ceased and their guitars were
silenced. It was only natural. He suddenly loomed up — squalid
and emaciated — in his long, plain blue habit, silent, like a specter,
from the wasteland inhabited by ghosts.

He went on his way leaving the superstitious countryfolk awed
and apprehensive.

He acquired an ascendancy over them without making any
effort to do so. In a primitive society in which, by reason of its
racial composition and the influence of the nefarious "holy mis-

452

sions," life rested on a basis of miracles they could not fathom, his mysterious mode of life began to create an atmosphere of supernatural prestige about him which, perhaps, aggravated his deranged temperament. Little by little all this domination which he unintentionally exercised on others seems to have taken hold on him. All the conjectures and legends by which he was soon surrounded stimulated the growth of his aberration. His madness acquired outward form. He saw it reflected in the intense admiration and unquestioning respect which in a short time made his word law in all disputes and quarrels and converted him into the supreme authority in all decisions. This attitude on the part of the multitude spared him the ordeal of trying to understand his own mental state, the painful effort of self-analysis and that obsessive introspection which drives an unhinged mind to madness. The multitude recast him in its own image, created him, enlarged him beyond all human proportions, and launched him upon a sea of errors two thousand years old. It needed someone who should translate its vague idealism and guide it along the mysterious paths that lead to heaven.

The evangelist emerged, but inhuman, an automaton. This agitator was a puppet. He acted passively, like a sleepwalker. But in his behavior he reflected the obscure, formless aspirations of three races.

And he acquired such dimensions that he projected himself into history. . . .

From the *sertões* of Pernambuco he proceeded to those of Sergipe, appearing in the city of Itabaiana in 1874.

He arrived there, as everywhere, unknown and arousing distrust by reason of his strange attire: a long, unbelted tunic, a hat with a wide drooping brim, and sandals. On his back hung a knapsack in which he carried paper, pen and ink, and two books, a *Brief Missal* and *The Hours of Maria.*

He begged his bread, but he always refused to take more than he needed for the day. He sought out the loneliest ranches. He never accepted any bed but the bare boards or, lacking this, the hard earth. He wandered about like this for a long time until he appeared in the *sertões* to the north of Bahia. His fame was growing. He no longer traveled by himself. The first of the faithful were following him on his uncharted route. He did not call them. They came of their own free will, happy to share with him his life of privation and suffering. For the most part they were the dregs of humanity, of doubtful antecedents, averse to work, a troupe of life's outcasts, adept in the ways of laziness and thievishness.

One of the disciples carried on his back the only temple that then existed of this puny new religion: a roughly carved cedar altar on which was an image of Christ. When they stopped along the roadside they hung it from the branch of a tree, and there they knelt in prayer. As they entered the hamlets and villages they bore it triumphantly aloft, intoning a chorus of litanies.

In 1876 the Counselor, as he was known, appeared in the town of Itapicuru de Cima. His fame had become widespread. A document published that year in the capital of the Empire bears witness to this:

> There has appeared in the *sertão* of the north a man who calls himself Antonio the Counselor, and who exerts a great influence on the lower classes, utilizing for this end his mysterious aspect and his ascetic habits, which make a great impression on the ignorance of these simple-minded people. He has let his hair and beard grow long, he wears a cotton tunic and eats very little, looking almost like a mummy. He goes about in the company of two women converts, and he spends his life praying and preaching and giving advice to the multitudes which gather to hear him wherever the priests permit it. By playing on their religious sentiments he attracts the people and does what he likes with them. He shows himself to be a man of intelligence, though devoid of culture.

These remarks, which were the exact truth, published in a journal hundreds of miles away, are eloquent testimony to the fame he was acquiring.

Meanwhile in this town of Itapicuru his extraordinary career almost came to an end. That same year, to the consternation of the faithful, he was arrested. This came about as the result of a false accusation which his strange life and past domestic difficulties justified to a certain point. He was said to have killed his wife and his own mother.

It was a gruesome tale. It was said that his mother hated her daughter-in-law and set about to work her ruination. With this in mind, she told her son that his wife was unfaithful to him; and as he demanded proofs of her guilt, she proposed to supply them without delay. She advised him to pretend that he was going away on a trip, but to remain in the neighborhood and at night he would see the seducer who was dishonoring his home. The poor wretch following her advice, rode several miles away from the town and then, taking a roundabout lonely route back, hid in a place he had selected where he could see what took place and act quickly.

There he remained hidden for hours until, late in the night, he saw a shadowy figure approach his house. He saw it creep up and climb into one of the windows. Before it could get through he felled it with a shot.

With one bound he was in the house, and with another shot he killed his wife, who was asleep.

Then he turned back to discover the identity of the man he had killed. And he saw, to his horror, that it was his own mother, who had disguised herself as a man to carry out her diabolical plan.

Aghast, crazed, he immediately fled, leaving everything he owned, to the *sertões* of the interior.

The popular imagination had begun to create a legend about his life, giving it a vigorous touch of tragic originality.

Nevertheless the fact remains that in 1876 the law laid hold of him just as the evolution of his spirit had reached its climax and he was sunk in a dream from which he was never again to awaken. The ascetic was emerging, in full stature, from the rude discipline of fifteen years of penance. He had reached perfection in his apprenticeship of martyrdom, a profession so highly recommended by the old Church fathers. It was the result of brutally binding himself over to hunger, thirst, fatigue, and every form of pain and misery. There was no suffering he did not know. His leathery skin was stretched over his insensible flesh like a battered and cracked coat of mail. It had been anesthetized by its sufferings. It was lacerated and scarred by disciplines more severe than a hair shirt; it had been dragged over the stones of the road, it had been charred by the blazing heat of the drought, numbed by the cold morning dew, had known only momentary rest in the bone-breaking beds of the rough hills.

His prolonged fasts brought him many times to the brink of death. The perfection of his asceticism would have surprised Tertulian, that gloomy advocate of the slow elimination of the flesh, "ridding himself of his blood, that heavy, importunate burden of the soul eager to flee. . . ."

For a person undergoing this training in suffering, that prison order was but a trifling incident. He received it with indifference. He forbade his followers to defend him. He gave himself up. He was taken to the capital of Bahia. There his strange appearance, his corpse-like face, as rigid as a mask, expressionless and unsmiling; his eyelids drooping over his sunken eyes, his strange garb, his revolting appearance, that of an unburied corpse, in the long tunic like a dark winding-sheet, and the lank, dusty hair falling about his shoulders, mingling with the unkempt beard which hung to his waist, made him the object of general curiosity.

As he was led through the streets people exclaimed and made signs to ward off the evil eye, while devout old women crossed themselves and fell back in fear.

The judges questioned him in amazement. He was accused of old crimes he had committed in his native region. He listened to the questions and accusations without answering a word, in stony silence. It was later learned that the guards who had brought him in had beaten him on the road. He did not voice the slightest complaint. His was the lofty indifference of a stoic. Only on the day he was to be embarked for Ceará — and I have this from a person of complete reliability — did he ask the authorities to protect him from the curiosity of the crowds, the only thing that bothered him.

On reaching his native town, the charges against him were proved to be groundless and he was placed at liberty. And that same year he appeared in Bahia once more among his followers, who had been waiting for him. His return, on the very day he had prophesied when he was arrested, so it was said, assumed the character of a miracle. His influence became thrice what it had been.

Then for a time (1877) he wandered about the *sertões* of Curaca, making his headquarters in Chorrochó, a village of a few hundred inhabitants whose lively fair attracted the majority of the people of that region of San Francisco. A beautiful chapel, still standing, tells of his stay there. And perhaps more deserving of veneration is a little tree at the entrance to the village which for a long time was the object of extraordinary devotion. It was a sacred tree. Its shadow cured the ills of the faithful; its leaves were an unfailing panacea.

The multitude launched a great series of miracles to which the unhappy wretch probably had never given a thought.

From 1877 to 1887 he wandered about those *sertões,* from one end to the other, even reaching the seacoast, in Villa do Conde (1887). There is probably not a city or village in this whole region where he did not make his appearance. Alagoinhas, Inhambupe, Bom Conselho, Geremoabo, Cumbe, Mucambo, Massacara, Pombal, Monte-Santo, Tucano, and other settlements saw him arrive, accompanied by the troupe of the faithful. In nearly all he left a trace of his passage: in one the rebuilt walls of a ruined cemetery; in another a restored church; farther on, a chapel, always beautiful.

His entrance in the towns, followed by the contrite multitude, in silence, bearing images, crosses, and banners of the Lord, was solemn and impressive. The people deserted their shops and farms. They swarmed into the place where he was, and for a time, overshadowing the local authorities, the humble, wandering penitent took command, became the sole authority.

Sheds covered with branches were erected in the public square, and in the afternoon the faithful intoned their prayers and litanies; and when the gathering was great a platform was constructed in the middle of the market-place so the words of the prophet could be heard from all sides and edify the faithful.

There he stood up and preached. It was an extraordinary experience, according to witnesses who are still living. It was a barbarous, hair-raising oratory, made up of fragments from the *Hours of Mary,* disconnected, abstruse, with astounding Latin quotations, pouring forth in disjointed phrases, a confused, tangled mixture of dogmatic advice, commonplace precepts of Christian morality, and weird prophecies.

It was grotesque and terrifying. Imagine a clown carried away by a vision of the Apocalypse!

Using few gestures, he would talk for a long time, his eyes fixed on the ground, without looking at the multitude, which was spellbound by the rush of words, which varied from nerve-racking exhortations to a wearisome singsong.

It would appear that he was often bemused by the effect of some significant phrase. He would pronounce it and then become silent, raising his head and suddenly opening his eyelids wide; then his deep black shining eyes could be seen, and the brilliant glitter of his glance. . . . Nobody dared to look upon him. The crowd, overawed, lowered its eyes, under the strange hypnotic spell of that terrible insanity.

It was on such occasions that this tormented wretch performed his only miracle: he managed not to make himself ridiculous.

In his preaching, in which he successfully competed with the wandering Capuchin fathers of the missions, he upheld a vague, incongruous system of religion. Whoever heard him could not avoid suggestive historical comparisons. On re-reading the unforgettable pages of Renan's *Marcus Aurelius,* in which he brings to life, through the power of his style, the mad leaders of the religious sects of the first centuries of Christianity, one can see in the Counselor's teachings the complete revival of their extinct aberrations. It would be impossible to find a more faithful reproduction of the same system, the same metaphors, the same hyperboles, almost the same words. It is a beautiful example of the similarity of evolutionary phases among peoples. This retrograde of the *sertão* is the living copy of the mystics of the past. One can experience, looking at him, the marvelous effect of a perspective of centuries.

He does not belong to our time. He belongs with all those stragglers whom Fouillée, in a felicitous phrase, calls the "runners on the field of civilization who fall farther and farther behind."

He was a dissenter cast in the same mold as Themison. He rose in rebellion against the Church of Rome, and he hurled invectives against it, employing its own arguments: it had forsaken its glory and was following Satan. His moral teaching was an interlinear translation of that of Montanus: chastity carried to the point of utter horror of woman, while at the same time there was absolute tolerance for free love, leading almost to the extinction of marriage.

In the Phrygian, as perhaps in the man from Ceará, this was the result of unhappy conjugal experiences. Both severely forbade the young women to do anything that enhanced their beauty. They fulminated against fancy wearing apparel, and both of them, above all, against elaborate hairdressing; and what is very curious — they both fixed the same punishment for this sin, the demon of the hair: a piercing crown of thorns for the offenders.

Beauty was, to them, a snare of Satan. The Counselor missed no opportunity to show his invincible repugnance for it. He never looked at a woman. He talked with his back turned even to pious old women who would have exercised a restraining influence on a satyr.

This similarity with the past grows even more impressive as one examines the absurd concepts of this mad apostle of the *sertões*. Like his predecessors, he appeared when it was believed that the world was coming to an end, that the millennium was at hand; and he had the same terror of the antichrist, whose presence could be felt in the universal collapse of life. The world was approaching its close. . . .

The faithful were to abandon all their possessions, all that might defile them with the slightest trace of vanity. As all worldly goods would be engulfed in the imminent catastrophe, it would be rash folly to treasure them. Let them give up their fleeting pleasures and make their lives a stern purgatory, unsullied by the sacrilege of a smile. The Judgment Day was at hand.

He prophesied years of disaster to follow one after another: [1]

[1] These prophecies were written out in a number of little notebooks that were found in Canudos. These I have quoted were copied from one of them that belonged to the adjutant of the officer in charge of the campaign.

. . . In 1896 a thousand flocks will flee from the meadows to the desert, and then the desert will become a meadow, and the meadow a desert.

In 1897 there will be much pasture and little stubble, and a single flock and a single shepherd.

In 1898 there will be many hats and few heads.

In 1899 the waters will turn to blood and a planet will appear in the east with a ray of sun that the branch will confront on the earth, and the earth in some spot will be confronted by the heavens.

There will come a great rain of stars and that will be the end of the world. In 1900 the lights will go out. God says it in the Gospels: I have a flock that is wandering outside the fold and it must be brought together so there will be but one flock and one shepherd.

Like those of old he believed he had been sent to do the will of God, and that it was Christ Himself who had prophesied his coming:

In the ninth hour, as He sat resting upon the Mount of Olives one of the disciples asked him: "Master, what shall be the sign of the end of the world?" And He answered: "There shall be many signs in the Moon and the Sun and the Stars. And an angel will be sent forth by My eternal Father, preaching at the gates, building towns in the desert, building churches and chapels, and giving advice. . . ."

Through all this wild maundering, together with the religious Messianic concept, there was the Messianism of the race, urging him on to rebellion against the republican form of government:

Verily, verily I say unto you, when nation shall rise against nation, Brazil against Brazil, England against England, Prussia against Prussia, from the depths of the sea Don Sebastian will come forth with all his army.

From the beginning of the world which he enchanted with all his army and restored in war.

And when he was enchanted he buried his sword in a rock, up to the hilt, and said: "Farewell, World."

Until a thousand and so many to two thousand years you will not come.

On that day when he comes forth with his army, he will put all those of this play Republic to the sword. The end of this war will come in the Holy House of Rome and the blood will run loin-deep.

Prophecy had, as can be seen, the same accent in him as when it first appeared in Phrygia, moving westward. It foretold the same Last Judgment, the downfall of the mighty, the destruction of the godless world, and the coming of the millennium.

Is there not to be seen in all this a marked trace of Judaism? It seems indubitable. This return to the golden age of apostles and prophets, this revival of old illusions, is nothing new. It is the ever recurring return of Christianity to its Hebrew cradle. Montanus is reproduced throughout history, changed in this respect or the other depending on the character of the different nations, but revealing in his very revolt against the ecclesiastical hierarchy, in his approach to the supernatural, in his vision of heaven, the outlines of the primitive dream of the old religion, before it had been distorted by the canonized sophists of the Church councils.

Following the example of his predecessors in the past, Antonio Conselheiro was a pietist, waiting for the coming of the reign of heaven on earth, which had been promised, ever delayed, and finally completely forgotten by the orthodox Church of the second century. His creed had little to do with Catholicism, which he hardly understood.

In keeping with the mission he had taken upon himself, after delivering these homilies, he ordered penances, which were generally to the benefit of the locality. Neglected churches were restored; abandoned cemeteries were repaired; beautiful new edifices were built. The stonemasons and carpenters worked for nothing; stores donated the materials; the multitude brought in the stones. For days on end the workmen busied themselves with their pious tasks, and their wages were credited to them in heaven.

When the work was finished the messenger of God suddenly departed — whither? Anywhere, taking the first road deeper into the *sertões*, over the endless plains, without even looking back at those who followed him.

He was unperturbed by the hostility of his dangerous adversary, the priest. According to reliable testimony, the clergy, in general, encouraged or at least allowed him to practice, without return of any sort, all those acts from which they derive their income: baptisms, confessions, feasts, and novenas. They showed indulgence toward the absurdities of the possessed saint, who at least helped them to eke out their meager sustenance. In view of this the archbishop of Bahia, in 1882, to bring to an end this tolerance, not to say barely disguised protection, sent out a circular to all the priests of his see:

> It has come to our knowledge that a person known as Antonio Conselheiro is going about among the parishioners of this see, preaching to the people who flock to hear him superstitious doctrines and excessively rigid moral concepts with which he is disturbing the consciences and undermining, not a little, the authority of the clergy in those regions. Therefore we order Your Reverence not to tolerate this abuse among your parishioners, advising them that we absolutely forbid them to gather to hear his preachings, for in the Catholic Church it is the mission of the ministers of religion alone to instruct the people, and a layman, however learned and virtuous, has no authority to do this.
>
> Meanwhile let this serve to increase your zeal in the exercise of your preaching duties so that your parishioners, properly instructed, will not be swept off their feet by every passing wind of doctrine. . . .

But the intervention of the Church was futile.

Antonio Conselheiro continued his mad apostolate without let or hindrance, through the *sertões*. And as though he wished to keep green the memory of the first persecution he had suffered, he always came back to Itapicuru, where the police authorities finally appealed to the government in a report which, after giving a brief summary of the antecedents of the agitator, says:

. . . He made his camp in this vicinity and soon he was building a chapel at the expense of the town.

Although this work may be an improvement, even a necessary one, for the town, it is not worth the agitation and unrest; and from the state the people are in, the apprehension of great disturbances is more than justified.

In order that you may judge what Antonio Conselheiro is, I need only tell you that he is followed by hundreds and hundreds of people who listen to him and follow his orders in preference to those of the parish priest.

There are no limits to their fanaticism, which is so great that it may be affirmed without fear of error that they adore him, as though he were a living God.

On the days of sermons, prayers, and litanies over a thousand people come together. In the building of this church, which involves weekly wages of almost a hundred thousand milreis, ten times the amount which should be paid, people from Ceará are employed, to whom he gives his absolute protection, tolerating and covering up their violations of the law, and this money comes from the credulous and ignorant, who not only do not work, but sell what little they have and even steal so that nothing may be lacking, without mentioning the large sums that have been collected for other buildings in Chorrochó, in the region of Capim Grosso.

Then it goes on to describe the latest outrage of the fanatics:

Owing to a misunderstanding between Antonio Conselheiro's followers and the priest of Inhambupe, they have armed themselves as though they were going into battle, alleging that they believe the priest is going to the place called Junco to kill him. It frightens those who have to go by to see those scoundrels armed with clubs, knives, daggers, shotguns, and God help anyone who is suspected of being hostile to Antonio Conselheiro.

As far as can be gathered, this report, couched in such alarming terms, received no answer. No measures were taken until the middle of 1887, when the diocese of Bahia intervened once more, the archbishop writing to the governor of the province to urge that measures be taken to curb "a person known as Antonio Vicente Mendes Maciel who is preaching subversive doctrines, and doing great harm to religion and the state, distracting the masses from their religious duties and dragging them after him, trying to convince them that he is the Holy Ghost, etc."

In the face of this complaint, the governor of that province addressed himself to one of the ministers of the Empire, asking that the madman be confined in an insane asylum in Rio. The Minister answered the governor, adducing the extraordinary argument that there was no vacancy in that institution, and the governor, in turn, communicated this cogent decision to the archbishop.

This was the beginning and the end of the legal measures taken during the Empire.

The Counselor continued his demoralizing apostolate without interference, acquiring an ever greater hold on the popular imagination. The first legends began to crop up. I shall not give a complete list of them.

He founded the settlement of Bom Jesus; and the astounded people told that on a certain occasion, when they were building the beautiful church that is there, ten workmen were struggling in vain to lift a heavy beam into place; whereupon the Chosen One climbed upon the wood and then ordered just two men to raise it up; and that which so many had been unable to do was done by the two, quickly, without any effort. . . .

Another time — and I heard this strange tale from persons who had not fallen under his spell — he came to Monte-Santo and ordered that a pilgrimage be made to the top of the mountain, where there was a little chapel. The ceremony began in the afternoon. The multitude laboriously toiled up the steep slope, chanting hymns of praise, stopping at the stations of the cross, imploring forgiveness. He marched at the head of the procession, grave, awe-inspiring, his head uncovered, the wind blowing his long hair about, supporting himself on his inseparable staff. Night fell. The penitents lighted torches, and the procession formed a luminous pathway along the ridge of the mountain. When they reached the cross at the summit, Antonio Conselheiro, panting, sat down on the first step of the rude stone stairway and fell into an ecstasy, raptly contemplating the sky, his gaze lost in the stars. . . .

The first wave of the faithful crowded into the little chapel, while the rest remained outside kneeling upon the jagged rocks.

Then the dreamer got to his feet, showing signs of great fatigue. Between the respectful rows of the faithful he made his way into the chapel, his head bowed in humility, drawing his breath with difficulty.

As he approached the altar he raised his pale face, framed by his disheveled hair. A shudder ran through the astounded multitude. Two tears of blood rolled slowly down the immaculate visage of the Blessed Virgin. . . .

These and other legends are still related in the *sertões*. It is only natural. Antonio Conselheiro summed up in his mad mysticism all the errors and superstitions that form the lowest common denominator of our nationality. He attracted the inhabitants of the *sertões*, not because he dominated them, but because they were dominated by their own aberrations. He was favored by his surroundings, and at times, as we have seen, he even achieved the absurdity of being useful. He was serving the ends of old, irresistible ancestral impulses; and dominated by them, he revealed in all his acts the placable disposition of an incomparable evangelist. In fact, his neurosis was benumbed by an astonishing placidity.

One day the priest of a congregation of the *sertões* saw arrive at his door a man, thin to the point of emaciation, exhausted, with long hair falling about his shoulders and a long beard down his breast: the traditional figure of the pilgrim, lacking neither the traditional cross hanging from the rosaries at his belt, the worn, dusty cloak, the canteen of water, nor the long staff. . . .

The priest offered him food; he accepted nothing but a piece of bread. He offered him a bed, but he preferred a board, on which he lay down without blankets, dressed, without even untying his sandals.

The next day this strange visitor, who until then had spoken few words, asked the priest to allow him to preach on the occasion of a feast that was to be held in the church.

"Brother, you are not ordained; the Church does not permit you to preach."

"Then let me perform the services at the stations of the cross."

"I cannot do that, either," answered the priest. "I am going to do that."

At this the pilgrim looked at him fixedly for a while and, without speaking a word, took from beneath his tunic a cloth. He brushed the dust from his sandals and departed.

It was the classic reproach of the apostles. . . .

Meanwhile the growing reaction he was encountering began to eat into his soul. Completely masterful by nature, he began to show irritation at the slightest obstruction.

Once, in Natuba, in the absence of the priest, with whom he was not on good terms, he ordered stones to be brought to repair the church. The priest arrived, saw that his sacred domains had been invaded, and in exasperation decided to put a stop to the infringement of his authority. Being a practical man, he appealed to the people's selfishness.

A few days before, the town council had ordered the inhabitants to pave the walks of their houses. The priest told the people they could use the stones that had been brought up for that purpose.

This time the Counselor did not limit himself to brushing the dust off his sandals. At the gates of the ungrateful city he uttered his first curse and departed.

Some time later, at the request of this same priest, a local political figure sent for him. The church was falling into ruin, the cemetery was becoming overgrown with weeds; the parish was poor. Only one who controlled the credulous as did the Counselor could repair this state of affairs. The apostle accepted the invitation, but he laid down his own terms, recalling with a haughtiness in contrast to his former meekness the affront he had received.

He was growing bad.

He looked upon the Republic with evil eyes, and preached rebellion against the new laws. From 1893 he assumed a belligerent attitude which was completely new. It began with a matter of slight importance.

The autonomy of the municipalities having been established, the town councils of the interior of Bahia posted on bulletin boards, which took the place of newspapers, edicts regarding the levying of taxes, and so forth.

When these innovations were introduced, Antonio Conselheiro was in Bom Conselho. The imposition of the tax exasperated him, and he planned an immediate answer to it. He gathered the people on a holiday and, amidst seditious shouting and volleys of rifle fire, he ordered the bulletin boards burned in a bonfire in the public square. His voice was heard above the "auto-da-fe," which the authorities were too pusillanimous to interfere with, openly preaching rebellion against the laws.

Later he realized the gravity of what he had done. Leaving the town, he took the Monte-Santo road, to the north.

The event produced a strong effect in the capital, and a considerable force of police was sent out to apprehend the rebel and dissolve the rioting groups, which at this time did not exceed two hundred. The police overtook them in Massete, a desolate desert spot between Tucano and Cumbe, in the foothills of the mountains of Ovo. The thirty members of the pursuing force attacked the crowd of miserable-looking penitents, certain of dispersing them with their first shots. They were dealing, however, with the fearless *jagunços*. They were completely routed and took to flight, their commanding officer in the lead.

Unfortunately this little battle was to be repeated on a larger scale many times later.

After their victory the faithful resumed their march, following the prophet in his hegira. They did not seek the towns as before. They made for the desert.

The rout of the troops would be followed by more vigorous persecutions, and with the protection of the wilderness they counted on being able to defeat their new adversaries by drawing them on into the hills. Without loss of time, eighty soldiers of the line set out from Bahia. But they did not proceed beyond Serrinha, where they turned back without venturing into the desert. Antonio

Conselheiro did not build up false hopes with this inexplicable retreat which saved him. He led the horde of the faithful, which was joined every day by dozens of proselytes, along the paths to the *sertão*, following a fixed route. He came to know the *sertão* well. He traveled it from one end to the other in an uninterrupted pilgrimage that lasted twenty years. He knew of hidden refuges where he would never be found. Perhaps he had marked them out earlier, foreseeing future vicissitudes.

He headed straight for the north. The faithful went with him. They did not ask where he was leading them. And they crossed steep sierras, sterile plateaus, and bare hills, on the march, day after day, in time to the chanting of hymns and the slow step of the prophet.

INDIAN AND WHITE MAN

To ATTEMPT TO REDUCE the native population of Latin America to a single type is as misleading as to look upon all the nations of this hemisphere as being the same. There is an initial error in the very word "Indian," because it gives rise to the thought of a possible connection with the inhabitants of the East Indies. The mistake dates back to Columbus, when the admiral believed he had reached Asia the day he landed in America. After that the Spaniards called the new continent the West Indies to distinguish it from the East Indies. As a matter of fact, our world was very different and very large. Within it there dwelt people of the most diverse races. Some had red skins, others were copper-colored; some were tall, others almost pygmies; some had straight hair, others curly. The state of cultural development they had reached varied greatly. In the jungle there were those who led a primitive existence, and in the highlands there were nations as advanced as the Aztecs and the Incas, although they represented two almost directly opposed ideas of social organization. Even today there are still native groups to be found in certain regions, such as the Amazon jungle, where the sociologist has an opportunity to observe the most primitive types of life; and, on the other hand, there are in Mexico, Ecuador, Peru, and Bolivia nations of Indians which have reached a point of development far above that of many groups of white peasants. It is entirely possible that the future will see the Indian completely absorbed in the "cosmic race" that is being formed in America, and that all that will be left will be touches of regional color like those which have persisted in certain regions of Europe such as Serbia, Holland, the Basque country. When this happens it will no longer be possible to speak of "Latin Americans," but of Argentines, Ecuadorians, Chileans, Venezuelans. Differences of racial stock, customs, climate will mold types as distinct as those of Europe. As a matter of fact, these differences already exist, and existed even before the arrival of Columbus. In Paraguay the Indian has disappeared as a race; the population is mestizo; but the Guarany language, which was that of the aboriginal inhabitants, still exists and is spoken by everyone there. Students of American folklore find in the dress of the Indians of Guatemala, in the music of the Quechuas of Bolivia and Peru, in the textiles of the Indians of Ecuador the most picturesque touches of color. Alongside this there is the struggle between the white man and the Indian. It is a drama that is economic more than racial. Exploitation by the rich, abuse of power by those in authority. One of these tragedies, with all the strange color of life near the polar regions, is that which the Chilean novelist Juan Marín paints in his book *Paralelo 53 Sur* (*Parallel 53 South*), from which the following pages are taken.

PARALLEL 53 SOUTH
JUAN MARÍN

Iₙ the hollow bowl of the sky there is no sun, only a cold metallic reflection, pale and leaden in hue. To the north water and sky vibrate in a silvery symphony. To the south the bluish tones predominate until they finally fuse above into the ermine of the mountains and the cotton of the clouds; below they darken until they are lost in the water.

The smoke of two or three fires in the village zigzags upward on the steps of the wind to float away like the hair of a drowning person in the transparent pools of the air.

Along the path that emerges from the woods, on the top of the hill, there appears first the pack-mule loaded with supplies and then the man on his horse.

"There comes José, there comes José!" shout the Indians, running out of their huts.

They raise their arms to the hill, yelling:

"Brandy! José!"

"Here comes our friend!"

From the cabins built of boards and tin and the skin tents come the Indian girls with their slanting almond eyes. Out come the old women with their skin like dried-up vegetable peelings, reeking of wolf and medicinal herbs.

Up from the beach come the Indian fishermen, leaving their rude canoes pulled up on the shore and bringing with them the gaping-mouthed, glazed-eyed fish.

"Brandy!"

Tonight there will be plenty of brandy.

"Brandy!"

Like a war-cry the word runs from hut to hut, arousing enthusiasm and appetite as it passes before each door.

"Brandy. Tonight the little port of Mejillones will be happy."

The horseman takes out a cigarette and slowly lights it. He is short and broad of shoulder. Across his freckled face the sensual mouth is like a thick gash. Reddish whiskers, as coarse as a horse's hair, cover his cheeks. He has been riding for three days to reach the village with his flour, sugar, coffee, and brandy. A few yards of gaudy cloth completes his stock. All this is to be exchanged for some dozens of otter hides or two-toned wolf pelts. He makes the trip every three months, crossing the steep Peñon range, where the snows spread their treacherous white carpet all the year, and following the narrow trails that wind along the Beagle Channel or cross the miry forests of Navarino Island. The winds smite him and the rains lash him. It is not a trip one would make for pleasure or sport. No. Only the ambition for money would make one endure such hardships. A good many years have passed since he began his trips through the islands and channels of the remote zone of the Magellan Straits, risking his life a hundred times. Now he finds it harder to endure the winters; the cold seeps into his flesh like water into the sand. That is why the rheumatism bites at his groaning bones with its stinging lash; only massage and brandy can soothe the gnawing ache.

While his horse descends the trail, still half an hour's ride from the village, José Alonso, between puffs at his cigarette, recalls the experiences of his wandering, adventurous existence.

He is forty-five years old and this trip is going to be one of the last. He can cast anchor at Usuaia or Magallanes and take up something new at which he won't have to work so hard. What the hell! He's put a few pennies aside, and it's time to start thinking about his old age. Managing a ranch wouldn't be a bad idea for the years to come. Twenty-five winters, not a single one more or less, he has spent in that blue and white hell of the islands of Tierra del Fuego.

A rush of memories descends upon him.

"Go along, Esperanza," he shouts at the mule, which, loaded down with the heavy sacks, is making little headway.

"Giddiap, you devilish beast. Don't you see your friends waiting for you down there? Can't you smell those Indian girls from here? Come on . . . come on!"

Like a mass of seaweed swept in by the tide and then washed out again, a wave of homesick longing rises from the depths of his soul.

He is a child once more in a sunny, noisy town of Andalusia. His mother used to lead him by the hand to the church on Sunday mornings along the road yellow with sun. The bells rang in the little church belfry and the girls, with a carnation fastened in their hair or holding a rose between their teeth, started for Mass; afterwards they sang the religious hymns, and later, in the afternoon, they danced with the boys in the meadow or fair grounds.

451

He felt vague, unconfessed desires growing within him and ripening in that fragrant, luminous atmosphere. At other times he went with his parents to a near-by town. Those visits to the city were like a dream of fairyland. His eyes stored up memories to last him for weeks. And nothing made him feel so sad as the return to the village in the orange-colored twilight, riding his little mule, alongside his mother's, while the first grains of wheat of the stars began to drop through the sieve of the sky.

"Get along, Esperanza, get along."

When he was ten years old they shipped him off with a family that was going to America. After failing to find anything in Buenos Aires, they came to Rio Gallegos.

He took a long draw on his cigarette and huddled down in his thick blanket.

There he began his travels through Argentine Patagonia, first as a peddler, then as storekeeper, herder, sheep-shearer, smuggler.

He tossed away his cigarette, which burned itself out in the wind, and, looking up at the sky, put spurs to his horse.

"We're just going to miss something good, old fellow. A little more and we'd be caught in a snowstorm."

A dark mass of clouds was piling up on the mountainside, and the air was charged with electricity. The temperature was dropping and a woolly mist was clouding over the windows of the day. Night began to fall.

Sharp glittering needles pricked his face which was blue with the cold. He wore heavy woolen gloves and a thick muffler around his neck. The blanket covered his legs half-way down his boots. It was the only way to ward off the cold of the islands.

"Get a move on, Sevillano, Esperanza."

The people of the village were now only a few yards away. "Rocha" the chief stepped out of the group and came forward with some of his men to meet the rider. Like enemies, the Indian and the white man looked each other over carefully, measuring each other's strength. Each knew the other's weakness. The Indian knew that the only object of the white man's trips was the otterskins, and he would hold out for the best possible price. The white man knew what the supplies he was bringing in meant to the tribe, and, above all, he knew that brandy is a key that opens many doors. After doing business together so many years, the Indians have come to feel a certain familiarity toward the red-headed trader, and he, in turn, treats them indulgently, like old friends. There are no real secrets between them, and this creates a kind of commercial climate in which satisfactory deals thrive.

Alonso had heard that the hunting season had been good these past months. This was the information he had picked up a few weeks earlier when he was in Ushuaia, in the "gringo" Sanders's cutter, buying provisions for his trip to Mejillones.

The load he was bringing in on his mule, he figured, should be worth at least half a hundred good skins. It wouldn't matter if he had to spend several days among the hunters. He'd finally win out, as long as there was still brandy in his jugs.

"Welcome, friend," said Rocha Calderon.

"Hello, chief. How are your people?"

He dismounted and one of the Indians took his horse by the bridle and the pack-mule followed toward the shed it already knew.

The circle of women then discreetly withdrew toward Rocha's house. The men began a vehement argument about the amount of rations to which they believed themselves entitled. A futile discussion, because in the end it would be the chief who would assign each his share.

In one of the poorer huts Rosa Cuyumaru, the wife of the fisherman, hastily finished braiding her hair. She squatted on the floor, on a sheepskin, looking at herself in a tiny mirror with a bright painted frame.

"José is coming, Rosa," said wan-looking Isabel from the doorway. Anemic and scrofulous, at sixteen she, like others, could bear witness to the Spanish trader's sexual prowess.

They came out of the house with their arms around each other's waist and eyes lowered, as was their habit.

José Alonso always stayed in the house of the chief, Rocha Calderon. It was the best house in the little port. It had a zinc roof and was divided into three rooms by wooden partitions. In one Rocha, his wife, and his many offspring slept. Another room was for the visitor, and the third, which was the largest, served as kitchen, dining-room, living-room, and court-room. There was little furniture; aside from the fireplace and the table of rough boards there were only two chairs and a half-dozen sheep hides scattered around the floor.

The snow was fleecing over the doorsteps and clinging to the posts as though trying to prop them up. The wind was howling. In the shed the Indians' horses whinnied at the new arrivals. In a little lean-to the old Indian women, together with Cuyumaru, the fisherman, stirred the big, blazing fire where the fish was beginning to boil. Among the women with their graying hair and slanting eyelids swarmed the children with their bowed legs and deformed torsos, like a mass of larva. In that atmosphere, heavy with smoke and strong smells, the wailing of the children, the coughing of the sick, and the barking of the innumerable dogs made up a disagreeable concert only slightly deadened by the roaring of the wind and the sea. Night had flung itself down upon the ocean, and the waves, as they broke against some uncharted cliff of the coast, might have been the resounding beat of the heart of that settlement lost in the austral seas.

At Rocha's house a jug of brandy was passing from hand to hand among those gathered there. In some of the young men that lowering silence which characterizes them was beginning to melt and they were noisily drinking each other's health in their tin cups or sea-shells.

José Alonso was dreadfully tired. With a taciturn air he approached the window, patched here and there with pieces of tin or strips of hide, which looked out over the bay with its half-blind eye. With his coarse hand he rubbed off the steam which had gathered on it and looked toward the beach through the feathers of snow that swirled about capriciously. He realized that he would have to drink with the Indians tonight; that was the only way to do business with them profitably. And he thought how dawn would find him, like all the other times, stretched out on the skins on the floor with his arms around some Indian woman, any one, the youngest or the most willing.

Just then Rosa, Isabel, Maria, and Luisa, all the young women of the tribe, passed in front of the window. Under their roughly tanned leather coats they were wearing their best dresses, of bright-colored percale. Their black braids were tucked under their wool caps, on which the snow was dropping its white feathers.

They came into the room.

"Good evening, friend."

"Hello, girls. I wondered where you were. I missed you."

A few minutes later all the Yahgans were squatting around the boiling kettle full of fish, sea-food, potatoes, and chunks of mutton which the old woman Pachamaru was stirring with a huge spoon.

Beside the window Rocha Calderon was arguing with the Spaniard.

"Only fourteen skins, friend, that was all we caught at Punta Abtao these weeks. You know, the otters have gone over to the Argentine side. How can I give you any more if I don't have them?"

José Alonso half-closed his eyes as he scratched his red whiskers indifferently. He lighted another cigarette and blew the smoke into the air.

"See here, Rocha, I've never gone away from here with the supplies I brought in. Do you want me to go back to Navarino with my load and have to turn over the flour, coffee, and brandy to those damned revenue officers or sell it to the telegraph agent of Yendegoia for whatever he wants to give me?"

Some of the Indians who were listening to the conversation began to talk excitedly among themselves in their harsh, guttural language.

Rocha made a strategic retreat to gain time.

Rosa had drawn away from her friends and came over beside the Spaniard. They stood framed in the semi-transparent rectangle of the window.

"Pedro have ten more hides hid in cabin. You give me pretty dress and bracelet and lots brandy and me tell you where are."

Alonso pretended not to have heard her. He slipped his arm around the woman's waist and kissed her mouth, which smelled badly.

"Fourteen and ten, that's twenty-four," he thought to himself.

"But that's not enough. I'm not leaving here with less than sixty hides. The gringo at Ushuaia wants fifty. If I don't bring them, good-by cutter, and good-by credit and supplies. Besides I have to allow five for the subcommissioner of the island, and at least five more for the Argentine customs inspector."

Filling his cup with brandy, he sauntered over to the chief and began to talk in a low voice, as though speaking to himself.

"No, my friend. I have to get at least eighty otter hides here, or if worst comes to worst, seventy and about twenty wolf-skins."

The Indian clasped his head in his hands. "But how, my friend, how? Where I going to get them for you?"

"Then why do I filthify myself, freezing and starving in this wilderness, traveling by night through these mountains which you couldn't even cross by day? You think I do it for the fun of it?"

"Listen, friend," said the chief, trying to talk.

But Alonso went on with his complaint. "What's in it for me if all the profit is to go to somebody else? It makes me mad to think that every time I come here there's the same argument."

The Indians, who had been listening to every word, called the chief over to one corner and began to whisper together eagerly. Then Rocha came back to the Spaniard.

"Look, friend, we going to give you all we have in camp. That's thirty skins. But besides supplies you leave ammunition for us in cutter. We no got bullets any more and you get cutter Williams or Sanders and take us Loberos Island in Martinez Channel."

The Yahgans and their women were laughing noisily and waving their arms about in nervous gestures. There must have been about twenty crowded together in the little house, a third of the population of Mejillones, which was all that was left of a tribe that was once powerful and occupied a large part of Patagonia and Tierra del Fuego.

Cuyumaru was the only one the brandy had turned somber. He lay stretched in a corner watching his wife, who had gone back to the Spaniard's side and was holding both his hands.

"You give more brandy Cuyumaru," she whispered to him, "and then you stay with me. Sleep together all night. I don't want you sleep again with Maria. You be with me all time and give me pretty things."

The young Yahgans had begun to sing their war-song, a lugubrious hymn filled with the echo of the sea and the loneliness of the mountains:

And from the heights of the mountain Alaru came down
And said to his men: We will go hunting
Alipentu, Alipenta.
Otumba miama ya.

The chief's son had taken out of a box the totem of the tribe, the head of a huge otter, stuffed by some rustic taxidermist and fastened to the end of a stick. The air was almost too heavy to breathe. To the smoke of the cigarettes and the smell of the soup bubbling in the pot there was added the stench of the bodies, which reeked of wolf grease and whale oil.

Alonso pulled away from Rosa's hands, for he could feel the eyes of the fisherman piercing his.

"Yes, Rosa, yes. We'll sleep together tonight."

Quietly he made sure that his knife was in its leather sheath and that his heavy revolver, loaded with bullets, was in his belt.

But the woman was stubborn and would not leave him.

"In cabin give you ten fine otter-skin. You give me red dress and bracelet and collar same as Isabel and Felicia."

The chief stood in the center of the room holding a jug of brandy in his hands. He was addressing some sort of prayer to the bewhiskered head of the otter. He was asking for good hunting in the coming months.

The noise of the savage song rose from the center of the room and rebounded from the zinc ceiling to lose itself like a rush of black cats down a snowy alley.

The tallow candle was guttering out in the neck of a bottle. Some of the Indians had taken hold of their women and were making for their huts. Through the window José Alonso saw them pass, bent over, shielding their eyes from the wind and the snow until they disappeared in the darkness. Other women came in, looking for their men, and in the confusion the majority of those drunken people had lost all notion of their taboos, and all contact with reality. All except Cuyumaru, the fisherman, the sad man of the tribe, the one who never laughed, because among all of them he was the only one in whose breast love had sunk its talons. Which unknown ancestor left in his fibers that romantic weakness of civilized men? What captain of a whaler, what Danish sea wolf, what sailor on some Chilean revenue cutter, left in the womb of his Indian grandmother that morbid tendency to dream, to dramatize his life and his love? "Sleepy One" his companions called him because he lived in a permanent, withdrawn dream. He used to be different; he liked to be alone, it is true, but he liked danger, too. The flint-tipped arrows of his bow never missed their mark on the heroic hunting expeditions; he swam like a fish and climbed swiftly to the highest peaks of the mountains. His father had said of him: "There'll be no better otter-hunter in all Mejillones than my young son Cuyumaru."

Until Rosa came into his life. She was a girl like any of the others of the tribe. He had never paid any attention to her. But one night when the tribe had made camp at Puerto Caracciolo, in Isla de los Ingleses, following a wolf pack, she came and lay down beside him. All she said to him was: "Cuyumaru, I want to sleep with you tonight."

And that night they slept together.

A strange spell seemed to have come over him since then — an unquenchable thirst for her caresses and her kisses and the touch of her body.

Now he was nothing but her slave. He knew that she was not faithful to him, that she had not been and never would be. For her, as for all those of her race, love was nothing but a physical act without psychological complications of any sort. It was the elemental pleasure of the flesh, which in the polar night seeks the contact of another body to vibrate with it in a purely animal delight and lose its numbness in warmth. It is the only joy they know.

But Cuyumaru, "the Sleepy One," did not understand this. And that night, while all were drinking, while Rosa was drinking and offering the white man her body in exchange for a few yards of bright cloth, his cup of bitterness overflowed. The tension had reached the breaking-point. The fumes of the orgy had penetrated to his soul.

"Rocha," he said, "give me brandy, more brandy. I want to be happy like the rest of you."

Clasping the totem of the tribe, he downed the fiery liquid, which ran burning through his body.

His wife looked at him and laughed.

"You, Sleepy One. You drink so much brandy! Look, look," she said to the others, "Cuyumaru drinking tonight more than ever. My husband want to get drunk, too."

She gave a loud drunken guffaw and the young and the old laughed with her.

Over the light eyes of the fisherman, as blue as though they were made of colored glass, flickered an ominous flame. He went over to the Spaniard, who was standing in the middle of the room, leaning up against the wall and surrounded by a group of Indians whose sleepy heads were growing foggy like the sea.

"José," he said, "me got many hides. If you want, you come my house and I give you."

José Alonso looked at him with a certain surprise. He had known the Indians for many years. He thought he understood them better than anybody else. Yet this Cuyumaru puzzled him.

Rosa had come over beside him and in a few minutes would be wanting to give herself to him under the blanket in some corner of this or another cabin. The Yahgan women had done this on all his trips. It is the custom. But some intuition warned him that danger threatened him tonight.

The fisherman turned away and walked toward the door.

"Now you know: you want hides, you come my house."

Alonso understood that this invitation was probably a trap. As far as he was concerned, there was no difference between Rosa and any of the other women. He had little desire for those greasy, foul-smelling bodies.

Caution kept him from going with the fisherman.

"We'll see about it tomorrow, Cuyumaru. Now let's have a drink, the last one."

The Indian turned back and, going over to his wife, said: "You drink, Rosa, you drink for me."

The woman held up the jug and drank until she had no breath left. The burning liquor ran through her like a tongue of fire. Then she laughed, saying:

"You know, Cuyumaru, tomorrow your wife have prettiest clothes in town and much brandy in house."

The Spaniard was benumbed with weariness from the nights he had been traveling without sleeping and half-stupefied by the liquor and the smoke. He yawned loudly, rubbing his heavy eyes with the back of his hand. He seemed to be seeing the Indian through a mist, yet he could distinguish the flame of hatred in his eyes.

"Cuyumaru," he said, "won't you have a drink with me?"

"You drink with Rosa. Cuyumaru give you hides for dresses you give her. Good night."

And he went out, raising the curtain of skin that hung before the door of the house, and a gust of wind and snow made the embers of the fire, where the remains of the feast were still steaming, blaze up.

The old women had already left, stumbling through the snow. The chief, Rocha Calderon, was sleeping with the ikon of the tribe clasped in his arms. His sons and older daughters were lying promiscuously here and there among the other Yahgans. Couples lay about under the skins, in shameless intercourse, to the complete indifference of the others.

The night was well advanced. Dawn was not far off. The snow had stopped. A cold, biting wind was blowing from the mountains and an icy crust was forming over the snow.

Rosa clasped her arms around the Spaniard.

"You sleep with me, won't you, José? Rosa yours. Spread out your blanket. . . ."

Her body was trembling with desire, and the excitement made it give off an acrid animal smell. Their mouths met in a long kiss. They lay down. A current of pleasant warmth ran through the man's legs. He sat up for a minute to blow out the candle. He took off his knife and his revolver and laid them beside his head. And then he turned to the woman.

Groans and monosyllables floated through the closely packed room. The drunken excitement of before was followed by snores and the droning mumbling of the drunk. The convulsive rhythm of the orgasm mingled with the heavy breathing of the sleepers. A dog barked in a near-by barn lot. And the crying of a child made a jangling reply.

José Alonso was soon sunk in sleep, but a sleep that had a life of its own, filled with absurd visions and broken fragments of his real or imaginary life, which appeared and disappeared in his memory like islands in a fog-bound sea. In this dream world he saw a child with bright eyes toiling up a high, steep mountain. It was hard for him to make the climb, but as he drew nearer the top the view that spread out before his enchanted eyes grew broader and more beautiful. At times the child and the man who was dreaming became the same person.

He saw many rivers which crossed the plain from every direction, tiny, like the veins on a baby's pale temple. In the distance all those blue threads came together in one broad stream that lost itself in the sea. Birds of shapes and colors never seen before flew through the transparent air, sometimes coming so near that they almost brushed him with their wings. He could see their bright round eyes, like glass beads, looking at him curiously, sometimes full of hatred, sometimes moist with tenderness. Ahead of him, in the distance, a woman with long, dark braids was going up the same path. From time to time she turned to look at him, stopped for a moment to see if he was following, and then began walking again, her sweet, thoughtful head bent forward. Behind the child an old man was painfully following. Again and again the child had to turn back to help him over the hardest stretches of the slope. Perhaps the man and the woman know one another but they cannot see each other for the child. The woman is the first to reach the summit, a peak where the wind howls and the stars are so close that it is frightening to see them spin in space like great golden tops. One can almost hear the whirring of their spindles.

When the woman reaches the top, she leans against a rock, with the sweet air of those nude figures in a pastoral painting. The child tries to hurry so he can reach her and bury his face in that beloved lap. But the climb is so hard, and besides that man behind him keeps him from going fast. He is always hearing his pitiful voice calling to him and seeing his tense arm raised in the air. Perhaps he is imploring help, perhaps he is threatening him. There is something about the gesture that the child cannot understand. There is one stretch that is particularly hard to cross; the earth seems to have been loosened there, and as he treads on it the stones slip and he is in danger of falling. The child would like to turn back, to go down again to the valley, which a sea of low clouds is already hiding from view. But as he looks down, his head begins to swim. He must go on, crawl along the narrow path, on his hands and knees, dig his fingers into the loose earth. There is a big jagged rock over which he must climb. It is perfectly plain that the rock is loose and that as soon as he takes hold of it it will start to roll. He cannot understand how the woman crossed it. Trembling with fear, the boy manages to clutch the rock and then, with a violent effort of all his muscles, he climbs upon it. His terrified eyes look out upon the vast space lying about him. Everything begins to whirl madly. And he feels that a gust of icy wind is sweeping him from his place and that he and the rock are rolling into the abyss. . . .

Alonso, in that intermediate zone that lies between reality and dreams, came back to earth. He turned over on the sheepskin that served him as a bed and, in mortal fear, stretched out his hand. A sharp, cold steel blade sank into his arm. Instantly he was awake. He tried to reach his revolver, but a lithe, powerful body pinned him down. The hot blood was staining the blanket and his face. His hands were held helpless by the body of his assailant. They struggled together, tense and wordless, in a duel to the death. But the noise of the struggle and the threshing of the bodies had awakened the woman. Rosa opened her eyes at the very moment her husband managed to get his strong hands about the Spaniard's neck. As swift as a tigress she snatched José's knife and sat up. The Yahgan's back made a splendid target. She raised her arm above her head and let it fall with swift, unerring aim. The sharp blade buried itself to the left of the backbone, between two ribs, up to the hilt. Not a sound did the Indian make. A great gush of blood burst from his mouth, drenching the face of his rival; then he rolled over on his side and lay there in an ever widening pool of blood. Alonso took two or three deep breaths, raising his hands to his throat as though feeling for an imagined dagger. The blood began to drip through the sleeve of his coat. In a few seconds he had passed from the fantastic world of dreams to the world of harsh reality.

"We've got to hurry, Rosa," he whispered.

He picked up his revolver and his dagger. He wrapped around him his blanket, from which gouts of blood were dripping, and they slipped out.

"Let's go to your cabin. Hurry!"

She took him by the hand and led him. Once there, she washed him and covered his wounded arm with strips torn from her clothes.

"Where are the skins?" he asked as soon as she had finished the simple treatment.

"Over here," she answered.

"You carry them to Rocha's barn and put them on my horse."

He slipped stealthily back to the house of the chief. Everything was just as it had been when they left. Nobody knew about the crime. He threw a sheepskin over the lifeless body and another over the pool of blood. He went into the little cellar beside the barn where the hides and provisions were kept. He could scarcely hold in his two arms the pile of skins he carried over to his horse. He saddled the mule and the horse, and loaded them, as best he could, with the skins and provisions.

"What luck," he muttered, "that there should still be a full jug of brandy. There's enough to get along for a few days."

Just then Rosa came in. Her face was transfigured by the crime or by passion. Her slanting little black eyes were blazing like live coals in the wan light of dawn. She was wearing her long skin coat, a cap over her head, and her hands were covered with heavy mittens. She had a bundle on her back. As Alonso mounted his horse, she took the mule by the bridle and with one swift leap was astride its back.

"Woman, what are you doing?" he stammered hoarsely.

"Me going with you," she answered. "You forget me kill him. How me stay here?"

The Spaniard realized that the die was cast and that, much as he hated the idea, his fate was linked to that of this headstrong, ambitious Indian woman. There was no time to waste arguing.

"Later on I'll find some way to get rid of her," he thought.

They got out on the trail and galloped swiftly up the mountainside. They had to make their escape before the tribe woke up.

The tribal law was an eye for an eye and a tooth for a tooth. Flint-headed arrows would rain down on the heads of the fugitives as the gnawing thoughts were raining on Alonso's conscience. It was not that the death of a man made much difference to him one way or the other. It was the presence of the woman whom he could hear galloping behind him. That was what upset and shamed him.

"Everything is all right as long as a fellow is by himself," he thought. "But the minute a woman steps in everything goes wrong."

The snow had hardened under the bitter morning wind, and the poor animals could hardly make it up the hill.

"If we manage to get to the woods before they find out what's happened, we'll be all right," said José.

"Which way you go?" shouted the woman.

"Which way would I go? Toward Navarino, of course."

"But you no see they follow us same way, and revenue officers in Navarino?" the woman excitedly answered.

He said nothing, but he realized that she was right. As a man, he felt humiliated in his pride, but he was obliged to give in.

"South, then?" he asked, yielding to her decision.

"First go south," answered Rosa. "We spend few days other side mountains, in middle of island, where no roads and nobody find us. There we wash our clothes, rest till your wound better, and then we go west."

"To the Sidney Ranch?" asked Alonso.

"Yes," she answered, "he your friend. Can help us leave island."
" 'Help us,' she said," he thought. "So this woman thinks we are
united for good. After all, she's right. If it hadn't been for her, I'd
be traveling in the other world by now."

They headed toward the mass of snow-covered mountains that
rose before them. There were no roads or paths there. Beyond the
forest came the bare rocks, the streams that roar down the hillside,
the snowstorms that bury whole forests, the stretches of swamps
in which age-old forests are transformed into inert matter, into
soft, clayey minerals.

Still farther, death howls in the distant blue of the mountains
that melt into the polar sky.

The man and the woman entered this infinite solitude, each
jealously guarding the secret of his ambitions and his fate.

THE NEGRO

THE IDEA OF BRINGING Negro slaves to America came in the early
years of the colony. It was sponsored by Father Las Casas, a contemporary of Columbus. The Christian zeal of this defender of
the Indians stopped short of the shores of Africa. But if the theory
was propounded by Las Casas, the business side of the enterprise
was carried on by the English and the French, who were then
engaged in piracy. The Caribbean became the hell of the Negroes
and the paradise of the slave-traders. Their boats arrived loaded
with black flesh, which was sold in the market-places of Cartagena, New Orleans, Jamaica. The Negroes constituted a solid
foundation for the French colony of Haiti. The plantations of cotton, sugar cane, and tobacco rested on a basis of slave economy.
The mines were worked with slave labor. Even in Buenos Aires
the slaves were sold in the open market, on the site of the present
Lesama Park. Brazil continued to be a great consumer of this
merchandise until late in the nineteenth century. The balance of

these enterprises is the Negro population of the United States, Brazil, and the Antilles. In the other countries of America the Negro has either disappeared or has mixed with the other races. In certain countries, such as Argentina, Chile, Bolivia, Uruguay, Paraguay, the proportion of colored blood is so slight as to be completely negligible.

The prejudice of the Spaniards against the Negro was quite as violent as that of the North Americans. Proof of race purity was required to enter the universities. In Brazil it was a common thing for a family to select one of its sons for the priesthood, for since only whites were admitted to the theological seminaries, a priest was a guarantee of racial purity for the whole family. But if this was the case among the upper levels of society – and at times even more so among certain groups of the poor gentry – there was always an indiscriminate zone where the white mixed freely with the Indian and the Negro. Besides there was the wide margin of illicit relations. And so the Negro gave a strong accent to this humanity. His laments in slavery, his wild rejoicing in liberty, the rhythm of his music, the voluptuousness of his dances, his laugh, with the one gold tooth gleaming in his white-paved mouth, his lithe arms swinging the machete or the oar, his back gleaming with sweat as he unloads the boats on the waterfront, his tales of witchcraft and devils, color the life of the tropics. The white still considers him the spawn of the Devil, and says:

> The whites go to glory,
> The mulattoes to heaven,
> The Negroes to purgatory,
> Not to say to hell.

And the Negro, who is nobody's fool, says:

> Whenever you see a white man
> Eating with a Negro,
> Either the white man owes him money
> Or the food belongs to the Negro.

But clashes between the two opposing colors has disappeared. Violence has been succeeded by verses.

A recent book which portrays the Negro with great power and emotion is *El pobre Negro* (*Poor Nigger*), the novel by the Venezuelan writer Rómulo Gallegos, from which the following episode is taken.

POOR NIGGER

RÓMULO GALLEGOS

MIDSUMMER EVE. In the cacao groves of La Fundación the slaves were working with might and main.

"This is the job for today," the overseer Mindonga had told them, pointing to a wide space overgrown with brush. "By evening you're to have this as clean as a dance floor, like this was the place where you're going to have the celebration this year. Hit those canes as though you were playing a tune on a drum."

Eager hands wield grub-hoe and machete without pause; but no one works so contentedly as Bad Nigger, for while the sharp blade in his powerful hands clears the field of brush, his thoughts are busy with the malicious couplets he has thought up for the night's celebration.

So satisfied is he with the work of his mind that, without slackening that of his arms, he begins to laugh, showing his strong white teeth, for it is impossible for him to keep quiet long:

"Oh, brothers, what verses I have thought up for tonight! Not a nigger or a mulatto anywhere in this part of the world that won't split his sides laughing seven days and seven nights when he hears me make my vows to St. John."

But the overseer, who allows no idling at the work and who winces every time he hears the word "mulatto," and who does not like this joking nigger anyway, calls out sharply:

"Swing that machete, flannel-mouth. All your strength goes to wagging that tongue of yours."

"What did I tell you?" grumbles Bad Nigger between his teeth. "That damned mulatto is always hounding me. One of these days he's going to get me at a bad moment, my patience will give out, and I'm going to bury this blade in his neck, even if they chop me to bits for it. These mulattoes behave like they were white. What am I doing? A poor Negro can't even talk to make his work easier. Damn that Father Las Casas for bringing us here. If the story that fellow from Coro, José las Mercedes, told when he was around here trying to get the slaves to rise is true. Maybe now I would be with him, shooting up the hills, if they hadn't got him in Panaquire, may he rest in peace! What a life! To have to plant and gather cacao for the white man, with your back bent at the orders of that mulatto."

An upstanding robust fellow, tireless at his work, always ready for a joke or a trick — it was from this and not because of a bad disposition that he had got his nickname — well built, proportioned like a statue and with extremely fine features for his race, this Negro was very popular with all the slaves, and the master thought a great deal of him.

When this was mentioned, the slave would say ironically:

"He is grateful to the animals who do good work. Just day before yesterday the black mule said to me as I was filling up its manger: 'Brother, the master appreciates us.'"

It was only the overseer Mindonga who could not bear him, and he was always picking on him for the least little thing, tormenting him so he would give him an excuse to use the whip on him. But the shrewd Negro saw through him, and as he knew that, even though the master was always kind to him, the smooth-tongued, tricky mulatto would always be able to show him that he was in the right, he never gave him an excuse to carry out his threats and merely muttered his complaints to himself. Besides he got over things quickly because he did not bear a grudge.

And his irritation that morning disappeared as soon as the overseer went to inspect the work the women slaves were doing.

Besides it would be hard for him to stay mad when that very evening the dance was to begin when the Negro forgets all his troubles. Tapipa and Roso Coromoto, the best drummers in all Barlovento, would have their drums in good shape, and if the master was generous, as he usually was and as he well might be this year with the good harvest, the old women slaves, who were no good for field work any more, would already be in the quarters preparing the corn and molasses liquor and the good things for them to eat at the dance, which would go on all night and all the next day.

"You swing your machete and keep your trap shut, Bad Nigger," he repeated to himself. "Tonight you'll have your fun dancing with that little black Saturna who has agreed to be your partner. And is she a fine-looking girl! You know, if I don't watch my step with that black girl, one of these days you're going to hear me saying to the master: 'Boss, sir, give me permission to marry that Saturna, for I can't keep my mind on my work any more on account of her.' Whoa there, Bad Nigger! What about maybe there's where the trouble with that yellow Mindonga comes from? Remember what they told you two days before yesterday? Suppose maybe it's true that the overseer is trying to meddle with that black girl? I'd better keep my eyes peeled. This very night I'm going to find out the truth and see if I'm going to have to sharpen up my machete for something besides chopping brush."

And now he kept quiet all the way down to the bottom of his soul, while the fumes of jealousy lent strength to his herculean arm moving the machete.

The rays of the sun were coming straight down through the motionless foliage. The slaves panted as they bent to the inhuman task. The bantering sparrows hopped about through the foliage of the tall guames and bucares that shaded the cacao grove, the agile, wary squirrels jumped from branch to branch, and the fallen leaves rustled as the snakes, driven from their nests, slipped away. One coiled and reared up before Bad Nigger, prepared to defend its nest, where it probably had its young. He cut off its head with one slash and the anger that was boiling in his breast muttered as he looked at the color of the snake:

"You would be yellow."

The sun was sinking behind the araguato trees, which are the color of the monkeys of this same name, who now came trooping back in noisy bands to the thick leafy trees where they spent the night. They were like a howling gust of wind sweeping through the forest, like the sound of a wailing multitude.

The long day's work was done and the overseer smiled perfidiously as he looked upon the wide space they had cleared of brush and snake-hills.

"This is what I call a good job," he said to the slaves who were busily finishing up. "You've earned your pleasure tonight, and tomorrow is another day."

The Negroes smiled back at him, thinking Mindonga was referring to the dance of the drums, and swinging the grub-hoes to their shoulders, they started off toward their quarters behind the overseer, who was on horseback. There were thirty of them, naked from the waist up, wearing nothing but pants rolled up to their thighs. But they were clothed in the human beauty of their powerful muscles, made sinewy with work, and the sweat of the day's toil adorned their black skin with bronze reflections in the sun.

They walked through the cacao plantation in Indian file down the path, which twisted, snakelike, through the staggered trees. They left the shade of the woods and came out upon the open banks of the Tuy. Down the slow-flowing muddy stream came a canoe. The boatmen, slaves of the Fundación de Arriba, shouted a greeting. They all belonged to Don Carlos Alcorta.

"Hello, friends."

"Hello, friends," came the answer. "Where do you come from?" "From Boca de Paparo," answered those in the canoe.

"Has the schooner sailed?" asked Mindonga.

"We left her riding at anchor, with all the cacao loaded, waiting for the wind to change."

And to their fellow slaves:

"Good-by, friends. We'll see you tonight at the dance."

"If God wills," answered those walking along the bank. "Bring along good verses to match Bad Nigger's. He's made up some dandies."

And Mindonga smiled perfidiously.

Down another pathway came the women carrying on their heads

the baskets of cacao they had gathered. Saturna led the group, and she smiled under the gaze of Bad Nigger. Her powerful limbs moved in a majestic, rhythmic sway as she balanced her load, and under her dirty blouse her virginal breasts with their erect nipples quivered. The eyes of the man who desired her fixed upon them and she made a gesture of modesty and showed her gleaming teeth, small and even as the grains of a well-filled ear of corn, in a wide smile as she remembered the dance she had promised him.

"I'm going to dance that weed-pulling nigger down tonight."

But as he kept staring at her, without saying a word, in contrast to his usual talkativeness, she became embarrassed and grumbled:

"Lord, what a man! Does he want to eat me with his eyes? Ave Maria Purísima."

Talking and bantering back and forth, the two rows of workers reached the patio of the plantation, where the cacao which had been spread out in the sun to dry during the day was already gathered into the sheds to keep it from the night dew. As the overseer dismounted he said to the slaves:

"All right. You've worked hard today and I know you're tired, so you don't have to say the Rosary tonight. And as soon as you've eaten you can all go to bed."

This was the humiliating fashion in which he treated them when the master was away; when he was there, on the contrary, he pretended to be kind to them. But now, in addition, they felt that they had been cheated, and they looked at one another, ask-ing silent questions, which only Bad Nigger ventured to put into words:

"To bed? And what about the dance we always have on this date?"

"I said this morning that the machete and grub-hoe were the only musical instruments there would be this year," answered Mindonga, more insolent and domineering. "The master doesn't want any more dances around here, because he doesn't feel like it. He's the boss and he doesn't have to give any explanations, any more than he would to a horse when he gets on its back. So you've heard what I said: every Negro to his pallet, and I don't want to hear a word out of anybody. Or I'll take my whip and make someone's back into a drum tonight. I wouldn't mind playing a tune on it."

But there were protests, even though they were only muttered ones:

"This is going too far. Now they've even taken away the dance, the only fun a poor nigger had."

"But twice as much work, and hard, like today."

"That's what being a slave is, all right."

"Nobody is one because he wants to be or if he can help it; nor should those of us who are be, for there's been laws about that since 1821. And the masters might obey them, for they're white and free, and they never did anything to get that way. And then they wonder why things happen."

"I don't believe the master had anything to do with this, myself," interrupted Bad Nigger. "This is the doings of that damned mulatto. Why, his name is almost *Mandinga*.¹ Because there's no harder wedge than one of the same wood. He's gone to Don Carlos with some kind of lie so he won't let us have the dance."

Tapipa, less excitable, more resigned and bitter, said:

"I wonder if it's because of the white blood in him."

"I don't know why it is, but the fact is that so far I've never seen a good mulatto. They just can't be. They're not one thing or another, and it's always the bad and not the good that comes out, because they're the Devil's work, for God doesn't do things on the sly, and when He's making something he doesn't mix up the recipes."

Roso Coromoto broke in, to egg him on and make him talk, since there was nothing else they could do for amusement:

"Stop talking about your betters, Bad Nigger. You're not too pure-blooded yourself. Don't you say yourself that all you'd have to do to look like a white man would be to paint yourself white because you don't have either the nose or the lips of a Negro?"

"Why, brother, till a little while ago you saw my father and mother around all the time."

"But in the house where your grandmother worked when she was a girl there weren't any Negro men."

---

¹ Devil.

472

"Oho!" exclaimed several of the group, resigned to the fact that the only fun they were going to have would be at the expense of their companion. "So that's how things are? What have you got to say to that, Bad Nigger?"

"You let me alone, boy. Don't you come messing with me now."

Tilingo went back to the subject that had started them off.

"What I want to say is that if the master didn't want us to have the dance, all right, he's the boss and he doesn't have to ask anybody's permission; but why did Mindonga, who must have known about it, wait till the last minute to tell us, fooling us as though we were children."

"Because he likes to humiliate us," answered Bad Nigger. "Can't you see he's mean just for the fun of it? But I swear by this cross," making a cross of his thumb and forefinger, "that I am going to dance tonight, even if it's on Mandinga's front doorstep."

Those who heard his oath were sure afterwards that the Devil had taken Bad Nigger at his word.

Men and women had already gone to their separate sleeping-quarters and were soon fast asleep, recovering the strength they had expended in the hard day's toil, when Bad Nigger, kept awake by his anger and resentment, began to hear the sound of a distant drum through the silence of the night.

He sat up on his pallet, listened attentively, and said to himself:

"That's coming from El Sitio, and that's where I'm going to be, no matter what it costs me."

He pulled from under the pallet the change of clothing and the new sandals which he had hidden there in readiness for his furtive escapade, and clutching them under his arm, he crawled to the door. He opened it cautiously, peered out into the empty patio, crossed it on tiptoe, climbed over the wall, and dropped into the field on the other side.

In the hot Midsummer Night the full moon shed its radiance over the hills and bathed the quiet guamo trees with its spectral glow. Everything about the quarters lay in silence and only in the distance could be heard the throbbing of the drum.

The dried leaves in the cacao grove were crackling under his feet, when he noticed that the sound of the drum was coming from a different direction. He stopped to see if he could locate it.

"It's not at El Sitio. It's at La Fundación de Arriba. Is it possible that they are letting them have a dance there and won't let us have one? It wouldn't surprise me, because Mindonga isn't in charge there. But if that's the case, I've just wasted my time getting up, for if that's where it is, the minute I show up there, they'll send me back so Mindonga can do a job on me. And won't he like that! Wouldn't it be better for me to go back? Wait a minute, Bad Nigger. It's not at La Fundación de Arriba, either. It's coming from the other side."

A goatsucker flew by, almost brushing his ear, and a shudder ran through him. Far away, in a tree on the other side of the Tuy, an owl hooted. Bad Nigger raised his right hand to the inseparable conjure-bag he wore around his neck, to ward off the spell of these unlucky birds, but the prayer he was about to say died on his lips as he noticed a strange thing that was taking place about him. With the passing of the clouds over the face of the moon the cacao grove was alternately bathed in splendor and in a wan pale light which broadened and then narrowed the field of vision as if by magic, making the silent loneliness of the spot even more frightening.

In the soul of the Negro the abysses of millenary superstitions opened wide. Those were ghosts moving among the trees, perhaps the souls in torment of old plantation slaves who were still working there, doing penance for the sins they had not confessed when they died, or perhaps they were the souls of the saved who were blocking his path so he would not go to the drum which Mandinga, who had taken him at his word, was playing at the door of hell.

He shivered and clutched tighter in his right hand the dirty conjure-bag which enclosed the protective powers of the piece of navel-string which kept him spiritually bound to his mother and protected him from harm and danger. And he murmured the prayer to keep off evil:

"Blessed Mother, you are at rest and I with you because of this by which you nourished me when I was in your womb. Keep me and hold me fast when I am about to fall, intercede for me with God in time of peril and the hour of danger."

And with this he resumed his crossing of the growing and shrinking grove, which seemed bewitched. He could not turn back because he realized that, despite his faith in the incantation, if he took one step back he would be seized by panic.

As for the sound of the drum, he could no longer tell from which direction it was coming. There were moments when he was not even sure there was such a noise anywhere. Yet he tried to persuade himself that he really was hearing it, and that it was a normal thing:

"Now it's coming from over at El Sitio again. It must be the wind that carries the sound from one direction to another as it shifts. . . . But there's not a breath of wind stirring, for not a leaf moves anywhere. There's a fox! Look at its eyes glowing like coals. Is it a fox? Was that someone laughing in there? I'm beginning not to like this too well."

He clutched the conjure-bag tighter to ensure its protection, and he tried to keep up his courage:

"Listen to that double drum! Doesn't it sound good! Hear that kettle-drum! What a time they must be having! Wonder where it is? It's not at El Sitio and it's not at La Fundación de Arriba, either. But if you walk straight ahead, without looking back, and ask the road which way to go and listen sharply, you get to Rome, they say. That's just the opposite of hell. There's that laugh again! Could that be Mindonga who's been sneaking along behind me through the trees? Mindonga — Mandinga — it sounds almost the same. Mindonga! Who ever heard of a Christian having a name like that! Though I doubt if that mulatto was ever baptized. Quit fooling, Bad Nigger, Mindonga has nothing to do with this. You swore you were going to a dance tonight, no matter where it was, and you have to keep your oath. Who said anything about being afraid? By the Holy Trinity and the Blessed Virgin of Carmen, mother of all men by the navel of Christ! Let's see if it's true the

Devil took me at my word. Tonight I dance to the music of that drum. It's coming from down there now, and there's where I'm going."

He strode firmly ahead, leaving the winding trail of the bewitched cacao grove, and came out on a broad, straight, cleared path, lined with thick mahogany trees evenly planted along the sides, whose pleached tops formed an arch above his head. He had almost reached the end when he stopped, saying to himself:

"But what am I doing here? This is the road to the Big House and I just realized it."

True enough, there was the master's house, built in a large open clearing and surrounded by gardens. On its weatherstained roof and on the pillars of the veranda the moon poured a flood of white light, and the silence of the night wrapped it around.

"There are the white folks sleeping so sweetly in their beds, with seven mattresses and their feather pillows," murmured Bad Nigger. "It won't hurt if I go on by, as long as I've come this way."

But then:

"Wait a minute. What's that moving on the porch? A white shadow that comes and goes. Suppose it's the master! Now it's stopped and it seems to be looking this way. Can it see me from where it's standing? I wonder if these white clothes are going to give me away. Look! It's not a real person. Look how it grows. Is it coming toward me? But it doesn't seem to move. Ave Maria Purísima. It's a ghost. Let me recite the Magnificat to it!"

Suddenly he shuddered, overpowered by blind terror. The shade, after stretching to a fantastic height, higher than the roof of the house, suddenly grew small and, without seeming to move, was out in the middle of the path, beneath the arch of the mahogany trees, and then, as though witchcraft were at work, it was coming toward Bad Nigger.

"Oh, sister," he babbled, shaking from head to foot, and clutching the conjure-bag in his right hand, convinced that he was face to face with the most terrifying ghost mortal eyes had ever beheld, "in the name of God, please let me by."

The vision gave a groan and dropped to the ground. Bad Nigger stood rooted in his steps, not daring to breathe. Then he muttered hoarsely:

"Listen to it moan. Like a real person."

As though drawn by a power stronger than his will, he took a few steps forward. The mysterious drum was beating in his temples.

Boom, boom, boom.

He stopped, and then said incredulously:

"Why, it's White Missy."

It was Ana Julia. She had stealthily left her bed, where she had been tossing about, unable to sleep, to see if she could find air. She was beginning to feel that choking sensation that preceded her attacks. She had walked about the veranda, like a restless spirit in the silence of the night, until suddenly the fascination of the dark breathless forest that lay about the house took possession of her soul. She stood for a moment at the top of the stairs that led to the proud mansion and then, in her folly, descended them, crossed the garden, and set out upon the path bordered by the mahogany trees. There she hesitated for a moment as she saw the white blotch of the fugitive's clothes, and then, overcome by the vertigo of her deep-seated disorder, she fell, her soul having fled, at the feet of the reckless slave. Her pale delicate face in the moonglow of the witching night still wore the stamp of gnawing pain, of deep, tormenting suffering. . . .

He had gazed upon the face of magic, and when this happens nothing is ever the same again. He was bewitched.

Dawn found him lying upon the side of a hill, face to the sky, dreaming with eyes open, spellbound, his brier-torn clothes soaked with dew. In his soul echoed the last words his lips had murmured before the enchantment:

"White Missy."

It was like the muddy waters of a mountain flood that little by little grow clear until they give back the pure tranquil reflection of the sky. Or like the radiant dawn of an unending day that has penetrated into a cave. What a beautiful, unforeseen happening, what a divine thing had suddenly taken place in his life!

Where had he wandered that glorious night? What soft grass carpeted that path he had traveled without tiring? His whole body bloomed with memories, and yet there was no one thing his memory could lay hold of. It was as though all that had happened to him had taken place in another man's dream.

The moon had walked beside him to light his wandering steps, and the clouds had parted to open a blue path dotted with tender stars. Because in his unexpected leap across the abyss wings had sprouted on the man's heels, and never again would he tread the hard earth or the thorny briers, but he would fly through the gentle air. And he seemed to melt into the glory of the dawn, all gold and glistening silk.

Below, while it was still dark, there had been the flickering of torches and the beating of drums through the hills. But it was the sound of a general returning victorious at the head of his troops, in a uniform of shining silk, with epaulets of gold, on a white charger shod with silver, naked sword flashing in the air. Below, the sea gave back the glittering reflection; through the hills came the rolls of the drums. From the highest peak a king gazed smiling upon his kingdom, which was the whole earth as far as the eye could reach. A man who was no longer black and who had never been a slave.

But all this took place in the dream of the other man. The one who was lying on the hillside only murmured over and over again: "White Missy."

But when a man goes beyond his boundaries there are always others who go out to hunt him back, and it was not to be wondered at that these should be the very slaves of La Fundación. Mindonga was urging them on like a pack of bloodhounds.

"This way. They've picked up the trail here."

They were already coming over the brow of the hill when the enchanted one got to his feet. At the head of the party came Tapipa and Roso Coromoto; and as he saw them so intent in their pursuit, he muttered:

"You, brothers?"

But instantly the great inward light that had come from the flight beyond the pale made him realize that what they were do-

ing was only natural, and he stood watching them affectionately
— they had not seen him yet — like friends he would never see
again.

"I'm telling you good-by, brothers," he said to himself. "For now
I belong to the world of free men, free, free. The men who have
taken to the hills that have been calling them this long time."

Then he slipped on hands and knees through the bushes till he
came to a wooded ravine that cleft the hillside, and through that
he quickly made his way, toward the sharp cliffs that rose up
abruptly before him, offering him refuge from his pursuers, for
only a man whose life was in danger would venture among those
rocky precipices.

But they picked up his trail and all morning he could hear
Mindonga's shouts urging them on:

"There he goes! There he goes!"

It was past noon when Tapipa, who was always ahead of the
party — not in the hope of catching him but, on the contrary, to
take another direction if he should see him — stopped on the summit of one of those cliffs and, waiting for the others and especially
the overseer, who was frenziedly whipping on the pursuit, said
when they had caught up with him:

"Bad Nigger is finished."

And he pointed out to the overseer a bush that hung over a cliff
that dropped sheer to the bottom of the chasm:

"Look. He's lost the protection of his mother, which has saved
him from harm and danger up to now. Look at his conjure-bag
caught on that bush. He has fallen into the bottom of that gorge."

It was not possible that anyone who had fallen down there
could come out alive, and Mindonga, after peering down the
chasm, beyond which it was impossible to go, in any case, finally
accepted Tapipa's explanation.

"Cut a pole and put a hook on the end of it and let's see if we
can bring up that mess of dung."

They did this and late that afternoon the overseer returned to
La Fundación, where Don Carlos Alcorta was impatiently waiting for him. All day he had done nothing but stride up and down
the courtyard where the cacao was spread to dry.

Mindonga dismounted and walked over to the master holding out the conjure-bag of the runaway. Don Carlos thought he meant that he had killed its owner and said to him:

"I wanted him alive."

Mindonga explained what had happened. There was a brief silence, which Don Carlos ended with:

"Throw that thing away."

But Tapipa, eager that the relic should not be profaned, broke in:

"Please, master, let me take it and bury it, for it's a sacred thing."

"Give it to him," said Don Carlos, who was in no mood to combat superstitions. And turning his back, he entered the Big House.

Tapipa did not bury the amulet, although he pretended he had. But he contributed to the growth of the legend that sprang up — according to which Bad Nigger had been carried off by the Devil because of his rash vow — by pointing out to his companions in superstition what was irrefutable proof:

"When I got to the top of that cliff you could still smell the sulphur Mandinga leaves behind him."

And all the others agreed that they too had smelled it.

THE CHACO WAR

The visitor to Bolivia is confronted by a landscape unlike any other in the world. Like the Grand Canyon or Yosemite Park it is a natural wonder. An Argentine novelist, of Jewish descent, said after visiting Bolivia: "The Book of Genesis must have been written in Bolivia." This observation coincides with Keyserling's: "Bolivia was made on the third day of Creation." This is the effect produced on persons of imagination and sensibility by this Republic without outlet to the sea, with its mountain ranges of unbelievable altitudes, its capital located 12,000 feet above sea-level, and its Lake Titicaca, a little fresh-water sea, situated at this same height on the slopes of the Andes. Victor Delhez, whose woodcuts are among the finest by any European artist of our times, came to Bolivia a few years ago. He was carried to this corner of the world by the tide of violence that has shattered the family of nations of the Western world. In his own country Delhez had illustrated *Les Fleurs du Mal* of Baudelaire and Dunsany's *Tales of a Dreamer*. In Bolivia he set about illustrating the New Testament. The figure of Christ appears against a background of Bolivian landscape. What Delhez has done in black and white another great European artist, Miguel Viladrich, of Catalonia, has done in colors. "Only in the canvases of El Greco," Viladrich said one day, "does one find certain of the colors that one sees in the plains and mountains around La Paz."

Not only is the landscape on a heroic scale, but it changes almost violently as it drops from the white summit of Potosí to the green hell of the jungle. All the climates of the world, all the trees are to be found on these mountains with their lodes of silver and tin. The old families of Bolivia eat from dishes of silver, and one of the ten richest men of America is Patiño, a Bolivian mestizo who controls the tin mines. There are, moreover, the most widely differing peoples in the population of Bolivia. In certain regions the language is Guarany, in others Aymará, in others Quechua. These are the three great branches of the native tree, which spread out in three different directions in the heart of old America. One of the civilizations which archæologists are studying now is that of Tiahuanaco. Standing around the lake, where they can still be seen, are the walls and pillars of its temples. Through its stone gates the forerunners of the Incas set forth to found their Empire when Europe was still submerged in dreams in the night of the Middle Ages. Then came the Spaniards, and in Chuquisaca, they built the most beautifully carved churches of the colony, and the university where people from Upper Peru, the Plata River region, and the north of Chile came to study. Then Bolivia became a mosaic of peoples frantically seeking a republic. It was there that Bolívar and Sucre received the final crown of victory at the end of the War of Independence. Bolívar was the Liberator; Sucre, the greatest general born on American soil.

But from then on, the Biblical background has been the scene of the fiercest struggles. Brutal dictatorships have flourished there for the past century. And to round out its tragic history, Bolivia had the Chaco War. The boundary dispute between Paraguay and Bolivia, or what was called "a boundary dispute," brought about a war of incredible ferocity between the two countries. In 1932 the dictator Siles mobilized his army, which was commanded by a German, General Kundt. The struggle, which began as skirmishes, grew until it acquired the proportions of a veritable holocaust. Peace was finally signed in 1935. The nature of the struggle in the Chaco desert, where the soldiers fought harder for a drink of water than for a thousand acres of land, is more vividly revealed in the episode of "The Well," from the book *Sangre de mestizos*, by the Bolivian journalist Augusto Cespedes, than in any history.

THE WELL
AUGUSTO CESPEDES

I AM *Miguel Najaya, sergeant in the Bolivian army, and I have been in this hospital of Tarairi for fifty days with an attack of beriberi due to vitamin deficiency, which is sufficient grounds, according to the doctors, for me to be evacuated to La Paz, my native city and my fond dream. I have been serving for two and a half years, and neither the bullet-wound I got in the ribs last year nor this fine case of beriberi have got me my discharge.*

In the meantime I get bored, wandering about among the specters in underdrawers who are the patients in this hospital, and as I have nothing to read in the sultry hours of this hell, I read myself, I re-read my diary. By stringing together the separate pages of this diary, I have managed to piece out of it the story of a well which is now in the hands of Paraguayans.

To me this well will always be ours, perhaps because of the agony it made us go through. Around it and within it a terrible

*drama in two acts was presented: the first, getting it started, and
the second, digging it out.*

This is what those pages say:

I

January 15, 1933. A summer without water. In this zone of the
Chaco, north of Platanillos, it almost never rains, and the little it
has rained has evaporated. To the north, to the south, to right or
to left, whichever way you look or walk through the almost incor-
poreal transparence of the forest of ashen tree-trunks, unburied
skeletons condemned to remain standing in the lifeless sand, there
is not a drop of water, which, however, does not prevent men at
war from living here. We live, wasted, unhappy, aged before our
time, the trees with more branches than leaves, the men with more
thirst than hate.

I am in charge of twenty soldiers, whose faces are splattered
with freckles, with scabs like disks of leather on their cheek-bones,
and eyes always bright with fever. Many of them had been sent
to the defense of Aguarrica and Kilometer Seven of the Saavedra
Alihuata Road, from which their wounds or sicknesses took them
to the hospital of Muñoz and afterwards to that of Ballivián.
When they recovered they were brought back, by way of Platanillos, to form part of the Second Army. They were attached to
the Engineers' Corps, where I was sent, too; we have been here for
a week now, close to Fort Loa, building a road. The country is
covered with thorny brush, labyrinth-like and colorless. There is
no water.

Ahead of us is a regiment which holds the hill that protects this
zone.

January 17 In the afternoon, amidst clouds of dust that perforate
the curving aerial paths that stretch to the pulp of the orange
sun, gilding the edges of the anemic foliage, the water-truck
arrived.

It is an old truck, its fenders all dented and twisted, the wind-
shield gone, one headlight held together by strips of tape, looking
as though it had been through a cyclone, and loaded with black
barrels. The cropped head of the driver looks like a gourd. He

shines with sweat and his shirt, open to the navel, reveals his wet breast.

"The creek is drying up," he announced today. "The water ration for the regiment is smaller now."

"This hauling water for the soldiers is going to turn me to water," added the helper who came with him.

He was as dirty as the driver; the latter was distinguished by reason of his shirt, whereas the former owed his personality to his greasy pants. He's tight, and he tries to beat me down on the ration of coca for my men. But once in a while he gives me a pack of cigarettes.

The driver tells me that at Platanillos they are thinking of moving our division farther up. This gives the soldiers food for talk. There's one from Potosí, Chacón, small, hard, and dark as a hammer, who voices the baleful question:

"Will there be water?"

"Less than here," is the answer.

"Less than here? Are we to live on air, like the caraguatas [1]?"

The suffering of the soldiers, which increases with the growing heat, is related in their minds to the relief the water, become an obsession, might give but does not.

Unscrewing the stopper of one of the barrels, they pour out our water in two gasoline cans, one for cooking, the other for drinking, and the truck drives on. A little water always spills out on the ground, wetting it, and swarms of white butterflies gather thirstily around the dampness. Sometimes I decide to be extravagant with a handful of water, and I pour it on the back of my neck, and some little bees, who live on God knows what, come and get entangled in my hair.

January 21   Last night it rained. During the day the heat was like a rubber suit. The reflection of the sun on the sand stabbed at us with its white darts. But at six o'clock it rained. We stripped and bathed in the downpour. Under our feet the warm mud slipped between our toes.

January 25   Again the heat. Again that dry, invisible flame which sticks to the body. It seems to me someone should open a window

---

[1] Plant with thorny leaves and succulent root.

somewhere to let in a little air. The sky is a huge stone in which the sun is set.

We live with axe and shovel under our arms. The rifles are half-buried under the dust in the tents, and we are nothing but road-builders cutting a straight line over the hill, opening a road, for what purpose we do not know, through the tangled brush, which shrivels with the heat, too. The sun burns everything. A field of hay which yesterday morning was yellow is white today, and dry, flattened out, because the sun has walked over it. From eleven in the morning until three in the afternoon it is impossible to work, for the hillside is like a furnace. During those hours, after searching in vain for a compact mass of shade, I stretch out under any tree, in the illusive shelter of branches which look like a diagram of twisted nerves.

The earth, without moisture to give it cohesion, rises like a white death, enveloping the tree-trunks in its dusty embrace, beclouding the network of shade, which is torn to tatters by the rushing torrent of sun. The gleam of the sun produces a magnetic vibration upon the profile of the near-by hayfield, which is rigid and pale as a corpse.

Prostrate, limp, we lie in the grip of the lethargy of the daily fever, sunk in a warm stupor against which the whir of the locusts, endless as time, saws back and forth. The heat, a transparent specter stretched face-down over the wasteland, snores in the shrilling of the locusts. They fill the woods, where they have their invisible, mysterious workshop with its millions of little wheels, trip-hammers, and whistles at work, which deafen the air for miles and miles around.

We, at the center of this exasperating polyphony, live a bare life of words without thoughts, hour after hour, watching in the colorless sky the rocking flight of the buzzards, which give my eyes the impression of decorative bird figures on an infinite stretch of papered wall.

In the distance, from time to time, come sporadic sounds of gunfire.

February 10 The heat has taken possession of our bodies, making them one with the inorganic laziness of the earth, turning them to dust, jointless, soft, feverish. They exist for us only by reason of the torment it causes us to transmit from the skin the sweaty awareness of the oven-hot kiss of the heat. We only come to ourselves at night. The day gives itself up in the great blaze of the sun's last crimson glow, and night comes determined to sleep, but it is beset on all sides by the pricks of endless animal cries: whistles, shrilling, cawing, a gamut of voices strange to us, to our upland, mountain ears.

Night and day. By day we are silent, but the words of my men awaken at night. There are some who are veterans, like Nicolás Pedraza, of Valle Grande, who has been in the Chaco since 1930, who helped build the road to Loa, Bolívar, and Camacho. He has malaria, and is as yellow and dry as a hollow reed.

"The *pilas*[2] have come up the trail from Camacho, they say," says Chacón, from Potosí.

"There's no water there, all right," speaks up Pedraza, in the manner of one who knows.

"But the *pilas* can always find some. They know these hills better than anybody else," interposes Irusta, a dour fellow from La Paz, with jutting cheek-bones and slanting eyes, who was in the battles of Yujra and Cabo Castillo.

At this a fellow from Cochabamba, nicknamed Cosñi, speaks up: "Yeah, that's what they say. . . . What about that *pila* we found at Siete dead of thirst when the creek was just a little way off, sarge?"

"That's right," I answer. "And there was that other one we found, by Campos, who got poisoned eating wild prickly pears."

"You don't die of hunger. But you do die of thirst. There in that field by Siete I saw our men sucking up mud the afternoon of the 10th of November."

Facts and words pile up and disappear. They pass like the breeze over the grass, without even moving it.

I have nothing else to put down.

February 6 It has rained. The trees look new. We've had water in our cisterns, but we haven't had bread or sugar. The provision trucks got bogged down in the mud.

---

[2] *Pila* or *patapila:* Paraguayan soldier.

February 10 They are moving us up twelve miles. The road we've cleared is not going to be used, but we'll cut another.

February 18 The driver with the torn shirt has brought us bad news. "The creek has dried up. Now we have to bring water from 'La China.'"

February 26 We didn't have any water yesterday. It is harder to bring it up because of the distance the truck has to travel. Yesterday, after chopping trees all day in the woods, we went down to the road to wait for the truck, and the last rays of the sun — rose-colored this time — tinted the earth-hued faces of my men, but they waited in vain for the usual noise to come down the dust of the road.

The water-carrier got here this morning, and a tumult of hands, jugs, and canteens, clashing loudly and angrily, sprang up about the water-barrel. A fight broke out that I had to settle.

March 1 A fair little lieutenant, with a full beard, has arrived at this post. He talked to me, asking me how many men I had in my squad.

"There's no water at the front," he said. "Two days ago two men got sunstrokes. We'll have to try to dig for water."

"At 'La China' they say they've dug wells."

"And they got water."

"They did."

"It's a matter of luck."

"Over this way, too, near Loa, they tried to dig some wells."

Whereupon Pedraza, who was listening to us, said that it was a fact, about three miles from here there was a hole that had been there as long as anyone could remember. It was just a few yards deep. Those who had dug for water there must have given up the idea. Pedraza thought it would be worth "digging a little more."

March 2 We've looked over the place Pedraza was talking about. There is a big hole there, almost grown over with brush, near a big *palobobo* tree. The blond lieutenant said that he would inform headquarters, and this afternoon we received orders to go on excavating the hole until we found water. I have assigned eight sappers to the work: Pedraza, Irusta, Chacón, Cosñi, and four other Indians.

II

March 3   The hole is about sixteen feet across and about sixteen deep. The ground is like cement. We have cleared a path right up to the spot and have made camp close by. We'll be able to work all day, for the heat is not so bad.

The soldiers, naked to the waist, shine like fish. Snakes of sweat with little heads of dirt run down their torsos. They throw down the pick, which sinks into the loose sand, and then let themselves down by a leather belt. The earth that comes out is dark, soft. Its optimistic color is a pleasant novelty along the edge of the cavity.

March 10   Forty feet. It looks as though we were going to find water. The dirt we bring up gets damper all the time. We have laid a floor over part of the well, and I had the men build a ladder and trestle horses of *mataco* wood so we can bring up the dirt by a pulley. The soldiers keep spelling one another, and Pedraza assures us that in another week he'll have the pleasure of inviting General X to "cool his arse in the water of the well."

March 22   I've been down in the well. On entering it, a sensation of almost solid contact runs up the body. Where the line of the sun stops, one has the feeling of a different kind of air, the air of the earth. As I go down in the shadow and touch the soft earth with my bare feet, I am bathed in coolness. I am about sixty feet down. I raise my head, and the black tube of the hole rises above me until it ends at the mouth, through which gushes the overflow of light from the surface. The bottom is muddy and the wall crumbles away easily at the touch. I have come out all muddy, and the mosquitoes have swarmed over me, making my feet swell.

March 30   It is a strange thing that is happening. Up to ten days ago we got almost liquid mud out of the well, and now it's dry dirt again. I've been down in the well again. The breath of the earth makes the lungs contract. The wall is damp to the touch, but on reaching the bottom I see that we have been digging through a layer of moist clay. I tell them to stop digging to see if in a few days water will begin to filter in.

April 12   A week went by and the bottom of the well was still dry. Then the digging began again, and today I went down. It is seventy-eight feet deep; everything is dark there, and only by the touch, like a person afflicted with night-blindness, can one make out the form of this subterranean womb. Earth, earth, thick earth which clenches its fists in the dark throes of asphyxiation. The earth which has been dug out has left in the hollow the specter of its presence, and when I strike the wall with the pick, it answers me with an echoless "toc-toc" which seems to hit against my breast.

While I was plunged in that darkness an old sensation of loneliness that had possessed me when I was a child, filling me with a strange fear as I crossed through the tunnel that perforated a hill near Capinota, where my mother lived, welled up in me again. I used to go into it cautiously, awed by the almost sexual presence of its terrestrial secret, watching the wings of the insects, crystalline insects, moving over the cracks in the earth against the light. It frightened me when I reached the middle of the tunnel, where the darkness became denser, but when I had passed it and found myself advancing faster and faster toward the brightness opening at the other end, a great joy came over me. This joy never reached to my hands, whose skin always recoiled at the touch of the walls of the tunnel.

Now I do not see the light ahead of me, but above me, high and out of reach, like a star. Oh, the flesh of my hands has grown used to everything, it is almost one with the earth's substance and no longer knows repugnance. . . .

April 28   I am afraid our search for water has failed. Yesterday we reached ninety-eight feet without finding anything but dust. We ought to stop this useless work, and I have sent a request for an interview to the captain of the battalion, who has given me an appointment for tomorrow.

April 29   "Captain," I said, "we've dug ninety-eight feet without striking water."

"But we must have water," he answered.

"Then let them try somewhere else, captain."

"No, no. Go on digging. Two wells ninety-eight feet deep won't give water. One a hundred and thirty feet deep may."

"Yes, captain."

"Besides, you may be going to strike it soon."

"Yes, captain."

"All right, then, another little effort. Our men are dying of thirst."

They are not dying, but they are agonizing every day. It is an unending torture, kept up from day to day with one jug of water to a soldier. My men, down in the well, suffer more from thirst than those outside, with the dust and work, but they have to go on digging.

I transmitted the order to them, and they voiced their useless protest. I managed to quiet them by offering them, in the captain's name, increased rations of coca and water.

May 9   The work goes on. The well is gradually acquiring a fearsome personality, real, voracious; it has become the boss, the unknown master of the sappers. As time goes by, the earth sinks deeper into them as they go deeper into it, becoming a part of them as by the force of gravity of a passive element, compact and endless. They advance along that road of night, through that vertical cavern, as in obedience to some sinister attraction, some inexorable law that condemns them to recede from the light, reversing the sense of their existence as human beings. Every time I look at them they give me the impression of not being made up of cells, but of molecules of dust, dirt in their ears, on their eyelids, in their eyebrows, in their nostrils, in their hair, their eyes, their souls filled with the dirt of the Chaco.

May 24   They have advanced several yards farther. The work is slow. One soldier inside digs, another one outside works the pulley, and pulls up the dirt in a bucket improvised from a gasoline can. The soldiers complain of asphyxia. When they work the air presses in on their bodies. Under their feet and around them and above them the earth becomes like the night. Somber, gloomy, taciturn, impregnated with a heavy silence, motionless and suffocating, a leaden mass piles up above the worker, burying him in darkness like a worm hidden in some geologic age, many centuries distant from the surface of the earth.

They drink the warm, heavy water of the canteen, which goes quickly, for although the "well-workers" get a double ration of water, it evaporates on their lips with that *black thirst*. With their bare feet they feel through the hot dust for the old coolness of the furrows they used to dig in the watered earth of the fields of their distant valleys, the memory of which still lives in their epidermis.

Then they dig, dig with their picks, while the earth slides down, burying their feet, but the water never appears. The water that we crave with the obsession of madmen may gush up in this voiceless, soundless hole.

June 5   We have gone down almost a hundred and thirty feet. To encourage my men I have gone down in the well to work, too. It seemed to me that I was falling endlessly, as in a dream. Down there I am forever separated from other men, far from the war, transported by the loneliness to a destiny of annihilation which strangles me with the impalpable hands of nothingness. No light can be seen, and the weight of the atmosphere presses in on all the planes of the body. The column of darkness falls vertically upon me and buries me, far from the ears of men.

I have tried to work, striking furious blows with the pick, in the hope of hurrying the passage of time with swift activity. But time is fixed and unchanging in this spot. If the light did not mark the change of the hours, time would stand still in this underground with the black uniformity of a dark room. This is the death of light, this is the root of that great tree that grows in the night and blots out the sky, covering the earth with mourning.

June 16   Strange things happen. This dark room enclosed in the bottom of the well reveals images of water through the reagent of dreams. The obsession of water is creating a peculiar, fantastic world which exists at a depth of a hundred and thirty-five feet and which reveals itself in a curious event that took place at this level.

Cosñi Herboso told me about it. Yesterday he had fallen asleep at the bottom of the cistern when he saw a serpent of silver begin to shine. He caught hold of it and it came to pieces in his hands, but others appeared and began to move about in the bottom of the well until they formed a spring of white, whispering bubbles which grew, lighting up the gloomy cylinder, like a magic serpent, which lost its stiffness to take on the flexibility of a column of water, on which Cosñi felt himself raised through the air until he came up to the surface of the earth.

And there, what a surprise! All the countryside had been changed by the touch of the water. Each tree had become a fountain. The hayfield was gone and in its place was a green lake where the soldiers were bathing in the shade of the willows. It caused him no surprise to see the enemy firing machine-guns from the opposite bank, and our men diving in the water after the bullets amidst shouting and laughter. All he wanted to do was drink. He drank from the fountains, he drank from the lake, submerging himself through countless liquid planes which lapped against his body, while the spray of the fountains wet his head. He drank, drank, but his thirst was not quenched by this water, so light and abundant, like a dream.

That night Cosñi had fever. I sent him up to the regiment's first-aid station.

June 24   The divisional commander stopped his car as he went by here. He talked to me, hardly able to believe that we have dug down almost a hundred and forty-eight feet, taking out the dirt pailful by pailful with a belt.

"You have to shout to the soldiers to make them hear when their turn is over, colonel," I said to him.

The colonel later sent back several packages of coca and cigarettes, and a bugle.

So we are tied to this well. We go ahead, or rather we go back to the bottom of the planet, to a geological era inhabited by darkness. It is the pursuit of water through an impenetrable mass. More withdrawn, more gloomy, dark as their thoughts and their destiny, my men dig on and on, digging air, earth, and life with the slow, spiritless activity of gnomes.

July 4   Can it be that there really is water? Ever since Cosñi's dream they all find it. Pedraza says he was almost drowned in a sudden gush of water that rose higher than his head. Irusta says his pick hit against some chunks of ice, and yesterday Chacón came out talking about a cave that was lighted up by the pallid reflection of the waves of an underground lake.

Do all this suffering, this seeking, this desire, all these thirsty souls gathered together in this deep hole, give rise to this florescence of springs?

July 16   The men are getting sick. They refuse to go down into the well. I have to make them do it. They have asked me to let them join the troops at the front. I have gone down again, and I have come up amazed and frightened. We are down almost a hundred and sixty-four feet. The air, which has grown blacker and blacker, closes in on the body, producing such a feeling of discomfort and uneasiness on every plane that it almost breaks the imperceptible thread that, like a memory, links the dwarfed being with the surface of the earth through that deep darkness which hangs over him like a leaden weight. No lowering tower of stone ever weighed with the somber gravitation of that cylinder of foul, hot air which slowly sinks downward. The men are the foundation. The arms of the underground earth smother the men; they cannot stay longer than an hour in that abyss. It is a nightmare. This earth of the Chaco is a strange thing, accursed.

July 25   The bugle — the gift of the division — is blown down the mouth of the cistern every hour to call the worker up. Its call must be like a gleam of light in the depths. But this afternoon, in spite of the bugle, nobody came up.

"Who's down there?" I asked.

"Pedraza."

They called him with shouts and the bugle. "*Tarariii!* . . . Pedrazaaaa!"

"Maybe he's gone to sleep."

"Or died," I added, and ordered them down to see what had happened.

A soldier descended, and after a long time, in the midst of the circle we formed around the mouth of the well, the body of Pedraza, half-asphyxiated, rose, fastened to the leather belt, hauled up by the pulley and pushed by the soldier.

July 29   Today Chacón fainted, and was lugubriously hoisted up like a hanged man.

September 4   Will there ever be an end to this? We no longer dig to find water, but in obedience to some fatal plan, some inscrutable design. The days of my soldiers are sucked into the maelstrom of this tragic hollow which swallows them blindly in its strange, silent growth, screwing them into the earth.

Up here above, the well has taken on the outlines of something inevitable, eternal and powerful as war. The earth which has been removed from it has piled up in thick lips, on which lizards and redbirds gather. When the digger appears at the well's mouth, a mixture of sweat and dirt, eyelids and hair white with dust, he seems to emerge from some remote Plutonian realm, like a prehistoric monster arising from primeval slime. Sometimes, just to say something, I ask:

"How about it?"

"Just the same, sarge, nothing."

Always nothing, just like the war. This nothing will never end.

October 1   We've been ordered to stop digging. After seven months' work we have not found water.

The appearance of the outpost has changed a lot. Log cabins have been built, and a battalion headquarters. We're going to start clearing a road toward the east, but our camp is to remain here.

The well, too, will stay here, abandoned, with its mute, terrible mouth and its sterile depth. This hole in our midst is always an intruder, a stupid enemy, but one that must be taken into account, as indifferent to our hatred as a scar. It is utterly useless.

III

December 7 (*Platanillos Hospital*)   The damned well was good for something after all!

My impressions are still clear, for the attack took place on the 4th, and on the 5th I came down with malaria and they brought me here.

Some prisoner captured at the front, where a legend had sprung up about the well, must have told the Paraguayans that behind the Bolivian positions there was a well. Spurred on by thirst, the Guaranys decided to attack.

At six in the morning the machine-guns began to gash the woods. We only realized that the forward trenches had been taken when we heard the fire of the Paraguayans less than seven hundred feet from where we were. Two Stokes grenades fell behind our tents.

I armed my sappers with their dirty rifles and deployed them for attack. Just then one of our officers came rushing up with a squad of soldiers and a machine-gun and ordered them to hold the line to the left of the well while we took over the sector to the right. Some of the men parapeted themselves behind the piles of earth that had been dug out. The bullets cut the branches with a noise like the slash of a machete. Two bursts of fire split the *palobobo* tree like an axe. The firing of the *pilas* grew heavier, and through the reports their savage shouts could be heard as they concentrated the fury of their attack on the well. But we did not yield an inch, *defending it as though there were really water there.*

The cannon balls plowed up the earth, the bursts of machine-gun fire split skulls and breasts, but we did not give up the well in five hours of combat.

By twelve o'clock everything had become vibrant silence. The *pilas* had withdrawn. Then we gathered up our dead. The *pilas* had left five, and among our eight were Cosñi, Pedraza, Irusta and Chacón, their breasts bare, their teeth showing, forever covered with dirt.

The heat, a transparent specter lying face-down over the hillside, was calcinating body and brain and making the ground crackle. To save the trouble of digging graves, I thought of the well.

We dragged the thirteen corpses to the edge and slowly pushed them into the opening, where, complying with the law of gravity, they tumbled over and disappeared, swallowed up by the darkness.

"Is that all there are?"

Then we shoveled in dirt, lots of dirt. But even so that dry well is still the deepest in all the Chaco.

THE GUARANY WORLD

WHEN ONE READS that during the second half of the last century the tiny Republic of Paraguay took up arms against Argentina, Brazil, and Uruguay together and held the armies of these three countries at bay for a long time, it becomes evident that this is a country with a strange heroic fiber in its make-up. The country was governed at the time by a dictator, Francisco Solano López, whom some have regarded as a madman, and others as a supremely brave leader of his people. The whole nation threw itself into the struggle with unparalleled bravery. With cannon mounted on rafts — six or seven logs fastened together with withes — they challenged the Brazilian fleet and even defeated it. When there were no longer any men left alive in the trenches the women rose up over the heaps of slain and fought the enemy with bottles and broken glass. It is said that in 1862, before the war, the population of Paraguay was over a million inhabitants. When it was over, only 170,000 women and 30,000 men remained. Even the children went to war. The blood of the youthful battalions stained the banner their schoolteacher bore in his hands.

But this is only one episode in the fabulous existence of Paraguay, for whom the tragic wheel of fate began to spin on the very day the Spaniards founded Asunción a little over four hundred years ago. Even then, to the accompaniment of duels and dagger-thrusts, the soldiers rose against the governor, and returned him to the King of Spain with ironical messages. The monarchs finally turned nearly the whole country over to the Jesuits, who founded a little socialist republic there which has given rise to some very picturesque literature. The Indians, however, revolted against the Jesuits, and in the eighteenth century the war of the "*Comuneros*" took place, and arrows flying gracefully through the air found their target in the fathers of the Company of Jesus. When the hour of independence struck for all the nations of Spanish America, Paraguay refused to link her fate to that of the Argentine and won

her freedom by herself. Then under the dictator Francia she isolated herself from the world in a proud anticlerical dictatorship.
The "President for life" had drunk freely of the writings of Voltaire and Rousseau, though, curiously enough, he had been educated in a Jesuit school.

There is not a single chapter in the strange and complicated
history of this land which might not serve as the background of
a splendid novel, the characters standing out against it in violent
relief. But perhaps the leading character has always been the
people. The aboriginal stock has been freely mixed with the Spanish strain, so that now it is rare to find anyone who is all Indian
or all white. All are mestizos. But in the streets and the market-
places, in the children's games, among the groups of women gathered together, sometimes in the Congress, and nearly always at
home the language that is spoken is Guarany. Even the direct
descendants of pure Spanish stock speak it. The best writers of
the country, who write in impeccable Spanish, talk Guarany with
their wives and children. A rich native tradition has been preserved in this language, but, besides, its vocabulary includes new
words that refer to the latest inventions of our day, built upon
Indian roots, without any admixture of Latin or Greek. The official
language is Spanish. Guarany is never taught in the schools. But
the child learns it in the street, from the lips of the servants, at the
table in his own home. Thus, even in words the strong personality
of the people of Paraguay is reflected.

Two scenes of the war against the triple alliance of Brazil,
Argentina, and Uruguay, from the book *Libro de los Heroes*, by
the Paraguayan author, Juan E. O'Leary, will give the reader an
idea of the intensity of the struggle.

OUR UNSUNG HEROES

JUAN E. O'LEARY

Wᴀʀ had been declared against the Brazilian Empire. The news reached Villarrica the afternoon of December 14, 1864. The town was in a state of great excitement. There was to be a meeting of the town council the next day at which the mayor would make a report on the situation and call on the inhabitants to take up arms in defense of their native land. The duties of normal life were forgotten, and everybody could talk of nothing but the dire news.

Yet, strangely enough, not a single sad or frightened face was to be seen. On the contrary, it seemed as though the news had come as a relief. War was a terrible thing, but war would bring to an end the armed peace that had existed for fifty years, during which we had been expecting, night and day, the deadly assault of our neighbors. And it was better once and for all to face the situation, prepared to triumph or die, than to live as we had, in a continual state of alarm.

The people were calm, sustained by a courageous optimism. They had no doubts of victory. They knew, by long experience, the Brazilians' lack of stomach for fighting. It would not be the first time that the perpetual ravagers of their beloved homeland had been punished.

That night in the family circles the comments continued. The children were startled by the talk of death, battles, destruction. It was all a riddle to them. They had come into a world of patriarchal peace, and they did not know that men killed one another like wild beasts. Their fathers, their older brothers, all their relatives, were speaking a strange language, hurling angry insults at the enemy, an enemy that was far away, that they had never seen. Even Grandfather, so mild, so kind, stirred restlessly in his great leather chair, recalling his exploits of long ago, when there had been war because of an invasion from the south. Everybody, the mothers, too, talked only of sacrifice, suffering, wounds, blood, with ever mounting agitation. Only the children were silent in the face of things they could not understand. And when they went to bed and closed their eyes, lulled to sleep by these martial dialogues, they dreamed of horrible things and had terrible nightmares.

The next day they did not go to school. And the happiness this produced stilled their fears for a little while.

Early in the morning the bells began to ring out wildly, calling the people together, and the beating of an old war-drum in the middle of the square indicated to all the meeting-place. By nine o'clock nobody was left in his house. All the dwellers of Villarrica were assembled at the foot of the flagpole.

The mayor read out the communication he had received to the effect that a state of war existed against Brazil, and that all citizens must be ready to defend their homeland. The country needed its sons. His words were heard in profound silence. When he had finished, the people answered him with a cry that broke from every throat, with a prolonged cheer which rose to heaven like a solemn oath. A few moments later the schoolmaster rose to speak. He recited the verses of the old national anthem, and then began to explain the full meaning of that war-hymn which had been so often repeated in the days of peace, and which was a sacred promise that must be kept in days of trial.

> Our arms, our lives, our all
> Are our country's to command.
> Woe to those who would
> Her sacred rights offend!

The hour had come to pledge their lives to the service of the common mother, so that the rights of the sovereign nation should not be outraged by a slave-ruling, rapacious monarch who after crushing a sister nation, Uruguay, was marching against us. Nobody could hesitate for a moment. The lion of our coat of arms, the symbol of the people of Paraguay, would roar its threat, as we had always promised:

The lion of Paraguay
Roars savagely and fierce
Against our nation's enemies,
Who seek her heart to pierce.

We had also promised to leave our children a great and beautiful country, swearing that we would never submit to the ambition of some foreign aggressor. And this was the moment to recall to memory that verse which contained both an obligation and a promise:

To our children we shall leave
A nation strong and bright;
Slaves we shall never be
Of some power's haughty might.

And as the schoolmaster repeated the words of the hymn, the listeners cheered him, full of emotion. That same day it was said that the teacher was leaving the school to enlist in the army. The children were amazed at this warlike spirit in one who until then had been so gentle, so harmless. It was a great sorrow for them to think that they were going to lose that good man who had always treated them with fatherly kindness.

When they went back to school, they found the teacher there just the same as other days. It seemed as though nothing had happened, that it had all been a dream and that things would go on in their little world just the same as always. But this was not the case. The teacher called them together in the patio of the school, and there he spoke to them as he used to do on national holidays. And then they heard from his own lips the dreadful truth. He had to leave them, he had to go to help defend the country. The supreme hour had come, and no one could fail to keep this rendezvous. If the fatherland was victorious, as it would be, and he lived, they would meet here again, to go on with their interrupted tasks. If he should die, he would know that at least in the memory of his students he would live on. . . . And he embraced each of them in turn, his eyes moist, trembling with emotion.

After this pathetic scene the school remained closed for a long time. And nothing more was known of the teacher. He disappeared in the uproar of battle.

II

The cruel war had pursued its course, and winning today, losing tomorrow, we had been slowly succumbing to the ever growing, ever renewed power of the Triple Alliance. At the beginning of 1869 Marshal López had returned once more to his former camp at Cerro Leon after the disaster of Lomas Valentinas. And while the invaders had busied themselves sacking Asunción and organizing a puppet government of traitors, he was at work recruiting a new army to continue resisting the invaders. By a miracle of his iron will, in May he had thirteen thousand men under arms again, mainly old men, young boys and wounded convalescents. With these he was to carry out the last campaign, the most heroic and bloody of all, in the hill country.

Caixas considered the war over and returned to his country. It fell to the lot of the cruel Count d'Eu to direct the allied army in the last act of the tragedy.

In July of that year López was defending the pass of Azcurra, and the enemy threatened him from Pirayú. The town of Piribebuy was at that time the provisional capital of the Republic as well as the stronghold that protected our rearguard.

The Count d'Eu, after long vacillation, decided on an encircling movement, to avoid a frontal attack and cut off our retreat. Early in August the Prince's troops began to move, first toward Sapucai, from there to Valenzuela, and then to Itacurubi.

On August 10 the allies were before Piribebuy. Over twenty thousand men and more than fifty cannon of the latest type surrounded the Paraguayan garrison, defended by 1,600 men and fourteen small guns. Early in the morning of the 12th a heavy bombardment signaled the beginning of the assault. From the heights around the town a blazing hail of cannon balls and howitzer shells fell upon the defenders of the little bastion, which in the meantime was greeting the approaching battle with gay bugle calls and loud cheers. At nine o'clock, under the bright sun, four strong allied columns converged on the fortress from all four sides.

It goes without saying that the first attacks were beaten off despite the small number of our defenders. General Mitre had already told the Count d'Eu a lesson he had learned from bitter experience: the allied soldiers were powerless against our defenses. But by using the stratagem of advancing under the protection of supply wagons loaded with alfalfa, the Brazilians were able to reach our lines and managed to open a breach to the southeast, which was the most vulnerable point of Piribebuy.

By this time it was eleven o'clock in the morning. Nearly all of our men had fallen. For some time the only ammunition for our cannon had been coconuts, and our women were trying to fight off the invader with broken glass, showers of sand, teeth, and nails. When the victorious invaders finally entered the town a pathetic sight met their eyes. Through the pall of smoke they saw emerge from the sector of our trenches that had been under the heaviest fire a group of little soldiers who by dint of great effort were bearing on a litter the exhausted, bleeding body of an old soldier. Crossing the square to the entrance of the church, they laid the wounded man down in the vestibule. He said a few words to the children, who clasped his hand and then returned to their posts.

Who was this man to whom his soldiers were so devoted? His white hair and emaciated body reflected innumerable hardships.

He had been in charge of the most dangerous sector of our defenses. He was in command of two battalions of boys from twelve to sixteen years of age. He was a top sergeant, but everyone used to call him Master Fermin. And truly he had the habits of a real teacher, to such a degree that the position he held with his youthful battalions was called the "school post." There were times when it really seemed like an open-air school. When their military duties were completed, these strange warriors laid their guns beside the breastworks and sat down on the ground in rows to listen to the teachings of the master. And Master Fermin spoke to them slowly, generally recalling the outstanding episodes of our national history, the brilliant past of Paraguay, its age-old struggle for liberty, its unwavering sacrifices to maintain its sovereignty, all of which was a lesson in patriotism for his hearers. And when he had finished these pleasant observations, they all stood up and sang the simple but moving verses of the national anthem.

On the afternoon preceding the final attack of the enemy this scene took place again. But this time Master Fermin spoke to his student soldiers of the sacred duty of dying in defense of one's country rather than suffer the humiliation of being subjected to a foreign power. And he concluded recalling to them the words of the national anthem, which they had learned in their homes, repeated at school, and now on the field of battle. As he concluded his last words, the children jumped to their feet and in ringing voices roared out this verse of the hymn:

> Die! Die! Die!
> Echoes loud and clear
> The proud voice of our nation
> That never has known fear.

With this they sealed the heroic promise that would soon be exacted by events.

Darkness brought the class to an end. And Master Fermin prepared himself for the trial of the following day. As the 12th of August 1869 dawned, the first cheers for the nation and Marshal López rang out from the "school post," which were loudly repeated throughout our lines to the accompaniment of the gay reveille. And it was there that the most savage fighting of the attack took place. Master Fermin had to withstand the fiercest onslaughts of the enemy, who, taking advantage of the terrain, were concentrating their strength at this point.

Wounded early in the battle, he watched nearly all his tiny soldiers fall, one after another. Those sublime children had learned the master's lessons and were carrying out the promise of our hymn:

> Die! Die! Die!

As the enemy prepared for the final attack, Master Fermin dropped to the ground, like a tower struck by lightning. He had managed to keep up until that moment, by a superhuman effort of the will, and he had been the soul of that desperate resistance. The gathering shadows of death closed in upon him. It was then that his pupils, in the hope of saving his life, carried him to the church. And the old man, in the midst of his agony, was granted the ineffable delight of knowing this proof of their love and devotion. He roused himself as they were leaving him to rush to their rendezvous with death long enough to clasp their generous hands for the last time.

III

There was not a single survivor of the "school post" — that is to say, the southeastern angle of the trenches of Piribebuy.

Master Fermin had his throat cut, as he lay dying in the church, by order of the Count d'Eu.

And this leader, so heroic and so beloved by his troops, was none other than the schoolmaster of Villarrica, whom we saw depart for war amidst the tears of his pupils. His name was Fermin López. His glorious but unknown career as a soldier received a martyr's crown.

THE WOMEN OF PIRIBEBUY

It was the 12th of August 1869. The cannon had been firing incessantly since dawn. Piribebuy was a mass of flame from the fires that had been started by the relentless allied bombardment.

The Count d'Eu was furious over the tenacious resistance of the besieged stronghold and at the losses he was suffering. Some means had to be devised to storm the Paraguayan trenches and take them by assault.

The truth of the matter was that this resistance was incomprehensible in the face of the facts. On the widespread circumference of the positions we were holding we had only 1,600 men, twelve cannon, and one howitzer. And the enemy was attacking on all sides.

But the hours went by without the enemy being able to observe any slackening of resistance on the part of the defenders of Piribebuy. As was said, His Imperial Highness was furious. It was the occasion of his military debut in Paraguay. The crown of Brazil was at stake. A defeat might entail the gravest consequences for him. . . .

He had to win. There could be no doubt of his success. He was accompanied by the two bravest generals of the Brazilian Empire: Osorio and Mena Barreto. And his troops, which outnumbered the enemy ten to one, were specially chosen veterans to whom the heroism of the Paraguayans was nothing new.

The strange thing was that reality had upset all his optimistic calculations. Piribebuy was holding out, holding out with savage force and decimating its attackers. Something had to be done.

Osorio suggested a mass assault, in which hand-to-hand fighting should decide the issue. His motto was the same as ours: Conquer or die. Just as in Humaitá, barely a year before, he wanted to storm our trenches and end once and for all this struggle to the death.

Osorio was the most reckless of all. He was sick; the wound he had received in Abay was not yet healed, and his natural irritability was further exasperated by the turn events had taken.

But the Count d'Eu, though upset, never lost his strong instinct of self-preservation. Osorio's bold plan did not appeal to him. Moreover, he did not for a moment forget the criticism Caixas had to endure as the result of Osorio's defeat at Humaitá. He did not want it said of him, too, that he had sacrificed the courageous gaucho of Rio Grande because he was envious of his glory.

The Paraguayans were not to be trifled with. Five years of experience had taught him that. Therefore, in view of all these circumstances, the Count d'Eu hit upon a more practical and less dangerous plan. He ordered all the supply wagons to be filled with hay and brought up to the front lines. Then they were to be driven at full speed toward the sectors of Piribebuy where the fighting was heaviest. Under cover of the wagons the different bodies of the attacking troops were to advance and attempt to force their way into the city through the breaches the sappers would try to open.

The big general attack was launched. The allies approached, protected from the fire of our artillery by their stratagem. But as soon as they emerged into the open field to charge, they were received with such a rain of fire that they had to withdraw.

Three times they were driven off and three times they were forced by their officers to renew the attack. In one of the charges Mena Barreto was killed by the accurate sharpshooting of a Paraguayan corporal by the name of Gervasio Leon. Osorio advanced over his body and reached our trenches.

By this time the situation inside Piribebuy was desperate. Our ammunition was gone, and our troops were unable to put up further resistance. Our famous marksman Major Hilario Amarilla had been loading his cannon for some time with coconuts, after having used up all the stones, broken guns, and pieces of bayonet he could find.

The commander of the city, Pedro Pablo Caballero, had exhausted every possible means of prolonging the resistance. He had neither soldiers nor ammunition left. And the enemy was storming the trenches.

The shelling grew heavier. There was not a place in the town that was not under enemy fire. The drama was approaching its end. But there was one more scene to be played out.

All the men were either dead or numb with fatigue, unarmed, helpless. But there were still a few hundred mothers who had witnessed the glorious agony of their sons. They remained to consummate the sacrifice, to sign with their blood that page of romantic heroism. And the women of Piribebuy rushed into the trenches to fight and die.

Arms? They were no longer necessary. Their object was to die, and for that the enemy's arms sufficed.

The cannon had become silent. The crack of the rifles was no longer heard. The Brazilians swarmed victoriously over our trenches. The sun gleamed on their sharp bayonets. They thought everything was over. . . .

A scream, a long scream of rage and despair, a many-voiced

shriek greeted the vanguard of the imperial forces as they penetrated into our positions. And this scream, which seemed to rise
from the bowels of the earth, was followed by a shower of empty
bottles and a cloud of sand which blinded the invaders.

It was the women of Piribebuy. Crouched in the bottom of the
trenches among the dead, they had not been noticed by the enemy.
And now they rose up, eager to fall beside those they had loved
in life, to accompany them on the final journey into the unknown.

With empty bottles, pieces of glass, nails, and teeth as their
weapons, they hurled themselves upon the enemy. The bottles
crashed over the black skulls, the broken glass slashed cheeks,
teeth tore away pieces of flesh, and fingernails scratched out eyes.

The soldiers of three nations, the seasoned soldiers of the Triple
Alliance, were powerless to defend themselves against the frenzy
of these half-starved women. They could not use their swords or
their bayonets against them. Blinded by the sand thrown into their
eyes, they slashed about them blindly, while the heroines of Piribebuy, their hands stained with blood, endeavored to avenge the
dead, who seemed to be following the struggle and who lay there
as death had overtaken them, their eyes still wide and angry, and
their fists clenched in fury.

"It was the siege of Saragossa all over again," wrote a Brazilian
historian, who could not help feeling the epic beauty of the scene.
Beyond doubt, it was an episode unrivaled by the most stupendous
in all history. Perhaps it was unmatched by anything in Saragossa,
or anywhere else, or at any other time.

The Count d'Eu mentioned it in his diary of the campaign, indifferently, to be sure, as might have been expected from that
monster of cruelty.

What was the end of that struggle between men who seemed
women and women who seemed men?

The heroines of Piribebuy were exterminated almost to the last
one. Those who survived were taken before His Serene Highness
and were made to witness the sacrifice of their companions, the
cutting of the throats of the wounded, the burning of the hospital
filled with wounded.

The wife of Colonel Caballero was forced to watch the torture of her husband, who because he had refused to surrender was tied hand and foot to the wheels of two cannon, stretched in the air, and then beheaded. And this was a scene that had not taken place in Saragossa. It was worthy of the barbarous days when the rude conquistadors treated the unhappy Tupac Amaru in much the same way.

Naturally, the Prince of Orléans makes no allusion to this in his campaign diary.

THE GUERRILLERO

During the past century civil war was a natural way of life in our America. There were passionate supporters of both sides, turbulent parties were formed, people gathered around a banner of any color to discharge a hail of lead upon their adversaries. It was a period during which the newly formed nations could offer their hot-blooded youth only the prospect of a rural existence without change or excitement. In the cities the light departed with the sun, there were no amusements, and at the sound of the vesper bell the family gathered to recite the Rosary. After the Rosary, bed. The romantics wrote love poems, argued politics, and in moments of exaltation "se pronunciaban"; that is to say, they declared war upon the government. Mountain and plain began to seethe with the movement of factious bands. Gay troops of riders raised clouds of dust along the roads or gathered at the entrance to the towns, drinking brandy from the bottle and shouting: "Long live the Liberals!" The horses neighed and pranced and the jet-bearded generals displayed their fanciest bandannas. It was the chance for the adventurous lad to become acquainted with the different parts of his country, to swim its rivers and to play the game of life or death according to the romantic code. The armies were masses of men and women in which the white young gentleman of the city and the Negro cane-chopper rode the wind of ad-

508

venture together. Almost nobody wore a uniform. In the tropical regions the men fought half-naked. When a revolutionary band defeated the government forces they stripped the prisoners of their official attire and then the rebels donned the uniform of the enemy, and the government soldiers were left in their underwear. On one occasion, when they sacked an upholstery and linen store belonging to a member of the opposition, the rebels made themselves shirts out of tablecloths and suits of brocade and velvet. In battle the women kept the cartridge-boxes filled, cared for the wounded, and cooked the food. They exposed themselves in battle more than the men. Anything was an excuse for a fight — a paper constitution, loyalty to a leader, a real or fancied offense to the family. There were acts of chivalry worthy of the days when knighthood was in flower, and others of unspeakable cruelty, as when the victim was sentenced to wear the "cachupina," which one author describes in these words: "It was a corset made of rawhide which was put on wet. As it dried, the skin shrunk and held the arms of the victim so rigid he was unable to move as it cut into his body." After the War of Independence, while the Church maintained its medieval privileges, the clergy found itself involved in the conflict. There were priests who were guerrilla leaders, and there were troops of rebel soldiers who entered the churches on horseback, committing acts of scandalous profanation.

But once the cities began to be lighted up at night, and the narrow, winding bridle-paths were superseded by highways and trains, and the law was able to assert itself against the political boss and his machine, intelligence was better able to control violence, and the sound of shooting grew more and more remote. Young men began to find other outlets than rebellion for their energies, and civil war began to be a tale of the past. But it has left behind a colorful tradition and a wealth of entertaining anecdotes which give our America a certain resemblance to medieval Europe, where so many picturesque bandits — whom we call knights — lent a background of barbaric charm to the history of the Western world. The last civil wars were those of Mexico. They have given rise to several admirable books, such as that by Martín

Luis Guzmán, *The Eagle and the Serpent,* from which the following episodes are taken.

PANCHO VILLA ON THE CROSS

MARTÍN LUIS GUZMÁN

THE CONVENTION was still in session when war broke out again. That is to say, the attempts at conciliation failed in practice before they failed in theory. To tell the truth, the reason they failed was that this was what the majority on both sides wanted. They had armies and they were close at hand, so how could they resist the temptation of putting them to fighting?

Maclovio Herrera, in Chihuahua, was one of the first to begin hostilities again, flouting Villa's authority.

"The damned son of a bitch," the Chief of the Division of the North fumed, "why, I made him! All he knows about fighting he learned with me. How does the treacherous, ungrateful cur dare to turn on me like that?"

His wrath was such that only a few days after Herrera's rising the troops Villa had sent in pursuit of him were hemming him in. The encounters were bloody, desperate. Both sides were Villa men, and it was a case of hurricane against hurricane. It was kill or be killed.

One of those mornings Llorente and I went to see Villa. It made our blood run cold to look at him. The glitter in his eyes made me realize suddenly that mankind is not of one species, but of many, and that these species are separated by limitless space, have no common denominator. An abyss cleaves them, and it may cause vertigo to look from one of these worlds to the other which lies opposite. As fleeting as a ripple on water there passed over my soul that morning, face to face with Villa, the giddiness of fear and horror.

To our "Good morning, general," he replied in a sinister voice:

510

"Not good, my friends. There are more hats around than we need."

I did not understand what he meant by the expression, nor do I think Llorente did, either. But whereas he selected the part of wisdom, keeping quiet, I asked with stupid, almost crime-provoking tactlessness:

"More whats, general?"

He took one step toward me and answered with the deliberation of a person who can barely control his anger: "More hats, my learned friend. Since when don't you understand the language of real men? Or don't you know that on account of Long-Ears (the damned son of a bitch, if once I get hold of him!) my boys are killing one another? Now do you understand why there are too many hats? Do I talk plain?"

I didn't say a word. Villa paced up and down the car, as if keeping time to the internal rhythm of his wrath. Every three steps he would say between his clenched teeth: "The damned son of a bitch. The damned son of a bitch."

From time to time Llorente and I exchanged glances, and finally, not knowing what to do or say, we sat down, close to each other. Outdoors the morning shone bright, its perfect harmony broken only by the distant noises and shouts of the camp. In the car, aside from the palpitations of Villa's rage, nothing was heard but the ticking of the telegraph apparatus.

Bent over his table, facing us, the telegraph operator worked on. His movements were precise, and his face as expressionless as his instrument. Several minutes elapsed in this fashion. Then the telegraph operator, who had been transmitting before, said, turning to his chief:

"I think they're here now, general."

Taking his pencil from behind his ear, he began to write slowly. Villa came over to the little table where the apparatus stood. His air was at once agitated and icy, impatient and calm, revengeful and indifferent.

He stood between us and the operator, in profile, leaning forward. On one side of the dark blotch of his silhouette against the wall the energetic line of his under-jaw and of his arm folded

511

across his breast stood out, and on the other, concluding the powerful angle that descended from his shoulder, the curved, dynamic outline of his pistol-butt. This morning, instead of his slouch hat, he wore a gray sun-helmet, with green facings on the brim. This headgear, always odd on him, seemed to me more absurd than ever that day. Strangely enough, instead of taking away from his height, it seemed to add to it. Seen close to, and against the light, his stature seemed to increase enormously; his body stopped all the light.

The operator tore off the pink pad the sheet on which he had been writing, and handed the message to Villa. He took it, but handed it back immediately, saying:

"You read it to me, friend, but read it carefully, for I think this means business now."

There was a sinister inflection in his voice, so portentous and threatening that it was reflected in the voice of the operator. Separating the words carefully and pronouncing every syllable, he began in a low tone: "I have the honor to inform you . . ."

As he read on, his voice grew stronger. The message, which was laconic, gave notice of the defeat that Maclovio Herrera had just suffered at the hands of the troops pursuing him.

Villa's face seemed to pass from the shadows into the light as he listened. But instantly, as he caught the final words, his eyes blazed again and his face flamed with his most terrible rage, his uncontrollable, devastating wrath. The commander of the troops, after giving the list of his casualties, had ended by asking instructions as to what to do with the hundred and seventy of Herrera's men who had given themselves up.

"What to do with them?" shouted Villa. "What a question! What should he do except shoot them? I honestly believe every one of my men is going bad, even the best ones I absolutely relied on. And if they're not, what in hell do I want with these generals that get friendly even with the traitors that fall into their hands?"

He said all this without taking his eyes off the poor operator, through whose pupils, and then through the telegraph wires, Villa perhaps hoped to make his anger reach the very battlefield where the corpses of his men lay.

Turning to us, he went on: "What do you think of that, gentlemen? Asking me what to do with the prisoners!"

But Llorente and I hardly returned his glance and, without answering a word, looked off into space.

This did not disturb Villa in the least. Turning to the operator, he ordered him:

"Come on, friend. You tell that damned fool I don't want him using up the wires on nonsense. He's to shoot the hundred and seventy prisoners immediately, and if he hasn't notified me in an hour that the order has been carried out, I'll come there myself and put a bullet through him so he'll know how to manage things better. You understand?"

"Yes, general."

And the operator began to write out the message.

At the first word Villa interrupted him:

"What are you doing, not obeying me?"

"I'm composing the message, general."

"What do you mean, 'composing'? You send that off the way I said it to you and that's all. Time wasn't made to be lost fooling with papers."

At this the operator put his right hand on the transmitter and, pressing the lever with his little finger, began to call: Tick-tick, tiqui; tick-tick, tiqui.

Between a pile of papers and Villa's arm I could see the knuckles of the operator's hand, tense and vibrant from the contraction of the tendons as they produced the homicidal sounds. Villa did not take his eyes off the movements that were transmitting his orders seven hundred miles to the north, nor did we. I kept wondering — with that stupid insistence we have in dreams — at exactly what moment the vibrations of the fingers were spelling out the words: "Shoot immediately." For five minutes that was a horrible obsession that blotted out every other reality, every other sensation.

After the operator had sent off the message, Villa seemed to grow more calm and sat down in an armchair near the desk. He sat there quietly for a little while. Then he pushed back his sun-helmet. Then he buried the fingers of his right hand in the reddish tangle of hair that hung over his forehead and scratched his head as though he were trying to get at some inward itching of the brain, of the soul. Then he sat quietly again. Perhaps ten minutes had elapsed.

Suddenly he flung round toward me and said: "What do you think about all this, friend?"

I answered evasively: "Were you talking to me, general?"

"Yes, to you."

Hedged in like this, I tried to turn it off, using the language of real men. "Well, there are going to be a lot of extra hats around, general."

"Maybe I don't know that. That wasn't what I asked you. What about the consequences? Do you think it's right or wrong, this business of the shooting?"

Llorente, braver than I, cut in ahead of me: "General," he said, "to be frank with you, I don't think that order is fair."

I shut my eyes. I was sure that Villa was going to get up — or without even getting up — and whip out his pistol to punish this criticism of his conduct in a matter which had flicked him on the raw. But several seconds went by, and then I heard Villa ask, without getting up, and in a voice whose calm contrasted strangely with the storm that had so recently preceded it:

"Well, let's see. Why don't you think my order was right?"

Llorente was so pale that it was hard to tell his skin from his collar. Nevertheless he answered firmly:

"Because, general, the message says the men surrendered."

"Sure. What of it?"

"When they are taken that way they shouldn't be killed."

"Why not?"

"That's why, general. Because they surrendered."

"You're a funny fellow. That's a good one. Where did you ever learn such things?"

My shameful silence had become unbearable. I broke in:

"I feel the same way, general. It seems to me that Llorente is right."

Villa enveloped us both in one glance.

"And what makes you think that, friend?"

514

"Llorente explained why: because the men surrendered."

"And I say again, what of it?"

As he repeated it this last time, a certain uneasiness was apparent which made him open his eyes still wider to take us both in with his restless glances. From the outside I could feel the pressure of this look of his, cold and cruel, and from the inside an irresistible impulse to talk, which was pricked on by the vision of the distant executions. I had to hit quickly on some convincing formula. "The person who surrenders, general, by doing so spares the life of others, since he renounces the possibility of dying fighting. And this being so, the one who accepts the surrender has no right to order the death sentence."

Villa looked at me steadily, and his eyeballs stopped rolling from one to the other of us. Jumping to his feet, he shouted to the operator: "Listen, friend, call them again, call them again."

The operator obeyed. Tick-tick, tiqui; tick-tick, tiqui.

A few seconds went by.

Villa inquired impatiently: "Do they answer?"

"I am calling them, general."

Llorente and I could not sit still, and we, too, came over to the instrument table.

Villa asked again: "Do they answer?"

"Not yet, general."

"Call louder."

The operator could not call louder or softer, but it was plain from the contractions of his fingers that he was trying to make the letters clearer and more exact. There was a short silence, and in a little while the receiving instrument began to tick.

"Now they're answering," said the operator.

"All right, friend, all right. Now you transmit as quickly as you can what I am going to say to you. Pay attention: 'Hold up shooting of prisoners until further orders. General Francisco Villa.' "

Tick, tiqui-tick, tiqui. . . .

"Finished?"

Tick-tiqui, tiqui-tick.

"All right, general."

"Now tell their operator that I'm right here beside the instrument waiting for the answer, and that I'll hold him responsible for any delay."

Tiqui, tiqui, tick-tick, tiqui-tick, tick. . . .

"Have you told him?"

"Yes, general."

The receiving instrument began to tick.

"What does he say?"

"He says he is going to deliver the message himself and bring the answer."

All three of us stood beside the telegraph table: Villa strangely restless; Llorente and I weak with anxiety.

Ten minutes went by. Tick-tiqui, tick, tiqui-tick.

"Are they answering?"

"It's not them, general. It's another station calling."

Villa took out his watch and asked: "How long ago did we send the first order?"

"About twenty-five minutes, general."

Turning to me, Villa asked: "Will the counter-order get there in time? What do you think?"

"I hope so, general."

Tick-tiqui, tick, tick. . . .

"Are they answering, friend?"

"No, general, it's somebody else."

Villa's voice was husky with an emotion I had never heard in it before, and it grew deeper each time he asked if the call was the answer to his counter-order. His eyes were riveted on the little lever of the receiving apparatus, and every time this made the slightest movement, he asked as though the electricity of the wires were reaching through to him:

"Is it him?"

"No, general, it's somebody else."

It had been twenty minutes since telegraphing the counter-order when finally the operator said: "Now they're calling," and picking up his pencil, he began to write.

Tick, tick, tiqui. . . .

Villa bent farther over the table. Llorente, on the contrary, seemed to stiffen up. I walked over beside the operator to read what he was writing.

Tick-tiqui, tiqui, tiqui, tick-tick. . . .

After the third line Villa could not curb his impatience and asked me:

"Did the counter-order get there in time?"

Without taking my eyes off the paper, I nodded my head.

Villa pulled out his handkerchief and mopped the sweat off his forehead.

We stayed and had dinner with him that afternoon, but he made no reference to what had happened that morning. Only as we were leaving, late that evening, Villa said, without any preamble:

"And thanks, friends, for that thing this morning, that business of the prisoners."

A PERILOUS SLEEP

THE NATURAL gifts that made Villa a vivid and entertaining talker were revealed to me one night in the little town of Guadalupe, in the state of Zacatecas.

Enrique C. Llorente, José Vasconcelos, and I had reached Guadalupe that afternoon. All three of us had come to talk with Villa about a number of different things and we planned to leave again in a few hours. Llorente was going to Washington, Vasconcelos to Aguascalientes; and I had to make a short trip to Chihuahua. After we had finished the official business, Villa said he would keep us company until our departure. But as the trains from Juárez and from Mexico City did not come through until one o'clock in the morning, in order to do this he had to give up his invariable habit of going to bed early. Such a delicate attention on his part surprised me beyond expression, for I knew him so well that I could not understand it. Partly because of his rude upbringing and partly because of his disposition, he was never polite to anybody. What was behind this unusual amiability? My astonishment and my suspicion — I could never free myself from my distrust of Francisco Villa — put me somewhat on my guard, and I watched the general with more than ordinary attention. I analyzed his least movement, I watched his gestures, I studied his expressions, his words.

Our conversation took place in a special car that Villa used for traveling or campaigning. The orderlies had cleared the table where we had eaten dinner. Villa's desk was closed. Every now and then the telegraph instrument clicked with what seemed to us idle messages going by. Through the little windows of the car we could see the pleasant valley, with its pools of water here and there, as it lay blue and mirror-like in the light of the moon. On the other side the silver of the moonlight and the ocher of the abrupt barren lands gave touches of enchantment to a landscape devoid of all beauty by the light of the sun.

The miracle of the autumn night finally took possession of us, and we stepped out on the platform to contemplate the vague, dreamlike confines that lay limitless beneath the nocturnal covering of the glittering sky. It was chilly. On one of the steps a sentinel stood guard, all wrapped up in a dark sarape, and humming an endless, melancholy air in a voice as light as the glow of his cigarette. Another, half stretched out on the platform, was sleeping with his head resting against the brim of his hat, which he had bent down to make a pillow. His breathing was so smooth and rhythmic that it seemed to be keeping time to the light-flooded night. The moonlight was so bright that we could see his chest rise and fall as he breathed. Villa had been looking at him ever since we came out, and he had not taken his eyes off him while Llorente, Vasconcelos, and I were admiring the view.

"What a mystery sleep is!" said Villa as we went back into the car. "What a mystery sleep is!"

And his restless eyes, always roving about as though possessed by terror, suddenly came to rest; they seemed to fix on some vague, distant point.

Sleep is the strangest and most mysterious thing there is."

Vasconcelos had pushed the back of his chair up against the desk. On the other side, to the left, Llorente's bust rose from behind the telegraph table. I sat directly across from Villa, and to be more comfortable I had tilted my chair back against the window-sill. As he talked, Villa seemed to be looking at me; through my eyes there passed that invisible ray by which he contemplated the images he was calling up.

"One time," Villa began, "when I was escaping with my pal Urbina, I found out that sleep is the strangest and most mysterious thing there is. For a week the mounted police had not let up for a minute in one of those brutal pursuits of theirs in which we came within an ace of being killed. My pal and I were hiding in the Durango sierra, and every day we thought they'd surely catch us as we slipped from one of our caches of provisions to another. We had left the last settlement we knew far behind us, the last wood-chopper's cabin, the last shelter of the forest guards. And yet it took us longer to dismount than for the mounted to appear and make us start our cruel journey over again. In all this time we had hardly rested or slept, and when we did, it was only for a few minutes. Our horses were ready to drop. Urbina was getting so worn out he'd doze off on his horse until he slipped out of the saddle. Several times I had to wake him up and talk to him and scold him so he wouldn't give up. In spite of my powers of resistance, I was getting utterly exhausted, and I couldn't get over my surprise that we couldn't shake the mounted off our heels. How did they do it? Had they planned it all out beforehand and sent men on ahead? Didn't they sleep, either? Didn't they rest?

"Finally one morning we thought we were safe. From the peak where we had managed to work our way through the heavy woods and thickets we could see the whole plain below, and there wasn't a sign of our pursuers. Two hours before anybody could find us we could see the approach, not only of a troop, but of a single rider, and we'd have time to climb farther into the sierra.

"We unsaddled. We fed the horses. We got ready to go to sleep.

"'Look, pal,' I said to Urbina, 'I guess there's no danger now. Still, I don't feel easy. One of us had better watch while the other sleeps, and then we'll change. You can go to sleep first while I watch. In two hours I'll wake you up and then I'll go to sleep.'

"All Urbina said was: 'All right, pal.'

"He couldn't keep his eyes open. He lay down, put his head on his saddle, and went straight to sleep.

"What a mystery sleep is! My pal slept just as calm and easy! There was nothing but peace and rest about him as he lay there. As I looked at him, I couldn't believe that for a week he had been within an inch of being killed or taken prisoner several times. It seemed to me that either I was dreaming then or I had been dreaming before. His breathing was even; his face had the repose of a man who has never known any danger. I remember he had on a pink shirt, and the button was off at the collar — I can still see it — and the folds of it would open and close with every breath. The light moving of the pink cloth on my pal's hairy black chest seemed to be such a part of the loneliness of the mountain, the quiet rustle of the trees, the steady munching of our drowsing horses, that I began to be afraid. The peace of his sleep terrified me, it was so different from that struggle to the death we had been mixed up in for so many years, God only knows why. And yet I couldn't take my eyes off that regular movement of Urbina's shirt, just as though I had been bewitched. Maybe I was beginning to go to sleep, too.

"But I came back to myself. To get away from that obsession I looked up. Away off, in the distance, down the mountain, where the mounted police might come, I saw a little white speck moving. But as I was still bewildered by the drowsiness that was overcoming me, I had to make an effort to realize what I was looking at in the valley. 'That's what it must be,' I said, and I jumped right up. Sure enough, it was the mounted. They were on our trail again; they'd soon be up to us!

"I shook Urbina.

"'Hey, pal, wake up, they're coming. Wake up, the mounted are after us.'

"But sleep is the queerest thing there is. My pal didn't hear me. His pink shirt kept on moving the same as before. There was the same peaceful expression on his face.

"To make time I went and brought up the horses and saddled

mine. All the time I kept calling my pal and shaking him with my foot. When I had my horse saddled, he was still asleep. I took hold of his head and shook it hard. He went right on sleeping just the same; his breathing didn't change at all, and to look at his face you would have thought that instead of pulling his hair and rubbing his ears I was smoothing his pillow so he would sleep better. When I saw that he wasn't waking up, I pulled the saddle out from under his head and started to saddle his horse. And all the time I kept yelling at him. When I had finished, I gathered up our guns and the sarapes. I rolled up our saddle-bags. I fastened everything to the saddles with the straps. . . . My pal didn't wake up. Then I began to call him as loud as I could. I yelled so loud that I didn't recognize my own voice. I had never heard my voice like that before and I never have since. And still my pal didn't wake up. Then I pulled out his pistol, lifted up his head with one hand, and with the other I fired off two shots right beside his ear. Urbina kept on sleeping. His breathing was just the same as when he went to sleep an hour before. His pink shirt barely moved.

"Afterwards, when I remember what an agony I went through that morning, I often think I should have lighted a match and held it in his hand until he woke up. But I didn't think of it then. The dark spot that was the mounted was getting clearer and clearer down below, and I couldn't think straight. Dimly I compared the helplessness of my pal with the danger that was flying toward us, and it seemed to me like a dream when your knees give way under you and you want to run and can't.

"Sleep is the most mysterious thing there is! I picked up my pal, threw him face-down across his horse, and tied him tight. Then I got on my horse and made for the sierra.

"That's the most terrible day I ever went through in my life. I had to look for the worst path I could find so as to throw the mounted off the track, and at the same time I had to watch out on those bad trails to keep my pal from getting hurt against the rocks and tree-trunks. Several times I had to double back on a trail and take another. Again I had to travel long distances on foot and open the way for Urbina's head, which was hanging over the side, or half carry his body in my arms. And I fled like that for more than three hours, more than six, more than eight. Finally, late that afternoon, I reached a place that offered some protection. I felt safe there and made camp.

"When I took my pal off the horse, his face was black with dust, and purple, for all the blood had rushed to his head. Yet he went right on sleeping, just as easy. I unsaddled the horses. I threw myself on the ground. I slept."

A long silence left Villa's last words echoing in our ears. Llorente, whose admiration for the guerrilla leader was boundless, smiled with an expression half moved, half triumphant. "What do you think of my man?" it seemed to say. Vasconcelos, who was always quick to show appreciation and respect for every manifestation of real humanity, whether fleeting or enduring, was pale with emotion. I just watched.

In a little while we heard the whistle of an engine. We got ready and went out. We said good-by alongside the train.

A few minutes later from one of the train windows I saw Villa pass by at a distance, with a woman who, I believe, had come in on the train from Juárez. To judge from her bearing and her silhouette she was young, perhaps pretty. Villa had an arm around her waist and was leading her toward his car.

Had he not said he would keep us company until the trains came in? So that was the real reason!

WHO'S WHO IN THIS BOOK

ALEGRÍA, CIRO. Born in La Libertad, Peru, 1909. Novelist, journalist, poet. Was imprisoned as an acting member of the Aprista party from December 1931 to July 1932, when he was freed by the revolution of Trujillo. Later, when this revolution had been put down, he was condemned to ten years of imprisonment, but after serving one year of his sentence he was exiled to Chile. There he received the award of the publishing house Nascimento for his novel *La Serpiente de oro*, which was published in English in 1943 under the title of *The Golden Serpent*. In 1941 he won first prize in the Latin-American Novel Contest sponsored by Farrar & Rinehart of New York for his book *Broad and Alien Is the World* (*El Mundo es ancho y ajeno*). — Author of: *La Serpiente de oro* (Chile, 1935); *Los Perros hambrientos* (1938); *El Mundo es ancho y ajeno* (1941).

ARGUEDAS, ALCIDES. Born in La Paz, Bolivia, 1879. Historian, novelist, diplomat. Studied social sciences at the Ecole Livre des Etudes Sociales in Paris. Secretary of the Legation of Bolivia in Paris (1910) and in London (1914); Consul of Bolivia in Paris (1925); Minister Plenipotentiary in Colombia (1929–30) and in Venezuela (1943). His *Historia General de Bolivia* (La Paz, 1922) was published in French (Paris, 1923). Other books of his have been published in Spain: *La Fundación de la república* (Madrid, 1921); *Los Caudillos Letrados* (Barcelona, 1923); *La Plebe en acción* (Barcelona, 1924); *La Dictadura y la anarquía* (Barcelona, 1926); *Pueblo enfermo* (Barcelona, 1934); *La Danza de las sombras* (Barcelona, 1934); *Raza de bronce* (Valencia, 1924).

CARRIÓN, BENJAMÍN. Born in Loja, Ecuador, 1898. Essayist, historian, diplomat, journalist. Professor of Sociology in the Central University of Quito, and Dean of the Faculty of Philosophy and Letters in the same university; Minister of Public Education

WHO'S WHO IN THIS BOOK

(1932–3), Consul of Ecuador in Le Havre, Secretary of the Legation in Lima, and Ambassador to Colombia. Author of: *Los Creadores de la Nueva America* (Madrid, 1930); *Mapa de America* (Madrid, 1930); *El Desencanto de Manuel García* (Madrid, 1931); *Atahuallpa* (Mexico, 1934); *Índice de la poesía ecuatoriana* (Santiago de Chile, 1935).

CASTAÑEDA ARAGÓN, GREGORIO. Born in Santa Marta, Colombia, 1887. Poet, short-story writer, journalist. Has been Consul of Colombia in Guatemala. Author of: *Máscaras de Bronce* (San Juan de Córdoba, 1916); *Campanas de Gloria* (San Juan, 1920); *Recortes de vida* (Baranquilla, 1922); *Náufragos de la tierra* (Bogotá, 1922); *Rincones del Mar* (Baranquilla, 1924); *Estampas de la España que se va* (Santiago de Chile, 1938), etc.

CESPEDES, AUGUSTO. Born in Cochabamba, Bolivia, 1904. Journalist, novelist. Assistant editor of the newspaper *La Calle* in La Paz. Author of a volume of short stories on the Chaco War entitled *Sangre de mestizos* (Santiago de Chile, 1937), and a novel, *Metal del Diablo*, dealing with the tin mines of Bolivia.

DA CUNHA, EUCLYDES. Born in Santa Rosa do Rio Negro, Brazil, 1866. Died in Rio de Janeiro, 1909. Sociologist, historian, journalist. *Os Sertões*, the best known and most popular of his works, has been, together with *Canaán*, the novel of Graça Aranha, the starting-point of the literary renaissance of Brazil. Author of: *Os Sertões* (1902), which has been translated into English with the title *Rebellion in the Backlands* (University of Chicago Press, 1944); *Peru vs. Bolivia* (1907); *Martín García* (1908); *Castro Álves e seu tempo* (1908); *A margen da historia* (1909).

ESTRADA, GENARO. Born in Mazatlán, Mexico, 1887; died in 1937. Diplomat, historian, essayist. Was Mexico's first delegate to the League of Nations, Mexican Ambassador to Spain, Minister to Turkey and Portugal. In Mexico he taught at the University of Mexico and was Minister of Labor. Outstanding among his publications are: *Poetas nuevos de México* (1916); *Visionario de la Nueva España* (1921); *Bibliografía de Amado Nervo* (1925);

Pedro Galín (1926); *Episodios de la diplomacia en Mexico* (1928); *Crucero* (1928); *Escalera* (1929); *Paso a nivel* (1933); *Senderillos* (1934).

GALLEGOS, RÓMULO. Born in Caracas, Venezuela, 1884. Novelist. In Madrid the Book of the Month Club awarded first prize to his novel *Doña Barbara*. This book, which is considered one of the outstanding works of Latin-American literature, was translated into English in 1931. Gallegos has been Minister of Public Education in Venezuela, Professor of History and Philosophy, and candidate to the presidency of the Republic. He was a voluntary exile in Europe during the dictatorship of Gómez. Numerous editions of his works have been published in Spain, Venezuela, and Argentina. His principal works are: *El Milagro del año* (drama, 1911); *Los Aventureros* (1913); *Reinaldo Solar* (1920); *La Trepadora* (1925); *Doña Barbara* (1929); *Cantaclaro* (1933); *Canaima* (1934); *Pobre Negro* (1937).

GRAÇA ARANHA, JOSE PEREIRA DA. Born in S. Luis do Maranhão, Brazil, 1868; died in Rio de Janeiro, 1931. Novelist, sociologist, journalist. His principal work is the novel *Canaán*, which was hailed as one of the masterpieces of our literature on its publication at the beginning of the century and placed its author among the first rank of Latin-American writers. It has been translated into several languages, and initiated a new current in Brazilian literature. His principal works are: *Esthetica da vida* (Rio, 1920); *O espirito moderno; Canaán* (1901); English translation of *Canaán*, Boston, 1920.

GUZMÁN, MARTÍN LUIS. Born in Chihuahua, Mexico, 1887. Novelist, journalist. Was a representative of the Progressive Party at the Convention of 1911, took part in the revolution against Huerta in 1913, lived in exile in Spain during 1915 and 1916. Has been Congressman, secretary of the University, Director of the National Library of Mexico. His book *El Aguila y la serpiente* (*The Eagle and the Serpent*) has been translated into English (New York: Alfred A. Knopf; 1930). His principal works are: *La Querella de México* (Madrid, 1915); *A orillas del Hudson*

(1922); *El Aguila y la serpiente* (Madrid, 1928); *La Sombra del caudillo* (Madrid, 1929); *Mina el Mozo* (Madrid, 1932); *Memorias de Pancho Villa* (4 vols., 1938).

HERRERA, FLAVIO. Born in Guatemala, 1895. Poet, novelist, lawyer, and teacher. Has been Professor of Penal Law at the University of Guatemala, and Chargé d'Affaires of the Legation of Guatemala in Costa Rica. Author of two volumes of short stories: *La Lente Opaca* (1921) and *Cenizas* (1923); several volumes of poetry: *El Ala de las montañas* (1921), *Sagitario* (1934), *Cosmos Indio* (1938), etc.; and two novels: *El Tigre* (1934) and *La Tempestad* (1940).

LATORRE, MARIANO. Born in Cobquecura, Chile, 1896. Short-story writer, journalist, teacher. Represented his country at the Book Fair in Bogotá in 1938. At the invitation of the Faculty of Philosophy and Letters of the University of Buenos Aires, he gave a course there in 1940 on Chilean Literature. Has received two literary awards in Chile: the Martínez Prize and the Athenæum Prize. Author of: *Paisajes Chilenos* (1910); *Cuentos del Maule* (1912); *Cuna de Condores* (1918); *El Romance del reloj cuco* (1920); *Ully* (1924); *Recuerdos de Rubén Guevara* (1925); *La Confesion de Tognina* (1926); *Collares* (1927); *Chilenos del Mar* (1929); *On panta* (1935); *Hombres y zorros* (1937).

LUGONES, LEOPOLDO. Born in Rio Seco, Argentina, 1874; died in Buenos Aires, 1938. Poet, essayist, historian, journalist. Was one of the leaders of the modernist movement in poetry in America. He was on the literary staff of the newspaper *La Nación* of Buenos Aires. He traveled extensively in Europe before the first World War, and on his return was appointed Director of the National Library. Among his abundant poetic productions the following books are outstanding: *Las Montañas del oro* (1897); *Los Crepúsculos del jardín* (1905); *Lunario sentimental* (1909); *Odas seculares* (1910); *El Libro fiel* (1912); *El Libro de los paisajes* (1917); *Las Horas doradas* (1922); *Romancero* (1924). The most notable of his prose works are: *La Guerra gaucha* (1905); *Piedras liminares* (1910); *Historia de Sarmiento* (1911); *El Imperio jesuítico* (1914); *Elogio de Ameghino* (1915); *El Ejército de la Iliada* (1915); *El Payador* (1916); *Las Industrias de Atenas* (1919); *El Ángel de la sombra* (novel), 1926.

LYRA, HEITOR. Born in Recife, Brazil, 1893. Historian, diplomat. Has been Chargé d'Affaires and councilor of the Brazilian Embassy in Germany, Chargé d'Affaires of Brazil to the Vatican, secretary of the Brazilian Embassy in London, and of the Brazilian delegation to the League of Nations. Author of: *Ensaios diplomaticos* (1922); *Arquivo diplomatico da independencia* (1922); *Historia de Dom Pedro II* (1939).

MANCINI, JULES. Born in Bogotá, 1875; died in Paris, 1928. Historian. He lived the greater part of his life in France. Only the first volume of his book *Bolívar y la emancipación de las colonias españolas,* which is considered one of the most important studies that has been written of Bolívar's life, has been published. The book was originally written in French, and was awarded the prize of the French Academy. The author himself translated his work into Spanish.

MAÑACH, JORGE. Born in Sagua la Grande, Cuba, 1898. Professor, statesman, writer. Was educated in Cuba, Spain, and the United States, where he was graduated from Harvard University; completed his studies at the University of Havana. Has taught at Columbia University, and is a professor in the University of Havana. Has held political posts in Cuba. One of the founders of *Revista de Avance.* Author of numerous essays and of *Martí el apostol* (1933), a biography of Martí soon to be published in English.

MARÍN, JUAN. Novelist, short-story writer, poet. This Chilean writer, who won recognition with his novela *Paralelo 53 Sur,* which received the Municipal Award of Santiago in 1936, was a medical officer with the Chilean fleet. His book on the Magellan Strait was written in the course of three trips with the fleet, on board the cutter *Micalvi,* the destroyer *Serrano,* and the cruiser

Latorre. In recent years Marín has been the Consul of Chile in Shanghai. His principal works are: *Looping* and *Aquarium,* volumes of poetry; *Alas sobre el mar, El Secreto del Dr. Baloux,* short stories; *Poliedro Médico, Ensayos Freudianos, El Problema sexual y sus nuevas formulas sociales, Hacia la nueva Moral,* essays; and *Margarita, el aviador y el médico; La muerte de Julián Aranda; Paralelo 53 Sur,* novels. He has also written a travel journal: *Clínicas y maestros en Inglaterra y Francia.*

MELÉNDEZ, JUAN. Born in Lima, Peru, about the middle of the seventeenth century. Dominican friar, author of *Los Tesoros verdaderos de las Indias,* which García Calderón considers "the fundamental work of religious history in Peru, an indispensable anthology and manual of Peruvian sanctity." Meléndez was supervisor of studies in the establishments of his order in Lima and Cuzco, and visitor of the dioceses of Peru. He went to Rome to arrange for the beatification of the Venerable Fray Vicente Bernedo, and to Spain to document and publish his book of the *True Treasures.* Three of Meléndez's works have been published: *Festiva pompa, Culto religioso, Veneración reverente, fiesta, clamación y aplauso a la feliz beatificación de la bienaventurada virgen Rosa de Santa María* (1671); *Vida Virtudes y Muerte del venerable padre y penitente siervo de Dios Fray Vicente Bernedo* (1675); *Los Tesoros verdaderos de las Indias* (1681).

MISTRAL, GABRIELA. Born in Elqui, Chile, 1889. Her real name is Lucila Godoy de Alcayaga. Poet, teacher, journalist. Was sent by the government of Chile to study the organization of libraries in Mexico (1922); Delegate to the Educators' Congress of Locarno; member of the international conference of university groups which met in Madrid in 1928; Professor of the History of Spanish Civilization at Barnard College, New York (1931); Secretary of the International Institute for Intellectual Co-operation of the League of Nations. She has been Consul of Chile in Madrid and in Lisbon, and is at present serving her country in this capacity at Petropolis, Brazil. Author of: *La Voz de Elqui* (1908); *Desolación* (New York, 1922); *Lecturas para mujeres* (Mexico,

1923); *Tala* (Buenos Aires, 1938); *Nubes blancas* (Barcelona, 1923).

NUCETE SARDI, JOSÉ. Born in Merida, Venezuela, 1897. Journalist and historian. Was secretary of the Venezuelan consulate in Berlin in 1937. Editor of the *Revista de Cultura Venezolana*. Author of *El Hombre de allá lejos* (1929); *El Escritor y civilizador Simón Bolívar* (1931); *Aventura y tragedia de Don Francisco Miranda* (1935); *Cuadernos de indagación y de impolítica* (1937).

OCAMPO, VICTORIA. Born in Buenos Aires, Argentina, 1891. Essayist. Editor of the magazine *Sur*, which also carries on many important cultural activities. She was educated in France and England, and has traveled widely in Europe and the United States. Author of: *De Francesca a Beatrice* (Madrid, 1924, with Introduction by J. Ortega y Gasset); *La Laguna de los nenúfares* (1926); *Testimonios* (1935); *La Langosta y los gangsters de las ediciones clandestinas* (1937); *Supremacía del alma y de la sangre* (1935); *Domingos en Hyde Park* (1936); *Testimonios (II)*, (1941); *San Isidro* (1943); *338171 T. E.* (essay on T. E. Lawrence) (1943).

O'LEARY, JUAN E. Born in Asunción, Paraguay, 1882. Historian, poet, professor. Has taught at the National College of Asunción, has been director of the National Archives of Paraguay, and Minister to Spain and Italy. His most important works are: *Historia de la triple alianza; Nuestra epopeya; El Paraguay en la unificación argentina; El Libro de los heroes; El Mariscal Solano López; El Centauro de Ybycui; Los Legionarios; El Heroe del Paraguay; Apostolado patriotico.*

PORRAS BARRANECHEA, RAUL. Born in Pisco, Peru, 1897. Historian, journalist, diplomat. Was a delegate to the Student Congress of Mexico in 1921. Is professor of the University of San Marcos, and director of the Colegio Universitario; Librarian of the Ministry of Foreign Affairs, 1922–6; Secretary of the Peruvian delegation to the Congress of Panama, 1926; delegate to the Congress of American Scholars of Seville, 1935; permanent delegate of Peru to the League of Nations. Author of: *El Periodismo en el Perú* (1921); *Lima* (1924); *Alegato del Perú en la cuestión de límites de Tacna y Arica* (1925); *Historia de los límites del Perú* (1926); *Mariano José de Arce* (1926); *José Antonio Barranechea* (1928); *Toribio Pacheco* (1928); *Pequeña Antología de Lima* (Madrid, 1935); *Cuadernos de historia del Perú* (Paris, 1936, 1937).

REYES, ALFONSO. Born in Monterrey, Mexico, 1889. Poet, essayist, diplomat. Minister Plenipotentiary of Mexico to Argentina (1924), France (1924), Spain (1926); Ambassador of Mexico to Argentina (1927 and 1936) and to Brazil (1930–6). Delegate of the University of Mexico to the International Congress of Sociology in Turin, representative of Mexico in the Seventh Pan-American Congress in Montevideo, and at the meetings of the P.E.N. Club in Buenos Aires (1936) and Havana, at which he presided (1941). At present director of the Colegio de Mexico. His most important works are: *Cuestiones estéticas* (Paris, 1911); *El Paisaje en la poesía mexicana del siglo XIX* (1911); *El Suicida, libro de ensayos* (1917); *Visión de Anahuac* (San José de Costa Rica, 1916); *Retratos reales e imaginarios* (1920); *Simpatías y diferencias* (5 series, Madrid, 1921–6); *El Cazador, ensayos y divagaciones* (Madrid, 1921); *Calendario* (Madrid, 1924); *Simples Remarques sur le Mexique* (Paris, 1926); *Las Jitanjaforas* (Buenos Aires, 1929); *A vuelta de correo* (Rio de Janeiro, 1932); *Rumbo a Goethe* (Buenos Aires, 1932); *Tren de ondas* (Rio de Janeiro, 1932); *La Crítica en la edad ateniense* (Mexico, 1941); *La Experiencia literaria* (Buenos Aires, 1942); *La Antigua retórica* (Mexico, 1942); *Los Nuevos argonautas* (Mexico, 1943); *Ultima Tule* (Mexico, 1942).

RINALDINI, JULIO. Born in Merlo, province of Buenos Aires, Argentina, in 1890. Critic, historian. His work has appeared in periodicals and journals of Argentina. He is considered one of the most capable art critics, and has devoted most of his effort to this field. His essay on the growth and development of Buenos Aires, published by the Argentine Commission for Intellectual Cooperation, has been translated into French and appears in the book *Quelques Regards sur l'Argentine*. Author of: *Toulouse-Lautrec* (Buenos Aires, 1942); *Auguste Rodin* (Buenos Aires, 1943); *Delacroix* (Buenos Aires, 1943).

RIVERA, JOSÉ EUSTASIO. Born in Neiva, Colombia, 1889. Died in New York, 1928. Poet, novelist. From the moment of its publication his book *La Voragine* assured him a place among the greatest novelists of our times. It has been translated into English, French, Russian, and German. It is known in English as *The Vortex*. In addition to his other works, Rivera left a drama in verse which has not yet been published. Author of: *Tierra de promisión* (sonnets) (1921); *La Voragine* (1924).

RODO, JOSÉ ENRIQUE. Born in Uruguay, 1872. Died in Italy, 1917. Essayist. Considered one of the great masters of the youth of Latin America. His influence made itself felt at the beginning of the century principally through two books which were widely read throughout Latin America: *Ariel* and *Liberalismo y Jacobinismo*. Two of his books have been translated into English: *Ariel* and *The Motives of Proteus*. Author of: *Rubén Darío* (1889); *Ariel* (1900); *Liberalismo y Jacobinismo* (1906); *Motivos de Proteo* (1909); *Cinco ensayos* (1911); *El Mirador de Próspero* (1913).

ROJAS, RICARDO. Born in Tucumán, Argentina, 1882. Historian, dramatist, poet, professor. Has been president of the University of Buenos Aires, professor and Dean of the Faculty of Philosophy and Letters. Has been director of the Biblioteca Argentina, a collection of masterpieces of Argentine literature, which has published 30 volumes. Rojas was awarded the Grand National Award of Literature for his *Literatura argentina*. His principal works are: Poetry: *La Victoria del hombre* (1903); *Los Lises del blasón* (1911); *La Sangre del sol* (1920); drama: *Elelin* (1929); *La Casa colonial* (1938); *Ollantay* (1939); historical and literary studies: *El Alma española* (1907); *El País de la selva* (Paris, 1907); *Cosmópolis* (Paris, 1908); *Blasón de Plata* (1912); *La Argentinidad*

(1916); *La Literatura argentina* (5 vols., 1917–22); *El Cristo invisible* (1927); *El Santo de la espada* (1933); *Retablo español* (1938); *Un Titán de los Andes* (1939); *Archipielago* (1942).

SANÍN CANO, BALDOMERO. Born in Rio Negro, Colombia, 1861. Critic, essayist, journalist, diplomat. Consul of Colombia in London (1911); professor at the University of Edinburgh (1919–20); Minister of Colombia to Argentina (1933); presided at the International Conference for Intellectual Co-operation (Buenos Aires, 1926); Representative in the Colombian Congress (1924–33); President of the University of Cauca (1940). For many years he was the correspondent of *La Nación* of Buenos Aires in Madrid, and later was a member of its editorial staff in Buenos Aires. Author of: *Administración Reyes* (Lausanne, 1909); *An Elementary Spanish Grammar* (Oxford, 1920); *Spanish Reader* (Oxford, 1920); *La Civilización manual y otros ensayos* (Buenos Aires, 1925); *Indagaciones e imágenes* (Bogotá, 1927); *Crítica y arte* (Bogotá, 1932); *Divagaciones filológicas y apólogos literarios* (Manizales, 1934); *Ensayos* (Bogotá, 1943).

SARMIENTO, DOMINGO FAUSTINO. Born in San Juan de la Frontera, Argentina, 1811; died in Asunción, Paraguay, 1888. Essayist, educator, journalist, statesman. His book *Facundo* is one of the greatest works written in Spanish in America. As President of the Argentine Republic, his work in the field of education was a great factor in the formation of his country. He was one of liberty's greatest champions. He traveled through Europe and the United States, studying the different systems of education. He was a friend of Horace Mann, and *Facundo* was translated into English by Mrs. Horace Mann with the title: *Life in the Argentine Republic in the Days of the Tyrants*. The most outstanding among his writings, which number more than thirty volumes, are: *Facundo* (Santiago de Chile, 1845); *Recuerdos de Provincia* (Santiago de Chile, 1850).

SOLANO, ARMANDO. Born in Paipa, Colombia, 1887. Journalist, statesman, diplomat. Has been Congressional Representative and Senator, and a member of the inner circle of the Liberal Party; special writer for the newspapers *El Espectador* and *El Liberal*. Was counselor of the Embassy of Colombia in Santiago de Chile. His most important books are: *Glosario sencillo* (1925); *La Melancolía de la raza indígena* (1929); *Prosas* (1936).

VASCONCELOS, JOSÉ. Born in Oaxaca, Mexico, 1882. Historian, essayist, philosopher, novelist. Was president of the University of Mexico (1920–4); Minister of Public Instruction (1920–5); candidate for president of the Republic (1929); in recent years, Director of the National Library of Mexico. While he was Minister of Public Instruction he was hailed in several countries of the continent as the master of the young generation. Outstanding among his writings are: *Pitágoras* (1916); *El Monismo estético* (1918); *Estudios Indostánicos* (1918); *Prometeo Vencedor* (Madrid, 1921); *La Raza cósmica* (Paris, 1925); *Indología* (Paris, 1927); *Aspects of Mexican Civilization* (Chicago, 1927); *Metafísica* (1929); *Pesimismo alegre* (Madrid, 1930); *Ética* (Madrid, 1930); *Sonata mágica* (Madrid, 1933); *Bolivarismo y Monroismo* (1934); *Ulises criollo* (1935); *La Tormenta* (1936); *Estética* (1936); *Breve Historia de México* (1937).

VERISSIMO, ERICO. Born in Cruz Alta, a small city in southern Brazil, 1905. Novelist, journalist, professor. Unable through lack of funds to study at the university, when he was seventeen years old he went to work in a grocery store, then in a bank, and finally in a drug-store. He worked in a book-store in Porto Alegre and later edited a magazine. He has published a volume of short stories, and the following novels: *Clarisa; Musica ao Longe* (1934), which won the Machado de Assis Prize; *Caminos cruzados* (1935), which won the Graça Aranha Prize; *Un Lugar ao sol; Olhai os Lirios do Campo;* and *O resto e' silencio*. He has also written children's stories and a biography of Joan of Arc. *Caminos cruzados* was published in English under the title *Crossroads* by The Macmillan Company in 1943; and the same house is bringing out a translation of *O resto e' silencio*.

INDEX OF AUTHORS

INDEX OF WORKS

A NOTE ON THE TYPE USED IN THIS BOOK

The text of this book is set in Caledonia, a Linotype face designed by W. A. Dwiggins. Caledonia belongs to the family of printing types called "modern face" by printers — a term used to mark the change in style of type-letters that occurred about 1800. Caledonia borders on the general design of Scotch Modern, but is more freely drawn than that letter.

Mr. Dwiggins planned the typographic scheme and designed the binding. The book was composed by The Plimpton Press, Norwood, Massachusetts, and printed and bound by The Haddon Craftsmen, Inc., Scranton, Pennsylvania.